WOMEN IN
COMMUNICATION

WOMEN IN
COMMUNICATION

WOMEN IN COMMUNICATION

A Biographical Sourcebook

Edited by Nancy Signorielli

Foreword by Alan M. Rubin

GREENWOOD PRESS
Westport, Connecticut • London

Library of Congress Cataloging-in-Publication Data

Women in communication : a biographical sourcebook / edited by Nancy
 Signorielli ; foreword by Alan M. Rubin.
     p. cm.
  Includes bibliographical references and index.
  ISBN 0–313–29164–0 (alk. paper)
    1. Women in communication—Dictionaries. 2. Communication
 specialists—Biography—Dictionaries. I. Signorielli, Nancy.
 P94.5.W65W667   1996
 302.2'092'2—dc20
  [B]   95–52756

British Library Cataloguing in Publication Data is available.

Library of Congress Catalog Card Number: 95–52756
ISBN: 0–313–29164–0

First published in 1996

Greenwood Press, 88 Post Road West, Westport, CT 06881
An imprint of Greenwood Publishing Group, Inc.

Printed in the United States of America

The paper used in this book complies with the
Permanent Paper Standard issued by the National
Information Standards Organization (Z39.48–1984).

10 9 8 7 6 5 4 3 2 1

To Robert, David, and Laura Jane

CONTENTS

CONTRIBUTORS

Alison Alexander (Ph.D. Ohio State University). Professor and Department Head, Henry W. Grady College of Journalism and Mass Communication, University of Georgia.

Carol A. Barbato (Ph.D. Kent State University). Assistant Professor, School of Communication Studies, Kent State University, Kent, Ohio.

Maurine H. Beasley (Ph.D. George Washington University). Professor, College of Journalism, University of Maryland.

Louise Benjamin (Ph.D. University of Iowa). Department of Telecommunications, School of Journalism, University of Georgia.

David S. Birdsell (Ph.D. University of Maryland). Associate Professor, School of Public Affairs, Baruch College, City University of New York.

Michael Breen (M.S. Syracuse University). Doctoral student, Syracuse University.

Elizabeth V. Burt (Ph.D. University of Wisconsin). Assistant Professor, School of Communication, University of Hartford.

Scott E. Caplan (M.A. University of Delaware). Doctoral student, Department of Communication, Purdue University, Lafayette, Indiana.

Ginger Rudeseal Carter (doctoral student, University of South Mississippi). Assistant Professor, Department of Journalism, Northeast Louisiana University.

Sheila Clough Crifasi (M.S. Boston University). Instructor, Department of Communication, University of Delaware.

Juliet Dee (Ph.D. Temple University). Associate Professor, Department of Communication, University of Delaware.

Julia R. Dobrow (Ph.D. The Annenberg School for Communication, University of Pennsylvania). Coordinator of Initiative on Children and Media, Department of Child Studies, Tufts University.

Patricia L. Dooley (Ph.D. University of Minnesota). Assistant Professor, Department of Communication and Journalism, University of Maine, Orono, Maine.

William P. Eveland, Jr. (M.A. Communication University of Delaware). Doctoral student, University of Wisconsin–Madison.

Elizabeth E. Graham (Ph.D. Kent State University). Associate Professor, Ohio University, Athens, Ohio.

Roger D. Haney (Ph.D. Michigan State University). Professor, Department of Journalism and Radio, TV, Film, Murray State University, Murray, Kentucky.

Margot Hardenbergh (Ph.D. New York University). Assistant Professor, Communication and the Arts Division, Marist College.

Beth Haslett (Ph.D. University of Minnesota). Professor, Department of Communication, University of Delaware, Newark, Delaware.

Carol Sue Humphrey (Ph.D. University of North Carolina). Associate Professor, Department of History, Oklahoma Baptist University.

Susan G. Kahlenberg (M.A. Communication University of Delaware). Doctoral student, Temple University, Philadelphia, Pennsylvania.

Sue Lawrence (Ph.D. University of Missouri-Columbia). Assistant Professor, Division of Communication and the Arts, Marist College.

Beth A. Le Poire (Ph.D. University of Arizona). Assistant Professor, University of California-Santa Barbara.

Candace Lewis (B.A. University of Delaware). M.A. student at The Annenberg School for Communication, University of Pennsylvania.

Suzanne Marcus (M.A. Syracuse University). Freelance Producer.

Douglas M. McLeod (Ph.D. University of Minnesota). Associate Professor, Department of Communication, University of Delaware.

Robert Miller (B.A. Yale University). Student, School of Law, University of Pennsylvania.

Johnna M. Moyer (B.A. University of Delaware). Student, School of Law, Catholic University.

John P. Murray (Ph.D. Catholic University). Professor and Director, School of Family Studies and Human Services, Kansas State University.

Amy I. Nathanson (M.A. Communication University of Delaware). Doctoral student, University of Wisconsin-Madison.

Christine L. Ogan (Ph.D. University of North Carolina). Professor, School of Journalism, Indiana University.

Norma Pecora (Ph.D. University of Illinois). Adjunct Assistant Professor, Ohio University, Athens, Ohio.

Elizabeth M. Perse (Ph.D. Kent State University). Associate Professor, Department of Communication, University of Delaware.

Alan M. Rubin (Ph.D. University of Illinois). Professor, School of Communication Studies, Kent State University, Kent, Ohio.

Wendy Samter (Ph.D. Purdue University). Associate Professor, Department of Communication, University of Delaware.

Amy Sarch (Ph.D. The Annenberg School for Communication, University of Pennsylvania). Assistant Professor, College of Staten Island, City University of New York.

Pamela J. Shoemaker (Ph.D. University of Wisconsin). John Ben Snow Professor, S. I. Newhouse School of Public Communications, Syracuse University, Syracuse, New York.

Jessica Staples (B.A. University of Delaware). M.A. candidate, Department of Communication, University of Delaware.

James W. Tankard, Jr. (Ph.D. Stanford University). Professor, School of Journalism, University of Texas-Austin.

Diane Zimmerman Umble (Ph.D. The Annenberg School for Communication, University of Pennsylvania). Associate Professor, Department of Communication and Theatre, Millersville University, Pennsylvania.

K. Viswanath (Ph.D. University of Minnesota). Assistant Professor, School of Journalism, Ohio State University.

Ellen A. Wartella (Ph.D. University of Minnesota). Dean, College of Communication, University of Texas-Austin.

Carol Wilder (Ph.D. Kent State University). Associate Dean and Chair, Communication Department, New School of Social Research, New York City.

Dorothy Zeccola (B.A. University of Delaware). M.A. student, Department of Communication, University of Delaware.

FOREWORD

This is a story of achievement. It is a compilation of essays about the lives and accomplishments of a group of communication professionals, women in communication. Those who are profiled in this book have had remarkable lives of achievement. Many have overcome obstacles that would not have been experienced by their male peers. They all have offered respected and valued professional service. They all have contributed to the discovery, synthesis, or application of knowledge about communication's significant role in society. They have done so primarily in academia, broadcasting, and journalism.

This book is an important biographic and bibliographic sourcebook. It includes an array of people in myriad positions. It also includes representative publications and other contributions. Many of those profiled have substantial academic credentials and come from that branch of the profession. They offer significant records of scholarly and administrative accomplishments. Others have gained recognition in the communication industry, politics, and public service.

All the women profiled in this book have furthered our understanding of the important role that communication plays in our lives and in the functioning of societies. They have been and continue to be important mentors to their students, apprentices, and colleagues. All their stories tell us about an interesting series of choices, obstacles, and opportunities. The profiles reveal how these professionals have achieved success despite the different expectations, demands, rewards, and recognition they experienced as compared with their male colleagues who occupied similar positions and enjoyed more favorable routes to success.

Most of the women included in this compilation are currently active professionals. Clearly, other deserving communication professionals could have been included. Some may find fault with who is omitted or who received briefer biographies. As with any project, space constraints made such choices difficult, even with the criteria used to make inclusion decisions.

In any event, this valuable work chronicles the lives of important professional role models for us all. These profiles document and preserve the significant contributions of women to communication and society. They are important historical records and socializing tools for our discipline.

Alan M. Rubin

ACKNOWLEDGMENTS

I truly enjoyed putting this book together and would like to thank everyone who helped bring it to press, especially each author and my editors at Greenwood. Special thanks to John Courtright, Betsy Perse, Edna Rogers, Alan Rubin, and Ellen Wartella for their advice. Thanks also to Myrna Hofmann and Laura Sowers for their help. Finally, thanks to my family, and particularly my children, who are always supportive of my work but who were especially helpful in the last hectic stage of proofreading and index-creating by providing encouragement, quiet, understanding, and hugs.

INTRODUCTION

Nancy Signorielli

Some would argue that communication is one of the oldest academic disciplines. As a field it covers many different areas, including rhetoric, interpersonal communication, group dynamics, journalism, broadcasting, and mass communication which, in this book, are examined from practical as well as theoretical orientations. Its rhetorical roots can be traced to Corax's *Art of Rhetoric* written in the fifth century B.C. Aristotle's *Rhetoric* (fourth century B.C.) is often noted as the most influential and notable of the early works in rhetoric (Becker, 1989). Johannes Gutenberg's invention, in 1457, of the movable-type printing press, which is generally said to mark the dawn of the Renaissance, is a critical juncture in the development of knowledge (Rogers, 1994).

Gutenberg's invention of a movable-type printing press was responsible for the eventual mass production of books and newspapers and the rise of journalism as a separate field of endeavor. Journalism has had a long and vibrant history. Forerunners to today's newspapers appeared by the middle of the 1500s when Venetians, using a coin called a *gazetta,* could purchase a sheet with news about the war in Dalmatia. Around 1625, *Corontos,* single sheets highlighting foreign news, were sold to the public in London. The *Daily Courant,* the first daily newspaper that recovered its costs from advertising, began publication in London in March 1702 (DeFleur & Dennis, 1988).

Newspapers appeared in the American colonies in the beginning of the 1700s, and by 1750 most Americans who could read had access to a newspaper. The press was extremely politicized in the years before the Revolutionary War. Numerous political pamphlets, including the Federalist Papers and the Declaration of Independence, were first published in newspapers and contributed to the push for independence (DeFleur & Dennis, 1988; Dominick, 1994).

The technological advances of the 1800s, including printing technology, the telegraph, railroads, and steamboats, greatly facilitated the growth of newspapers. During the 1830s, the first mass newspaper, the *New York Sun,* began publication. Incorporating interesting stories about local happenings and sold by newsboys for a penny, the *Sun* put newspapers within everyone's means. Another key factor in the growth of journalism and newspapers was the increased emphasis on sensationalism, crime, and human interest stories, dubbed Yellow Journalism. Newspapers reached their peak of popularity by World War I. The Great Depression coupled with the rise of radio (and later television), which competed with newspapers for advertising dollars, led to reduced circulation and the eventual consolidation of the nation's newspapers (DeFleur & Dennis, 1988; Dominick, 1994).

The growth of the nation's newspapers was coupled with the academic study of journalism. Although the study of journalism at the university level was first proposed in 1869, the first courses in journalism were not offered until the early 1900s (Rogers, 1994). A key figure in the development of journalism education was Willard Grosvenor ("Daddy") Blyer, who began offering courses in journalism at the University of Wisconsin in 1905 (Troldahl, 1989). Under Blyer's direction, journalism became a department at Wisconsin in 1912 and a school in 1927 (Rogers, 1994). Blyer made three major contributions to the study of journalism and, indirectly, to the development of the discipline of communication. First, he incorporated the methods of the behavioral sciences; second, he studied public opinion; and third, he received approval for a doctoral program whose primary focus was in an existing field, such as political science, but with a minor focus in journalism (Troldahl, 1989). Most importantly, those who studied with Blyer at Wisconsin passed on his legacy.

The earliest roots of the study of communication, and particularly the mass media as a social science, can be traced to the late 1930s and the 1940s with the work of George Gallup and particularly Wilbur Schramm (Rogers, 1994; Troldahl, 1989). Four studies conducted during this era were of considerable importance in furthering our understanding of the media. First, the Payne Fund studies, conducted between 1929 and 1932, examined, in 13 separate studies, how the movies influenced children (Charters, 1933). Second, the aftermath of Orsen Welles' rendition of H. G. Wells' *War of the Worlds* on CBS's "Mercury Theatre on the Air" was examined by the Office of Radio Research at Princeton University (Cantril, 1940). Third, voter behavior in the 1940 presidential election was analyzed in *The People's Choice* (Lazarsfeld, Berelson, & Gaudet, 1948). Finally, Herta Herzog* conducted the first study in uses and gratifications, examining listeners and nonlisteners of radio daytime serial dramas (Herzog, 1942–1943).

World War II provided an opportunity for researchers from numerous disciples to gather together to promote the war effort and further the study of communication. Ev Rogers (1994) reflects on the importance of this decade for the study of communication. Scholars, including Kurt Lewin and Paul F. Lazarsfeld, immigrated from Europe. Others, such as Harold D. Lasswell and Carl I. Hovland, became interested in communication. Wilbur Schramm brought his knowledge of communication to the Office of War Information and the Office of Facts and Figures and with other notable scholars in Washington during the war years effectively developed his approach to the discipline of communication. Critical studies in communication conducted during World War II include the early study of persuasion in the analysis of the "Why We Fight" training films. These films were produced to give young American recruits background information on the international events leading up to the war and the United States' involvement in it (Hovland, Lumsdaine, & Sheffield, 1949).

The years after World War II further differentiated the study of communication from the social sciences from which it emerged—psychology, sociology, and particularly political science. Doctoral programs in communication were first instituted at the large land-grant institutions in the Midwest (Illinois, 1947; Iowa, 1943; Minnesota, 1951; Wisconsin, 1950) and on the West Coast (Stanford, 1952) and were followed by institutes for the study of communication research, such as the Institute for Communication Research at the University of Illinois (Rogers, 1994). The explosion of distinct departments of communication in American universities took place during the 1960s and 1970s. Lowery and DeFleur (1995) note that there are now more than 2,000 distinct departments and schools of communication throughout the country. Moreover, about 5 percent of the bachelors' degrees awarded each year are in communication-related disciplines.

Although the discipline's roots can be traced back for centuries, most would agree that the study of communication as we know it today is relatively new. Thus, few detailed histories of the discipline exist. Rogers (1994) traces communication to Charles Darwin, Sigmund Freud, and Karl Marx and notes its emergence into a full-fledged discipline in the years following World War II with the work of Wilbur Schramm and his establishment of the Institute for Communication Research at the University of Illinois in January 1948. Consequently, many of the key scholars in the discipline today are now at the prime of their careers. Similarly, as the industry grew with the explosion of technological advances after World War II, key figures in the industry (those who are most prominent in television, radio, and journalism) now are also at the apex of their careers.

Relatively few women were actively involved in the early or formative years of the discipline of communication. Two women, Ruth C. Peterson and Dorothy P. Marquis, were among the researchers working on the Payne Fund Studies, and two, Hazel Gaulet and Herta Herzog, were active with Lazarsfeld's Office of Radio Research Project. Although Margaret Mead was among the "invisible college of scholars" with whom Wilbur Schramm regularly met during his World War II years in Washington, and the only woman included in Rogers' (1994) list of the principal figures in the history of communication study, Professor Mead is not typically regarded as a communication scholar. Aside from the relatively small number of women, many of whom are included in this collection, who were active in the growth of newspapers and journalism during the 1800s and early 1900s, most of those in the present volume are now actively working in the field, for only a few women were active in the discipline before the 1960s and 1970s.

The growth of women in communication is also mirrored in the field's professional organizations. Two of the three major professional organizations in communication were started in the early 1900s—the Association for Education in Journalism and Mass Communication (AEJMC) and the Speech Communication Association (SCA). Although the founders of the Speech Communication Association (originally the National Association of Teachers of Public Speaking) were all men, the first woman president (Henrietta Prentiss of Hunter College) was elected in 1932 and the second female president (Maud May Babacock of the University of Utah) took office in 1936. Since the 1930s a woman has been elected president of SCA about once every ten years. On the other hand, the Association for Education in Journalism and Mass Communication did not elect a woman to its presidency until 1979 when Mary A. Gardner of Michigan State University was elected president of what was then called the Association for Education in Journalism. The next woman president of AEJMC (Sharon M. Murphy* of Marquette University) was elected in 1987. Since 1990, however, seven women have been elected president of this organization, including the 1996 president, Pamela Shoemaker.* The International Communication Association (ICA), formed in 1950, elected its first woman (Brenda Dervin*) as president in 1985–1986. With a pattern similar to AEJMC, the 1990s have seen a number of women elected as president of ICA.

Over the past 25 years, the steady growth of women in communication has paralleled, or even exceeded, the growth of women in other academic disciplines. At most universities, women make up about half of all undergraduate and graduate students in communication departments. Moreover, as noted above, women are extremely active in the field and professional organizations, and many women have risen to prominence in the field. Again, most of these women are now at the apex of their careers, and it is this group that is highlighted in this collection.

When approached by the Greenwood Publishing Group to edit this biographic sourcebook, I realized that indeed there was a need to bring together information about the key women in communication—pioneers in journalism, broadcasting, publishing, and of course scholars in both mass and interpersonal communication. My assessment of the need for this book arose in part from the myriad of calls I receive each semester from students around the country asking to interview me about my role in the discipline, my personal life, and how my personal life and professional life complement each other or are kept in perspective. In the course of these discussions, the students (who typically were conducting interviews of women communication scholars as part of a class project) would say that it was almost impossible to find any information about women, particularly the most active contemporary women, in the discipline.

The questions that then arose were, who should be included, how should the women be selected, who should write about them, and what should they write about? Working with Mildred Vasan, my editor at Greenwood Press, we decided that three groups of women—the pioneers (in journalism, broadcasting, and scholarship), the current key professionals in the industry, and the current scholars in mass and interpersonal communication—should be highlighted in the collection. The final selections were made with a peer review process in which a number of well-known and respected scholars in communication (communication journal editors, past presidents or fellows of the International Communication Association and the Speech Communication Association, etc.) were asked to nominate women to be included in this reference work.

We first focused on scholars and professionals in communication. In addition to the peer review process, the research of Hickson, Stacks, and Amsbary (Active Prolific Female Scholars in Communication, *Communication Quarterly,* 1992, 40, no. 4, 350–356) was used to supplement the peer nominations with basic statistics regarding publication records. The final selection of 48 biographies included those women who were consistently nominated by this group of renowned, respected, and publicly acclaimed scholars.

So many of our active women scholars were nominated for inclusion in the book that only a fraction could be selected for a full biography because of space limitations. Consequently, we decided to include an appendix highlighting as many of the entire group of scholars as possible. This appendix consists of short essays that provide basic background information about these scholars. It was felt that this appendix could be used to recognize the large number of women who have considerable stature in the field as well as a number of women who could be labeled as the "up and coming stars" in the field.

The second group of biographies describes key professionals in the industry who were also selected through the peer review process. This group does not include those women commonly characterized as "talent" (e.g., Oprah Winfrey, Roseanne, etc.). The third group, pioneers in journalism and broadcasting, were selected by examining a number of existing biographical collections to find those women who seem to have made sizable contributions to the field and for whom it could be argued that the collection would be less useful if they were omitted. In addition, most of the existing biographies did not go into as much detail as this book or focused on different aspects of their lives.

Naturally, arguments could be made about why some women were included and others excluded. In terms of the current scholars, the Appendix will provide a way to include information about more women. Unfortunately, because of space limitations this section could not be readily expanded to include those women who are of more historical interest as well as the current professionals in the industry.

The contributors to this volume are an impressive group in their own right. They include current scholars in the history of journalism as well as scholars in the more general fields of mass and interpersonal communication. Biographers also include a number of recent Ph.D. students as well as current graduate students.

Biographers were asked to focus on each woman's scientific and professional contributions to the field. Most also conducted personal interviews to gather all the information they needed to write a full account of the woman's life and work. Each biography is structured similarly and focuses on the following areas:

1. Family background (date of birth, parents, siblings, marriage, children, etc.)
2. Education
3. Career development (mentor if appropriate) or marriage and career
4. Major contributions and achievements
5. Critical evaluation of contributions and achievements
6. Integration of Personal and Professional Life
7. Selected bibliography (including the most important publications)

This sourcebook consists of a series of entries focusing on the life and work of contemporary professionals and scholars in the fields of interpersonal, organizational, and mass communication as well as key figures in the history of journalism and a small, elite group of professionals who have made an important, far-reaching, significant, and consistent contribution to the field. As many of these women's lives are interconnected, asterisks have been used to cross-reference entries. The entries thus serve to document and evaluate the diverse contributions of women in communication.

REFERENCES

Becker, S. L. (1989). The rhetorical tradition. In S. S. King (ed.), *Human communication as a field of study: Selected contemporary views.* (pp. 27–42). Albany, N.Y.: State University of New York Press.

Cantril, H. (1940). *The invasion from Mars: A study in the psychology of panic.* Princeton, N.J.: Princeton University Press.

Charters, W. W. (1933). *Motion pictures & youth: A summary.* New York: Macmillan Co.

DeFleur, M. I., & Dennis, E. E. (1988). *Understanding mass communication.* Boston: Houghton Mifflin.

Dominick, J. R. (1994). *The dynamics of mass communication.* New York: McGraw-Hill.

Herzog, H. (1944). What do we really know about daytime serial listeners. In P. F. Lazarsfeld & F. N. Stanton (eds.), *Radio Research, 1942–43.* New York: Duel, Sloan & Pearce.

Hickson, M., III, Stacks, D. W., & Amsbary, J. H. (1992). Active prolific female scholars in communication, *Communication Quarterly,* 40(4), 350–356.

Hovland, C. I., Lumsdaine, A. A., & Sheffield, F. D. (1949). *Experiments on mass communication.* Princeton, N.J.: Princeton University Press.

Lazarsfeld, P. F., Berelson, B., & Gaudet, H. (1948). *The people's choice*. New York: Columbia University Press.

Lowery, S. A., & DeFleur, M. L. (1995). *Milestones in mass communication research.* 3rd ed. White Plains, N.Y.: Longman.

Rogers, E. M. (1994). *A history of communication study: A biographical approach.* New York: Free Press.

Troldahl, V. C. (1989). The social scientific roots of the mass communication tradition. In S. S. King (ed.), *Human communication as a field of study: Selected contemporary views.* (pp. 42–56). Albany, N.Y.: State University of New York Press.

MARY CLEMMER AMES (1831–1884)

Patricia L. Dooley

Nineteenth-century political journalist, poet, and novelist Mary E. Clemmer Ames Hudson was one of a small number of women who worked in that era's male-dominated field of mainstream political journalism. Perhaps best known for her political columns, published for more than ten years starting in 1866 in the New York *Independent,* she also worked for other newspapers, and published poetry as well as several novels. An astute, and sometimes caustic, political observer of the Washington political scene, she was popular not only with newspaper readers, but also with her publishers, who valued her for her ability to attract patrons. In addition, her columns explored topics related to the concerns of women and other groups, such as the recently freed slaves. While she didn't shy away from writing scathing critiques of the country's leaders, she found the notoriety her writing garnered uncomfortable.

In response to her popularity, New York *Independent* and Brooklyn *Daily Union* publisher Henry C. Bowen paid her $5,000 for her services in 1872, said to be the highest annual salary paid to an American newspaperwoman up to that time. Although a supporter of woman's suffrage, Clemmer did not take an active part in the movement, nor did she eschew mainstream journalism in favor of setting up her own periodical, as did many of the more militant women journalists of the period. While long noted as an important nineteenth-century journalist, historians have generally not regarded her to be as influential as some of her contemporaries in furthering the interests of women journalists.

FAMILY BACKGROUND

Born on May 6, 1831, Mary Clemmer spent her early life in Utica, New York, the town in which she was born. She was the eldest of the children who lived to maturity, and her parents, Abraham and Mary Kneale Clemmer, provided her and her three sisters and two brothers with a modest but intellectually stimulating family life. Her father's family, of Alsatian Huguenot origin, came to America long before the American Revolution. Said to be handsome but impractical, Abraham Clemmer often experienced difficulty as he sought to make a living as a tobacconist, grocer, and merchant. Mary's mother came to Utica from the British Isle of Man in 1827. Possessed of an artistic and religious temperment, she passed these traits on to her daughter Mary.

EDUCATION

The family's modest circumstances provided the Clemmer children with only the most basic formal education. After the family moved to Westfield, Massachusetts, in 1847, Mary attended Westfield Academy. Upon completing her studies there, she was denied further opportunities for formal schooling. But her parents fostered a home environment that was conducive to the development of their children's talents, and she was allowed to indulge freely in various intellectual and artistic pursuits. She composed poetry at an early age and read voraciously, especially history and English and French memoirs. In addition, she was encouraged to think of her work as suitable for public consumption. Her earliest formal contact with journalism apparently occurred when a Westfield teacher encouraged her to send one of her poems to Samuel Bowles for publication in the *Springfield Republican.*

MARRIAGE AND CAREER

Mary Clemmer was married for the first time in 1851 at age 20 to Methodist minister Daniel Ames. The union was not a happy one, and the couple lived apart periodically until they separated permanently in 1865. Ames' ministerial calling took him west for several years, including Knowlesville, New York (1854–1856) and Winona, Minnesota (1857–1859). Returning east in 1860, he served for about a year as principal of a boys' school in Jersey City, New Jersey, and then briefly at Washington, D.C. Next, he accepted a federal post at Harpers Ferry, Virginia, where Mrs. Ames witnessed the town's bombardment and surrender, and was a prisoner of the Confederates for a time. Her biographers claim she was so desperately unhappy in the marriage that she at times contemplated suicide, and the couple finally divorced in 1874.

Clemmer began to pursue a writing career in about 1859, when, while living in New York, she began contributing letters to the *Utica Morning Herald* and *Springfield Republican.* During the next several years, she made friends who aided her in her quest to become an established journalist and literary writer. In New York, for example, she befriended Alice and Phoebe Cary, who welcomed her into their literary circle. During the war, when she lived for a time in Washington, working in army hospitals, she became acquainted with certain congressmen and senators and their wives, including Congressman Portus Baxter and Senator Justin S. Morrill of Vermont. She published her first of three novels in 1864, a work entitled *Victoire* that failed to receive much notice.

After separating from her husband for the last time in 1865, Clemmer began to pursue a writing career more seriously. She resumed writing under her given name and returned to Washington, where she launched her career at the New York *Independent,* a post she would hold for more than a decade. In addition, her writing was periodically published in other newspapers in New York and Ohio.

While Clemmer's journalism afforded her a comfortable living, she at times expressed a certain amount of distaste for the field. Believing poetry and fiction-writing to be a higher calling than journalism, she sometimes substituted her poetry for columns in the *Independent.* In 1871 she published the most successful of her three novels, a work entitled *Eirene; or, a Woman's Right,* which drew on her wartime experiences at Harpers Ferry. Her 1873 book, *A Memorial of Alice and Phoebe Cary,* was praised by the *Nation*'s reviewers as one of her best works, and in 1883, a collection of her poems entitled *Poems of Life and Nature* was published.

Throughout her career, Clemmer exhibited a strong commitment to furthering the interests of women, including those who worked outside their homes. But while she supported the concept of the independent career woman, she also frequently wrote that domestic life was woman's highest calling, and expressed discomfort with the fame her career had brought her. In reaction to the almost instant notoriety her newspaper columns brought her, she complained, "Fame is a curse which soils the loveliness of the womanly name by thrusting it into the grimy highway, where it is wondered at, sneered at, lied about, by the vulgar, the worldly, and the wicked."

In 1876 Clemmer bought a mansion on Capitol Hill, where she brought her aging parents to live. The previous year she had begun suffering from headaches so severe that her work output was affected, and in January 1878, her writing career was nearly ended when her skull was fractured in a carriage accident. Her biographers write of the extreme physical discomfort she endured as she struggled to continue her work.

In 1883 Clemmer married Edmund Hudson, a noted Washington journalist who edited the *Army and Navy Register.* When the two returned from a European wedding tour that autumn, her health was improved. But soon afterward, she was stricken with paralysis; she died eight months later of a cerebral hemorrhage at her Washington home.

MAJOR CONTRIBUTIONS AND ACHIEVEMENTS

Clemmer's "Woman's Letter from Washington" first appeared in a March 1866 issue of the New York *Independent.* An influential weekly religious periodical with informal ties to the Congregational church, the widely circulated

Independent covered general news and commentary about political affairs from a Radical Republican perspective.

Clemmer focused on a wide variety of topics in her columns, which ranged from government, politics, political and ethical philosophies, politicians, and the plight of certain groups of people to descriptive commentaries on places she visited both inside and outside the Washington area. Subjects she frequently wrote about were justice for the recently freed slaves, her devotion to Republican principles, descriptions of Congress and its leading members, the need for improved morality in Washington, and women government workers. During the first several months of her columns, for example, she wrote about the anniversary of President Lincoln's assassination, Mount Vernon, a recent presidential veto, the death of Senator Foot of Vermont, a physical description of the House of Representatives and its speaker, springtime in Washington, and the anniversary of the abolition of slavery.

Although by modern journalistic standards Clemmer's writing is overly ornate, her descriptions of people, places, and events offered her readers vivid portraits of her subjects. For example, a column on an Ohio congressman described how he appeared when irritated: "When angered, he looks like a pugnacious mastiff. He seizes his foe with a merciless grip, and, like other mastiffs, his bark is not half as bad as his bite."

Although at first a backer of President Ulysses S. Grant, as the scandals associated with his administration unfolded, she increasingly attacked him, especially the "cronyism" that led to his appointment of corrupt officials. Following the Grant administration, she staunchly supported President Rutherford B. Hayes, often writing about his wife Lucy, whom she admired greatly. Skeptical of both presidents James Garfield and Chester A. Arthur, she especially disliked Arthur because of his stand on the involvement of women in politics. In response to Arthur's criticism of women lobbyists, she wrote, "The question is not whether women shall or shall not influence public events, but, their powers being an acknowledged fact, the question is whether that power shall be subtle, secret, unacknowledged, equivocal, or whether it shall be legal, legitimate, open, honorable as the sunlight."

The success with readers which such writing brought was noticed. For example, after publishing her columns for a time, a letter she received from the *Independent*'s managing editor quoting editor Theodore Tilton's glowing evaluation of her work said, "I find also in my travels much commendation expressed of Mrs. Ames' letters. She is your card, and she is a trump."

In 1869 Clemmer began a three-year hiatus from the *Independent* by going to work for its publisher Henry C. Bowen at his Brooklyn *Daily Union.* Besides her daily column, the *Union* published Clemmer's book reviews and various editorials on politicians and events. In addition, she performed various business-related tasks. It was this job that was to pay Clemmer the $5,000 yearly salary. Two volumes of her newspaper columns, *Outlines of Men, Women, and Things* and *Ten Years in Washington,* were published in the early 1870s, and her columns were also published periodically in the Cincinnati *Commercial,* calling further attention to her journalistic career.

CRITICAL EVALUATION OF CONTRIBUTIONS
AND ACHIEVEMENTS

Clemmer is an important figure in the field of nineteenth-century political journalism, and her career also likely contributed to the advancement of women writers, especially women journalists.

Because of the *Independent*'s reach into the community, and because of her popularity, Clemmer's column probably served in the long run to advance the interests of political journalists, who during the post–Civil War period aspired to status as the citizenry's chief purveyors of political information.

As her popularity grew, politicians sought her favor, providing evidence that women journalists could become figures of importance in the largely male world of politics and political journalism.

Clemmer distinguished herself among the approximately 20 women who in the 1870s sought to become regular members of the largely male Washington press corps in the post–Civil War era. Refusing to conduct herself like many of her female journalistic peers, she published her work under her own name. Many other popular women journalistic writers of the era wrote under assumed names. Sara Willis Parton, for example, wrote under the pseudonym "Fanny Fern," and Sara Clarke Lippincott signed her columns "Grace Greenwood."

Clemmer wrote about certain women journalists she admired, as well as those she disdained. Among the women journalists she held up as models for others were Grace Greenwood, Margaret Ossoli Fuller, and French journalist Madame Guizot. Those she chastised most severely she referred to as "Jenkins," women who wrote largely on topics she considered trivial, such as fashion and gossip.

She argued that women were of a higher moral fiber than men and were thus specially equipped to serve as Washington correspondents, whose job, she said, was to critically observe and write about government and those who lead it.

Clemmer gathered material for her columns not only through her visits with the many friends she made in the capital, but also by the long hours she sat in the Congress's women's gallery. She refused to sit in the reporter's gallery, determined not to model her behavior on that of her journalistic male counterparts.

In addition to these contributions, Clemmer's writings are important historical documents that provide portraits of the period's gender relations, as well as the conditions under which various groups worked and lived, particularly women and blacks. For example, in one column that described the communication style of a particular senator involved in a conversation on a public matter at a dinner party, she observed how he changed his demeanor when encountering a woman. She said, "But when the gentleman turned to address her, he altered his voice, he changed his manner, as with one vast effort he dropped to the level of small talk. And, oh! What do you think was the first thing he told her? A fib, of course. He told her she 'looked charming,' the poor thing, standing there, faded and jaded, in the pitless gaslight.'' She expressed her fear that it would be a long time before men realized women's potential, and she thought them ridiculous for treating women differently.

INTEGRATION OF PERSONAL AND PROFESSIONAL LIFE

Despite her expressed belief that the domestic life was women's highest calling Clemmer doggedly pursued a full and rather complex public life, seemingly putting career ahead of home. She often wrote about the need for women to be financially independent, and spoke on their behalf in terms of their treatment in the workplace.

Throughout her life and career, Clemmer confronted tensions that contemporary women journalists still face, such as how to be part of the journalistic fold without being criticized for not being feminine enough. Her career embodied an ideology that resisted constructions of mainstream journalism as a male field. While it would take generations for women to become more fully accepted in the journalistic fold, scholars and professionals seeking insight into the history of women in journalism ought to look not just at the examples of the century's more militant women journalists, but at journalists such as Mary Clemmer as well.

REFERENCES

Andrews, J. C. (1971). Mary E. Clemmer, *Notable American women, 1607–1950: A biographical dictionary,* vol. 1. (pp. 40–42). Cambridge, Mass.: Belknap Press of Harvard University Press.

Arthur's Home Magazine. 1884, December. Mary Clemmer, 670–672.

Beasley, M. H. (1978). Mary Clemmer Ames: A Victorian woman journalist. *Hayes Historical Journal,* 5763.

Beasley, M. H. (1983). Mary Clemmer Ames. *Dictionary of Literary Biography,* vol. 23. *American newspaper journalists, 1873–1900.* (pp. 3–7). Detroit, Mich.: Gale Research Co.

Bolton, S. K. (1884, August 28). Our Mary Clemmer. *Independent,* 1.

Bonner, S. (1875, February). Mary Clemmer. *The Cottage Hearth,* 29–30.

Cincinnati Commercial. (11 February 1878). Mary Clemmer, 5.

Hudson, E. (1885). *An American woman's life and work: A memorial of Mary Clemmer.* Boston: Ticknor & Co.

Literary News. (September 1884). Mary Clemmer Hudson, 263–264.

Washington (D.C.) Evening Star. (1884, August 19). Death of Mary Clemmer Hudson, 1.

Whiting, L. (1884). Mary Clemmer, in *Our famous women: An authorized record.* Hartford, Conn.: Worthington.

Manuscripts

A collection of letters written to Clemmer and a file of her columns are located at Rutherford B. Hayes Library, Fremont, Ohio.

Selected Publications

Victoire. (1864). New York: Carleton.
Eirene; or, A woman's right. (1871). New York: Putnam's.
A memorial of Alice and Phoebe Cary with some of their later poems. (1873). New York: Hurd & Houghton; London: Low; Houghton.
Outlines of men, women and things. (1873). New York: Hurd & Houghton.
His two wives. (1875). New York: Hurd & Houghton.
Ten years in Washington: Life and scenes in the national capital as a woman sees them. (1875). Hartford, Conn.: Worthington.
Memorial sketch of Elizabeth Emerson Atwater: Written for her friends. (1879). Buffalo, N.Y.: Courier Co.
Poems of life and nature. (1883). Boston, Mass.: Osgood.

SANDRA JEAN BALL-ROKEACH (1941–)

Amy I. Nathanson

Sandra Ball-Rokeach has made major contributions to communication and sociology through her work on the mass media, violence, and values. A self-labeled social analyst, Ball-Rokeach has resisted adhering to formal disciplinary boundaries so that she may speak to a larger audience who shares an interest in the social world regardless of their academic titles. She has a fascination for social issues, and her professional work is an extension of a deep-rooted intellectual curiosity. Her accomplishments and recognition were achieved despite the constant battles she faced as a woman in a male-dominated profession. She achieved success through perseverance and dedication, and is an inspiration for other women who face the challenge of proving themselves intellectually in a sexist environment.

FAMILY BACKGROUND

Sandra Ball-Rokeach was born in Ottawa, Canada, on October 27, 1941. The second born of four children, she was reared by her English parents. Prior to her marriage, Ball-Rokeach's mother, Ailsa Mary Neill, had completed some high school and worked at the telegraph in England. Ball-Rokeach's father, Leslie Wilson, earned his Ph.D. at the University of Manchester and worked as a physicist.

Ball-Rokeach received different messages from her parents regarding her career aspirations. Her mother was very supportive and encouraged her to go as far as she wanted professionally. Ball-Rokeach believes her mother identified with her, and wanted her daughter to accomplish what she herself had not had the opportunity to complete. In contrast, her father did not take his daughter's professional dreams as seriously. In his eyes, Ball-Rokeach should have been satisfied playing the part of a nice, happily married girl. Concerned that his daughter was rejecting her traditional sex role, Leslie Wilson was slow to see Ball-Rokeach as anything other than a homemaker.

Despite their opposite reactions to their daughter's vocational desires, Ball-Rokeach's parents were both very independent people who encouraged their children to explore and develop their own interests. As a result, Ball-Rokeach learned to value independence over orthodoxy and thus pursued a nontraditional career.

EDUCATION

Ball-Rokeach attended public schools throughout her education. She went to elementary school in College Park, Maryland, where she was a good student and was an active member of the boys' hardball team. Emulating their parents' commitment to independence, Ball-Rokeach and her sister comprised the entire female segment of the team. In the midst of her elementary school career, Ball-Rokeach's family moved to Altadena, California, where she completed both elementary and junior high school.

Always an observer of intergroup interactions, Ball-Rokeach believes she was born a sociologist of sorts. Her preadolescent years were particularly important to the young sociologist and taught her a number of lessons regarding the influence of social factors on intergroup behavior. Although not yet aware of the different treatment allotted to males and females, she had begun to take notice of how members of different socioeconomic and racial groups received inequitable attention.

Ball-Rokeach admits that her awareness of prejudicial treatment targeted at certain groups often transformed her from a well-behaved student to a "terror" who was not afraid to wreak havoc in the classrooms of teachers she did not respect. She remembers one incident in which she instigated a bunny-hop that led her peers out of the classroom of a disrespected teacher, into the hallway, and back into the room through a different door. Unfortunately, she also led her classmates to bunny-hop right into the school principal on the second round of their prank, a maneuver that landed the children in the vice-principal's office. As punishment, the school decided to expel the lower-class participants and only reprimand the middle-class Ball-Rokeach. But Ball-Rokeach contested their decision, announcing that if the others were going to be expelled, she too should be asked to leave. This early fight against social class prejudice ended up in a victory for Ball-Rokeach, for none of the children was expelled for the incident.

Ball-Rokeach credits her parents, whom she remembers as very fair people, for instilling in her the keen sense of justice that motivated her protest against the school's actions. Her parents' influence on her development as an independent, free-thinking individual was also apparent during her junior high school years. She remembers having difficulty accepting the behavior promoted by certain cliques, such as drinking, smoking, and sexual activity. Unlike the rest of her peer group, she did not embrace these ideals and, therefore, made a conscious effort to break away from the cliques. Although the social consequences of her move were difficult to face, she soon established her own following when others in her peer group also broke away from the cliques and joined her.

Looking back now, Ball-Rokeach believes that her deliberate separation from the cliques was fundamental to shaping her life course. Perhaps the positive consequences of her decision gave her the strength and confidence to fight the battles she would wage as a woman working in the male-dominated world of academia.

Ball-Rokeach attended two different high schools before she received her diploma. Although she began her high school career in a good public school in Pasadena, she graduated from a San Diego high school, where she studied with children whose families lived and worked on the Southern California ranches. Unfamiliar with this group of people, Ball-Rokeach was fascinated by the lifestyle of these "ranch kids." While she does not praise the education she received at this school, she appreciates the opportunity it gave her to interact with and learn about a completely new circle of people.

In 1959 Ball-Rokeach entered San Diego State University, where she was a triple major in sociology, English, and history. Although the workload was demanding, she enjoyed majoring in three different subjects. Many of her friends were English and history majors who enjoyed school, and, as a result, much of her social life centered around discussions and activities relating to school. In addition to these intellectual activities, Ball-Rokeach also maintained a full extracurricular life, spending as much time as possible outdoors, where she could stay in touch with nature. During college, she lead a well-balanced life, and thus she strove to learn as much as she could while still taking the time to enjoy herself.

Although she liked her English and history classes, Ball-Rokeach could not envision how these majors would culminate in a meaningful career. However, she believed that she could make a purposeful contribution to sociology, an area she saw as "primitive" and relatively unexplored. Reflecting on her first sociology class, she remembers thinking the material was "so stupid" and that so little knowledge had been accumulated. As a result, she believed she could truly make her mark in sociology. Although she considered other careers (among them the law, medicine, and professional tennis), she found the lifestyle of the college professor most appealing because it would allow her to more easily maintain the quality personal life she had led during her college years.

The vocational possibilities, combined with her long-standing interest in the social world, led Ball-Rokeach to seriously consider attending graduate school in sociology. In her senior year of college, Ball-Rokeach transferred from San Diego State to the University of Washington in order to get a taste of the leading department in sociology at that time. After earning her Bachelor's degree in sociology from the University of Washington in 1963, she decided to continue in the program. Although her major specialization during her graduate career was social psychology and deviance, Ball-Rokeach admits that her first and most enduring intellectual love was theory. To this day, she continues to seek an elegant, yet uncomplicated, conceptual framework for understanding sociology.

Ball-Rokeach faced many challenges as a female graduate student, most of them initiated by professors who refused to take her interests seriously. She reports that most women were simply not respected in academia, and instead of pursuing a professional career were expected to marry and have children. Her professors went so far as to tell her that she should crop her hair, put on glasses, and wear a barrel if she wanted to be taken seriously. As one of the first women to endure this sexist academic environment, Ball-Rokeach had no support group to help her face the challenges associated with being a minority. She also had no positive female role models. There were very few females in academia, and those few she did encounter were unwilling to identify with any collective goals of women and denied that there were any structural barriers to their advancement.

Despite these obstacles, Ball-Rokeach enjoyed a productive graduate career. Her Master's thesis explored the idea that leadership is not characteristic of certain individuals, but that situational demands determine who assumes that role. She successfully challenged the notion that leaders are born and in so doing confirmed that context is a defining element of leadership. Still fascinated by the problem and effects of context, Ball-Rokeach's dissertation involved an experiment that tested people's reactions and adaptations to a structurally ambiguous situation. Although her professors were wary of her ability to undertake the ambitious design, she saw the project through to its successful completion. Ball-Rokeach remembers that her dissertation was the most rewarding part of her graduate career because it allowed her to devote concentrated time to a project that she found fascinating but had to fight to complete because others considered it undoable and consequently very rebellious.

CAREER DEVELOPMENT

Ball-Rokeach secured her first job at the last minute, overcoming challenges related to sexism. Despite her stellar graduate school record, for employers the most glaring aspect of her file was her gender. Ball-Rokeach explained that, during this time, individuals did not apply for advertised university jobs. Instead, department heads controlled their students' job placement by recommending individuals for positions. Although women were consistently the strongest performers in graduate school, Ball-Rokeach says that, for the most part, men received interviews at the top-level institutions while highly qualified women were overlooked.

According to Ball-Rokeach, the individuals who controlled this process did not take her interest in academia seriously, assuming instead that she would get married and raise a family. Nevertheless, she persisted and finally convinced them that she was worthy of more serious treatment. Finally, in 1967 she obtained a job as an assistant professor at the University of Alberta in Edmonton, Canada. After one year there, she was recommended by her graduate school adviser, Otto Larsen, to serve as co-director of the Mass Media and Violence Task Force for the National Commission on the Causes and Prevention of Violence, a position she held from 1968 to 1969.

Ball-Rokeach characterizes her time spent working as co-director of the Task Force as "revolutionizing." Although she had physically separated herself from the academic environment, her mental devotion to her field remained intact and colored her interpretation of the experience. She was fascinated by the power structures of the corporate world. Working alongside politicians, lawyers, and other influential people, she learned a tremendous amount about power dynamics and the communication processes that characterize and perpetuate power structures. Just as she had done as a child, Ball-Rokeach played the role of observer, this time turning a professional assignment into a sociological case study of the corporate world.

Ball-Rokeach admits that she found the nature of her assignment "boring." Although she was not especially interested in the psychology of media effects, the results of the report sparked considerable national interest. The report was the first to suggest that the mass media do in fact make children more violent. This conclusion prompted President Richard Nixon to accept the recommendation of Senator Pastore to appoint the Surgeon General's Scientific Advisory Committee to investigate the issue further.

After serving on the Task Force, Ball-Rokeach returned to the University of Alberta for one more year. She then accepted a job as a political sociologist at Michigan State University, where her future husband, Milton Rokeach, was a professor of psychology. She then spent two years as a visiting professor at the University of Western Ontario until 1972, when she and her husband moved to Washington State University where they remained for the next 14 years. After having moved around the country for most of her life, Ball-Rokeach said it was good finally to settle down for a while. As a member of the highly regarded Sociology Department, Ball-Rokeach remembers that Washington State was a great place to be and felt satisfied working with the department's high-quality, supportive faculty.

In 1986 Ball-Rokeach made a major career decision by joining the faculty at the University of Southern California, where she currently holds positions in The Annenberg School for Communication and a courtesy appointment in the Department of Sociology. Prior to her move, Ball-Rokeach's sociological approach was often pursued independently of mass communication. However, she had never lost interest in studying the social power of the mass media. Needing to prioritize her research interests, she decided to focus on the mass media and accepted the position with The Annenberg School, a move that culminated in her appointment as doctoral program chair in 1992 and co-director of the School of Communication in 1994.

At the private University of Southern California, Ball-Rokeach realized, with some discomfort, that many economically advantaged undergraduates define the teacher-student relation as a provider-customer relationship. This realization came at the same time that she found it increasingly hard to distinguish most universities from the corporate world. Nevertheless, Ball-Rokeach believes the struggle to place academic over corporate values is worth it. In her mind, the move to USC was valuable. In particular, she praises the university's resources as well as the high quality of the doctoral students. Despite the inconveniences of living in Los Angeles, she finds the turbulent city a fascinating place to live and work.

MAJOR CONTRIBUTIONS AND ACHIEVEMENTS

Ball-Rokeach's early work in mass communication focused on the role of the mass media in legitimizing and perpetuating violence in American society. Her work as co-director of the Task Force on Mass Media and Violence for the National Commission on the Causes and Prevention of Violence with Robert K. Baker culminated in a massive, 600-page report titled "Violence and the Media," which now serves as a landmark publication in the mass communication field. Within this volume, the results of a content analysis of prime-time television programs conducted by Professor George Gerbner and his colleagues at The Annenberg School for Communication, University of Pennsylvania, findings from a nationwide survey of Americans' beliefs about and experience with violence. This comparison of the real world with the media world revealed startling discrepancies between the two in terms of the prevalence of violence. Overall, televised violence occurred much more frequently than real-world violence during 1968 and 1969. However, the two worlds showed remarkable similarity among respondents who preferred violent media content, had more actual experiences with violence, and subscribed to norms that tolerated violence.

Baker and Ball-Rokeach (1969) concluded that television can legitimize and reinforce both violent beliefs and violent actions. They also suggested that the long-term effects of exposure to televised violence may even condition nonviolent viewers into accepting and subsequently enacting violent behavior. By highlighting the role of television in reinforcing and even instilling in viewers violent beliefs and tendencies, this project forced other researchers to reexamine the power and influence of the mass media in contemporary society and served as an inspiration for a number of research projects sponsored by the Surgeon General (1972) on the relationship between television and social behavior.

Although she was asked to write a report on the psychological effects of televised violence, Ball-Rokeach preferred to take a sociological perspective in her own work. Concerned with macro-level legitimizations of violence, she also investigated the value systems of groups that typically engage in violent acts. Initially, she addressed "subculture theories," giving particular attention to that espoused by Wolfgang and Ferracutti (1967). She challenged the subculture of violence thesis (see Ball-Rokeach, 1973) by refuting its claim that violence is performed by individuals whose attitudes and values are different from those of nonviolent persons. Her analysis subsequently became a widely contested publication on both theoretical and methodological grounds.

Among this study's most recognized contributions is its unique conceptualization of values. Rather than having respondents answer "one-value questions" in which distinct values are evaluated one at a time, Ball-Rokeach used the Rokeach Value Survey (1967), which asks participants to rank values so that their relative importance can be assessed and a hierarchy of values can be assumed. This concept of value hierarchies guided her later work, prompting her to investigate the stability of American values over time (see Rokeach & Ball-Rokeach, 1989). This work measured societal values over a 13-year period and found that, overall, American values remained relatively stable, but that the ranking for "equality" declined rather quickly and dramatically. Ball-Rokeach explains that the drop in equality is a particularly important finding, given that rankings of the value are positively correlated with favorable attitudes and behavior regarding such issues as civil rights and gender equality. In conjunction with this piece, she offered a formal explanation for why societal values remain stable and what may prompt them to change using the post-hoc critical analysis she conducted with Irving Tallman on the civil rights movement as her theoretical base (see Ball-Rokeach & Tallman, 1979). This line of research suggested that changes in society's collective value systems occur when individuals engage in moral self-confrontations and discover inconsistencies either within their value systems or between their values and behaviors.

These ideas laid the groundwork for the massive, nationwide experiment she conducted with Milton Rokeach and Joel Grube which tested the influence of television on American values (Ball-Rokeach, Rokeach, & Grube, 1984). Their Great American Values Test investigated the possibility that television prompts changes in societal value systems by endorsing certain values, thereby leading viewers with incompatible values to modify their beliefs in order to remain consistent with the televised norms. In addition to incorporating a belief system theory grounded in what they called self-confrontation, this study also used a revised version of a dependency model of mass media effects that Ball-Rokeach had first introduced eight years previously (see Ball-Rokeach & DeFleur, 1976). The elaborated model provided a framework for understanding both media exposure and media effects in terms of the nature and intensity of individuals' dependency relations with the media. The experiment provided the first empirical test of hypotheses derived from this model.

To examine television's impact on viewers' value systems and accompanying behaviors, Ball-Rokeach, Rokeach, and Grube wrote and produced a 30-minute television program called "The Great American Values Test," which featured "Lou Grant" star Ed Asner and then anchorperson of ABC's "Good Morning America" Sandy Hill as co-hosts. In 1979 this show was simultaneously aired on all three of the local commercial stations in the Tri-Cities area of eastern Washington. The first half of the program featured a general discussion of values: what they are, how they are measured, and some of the findings regarding value differences between members of various demographic groups. The second half of the program provided viewers with a more detailed review of results from these studies, pointed out some of the inconsistencies, and encouraged the audience to interpret the findings. This part of the program was designed to prompt viewers to reflect on their own value systems and to evaluate their internal consistency and compatibility with idealized concepts of self.

The results from this massive project suggested that television has the potential to influence and shape viewers' attitudes, values, and especially their behaviors. However, these findings did not support the all-powerful conception of the mass media upheld by direct effects models such as the magic bullet theory. Rather, the results from the Great American Values Test suggested that individual variables, such as media dependency and viewing habits, are also important determinants of the extent to which television maintains its influence.

This study was important not only because it empirically demonstrated the long-term effects of television on viewers' attitudes, values, and behaviors, but also because it used a natural setting in which viewers had the option of exposing themselves to the stimulus. As a result, the process of selective exposure (a phenomenon that necessarily accompanies television viewing behavior) could be addressed in their discussion of mass media effects. The external validity of the Great American Values Test allowed the researchers a unique opportunity to examine mass media effects as they most naturally occur. Ball-Rokeach reports that the study was ideal because it overcame all of her own objections to research. Today, she considers the project to be one of her biggest accomplishments.

Looking toward the future, Ball-Rokeach hopes to outline the theoretical development and empirical support of media systems dependency theory in one book, as well as integrate value theory and research into that framework. On a larger scale, she hopes to better understand the causes and implications of our dynamic society. Challenged by its continual reorganization, she is particularly interested in how communication phenomena affect the potential and actuality of societal transformation.

CRITICAL EVALUATION OF CONTRIBUTIONS
AND ACHIEVEMENTS

Although Ball-Rokeach's theoretical contributions to the conceptualization of values have been very well received, her methodological tactics have been the subject of some controversy. One such criticism came from Schuman, Steeh, and Bobo (1990) and is aimed at her endorsement of ''two-value questions'' (in which subjects are forced to select one of two desirable options) as a superior means of tapping respondents' values over other survey formats. Rokeach and

Ball-Rokeach (1989) admit that they "assume that responses to two-value questions will come closer to the 'truth' than will responses to one-value questions because two-value survey questions will activate, as in real life, a person's value priorities rather than how the person feels about one value considered in isolation" (p. 780). However, Schuman et al. (1990) argued that this assumption was not justified in Rokeach and Ball-Rokeach's interpretation of attitude data collected for Schuman, Steeh, and Bobo's 1985 publication, and led them to regard only some of the 1985 findings (that is, responses elicited from two-value questions) as meaningful.

Schuman et al. (1990) claimed that Rokeach and Ball-Rokeach's selective interpretation of their data not only was a bad decision, but was also poorly conducted and flawed. They argued that Rokeach and Ball-Rokeach's erroneously labeled one item (tapping attitudes toward desegregation) a two-value question when in reality it presented respondents with three alternatives: one supporting desegregation, one supporting strict segregation, and one supporting something in between these extremes. While Rokeach and Ball-Rokeach concluded that the general trend they observed during 1971 and 1974 toward choosing the middle alternative indicated a decline in egalitarian values, Schuman et al. argued that they had ignored more genuine two-value questions in the attitude survey which indicated a trend toward egalitarian values. Given that a consensus regarding the proper operationalization and measurement of values has not yet been reached, it is not surprising that Schuman et al. and others (e.g., Magura, 1975) have leveled methodological criticisms against Ball-Rokeach's work on values. Despite the criticisms, there is little doubt that she has made significant contributions to research on values. Her work—and the criticisms of it—have inspired further debate and research, which will ultimately facilitate the development of a more refined notion of values.

Ball-Rokeach's work in mass communication has been criticized on a more general level for failing to say anything new. Ball-Rokeach accepts this criticism and recognizes the challenge she and other scholars face in making meaningful contributions to our collective knowledge. Her "relational mode of analysis" has also been subject to some debate from media effects scholars because of its nontraditional approach. Most media effects research is conducted from a micro-level perspective that centers on the individual's psychological reactions to media content. However, Ball-Rokeach's analysis focuses on the relationship between the media and their audiences rather than on the characteristics of either element alone. Ball-Rokeach's explication of this interrelationship has been criticized for lacking clarity. Given that her approach asks readers to consider media effects in a way that is not commonly attempted, Ball-Rokeach understands and accepts the critique. In response, she has challenged herself to be so clear in her explications that subsequent debates of her work may evolve from a level of shared understanding rather than digress into arguments regarding the proper interpretation of her conceptual framework.

INTEGRATION OF PERSONAL AND PROFESSIONAL LIFE

Ball-Rokeach met her husband, Milton Rokeach, when she was fresh out of graduate school and working as the co-director of the Task Force. She was familiar with his work in psychology and had admired its eloquence. Believing that the report would benefit from his contributions, she called him to ask if he would author a paper for the project, a request that he subsequently refused. Nonetheless, the two remained in contact and built a relationship that lasted 20 years until Rokeach died in 1988.

As a couple in academia, the two faced a number of unique challenges. In particular, Ball-Rokeach was concerned that her relationship with the older, established Rokeach would lead others to assume that she was his student and that their relationship gave her certain professional advantages. Wanting her own independent recognition, Ball-Rokeach refrained from collaborating with her husband on research until later in her career, after she had already established a name for herself. Their involvement in academia also made it difficult for them to secure desirable jobs at the same institution. Fortunately, the two were not competing for positions within the same department. Nonetheless, Ball-Rokeach notes that sacrifice and compromise were necessary survival tactics for maintaining their happy marriage.

Their 23-year age difference also presented challenges for them. Although Rokeach was unusually committed to racial and social equality, he had difficulty understanding the struggles that women endured in a patriarchal society. Ball-Rokeach remembers one incident in particular that she felt was indicative of larger issues surrounding their relationship. Ball-Rokeach was in the kitchen washing the dishes while Rokeach was looking over a draft of something she had written. Rokeach was irritated that his wife had asked him to review a paper that had spelling errors and uncrossed t's, and made it clear that he would not read imperfect copies of her work. Ball-Rokeach retaliated by pointing out that while he was reading her paper, she had been re-washing pots that he had left ''imperfect''—she questioned why she had to be perfect in both the domestic and professional domains while he was allowed to be sloppy in one area. Rokeach rejected her analogy and implied that he simply did not have to meet domestic standards, but that she was in fact subject to criticisms from both the domestic and the professional worlds. The incident ended in laughter when Rokeach finally realized that he was upholding a sexist double-standard. For Ball-Rokeach, however, it highlighted the sentiment endorsed by Rokeach and others of his generation regarding the privilege of men to prioritize their responsibilities over women's challenge to meet the standards of both worlds simultaneously.

Although the two had what Ball-Rokeach describes as ''knock-down-drag-out fights'' regarding these sorts of issues, ultimately, Rokeach made tremendous strides in understanding the need to fight for women's rights.

As a wife and stepmother, Ball-Rokeach endured a number of medical crises involving her family. Rokeach's youngest daughter was diagnosed with leukemia, and Rokeach was seriously ill for 12 years. During this time, Ball-Rokeach's family remained her first priority, which precluded her from making many professional commitments. Her coping strategy during this stressful time was to work as hard as she could during reprieves from medical crises and then devote her attention to her family during times of illness.

Despite the hardships of her personal life, Ball-Rokeach has resisted taking herself or her work too seriously; instead, she has sought to have fun with her work. She tells her students that it is more important for them to love the questions they ask rather than the answers they receive so that their research remains interesting and personally relevant. She urges them to resist rigid, formal boundaries that may discourage their creative inquiries. Her commitment to this lesson is evident in her own work, for she has integrated ideas formally existing in distinct disciplines within a more encompassing approach. She feels that questions posed within academic "cubbyholes" become boring, mechanical, and often unworthy of reply.

Certainly, defying boundaries has not been unusual for Ball-Rokeach. Her commitment to independent thought has shaped both her personal and professional life by urging her to pursue interests and ideas that might otherwise remain unchallenged by more traditional perspectives. Her success is testimony to the value of perseverance and a strong professional commitment, and serves as an inspiration for others who must endure similar challenges. Her scholarly contributions continue to enrich our collective understanding of human society.

NOTE

All quotations and biographical information not otherwise referenced are drawn from telephone interviews with Sandra Ball-Rokeach conducted by the author on June 5 and June 9, 1994.

REFERENCES

Baker, R. K., & Ball, S. J. (1969). *Violence and the media.* Washington, D.C.: Government Printing Office.

Ball-Rokeach, S. J. (1973). Values and violence: A test of the subculture of violence thesis. *American Sociological Review,* 38, 736–749.

Ball-Rokeach, S. J., & DeFleur, M. L. (1976). A dependency model of mass media effects. *Communication Research,* 3, 3–21.

Ball-Rokeach, S. J., Rokeach, M., & Grube, J. W. (1984). *The great American values test.* New York: Free Press.

Ball-Rokeach, S. J., & Tallman, I. (1979). Social movements as moral confrontations: With special reference to civil rights. In M. Rokeach (ed.), *Understanding human values.* (pp. 82–94). New York: Free Press.

Magura, S. (1975). Is there a subculture of violence? *American Sociological Review,* 40, 831–835.

Rokeach, M. (1967). *Value survey.* Sunnydale, Calif.: Halgren Tests.

Rokeach, M., & Ball-Rokeach, S. J. (1989). Stability and change in American value priorities, 1968–1981. *American Psychologist,* 44, 775–784.

Schuman, H., Steeh, C., & Bobo, L. (1985). *Racial attitudes in America: Trends and interpretations.* Cambridge, Mass.: Harvard University Press.

Schuman, H., Steeh, C., & Bobo, L. (1990). A clarification. *American Psychologist,* 46, 674–675.

Surgeon General's Scientific Advisory Committee on Television and Social Behavior (1972). *Television and growing up: The impact of televised violence.* Report to the Surgeon General, United States Public Health Service. Washington, D.C.: Government Printing Office.

Wolfgang, M., & Ferracutti, F. (1967). *The subculture of violence: Towards and integrated theory in criminology.* New York: Tavistock.

Additional Representative Publications by Sandra Ball-Rokeach

Ball-Rokeach, S. J. (1971). The legitimization of violence. In J. F. Short and M. E. Wolfgang (eds.), *Collective Violence.* Chicago: Aldine.

Ball-Rokeach, S. J. (1973). From pervasive ambiguity to a definition of the situation. *Sociometry,* 36, 378–389.

Ball-Rokeach, S. J. (1976). Receptivity to sexual equality. *Pacific Sociological Review,* 19, 519–540.

Ball-Rokeach, S. J. (1985). The origins of individual media system dependency: A sociological framework. *Communication Research,* 12, 485–510.

Ball-Rokeach, S. J., & Cantor, M. G. (eds.). (1986). *Media, audience and social structure.* Beverly Hills, Calif.: Sage.

Ball-Rokeach, S. J., & Loges, W. E. (1994). Choosing equality: The correspondence between attitudes about race and the value of equality. *Journal of Social Issues,* 50(4), 9–18.

Ball-Rokeach, S. J., & Loges, W. E. (1996). Making choices: Media roles in the construction of value-choices. In C. Seligman, J. Olson, & M. Zanna (eds.), *Values: The Ontario Symposium* Vol. 8 (pp. 277–298). Hillsdale, N.J.: Erlbaum.

Ball-Rokeach, S. J., Power, G. J., Guthrie, K. K., & Waring, H. R. (1990). Value framing abortion in the United States: An application of media system dependency theory. *International Journal of Public Opinion Research,* 2, 249–273.

DeFleur, M. L., & Ball-Rokeach, S. J. (1989). *Theories of mass communication,* 5th ed. New York: Longman.

Loges, W. E., & Ball-Rokeach, S. J. (1993). Dependency relations newspaper readership. *Journalism Quarterly,* 70, 602–614.

MARGARET BOURKE-WHITE (1904–1971)

Ginger Rudeseal Carter

The photojournalism career of Margaret Bourke-White spanned more than 30 years at a time when women were not accepted in the field. Hers was a career of milestones: She was the first woman to be certified as World War II correspondent, later photographing a bombing raid and a prison camp liberation. *Life* magazine featured her work on its first cover and offered her the first mission to the moon as soon as transportation could be arranged. She interviewed and photographed Gandhi just hours before his assassination in India. Her career ended by a battle with debilitating Parkinson's disease, Bourke-White continued to be a fighter, undergoing experimental brain surgery twice, then writing her autobiography.

Through her innovative photography and writing, Margaret Bourke-White brought photography respect as an art form and as a medium of communication; her independent lifestyle pointed the way toward greater personal and professional freedom for women (Daffron, 1986). All this came from a fascination with her father's business and a love of snakes.

FAMILY BACKGROUND AND EDUCATION

Margaret Bourke White (she added the hyphen after her first divorce) was born on June 14, 1904, in Bronx, New York, the second of three children of Minnie Bourke and Joseph White. The family moved to Bound Brook, New Jersey, two years later. The day of Maggie's birth was also her parents' wedding anniversary and Flag Day. Minnie Bourke and Joe White were lovers of the outdoors; Joe was also an avid amateur photographer. In her biography *Portrait of Myself* (1963), Bourke-White wrote that her parents' interest in natural history was so lasting that "it nearly made a biologist of me instead of a photographer"

(Bourke-White, 1963). She planned to become a herpetologist, studying snakes and traveling around the world, "doing all the things women never do." Bourke-White collected snakes and turtles, housing them in wire cages built by her father.

Her father's influence as an engineer (he was an inventor who later invented a portable printing press for use in World War I) would also have a profound effect on Bourke-White's later photographs. In her autobiography, Bourke-White recalled visiting factories with her father, watching the blackness of the factory being broken by the "sudden magic of flowing metal and flying sparks." It was a memory, she wrote, that was so vivid and so alive it shaped her whole career.

As a child, Bourke-White was not interested in photography, even though her father enjoyed it. Her love was reptiles. After winning a coveted school essay contest her sophomore year at Plainfield High School in New Jersey, Bourke-White wrote that she used her $15 prize money to purchase three books: The Dickerson *Frog Book,* the Holland *Moth Book,* and the Ditmars *Reptile Book.*

EDUCATION AND FIRST MARRIAGE

Bourke-White enrolled at Columbia University in 1923, but at the end of her first semester, her father suffered a stroke and died 24 hours later. Joseph White's death left Bourke-White without her beloved father, the major influence of her life; his death also left the family without money. Bourke-White borrowed money from a family friend to complete her freshman year at Columbia, working odd jobs to make extra cash.

Two things happened after her father's death that profoundly changed Bourke-White's life. First, she took up photography, her father's favorite hobby. Second, she took an art class that allowed her to study with renowned photographer Clarence White. A leader in the pictorial school of photography, White taught photography as an art form rather than a documentary photography style. In his class, Bourke-White experimented with gauzy, soft-focus photography that looked like a watercolor painting. Minnie White, still suffering financially from her husband's death, scraped together $20 and bought her daughter a second-hand Ica Reflex camera with a "crack straight through the lens." Bourke-White would use that camera for the next six years.

After a summer as a photographer and nature counselor at a camp in Connecticut, Bourke-White, using money loaned her by family friends, transferred to the University of Michigan in Ann Arbor, where she enrolled in the herpetology program to study with zoologist Alexander Ruthven. There Bourke-White studied hard, taking photographs for the school yearbook and newspaper for extra cash. One day while walking into the student cafeteria, she was literally trapped in a revolving door by Everett Chapman; he wouldn't let her out of the door, she wrote, until they scheduled a date. A graduate engineering student, "Chappie" reminded her of her late father, Bourke-White recalled in her au-

tobiography. They fell in love and were married on Friday, June 13, 1924—
one day before Bourke-White's twentieth birthday. An omen preceded the wedding when, the night before, as Chappie put the finishing touches on the hand-
made ring, it broke into two pieces. This, Bourke-White wrote, was a sign of
the next two years to come.

After a short honeymoon, Mr. and Mrs. Everett Chapman moved to Indiana
where Chappie taught at Purdue and Margaret continued her studies. Since
Bourke-White was older than her fellow students, and married as well, making
friends was difficult. The Chapmans moved from Purdue to Cleveland, Ohio in
1925; by day Bourke-White worked at the Cleveland Natural History Museum,
and in the evenings she took classes at Case Western Reserve University. This
was her fourth college in four years. Working women were rare in 1926, and
Bourke-White wrote that she took the job to make sure she could support herself.
The next year, her marriage failing, she left Chapman and transferred to Cornell
University in Ithaca, New York, "for its beautiful waterfalls and campus."
There, at the suggestion of Ralph Steiner, with whom she had studied in Clarence White's class, Bourke-White shifted from the soft-focus style of photography to an opposite style that made building photographs look like paintings.
That Christmas she sold copies of her photographs to students. While at Cornell,
she was hired to shoot the cover photographs of the Cornell alumni magazine
each month. She recalled in her book that alumni who worked in architecture
said she had promise in the growing field of architectural photography, but she
wanted a second opinion. In a career-shaping move, Bourke-White took her
portfolio to New York during Easter vacation to architect Benjamin Moskowitz;
she caught him as he was leaving to get his commuter train. Bourke-White
showed him her photos as they waited for the elevator. Moskowitz missed the
train, called in his associates, and Bourke-White left the office with the assurance
that she could "walk into any architect's office in the country with that portfolio
and get work." Herpetology was abandoned, and after graduation a few months
later, Bourke-White moved back to Cleveland, divorced Chapman at City Hall,
legally changed her name to Margaret Bourke-White, and opened the Bourke-
White Studio.

CAREER DEVELOPMENT

Bourke-White's first job was to photograph a school for two Cornell alumni;
they had already hired three photographers who had not worked out. Her photographs put the school in a bright new light, bringing cash to Bourke-White
Studios. She learned more about her business through trial and error, developing
and printing her photographs in her tiny one-room apartment.

Bourke-White met the man who would become an important early mentor on
a windy day in Cleveland in 1928. Traveling without a camera, she spotted an
elderly preacher on a soapbox, bellowing to the pigeons in the square. Bourke-
White ran into an adjacent camera store and borrowed a camera for the photo-

graph; when she returned it, she met Alfred Hall Bemis. For the next two years, Bemis and his technician Earl Lieter would be her technical advisers, teaching her about developing, flash photography, and printing. Bemis and Lieter also helped her in early photo shoots for John Hill, one of the founders of the Hill and Knowlton Public Relations firm. Hill, engaged in the new field of corporate publicity, hired Bourke-White to photograph the buildings of his clients, including the Union Trust Bank. According to his autobiography, Hill also helped her gain entrance to the photo shoot she had desired since returning to Cleveland—the Otis Steel Mill. Armed with a letter of introduction and her portfolio, Bourke-White persuaded Otis Steel president Elroy Kulas that his mill was indicative of the hope in America. Kulas gave Bourke-White the run of his establishment while he was away in Europe for the next five months.

During that time, Bourke-White and Bemis visited the mill nightly, but the shots lacked the intensity and color of the steel ''pours.'' Two traveling salesmen, who were Bemis' acquaintances introduced her to two new products for photographs which produced startling results. The first innovation, fill lighting using flares designed for movie stunts, allowed Bourke-White to photograph the path of sparks; this was the first time sparks had ever been recorded with a still camera. The second was a more sensitive Agfa Gaevert paper that gave the final prints the contrast they had lacked. When Kulas returned, he paid Bourke-White $1,600 for her photographs and published a special report for stockholders called *The Story of Steel.* A photo of the mill's 200-ton ladle won Bourke-White first prize at the Cleveland Museum of Art Show in May 1928. Representatives from other steel mills asked Bourke-White to photograph their operations. Most poignantly Bourke-White felt a kinship with her late father which she had never before experienced. She wrote that she felt his presence while she worked.

Early in 1929, she received a telegram from Henry Luce, founder of *Time* magazine, inviting her to come to New York at his expense. Bourke-White later wrote that at first she thought about declining the interview; *Time* only photographed political figures, and she was not interested in that. It took only a few minutes into the meeting with Luce and his associate Parker Lloyd-Smith, however, to discover that she was wanted for her industrial photography skills. Luce was launching a new magazine, which would later be named *Fortune,* and he wanted to include her innovative, dramatic photos of industry. Bourke-White was hired, moved temporarily to New York, and on July 4, 1929, embarked on her first assignment: shoemaking in Lynn, Massachusetts. This assignment was followed by orchid raising in New Jersey and meatpacking in the Chicago stockyards. Not only was she doing what no woman had done before, Bourke-White was also shooting photos of subjects few men had photographed in the past.

It was at one such shoot for a future issue of *Fortune* that Bourke-White missed one of the greatest news stories of the century. That day, in October 1929, Bourke-White and an assistant were in Boston photographing the interior of a bank at night; vice presidents lingered late that day, darting in and out of the photos. Bourke-White wrote that when she inquired about the lateness of the employees, one responded, "Didn't you know, the bottom dropped out." Bourke-White wrote that she had been studying a football guidebook for a date and had not seen the evening's papers. She had missed the news, and she was probably the only photographer inside a bank that fateful night.

In spite of the crash of 1929, *Fortune* made its debut in February 1930. For the next six years, Bourke-White worked as a photographer for the magazine as well as for advertising agencies. Her photographs, which she had once sold for $10, now commanded more than $100 each. She was almost as well known for her personal adventures as her photographs. She dressed very dramatically—designer hats, stunning colors—and even used camera cloths that matched her accessories. Goldberg (1986) wrote that Bourke-White "willingly collaborated in the creation of the Bourke-White legend." Since her return to Cleveland, she had a particular style about her: she raced around the world, dangled from skyscrapers, and worked day and night. She was "totally dedicated and utterly fearless" (Goldberg, 1986).

Bourke-White's work for *Fortune* brought her another coup in June 1930 when she accompanied her editor, Parker Lloyd-Smith, to Germany and Russia. The USSR had begun its Five-Year Plan for industrialization in 1928 and had not allowed any photographs of the process. Yet when *Fortune* expressed interest in documenting the advancement, the Russians encouraged the magazine to send Bourke-White, whose industrial photos were world-famous. When she arrived in the country, she was made a guest of the government. Her work appeared in *Fortune,* and it was followed by her first book, *Eyes on Russia,* which appeared to good notices in 1931. Combined with her *Fortune* assignments, this book made Bourke-White the best known photographer in America. She returned to Russia twice more in the next two years. Interestingly enough, on these subsequent trips, Bourke-White brought along a movie camera and sold her footage. The film was made into two short travelogues titled *Eyes on Russia* (which she narrated herself) and *Red Republic.* Bourke-White, however, chose to stay with still photography.

Back from Russia, Bourke-White returned to advertising work and photographed airplanes in flight for Eastern Airlines advertisements; she had invited her mother, Minnie, to fly on one of the planes. Minnie maintained an active lifestyle at age 66 and was taking classes at Columbia University. Just two days before she was to fly for the first time, Minnie announced her plans to her classmates, collapsed on the floor, and never regained consciousness. She died two days later.

Bourke-White's photographic style began to change in early 1936 when she met author Erskine Caldwell at a cocktail party. Caldwell had written the hugely popular *Tobacco Road* and was looking for a photographer to accompany him through the South, taking photos for a new book. Bourke-White got the job, although she was told that Caldwell did not like her work. They planned to begin the work in Augusta, Georgia on June 11, 1936. Needing to close her studio and home before she left on the shoot, Bourke-White called Caldwell in

Wrens, Georgia, asking for a one-week extension, whereupon he promptly called off the project. She wrote that she packed everything and took a midnight plane to Georgia, sent Caldwell a letter of apology, and they made up. After a rocky start, they traveled across Georgia, Alabama, Mississippi, South Carolina, Louisiana, and Arkansas, photographing and writing about the sharecroppers in the region. The book, *You Have Seen Their Faces,* was published in 1937 with a joint credit line. Although the book sold well, it was unpopular in the South because of the stereotypical portrayal of Southerners; many called its contents propaganda. This book, followed by James Agee and Walker Evans' *Let Us Now Praise Famous Men* (1941), is considered the first in a new era of documentary photographic projects (Stott, 1977). Bourke-White wrote that this project changed her style of photography forever.

Other changes were in store for Bourke-White. When she returned to New York in the fall of 1936, Henry Luce sent her out on her first assignment for *Life* magazine; Luce wanted a "photo essay" of Fort Peck Dam in Montana. She photographed the vast structure in her signature architectural style and then documented the way of life in the small Montana town of New Deal. The photo of the dam was the first *Life* cover on November 23, 1936; her photo essay of the people in the town both on the job and off took up the first nine pages, causing the editors to note that her work was "a revelation."

Bourke-White became one of four photographers listed on *Life*'s masthead, and the only woman photographer with a continuing by-line. She photographed the Louisville, Kentucky, flood of 1937 and documented the tyrannical empire of Boss Hague in Jersey City. In July 1937, *Life* sent Bourke-White to the Arctic with a day's notice, sailing with the governor-general of Canada, Lord Tweedsmuir; later, she flew above the Arctic Circle and photographed it, the first woman ever to do so. Her trip was punctuated with telegrams from Caldwell. The two began a romantic relationship in February 1937, although he was still married. That summer, Caldwell sent a telegram to the Arctic, addressed to "Honeychile, Arctic Circle." It pressed on: "Come home and marry me, signed Skinny." She stayed on assignment, returning home when the assignment was completed. *Life* featured two photo essays by Bourke-White in its next issue.

Caldwell loved "Kit," his nickname for Bourke-White, but he was married. His wife, Helen, divorced him on April 18, 1938, after she met Bourke-White. In the meantime, the two had traveled to Czechoslovakia and written *North of the Danube,* which was published to good reviews in 1939. On their return from Europe, Bourke-White recalled in her autobiography, reporters hounded them about the rumors of their impending marriage. Finally, on February 27, 1939, Caldwell and Bourke-White were married by a justice of the peace in a small church in Silver City, Nevada at sundown. They honeymooned in Hawaii and then settled in Darien, Connecticut. They planned to start a family, hoping for a baby daughter who would be named Patricia.

That fall, Bourke-White left for London where she photographed the blacked-out streets of London; then she traveled to Romania, Turkey, and the Middle

East. On her return, she and Caldwell embarked on a cross-country trip where they documented how Americans felt about the war. The result, a book called *Say, Is This the USA?*, was published in 1941. Bourke-White wrote that the photographs were not her best. She and Caldwell were beginning to experience trouble in their marriage, but still, in 1941, they traveled to war-torn Russia, where that July Bourke-White photographed German bombing raids on the Kremlin. A month later, she photographed Joseph Stalin. The couple returned to the states where they both entered the lecture circuit. Their marriage, however, had begun to crumble. By the time of the bombing of Pearl Harbor in 1941, the two were leading separate lives. Bourke-White wrote in her autobiography that she knew she needed to be of service to her government. Caldwell had a lucrative movie offer from Hollywood. She added that they "had five good, productive years," but she was relieved when it was over. They divorced in 1942.

That fall, Bourke-White was sent on the assignment of a lifetime: *Life* had arranged with the U.S. Air Force to accredit her as a war correspondent, the first woman to receive that honor. Bourke-White held the assimilated rank of lieutenant. While accredited, she photographed Prime Minister Winston Churchill on his sixty-eighth birthday; the photo of Churchill, birthday carnation in his pocket, ran on the cover of *Life*. Bourke-White also photographed Ethiopian King Haile Selassie and was given the honor of naming a B-17 bomber, known forever after as "the Flying Flitgun."

Although the Air Force allowed Bourke-White access to most aspects of the war's battles, it refused to allow her to fly on a B-17. She wrote in her autobiography that she wanted, more than anything, to photograph a bombing raid. In early 1943, she began the trip to Africa by Navy transport; in the middle of the night, the transport carrying Bourke-White and 6,000 others "because sea travel was safer" was torpedoed. She survived on a crowded lifeboat, taking pictures of the rescue on the one camera she had slipped into her *musette* bag in place of food rations. After Bourke-White was rescued, she was taken to the Algiers villa of General Jimmy Doolittle to recuperate. There, she received permission to go on that bombing raid since "she's gone through everything else." To prepare for the mission, Bourke-White had to learn to use the oxygen supply, replace the five cameras lost at sea, and prepare for the heat-and-cold extremes she would face while flying at 15,000 feet.

January 27, 1943, was the day of the bombing mission, and Bourke-White wrote that the day was bright and clear; she was assigned to a squadron assigned to bomb a major German air base in Tunis. Flying in the lead ship, she filmed the crewmen at work as well as the bombs falling. Her plane was hit twice in the raid, and two others on the mission were shot down. She wrote in her autobiography that she never thought about the fact that she, too, might not return. *Life* ran the photo essay in its next issue, proclaiming on the cover "*Life*'s Bourke-White Goes a Bombin' " and pictured her in her flight suit. That photo graced the back flap of *Portrait of Myself*.

Bourke-White documented two more major missions during World War II. After viewing war from the air, she joined the ground troops in Italy for the "caterpillar view," where she met and fell in love with Major Jerry Papert, who begged Bourke-White to marry him. She stalled, and tragically, he was captured by the Germans and died when the field hospital in which he was sequestered was bombed.

Bourke-White followed his death with a photo essay on the staff of the field Army hospital working in Italy in 1944; the photos were lost in the mail and never found or published. She later published a book of her photos from this mission titled *They Called It "Purple Heart Valley"* (1944). The work was similar in style to the work she pioneered with Erskine Caldwell, only Bourke-White now wrote the text as well as photographing the soldiers.

Her final mission in 1945 was to accompany General George Patton's army on its final march across Germany. On this mission, Bourke-White saw the Nazi work camps and offices. She was with Patton's troops when they liberated the camp at Buchenwald; Patton ordered the 1,000 people of the town of Weimer to see what had happened so close to their homes. Bourke-White photographed the atrocities as well as the faces of the people in the town as they viewed the destruction. Her book *"Dear Fatherland: Rest Quietly"* spoke to the social necessity of war, reminding people to remember what people had sacrificed. Perhaps the most touching connection of this final assignment was that Bourke-White was of Jewish ancestry; her father was Jewish. Although Bourke-White rarely spoke of or even acknowledged her heritage, photographing Jews who had died at the hands of others could not have been an easy assignment. Her book was used as part of the evidence at the Nuremburg trials.

Bourke-White left her World War II duties at the rank of lieutenant colonel. Her work touched millions through her books and *Life* magazine photo essays. Upon her return to the United States, she was still *Life*'s star photographer. She continued to travel the world, write, deliver lectures, and take photographs; at age 42, she had traveled more than she ever dreamed she would as a child. She was, without question, the most influential and important photographer in the world.

Her first postwar *Life* assignment was in India, where in 1947 she examined the developing nation as it struggled to split from Great Britain. There she met Mohandas K. Gandhi, the leader of the nonviolent revolt. Bourke-White wrote in her book *Halfway to Freedom* that she considered herself fortunate to have witnessed and been able to document the historic early days of these two nations: India and Pakistan. In these countries Bourke-White experienced death, life, hunger, sickness, and strength. The photos in the book, taken during this and a subsequent trip, show the concern in the faces of the people.

Bourke-White wrote that Gandhi taught her an invaluable lesson about understanding a subject when he insisted that she learn to spin thread before she could photograph him spinning. It took two afternoons during a tight deadline time, but Bourke-White learned. She wrote that she was as close to awe as she had ever been when she was introduced to Gandhi. Given only three chances to photograph him, she succeeded on the third try; the photo she took is one of the most famous of the Indian leader. She returned to the states with her photos and notes and began *Halfway to Freedom* but found she had insufficient information to write.

Bourke-White returned to India in 1948 to find the country in the midst of a holy war. On the final day of her second visit, she met with Gandhi who at 78 was pale and frail, for he had been fasting. She interviewed him, telling him about *Halfway to Freedom.* Gandhi told Bourke-White that he had given up hope. They parted that afternoon, and Bourke-White wrote that she called "good-bye and good luck as the two parted." Hours later, on the way to evening prayers, Gandhi was assassinated. Bourke-White had received the last interview he had given. She remained in India a few more days, photographing the frenzy following the death; she also photographed the funeral pyre. *Halfway to Freedom* was completed and published in 1949.

Dangerous assignments—first to the underground gold mines of South Africa, next to the jungles of Korea, and then to anti-American rallies in Japan—continued to beckon Bourke-White. With each assignment, she took the art of photojournalism to a new level while completing assignments no woman had ever attempted before. The photo which she wrote was "the most significant in her career" was taken in Korea, where she accompanied a released Korean prisoner to a reunion with his family. She wrote, "In a whole lifetime of taking pictures, a photographer knows that he will take one picture that seems the most important of all. And you hope that everything will be right." That afternoon, it was. She photographed the reunion of Nim Churl-Jin and his mother, who had thought her son was dead.

Bourke-White returned to her home in Darien in January 1953. That summer, she completed a photo essay on Jesuits for *Life.* This became her last book, *A Report on the American Jesuits,* written with John LaFarge.

Late that summer, Bourke-White wrote that she could no longer deny that something was wrong with her physically. She had developed "staggers" after she rose from sitting while on assignment in Korea. The staggers were more embarrassing than anything else, she added; they were accompanied by a dull ache in her leg that wouldn't go away. By that summer, she had trouble moving, and the pains were in her arms and shoulders. What Bourke-White did not know was that she was in the early stages of Parkinson's Disease, a neurological disorder that attacks the brain and affects movement. Parkinson's leaves the mind intact but the body helpless; she was no longer "Maggie the Indestructible." She called the disease "My Mysterious Malady" and wrote about it in the final chapters of her autobiography. She undertook physical therapy, but her weakening condition forced her retirement from *Life* in 1957, 21 years after her first cover photo. Between 1955 and 1962 she wrote *Portrait of Myself* at home in Darien. During that time, she underwent two experimental brain operations to slow the spread of the disease. In 1959, Bourke-White allowed *Life* photographer Alfred Eisenstaedt to document her life after the operation; his photo essay was turned into a television movie, "The Margaret Bourke-White Story," starring Teresa Wright and Eli Wallach. She even served as a technical adviser to the filming.

Through the 1960s she fought the disease, writing at home and trying new experimental treatments. In 1971 Bourke-White fell, cracked several ribs, and was confined to Stamford Hospital. She died on August 27 of complications from Parkinson's; ironically, the big-picture *Life* magazine that had been Bourke-White's passport to the world went out of business the next year. Her photographs were donated to Syracuse University after her death.

Margaret Bourke-White wanted a life of travel and adventure, and she lived an incomparable life. She wrote that she did not like closed doors and always fought to get through them. This tenacity helped her land assignments that made her the envy of photographers—men and women alike—everywhere. Today, her work lives on at Syracuse University, where her photos are housed. Most of all, the doors she opened for photographers and journalists changed the field of documentary photography forever and created the field of photojournalism.

Bourke-White once wrote, "You are responsible for what you have done and the people whom you have influenced. In the end, it is only the work that counts." Her work, and her life, more than reflected that philosophy.

REFERENCES

Beasley, M., & Gibbons, S. (1993). *Taking their places: A documentary history of women in journalism.* Washington, D.C.: American University Press.

Bourke-White, M. (1942). *Shooting the Russians.* New York: Simon & Schuster.

Bourke-White, M. (1949). *Halfway to freedom.* New York: Simon & Schuster.

Bourke-White, M. (1963). *Portrait of myself.* New York: Simon & Schuster.

Caldwell, E., & Bourke-White, M. (1937). *You have seen their faces.* New York: Viking Press.

Daffron, C. (1986). *Margaret Bourke-White: Photographer.* New York: Chelsea House Publishers.

Goldberg, V. (1986). *Margaret Bourke-White.* New York: Harper & Row Publishers.

Marzolf, M. (1977). *Up from the footnote.* New York: Hastings House.

Stott, W. (1977). *Documentary expression and thirties America.* New York: Oxford University Press.

Books and Photographic Essays by Margaret Bourke-White

The Bourke-White photography archive is housed at Syracuse University.

Bourke-White, M. (1931). *Eyes on Russia.* New York: Simon & Schuster.

Bourke-White, M. (1942). *Shooting the Russians.* New York: Simon & Schuster.

Bourke-White, M. (1944). *They called it "Purple Heart Valley."* New York: Simon & Schuster.

Bourke-White, M. (1946). *Dear fatherland: Rest quietly.* New York: Simon & Schuster.

Bourke-White, M. (1949). *Halfway to freedom.* New York: Simon & Schuster.

Bourke-White, M., & Lafarge, F. (1956). *A report on the American Jesuits.* New York: Farrar, Straus, & Cadahy.

Caldwell, E., & Bourke-White, M. (1937). *You have seen their faces.* New York: Viking Press.

Caldwell, E., & Bourke-White, M. (1939). *North of the Danube.* New York: Viking Press.

Caldwell, E., & Bourke-White, M. (1941). *Say, is this the U.S.A.?* New York: Viking Press.

HELEN GURLEY BROWN
(1922–   )

Candace Lewis

There is a photo of Helen Gurley Brown lying poised in a leopard-skin blouse and short black skirt, her hand draped over an embroidered pillow. "Good girls go to heaven," the pillow reads. "Bad girls go everywhere" (*Psychology Today,* 1994, p. 23). For the past 30 years, Brown has gone places, reigning as the editor in chief of *Cosmopolitan,* a women's magazine known for the sexy models that grace its covers. Had it not been for Brown, however, such covers would never have graced the magazine.

The concept of the quintessential *Cosmo* girl as a sexy, fleshy model was developed and offered in her first book, best-seller *Sex and the Single Girl.* The book, based on her experiences as a young, single, working woman, discussed matters of life, love, sex, money, and work. Although the book created quite a stir and scandal in the context of 1962 norms regarding proper behavior for young women, it was also thought to present honest and true-to-life advice. Through this book, Brown cultivated a career offering the advice she had accrued throughout her life, from her humble beginnings in Arkansas to her days as a single, working woman with an advertising career.

CHILDHOOD AND EARLY CAREER IN ADVERTISING

Helen Gurley, the second daughter of school teachers Ira and Cleo (née Sisco) Gurley, was born in Green Forest, Arkansas, on February 18, 1922. Her early life was wrought with financial insecurity, inspiring her to go places beyond those offered by her Ozark Mountain family. Brown did not like the kind of life—hillbilly, ordinary, and poor—that seemed to be programmed for her, and from the time she was 7 she knew she wanted something else (Brown, 1982). Her desire for a better life led her to become friends with children of wealthier families in Little Rock, Arkansas, as she grew up. She became quite adept at pleasing the parents of her wealthy classmates. She found that fraternizing with the rich provided a way to eat good food, visit great houses, and try on the beautiful clothes in her friends' mothers' closets (Brown, 1982).

Of her own mother, Helen speaks fondly, praising her mother's encouragement to use her brain and work to get ahead—advice that most mothers did not give to daughters in those days (Brown, 1982). She also credits her mother with cultivating Helen's preoccupation with beauty. "My mother," she explains, "had terrible hang-ups about beauty because of being compared to a ravishing younger sister, [and she] dutifully passed on all her beauty anxieties to me . . . Sometimes my mother would peer closely at me and say, 'I really do think you're getting better-looking every day,' meaning, unmistakably, 'You've got a long way to go, baby!' " (Brown, 1982, p. 115). Helen, now a "baby neurotic" about her looks, says she grew older being conscious about her looks and never stopping her attempts to improve them.

As an adolescent, Helen's desire for a life bigger than the one Arkansas offered was fueled by the movies and film celebrities. When she was about 12, she used to sit, on summer nights, out on the porch of her grandmother's house in Osage, Arkansas (population 40), star gazing and dreaming about life in Hollywood. She and her sister Mary faithfully read *Silver Screen, Photoplay,* and *Movie Mirror* and saved all the pictures they could find of Joan Crawford, Jean Harlow, and Clark Gable. "Hollywood was as far off as Mars, of course, but I'm *certain* that longing-lonely time was, in an odd way, the beginning of my 'drive' " (Brown, 1982, p. 20).

Hollywood was in her reach, however, when she and her family moved to Los Angeles, California. There she attended high school and, upon graduating, attended a semester at Texas Women's University on a scholarship before returning to Los Angeles for business school. Work, not scholarship, was the norm in Helen's upbringing. "There was never any question that I had to work—my sister Mary [crippled by polio at age 19] telephoned people from her wheelchair [for a survey and polling company] to see what radio show they were listening to (pay: forty cents an hour)," she recalls. "Mother pinned tickets on merchandise in the marking room of Sears Roebuck; and we couldn't have managed without my eighteen-dollar-a-week salary" (Brown, 1982, p. X).

Helen began her working career at age 18 as secretary to an announcer at a Los Angeles radio station. It was there that she first encountered sexism and sexual harassment. At the radio station, male workers engaged in a game called scuttle, the object of which was to get the panties off one or more secretaries a day (Brown, 1985). As she later recalled, she was fairly ignorant about the harassment and discrimination in such behavior. It went unnoticed because at that time women were not educated or very conscious of such things (Brown, 1985). Sixteen secretarial jobs later, Helen arrived at the Los Angeles advertising agency Foote, Cone & Belding, as secretary to executive Don Foote. Impressing her boss and his wife with her letter-writing style, she was permitted to write ad copy during Christmas seasons, and, after winning a *Glamour* magazine writing contest, she was given an agency copywriting position in 1953.

The job, Helen reminisces, was her "breakthrough job." The position was not a "breakthrough" just in terms of her career, however; it also represented her ability to break through the trenchant sexism that existed in advertising during this era. Women in advertising reported "vulnerable opposition" to women's presence in any capacity other than clerical work. Agencies preferred men, and women were warned that succeeding in advertising would depend upon their concentrating on their work "to the exclusion of everything else . . . home, heart interest, and children" (Beasley & Gibbons, 1993, pp. 14–15). Helen's recollections of her advertising career indicate that she experienced such attitudes and that she did concentrate on her career to the exclusion of marriage and childbearing: "my six *male* co-workers used to growl when they saw me curved over my typewriter at 5:30 PM when they went home . . . to spend the evening with their families," she writes. "One of them even complained to our boss that I was taking advantage of the rest of them because I wasn't married and didn't have to go home" (Brown, 1982, p. 50). Helen remained resilient to such sexism and admitted later that she was unsure whether she was sorry so few women were in advertising: "I had this heady job [at Foote, Cone & Belding], tons of special attention for being the only woman, and all nine male copywriters all to myself" (Brown, 1985, p. 118).

After ten years at Foote, Cone & Belding, in 1958 Helen became an advertising writer and account executive at Kenyon & Eckhardt, a Hollywood advertising agency. During her four years at the agency, two other female copywriters and she were supervised by 15 successive male copy chiefs. Despite the discrimination, she was recognized for her work, receiving the Francis Holmes Achievement award for outstanding work in advertising from 1956 to 1959.

While working at Kenyon & Eckhardt, she also met David Brown, a film, theater, and television producer later responsible for such films as *The Sting, Jaws, Cocoon,* and *Driving Miss Daisy.* Helen knew she wanted to marry David the night they met. Having grown up in the Depression and having to help support her mother and sister gave Helen a sense of whom she wanted to marry. Her husband had to be dynamic; a box boy at the A&P just would not do. David Brown was that kind of man (Brown, 1982). They married on September 25, 1959, when Helen was 37 years old; it was her first marriage—though admittedly not her first lover—and his third.

Prior to their marriage, David helped Helen with her work by providing concrete suggestions about her television and print ad assignments. His contributions to her work became even more valuable and influential when her job at Kenyon & Eckhardt was in jeopardy. In 1960 David had read some of Helen's old letters to a past boyfriend and had encouraged her to write a book. With her job in question, writing a book seemed an ideal way to keep busy. David struck on an appealing topic, one Helen felt she could write about easily and with authority. His idea was to write about "how a single girl goes about having an affair, how she clears the decks for action. What does she do with the guy she's already seeing? What's the best place to consummate this affair? What's her life like? What kind of person is she? I said, 'My God, that's my book, that's my book!' " (Lewis, 1981, pp. 25–26). Helen notes that although the book had a light touch, it turned out to be much more sincere and serious than originally planned.

Sex and the Single Girl (1962) became an international best-seller, remaining on best-seller lists well into 1963. It also became a motion picture feature starring Natalie Wood and Tony Curtis. The book—a compendium of Helen's advice on matters of sex, work, money, affairs, and clothes—captured the growing mood of independence and excitement that greater earning power was heralding for so many women across the globe. It also expressed Helen's views about sex—views that were "downright revolutionary for her time," as a *Playboy* interviewer noted. "At a time when Mamie Eisenhower was still on the most-admired list. When women's magazines were printing recipes and family homilies, when men's sexual behavior was barely discussed in major publications and women's wasn't even acknowledged, Helen Gurley Brown was saying some unsettling things" (Lewis, 1981, p. 24). In short, in her book she was calling for the overhaul of American abortion laws, discussing diaphragms, and saying that girls who get pregnant were jerks (Lewis, 1981). The book transformed Helen into a modern pundit for a multitude of lonely and bewildered American women.

ARRIVING AT *COSMOPOLITAN*

That her readers were bewildered about sex and relationships was without question. Soon after her book's publication, Helen was inundated with mail from young women seeking advice about their love lives. Reading it, her husband suggested that she start a magazine offering stories that addressed the women's concerns. Together they drafted a simple proposal based conceptually on the philosophies she had put forth in her book. The magazine would advise young women readers how to get the most from their lives, how to improve themselves, and how to live their *own* lives instead of living vicariously through a man. Riding on the wave of Helen's recent success and using some of David's entertainment industry contacts, David took the prospectus to several publishers, including Hearst Publications. At the time, one of Hearst's publications was the floundering magazine, *The Cosmopolitan*. Established in 1886, the magazine was purchased by William Randolph Hearst in 1905, and featured fictional stories and pieces. By the late 1950s, however, the market for the fiction magazine genre had diminished, and the Hearst Corporation, not willing to incur the risk of starting up a new magazine, saw in David and Helen's proposal a last chance for *The Cosmopolitan*. Thus, they handed the feeble magazine over to the successful female author and gave her a free hand to reformat the magazine's content and layout (Braithewaite & Barrell, 1979; Brown, 1982).

Never having set foot in a magazine office except for a few minutes at *Glamour* when she won a writing contest in 1953, Helen arrived at *The Cosmopolitan* in 1965 as editor-in-chief. Although she knew nothing about handling people (she had never had her own secretary), she now had to lead 34 people. "The night after my first day at *Cosmo*, I slipped out of bed around midnight and curled up in a little ball under David's desk! David found me around 4 AM and got me back to bed" (Brown, 1982, p. 55). Given her admitted lack of experience, as well as her gender, Helen's position was an extraordinary feat. When Helen became *Cosmo*'s editor, the norm of magazine publishing was that women rarely rose to top editorial positions even if the publication was aimed at female audiences (Beasley & Gibbons, 1993). Even in 1977, after the women's liberation movement, 73 percent of key magazine editorships were still held by men. In 1973 a majority of those women who were magazine editors used men's first names, initials rather than a first name, or names applicable to either sex (Butler & Paisley, 1980). Helen Gurley Brown, however, wanted to go places, and she would take her magazine with her, revitalizing its content, and, consequently, reviving its circulation and advertising sales.

SIGNIFICANCE OF HELEN'S INFLUENCE ON *COSMOPOLITAN'S* CONTENT

Helen's key editorial position enabled her to tailor *Cosmopolitan*'s content to modern women's needs and thus to shatter iconoclastically many of the old values women's magazines had previously maintained. With no women in influential positions, the articles and fiction featured in women's magazines prior to the mid-1960s upheld an age-old formula that advanced and reinforced the myth or "cult" of true womanhood: that women should exemplify piety, purity, submissiveness, and domesticity (Beasley & Gibbons, 1993, p. 8). Popular women's magazines like *Family Circle, Good Housekeeping, Ladies Home Journal, Better Homes and Gardens, Redbook, McCall's,* and *Woman's Day*—known as "women's service books" and the "Seven Sisters" in industry lingo—implied that housekeeping and having a happy family and a satisfied husband were a woman's means to self-fulfillment and happiness (Beasley & Silver, 1977, 1993). Besides highlighting women's roles as caregivers and servants, such magazines also emphasized women's roles as consumers, marketing home and beauty products to better serve women's households or their appearance.

By the early 1960s, however, declining sales indicated there were too many women's magazines with similar formulas that were not being well received by a newer generation of women. Newer consumers perceived such publications at worst as "tired and dowdy," at best as "old-fashioned" (Beasley & Silver, 1977; Kastor, 1984). With the success of *Sex and the Single Girl* as well as the myriad requests for advice it inspired, Helen sensed she had a finger on the pulse of this newer generation of young women. Rather than using the tired tales of married women with a husband, children, and middle-class household that had been so frequent in women's magazines (Bailey, 1969), she exerted her power as editor-in-chief to tailor *Cosmopolitan*'s content to young women who were interested in their lives and the world outside of their homes, in self-improvement and their careers, in their appearance and their relationships. Fashion and home interests were accorded minimal copyspace, and babies were "definitely out" (Braithewaite & Barrell, 1979, p. 51).

Cosmopolitan was edited to be a resource for young women of the day, talking to them in an honest voice with a personal and friendly tone. Indeed, the tone was that of a perennial older sister from Little Rock, Arkansas, who wanted only the best for her younger sisters. Helen achieved such a voice by editing the magazine through feeling a sense of companionship and similarity with her readers. Such feeling worked: when Helen assumed her position, *Cosmopolitan*'s circulation was 600,000; in less than seven years, it topped 1.5 million.

Revitalized by Helen's editorship, *Cosmopolitan* cultivated a bright and breezy style but one that also told its readers, in Helen's words, "Do your own work . . . make your own money, use your talent, live up to your potential. That, to me, is a very moral message, and that's in every page of *Cosmo*" (*Psychology Today,* 1994, p. 70). The magazine soon developed an archetype of its reader, the Cosmo girl. She was "out to attract men, hold down a good job, make the best of herself, and, not least, improve her sex life," but she needed "help and advice on those aggravations like jealousy, envy, and a feeling of just not being up to it that hits us all too often" (Braithewaite & Barrell, 1979, pp. 49 and 53). As the magazine flourished with the voice and direction Helen brought to it, its cover models began to reflect this female archetype. Gracing the checkout counters of supermarkets across the United States, *Cosmo*'s circulation soared after its re-launch; 93 percent of its sales derived from "bookstall" rather than subscription sales, a figure similar to the circulation statistics of today (Braithewaite & Barrell, 1979; *Cosmopolitan,* 1995b).

Although selling to women at grocery checkouts was a successful marketing tactic, it was not without criticism. Following the 1963 publication of *The Feminine Mystique* by Betty Friedan, herself a former women's magazine journalist, women were becoming increasingly aware of their exploitation as consumers and housewives (Beasley & Gibbons, 1993). Writer Nora Magid's analysis of women's magazines, for example, indicted selling women's magazines in the supermarket: "an environment which invites high sales. . . . Located right at the site of purchase . . . the homemaker is told that the magazine is a vital purchase in her grocery cart" (quoted in Beasley & Silver, 1977, p. 94). While Helen's fresh editorial content had caused waves and heralded change among the women's magazines, feminist critics found fault with the magazine's tendency to overinstruct readers on how to become some stereotype of a woman they might not be naturally (Beasley & Gibbons, 1993). Therefore, in 1970 a group of feminists visited Helen in order to convince her to reduce the *Cosmo* reader's anxiety about aspiring to be some archetype she was not and to increase encouragement of the reader's pride and acceptance of her true self and her own talents.[1]

COSMOPOLITAN TODAY

Nearly 20 years after the feminists visited Helen, female members of an American Society of Magazine Editors' forum concurred that "women are as traditional now in their wants and in their wish list as they have ever been. . . . They want family, they want love. . . . if you're operating in the mass market you've really got to bear [those desires] very, very much in mind" (Beasley & Gibbons, 1993, p. 218). Helen Gurley Brown has not forgotten the mass market of young women to whom she gears her magazine. Indeed, as the editorial director of *Cosmo*'s 28 international editions, she has even kept in mind that the young Cosmo girl wants the same things whether she is Australian or Brazilian. These international editions have positioned *Cosmopolitan* as the largest selling young women's magazine in the world, its international audience exceeding 24 million monthly readers (*Cosmopolitan,* 1995b). Several of these global editions—Australia, Brazil, France, Italy, Latin America, and Great Britain—have already celebrated their twentieth anniversaries.

Besides its international descendants, *Cosmo* has also inspired several spinoff magazines in the United States. In 1970, for example, *New Woman* was launched to compete with *Cosmopolitan,* and in 1980, *Woman* magazine hit the presses to do the same. Most notable of the *Cosmo* spinoffs, however, was the publication of *Playgirl* magazine in response to the overwhelming sales of the 1972 *Cosmo* issue featuring a full center layout of Burt Reynolds in a coy nude pose (Braithewaite & Barrell, 1979, p. 55).

Cosmopolitan, despite any spinoffs or competition, continues to succeed today as one of the most highly circulated women's magazines in the United States. Monthly, it sells over 2.6 million copies, and 72 percent of those sales are from newsstand purchases. Thus, it is one of the top magazines for single-copy sales in the United States (*Cosmopolitan,* 1995b).

Cosmopolitan has extended itself into other profitable markets. It is now a leading U.S. exercise video producer, and it also markets eyewear, sportswear, and a paperback series with Avon Books. Helen, too, has continued to produce along with her work maintaining the magazine's editorial content. Following *Sex and the Single Girl,* she wrote *Sex and the Office* (1965), *Helen Gurley Brown's Outrageous Opinions* (1967), *Helen Gurley Brown's Single Girls Cookbook* (1969), *Sex and the New Single Girl* (1970), *Having It All* (1982), and *The Late Show: A Semi-practical Guide to Growing Old* (1993).

---

[1]As a result of their visit in 1970, *Cosmopolitan* ran excerpts from Kate Milett's *Sexual Politics* later that year.

In recognition of her work at *Cosmopolitan,* she was awarded distinguished achievement awards in journalism from the University of Southern California (1971) and Stanford University (1977), and granted a special award for editorial leadership by the American Newspaper Woman's Club in 1972. In 1985 she was awarded the New York Women in Communications Award, and she was honored at Northwestern University's Medill School of Journalism with the establishment of the Helen Gurley Brown Research Professorship. In 1988 Helen was inducted into the Publisher's Hall of Fame—the result of many years she spent applying herself in order to avoid or, as she puts it, to "run scared" from the humble beginnings she did not want to be her end. Indeed, Helen has brought herself very far from such beginnings, and, importantly, not by being one of those "good girls" who go to heaven" as her embroidered pillow indicates. Instead, Helen Gurley Brown capitalized on her experience as a "bad girl"— as a single, working woman having premarital sex in an era when most women were neither single, working, nor willing to talk about sex—and on her experience as an editor who overthrew the traditional content of women's magazines and the traditional gender norms of editing employment. Helen Gurley Brown is living proof that "Bad girls go everywhere." As she herself has acknowledged: "I am crafty, but who ever really believed only the Cream-of-Wheat inherited the earth?" (Brown, 1982, p. 3).

REFERENCES

Bailey, M. (1969, Summer). The woman's magazine short-story heroine in 1957 and 1967. *Journalism Quarterly,* 365.

Beasley, M., & Gibbons, S. (1993). *Taking their place: A documentary history of women and journalism.* Washington, D.C.: American University Press.

Beasley, M., & Silver, S. (1977). *Women in media: A documentary source book.* Washington, D.C.: Women's Institute for Freedom of the Press.

Braithewaite, B., & Barrell, J. (1979). *The business of women's magazines: The agonies and the ecstasies.* London: Associated Business Press.

Brown, H. G. (1962). *Sex and the single girl.* New York: Avon Books.

Brown, H. G. (1982). *Having it all.* New York: Pocket Books.

Brown, H. G. (1985, July). "What the women's movement means to me." *Ms.,* 14, 118.

Brown, H. G. (1993). *The late show: a practical, semi-wild survival guide for every woman in her prime or approaching it.* New York: Avon Books.

Butler, M., & Paisley, W. (1980). *Women and the mass media: Sourcebook for research and action.* New York: Human Sciences Press.

Cosmopolitan. (1995a). *Cosmopolitan* media kit: Editorial research and mission statement. New York: Hearst Publications.

Cosmopolitan. (1995b). *Cosmopolitan* media kit: Audience research and circulation profile. New York: Hearst Publications.

Cosmopolitan. (1995c). Helen Gurley Brown's biography. Fax transmission. New York: Hearst Magazines.

Finke, N. (1990, April 20). Birthday girl: The times are changing, but not *Cosmo,* still hot after 25 years. *Los Angeles Times,* E1.

Harper's Bazaar. (1983, August). The single girl's guru. 40.

Johnson, S. (1993). Magazines: Women's employment and status in the magazine industry. In P. J. Creedon, ed., *Women in mass communication: Challenging gender values.* 2nd ed. (pp. 134–153). Newbury Park, Calif.: Sage.

Kastor, E. (1984, May 7). The renaissance of women's magazines. *Washington Post,* C5.

Lewis, R. A. (1981). Helen Gurley Brown: *Playboy* magazine interview. *Playboy Interviews.* (pp. 24–36). New York: Playboy Press.

Psychology Today. (1994, March/April). Interview: Helen Gurley Brown, bad girl. 27, 22–24, 70–71.

JUDEE K. BURGOON
(1948–   )

Beth A. Le Poire

> They are earnestly telling you something they are telling you about themselves they are telling you with all their might something they want you to know and the story is not them it is the movement the twisting mouth the eyes trying to pinion you the face crying for attention the shoulders squared the breath fast and even to push forth the words that don't matter only the gesture does.
>
> —Alexandra Grilikhes
> (*The Women's Review of Books,* March 1985)

Recognized internationally as an outstanding nonverbal and relational communication scholar, Judee Burgoon has contributed considerably to the discipline of communication. Her work on relational communication, expectancy violations theory, the social meanings model, and her newest interaction adaptation theory, in particular, provide significant and heuristic contributions to the study of the functions of communication behavior within interpersonal relationships. She has received 12 top paper awards from national and international conferences, as well as five teaching awards from universities and national organizations. In addition, she has been recognized as an ICA (International Communication Association) fellow, an honor reserved for only about 30 of the field's outstanding scholars. She clearly has had a large impact on the field of communication, both for her own scholarship and as a mentor of young scholars.

FAMILY BACKGROUND

Judee Kathelene Stringer was born in Ames, Iowa, on February 5, 1948. Her father, Joseph Kenneth Stringer II (known as Ken), was a man of many vocations and avocations—owner of a cab company, car salesman, owner of an auto dealership, landlord, realtor, inventor, owner of an art shop, and at one time, a member of the Iowa State Legislature. Ken was responsible for the unique spelling of Judee's name. Her mother, Mary Elene (Polly) Parrott, graduated from Iowa State with an undergraduate degree in home economics. She was a diligent homemaker who raised five children (of whom Judee was the oldest); she also had a high appreciation for education and encouraged all of their children to do well in school. Judee had two sisters and two brothers, Della, Marilyn, Ken, and Warren. She notes that her family contributed to her academic achievements. Her father, she said,

worked six or seven days a week. His work ethic and entrepreneurial activities became a model for me of immersing oneself in work, and my first job, at age 13, was doing bookkeeping for the gas station he owned. He was also a man very much interested in issues, ideas, and politics. Early on, he encouraged me to write, at times even hiring me to produce speeches for use in his political campaigns.

EDUCATION

Burgoon's interest in communication began with a ninth grade speech course. She describes her teacher, Miss Beck (who also directed the voice choir), as a wonderfully inspiring teacher. This class propelled her into debate and theater in high school. She continued her interest in written and oral communication when she returned to her parents' alma mater, Iowa State University, to double-major in speech and English and double-minor in social studies and education. She graduated, summa cum laude, in 1970. After graduation, Judee taught for a year while her first husband, Charles Heston (whom she quips she married for his name), finished his degree at Iowa State. Judee and Charles then moved to Normal, Illinois, where she completed a Master of Science in communication at Illinois State University in 1972 under the direction of James McCroskey. His biggest contribution to her education, according to Judee, was instilling a value for productivity.

Heston and she divorced in 1972 and Judee began studies toward her doctorate at Florida State. She completed her degree at West Virginia after moving there to take a teaching assignment that opened up midsemester. At West Virginia she was offered an All-University Fellowship for graduate education in both communication and educational psychology. She had two advisers: William B. Lashbrook (a.k.a. Brad) in communication, and Roger McAvoy in education. Judee reports that Lashbrook had a major influence on her thinking and approach to scholarship. She describes him as a very abstract and analytical thinker who pushed all of his students to think in those terms. He "dragged us screaming and kicking into research methods and ignited our enthusiasm." Her focus on social science methods is very evident in her work, the program in which she is currently employed, and her mentoring.

In 1974, at the age of 26, Judee was awarded a doctorate of education from West Virginia University in communication and educational psychology. These were quite a number of marked achievements for one so young—three advanced college degrees, two of which were double-majored, as well as a year of teaching experience. Although Michael Burgoon, then an assistant professor in communication at West Virginia, did not directly advise Judee, she considered him her other primary mentor. They had met prior to their joint time at West Virginia, and they married in 1974, after Judee received her doctorate.

CAREER DEVELOPMENT

In 1974, after completing her doctorate at West Virginia, Judee took a job as assistant professor of speech and director of forensics at the University of Florida. Between 1974 and 1977 she taught a number of courses, including theories of human communication, discussion methods, argumentation, advanced argumentation, nonverbal communication (and research), multivariate research methods, and interpersonal communication. In the spring of 1977, she took a leave of absence to be a visiting professor at Michigan State University.

In the fall of 1977 the Burgoons moved to New York City where they lived for a year. During this time Judee was vice president of the National Center for Telephone Research at Louis Harris and Associates (a marketing research and opinion polling firm). Her foray into media research began when she was put in charge of Gannett's newspaper research. This association grew into a long-term consulting arrangement with various media organizations. She was one of the six people responsible for the initial concept and design research on *USA Today*. (To date, she and Michael have conducted research for over 100 media properties as well as continuing to work with *USA Today*.) While in New York she also did free-lance writing for Random House and Latham Publishing and taught small-group communication as an adjunct assistant professor at Hunter College.

The Burgoons next moved to Michigan State University (Michael's alma mater) where she and Michael remained until 1984. Judee was an assistant professor from 1978 to 1980 when she received tenure and was promoted to associate professor. From 1980 until 1983, she was director of graduate studies in communication. At Michigan State, she taught a range of courses, including, but not limited to, nonverbal communication, metamessages and relational messages, and univariate and multivariate research methods.

In 1984 the Burgoons joined the Department of Communication at the University of Arizona. Judee was hired at the rank of full professor and soon became the director of graduate studies. She was only 36. With a teaching load similar to her previous appointments, Judee also became a member of the faculty of the Arizona Executive Program and Executive Development Program in the College of Business and Public Administration, as well as a member of the interdisciplinary committee on environment and behavior. In the fall of 1989,

Judee took a sabbatical as a visiting scholar in psychology at Harvard University. While there, she honed her methodological skills, working with Robert Rosenthal and Ellen Langer.

MAJOR CONTRIBUTIONS AND ACHIEVEMENTS

Judee Burgoon is one of the top scholars in communication in terms of research productivity and publications. As a testament to this fact, she was named an International Communication Association (ICA) fellow (the second woman to receive this distinction) and was recently elected to the Society for Experimental Social Psychology. She consistently publishes in the top journals in communication and psychology. Her publication record includes 7 books, more than 130 refereed journal articles, and 20 book chapters. In addition, she has served on the editorial board (or as an editorial consultant) for eight major journals in communication and psychology, including *Human Communication Research, Communication Monographs, Communication Research, Quarterly Journal of Speech, Journal of Nonverbal Behavior,* and the *Journal of Social and Personal Relationships*. Most notably, she recently completed a highly commendable tenure as editor of one of the premiere journals in communication—*Communication Monographs*.

These accomplishments reflect her ability to conduct first-rate research as well as inspire and influence other scholars. In addition, she has an impressive record of intramural and extramural funding for 24 projects from agencies and sponsors ranging from Gannett Company, Inc., to the Army Research Office and the National Institute of Mental Health.

Relational messages. Judee Burgoon's primary research focus is relational messages and nonverbal communication. Not surprisingly, her work on relational communication (Burgoon & Hale, 1984, 1987) is one of her greatest contributions. Her work focuses on how communication functions to define the nature of all relationships. Relational messages are implied messages above and beyond the content of the message and indicate how individuals feel about themselves in the relationship, about their partner in the relationship, and about the relationship in general. Burgoon's work extended previous theorizing (e.g., Bateson, 1958; Watzlawick, Beavin, & Jackson, 1967). Burgoon and Hale proposed that up to 12 relational messages (dominance, formality-informality, composure, similarity, task-social orientation, equality, emotional arousal, and intimacy, which includes the subthemes of affection-hostility, inclusion-exclusion, involvement, depth-superficiality, and trust) could accompany any message. This view expanded the understanding and theorizing about relational messages and their impact on relationships in general, and has been highly heuristic as a theoretic and research tool.

Social meanings model of nonverbal communication. Burgoon's work on relational messages led to a social meanings model of nonverbal communication (e.g., Burgoon, 1991; Burgoon, Buller, Hale, & deTurck, 1984; Burgoon, Coker, &

Coker, 1986; Burgoon & Newton, 1991; Burgoon, Newton, Walther, & Baesler, 1989; Coker & Burgoon, 1987). According to this view, some nonverbal behaviors comprise a socially shared vocabulary analogous to verbal communication. Regularly used behaviors among members of a social community are presumed to be intentional acts (although any particular enactment need not be intentional), and have consensually recognizable interpretations. As with verbal language, a given behavior may have multiple meanings, but the range of possible interpretations is finite and fairly limited.

This model encourages nonverbal scholars to examine a host of behaviors in combination (e.g., involvement expression, for instance), instead of looking at one or two nonverbal behaviors and their relation to communication outcomes. This is methodologically as well as theoretically sound in that examining many behaviors in combination, rather than looking at one behavior at a time, provides a more stable estimate of the true communication effects of the construct.

Burgoon also has had a significant impact on the way nonverbal researchers conduct their research. She and Jim Baesler (Baesler & Burgoon, 1987; Burgoon & Baesler, 1991), for example, discuss the benefits and drawbacks of measuring global percepts (overall perceptual judgments not directly observable through behavior but rather inferred, such as kinesic involvement), or macro-measures (measures that include behavioral indices but still call for some judgment, such as vocal variety) and micro-measures (direct behavioral indicators that are directly observable, such as forward body lean or amount of eye contact).

The importance of Burgoon's work in the nonverbal arena is found in her nonverbal textbook, co-authored with former students David Buller and Gill Woodall (Burgoon, Buller, & Woodall, 1989). This book divides the study of nonverbal communication into two primary units: *structure* (e.g., kinesics, vocalics, physical appearance, proxemics, haptics, chronemics, and artifacts) and *function* (e.g., impression management, relational communication, deception, social influence, and emotional expression).

Expectancy violations and adaptation processes. Other contributions include Burgoon's explication of expectancy violations theory, as well as her ensuing work on reciprocity and compensation interaction patterns. Her work on expectancy violations theory, initially explicated in an attempt to deal with the conceptual shortcomings of equilibrium theory (Argyle & Cook, 1976; Argyle & Dean, 1965) and the arousal-labeling model (Patterson, 1985), now spans nearly two decades. Expectancy violations theory was initially designed to deal with nonverbal proxemic violations (Burgoon, 1978), but has recently been expanded to account for a number of other types of violations, including involvement violations in general (Burgoon & Hale, 1988; Burgoon, Newton, Walther, & Baesler, 1989).

Mentoring. Dr. Burgoon's research assistantship model is greatly responsible for the success of her students. Her typical doctoral student, for instance, is given direct training in every aspect of research, from prospectus writing through the design and execution of experiments, data management, data analysis, and report writing. Her belief in her students' abilities, combined with a critical eye, careful sculpting, and insightful mentoring, has created successful apprenticeships resulting in scholars with theoretical foci, good academic values, and the ability to conduct research.

CRITICAL EVALUATIONS OF CONTRIBUTIONS AND ACHIEVEMENTS

The major criticisms of Burgoon's work revolve around (1) the explanatory calculus of expectancy violations theory (with a counter-explanation offered by Cappella and Greene's [1982, 1984] theory of discrepancy arousal), (2) problems revolving around failure of the model to explain reciprocity and compensation outcomes, and (3) her work on nonverbal indices of arousal.

Patterson's (1985) critique of intimacy models included one of Burgoon's models. He presents three criticisms of her model. First, research supporting the model has been partial and inconsistent. Second, the model is complex, which may result in confounding and interacting variables obviating firm conclusions. Third, the original model included distance violations only. (Burgoon and Hale's [1988] subsequent work has extended the model to deal with immediacy violations.)

Some would argue (e.g., Cappella & Greene, 1982, 1984) that discrepancy arousal theory was posited as a way to deal with the complexity of expectancy violations theory (Street, personal communication, 1991). Discrepancy arousal theory, however, was offered as a more parsimonious explanation and argues that arousal does not simply mediate outcomes of discrepancies, but actually moderates communication outcomes. Specifically, small changes in involvement behavior are said to lead to small arousal changes and no change in the partner's behavior. Moderate changes in involvement, on the other hand, are expected to lead to moderate changes in arousal and positive emotions and approach behavior. Finally, large changes in involvement are assumed to be followed by large aversive changes in arousal and subsequent decreases in involvement (or avoidance behavior). Thus, this model is less cognitive, more physiological, and simpler than expectancy violations in terms of fewer explanatory mechanisms.

Le Poire and Burgoon (1994) recently compared both models. Unfortunately, neither model was totally supported because all communication changes (whether predicting reciprocity or compensation) were met with reciprocity. Nevertheless, discrepancy arousal theory was more predictive of actual communication outcomes if the troublesome variable of arousal was removed.

To deal with these findings, as well as those in another expectancy study (Burgoon et al., 1992), interaction adaptation theory was developed (Burgoon, Dillman, and Stern, 1995). This theory posits that (1) there is innate pressure to adapt interaction patterns (regardless of reward level, violation, etc.), and (2) "at the biological level, the inherent pressures are toward entrainment and synchrony, with the exception of compensatory adjustments that insure physical safety and comfort'' (Burgoon, Dillman, and Stern, 1995). Thus, this work extends beyond violations of expectancies theory to argue that, in general, interactants are pressured to converge toward the communication style of their partners. This offers an important touchstone from which to understand the research of reciprocity and compensation in many situations.

Most recently, Sparks and Greene (1992) have criticized Burgoon's work on nonverbal expressions of arousal (see Burgoon, Kelley, Newton, & Keeley, 1989; Burgoon, Beutler, Le Poire, et al., 1993; Burgoon, Le Poire, Beutler, et al., 1992; and the rejoinder by Burgoon and Le Poire, 1992). Burgoon et al. (1989) originally advanced a two-dimensional view of arousal (high-low, positive-negative) to determine whether nonverbal indices could discriminate arousal intensity and arousal valence. Sparks and Greene (1992) argued that this piece fell short of its objectives because it did not measure physiological arousal as a criterion of interest. Burgoon and Le Poire (1992) proferred that this was not the primary objective of the study, and that unobtrusive nonverbal measures are reliable, distinguish differing forms of arousal, and prove useful as predictors. Consequently, nonverbal measures may obviate the need for obtrusive physiological indicators.

In sum, the fact that Burgoon's work has been criticized on both theoretical and methodological grounds speaks to its impact on the field of communication. Her work on relational messages, the social meanings model, expectancy violations theory, and interaction adaptation theory serve as models and references for many scholars of nonverbal communication in particular and communication in general. Her work will continue to elicit further thinking and research, whether through support or criticism.

INTEGRATION OF PERSONAL AND PROFESSIONAL LIFE

Judee Burgoon has been able to integrate her personal and professional life. She is married to another communication scholar, Michael Burgoon, and they have had a productive union—both personally and professionally. Their long-awaited daughter, Erin, was born in 1984. In addition, they have co-authored over 40 book chapters, articles, and books. Despite the prolific nature of their professional activities, Judee and Michael attempt to maintain a balanced home life—they spend time with their daughter, golf, hike, and also visit with Michael's mother, who lives in Tucson. With regard to Erin, Judee says, ''Of all the things I've accomplished, she matters the most.'' Judee and Michael also try to be involved in activities with their graduate students and other faculty. The department seems to follow a ''work hard–play hard'' mentality that has helped build a sense of community among the students and faculty.

During their tenure at the University of Arizona, the Burgoons have had a significant impact in shaping a communication department focused on social science—Michael, in his seven-year role as department head, and Judee, as director of graduate studies. With its shift from a Fine Arts unit known best for its service teaching and oral interpretation emphasis to an emphasis on communication theory and research, coupled with a strong value for scholarly productivity, the department and its students have prospered. In addition, based on their high ideals and standards the Burgoons have built a program of bright and highly skilled graduate students who produce top papers at national and international conferences across the country and have been hired in positions at major universities. Judee's Ph.D.s, for example, hold faculty positions at Northwestern University, Pennsylvania State University, the University of New Mexico, the University of Georgia, Texas A & M, the University of Arizona, Arizona State University, the University of California at Santa Barbara, and the University of Delaware. Judee is given a great amount of credit for the program's accomplishments.

In sum, the field of communication has been significantly enriched by the work of Judee K. Burgoon. Her insights into interpersonal and nonverbal communication in general, and relational communication, expectancy violations, social meanings, and interaction adaptation in particular, have been very influential in the field. That, combined with her extensive mentoring, is the strong legacy of excellence in research she leaves for the field.

REFERENCES

Andersen, P. A. (1985). Nonverbal immediacy in interpersonal communication. In A. W. Siegman and S. Feldstein (eds.), *Multichannel integrations of nonverbal behavior.* (pp. 1–36). Hillsdale, N.J.: Lawrence Erlbaum.

Argyle, M., & Cook, M. (1976). *Gaze and mutual gaze.* Cambridge: Cambridge University Press.

Argyle, M., & Dean, J. (1965). Eye-contact, distance, and affiliation. *Sociometry, 28,* 283–304.

Baesler, J. B., & Burgoon, J. K. (1987). Measurement and reliability of nonverbal behavior. *Journal of Nonverbal Behavior, 11,* 205–234.

Bateson, G. (1958). *Naven.* 2nd ed. Stanford, Calif.: Stanford University Press.

Burgoon, J. K. (1978). A communication model of personal space violations: Explication and an initial test. *Human Communication Research, 4,* 129–142.

Burgoon, J. K. (1983). Nonverbal violations of expectations. In J. M. Weimann & R. P. Harrison (eds.), *Nonverbal interaction.* (pp. 77–111). Beverly Hills, Calif.: Sage.

Burgoon, J. K. (1991). Relational message interpretations of touch, conversational distance, and posture. *Journal of Nonverbal Behavior, 15,* 233–259.

Burgoon, J. K., & Aho, L. (1982). Three field experiments on the effects of violations of conversational distance. *Communication Monographs, 49,* 71–88.

Burgoon, J. K., & Baesler, E. J. (1991). Choosing between micro and macro nonverbal measurement: Application to selected vocalic and kinesic indices. *Journal of Nonverbal Behavior, 15,* 57–78.

Burgoon, J. K., Beutler, L. E., Le Poire, B. A., Engle, D., Bergan, J., Salvio, M., & Mohr, D. C. (1993). Nonverbal indices of arousal in group psychotherapy. *Psychotherapy, 30,* 635–645.

Burgoon, J. K., Buller, D. B., Hale, J. L., & deTurck, M. A. (1984). Relational messages associated with nonverbal behaviors. *Human Communication Research,* 10, 351–378.

Burgoon, J. K., Buller, D. B., & Woodall, G. (1989). *An introduction to nonverbal communication.* Boston: Houghton Mifflin.

Burgoon, J. K., Coker, D. A., & Coker, R. A. (1986). Communicative effects of gaze behavior: A test of two contrasting explanations. *Human Communication Research,* 12, 495–524.

Burgoon, J. K., Dillman, L., & Stern, L. A. (1995). *Interpersonal adaption: Dyadic interaction patterns.* New York: Cambridge University Press.

Burgoon, J. K., & Hale, J. L. (1984). The fundamental topic of relational communication. *Communication Monographs,* 51, 193–214.

Burgoon, J. K., & Hale, J. L. (1987). Validation and measurement of the fundamental themes of relational communication. *Communication Monographs,* 54, 19–41.

Burgoon, J. K., & Hale, J. L. (1988). Nonverbal expectancy violations: Model elaboration and application to immediacy behaviors. *Communication Monographs,* 55, 58–79.

Burgoon, J. K., & Jones, S. B. (1976). Toward a theory of personal space expectations and their violations. *Human Communication Research,* 2, 131–146.

Burgoon, J. K., Kelley, D. L., Newton, D. A., & Keeley, M. P. (1989). The nature of arousal and nonverbal indices. *Human Communication Research,* 16, 217–255.

Burgoon, J. K., & Le Poire, B. A. (1991). Effects of communication expectancies, actual communication, and expectancy disconfirmation on evaluations of communicators and their communication behavior. *Human Communication Research,* 20, 67–96.

Burgoon, J. K., & Le Poire, B. A. (1992). A reply from the heart: Who are Sparks and Greene and why are they saying all these horrible things? *Human Communication Research,* 18, 472–482.

Burgoon, J. K., Le Poire, B. A., Beutler, L. E., Bergan, J., & Engle, D. (1992). Nonverbal behaviors as indices of arousal: Extension to the psychotherapy context. *Journal of Nonverbal Behavior,* 16, 159–177.

Burgoon, J. K., Manusov, V., Mineo, P., & Hale, J. L. (1985). Effects of gaze on hiring, credibility, attraction, and relational message interpretation. *Journal of Nonverbal Behavior,* 8, 133–146.

Burgoon, J. K., & Newton, D. A. (1991). Applying a social meaning model to relation message interpretations of conversational involvement: Comparing observer and participant perspectives. *Southern Communication Journal,* 56, 96–113.

Burgoon, J. K., Newton, D. A., Walther, J. A., & Baesler, E. J. (1989). Nonverbal expectancy violations and conversational involvement. *Journal of Nonverbal Behavior,* 13, 97–120.

Burgoon, J. K., Stacks, D. W., & Burch, S. A. (1982). The role of interpersonal rewards and violations of distancing expectations in achieving influence in small groups. *Communication,* 11, 114–128.

Burgoon, J. K., Stacks, D. W., & Woodall, W. G. (1979). A communicative model of violations of distancing expectations. *The Western Journal of Speech Communication,* 43, 153–167.

Burgoon, J. K., & Walther, J. B. (1990). Nonverbal expectancies and the evaluative consequences of violations. *Human Communication Research,* 17, 232–265.

Burgoon, J. K., Walther, J. B., & Baesler, E. J. (1991). Interpretations, evaluations, and consequences of interpersonal touch. Manuscript submitted for publication.

Cappella, J. N., & Greene, J. O. (1982). A discrepancy-arousal explanation of mutual influence in expressive behavior for adult and infant-adult interaction. *Communication Monographs, 49,* 89–114.

Cappella, J. N., & Greene, J. O. (1984). The effects of distance and individual differences in arousability on nonverbal involvement: A test of discrepancy-arousal theory. *Journal of Nonverbal Behavior, 8,* 259–285.

Coker, D., & Burgoon, J. K. (1987). The nature of conversational involvement and nonverbal encoding patterns. *Human Communication Research, 13,* 463–494.

Hale, J. L., & Burgoon, J. K. (1984). Models of reactions to changes in nonverbal immediacy. *Journal of Nonverbal Behavior, 8,* 287–314.

Le Poire, B. A. (1991). Orientation and defensive reactions as alternatives to arousal in theories of nonverbal reactions to changes in immediacy. *Southern Communication Journal, 56,* 138–146.

Le Poire, B. & Burgoon, J. K. (1994). Two contrasting explanations of involvement violations: Expectancy violations theory versus discrepancy arousal theory. *Human Communication Research, 20,* 560–591.

Patterson, M. L. (1985). An arousal model of interpersonal immediacy. *Psychological Review, 83,* 235–245.

Sparks, G. L., & Greene, J. O. (1992). On the validity of nonverbal indicators as measures of physiological arousal: A response to Burgoon, Kelley, Newton, and Keeley-Dyreson. *Human Communication Research, 18,* 445–471.

Stacks, D. W., & Burgoon, J. K. (1981). The role of nonverbal behaviors as distractors in resistance to persuasion in interpersonal contexts. *Central States Speech Journal, 32,* 61–73.

Street, R. L., Jr. (1995). Personal communication, Texas A&M University.

Watzlawick, P., Beavin, J. H., & Jackson, D. D. (1967). *Pragmatics of human communication: A study of the interactional patterns, pathologies, and paradoxes.* New York: W. W. Norton.

JOANNE CANTOR
(1945–)

Amy I. Nathanson

Joanne Cantor has made significant contributions to the literature in both mass communication and child development. Her research on children's emotional reactions to the mass media was the first to interpret the emotional effects of media from a cognitive developmental perspective—a link that continues to inform current research and theory. Her present work on media violence tackles questions about ratings and advisories that have previously gone unanswered and includes an assessment of the use of ratings and advisories based on the largest random sample of television programming ever collected. Her concern with producing theoretically important and socially relevant findings is evidenced by the influence her work has had on scholars, lawmakers, and the general public. Her genuine fascination with her work has resulted in over 60 publications and has gained her national recognition as an expert on children and television.

FAMILY BACKGROUND

Joanne Cantor was born in Newport News, Virginia, on April 25, 1945, but grew up in suburban Washington, D.C. The youngest of three children, Cantor was raised by Irving (or "Chips") and Elizabeth Mandel Cantor. Reflecting on her upbringing, Cantor likens her experience to the family life portrayed on popular 1950s sitcoms. Her family seemed typical in that her father worked and her mother stayed at home to raise the children.

Cantor's extended family was far from typical, however. It included many "professionals" such as lawyers and doctors. Even both of her parents earned advanced degrees. Her father received his B.A. and L.L.B. from Cornell University and worked as a building contractor as well as provided some legal services. Her mother earned her B.A. from Barnard College and, after many years as a homemaker, went back to school to earn her Master's in social work from Catholic University. She then worked full time as a social work administrator.

Her mother served as her role model by demonstrating how a woman could achieve professional success, contribute to society, and still put her family first. Before studying for her Master's while a full-time housewife, Elizabeth Cantor was an active participant in many volunteer organizations, often being elected president of these groups. Her mother's successful balance of both professional and family demands set a standard that Cantor would later emulate in her own life.

Although Cantor's parents always encouraged their children to pursue an education, they were a bit wary of her desire to go into academia. After all, Cantor would be exploring unfamiliar territory, for no one in her family had ever studied for a Ph.D. Even more troubling was their apprehension that Cantor would become too career-oriented and never marry and have a family. Their concerns notwithstanding, Cantor's parents always remained supportive of her achievements.

EDUCATION

Cantor's primary and secondary education was earned in the public schools of Washington, D.C. She enjoyed elementary school and aspired to teach whichever grade she was currently in at the time.

During high school, Cantor especially enjoyed her English, math, biology, and language classes. At this time, she thought she might like to teach languages; however, she was also considering a career as a secretary. As a result, she took shorthand and typing classes and even landed her first summer job working as a secretary in the office of Newton Minow—the chairman of the Federal Communications Commission who became famous for branding television a "vast wasteland."

Cantor remembers having some great teachers in high school who inspired her commitment to learning. In particular, she valued the teachers who encouraged students to go beyond curriculum requirements and think independently. Although some of her teachers were rigid and even bigoted (one English teacher was displeased with Cantor for completing book reports on famous African Americans), Cantor assesses her precollegiate education as excellent.

Like her father, brother, and sister, Cantor attended Cornell University. Consistent with her high school interests, she majored in French literature and planned to teach language at the high school level. However, she admits that she was not especially interested in her major and, like many of the other women in her cohort, assumed she would eventually be a full-time mother and housewife.

Unlike high school, college was disappointing to Cantor. The self-confidence she had gained in high school was undermined by arrogant and sometimes sexist professors and teaching assistants who often assumed that whereas men attended college to prepare for careers women enrolled to find a husband. Cantor remembers that many professors treated women as though they were simply taking up classroom space rather than serving as competent and motivated members of the academic community.

After enduring four years in this uninspiring environment, Cantor awoke to the realization that teaching language was not for her. She decided not to enroll in Yale's Master's of Arts in Teaching program when she graduated from Cornell in 1967. Instead, she headed for Paris with her college roommate where she found a job as assistant to the casting director of Twentieth-Century-Fox France. But after a year and a half, she became bored with her work and decided to return to school. Unfortunately, her college training had only prepared her for graduate work in areas she no longer found interesting. However, she had read about Marshall McLuhan's work in the newspapers and was intrigued by the emerging field of communication. Although she had no formal training or background in communication, she applied and was accepted at The Annenberg School for Communication at the University of Pennsylvania in Philadelphia.

At Annenberg, Cantor quickly developed an interest in quantitative social science research thanks to Dolf Zillmann's introductory statistics course. Not only did she find statistics to be a fascinating approach to knowledge, but she was also intrigued by Zillmann's research. Cantor became Zillmann's advisee and research assistant. Although she had only planned to get her M.A., her enthusiasm for her work and subject area led her to reconsider. After receiving her Master's in 1971, Cantor moved to Indiana University when Zillmann accepted a position there, and she received her Ph.D. in 1974.

During this time, Cantor's research explored a variety of communication phenomena, as evidenced by the topics of her Master's thesis and doctoral dissertation. Her M.A. thesis, "Induction of Curiosity via Rhetorical Questions and Its Effect on the Learning of Factual Materials," which was later published, showed that the addition of rhetorical questions to a lecture can increase the amount students learn from it. Her dissertation, "Imitation of Aggression as a Function of Exposure to a Model's Emotional Expressions Contingent upon His Performance of Aggressive Acts," suggested that the emotional expressions of a model may stimulate imitation—whether the emotions are positive or negative. In other work, she studied aggression, the psychology of humor, the impact of message variables on persuasion, and excitation transfer effects (Cantor, Zillmann, & Bryant, 1975; Zillmann & Cantor, 1972, 1974, 1976). By the time she earned her Ph.D., Cantor already had nine articles published or in press in scholarly journals.

As a female graduate student, Cantor encountered a number of challenges related to sexism. In addition to suffering sexual harassment from one professor, she endured criticism from some male graduate students who refused to accept her competence. As the teaching assistant in a graduate-level statistics class, she faced a particularly hostile male student who believed that no woman could ever teach him anything to do with numbers. This student prepared questions he believed would stump Cantor and spent class time challenging her to respond. Cantor's persistence paid off, however, as the students soon realized that they needed her help to understand the material. Although Cantor has spent much time in the public eye, she remembers this class as her toughest audience. Today, memories of this experience help her maintain her confidence by reminding her of the challenges she has met and successfully overcome.

Although some of her male counterparts and superiors were skeptical of women's place in academia, Cantor remembers that Zillmann was especially encouraging of her work. Because there were no female role models for Cantor in her area, Zillmann's confidence was especially important to her. Rather than adopt others' sexist attitudes, Cantor chose to trust his faith in her ability and remained determined to continue her studies.

Cantor cites her participation in research as among her most rewarding experiences during graduate school. She enjoyed all facets of the research process—from developing an idea to reporting and interpreting the results. In addition, the collegiality she gained from working as a team player enhanced her enjoyment of the intellectual process.

CAREER DEVELOPMENT

In 1974, after earning her Ph.D., Cantor accepted a position as assistant professor in the all-male Department of Communication Arts at the University of Wisconsin at Madison. She received tenure in 1978 and remains on the faculty.

Upon arriving in Madison, Cantor was the first to introduce social scientific methods to the department's "Radio-TV-Film" concentration. Given the unfamiliarity of her approach, students initially met her self-designed classes with hostility. Despite this opposition, Cantor always felt supported by her colleagues and was ultimately responsible for founding the department's social scientific "media effects" specialization.

As a new faculty member, Cantor recalls that she was naive about the tenure process and had not created any long-term career goals for herself. She was simply interested in conducting research and teaching in her area of specialization. Her interest in and dedication to her research were reflected in her remarkable productivity, which easily earned her tenure in just four years. Cantor admits that she achieved tenure before realizing the challenge and stress that is supposed to accompany the process.

Shortly after receiving tenure, Cantor was given a number of administrative opportunities. She served as her department's director of graduate studies during the 1979–1980 academic year and then as associate chair from 1980 to 1983. While serving as acting chair in 1988, she became pregnant. In 1989—nine months after her son was born—she became department chair, and one year later, she accepted the position of associate dean of the College of Letters and

Science with responsibility for all of the college's social science departments and programs. After completing a four-year term, she decided to return to full-time teaching and research to take advantage of the tremendous research opportunities that were coming her way. Despite her active participation in administrative work, Cantor's primary interest has always been in teaching and research. She says that she accepted the initial administrative positions not out of any particular interest, but because the jobs needed to be done.

Cantor admits that throughout her educational and career development she has never been especially driven or ambitious. Her productivity is the result more of her fascination with her work than of any intense drive to succeed. Her enthusiasm has won her great opportunities that have resulted in important publications. But, as Cantor puts it, her career success is more of a "side effect" of her genuine interest in her research questions (Wheatman & Hamele, 1995).

MAJOR CONTRIBUTIONS AND ACHIEVEMENTS

Although Cantor has studied a wide range of topics, she is most widely recognized as an expert on children's fright reactions to television. She first thought of studying the area when listening to her graduate students talk of their own children's fright responses to television. Having remembered her own media-induced fright experiences, Cantor decided to explore this issue more systematically. Despite the abundance of anecdotal reports of fright reactions to television, Cantor was surprised to notice the literature's lack of interest in this topic.

In her proposal to the National Institute of Mental Health, Cantor expressed her interest in explaining children's fright reactions to television by using Piaget's stages of cognitive development. To Cantor, it seemed obvious that the way children perceive and comprehend the world would be related to what scares them. However, no one had ever made this connection before. The series of nine studies was funded in 1981, and, although it was only slotted as a three-year program of study, the grant marked the first installment in over a decade of scholarly work on the topic (see Cantor, 1994 for a review).

Cantor's research was the first to provide a theoretical explanation of why different media depictions are frightening to children of different ages. When placed in a cognitive developmental framework, the age-related differences in children's reactions to the same mediated message finally became understandable. This research answered questions that had never been addressed before. It advanced the literature as well as provided information to parents who were perplexed by their children's reactions to seemingly unthreatening images. Rather than examine media messages from an adult's view, Cantor sought to understand them from a child's qualitatively unique cognitive perspective. In most of her research, Cantor has taken into account her sample's cognitive capacities and linked them to any observed effects (see Cantor, Wilson, & Hoffner, 1986; Hoffner & Cantor, 1985, 1990; Hoffner, Cantor, & Thorson, 1988).

One important extension of Cantor's work on children's fright reactions to television has been in developing coping strategies for handling undesirable reactions (see Cantor & Wilson, 1984, 1988; Wilson & Cantor, 1985, 1987; Wilson, Hoffner, & Cantor, 1987). As with her other research, Cantor adheres to a developmental perspective to understand the effectiveness of certain techniques for helping youngsters deal with the stress imposed by disturbing media images. She has discovered that coping strategies must cater to the child's level of cognitive sophistication in order to be useful. In addition to lending more support to her proposed link between cognitive development and media effects, this work has tremendous practical appeal by offering real solutions for dealing with the sometimes unpleasant side effects of watching television.

One of the major goals of Cantor's research is to provide information that will be useful to all people—from scholars to parents to lawmakers. This concern for practicality is evident in the book she is currently writing with parents as the target audience. Her book will tell parents about her 15 years of research findings on children's fright reactions to television and provide advice on how to anticipate, understand, and prevent or ease these unwanted emotional responses.

Methodologically, Cantor has improved techniques for assessing young children's cognitive and emotional reactions to the media. Aware of the difficulty young children have in articulating their emotions, she developed visual aids to help them report their feelings. Cantor pairs response options such as "happy," "sad," and "angry" with drawings of faces that represent each emotion. Children are thus able simply to point to the face that represents how they feel rather than having to verbalize their thoughts. Cantor also assesses the intensity of the young child's response by asking follow-up questions in a similar fashion. The size of both the pictures and the writing increases with the intensity of the responses, thereby allowing children to indicate the degree to which they were affected by pointing at a particular image. Cantor also supplements these self-reports with physiological measures and by videotaping and later coding children's facial expressions while viewing.

Cantor is making significant contributions to understanding children's reactions to media violence. She is presently working on the Independent Television Violence Assessment, which is funded by the National Cable Television Association and coordinated by the nonprofit group "Mediascope." Her responsibility in this three-year project is to assess the use and influence of ratings and advisories. This landmark project will analyze data from the largest and most extensive random sample ever collected on television programming. The influence of this research will be great, for its results will be presented to Congress, to the general public, and to the industry so that more effective rating and advisory systems can be designed. Cantor is pleased with the practical applications of this massive project. She is hopeful that its very existence—and the fact that the cable industry is supporting the overall four-university research program with a $3.3 million grant—reflects the industry's desire to help find solutions to the problem of media violence.

Cantor's interest in media violence has also inspired her to attack another research area—the attractions of violent media. With the support of the Harry Frank Guggenheim Foundation, she has completed a chapter that explores why children choose to watch violent television (Cantor, in press). This project fits neatly into one of Cantor's major research objectives: to understand the motivations behind the viewing of television entertainment. For Cantor, discovering why individuals spend an extraordinary amount of time and money on mediated images is not only a fascinating question, but is also revealing of the human psyche. Understanding our interest in potentially upsetting images, such as violence, is even more perplexing and intriguing.

In addition to conducting her own research, Cantor has served as a research adviser and consultant for a number of projects undertaken by her local public television station, WHA-TV. Currently, with funding from the National Science Foundation, she is evaluating the impact of the Wisconsin-based children's series "Get Real!" on attitudes toward gender roles, racial tolerance, and science. Cantor is a firm supporter of children's educational programming like "Get Real!", citing the long-term, pro-social benefits of such shows. She has also helped implement WHA's community outreach survey on adolescents and violence, using samples of children from correctional institutions, 4H groups, and high schools.

The theoretical and practical applications of Cantor's work have earned her many academic awards and much public attention. In addition to receiving numerous invitations to speak at scholarly events, she is frequently quoted in the press and appears regularly on television and radio news and talk shows. Cantor states that although it was a bit embarrassing to be named one of the "25 smartest people in Madison" by *Madison Magazine* last year, she feels good about her recognition as a leading national expert on television and children.

Cantor is especially proud of her research that has sought both theoretical advancements and social relevance. The awards she has received are not as meaningful to her as learning that her work has touched others in some way. The tremendous impact she has had on others is reflected in reports on the outstanding quality of her former graduate students' work. For Cantor mentoring graduate students is one of the most enjoyable and rewarding parts of her career. The success and accomplishments of her graduate students are part of her contribution to the field and reflect the quality of her own work.

CRITICAL EVALUATION OF CONTRIBUTIONS AND ACHIEVEMENTS

Given her empirical approach to the study of media effects, Cantor has sometimes been criticized by those outside of the social science area for being "too quantitative." Although she remains faithful to her approach, she has tried to address some of the concerns of these alternative perspectives so that her findings can speak to a diverse audience.

Lending a critical eye to her own work, Cantor recognizes the limits of her experimental and survey research. If she had unlimited funds, she says she would have her experimental stimuli professionally written and produced in order to reduce threats to external validity. To extend the generalizability of her survey work, Cantor hopes to work in the future with national random samples.

Despite the limitations imposed by budgetary constraints, Cantor's work has demonstrated remarkable reliability. Her cognitive developmental approach to exploring children's understanding and reactions to mediated messages has repeatedly found support in a wide variety of situations and continues to inform our understanding of both child development and media effects.

INTEGRATION OF PERSONAL AND PROFESSIONAL LIFE

Cantor reports that being single and a workaholic benefited her early professional life. Without any outside distractions, she was able to devote full-time energy to her work, resulting in dozens of publications. However, after earning tenure and feeling satisfied with her career, Cantor decided to devote more attention to her personal life. She alerted friends that she was interested in meeting new people and soon met her future husband—the assistant attorney general for the State of Wisconsin, Robert W. Larsen—on a blind date in April 1981. They were married that August.

Cantor and Larsen have managed their dual-career marriage by splitting household and parenting responsibilities equally. Cantor feels very lucky to have a happy marriage and relishes the time she spends with her family after a full day of work. The mental change of pace offered by her family life makes her even more productive when she shifts her attention back to work. She believes that her rewarding personal life has given her a more positive outlook in general, thereby allowing her the increased energy and creativity that was once consumed by stress during her self-proclaimed workaholic days.

Cantor reports that her personal happiness is more important to her than any career achievement. Her family is her number-one priority, and she gladly makes professional sacrifices to maintain that focus. Since beginning her family, she travels less for professional activities, seldom misses a dinner at home with her family, and has tried to avoid tackling too many responsibilities that could infringe on her personal life. She accepted the position of associate dean when her child was a year old and only after she was assured that she could leave work by 3:00 P.M. four days a week during her first year in the position. In her research, Cantor tries to accept only those new commitments that will be especially rewarding to both her professional and personal development.

Spending quality time with her seven-year-old son, Alexander Cantor Larsen, has also given Cantor new ideas and insights into her research. She watches television with Alex and discusses the programs with him, but she never uses him as a "guinea pig" for her work. Her work on children's fright reactions to television has made her particularly sensitive to scary television content—an awareness that prompts her to shelter Alex from potentially upsetting shows. Cantor suspects that her concern has also led to Alex's own avoidance of scary programs.

Cantor's recreational activities also center around her family. She enjoys doing arts and crafts projects with her son and sailing with her husband in competitive races. Before her marriage, Cantor was quite active politically. She volunteered her expertise in communication to political causes and did everything from designing and running polls for congressional candidates to writing speeches and advertisements for local mayoral candidates. Today, she is concerned primarily with women's issues and offers her support whenever possible. When enjoying time alone, Cantor likes to read, especially books by and about women.

Cantor hopes to be remembered as a person who successfully managed both family and professional demands. Perhaps her success in each domain has allowed her a fresh perspective to tackle the demands of the other one. As a parent, she recognizes the need for practical research that can address the everyday struggles of child rearing. As a researcher, she understands the importance of advancing theory by posing well-articulated questions and carefully designing studies to address them. Her commitment to these concerns has yielded two decades of research that speaks to both academic and general audiences and continues to benefit us today.

NOTE

All biographical information not otherwise referenced is drawn from interviews with J. Cantor conducted by the author in August 1995.

REFERENCES

Cantor, J. (1994). Fright reactions to mass media. In J. Bryant and D. Zillmann (eds.), *Media effects: Advances in theory and research*. (pp. 213–245). Hillsdale, N.J.: Erlbaum.

Cantor, J. (in press). Children's attraction to violent television programming. In J. Goldstein (ed.), *Attractions of violence* (volume supported by the H. F. Guggenheim Foundation).

Cantor, J., & Wilson, B. J. (1984). Modifying fear responses to mass media in preschool and elementary school children. *Journal of Broadcasting, 28*, 431–443.

Cantor, J., & Wilson, B. J. (1988). Helping children cope with frightening media presentations. *Current Psychology: Research and Reviews, 7*, 58–75.

Cantor, J., Wilson, B. J., & Hoffner, C. (1986). Emotional responses to a televised nuclear holocaust film. *Communication Research, 13*, 257–277.

Cantor, J. R., Zillmann, D., & Bryant, J. (1975). Enhancement of experienced sexual arousal in response to erotic stimuli through misattribution of unrelated residual excitation. *Journal of Personality and Social Psychology,* 32, 69–75.

Hoffner, C., & Cantor, J. (1985). Developmental differences in responses to a television character's appearance and behavior. *Developmental Psychology,* 21, 1065–1074.

Hoffner, C., & Cantor, J. (1990). Forewarning of threat and its successful outcome: Effects on children's emotional responses to a film sequence. *Human Communication Research,* 16, 323–354.

Hoffner, C., Cantor, J., & Thorson, E. (1988). Children's understanding of a televised narrative: Developmental differences in processing of video and audio content. *Communication Research,* 15, 227–245.

Wheatman, C., & Hamele, A. (1995, Spring). [Out-takes from interview with Joanne Cantor.] *The golden choice.* [Videotape]. Museum of Science and Industry, Chicago.

Wilson, B. J., & Cantor, J. (1985). Developmental differences in empathy with a television protagonist's fear. *Journal of Experimental Child Psychology,* 39, 284–299.

Wilson, B. J., & Cantor, J. (1987). Reducing children's fear reactions to mass media: Effects of visual exposure and verbal explanation. *Communication Yearbook 10.* (pp. 553–573). Beverly Hills, Calif.: Sage.

Wilson, B. J., Hoffner, C., & Cantor, J. (1987). Children's perceptions of the effectiveness of techniques to reduce fear from mass media. *Journal of Applied Developmental Psychology,* 8, 39–52.

Zillmann, D., & Cantor, J. R. (1972). Directionality of transitory dominance as a communication variable affecting humor appreciation. *Journal of Personality and Social Psychology,* 24, 191–198.

Zillmann, D., & Cantor, J. R. (1974). Rhetorical elicitation of concession in persuasion. *Journal of Social Psychology,* 94, 223–236.

Zillmann, D., & Cantor, J. R. (1976). Effects of timing of information about mitigating circumstances on emotional responses to provocation and retaliatory behavior. *Journal of Experimental Social Psychology,* 12, 38–55.

Additional Representative Publications by Joanne Cantor

Cantor, J., & Reilly, S. (1982). Adolescents' fright reactions to television and films. *Journal of Communication,* 32, 87–99.

Cantor, J., & Sparks, G. G. (1984). Children's fear responses to mass media: Testing some Piagetian predictions. *Journal of Communication,* 34, 90–103.

Cantor, J., Sparks, G. G., & Hoffner, C. (1988). Calming children's fears: Mr. Rogers vs. The Incredible Hulk. *Journal of Broadcasting and Electronic Media,* 32, 271–288.

Hoffner, C., Cantor, J., & Badzinski, D. M. (1990). Children's understanding of adverbs denoting degree of likelihood. *Journal of Child Language,* 17, 217–231.

PEGGY CHARREN
(1928–   )

Ellen A. Wartella

Perhaps more than any other person, Peggy Charren has been the guiding light behind the last 30 years of discussions about children's television. From a "Boston housewife" who organized a small group of parents concerned about television and children in 1968 out of the living room of her house in Newtonville, Massachusetts, Peggy Charren, as head of Action for Children's Television (ACT), became the insistent force behind the policy debates that led to the 1990 Children's Television Act. Today Charren, as a senior scholar at Harvard University, continues to speak out as an advocate for more and better children's television and is pursuing ways to strengthen the 1990 act as one of the leading children's advocates in the country. Moreover, public advocacy groups in other countries as far flung as Japan, Britain, and Australia count Peggy Charren as the inspiration and ACT as the model for advocacy of better quality children's television everywhere.

FAMILY BACKGROUND

Peggy Walzer Charren was born on March 9, 1928. Her father, Maxwell, was in the fur business, and her mother, Ruth, was a pianist who had studied at the Julliard School. In addition to Peggy, they had a second daughter, Barbara, Peggy's junior by three years. Her father received his degree from New York University, and her mother left Julliard before receiving her degree.

Charren's family was politically progressive, and her upbringing in Manhattan was that of a well-educated upper-middle-class child from the upper west and then east side. Her background, including both the arts and politics, continued to be part of her life's work. In addition, her family, their friends, and her various school and vacation activities ensured that throughout her life

Charren would have access to people in the media and in politics. The circles in which she traveled were populated by many who became media producers and industry personnel. Growing up in Manhattan was clearly an advantage for her future interests in media and policy.

EDUCATION

Charren attended the New York City public schools (PS 9 for elementary school) and later Hunter College High School on the upper east side. Her high school years spanned the war years, and Hunter was an all-girls school at the time. As she put it, "the only male at school was Jimmy, the elevator man." It was also in high school that she began attending the Ethical Culture Center on the upper west side, a place to debate social issues and have a chance to meet other young people, particularly young men.

She attended Connecticut College, graduating with a B.A. in English in 1949. As she puts it, "I don't really think I had a career ambition ... I wanted to work, but I don't think I thought of a grand design, it was much more haphazard than that." Indeed, after she finished college, she went to an employment agency to get her working start as quickly as possible.

MARRIAGE AND CAREER

When Charren graduated from college she was offered three jobs, one at the J. Walter Thompson Advertising Agency, one at the Advertising Council, and one at WPIX-TV. She took the one at WPIX to work as a script typist; but she was a bad typist and lasted only two weeks at that job before becoming head of the film department at the station. Her job was varied. She was in charge of keeping track of the syndication to other television stations around the country of films to which WPIX owned the rights. At other times she called the shots in the control room, held talent shows for live programs, and escorted visitors to the studio (memorably, the singer Edith Piaf). Having found an interesting job in television, which was then a very new medium, she was the envy of her friends.

When she met and then married Stanley Charren in June 1951, she quit her job at WPIX to move with him to Providence, Rhode Island. Stanley was an engineer by education (Brown and then Harvard universities) and an entrepreneur by inclination. During their time in Rhode Island, he worked in a measuring equipment business, while she found a variety of jobs, moving with him to Boston a few years later, in 1954. The jobs she held before her first daughter, Deborah, was born in 1956 included working for the *Mathematical Review,* an academic review journal in Providence; opening an art gallery while there; and then, in Boston, working at a variety of jobs at Harvard, including serving as an assistant in a psychology laboratory.

During these years, while spending most of the time as an at-home mother, raising her two young daughters, Charren continued to work in one of her two great loves, books. Her life took a different turn following a quite mundane event: her attendance at a book fair at her daughter's school in the mid-1950s. Her dismay at the poor quality of the fair combined with her love of children's literature led her and her neighborhood friend to organize Quality Book Fairs for schools in the Boston area. This career lasted until her second daughter, Claudia, was born in 1964.

In the early 1960s, Charren became involved in the Newton Creative Arts Council in her community as a volunteer organizing arts events for the community. That stint lasted about two years and gave her access to the WGBH public television community in Boston.

By 1968, as Charren put, she found herself with "lousy daycare and this wonderful sense of how to turn kids on to breathtaking moments of drama and literature and there was TV with wall to wall monster cartoons . . . it was 1968 and I looked at that screen and said why don't I get some book-based programs on TV." Thus, her frustrations over the programs her young children were watching on TV, together with her love of children's books (today she continues to collect first editions and rare editions of children's literature) and her history of volunteer community efforts in the arts, became the genesis of her concern about children's television. Her activism in the television arena was not as a censor, but as someone who wanted to help get "good" literature to children— to bring to children what she had done with book fairs in her hometown and provide them access to the best in children's literature.

And so in 1968 she brought together a variety of friends—community people, someone from the public broadcasting station, the head of the English Department in the Newton school system, and a variety of interested parents. Over the course of several meetings at which they talked about what they would like to see on television, Action for Children's Television was born.

For Charren, ACT (she came up with the acronym) represented another good cause that she thought would take up her time and energy until she returned to her book fair business when her younger daughter started school. From the earliest meeting her friends were skeptical that a group of concerned parents in Newtonville, Massachusetts could affect the television industry, which was centered in New York, Los Angeles, and Washington.

From the beginning, Charren thought ACT could be a potent force. The group that first year registered as a 501c3 nonprofit organization. Between 1969 and 1970, Charren and ACT discovered the Federal Communications Act of 1934 and the public interest responsibility of broadcasters. When Charren realized the group needed money, she scoured magazine stories on how to apply to foundations for grants and which foundations were interested in which issues, and bought a manual on how to write grant applications. She applied for a grant to the John and Mary Markle Foundation whose new executive director, Lloyd Morrisett, had expressed an interest in funding television studies and groups. In

1970 ACT was awarded a two-year grant totaling $165,000 to work on improving children's television.

From the start, Charren also knew how to reach the networks and garner publicity for ACT. It was during this two-year period as well that ACT wrote to the heads of all three television networks in New York, asking to meet with them to discuss children's television. CBS responded with an appointment. Charren and several of her colleagues arranged to meet with CBS in New York and with a reporter at the *New York Times* after the meeting. When she and her colleagues showed up at CBS, a lower level bureaucrat met with the women to show them clips of current CBS shows and discuss what CBS was doing about children's television. Charren and the others in the ACT group listened patiently and pointed out that CBS and the other networks were not doing enough for children, that there were too few choices, no news show, not enough diversity, and too many, indeed almost all, cartoon shows. Charren then asked if Mike Dann was available. (Dann was the network programmer whom she knew as a fellow summer vacationer at Martha's Vineyard, whose wife she knew as part of a group with which she had gone bird watching.) He met with the group and during that discussion, Charren pointed out ACT's concerns about choice and diversity in children's programming. She noted that the network's lack of a vice president in charge of children's television suggested their disinterest. Dann was impressed and later expressed his approval to the same reporter from the *New York Times* with whom the group had talked after the meeting with CBS. Thus, in that one day, Action for Children's Television visibly got its agenda into a *New York Times* story and also attracted the attention of a major network.

The next step was to move more directly into the policy arena. ACT did that in February 1970 with a visit to the Federal Communications Commission (FCC) with a one-page petition requesting that the FCC examine the quality of children's TV. (As Charren remembers it, the night before the trip, a lawyer friend had given her a copy of the format at the top of the page to be used in making a filing before the Commission. Charren spent the evening retyping ACT's one-page list of concerns about children's TV.) During Charren's FCC visit, she and a few of her colleagues in ACT met with six of the seven commissioners, including the FCC chairman Dean Burch. Clearly, the group was persuasive, since that one-page petition became the basis of the FCC Notice of Inquiry into Children's Television released in March.

From the time of that Notice of Inquiry through the 1974 Children's television rule-making by the FCC, the 1978 Federal Trade Commission investigation of children's television advertising, the FCC filings in 1983 and 1984 which had the FCC investigate program-length commercials, and the myriad of congressional investigations into children's television which culminated in the 1990 Children's Television Act, Charren and ACT have been at the center of the policy debates about children's television. Moreover, during this time Charren became the spokeswoman and advocate for better and more quality children's television.

IMPACT ON THE FIELD

The passage of the Children's Television Act of 1990, the first federal policy regarding children's television, was the culmination of ACT's lobbying efforts. The act established each station's obligation to serve the educational and information needs of children; it placed specific limits on the amount of advertising permitted during children's programs; it directed the FCC to rule on the question of whether or not to allow children's program-length commercials; and it established a National Endowment for Children's Educational Television to seed independent productions of quality children's educational shows. Charren maintains that, with the passage of this legislation, ACT had accomplished its goals. She says, "even though their airwaves weren't working as they should be, it seemed to me that it was the beginning of a process that other constituencies should get involved in and as a mandate it was just what ACT did, other people could now help move children's television forward." In February 1992, ACT closed its doors: its job was done.

At every major step along the route to the 1990 Children's Television Act, Charren and ACT were there, petitioning the FCC, testifying at congressional hearings, being interviewed in the press regarding new developments, such as the growth of toy-related programming in the 1980s, and generally being very public critics of commercial television advertising practices and supporters of quality children's television shows on cable and on public television or wherever they found them. The omnipresence of Charren as *the* children's television advocate is clear in all public reviews and discussions about children's television in the past 25 years or more. Charren has kept the children's television issue on the public agenda, and while the practices of the networks regarding children's television have ebbed and flowed over the years (with more diverse and quality programs following threats to regulate children's TV and the passage of the 1990 Act), Charren has been a constant observer of the scene. Peggy Charren has become synonymous with children's television advocacy in this country.

As founder of ACT, Charren eventually came to lead a 10,000-member nonprofit organization that worked to encourage quality children's television, program diversity, and the elimination of excessive commercialization of children's TV. Along the way, she co-authored several books about children and television, including *The TV Smart Book for Kids* (E.P. Dutton, 1986) and *Changing Channels: Living (Sensibly) with Television* (Addison-Wesley, 1983). She has also received six honorary degrees from, among others, Bank Street College of Education, Emerson College, and Tufts University, and now sits on ten national advisory boards. She has won numerous awards, including a special Peabody Award in 1992 and a National Academy of Television Arts and Sciences Trustees Emmy in 1988. She has lectured at prestigious universities here and around the world. Today, Peggy Charren is a visiting scholar in education at Harvard University's Graduate School of Education. She continues to serve as a media consultant on children's television issues as well as an advocate for quality children's media. Her influence has been, and continues to be, profound in this arena.

CONSTANCE (CONNIE) YU-HWA CHUNG (1946–   )

Susan G. Kahlenberg

Connie Chung is one of the United States' foremost women broadcasters. Chung earned her position as co-anchor on the CBS nightly network news with Dan Rather and as anchor of "Eye to Eye with Connie Chung," a prime-time news hour, through hard work and dedication with gracious aggressiveness and intelligence. Connie, an Asian-American, was the first woman to co-anchor the nightly network news since Barbara Walters in 1976 and one of the highest paid women in television news. She gained widespread popularity and respect; her Q rating (a measure of the popularity of a product or television personality) was one of the highest of all news broadcasters. Moreover, *U.S. News & World Report*'s 1990 Best of America survey listed her as "favorite interviewer." Connie Chung has received many awards and honors, including three Emmy Awards, a George Foster Peabody Award, two American Women in Radio and Television National Commendation Awards, a 1991 Clarion Award, a 1991 Ohio State Award, and a 1991 National Headliner Award. She is a strong role model for women in contemporary society. Chung has clearly demonstrated that women can be successful in both career and marriage; she has been married to Maury Povich, the host of "The Maury Povich Show," since 1984. She has also made tremendous strides for women in television by challenging the assumptions of traditional female roles in American society. Her achievements in television news have undoubtedly encouraged more women to enter this traditionally male profession.

FAMILY BACKGROUND

Constance Yu-hwa Chung was born on August 20, 1946 in Washington, D.C., the tenth and youngest child of Margaret and William Ling Chung. She is the only member of her immediate family who was born in the United States. Connie's parents moved to the United States in 1944 from Shanghai, China. During World War II, living conditions in Shanghai were appalling. Five of the first nine Chung children died in infancy. William, a member of the Nationalist party and a diplomat in Chiang Kai-shek's government, moved his wife Margaret and their four children from Shanghai to the suburbs of Washington, D.C, where he believed his family would have a better life and more fruitful opportunities. He worked at the United Nations until 1949 when the communists took over China and he was forced to give up his job (Brin, 1984). He then went into accounting and worked two jobs as a financial manager to support the family (Brin, 1984; Hickey, 1993; Wallace, 1985).

Most of Connie's memories from childhood are happy ones. She describes her family as big and wonderful (Malone, 1992). At times Connie felt inferior to her sisters because she was the only child in her family not born in China. But her sisters shared memories of China with Connie, which made her feel included and knowledgeable about their birthland. While at home, Connie spoke Chinese, the language spoken by all the Chungs (Malone, 1992).

EDUCATION

During elementary school, Connie was a shy, quiet child who was often intimidated by her four older sisters. One of her teachers in school wrote on her report card, "speaks too softly," which devastated her (Kaiser, 1988; Malone, 1992). Thereafter, she made more attempts to speak up and out. Overall, Connie considered herself "a regular goody-two-shoes," who, like many girls, fantasized about becoming a ballerina (Malone, 1992; Salisbury, 1985).

As a child, Connie developed a strong work ethic from her parents, whom she admired and respected. In an interview with Mary Hickey (1993), Chung acknowledged that both her parents worked very hard to succeed in the United States. Thus, they had high expectations for each of their daughters. In Chinese culture, sons are highly valued by the family unit. As the youngest child, Connie wanted to be her father's son and perpetuate the family name (Hickey, 1993). This desire was one contributing influence toward her educational success.

In high school, Connie overcame her shyness and became active in school plays, variety shows, and student government. She was raised reading the *Washington Post* and developed a strong interest in government affairs. She claims that "you can't grow up in Washington, D.C., and not be extremely aware of what's going on on Capitol Hill. It's part of local news, in addition to being network news. You can't grow up like I did without developing an interest for how this country works" (Paisner, 1989, p. 219).

Connie Chung attended the University of Maryland at College Park from 1965 to 1969, originally majoring in biology. In the summer between her junior and senior years, she worked as a summer intern writing speeches and press releases for Seymour Halpern, a Republican congressman from New York (*Current Bi-*

ography Yearbook, 1989). When she returned to college in the fall, she switched
her major to journalism. After experiencing the excitement of watching politics
at work, Chung found that "dissecting frogs lost its appeal" (Malone, 1992, p.
15; Paisner, 1989). She stopped working in the laboratory and accepted a part-
time job as a copy clerk at WTTG, a Metromedia-owned television station in
Washington, D.C., in hopes that it would turn into a full-time job after graduation. She desperately wanted a job in broadcasting and was willing to do odd
jobs around the station just to be affiliated with the media.

Upon graduation, Chung was awarded a certificate of recognition for outstanding scholarship in her journalism classes (Malone, 1992). In retrospect, Chung
believes she should have majored in history or English instead of journalism.
In an interview with Helen Chang, a reporter from *Savvy,* Connie claimed that
majoring in journalism was not challenging and demanding. "[As a journalism
major], you learn a little bit, but you'd learn just as much on the job or by
taking a summer internship in television or radio" (Chang, 1986, p. 29). In
short, she found her experience as a journalism major unrewarding when compared to her summer internship with Seymour Halpern or her future reporting
experiences with CBS or NBC.

In addition to holding a Bachelor of Arts degree in journalism from the University of Maryland, Chung has received a Doctor of Humane Letters from
Brown University; an honorary doctorate in journalism from Norwich University, Northfield, Vermont; an honorary doctorate from Providence College,
Rhode Island; and an honorary Degree of Laws from Wheaton College, Northfield, Massachusetts (*Connie Chung,* 1994).

CAREER DEVELOPMENT

Connie Chung's objective, after graduating from the University of Maryland,
was to become a full-time reporter at a television station in Washington affiliated
with a large network. She became newsroom secretary for WTTG-TV because
it was the only full-time offer she received. She quickly advanced to news writer,
where she developed her reporting skills (Paisner, 1989), and eventually to an
on-air reporter. By 1971 hard work, brains, and charm made Chung a reporter
for CBS's Washington, D.C., affiliate. This, Connie claims, was her dream job
(Malone, 1992).

Chung had enormous drive, ambition, and ability, but affirmative action also
helped her enter this traditionally white male profession (Malone, 1992). In 1971
the Federal Communications Commission began pressuring networks to hire
more minorities. Chung was one of four women hired by CBS news. In an
interview with Daniel Paisner (1989), Chung said that "there were always distinct and clear permutations and combinations of women that were appropriate
at that time to hire. In other words, a Chinese woman, a black woman, a nice
Jewish girl, and a blond shiksa. Perfect. And so they [CBS] took care of years
of discrimination" (p. 221).

Those who believed Chung's hiring at CBS was mere tokenism soon realized that Chung was a tenacious worker who was willing to cover any assignment and work long, grueling hours. She worked as a rookie with "heavyweights" such as Dan Rather, Roger Mudd, Marvin Kalb, Daniel Schorr, and Walter Cronkite. At the time, Rather was a CBS reporter covering the White House, and he was impressed by Chung's professional attitude. He commented that "no assignment was too gritty or grimy, no weather was too inclement to send her [Chung] out" (Smith, 1983, p. 32).

Chung compensated for her inexperience with aggressiveness, motivation, and hard news reporting. Richard Cooper, a colleague of Connie's during the 1970s, commented that "she [Connie] was small and pretty, but she could elbow with the best of them. She was not some flower one could push aside" (Waters, Friendly, & Howard, 1983). If anything, her petite, attractive appearance and assertiveness increased her popularity. It did not negatively affect her professional reputation with viewers or colleagues. In addition, being a woman in a traditionally male profession did not affect the quality of Chung's work. Her news stories and reporting style were competitive with those of her male colleagues. CBS News regularly sent two or three reporters out on the same story to compete against other networks as well as each other. The best story would be broadcast on Walter Cronkite's show that night. More often than not, Connie's story would air (Ryan, 1988). Overall, her performance as a CBS reporter from 1971 to 1976 demonstrated that she was an important asset to any news station.

Chung's first big assignment as CBS network correspondent was to cover the presidential campaign of George McGovern, Democratic senator from South Dakota. She was, however, the "low person on the totem pole." According to Dan Rather, she was "right at [McGovern's] elbow every second" (*Current Biography Yearbook,* 1989, p. 107). Chung's second big assignment was covering the Watergate affair. She was part of a team that followed stories on several key figures in the scandal, including John Dean, John N. Mitchell, Richard G. Kleindienst, John D. Ehrlichman, and H. R. (Bob) Haldeman (*Current Biography Yearbook,* 1989). During her coverage of Watergate, Chung was noted by other reporters as indefatigable. Her work as news reporter dominated her life, and she often worked on little sleep in order to get an important interview. For example, Connie would wait outside McGovern's home before dawn and one morning she staked Bob Haldeman out at church to get an interview (Malone, 1992; Paisner, 1989; Waters, Friendly, & Howard, 1983). Chung's persistence, determination, and excellent news reporting skills earned her the number one reporter position in her third big assignment—covering the confirmation of Nelson Rockefeller as vice president under Nixon's successor, Gerald Ford. She immersed herself in the assignment, becoming a virtual encyclopedia of knowledge on Rockefeller (*Current Biography Yearbook,* 1989; Smith, 1983).

Chung claims that her five years as a CBS news reporter were the high points of her career (Chang, 1986). Chung not only pursued her fascination with politics and the media, but also proved to her colleagues and the American public

her strong capabilities and credibility as a woman news reporter. During the
next 23 years of Chung's career, she established herself as one of the most
talented and popular television news reporters.

MAJOR CONTRIBUTIONS AND ACHIEVEMENTS

In 1976 Connie was offered a position anchoring the local news at KNXT-
TV in Los Angeles, a station owned and operated by CBS. The station had
slipped behind the local ABC and NBC affiliates, and Connie was expected to
raise the ratings (Malone, 1992). Suffering from restlessness, boredom, and a
post-Watergate letdown, Connie accepted CBS's offer to anchor in California.
With hard work and a warm, straightforward manner, Connie won herself a
loyal following and managed to make a significant change at KNXT. She anchored the 11:00, the early 6:00, and the 4:30 newscasts, and raised the ratings
at KNXT from last to a strong second (occasionally receiving the number one
rating) (Paisner, 1989). Connie became a local hero; her face was plastered on
billboards, at the backs of buses, and in newspaper advertisements (Kaiser, 1988;
Paisner, 1989). By 1983 she became television's highest-paid local newswoman,
with an estimated salary between $600,000 and $700,000 a year (Chang, 1986;
Kaiser, 1988).

After seven years in California, Connie was eager to report again on national
politics instead of local news. She was especially eager to report on the 1984
presidential race for a national network. Connie told *New York,* ''I could see
1984 tap-dancing its way into my heart and not being able to really grasp it''
(Smith, 1983, p. 32). Through negotiations, Connie accepted a contract offer
with NBC, even though it meant a drop in salary and leaving CBS (Malone,
1983). Despite these disadvantages, the move offered Chung the opportunity to
report on politics for a national network. It also provided Chung the challenge
of raising the ratings of the ''Early Today Show'' or ''News at Sunrise,'' which
preceded the 7:00 A.M. ''Today Show.'' She replaced Jane Pauley and Bryant
Gumbel as sole anchor of NBC's 6:00–7:00 A.M. program ''News at Sunrise''
(Buchalter, 1983). Chung also substituted for Tom Brokaw on the weekday
evening news, sole anchored the Saturday evening network news, and did 90-
second news briefs for NBC at night (Malone, 1992). This was one of the most
arduous work schedules in television broadcasting. As Charles Kaiser (1988)
claimed, ''Doesn't this sound like the portrait of a driven woman?'' (p. 222).

For the second time in her broadcasting career, Connie's talent and skill as a
news anchor raised the ratings of a faltering program. ''Early at Sunrise'' drew
high ratings and rose to the top of the scale, occasionally tying at first position
with CBS's ''Early Morning News'' (Malone, 1992; Waters et al., 1983). In
addition, Chung was respected by her co-workers, who claimed she offered
continuous praise, motivation, and a good example, and by national viewers,
who were captivated by her grace and cool manner (Salisbury, 1985). ''She
doesn't have the pomposity that a lot of people in this business have,'' said

CBS producer Andrew Heyward (Hickey, 1993). Chung's status as a rising network star was again confirmed through her success.

After two years of anchoring "Early at Sunrise," Chung was given a new challenge—co-anchoring a new prime-time magazine show, "American Almanac," with Roger Mudd (*Harpers Bazaar,* 1985). This was a monthly series representing NBC's fourteenth attempt to create a competitive prime-time news magazine (*Current Biography Yearbook,* 1989). "American Almanac," however, was never assigned a weekly slot and was withdrawn after a few months due to low ratings. It resumed under the name "1986," with Chung and Mudd as co-anchors; it ran for approximately six months and was again canceled due to low ratings (Malone, 1992).

Despite this professional setback, Chung was still considered an important asset to the NBC news staff. She was popular with viewers and had a strong reputation as a broadcast journalist. In 1987 she visited China for the first time with NBC news and broadcast several programs live from Beijing and other cities (*Current Biography Yearbook,* 1989; Malone, 1992). While in China, she tracked down her relatives, went to her grandparents' graves, learned how World War II and the Cultural Revolution had affected her family, and prepared a special broadcast on her experience for NBC. "It was the most rewarding experience I've ever had," said Chung to an interviewer with *Parade Magazine* (Ryan, 1988, p. 25). "I think it [the broadcast] was meaningful to the viewers, because it was *my* family. My life has been much more defined by my roots since that experience" (Ryan, 1988, p. 25).

In addition to this special broadcast, Connie anchored five one-hour series of single-subject documentaries for NBC; "Life in the Fat Lane" (fad diets and their negative effects); "Scared Sexless" (AIDS and how it affects sexual mores); "Stressed to Kill" (stress-related illness); "Guns, Guns, Guns" (the easy accessibility of handguns in the United States); and "Everybody's Doing It" (a report on aging) (Appelo, 1988; *Current Biography Yearbook,* 1989; Malone, 1992). These one-hour documentaries included investigative reporting as well as commentary and interviews with television and film celebrities. Although Tom Shales, a TV critic from the *Washington Post,* and other reviewers were extremely critical of these so-called "gaudy" prime-time documentaries, they were very successful and received high ratings (*Current Biography Yearbook,* 1989). Furthermore, Chung's popularity increased because she switched from her no-nonsense news delivery to a lighter, more humorous style, which matched the frothy image of these specials (Malone, 1992). She was praised by producers for having the ability to project two different on-air images. The special "Scared Sexless" was the highest rated NBC News special in ten years (*Current Biography Yearbook,* 1989).

Chung, nevertheless, did not entirely abandon her straightforward manner of delivering the news. She continued to prove her excellence as a serious broadcaster by obtaining the first interview with Jesse Jackson (a presidential candidate at the 1988 Democratic convention) (*Current Biography Yearbook,* 1989;

World Book Encyclopedia, 1991). She was also the first newsperson to speak with John F. Kennedy Jr., following his speech introducing Senator Edward M. Kennedy at this convention (*Current Biography Yearbook,* 1989).

In 1989 Chung stunned television viewers and insiders by accepting a contract offer from CBS News. Connie's contract offer was partially the result of Diane Sawyer leaving CBS News for a lucrative offer at ABC News. As a result, CBS offered Connie an irresistible opportunity and challenge at their network. For approximately $6 million over three years, Connie would anchor the Sunday evening news, substitute for Dan Rather on the nightly network news, and anchor the magazine style show "West 57th," which was later substituted with "Saturday Night with Connie Chung" (Malone, 1992; McMurran, 1989; *People,* 1989). At the end of its first season, "Saturday Night with Connie Chung" was scheduled for a more favorable evening and was renamed "Face to Face with Connie Chung" (Malone, 1992). This prime-time magazine program became a series of specials in 1991.

Accepting the CBS offer and leaving NBC News was a risk for Chung. According to Malone (1992), "NBC and ABC vied for first place, and CBS occupied the bottom rung" (p. 115). Chung's offer at CBS demonstrated that women broadcasters had earned respect in the television industry. According to Judy Flander (1985), during the 1970s the news was dominated by white males. There were virtually no minorities in top or middle management, making news decision-making policies, as newspeople, or as anchors of news programs. Women were "a minority within a minority . . . and their visibility stems[ed] from 'fringe anchor jobs'—in the morning, on weekends" (Flander, 1985, p. 153). Twenty years later, however, women have negotiated for high salaries, more responsibilities, and stronger positions within the network.

Connie Chung is one woman who has largely influence, challenged, and changed women's roles as television broadcasters. Her contributions, achievements, and popularity with audiences are tremendous. As *Time* magazine notes, "the battle over Chung [when she left NBC for CBS in 1989] illustrates even more vividly how much clout TV news stars can wield when they have reached a certain level of audience recognition" (Zoglin, 1989, p. 71). Newswomen have more control over what programs or news slots they anchor and how much money they are paid. Even though newswomen like Connie Chung still may receive more public scrutiny over their appearance and their private lives than newsmen, they have earned more widespread respect for their talent.

Throughout Chung's career, her goal was to anchor the network nightly news. Barbara Walters briefly co-anchored the ABC network news show with Harry Reasoner in 1976 (Conant, 1990; Waters & Rogers, 1993). For more than 15 years, however, all three network nightly news shows were anchored by men, and Connie did not expect her goal to become a reality. However, on June 1, 1993, Chung joined Dan Rather as a co-anchor of the CBS evening news. Her appointment as co-anchor was a strategic attempt by CBS to increase the ratings of the evening news (Landler, 1993). Although CBS claims that the coanchorship was Rather's idea, some speculate that Chung was assigned to the nightly news because of her high Q rating (recognizability to viewers as an Asian-American TV star), and natural warmth and appeal to all viewers, especially female and younger viewers (Andersen, 1993; Landler, 1993; Waters and Rogers, 1993). Rather has been criticized by TV critics as wooden, stiff, tense, and unpredictable (Katz, 1993). Landler (1993) commented that "viewers seem[ed] to prefer Jennings' [of ABC] silken style to Rather's this-just-in tone" (p. 33). Thus, the two distinct personalities of Chung and Rather were expected to be a good balance at the anchor desk.

Besides co-anchoring the nightly news, Chung also anchored "Eye to Eye with Connie Chung," a prime-time news hour that premiered on June 17, 1993 (replacing Chung's previous Emmy Award-winning CBS news prime-time series "Face to Face with Connie Chung") (*Connie Chung,* 1994). This prime-time magazine show received strong ratings and was competitive with other magazine-style news programs.

As a broadcast journalist, Connie is best known for her memorable interviews. Tom Brokow calls Connie a "winning interviewer: she has the ability to get people to sit down and talk, and pursue the salient points in a tough but still engaging way" (Kaiser, 1988, p. 166). She was the first TV journalist to interview Los Angeles Lakers' star Magic Johnson after his announcement that he had the AIDS virus. She conducted the first and only one-on-one interview with Captain Joseph Hazelwood of the Exxon *Valdez.* She also interviewed Michael Durant, a U.S. pilot captured in Somalia; Roger Clinton, the brother of President Bill Clinton; Heidi Fleiss, a convicted Hollywood madam; as well as Newt Gingrich's mother (Younger, 1994). Her dream would be to interview Barbara Walters and make her cry on camera, since Walters once jokingly commented that she would die if one more person cried while she was interviewing them (Younger, 1994).

Chung's investigative reporting on the potential dangers of breast implants sparked a nationwide medical controversy. In addition, she won a Silver Gavel award from the American Bar Association in 1991 as the first network TV correspondent to report on the debate surrounding testing convicted rapists for AIDS (*Connie Chung,* 1994; Younger, 1994).

CRITICAL EVALUATION OF CONTRIBUTIONS AND ACHIEVEMENTS

Being a prominent television star, Chung has received criticism from the public and media critics throughout her career. She received the harshest criticism of her career in 1991, when she announced plans to reduce her work schedule to try to start a family. This plan involved abandoning "Face to Face with Connie Chung," the successful prime-time magazine show (Hickey, 1994). Critic Gail Collins felt Chung owed it to her colleagues at "Face to Face" to figure out whether she could dedicate the long hours and extra work to the show before starting it (Collins, 1990).

High-achieving women often have conflicts balancing career and family. As Chung said, "Many [career] women of my generation felt that if we took time off to have a child, our careers would suffer" (Hickey, 1993, p. 68). So many women delay marriage and starting a family until they have job security and a strong reputation. Even then, "the public has an insatiable curiosity about how they are coping with their careers and marriages because their stories mirror the changes that are taking place in their audience's own lives" (Conant, 1990, p. 61).

Since the advent of the women's movement, women have been fighting for equal opportunities and employment in traditional male occupations. Unfortunately, even though women are succeeding in traditional male occupations like broadcast journalism, there is still a double standard. Women are expected to balance their career, marriage, and family at the same time, without taking time off from their careers. When women take time off from their careers for personal reasons, they are often criticized and their achievements devalued.

Chung's decision to leave "Face to Face" and start a family, however, should not devalue her achievements and contributions in broadcast journalism. For much of her career, marriage and family were secondary. Her decision to re-evaluate her priorities and commit more time to her private life should be respected and supported by her fans and critics. As Chung said, "there's no perfect time to have a baby. I kept waiting for the right moment, and there was always something stopping me: another big story, another convention, another new magazine show" (Hickey, 1993, p. 68). There will always be career opportunities for television stars like Connie Chung, but a woman cannot always bear children.

Chung has also been criticized by network insiders for her broadcasting style. She may be captivating and charming on screen, but she is rumored to be heavily produced. Furthermore, colleagues claim Connie is an unreliable "on-the-air ad libber." According to Steve Friedman, executive producer of the "Today" show, it is dangerous to put Connie out on location without a script (Andersen, 1993). An anonymous NBC insider claims Connie once refused to go on the air without a script when she was co-anchoring with Bryant Gumbel on the "Today Show." Gumbel then accused Connie of not being a team player (Kaiser, 1988).

Even if Chung reads directly from a teleprompter or has to be heavily produced, it is important to note that her instincts are strong and that she writes virtually all of her own scripts. Daniel Paisner, in his book *The Imperfect Mirror,* describes the amount of hard work and energy Chung devotes to writing the perfect script. "Connie is meticulous and exacting in her choice of words; if she were working on a traditional typewriter, her wastebasket would be filled with the crumpled stops and starts" (Paisner, 1989, p. 239). Furthermore, producers typically prepare initial background research and possible interview questions. Chung, however, prepares her own interview questions based on her research and instincts, only occasionally supplementing them with the producer's ideas (Younger, 1994).

INTEGRATION OF PERSONAL AND PROFESSIONAL LIFE

Chung devoted the beginning of her career entirely to her work, despite her parents' hopes that she would marry (Malone, 1992). Although she went out socially, she did not want to devote much time to a romantic relationship. At that point in her career, her work was her passion (Malone, 1992). She claims, "I was always climbing, you know, clawing, trying to get to the next step [in my career]. So I think what it is is it [marriage and children] didn't enter into the picture for me for so many years" (Paisner, 1989, p. 142). In addition, Chung would not date men connected with her news assignments, which eliminated many men with whom she regularly interacted (Malone, 1992).

Connie Chung met her husband Maury Povich in 1969 when he was the popular host of "Panorama," a midday talk show on WTTG-TV in Washington, D.C. (Malone, 1992; McMurran, 1989). Like Connie, Povich was born and raised in Washington, D.C. His father, Shirley Povich, is a long-time sports writer for the *Washington Post*. Povich has two daughters, Susan and Amy, by his first wife, Phyllis Minkoff.

A year after Connie joined KNXT, Povich was also hired to anchor with her on the 5:00 P.M. newscast (Malone, 1992). After six months in Los Angeles, Povich was fired when the ratings of his program failed to improve. That same week, his marriage broke up, leaving Maury devastated. Chung supported Povich emotionally, and the two became close friends (Malone, 1992; Wallace, 1985). Eventually, Chung and Povich became romantically involved, but most of their time was devoted to their careers. In 1978 Povich accepted an offer at a San Francisco station, but returned two years later to the East Coast, first as newscaster on KYW in Philadelphia and then as host of "Panorama" in Washington, D.C. (McMurran, 1989; Wallace, 1985).

Chung claimed, "I truly knew from the beginning that Maury was the one, but I just didn't have it in me to commit myself" (McMurran, 1989, p. 120). Connie and Maury became frequent fliers on the Los Angeles-San Francisco route, but the romance cooled when he headed back east. They became pen pals and began seeing other people. However, after six months they reevaluated their lives, resumed their long-distance relationship, and became frequent fliers again (Wallace, 1985).

In 1983 Chung accepted a contract with NBC and moved to New York. For more than a year, she would fly to Washington late Saturday night and hurry back late Sunday afternoon to be at work early Monday morning (McMurran, 1989). When asked by reporters and fans whether she moved back east to be with Povich, Chung replied, "Would anyone ask a man if he were moving to

be nearer a woman? Or would they just assume it was a career choice?'' (Buchalter, 1983).

On December 2, 1984, Connie Chung and Maury Povich were married in
Connie's New York apartment. Two years after their marriage, Maury obtained
an anchor position on New York's FOX Channel 5 as well as a host position
on FOX's ''A Current Affair,'' a controversial tabloid-TV show (Malone, 1992,
McMurran, 1989). Finally, the couple's commuting relationship ended. After
their marriage, Chung triumphantly declared that Povich was the most important
thing in her life; her career was secondary (Malone, 1992). The couple was no
longer willing to cut their private life to accommodate their professional goals.
Nevertheless, Chung's popularity continued to increase, and her professional
career soared on toward greater heights.

Connie claims that Maury has helped her realize that life exists beyond her
career. ''If it weren't for Maury, my life would have been completely consumed
by work. He's really taught me how to relax and enjoy living,'' claims Connie
(Hickey, 1993, p. 67). Since their marriage, both of their careers have been
falling more in sync. In 1990 Maury left Channel 5, published a book about his
life experiences hosting ''A Current Affair,'' and started his own talk show,
''The Maury Povich Show.'' Around the same time, Connie left NBC for a
lucrative, $6 million contract with CBS co-anchoring the nightly network news,
a job she never thought would fall to a woman in her lifetime (Wallace, 1985).

Povich has been completely supportive of Chung's broadcasting career. He
has always respected Chung for her career decisions, even when they led her to
postpone their plans to have children (McMurran, 1989). Overall, the couple
believes that being in the same business has helped their relationship grow
strong. They have developed pride in each other's work and success, as well as
a great understanding and empathy when things at work are difficult (Wallace,
1985).

Connie Chung is a remarkable woman. In her career as a broadcast journalist,
she has had a large impact on the field of communication. Her cool, serene,
straightforward manner as a newswoman has earned her high ratings and popularity. In addition, her sense of humor, forays in Yiddish, and outbursts of
laughter on appearances with Dave Letterman have shown that Chung has a
great personality. As she states, ''inside me, there's a stand-up comic screaming
to get out'' (Ryan, 1988, p. 24). Although Chung has experienced professional
and personal setbacks, her overall image as an accomplished, successful woman
has remained. Americans have watched her develop as a journalist over the
years. An excellent interviewer, a thorough investigator, and a hardworking journalist, Connie Chung has become one of America's favorite television personalities. Through her achievements and contributions as newswoman, she has
opened many doors for women in the field of broadcasting.

ADDENDUM

Connie Chung has recently been dismissed from the "CBS Evening News" and her host position on the prime-time series "Eye to Eye with Connie Chung" (Kennedy, 1995; Levitt & Matsumoto, 1995). Instead of accepting CBS's offer to anchor on weekends and to occasionally sub for Dan Rather, her former co-anchor, Chung has asked to be released from her contract (Kennedy, 1995). To date, Chung has not accepted any offers from other networks. Meanwhile, Connie and her husband have adopted a baby boy, Matthew Jay Povich.

REFERENCES

Andersen, K. (1993, May 31). Does Connie Chung matter? *Time*, 71.
Appelo, T. (1988, April). Anchors aweigh. *Savvy*, 46–47, 83.
Brin, D. (1984, December 2). Connie Chung. *New York Daily News*, 3.
Buchalter, G. (1983, June 13). To wake up its sluggish *Early Today* Show, NBC anchors its hopes on Connie Chung. *People*, 34–35.
Chang, H. K. (1986, February). The prime time of Connie Chung. *Savvy*, 26–29.
Collins, G. (1990, December). Chung's choice. *Working Woman*, 110.
Conant, J. (1990, August). Broadcast networking. *Working Woman*, 58–61.
Connie Chung [publicity material]. (1994, August). New York: CBS News.
Current Biography Yearbook. (1989). New York: H. W. Wilson.
Flander, J. (1985, July). Women in network news. *Cosmopolitan*, 152–155.
Hickey, M. C. (1993, October). This is her life. *Ladies Home Journal*, 64–68.
Kaiser, C. (1988, November). Here's Connie. *Vanity Fair*, 165–167, 222.
Katz, J. (1993, October 14). Over to you, Dan: How Cronkite's heir became Chung's sidekick. *Rolling Stone*, 44–45, 130.
Kennedy, D. (1995, June 2). Anchor away. *Entertainment Weekly*, 12.
Landler, M. (1993, May 31). Can a second anchor steady the CBS evening news? *Business Week*, 33.
Levitt, S., & Matsumoto, N. (1995, July 3). Call her mom. *People*, 41.
Malone, M. (1992). *Connie Chung Broadcast Journalist.* Hillside, N.J.: Enslow.
McMurran, K. (1989, April 10). Two hearts, beating in prime time. *People*, 116–117, 119–120, 122.
The new achievers: Success & glamour. (1985, October). *Harper's Bazaar*, 218, 284.
Paisner, D. (1989). *The imperfect mirror: Inside stories of television newswomen.* New York: William Morrow.
Ryan, M. (1988, May 29). Inside me, there's a stand-up comic screaming to get out. *Parade Magazine*, 24–26.
Salisbury, A. (1985, August 31). The price of ambition: She hasn't found time yet to live with her husband. *TV Guide*, 12–15.
Smith, D. (1983, August 8). Waking up with Connie Chung. *New York*, 30–33.
Wallace, C. (1985, June 10). D. C. newsman Maury Povich anchors NBC's Connie Chung after a longtime cross-country romance. *People*, 151–153, 156, 158.
Waters, H. F., Friendly, D. T., & Howard, L. (1983, August 15). NBC's early-morning star. *Newsweek*, 77.

Waters, H. F., & Rogers, P. (1993, May 31). TV: Anchors adrift. *Newsweek,* 60–61.

Who's who in America. (1990–1991). Wilmette, Ill.: Marquis Who's who.

The wooing of Diane Sawyer sparks a fierce network battle. (1989, April 10). *People,* 124.

World Book Encyclopedia. (1991). Chicago, Ill.: World Book.

Younger, J. D. (1994, May/June). Connie Chung knows news. *Amtrack Express,* 30–33.

Zoglin, R. (1989, April 3). Star wars at the networks. *Time,* 70–71.

RUTH FRANKLIN CRANE (1902–1989)

Norma Pecora

> What *would* a modern woman do without a radio set! As soon as a
> new idea in foods, or fashions, or home management comes along,
> it's incorporated in some one of the many women's programs. There
> are many, many women whose work it is to see that these new ideas
> are spread.
>
> Sometimes these unknowns of the air become as familiar to them
> as family friends. (Sharman, 1930)

"Mrs. Page" of "Mrs. Page's Household Economies," for almost ten years, was a broadcasting pioneer named Ruth Crane.[1] The program was a combination of what we would now define as product endorsements or perhaps program-length "infomercials" and advice for the American woman on how to use the myriad of new consumer products available in the 1920s and 1930s—as well as a friendly voice into her kitchen.

An often overlooked form of broadcast programming, women's service programs like "Mrs. Page's Home Economies" brought information and companionship to the woman at home. Defined as the "housewife's electronic liberator" (in Rouse, 1979), the tradition of these programs has continued with network programs such as "Good Morning America" (ABC), "Today" (NBC), and "This Morning" (CBS) and local or cable programming and syndicated shows like "Working Women" (Allbritton Television). Generally scheduled in the morning or early afternoon hours, these shows had, and still have, several advantages. First, they tend to be "budgetless" (Accomplishments, n.d.) and, second, they offer a niche audience of consumers to advertisers (Meehan, 1993;

"Women" working, 1995). Women's household or service programs, unlike serials, soaps, dramas, or news shows, fill air time with minimal investment in staff and for little cost. Such shows often rely on a limited staff—sometimes just one person—to write, produce, and perform; guests willing to serve for media exposure; and product manufacturers eager to contribute goods and services for name-recognition. In fact, some programs, such as "Mrs. Page's Household Economies," were virtually all advertisements delivering an audience of women to advertisers for products as diverse as dog food and beauty aids.

Ruth Crane began her career in 1929 working for WJR-Radio in Detroit, Michigan, as the women's program director and commercial editor. She moved to Washington, D.C., in 1944 to continue that role at WMAL radio and television until her retirement in 1955. She began as "Mrs. Page" in Detroit and moved to Washington, D.C., with "Modern Woman" and "Shop by Television," a forerunner of the home shopping networks popular today. Crane is rather typical of many of the women who worked in early radio and television. When she entered the broadcasting business, female employees were few and often limited to daytime homemaking programs. Although they often had a background in journalism or theater, they rarely were allowed work as journalists. As Crane wrote in the 1960s:

In the late 20's we could be heard here and there over the U.S. giving housekeeping shortcuts, recipes, club news, along with do-gooding and a little apron-pocket philosophy. That was what the station managers and our advertisers wanted and that was what we did. (Schaefer, n.d. [a])

As late as 1956, when television was well established as a medium, there were still over 851 women commentators on many local radio stations (Money and Martha, 1956). Because Crane was not among the very "firsts," and she was local, not national, she has received little attention.[2] However, she is interesting for her dedication to bringing professionalism to the women in broadcasting and recognition and stature to the programs that devoted their time to "apron-pocket philosophy."

FAMILY BACKGROUND, MARRIAGE, AND EDUCATION

Quoted as saying "Well, you have to be born somewhere," Crane was born in 1902 in St. Louis, Missouri. In 1925 she married an advertising executive, Gilbert S. Crane, and they moved to Detroit, Michigan. Four years later he died, leaving Crane a young widow. In November 1945, she married William H. Schaefer, an auto executive from Detroit (Schaefer, n.d. [a]).

Crane and Schaefer had what is now called a "commuter marriage." She had moved to Washington, D.C., in 1944, and Schaefer remained in Detroit until his retirement. She once described the marriage as "a wonderful arrangement. . . . We see each other whenever we can and have a perfectly grand time together. Neither of us gets in the other's way, and we're both pleased with the set up'' (Ruth Crane, 1948).

Crane began her education in Missouri, first at Drury College and then at the University of Missouri. After one year, she moved to Chicago to attend Northwestern University. She attended classes from 1921 to 1925 at both Northwestern and the Chicago Art Institute. Training in journalism, theater, and advertising, she continued to take courses at Wayne State University after her move to Detroit (Press Release, n.d.).

Like many women, college and a husband prompted Crane's early moves: first to Chicago and then to Detroit. One can only speculate on the reason for her move to Washington, D.C. She appeared to have a well-established professional career and personal life in Detroit, but nonetheless she left for Washington, D.C., in the mid-1940s. Our only clue to the motivation for this move are in comments she made later and in the climate of the time. In an oral history interview (1975), Crane spoke of Washington as ''fascinating'' where ''a whole new world opened up'' for women after World War II (Press Release, n.d.).

David Brinkley, in his book *Washington Goes to War,* also spoke of the excitement and social life that attracted many to the nation's capital during World War II. According to Brinkley, the wealthy and ambitious moved to Washington where they could ''party with a purpose'' and, in some cases, move into a society where they could be more easily accepted, unlike the already well-established social order of New York or Chicago (p. 178). Young women moved there for the many clerical jobs, and the eligible young men mustered to support the war effort (p. 108). One can presume Ruth Crane moved there to be a part of this excitement and the growing community of journalists.

CAREER DEVELOPMENT

Like many women working in early broadcasting, Crane began in journalism—as a correspondent for the local county newspaper and the school paper while still in high school, and then as a staff writer on the campus newspaper at Northwestern University. She later moved into advertising. Her first job out of college was writing advertising copy for Hart Publishing Company in Chicago. In 1927, after moving to Detroit, she was employed by the Pauline Arnold Research Organization conducting consumer research.

Ruth Crane spoke of her career in broadcasting as serendipitous. Offered the choice of two jobs in 1929, one as a fashion writer and the other with a radio station, Crane chose the radio job. In retrospect, it was a strategic move, for the radio business was one of the few to survive and even expand during the Depression years (Crane Schaefer, 1975). Her later move to Washington, D.C., in 1944 was described as a ''desire to be closer to the action'' (Schaefer, n.d. [a]), and she maintained that her career in television began simply because she was ''there'' (Crane Schaefer, 1975; Schaefer, n.d. [a]).

Radio

Crane's career in broadcasting began when she made the pragmatic choice of a short commute to work. Hired by Leo Fitzpatrick at WJR in Detroit, later head of the National Association of Broadcasters, she was told to create a job for herself. At this time, 1929, few of the jobs in radio were well defined. Crane noticed that the salesmen at WJR would return to the station after selling radio time and attempt to sell the sponsor's product with no thought to the advertisement. With her background in copy writing and consumer research, she saw the importance of commercials and was dismayed by the casual way advertising was treated at the station. By default she became commercial editor, writing advertising copy, selling radio time, servicing accounts, and announcing on-air.

Her first title, "Women's Program Director," came with little money and less respect. Although she became "Commercial Director" soon after she was hired, no money was added to the position, only additional work. In the 1975 oral history interview, she was asked about the respect accorded to women on radio. She stated:

I've checked this with many other women who were in radio and TV too. I think a phenomenon of the early days of both radio and TV—and, for all I know it still exists— is that the Women's Director who had her own shows was inescapably considered a character by her station associates . . . oddly the lowest branch on the organization tree was usually that of the woman who did foods, children's programs, women's activities and so on, no matter how well sponsored and notwithstanding this woman in almost all cases was her own complete staff—writer, program director, producer, public relations, innovator, outside speaker, often saleswoman for her own sponsors, radio or TV and sometimes both. (Crane Schaefer, 1975)

In addition to her advertising duties and her position as women's program director, Crane replaced the woman who was hosting "Mrs. Page's Household Economies" which aired six days a week. Described as 15 minutes of "worthwhile information" about the things that women use and need in their home (Of Interest, n.d.), the program format was the presentation of about seven, noncompetitive products on any given day. Products included: Ohio China Company, Detroit White Lead Works, Malt-O-Meal, Red Heart Dog Food, Colonial Dames Beauty Aids, Japanese Crab Meats, Mullers Chicory, Drums Cleaner, Rapinwax Paper, Scot Towels, Colman's Mustard, Win-You Food Products, Quaker Macaroni Products, Burnham and Morrill Food Products, Junket Mix, Western Growers Association, ABC Coal Range, and the Household Finance Corporation (from WJR promotional material, circa 1938). The show reached five states and parts of Canada, and, when Crane left, Agnes Clark assumed the "Mrs. Page" name and continued the program at least until 1949 (Garver, 1949). This practice of using pseudonyms was common. Crane used several during her time at WJR, including from time to time Alice Franklin, her birth name.

In 1944 Crane moved to WMAL radio in Washington, D.C., an affiliate owned by the *Evening Star* newspaper. Although both WJR and WMAL were network-affiliated stations, Crane's programs were not nationally distributed. At WMAL she was again the director of women's activities and was now responsible for "The Modern Woman," a daily, half-hour, morning program. Her program expanded to include interviews with local personalities, visiting Hollywood stars, national political figures, and international dignitaries. This access to celebrities was clearly part of the attraction of the Washington, D.C., market to her. As she said of her experience,

[C]ompared to my background in Detroit particularly where we were supposed to be interested mainly in housewifery, . . . one had entree to many, many things going on. Here we were more or less a part of the action rather than reporting the action. There are and were so many people resident here—so many politicos, Ambassadors and that sort of thing. (Crane Schaefer, 1975)

"Modern Woman," Crane's radio program, went on television in 1947 as the first televised woman's program in the Washington, D.C., market,[3] and for the next nine years she had both a daily radio and television program on the air. According to Crane, she was the one to make the transition from radio to television because she was "there." The station found it most efficient to use the radio staff for the new television programming. The transition was easy because it was only a matter of learning to do and show as well as talk (Schaefer, n.d. [a]). A *Variety* review of the television version of "Modern Woman" stated that it was only "natural" that her morning radio program be adapted to television (The Modern Woman, 1951).

Television

While other women's programs claimed "firsts" on television, Crane's was the first in the D.C. market and among the most popular both with advertisers and audience. One *Variety* reviewer wrote,

To give a true picture, one should appraise a week's run in order to show producer's [Crane's] deftness in meeting topics of the day and in varying structure.

Typical show caught features a succession of guests. Ted Mack, in town to rehearse the VIP version of his "Amateur Hour." p.a.'ed the plug benefiting the USO. Jane Hilder, local remedial reading expert, demonstrated her technique with one of her pupils, a poised and winning nine-year-old lad. Then Carolyn Hagner Shaw, editor of capital's "Social List" and authority on protocol, presented the AAA award to the "courteous driver of the week," a regular Wednesday feature of show.

Interspersed with the public service aspects are fashions and a cooking interlude, opportunity not only to provide some culinary hints, but also to integrate commercials into
show. (The Modern Woman, 1951)

With only one week's warning from her station manager, in November 1947
Crane made the move to television. She filled the half-hour by writing and
performing a skit on Christmas shoppers; her second show was much more
typical of future programs, and included the television debut of Margaret Truman, daughter of the president (Schaefer, n.d. [a]; Truman, 1956). Over the
years, whoever was in town was fair game. A partial list of guests included
representatives of the women's branches of the armed services; political figures;
society maven Perle Mesta; and Hollywood stars such as Douglas Fairbanks,
Jr., Veronica Lake, and Debbie Reynolds (Commercials à la Crane, n.d.). Crane
also supported various civic and volunteer organizations by giving publicity to
their groups, receiving awards for her work from the District of Columbia Community Chest, the Washington Heart Association, and the National Safety Council, to name a few (Press Release, n.d.).

To encourage interest in television and to bolster television sales, Crane devoted an hour of time on her television show to local women's clubs. A limited
number of the club's members were invited to participate in the WMAL studio
in trade for publicity and recognition for the club. In trade, other members were
obligated to have "TV teas" in their home for members who were not invited
to the studio. Those who did not have a television, of course, had to buy one
for the event, as did those on the program whose family wanted to watch (Crane
Schaefer, 1975).

In November 1949 Crane added a truly innovative television program to her
schedule. The harbinger of current home shopping networks, "Shop by Television" was a very simple concept of a direct retail or shopping service using
television and telephone. Aired at 7:30 P.M. on Tuesday nights by WMAL-TV
and sponsored by Hecht's department store, the program was built on the appeal
of newspaper advertisements, window shopping, and mail order catalogs—all
of which Crane recognized as important to a good selling program (Press Release, n.d.). Each week products would be demonstrated by Crane and her announcer, Jackson Weaver. With telephone operators on stage, audience members
could call in their order from home. The program was initially scheduled to run
only for the 1949 Christmas season but was so successful it continued for four
years and the number of telephone order-takers was increased from the initial 3
to 40. For a time it became the model for similar programs nationwide.

In 1953 as old theatrical releases became entertainment fare on television,
"Modern Woman" was replaced by "Hollywood Matinee" with Ruth Crane
as hostess. This was a film show that enjoyed high ratings with national and
local commercial participation. However, Crane still conducted interviews with
visiting celebrities and people in the news in a guest-time segment (Press Re-

lease, n.d.). Little is available on this program except it continued for a time after Crane's retirement in 1955, with Lynn Hart as the host.

Crane also covered special events such as the visit of British royalty in 1951 and the presidential inauguration of 1953 (Press Release, n.d.).

She retired in 1955 after 26 years in broadcasting.[4]

MAJOR CONTRIBUTIONS AND ACHIEVEMENTS

Crane made two contributions to American broadcasting. First, she sought to gain professional recognition of women in broadcasting through her organizational activities and her programs. Second, she took her role as mentor seriously, encouraging and training young women; she also coached people on the use of both radio and television.

In recommending Ruth Crane for national ''Advertising Woman of the Year'' (she had won the local award twice—1949 and 1953), an unidentified writer said the following of Crane.

As one of the charter members of the Association of Women Broadcasters of NAB [National Association of Broadcasters], as a national officer ever since its inception and particularly as National President for a two-year term, Miss Crane has been instrumental in formulating policies of the organization and the industry, has established practices and patterns now followed by many women broadcasters and has been a source of inspiration and information to innumerable individual women broadcasters, both experienced and inexperienced. (Women's Advertising Club, 1950)

Recognizing the context of this quotation and the distinct possibility of embellishment, we can nonetheless see that Ruth Crane's contribution to professional organizations at a local and national level was impressive. As the following chronology demonstrates, during her years in Detroit and Washington, D.C., she held seven offices in the major professional women's broadcasting organizations.

PROFESSIONAL ORGANIZATIONS
1929–1955

No date	District representative	American Women in Broadcasting, Detroit
1945–1946	President	Women's Advertising Club of Washington
1947–1949	President	Association of Women Broadcasters (later Association of Women in Radio and Television)
1947–1950	Secretary	American Newspaper Women's Club
1949–1950	First Vice president	Women's National Press Club

1949		Advertising Woman of the Year: Women's Advertising Club of Washington
1950–1951	Vice president	Women's National Press Club
1953–1955	President	American Newspaper Women's Club
1953		Advertising Woman of the Year: Women's Advertising Club of Washington

Although little information is available on Crane's political agenda for women in broadcasting, we can speculate that her position of leadership in these organizations was significant. The unidentified writer cited above notes Crane's "contributions to the profession of radio advertising and [how she] has worked toward advancing the standing and progress of women in it" (Women's Advertising Club, 1950). A WMAL biography (Press Release, n.d.) commented on her interest in "women's legal status, opportunities and program in civic, political and business worlds."

Clearly, Crane realized the lack of recognition given women in the broadcast industry. Often she commented on their unequal treatment and the lack of respect for their work. She commented on the issue in an unpublished history of the National Women's Club (circa 1968).

Outside of the basic women's interest field it was accepted that men's voices were preferred on the air both for tone and authority. Women listeners would be jealous of us, it was said, in any more worldly role. Men's voices were more believable. Radio was then and still is generally held to be a man's world.[5]

At another point she stated:

An anomoly [sic] however—a curious double standard, is that usually the woman broadcaster on the station staff, doing radio or TV or both—must constitute in herself a whole Woman's News Bureau. Household, food, children, fashion, health, social service, society, civic events, White House, press conferences, promotional meetings, theater—the whole raft of "women's interest" comes in the purview of this broadcaster-writer-producer usually with little or no help; And in addition she feels she must belong to and often hold office in professional organizations, make speeches and publicity appearances, attend social events. In most cases [the] men [of radio-TV] work their scheduled hours, and that's that. (Schaefer, n.d. [b])

Not only did Crane advocate respect for women in the broadcast industry, but she also acknowledged the problems within the profession itself. There has been a tradition of discord between "print journalists" and "broadcasters." It was not until 1944 that the Women's Nationai Press club officially included women broadcasters to what Crane perceived as "professional journalistic standing" (Schaefer, n.d. [a]).[6]

Along with recognition and respect for women in the industry, regard for the audience was also important to Crane. She felt that the information women's programs offered their audience was important and of value and that the audience deserved to be treated with respect. When a colleague from the American Women in Broadcasting commented "disdainfully" on women "telling how to revivie [*sic*] a wilted lettuce leaf," Crane was "irate" (Crane Schaefer, 1975). She believed strongly that radio served as a friend to many women isolated at home and that the information dispensed was useful. As she said about the "wilted lettuce":

I didn't think then, and still don't, that the only really proud function of women on the air is to deliver what the newcomers at that time and perhaps still do call hard news. There is a lot of other information, as is well known and practiced, that women find interesting and beneficial when expounded by an expert. (Crane Schaefer, 1975)

This philosophy was evident in the material she "expounded" on her shows. While the programs included consumer information, Crane's programs also discussed world events, civic affairs, public service issues, the arts, and society. Crane, like other women broadcasters of radio and early television, saw her role as commentator and took her responsibility, as well as her audience, seriously. Crane advised others not to "underestimate the I.Q. of [the] women listeners" (Press Release, n.d.).

The second major way in which Crane contributed to the broadcast industry was as mentor. She trained others in both the business of broadcasting and the use of the medium. By the early 1950s college-level broadcasting programs were well established as training grounds. Prior to World War II, however, there were few formal programs in broadcasting, and many of the early broadcasters received their training through day-to-day experience or in another medium such as vaudeville or the theater. In addition, politicians and world leaders found that the new medium was ideal for promoting a cause, particularly in the Washington, D.C., area where their audience was often other newsmakers. Television was beginning to set the agenda for public debate. Politicians wanted to know the best way to use this new medium, and Crane was willing to work with them.

At the college level, Crane lectured to one of the first classes in broadcasting taught at the University of Michigan. Later, she lectured at a variety of colleges and universities, including Southeastern University, American University, and George Washington University (Women's Advertising Club, 1950; Press Release, n.d.). In addition to classroom lectures, her staff included students from places like Bard College, Syracuse University in New York, and from her alma mater, Northwestern University (Women's Advertising Club, n.d.).

Crane led both formal and informal training sessions and wrote on the subject. In 1952 several magazines reported on seminars offered by WTOP-CBS in Washington, D.C., for politicians and the advice the United Church of Christ gave its constituents on how best to use the medium of television (TV Training,

1952; TV's School for Candidates, 1952). Crane, however, had been doing such training well before 1952. Her 1930 advice for those who believed they had the talent to be radio stars offers us insight into the demands of early radio.

[T]o win a place on a commercial program, the entertainer must be sold to the station and to the advertisers, must have a sure-fire act that cannot fail to sell him and the product he represents to the radio audience.

An enterprising station endeavors to keep its programs well-balanced, full of variety and pep and free as possible from lengthy conversation or dialogue. (Franklin, 1930)

Her later advice to those using television was to "Be yourself and enjoy yourself!" (From the Modern Woman, n.d.).

Crane's success was not only in the area of radio and television commentary; she was also highly regarded in the advertising industry, having twice been awarded "Advertising Woman of the Year" by the Washington Women in Advertising (in 1949 and again in 1953). She began as a copy writer in Detroit and continued to write much of the advertising material she used on-air. Like her programs, her approach to copy writing was based in her consideration of the audience: "My copy must be interesting, must be presented from the standpoint of the listeners' own experience, must contribute to them . . . must not insult their intelligence" (Press Release, n.d.).

Through her organizational leadership, her professional presence, her achievements as a mentor, and her contributions to programming and advertising, Ruth Crane played an important part in early broadcasting. Whether it was serendipity, fate, or clever career decisions, she was a successful woman in broadcasting from 1929 to 1955, with a daily program on both radio (26 years) and television (9 years).

CRITICAL EVALUATIONS OF CONTRIBUTIONS AND ACHIEVEMENTS

Although not one of broadcasting's "firsts," Ruth Crane was very much a part of early broadcasting and accepted its structure as commercially driven without question.[7] At the time she entered the field, it was a well-established commercial medium. Most of the debates on the use of radio and the possibilities for financing it were won or lost; the economics were tied to the growing consumer markets. As a strong advocate of what was seen as "free" broadcasting (The Lady Is a Huckster, 1954) and with her background in advertising and copy writing, Crane never questioned the role of a commercial-based system. To her, the relationship between sponsor and radio was "natural," and programs such as "Mrs. Page's Household Economies" served an important function. A 1925 promotional for the program stated its objective—"to sell merchandise to women. . . . Fifteen minutes of worthwhile information about the things that women use and need in their homes" (Of Interest to Men, n.d.). She continued this tradition when she was "Mrs. Page" and later with "Modern Woman" and "Shop by Television."

Programs like "Mrs. Page's Household Economies" increased in value to broadcasters and advertisers as the female audience expanded and as the importance of radio to sell national-brand consumer goods for mass consumption was recognized. Even though these programs had a smaller audience than the prime-time evening entertainment, as one radio manager noted, women's and farm programs were among the best-selling shows, particularly outside the major markets. Advertising sales connected with these program types were in "reverse-ratio . . . constantly at, or near, the top of the revenue ladder" (The Lady Is a Huckster, 1954). The commercial dollars that the shows attracted easily offset the low production costs and returned a reliable profit. "Shop by Television," a program Crane and others characterized as innovative, was nothing more than a half-hour of advertisements for consumer products and Hecht's department stores. Television simply added the advantage of visually demonstrating a product to the format of "Mrs. Page's Household Economies."

As a woman in communications, Ruth Crane recognized the inequities of the industry, but one must be cautious of the dangers inherent in hindsight. In her writings, she spoke of the advantages offered to men in the business. She was concerned with the lack of respect for women, and she expressed dismay over the unequal treatment of women: men had less responsibility and higher pay, and there were limited opportunities for many women in broadcasting during her tenure. In the 1975 oral history interview, she voiced her hope that such attitudes had changed since her retirement. However, her response to these problems appears to have been simplistic: allowing more women through the gates would change the situation. In fact, in the conclusion of the oral history interview, she alludes to the changes she believes have come about simply because women are more evident.

Because Ruth Crane was not among the "first of the firsts," our recollection of her is limited. What we know of her we know from press releases and her few writings that have survived. We have no record of her work behind the scenes, in meetings, in negotiations, or in speeches. We can only know from what is available that she was an attractive, articulate woman who appears to have been well suited for a time in history when radio and television were attempting to establish a persona. As for her contribution to that persona, she brought to the audience a friendly voice; to the medium a respectable ambassador; and to the advertiser the modern woman.

Ruth Franklin Crane Schaefer died on June 10, 1989 at the age of 87.

NOTES

1. This, like much of the information in this biography, comes from one of the few sources of information available on Ruth Crane Schaefer. These are an oral history conducted in 1975; an undated nominations speech for Advertising Woman of the Year

1950; an undated bibliography from WMAL; and two versions of an undated, unpublished manuscript for a history of the Women's National Press Club.

Unfortunately, much of what is written about her centers on program anecdotes: losing scripts, breaking "unbreakable" dishes, and collapsing chairs.

2. The exceptions are several book chapters based on the material in her oral history: Beasley and Gibbons (1993); Heinz (1979); and Hosley and Yamada (1987).

3. Although she claimed "everything was a 'first' in those days," her "firsts" were then listed as having "been nipped twice on the same program by a Seeing Eye Dog . . . to cook an octypus on TV . . . to stage a real surprise bridal shower" (Schaefer n.d. [a]).

4. Of her retirement she said she was now "just a viewer" as one would say "just a housewife." However she had an interesting criticism of the "Happy Talk" news format popular at the time of the interview. "From the viewing side, a real annoyance to me, and to a lot of other people too, I think, is the joshing that goes on between announcers which may be side-splitting but is usually unintelligible to those in front of their sets. Your little fun isn't important to us who are anxiously awaiting the weather report or more important news especially when we don't know what the giggling is all about."

5. This section was edited from the final version.

6. For an interesting discussion of the Women's National Press Club see Beasley, "The Women's National Press Club" in *Journalism History,* 15(4), 112–121.

7. WJR-Detroit went on the air May 1922 and was one of the first to be an affiliate of the NBC network.

REFERENCES

Accomplishments: Unpublished report. (no date). Broadcast Pioneers Library; University of Maryland: College Park, Md.

Albig, W. (1939). *Public opinion.* New York: McGraw-Hill Book Co.

Arell, R. (1937, November). Silent voices. *Independent woman.*

Beasley, M. (1988). The Women's National Press Club: Case study in professional aspirations. *Journalism History,* 15(4), 112–121.

Beasley, M., & Gibbons, S. J. (1993). *Taking their place.* Washington, D.C.: American University Press.

Brinkley, D. (1988). *Washington goes to war.* New York: Alfred A. Knopf.

Commercials à la Crane. (no date). Broadcast Pioneers Library; University of Maryland: College Park, Md.

Crane Schaefer, R. (1975, November 18). Interview by Pat Mower. Broadcast Pioneers Library, Oral History Collection; University of Maryland: College Park, Md.

Experience necessary. (1948, August 9). *Newsweek,* 59.

For the Girls at Home. (1954, March 15). *Newsweek.*

Franklin, A. (1930, November). I want to get on the radio. *Radio Gossip,* 28.

From the modern woman: Some timely suggestions on: How radio and television can help you. (no date). Broadcast Pioneers Library; University of Maryland: College Park, Md.

Garver, R. (1949). *Successful radio advertising with sponsor participation programs.* New York: Prentice-Hall.

Good TV Business. (1950, June 26). *Newsweek.*

Heinz, C. (1979). Women radio pioneers. *Journal of Popular Culture,* 22(2), 305–314.

Hettinger, H. S. (1933). *A decade of radio advertising.* Chicago: University of Chicago Press. (Arno Press. History of Broadcasting: Radio to Television, reprint 1971).

Hettinger, H., & Neff, W. (1938). *Practical radio advertising.* New York: Prentice-Hall.

Hosley, D. H., & Yamada, G. K. (1987). *Hard news: Women in broadcast journalism.* Westport, Conn.: Greenwood Press.

The lady is a huckster. (1954, October 16). *TV Guide.*

Meehan, E. (1993). Heads of household and ladies of the house: Gender, genre, and broadcast ratings, 1929–1990. In W. Solomon, & R. McChesney (eds.), *Ruthless criticism.* Minneapolis: University of Minnesota Press.

The Modern Woman. (1951, January 24). *Variety,* 181(7), 26.

Money and Martha. (1950, June 26). *Newsweek.*

Of interest to men about women . . . (no date). Broadcast Pioneers Library; University of Maryland: College Park, Md.

Press Release: Ruth Crane. (no date). Broadcast Pioneers Library; University of Maryland: College Park, Md.

Rouse, M. G. (1979). Daytime radio programming for the homemaker, 1926–1956. *Journal of Popular Culture,* 22(2), 315–327.

Ruth Crane. (1948, January 26). *Broadcasting/Telecasting,* 48+.

Schaefer, R. C. (no date [a]). Our radio and TV members. Women's National Press Club. Unpublished manuscript; National Press Club Archives: Washington, D.C.

Schaefer, R. C. (no date [b]). Suggested preface to Radio-TV Section. Women's National Press Club; Unpublished manuscript; National Press Club Archives: Washington D.C.

Sharman, O. (1930, October). Radio—and the woman's world. *Radio Gossip,* 6.

Shop by Television. (1950, January 11). *Variety,* 177(5), 29.

Smulyan, S. (1994). *Selling radio: The commercialization of American broadcasting 1920–1934.* Washington, D.C.: Smithsonian Institute Press.

Sponsors show confidence by signing up for television. (1974, November 2). *Washington Post,* 41.

Sterling, C. H., & Kittross, J. M. (1990). *Stay tuned: A concise history of American broadcasting.* 2nd ed. Belmont Calif.: Wadsworth Publishing Co.

That Woman at WNEW. (1949, February 21). *Newsweek.*

Truman, M. with M. Cousins. (1956). *Souvenir.* New York: McGraw-Hill Book Co.

TV training. (1952, May 26). *Newsweek,* 63+.

TV's school for candidates. (1952, May 24). *Business Week,* 120+.

Vaughn, M. (1989, June 12). Broadcast pioneer Ruth Crane. *Washington Times,* B:4.

"Women" working. (1995, January 16). *Broadcasting & Cable,* 117.

The Women's Advertising Club of Washington, D.C. (no date). Advertising Woman of the Year. Broadcast Pioneers Library; University of Maryland: College Park, Md.

DOROTHY DAY (1897–1980)

Pamela J. Shoemaker and Michael Breen

"What did the women do after the crucifixion? The men were in the upper room praying and the women, by their very nature, 'had to go on with the business of living.' They prepared the spices, purchased the linen cloths for the burial, kept the Sabbath, and hastened to the tomb on Sunday morning. Their very work gave them insights as to time, and doubtless there was a hint of the peace and joy of resurrection to temper their grief'' (Dorothy Day, writing in *The Catholic Worker,* cited in Quigley & Garvey, 1982, p. 36). Ever the pragmatist, Dorothy Day was a "Martha" of her day, who not only saw the work to be done but, unlike Mary, instead of bemoaning the lack of help, set to with a will and accomplished much in the process. The "business of living" for her was to lead her into a remarkable journey that resulted in her launching her own newspaper, *The Catholic Worker,* and becoming a profound influence on her church and on society.

FAMILY BACKGROUND

Dorothy May Day was born in Brooklyn on November 8, 1897, in the urban environment where she would be raised and to which she dedicated her life and her work. She lived and worked in New York City most of her life, but spent some time in Berkeley as a child, and as an adult lived for a time in Chicago and New Orleans (Miller, 1982).

She was the third of five children, the second daughter of John and Grace Day, and, although relations with her mother were good, her father was a distant and disapproving figure. Grace Day was generally called "Mother Grace" and was a continuous presence in Dorothy's life. Her father, a sports journalist with a very strong interest in horse-racing, was not comfortable around Dorothy and her frequently radical ideas. Even as a child, Dorothy frequently got into "trouble" at school or home, showing an early interest in sex and enjoying shocking adults with lewd gestures and language or petty thefts (Miller, 1982, p. 3).

As a more mature Dorothy embraced the radical ideas of communism and then later converted to Catholicism, her father gave up on her. As Dorothy wrote in her autobiographical book *The Long Loneliness,* she believed that her ideas brought her father great unhappiness. Her father believed that Dorothy and her friends were endangering the country with their radical ideas and communist leanings (Day, 1952b). She was not close to her family for most of her life. When she was first put in prison for demonstrating for the women's suffrage movement in 1917, no one from her family contacted her. In the late 1930s, her father wrote to a relative that Dorothy was "the nut of the family. . . . I wouldn't have her around me" (Miller, 1982, p. 311).

Little wonder that Dorothy claimed no status from her family background. Her father's family was Scots-Irish, and her great-grandfather James McElwee had fought in the Revolutionary War, but she never pursued membership in the Daughters of the American Revolution (Miller, 1982, p. 2). Grandfathers on both sides of her family had fought in the Civil War, the Scots-Irish side backing the Confederacy and her mother's English family the Union side (Coles, 1987, p. 1).

Religion, which played such a major part of her adult life, was only a minor force as she was growing up. When about 7 or 8 she found a Bible—the first she had seen—in the attic of their rented house in Berkeley and spent hours reading it, not remembering what it said, but feeling a sense of holiness from it. The family were not regular churchgoers, and at one point she claimed her father was an atheist (Miller, 1982, p. 5). When the family moved to Chicago, the local Episcopalian pastor asked her mother if the children could attend church—her mother was raised Episcopalian—and Dorothy seemed to enjoy the church services (p. 18). When she was 16, Dorothy and her mother dabbled briefly in Christian Science, but she did not attend the church and declared herself "sick and tired of religion" (Miller, 1982, pp. 28–29).

EDUCATION

Day's favorite courses in high school were English, Latin, and Greek; she went so far as to translate a ten-cent copy of the New Testament from Greek to English (Miller, 1982, p. 27). One suspects that her real education came from the books she read on her own, including Spencer, Darwin, Huxley, Kant, Spinoza, Jack London, and Upton Sinclair.

In 1914 she won a $300 Hearst scholarship and took the train from Chicago to Urbana to attend the University of Illinois. She looked forward to independence from her family and at 16 years of age felt mature (Merriman, 1994). College was a disappointment to her, possibly because she had no real idea of what she wanted to study or why she was there beyond wanting to read and write more. She declared English to be foolish because of the emphasis on reading poetry aloud. History required too much rote memorization, biology was uninteresting, and Latin, a favorite in high school, was boring. She took 16 classes during her two years at Illinois, failing biology and getting Cs and Bs in her other classes. She attended only those classes she found interesting (Miller, 1982, pp. 32–33).

Her college days were less devoted to her curriculum than to stretching her wings of independence. As in high school, she led an isolated existence, interacting with few of her peers, probably because she thought she had little in common with them. She believed herself to be large and plain and seemingly went out of her way to avoid socializing. Her classmates were interested in sports, sororities, and other activities Day judged banal.

She retreated into more reading, consuming "Big" Bill Haywood on the Industrial Workers of the World, Arturo Giovanitti, "mother" Jones, Elizabeth Curley Flynn, Carlo Tresca, and nineteenth-century Russians, including Artsybashev, Turgenev, Gorki, Chekhov, Andreyev, Tolstoi, and Dostoevsky. Sometimes she bought so many books that she didn't have enough money to buy food (Miller, 1982, pp. 34–35).

When a professor declared that religion was only for the weak-minded, Day decided to cut it out of her life. She openly criticized those who were pious and began deliberately swearing in order to shock those around her (Miller, 1982, p. 34).

Writing was her primary creative outlet; she worked for both *The Daily Illini* and the local Urbana newspaper. She also joined a university writing club, the "Scribbler." Toward the end of her time at the university, Day became the book critic and reviewer for the Chicago *Examiner*.

CAREER DEVELOPMENT

Day left the university in 1915, when her father left Chicago to work on the New York *Morning Telegraph*. Armed with her newspaper clips, Dorothy sought work as a journalist, but most editors wouldn't even talk with her, saying that she "was very young and that newspapers weren't the place for young girls" (Miller, 1982, p. 55).

She did find work but not in mainstream journalism. Her first job was with the socialist newspaper the *Call*. She persuaded Chester Wright, the editor, to take her on for $5 a week, the wage she might earn in a factory. Wright said that if Dorothy could live on $5 a week for one month, he would hire her. He must have been satisfied that this young woman belonged on his newspaper, because at the end of the month, he raised her pay to $12 (Miller, 1982, p. 5). Her first stories in the *Call* were about how she managed to survive on that $5 weekly wage, even though she had moved out of the family residence because of her father's disapproval.

The *Call* advocated no single coherent socialist philosophy; instead, it supported four causes—the American Federation of Labor, the Amalgamated Clothing Workers, the IWW (known as the "Wobblies"), and the anarchist point of view. Day attended many lectures by radicals to acquaint herself with their views, including the Birth Control League. She was assigned to cover the prison release of a woman who worked for a clinic that advocated birth control. The *Call* wanted her to describe the pain and suffering that the woman had endured, but Day found little of either. "I realized that I was distorting the truth, and it sometimes irked me that my job was always to picture the darker side of life, ignoring all the light touches, the gay and joyful sides of stories as I came across them" (Day, 1924; Miller, 1982, p. 64). She left the *Call* after being criticized by a fellow reporter for slapping an anarchist who accosted her at a dance.

Her next job was working for the *Masses,* edited by Max Eastman, who was a graduate student at Columbia University and the assistant of John Dewey. When a co-worker told her that he was "an ardent feminist and an unqualified advocate of 'sex for the single girl,' " Day told him that he was lying, that "she recognized an 'intellectual' approach to seduction when she saw one, and where she was concerned, she would just as soon be the object of a more primitive technique" (Miller, 1982, p. 81).

Unfortunately, the *Masses* was short-lived, having lost its mailing permit. Its successor was the *Liberator,* "the American voice of the Russian Revolution," but in 1917 Day's part-time responsibilities on the *Liberator* were not as extensive as in the closing days of the *Masses,* and she left journalism for a time. She and her sister Della began nurses' training, but it was not for Dorothy. She went back into journalism after moving with Della to New Orleans in the fall of 1923. She worked for the New Orleans *Item,* with her special qualification being that she would work as a taxi dancer and write a series of articles on these places of sin (Miller, 1982, p. 160).

While she worked for the *Item,* she published her book *The Eleventh Virgin,* (1924), which, though not a critical success, did bring in $2,500 for the movie rights. Although the movie was never made, the money allowed Day to move back to New York and buy a "shack" along the ocean where she could write, primarily articles for newspapers and magazines (Miller, 1982).

In 1924 Day met Forster Batterham, an Englishman and self-proclaimed anarchist. He lived with her much of the time she was at the beach house and became her common-law husband. In June 1925 Day discovered that she was pregnant with his child. The pregnancy was a source of joy for Day, and she began to visit the Catholic chapel near her house. Her daughter, Tamara Teresa, was born on March 3, 1926. Forster did not approve of Day's interest in religion or her decision to have Tamara baptized and to undergo religious training herself. His anger led him to leave her and Tamara many times and then to return. By 1929 Day had ended the relationship.

Money was a problem during the early years of Tamara's childhood. Caring for her daughter left Day little time to write. She worked at a number of odd jobs, including synopsizing novels for MGM for $6 each, and she wrote movie dialogue for the Pathé Motion Picture Company for $125 a week. But she also managed to work for the Anti-Imperialist League, a communist affiliate, doing publicity about U.S. aggression in Nicaragua (Miller, 1982, p. 200). For *Commonweal* she wrote about her and Tamara's increasing piety. Motherhood was a significant event in her life. As June O'Connor, a scholar of feminist religious ethics, sees it, Day was "a person impelled by religious and ethical concerns who felt she had something distinctive to say about social issues precisely because of her experiences and perspectives as woman and mother" (1991, p. 2).

A very influential person in Day's career was Peter Maurin. He and Day had similar views on social issues and were both Catholic, although Maurin said that Dorothy had not been properly instructed in Catholicism and took it upon himself to correct that deficiency. Maurin encouraged Day to begin her own newspaper to talk about social issues within the context of Catholicism. *The Catholic Worker*—the Catholic response to the communist *Daily Worker*—began as an eight-page, tabloid paper with 2,500 copies printed for $57, with the first issue coming out on May Day 1933. Day decided to sell it for one cent, a rate that would qualify for a second-class mailing permit, but also make it available to the poor. The paper ran mostly on donations, large and small. By September, the press run had increased to 20,000 and by December 1934 to 60,000. It topped the 100,000 mark in the 1980s and is still publishing.

The paper's editorial stance was simultaneously socialist and strictly in compliance with Church doctrine, although it had no formal relationship with the Church (Roberts, 1984, p. 3). Day and Maurin attacked traditional middle-class Catholic values and argued for the laity to take on more responsibility for helping those in need. They were pacifist, even during World War II. They worked for change within the capitalist system, a change toward a more communitarian society (Miller, 1982, p. 428).

In their first editorial, Day and Maurin wrote:

It's time there was a Catholic paper printed for the unemployed.
The fundamental aim of most radical sheets is the conversion of its readers to radicalism and atheism.
Is it not possible to be radical and not atheist?
Is it not possible to protest, to expose, to complain, to point out abuses and demand reforms without desiring the overthrow of religion?
In an attempt to popularize and make known the encyclicals of the Popes in regard to social justice and the program put forth by the Church for the "reconstruction of the social order," this news sheet, *The Catholic Worker,* is started. (Roberts, 1984, p. 3)

Although she was accused of being soft on communism, nothing could have been further from the truth. As her biographer, William Miller, put it, "The personalist position of Peter Maurin and Dorothy Day, as they had applied it to the conditions of life in the twentieth century, was the most fundamental and clear-cut anticommunist idea and program that had been defined by an American Catholic voice'' (Miller, 1982, p. 434).

Day established Catholic Worker houses in several cities and ''agronomic universities'' in the countryside—farming communities for those who preferred a rural to an urban environment. Both the houses and the farms provided clothing, food, and lodging for those who needed it. And through it all—through editing the newspaper, administering the houses and farming communities, and increasingly traveling to talk about the Catholic Worker movement—Dorothy Day lived the life of a Catholic Worker. She wore the clothes and ate the food that her organizations made available to the poor.

She worked because there was work to be done; the poor must be clothed and fed. Their concerns and issues must be championed. Day continued to write books and shorter pieces in order to have money for Tamara. Yet, she would have been uneasy with the concept of her having a *career,* in the sense of being concerned about her own advancement, development, reputation, and success (O'Connor, 1991, p. 31). For Dorothy Day, her work was her life and her life was her work.

MAJOR CONTRIBUTIONS AND ACHIEVEMENTS

Dorothy Day died on November 29, 1980 of heart failure. Her legacy is not *The Catholic Worker* newspaper or any of the numerous Worker organizations she helped found. Rather it is a shift in the way in which American Catholics looked at their world. She was committed to advocacy journalism as the social activist's prime tool. Journalism could be used ''to move the heart, stir the will to action; to arouse pity, compassion, to awaken the conscience'' (Roberts, 1984, pp. 67–68). She believed that the purpose of *The Catholic Worker* was to influence its readers' opinions. In the terms of Johnstone, Slawski, and Bowman's (1972) conceptions of the journalist role, Day was a ''participant'' in the news, not a ''neutral.'' She believed in uncovering the story and developing the worldview of her readers. She valued interpretation over getting the story out quickly (Roberts, 1984, p. 69).

In addition to editing the newspaper, for 40 years Day traveled the country, talking with thousands of people about her causes. She raised money that kept the newspaper and the Worker houses running; she raised the consciousness of two generations of Americans, and her influence extends to two generations of social activists. The roots of today's peace movement and of those concerned with social justice lie with Dorothy Day. ''Day and her colleagues were the single unbroken pacifist link in the United States over the past five decades, as they remain'' (Roberts, 1984, p. 173).

Although Day was banned as a speaker by several bishops and criticized by many of the clergy, her work was never openly attacked by the Catholic Church and no attempt was made to stop her. Nancy Roberts (1984, p. 108) gives two reasons for this: ''There was the doctrinal purity of the Catholic Worker philosophy, with its irrefutable sources, the same as the Church's. And the hierarchy could not fault Day's emphasis on the works of mercy, or her active resistance to the works of war, positions rooted in the Gospel command to love one another.''

In addition to her articles for newspapers and magazines, Day also wrote a series of books that, taken collectively, serve as her autobiography. *The Eleventh Virgin* (1924) was her first book, a thinly disguised description of her life before she met Peter Maurin and then began *The Catholic Worker*. The heroine is "June," an adolescent who experiences her awakening sexuality, loves, has an abortion, but still hopes for a conventional marriage (Miller, 1982, pp. 13–14). A *New York Times* book reviewer criticized the book on structural grounds, but praised it as an honest look at modern life. Later, Day said she was embarrassed by the book, with its description of her unconventional life before converting to Catholicism (O'Connor, 1991, p. 15).

The second of the autobiographical books was *From Union Square to Rome* (1938), Day's story of how she came to the Church from a communist background. *The Long Loneliness: The Autobiography of Dorothy Day* (1952) continues a description of her religious conversion and omits details of her life that were not on the path to Catholicism (O'Connor, 1991, p. 14). *Loaves and Fishes* (1963) is Day's description of *The Catholic Worker* as newspaper and social movement. Taken together, the four books provide a "lens by which we are able to see Dorothy Day in her multiple identities and thus answer questions about her self-understandings and moral sensibilities. In distinctively different ways, each lends insight into Dorothy Day's moral concerns, convictions, and commitments" (O'Connor, 1991, p. 14).

CRITICAL EVALUATION OF CONTRIBUTIONS AND ACHIEVEMENTS

Day's biographers are largely fans. Miller (1982, p. 391) says of her fundraising, "As a successful beggar, Dorothy had few equals. . . . [T]he many small donations that came from those who were themselves almost impoverished. Dorothy well knew these people and she was determined, in her own poverty, to be faithful to the trust they had in her."

Roberts (1984, p. 173) writes that "Dorothy Day's dealings with the Catholic Church paralleled in many ways Christ's relationship with the religious hierarchy of His age. In fulfilling Church law, she ultimately relied on conscience and emerged as probably the greatest lay influence on the Roman Catholic Church in this century."

O'Connor (1991, p. 11) says that Day "is widely known as a social critic, protester, and dissenter, as anarchist, pacifist, and Communist become Catholic, as advocacy journalist and editor of *The Catholic Worker* newspaper, as founder of numerous houses of hospitality for the homeless, as single parent, working mother, and grandmother. Some would add to this list the label saint."

Goetz (1984, p. 2) has said that "Dorothy Day moved through her long life as a kind of conscience for American Catholics." *The Catholic Worker* touched thousands of people, compared by Colman McCarthy to "a prowling animal outside the doors of our dead and lazy institutions. . . . [It] has awakened Americans to the plight of the poor, and to other issues of social justice and peace" (Roberts, 1984, p. 4). Modern Catholic peace activists such as Fathers Daniel and Philip Berrigan, Thomas Cornell, Eileen Egan, James W. Douglass, James Forest, and Robert Ellsberg have "acknowledged their debt to her relentless Christian witness. And the American Catholic bishops praised Dorothy Day's exemplary peace activism in their 1983 pastoral letter which condemned the use of nuclear weapons as immoral" (Roberts, 1984, p. 4). Catholic historian David J. O'Brien has called Day "the most significant, interesting, and influential person in the history of American Catholicism" (Roberts, 1984, p. 4).

As a model for today's women, Day is a mixed case. Although she marched in the first suffrage demonstration in Washington, D.C., and was thrown in jail because of it, Day said she was at the demonstration for the experience and had little support for the suffrage cause. She never exercised the right to vote, even though she also lived through the women's movement of the 1960s and 1970s. O'Connor (1991, pp. 38–39) writes that Day was not only "not an advocate of women's suffrage, she was not a feminist in any self-conscious, intentional, or public way. She spurned sociopolitical feminism, refusing to march on behalf of women's rights; she was no closet feminist either, since she regularly critiqued the movement in both its early and later twentieth-century forms as being too self-centered."

Day held many traditional ideas about gender roles, yet O'Connor judges her to have a hidden feminist dimension,

for her work is punctuated with observations and recommendations that clearly reflect a critical eye with respect to injustice in sex roles and a desire to expand and improve opportunities for women and men alike. . . . She became a voice on behalf of laborers, pacifists, and nonviolent protesters for social change, the majority of whom were men. But along the way Day did voice some critical complaints about inequities between the sexes, illustrating affinities with the feminist critique, and she placed theological as well as social and personal value on the fact that a greater balance or integration of gender roles was possible and desirable. (O'Connor, 1991, pp. 38–39)

But her impact extended beyond Catholicism to all areas of social justice and peace. American Catholic social teaching had "shared generally in a passivity and lack of social vision. Dorothy Day was a notable exception to this general malaise. Both before and after her conversion to Catholicism, she reflected upon and responded actively to the social and religious sensibilities of her age" (Merriman, 1994, p. 4). She chose a life not easily adopted by someone raised in the middle class. She lived among the urban poor, among the people she wanted to help. "She and her fellow Catholic Workers are not the kind of reformers who live in one world while hoping to change another" (Coles, 1987, p. 111). *The Catholic Worker* held to its editorial line for decades: "The personalist, communitarian Christianity, voluntary poverty, pacifism, and nonviolent social justice activism" (Roberts, 1982, p. 3).

Upon her death, her obituary appeared in many mainstream publications, including the *New York Times, Washington Post, New York Review of Books, Nation, New Republic, Time, Newsweek, America,* and *Commonweal.* The *New York Times* acknowledged her "seminal role in developing the social and economic thinking of a generation of American priests and laymen." The *Washington Post* described her as a "towering figure in twentieth-century American radicalism" (Roberts, 1984, pp. 4–5).

INTEGRATION OF PERSONAL AND PROFESSIONAL LIFE

Robert Coles (1987, p. 111) has written that "nothing mattered more to Dorothy Day than the way she lived her life. She was interested in books and ideas, but for her the rest of a life is its everyday moral texture—what one does, finally with all the hours of each day." Reading and writing were constants in her life. Aside from a brief stint as a nurse, she made a living from her writing.

Her first love was Lionel Moise, an orderly at the hospital where both worked. They lived together for a time, but he ordered her from the apartment. It is not clear why, but it may have been because of her strong personality—he could not "own" her in the way that he owned other women. When Day realized that she was pregnant, she delayed telling Moise for three months. When he found out, he insisted that she get an abortion. When she got back to their apartment, she found a note saying that he was leaving. She soon after married Barkeley Tobey, but the marriage lasted less than one year.

By far the two most important relationships in her life were with her common-law husband Forster Batterham and her working relationship with Peter Maurin. Both Forster and Dorothy had strong feelings about the social injustices they saw, but whereas Forster withdrew from the world to escape injustice, Dorothy was compelled to action (O'Connor, 1991, p. 24). Peter Maurin shared Day's interests in a Christian social vision, but he was most interested in the plight of those in rural areas, whereas Day was drawn to those working in factories and living in slums (O'Connor, 1991, p. 24). Although Maurin helped Day found *The Catholic Worker,* she quickly realized that it would be her leadership that would make it a success. She often used her earnings from other writing projects to print the newspaper.

As for her relationships with women, she was close to her sister Della, but no single woman gets the attention in Dorothy's autobiographical books that Forster and Peter Maurin did. "Dorothy seems to have lived in a primarily male world, both as a radical reporter and, later, as a radical Christian and editor. Her story is notable for its dearth of discussion about living female role models, friends, or confidants" (O'Connor, 1991, pp. 25–26).

CONCLUSION

This remarkable woman, once described by Evelyn Waugh as "an autocratic saint who wants us all to be poor," was a woman ahead of her times, a prophet who walked a long and often lonely road, in fidelity to a gospel to which she was passionately committed. Dorothy Day was probably the most influential woman in the American Church of the twentieth century, a fact made all the more remarkable by her lack of interest in women's issues.

In a very patriarchal world at a time when women, like children, were expected to be seen and not heard, Dorothy Day was a loud and clamoring voice for the voiceless. In her life, her writings, and her work she gave expression to the cry of the poor, those who are trammeled on by the bulk of society, those who are born only to live and die in abject poverty.

Dorothy Day was a faithful Catholic in the very best sense of that term. She saw the splendor of what the Church had to offer in terms of vision and possibility for humanity, but she was also very willing to voice her opinion when she saw injustice within the institution. Dorothy Day—woman, thinker, lover, leader, saint; a rare mix of qualities and talents combined with a fearless conviction about what was right and necessary and—despite her lack of interest in women's issues per se—made her a wonderful role model for men and women of all times.

REFERENCES

Coles, R. (1987). *Dorothy Day: A radical devotion*. Reading, Mass.: Addison-Wesley Publishing Co.

Day, D. (1924). *The eleventh virgin*. New York: A. & C. Boni.

Day, D. (1928, June). Having a baby. *New Masses*, 5–6.

Day, D. (1928, July). Girls in jail. *New Masses*, 14, 15.

Day, D. (1938, 1978). *From Union Square to Rome*. New York: Arno Press.

Day, D. (1938, September). Explains CW stand on use of force. *The Catholic Worker*, 1, 4, 7.

Day, D. (1939). *House of hospitality*. New York: Sheed & Ward.

Day, D. (1942). Fight conscription. *The Catholic Worker*.

Day, D. (1943, January). If conscription comes for women. *The Catholic Worker*, 1, 4.

Day, D. (1951, May). The incompatibility of love and violence. *The Catholic Worker*, 1–2.

Day, D. (1952a). A Catholic speaks his mind. *Commonweal*, 55, 640–641.

Day, D. (1952b). *The long loneliness: The autobiography of Dorothy Day*. San Francisco, Calif.: Harper & Row.

Day, D. (1953, July–August). Meditation on the death of the Rosenbergs. *The Catholic Worker*, 2, 6.

Day, D. (1954, February). The Pope and peace. *The Catholic Worker*, 1, 7.

Day, D. (1955). Conscience and civil defense. *New Republic*, 133–136.

Day, D. (1957, July–August). Dorothy Day writes from jail. *The Catholic Worker*, 1, 6.

Day, D. (1963). *Loaves and fishes*. San Francisco, Calif.: Harper & Row.

Day, D. (1964, April). Mystery of the poor. *The Catholic Worker, 2*, 8.

Day, D. (1970, August). Anarchism through peace. *The Catholic Worker* [Australia], 3–4.

Day, D. (1973). A reminiscence at 75. *Commonweal, 98*, 424–425.

Ellsberg, R. (ed.). (1983). *The selected writings of Dorothy Day*. New York: Alfred A. Knopf.

Goetz, J. W. (1984). *Mirrors of God*. Cincinnati, Ohio: St. Anthony Messenger Press.

Johnstone, J. W. C., Slawski, E. J., & Bowman, W. W. (1972). The professional values of American newsmen. *Public Opinion Quarterly, 36*, 522–540.

Merriman, B. O. (1994). *Searching for Christ: The spirituality of Dorothy Day*. Notre Dame: University of Notre Dame Press.

Miller, W. D. (1982). *Dorothy Day: A biography*. San Francisco, Calif.: Harper & Row.

O'Connor, J. (1991). *The moral vision of Dorothy Day*. New York: Crossroad Publishing Co.

Quigley, M., & Garvey, M. (eds.). (1982). *The Dorothy Daybook*. Springfield, Ill.: Templegate Publishers.

Roberts, N. L. (1984). *Dorothy Day and the Catholic worker*. Albany, N.Y.: State University of New York Press.

BRENDA L. DERVIN
(1938–   )

Carole A. Barbato

Risk taker, daredevil, independent, diverse thinker, and survivor are some words that can be used to characterize both the personal and professional life of Brenda L. Dervin. Her research defies categorization using the traditional research paradigms of the field. She has chosen not to follow but rather to forge a new path, teetering on the edge. Her personal life also marks the characteristics of a risk taker. Although life has given Dervin more tragic experiences than anyone should have to endure, she has taken each situation and turned it into a positive outcome. Most of us would be devastated by any one of these experiences and justifiably so, but Brenda Dervin refused to yield. These experiences have influenced her research and her research has influenced the direction of the field toward the dialogic.

FAMILY BACKGROUND

Ermina Diluiso was the third of seven children of Italian immigrants. She became pregnant as a teen, and knowing her family's feelings about unwed mothers she hid her pregnancy from everyone but her sister. On November 20, 1938, in Beverly, Massachusetts, a baby girl was born to this unwed teenage mother. Ermina's father ordered the baby out of the house, so Ermina's brother took the baby girl to a hospital. The baby was later sent to an orphanage where she would stay for six and a half years. She became a ward of the Catholic Church, and the Church would baptize her Rita Mary Diluiso. While at the orphanage, this young child was physically and emotionally abused, being locked for hours at a time in a closet. Because of this trauma, until she was adopted, she did not speak to anyone and would not let others touch her. When Rita Mary was six and a half years old, an executive of Allied Artists, a motion picture firm, noticed this petite, frail, but beautiful child during one of his charity visits to the orphanage. The man was John Jordan Dervin. Later he and his wife, Marjorie, would adopt this child.

John Jordan and Marjorie Dervin picked up the child at a Boston train station with a car full of toys, gifts, and new clothes much too big for the undernourished, frail child. The orphanage had outfitted the child for the trip with one new outfit and an empty suitcase. The couple looked dashing in their fine clothes and fancy car, the child thought. The couple named the little girl Brenda Louise Dervin. She went to live with her new parents and brother, Johnny, in a beautiful home in Newton Center, Massachusetts, a suburb of Boston. It should have been the beginning of a wonderful life for the orphaned child, but this story was not to have a Hollywood ending.

John Dervin was first-generation Irish Catholic, and Marjorie was second-generation Irish/English descent. Both were struggling to fit into the upper class Boston society they found themselves in because of John's position in the motion picture industry. Although John attended Boston College for a couple of years and Marjorie attended a teachers' college, neither had much background for the life they were leading. They joined the Book-of-the-Month Club because it was the thing to do, but they rarely read the books. The family received a state-of-the-art phonograph as a gift from Charlie Chaplin. They played show tunes for their pleasure and kept a classical record collection that at the time was impressive, but they did not play any of these records and just displayed them for others to see. John was a charitable and socially conscious man, but both John and Marjorie were more concerned about what was socially appropriate than what they believed was right. This would bother their daughter, Brenda, and would later influence her work and her choices in life.

Although John wanted to adopt this little girl, Marjorie was more obsessed with their adopted and ailing son, Johnny. Marjorie became physically and verbally abusive toward Brenda. Although John was a kind and gentle man, he did not intervene, and so after great difficulty learning to read, Brenda retreated to books. Books were her best friends as she was growing up, and they continued to be her only best friends until she went to graduate school in Michigan. Brenda's daredevilishness was played out when she was a teenager, particularly after the family moved to Port Washington, New York, and lived in an apartment complex on Manhasset Bay. Against orders she would swim across the bay and sail out into dangerous Long Island Sound.

At the young age of 32 years, Brenda Dervin was stopped in her tracks with the news that she had cancer. She claimed that this event caused her to pause and take stock of her life and to understand that her shaky beginnings had contributed a host of physical and emotional struggles. At the age of 36 she searched for her roots, and it was at that time that she learned about her mother, Ermina. Although she never met her birth mother, who by then was deceased, she has maintained contact with Ermina's other two daughters, Diane and Sandra—her half-sisters—sharing important family times that had been missed through the years.

EDUCATION

Because of her adopted brother's health, Brenda Dervin moved quite a bit during her school years, attending nine schools during the first twelve years of her education. She went to schools in Newton Center, Massachusetts; Flushing, New York; Tucson, Arizona; Coral Gables, Florida; and, finally, back east to Roslyn and Port Washington, New York. During all of these moves, Brenda was shy, reclusive, and not a particularly good student, although she was always passionate about writing. In fact, when she was in fifth grade, she asked her parents for a typewriter so that she could express herself in writing. It was not until eleventh grade, after moving back to New York, that she decided she would be aggressive about being the *best* in her classes and would become actively involved in school activities. She did just that. She was editor of the yearbook, wrote for the school paper, and became a member of many school organizations. She also was the organizer of the senior prom. She said that there were three high school teachers who "saw through the mess that was me" and tried to encourage her to live up to her potential as a student and a person.

Although she was accepted at the University of Wisconsin, School of Journalism, John and Marjorie would not permit Brenda to go there. They wanted her to attend a college because it was what was expected of them, and they felt it would be important if she was to find a good husband. They would only permit her to attend Cornell University because it had a home economics department. She attended Cornell from 1956 to 1960. While she did not like the traditional home economics classes, Dervin found that she excelled in the social sciences and philosophy, and she developed a close relationship with a social scientist mentor on the College of Home Economics faculty. Dervin graduated from Cornell in 1960 with a bachelor of science degree in home economics, with an emphasis on journalism. It was there that she first thought of graduate school in communication. Although Cornell was intellectually stimulating for Dervin, it was not until she began her doctoral degree program that she realized her strengths as a student scholar.

In 1965 she began her graduate program at Michigan State University (MSU) in communication research, receiving her Master of Science degree in 1968 and her Ph.D. in 1971. Aside from involvements in studies and research, Dervin termed contact with foreign students as the significant experience at MSU. Dervin worked with the MSU/U.S. Agency for International Development (AID) communication training workshops for foreign students studying in the United States, and she developed close relationships with many of the foreign graduate students in MSU's communication program. As a result, Dervin has been absorbed by international issues ever since and gained as one of her closest friends and colleagues Luis Ramiro Beltran, sometimes called the father of communication research in Latin America.

CAREER DEVELOPMENT

After graduating from Cornell University, Dervin followed a husband to Washington, D.C. With a recommendation from Cornell, she became public relations assistant for the American Home Economics Association from 1961 to 1962. She had a wonderful role model for a boss; a strong, positive woman and a marvelous public relations director. Later, Dervin lived with her husband in Milwaukee, Wisconsin, from 1963 to 1965 where she worked as a communication specialist for the Center for Consumer Affairs at the University of Wisconsin Extension. It was here that she began to develop seriously her social consciousness.

Dervin was a teaching assistant and instructor for the Department of Business Law and Office Administration at Michigan State University from 1966 to 1967 and was a research associate or teaching assistant for the Department of Communication from 1966 to 1970. In 1970 she was resident lecturer and coordinator for the MSU Agency for International Development communication workshops.

Dervin accepted her first university teaching position as an assistant professor at Syracuse University in the School of Information Transfer in 1970 before completing her doctoral degree. She was an assistant professor at the University of Washington from 1972 to 1986. Unknown to her at the time she accepted the position, she arrived to a ''climate of assault,'' as many of the faculty had not supported her candidacy. Being one of a few women in the department, she found the atmosphere oppressive. However, it was there that she met and was befriended by Richard Carter, a man whom she deeply admires. She describes Carter as an honorable man and an independent thinker. Dervin credits him with helping her to become a methodologian and to explore philosophical issues, gap bridging, and theories of communication. Dervin was promoted to associate professor in 1977.

In 1986 Dervin accepted a position as full professor and chairperson of the Department of Communication at Ohio State University (OSU). Her mandate was to put the department ''on the map as one of the best communication departments in the country.'' After a stressful period of organizational change, the faculty worked together to accomplish this goal, revising its entire graduate curriculum and developing a program that focused on substantive depth and methodological breadth. Dervin assesses the efforts as successful, citing evidence from a departmental self-study and from national rating lists. More important than the ratings, Dervin points to how the OSU faculty worked together to build the department as a stimulating place where people honor excellence and depth as well as the building of bridges across diverse methodologies. It is at OSU that Dervin said she has felt privileged to be involved in a genuine community of scholars. She stepped down as chairperson in 1988 but continues to serve the university as a full professor.

MAJOR CONTRIBUTIONS AND ACHIEVEMENTS

Dervin has produced some 60 journal articles and book chapters in her areas of speciality. Her work addresses many eclectic topics: information equity, information seeking and use, public communication campaigns, health communication, media use and production, telecommunication use, communication and development, communication system design, audience reception, feminist scholarship, and research methodologies.

Dervin, however, categorizes herself as being on one expanding path, starting first with issues of information poverty among those whom society labels poor, then moving to concerns of information poverty as it impacts all citizens. From here she began to address concerns of communication/information system design—how to design and implement effective and equitable systems. This led her to issues of the impact researchers have on system design and thus to the development of methodological approaches for what she labels giving voice to those without voices and treating the research situation as a communication situation. This led to her efforts to influence methodological approaches that address users/audiences/citizens/patients/patrons in all communication contexts, which in turn led to her vision of the communication field as finding unity in its diversity by developing new and genuinely communication-based methodological approaches.

Dervin's concern for those whom society labels as poor began, of course, in her first jobs in Washington and then Wisconsin, and continued with her work on the urban poor at Michigan State (see Dervin & Greenberg, 1972; Greenberg & Dervin, 1970a, 1970b), and with her dissertation, which focused on the information behaviors of black low-income adults (Dervin, 1971). Dervin characterizes her dissertation as her last great research embarrassment, for in retrospect it did not give voice to those without voices. Rather, it imposed a rigid voice on them, proving yet again that people who are more like us (the privileged) communicate and use information like we do. While from a system perspective this may be empirically accurate under some conditions, Dervin says, it provides no guidance for the design of effective and efficient communication/information systems and instead reifies existing inequities (Dervin, 1989a, 1989b, 1994).

For more than two decades Dervin has dedicated her work to developing a programmatic series of studies and projects analyzing the problems and potential of communication/information system designs. Her primary mission in this series of studies has been to explore an alternative way to explain the information/ knowledge gap hypothesis. She has argued that the researcher perpetuates inequities among system users by defining differences among them through traditional measures (e.g., demographic and personality variables) which mirror system structures. This view defines users in system terms with predictable blame-the-victim results. Dervin rejects this assumption and the traditional definition of the "user/receiver." She has summarized her perspective in the following way: "Traditional user categories lead us to a view of communication systems that makes haves and have-nots inevitable" (Dervin, 1989b, p. 218). Dervin does not suggest that traditional categories have no role, but she rejects their usefulness if one is interested in effective system design. She calls instead for communication-based categories that focus on how humans use communication/information to make sense of their worlds.

To this end, Dervin has worked since 1972 on the development of a methodological approach she calls "Sense-Making," which consists of an elaborate set of assumptions, a theory, and a set of data collection and data analysis methods, all oriented to systematically giving voice to the unvoiced, or hearing users/audiences on their own terms. The approach is built on several core philosophical premises. The most important is the idea that communication is what humans do to bridge gaps between order and chaos, chaos and order. Thus, Dervin categorizes Sense-Making as a methodology between the cracks because instead of focusing on individuals or structures, interpersonal or mass, authority or freedom, Dervin has accepted both ontological and epistemological order and chaos and mandates a focus on communicating as the in-between (Dervin, 1991, 1993, 1994). Sense-Making implements concepts related to time, space, and movement into an analytic based on the metaphor of a person moving through time-space to bridge gaps (Dervin, 1989a, 1992).

One of Dervin's major accomplishments has been the development of a series of alternative predictors of information/communication behaviors—alternatives that tap into the worlds of actors on their terms. One example is an often used measure in Dervin's studies called "situation movement state," which focuses on how the actor sees her situation in terms of movement: no road ahead, more than one road ahead, one road but blocked, one road but being dragged down it. In a series of test studies in a variety of contexts (e.g., health, library use, phone use, media use), Dervin has pitted these alternative predictors of information seeking and use against traditional predictors and found that the alternative predictors offered more predictive and explanatory power in attempts to understand users (e.g., Atwood & Dervin, 1981; Dervin, Nilan, & Jacobson, 1981). From this she has concluded that there are universals in how humans make sense of their worlds, universals that allow diverse humans to connect with each other despite their differences; universals that can be systematically used in system design. These universals, she suggests, come from focusing on processes and procedures rather than states and entities.

It is at this juncture that Dervin's work intersects with her impact on the field of communication generally. She has been an advocate for analyzing communication communicatively. She has posited that the only way to move the field forward is to look at communication as verbs and not nouns (Dervin, 1993). "No matter what stripe the scholars in the field wear, at some point all of them can be heard talking communicatings [*sic*] rather than communication'' (p. 52). From Dervin's perspective, one of the difficulties is that the communication field mirrors the noun categories of its parent disciplines in its effort to develop theories. As a result, the field's diversity seems like a Tower of Babel. Dervin proposes that it is only in developing communication analytics that unities can be found in the diversity.

One way in which Dervin has tried to exemplify this central point has been to address the contributions feminist scholarship can make to the field of communication. Dervin has never considered herself a feminist scholar, but she was drawn to understanding feminist scholarship when she interpreted Timothy Haight as categorizing her work as feminist in his 1983 article in the *Journal of Communication*'s ''Ferment in the Field'' issue. After study, Dervin concluded that feminist scholarship provides an exemplar of the contribution diversity can make to the field because feminist scholarship addresses the central issue of opening up a space for women's voices. For Dervin, feminist scholarship provides an example of substantive depth with methodological breath ''using whatever method and perspective in whatever discipline needs to be brought to bear in order to pursue its aims'' (Dervin, 1987, p. 109).

The same search for substantive depth and methodological breadth has guided Dervin's service as a leader in the field of communication. Believing that the field needs to develop new ways of listening to its diversity in order to move toward unity, as program chair for the 1985 meeting of the International Communication Association (ICA), Dervin organized what is now recognized as the landmark ICA conference encouraging paradigm dialogues in communication. With the theme of the conference, ''Beyond Polemics: Paradigm Dialogues,'' she implemented a rule that each division and working group define its own paradigm dialogue on its own term. From Dervin's perspective, one must move to unity in communication, and this was a first step. At this conference she found funds to encourage the participation of two leading sociologists, Stuart Hall (Marxist cultural theory) and Anthony Giddens (structuration theory). These theorists continue to influence communication theory and research.

Using this same philosophy, Dervin has made extensive contributions as an editor in the field of communication. She edited 14 volumes as series editor for Ablex from 1986 to 1992 and assisted an additional 70 monographs and texts into press. She was co-editor of the Progress in Communication Sciences' series, volumes II–XI, from 1980 through 1993, where each volume brought together in-depth state-of-the-art reviews focusing on a diverse selection of communication phenomena. Similarly, the two co-edited volumes arising from the ICA 1985 meeting *(Rethinking communication, Volume 1: Paradigm issues; Rethinking communication, Volume 2: Paradigm exemplars)* have been cited as examples of the rich and diverse research of the communication field.

Dervin has served the field of communication in a variety of organizational capacities. In 1986 she was the first woman elected president of the International Communication Association as well as its first woman fellow. She served as a member of the ICA Executive Committee and Board from 1983 to 1988 and has been an active member of several divisions in the association.

She has also been an active member of the Association for Education in Journalism and Mass Communication serving as head of its Theory and Methodology Division in 1978. She is a long-time member of the Union for Democratic Communication, and a founding member of the International Society for Panetics. She is currently serving as one of eight U.S. representatives on the governing council of the International Association for Mass Communication Research, where she has been instrumental in founding its book series mandated to cover communication scholarship worldwide. Dervin has also served as editor, contributing editor, and reviewer for numerous journals.

CRITICAL EVALUATION OF CONTRIBUTIONS AND ACHIEVEMENTS

A July 1994 on-line search showed that Dervin's solo or senior authored work has been cited 322 times in Social Science Citation Index, with about 50 percent of these citations coming from journals in the fields of information and library science. Dervin's remaining citations appear in communication journals, with about 15 percent appearing in varied journals of other fields: education, public health, sociology, psychology and psychiatry, social work, public policy, planning, and development. In addition, Dervin's work has won four top paper awards in three of ICA's divisions (Atwood & Dervin, 1981; Dervin, Harlock, Atwood, & Garzona, 1980; Dervin, Jacobson, & Nilan, 1982; Dervin, Nilan, & Jacobson, 1981) and has been supported by almost $750,000 in grants and contracts.

Despite this attention to Dervin's work, those who study communication in a traditional communication program teaching traditional communication paradigms could well miss the contributions of Dervin's work to the field. She has tried to move the field into an arena in which many in the communication field do not want to go. The 1985 International Communication Association Conference and people's reactions to it are a prime example. The 1985 ICA conference on "Paradigm Dialogues" followed the dialogue started in the 1983 *Journal of Communication* article, "Ferment in the Field." Although many praised Dervin's organization of the ICA conference as an act of "genuine intellectual courage" (Hall, 1989, p. 50) and as the beginning of the communication field's acceptance of pluralism, others noted that her work was an attempt to encourage divergence rather than convergence toward a universal "theory of communication" (see Berger, 1991). Dervin thinks this criticism misses the point. She would argue that "it is useful to reach for a universal perspective but it will be a universal perspective of a different kind—a communication kind." It is the difference between looking at communication as noun versus verb.

The *Progress in Communication* series she edited for ten years is testimony

to her risk-taking behavior and her "healthy tolerance for ambiguity" which
Gerald Miller (1981) claimed would be necessary to survive in the communication field. These works, however, received mixed reviews regarding their contribution and impact on the field. Two reviews are representative of this
reception in the field of communication.

Brown (1987) remarked that the articles in Volume 7 did not live up to the
editors' claim of providing state-of-the-art reviews of literature in the fields of
communication and information sciences. However, he suggested that "each
chapter provides an interesting and often thought-provoking perspective on a
particular topic" (p. 181). James Miller (1985) was equally harsh in his review
of the fourth volume. He suggested that "with this volume as evidence, however, neither the coherence of the field nor the productivity of its practioners is
especially well demonstrated" (p. 180).

Others characterize these volumes differently. Agostino's (1981) review of
one of the volumes in the series noted that "in all, this is an insightful and
thought-provoking book representative of the variety of topics, approaches, and
quality of academic research in the communications field" (p. 438). Also, Wigand (1985) praised the editors' attempt to pull together disparate views of
research. He concluded, "Together they constitute a whole, are challenging,
provide useful recommendations and suggestions for further exploration, and
can be recommended to the communication scholar and student" (p. 204).

When *Rethinking Communication,* Volumes 1 and 2, first appeared in print,
they received only lukewarm reception from communication critics but praise
from those in political science and sociology. McQuail (1990) accused the authors of rehashing the same old paradigm arguments. He further noted: "The
terms of the 'paradigm debate' as it is conducted in these volumes do not ex-
haustively map the alternatives facing communication researchers" (p. 132). He
did concede, however, that the volumes offered a diverse and rich exploration
of the field. He stated that "the reader may wish to use this volume simply as
a mine of generally high quality 'state of the arts' treatment of selected problems
in the field" (p. 132).

Littlejohn (1991) also gave a lukewarm endorsement for the volumes. He
stated that Volume 1 on paradigm issues presents "five fairly distinct positions,"
thus "demonstrating the problem of diversity in the field." He concluded: "It
is doubtful that this volume accomplishes dialogue in any fresh way, but in
general it is a fruitful addition to the growing metatheoretical literature relevant
to our field" (p. 491). Regarding the second volume on "paradigm exemplars,"
he criticized the editors for presenting the articles in alphabetical order rather
than clustering the essays according to the heuristic matrix developed by the
editors. The editors abandoned the matrix because they did not want to replicate
existing category schemes and deemed the exercise premature. Given all this,
Littlejohn still praised the group of essays as excellent.

Berger (1991) further questioned the lack of "field defining theories" by
communication researchers. Although the volumes demonstrate the diversity of

the field, Berger noted, the diversity represented in these volumes might be a concern for the future of the field: "Although specialization is almost an inevitable consequence of growth, the fact that there is no particular theoretical paradigm or touchstone theories around which communication researchers might organize their efforts is at least one source of concern" (p. 101). He concluded that other disciplines have a high degree of specialization but still manage to organize their research under "touchstone" theories or paradigms.

On the other hand, Vuchinich's (1990) review in *Contemporary Sociology* argued that the book was a "stimulating collection" and a "pleasure to read; it bristles with fresh ideas and important new applications in the context of solid methodology." He concludes that "the book will be useful to scholars of all stripes interested in communication" (p. 740). Mishler (1990) recognized the *Rethinking Communication* series as an "exemplar" for "clarifying and comparing alternative research models" in the field of communication (p. 421). And in a ten-year followup to the now classical contribution of the "Ferment in the Field" issues published in the *Journal of Communication,* the *Rethinking Communication* volumes are cited by a number of authors as being instrumental in shaping theory building and defining the future of the field (see *Journal of Communication,* 1993, edited by Levy and Gurevitch).

Perhaps Dervin's most influential and accepted work has been on the knowledge/information gap concept. Her research has been impressive and has been cited numerous times by others doing research on the effects of the "information gap" in the field of communication and in a variety of other disciplines. Agostino (1981) noted that Dervin's "Communication Gaps and Inequities" article published in the *Progress in Communication Sciences: Volume II,* is elemental and bold. He also stated that it is a "crisp summary of research into information inequities and a strong argument for shifting explanation for these gaps from analysis of the receiver to the source" (p. 438). This break from the traditional way of looking at the "information poor" was further supported by Freshley's (1982) review: "Dervin dashes such traditional assumptions as 'information availability leads to understanding' and deals with the contradiction of absolute information existing while the communication process posits that people subjectively perceive the world" (p. 223). Her "Sense-Making model" has been cited in the communication field (e.g., Ettema, Brown, & Luepker, 1983; Hoijer, 1992; Moffit, 1994) and in a variety of journals in a variety of other fields (e.g., Raviv, Maddyweitzman, & Raviv, 1992; Winkleby, Flora, & Kraemer, 1994). This work is most frequently cited in information and library science (e.g., Bruce, 1994; Gammack, 1994) and has been the subject of in-depth reviews in that field. Savolainen (1993), as one example, reviewed and assessed "the sense-making theory of Brenda Dervin . . . as an inspiring critique addressed to the limitations of the traditional intermediary-centered approach [to information seeking and use]" (p. 13).

INTEGRATION OF PERSONAL AND PROFESSIONAL LIFE

Being orphaned and feeling so alone growing up as a child, Brenda Dervin learned to become independent minded and a radical thinker. It was these life experiences that have given passion to her work not only in theory development but also in her tolerance for multiple methodologies, her emphasis on the dialogic, and her "healthy tolerance for ambiguity" in the field of communication.

Her independence and philosophical thinking had its roots in the small, abused, orphaned girl, and the adopted daughter who wasn't wanted by her adoptive mother. She said that the "moving passion of my work which is the design of theory, methodology, method and practice for responsive systems or dialogic communication comes from these roots." She wanted desperately as a child to understand the actions of her abusers and to forgive them. At a very young age, she knew instinctively the importance of the dialogic, of communication as the start of the healing process. The abuse Dervin endured caused her to retreat within herself and to be self-reflexive. Thus, writing became an important means of self-expression, and this began her analysis of events or her attempt to make sense out of something that made no sense. Furthermore, the long-lasting physical and emotional damages from these early years have provided her, Dervin says, with a "special kind of understanding of human struggles and with a personal platform from which to challenge the all-too-facile imposed understandings of so-called experts." As a result, the theme of giving voice to the unvoiced is seen throughout her research efforts and her life choices. Her work with the urban poor, international students, the Sense-Making model, and her views of feminist scholarship all reflect this passion which began from these early life experiences.

As a communication specialist for the Center for Consumer Affairs, Dervin began to develop her social consciousness. It was here that she wrote her first book, *The Spender Syndrome* (1965). This book was a compilation of case studies of people with consumer problems. She was asked to design programs to help poor people spend their money more wisely. She began to think, "Why should people who are poor have to be more disciplined than people who are rich?" This peaked her social consciousness and began her quest for seeing things from the users/receivers' perspective, not the researchers' dominant view.

Her feminist perspective had its origins in her experiences living with her adoptive mother who was concerned primarily with appearances and living for men, and in a world where it seemed (and often still does) that "every inch of the female journey is a struggle with discourses of oppression." Because of these experiences she feels it is her responsibility to tell the "emotional truth" rather than merely "working smart." Feminist scholarship, then, can be an exemplar by giving humanity voice, according to Dervin.

Being befriended by and working with international students at MSU, Dervin soon refined her social consciousness, and it was the first time she felt that she belonged. She recalls, "No one belonged so we all had to be tolerant of each other. We were all so different so we had to use communication deliberately to 'bridge gaps.' " It was from this experience that Dervin began to think about communication as procedure.

Marxist thought and critical theory and philosophy were also introduced to her at Michigan, even though it was not part of the graduate curriculum. When she found it difficult to be accepted by most of the U.S. male graduate students at Michigan, it was the male foreign students who came to her rescue. She was absorbed into their worlds and became interested in international issues because of this positive experience. According to Dervin, these influences forced her to explore Marxist thought and critical theory, and to develop an intellectually informed social consciousness.

Being befriended by Richard Carter also had a significant influence on Dervin's philosophical development. She said that it was Carter's work that directed her to look at communication as behavior and started her on the journey to the development of Sense-Making.

The 1985 International Communication Association conference she planned was a turning point in her life as well as the field of communication, enabling her to put into practice her theory of working in the dialogic. It was the first step at achieving her dream of "honoring intellectual depth and methodological diversity." It was also this conference that began to legitimize critical and feminist scholarship in her field so that she did not feel so intellectually alone. The conference both opened her to the work of Giddens and Hall and gave her the privilege of knowing them personally. She says: "They provided me with a vision of how one can struggle to live one's life and one's work as an honorable, committed, and rigorous scholar."

It was at Ohio State that Dervin says she found a "genuine place of intellectual stimulation," a place where exchanges between supposedly different and sometimes competing approaches and foci "enabled her own work and that of her graduate students and colleagues to soar."

When asked how she would like to be remembered, she answered: "Someone who was absolutely passionate for and who lived and practiced in alliance with her philosophy and theory. A person who pursued in every way a dialogic or a communication approach to communication." She has done just that through her mentoring, her life work and writing, and her research.

The end of the story has not been lived out. The degree to which Dervin is able to achieve her goal for the field in truly accepting the "diversity of methodological perspective" has yet to be realized; but knowing the life and tenaciousness of Brenda Dervin, we know she will never give up trying. As she concluded: "Maybe the end of the story will be a good one." If Brenda Dervin has anything to do about it, it will.

AUTHOR'S NOTE

All biographical information was obtained from three interviews/conversations the author had with Dr. Brenda L. Dervin on July 18, 22, and 27, 1994. During these interview sessions, Professor Dervin also reflected on and discussed with the author her philosphical ideals, her contributions to the field, and her achievements. The author would like to express her appreciation to Dr. Dervin for her openness, thoughtfulness, and patience. Furthermore, the author would like to express her sincere gratitude for Dr. Dervin's comments and suggestions on an earlier draft of this chapter.

REFERENCES

Agostino, D. (1981). [Review of *Progress in Communication Sciences: Volume II*]. *Public Opinion Quarterly, 45*, 437–438.

Atwood, R., & Dervin, B. (1981). Challenges to socio-cultural predictors of information seeking: A test of race vs. situation movement state. In D. Nimmo (ed.), *Communication Yearbook 4.* (pp. 549–569). New Brunswick, N.J.: Transaction Books.

Berger. C. R. (1991). Communication theories and other curios. *Communication Monographs, 58*, 101–113.

Brown, D. (1987). Twin aims [Review of *Progress in communication sciences: Volume VII*]. *Journal of Communication, 37*, 178–181.

Bruce, H. W. (1994). A cognitive view of the situational dynamism of user-centered relevance estimation. *Journal of the American Society for Information Science, 45*, 142–148.

Dervin, B. (1965). *The Spender Syndrome: Case studies of 68 families and their consumer problems.* Madison, Wisc.: University of Wisconsin Extension.

Dervin, B. (1971). Communication behaviors as related to information control behaviors of black low-income adults. Ph.D. diss., Michigan State University, 1971. *Dissertation Abstracts International, 32A*, 7021.

Dervin, B. (1987). The potential contribution of feminist scholarship to the field of communication. *Journal of Communication, 37*, 107–120.

Dervin, B. (1989a). Audience as listener and learner, teacher and confidante: The sense-making approach. In R. Rice & C. Atkins (eds.), *Public communication campaigns.* (pp. 67–86). 2nd ed. Newbury Park, Calif.: Sage.

Dervin, B. (1989b). Users as research inventions: How research categories perpetuate inequities. *Journal of Communication, 39*, 216–232.

Dervin, B. (1991). Comparative theory reconceptualized: From entities and states to processes and dynamics. *Communication Theory, 1*, 59–69.

Dervin, B. (1992). From the mind's eye of the user: The sense-making qualitative-quantitative methodology. In J.D. Glazier & R. R. Powell (eds.), *Qualitative research in information management.* (pp. 61–84). New York: Libraries Unlimited.

Dervin, B. (1993). Verbing communication: Mandate for disciplinary invention. *Journal of Communication, 43*, 45–54.

Dervin, B. (1994). Information ↔ democracy: An examination of underlying assumptions. *Journal of American Society for Information Science, 45*, 369–385.

Dervin, B., & Greenberg, B. S. (1972). The communication environment of the urban poor. In F. G. Kline & P. J. Tichenor (eds.), *Current perspectives of mass communication.* (pp. 195–233). Newbury, Calif.: Sage.

Dervin, B., Grossberg, L., O'Keefe, B. J., & Wartella, E. (1989). *Rethinking communication, Volume 1: Paradigm issues.* Newbury Park, Calif.: Sage.

Dervin, B., Grossberg, B. J., & Wartella, E. (eds.). (1989). *Rethinking communication, Volume 2: Paradigm exemplars.* Newbury Park, Calif.: Sage.

Dervin, B., & Hariharan, U. (eds.). (1993). *Progress in communication sciences: Volume XI.* Norwood, N.J.: Ablex.

Dervin, B., Harlock, S., Atwood, R., & Garzona, C. (1980). The human side of information: An exploration in a health communication context. In D. Nimmo (ed.), *Communication Yearbook* 4. (pp. 591–608). New Brunswick, N.J.: Transaction Books.

Dervin, B., Jacobson, T., & Nilan, M. (1982). Measuring information seeking: A test of a quantitative-qualitative methodology. In M. Burgoon (ed.), *Communication Yearbook* 6. (pp. 419–444). New Brunswick, N.J.: Transaction Books.

Dervin, B., Nilan, M., & Jacobson, T. (1981). Improving predictions of information use: A comparison of predictor types in a health communication setting. In M. Burgoon (ed.), *Communication Yearbook* 5. (pp. 807–830). New Brunswick, N.J.: Transaction Books.

Dervin, B., & Voigt, M. J. (eds.). (1980 through 1989). *Progress in communication sciences: Volumes II through IX.* Norwood, N.J.: Ablex.

Ettema, J. A., Brown, J. W., & Luepker, R. V. (1983). Knowledge gap effects in a health information campaign. *Public Opinion Quarterly, 47,* 516–527.

Freshley, D. (1982). [Review of *Progress in communication sciences, Volume II*]. *Quarterly Journal of Speech, 68,* 223–224.

Gammack, J. (1994). Information in action: Soft systems methodology. *Systems Practice, 7,* 222–224.

Greenberg, B., & Dervin, B. (1970a). Mass communication among the urban poor. *Public Opinion Quarterly, 34,* 224–235.

Greenberg, B., & Dervin, B. (1970b). *Uses of the mass media by the urban poor: Findings of three research projects.* New York: Praeger.

Hall, S. (1989). Ideology and communication theory. In B. Dervin, L. Grossberg, B. J. O'Keefe, & E. Wartella (eds.), *Rethinking communication, Volume 1: Paradigm issues.* Newbury Park, Calif.: Sage.

Hoijer, B. (1992). Sociocognitive structures and television reception. *Media Culture and Society, 14,* 583–603.

Levy, M. R., & Gurevitch, M. (eds.). (1993). The future of the field I [special issue]. *Journal of Communication, 43(3).*

Littlejohn, S. W. (1991). [Review of *Rethinking communication: Volumes 1 & 2*]. *Quarterly Journal of Speech, 77,* 490–493.

McQuail, D. (1990). Paradigmatic guidance [Review of *Rethinking communication, Volumes 1 & 2*]. *Journal of Communication, 40,* 130–132.

Miller, G. (1981). " 'Tis the season to be jolly": A yuletide 1980 assessment of communication research. *Human Communication Research, 7,* 371–377.

Miller, J. (1985). Conventional rules [Review of *Progress in communication sciences, Volume IV*]. *Journal of Communication, 35,* 180–184.

Mishler, E. G. (1990). Validation in inquiry-guided research: The role of exemplars in narrative studies. *Harvard Educational Review, 60,* 415–442.

Moffit, M. A. (1994). Collapsing and integrating concepts of public and image into a new theory. *Public Relations Review, 20,* 159–170.

Raviv, A., Maddyweitzman, E., & Raviv, A. (1992). Parents of adolescents—help-seeking intentions as a function of help sources and parenting issues. *Adolescence,* 15, 115–135.
Savolainen, R. (1993). The sense-making theory—reviewing the interests of a user-centered approach to information seeking and use. *Information Processing and Management,* 29, 13–28.
Vuchinich, S. (1990). [Review of *Rethinking communication*]. *Contemporary Sociology,* 19, 740–741.
Wigand, R. T. (1985). Diversity, coherence [Review of *Progress in communication sciences, Volume V*]. *Journal of Communication,* 35, 202–204.
Winkleby, M. A., Flora, J. A., & Kraemer, H. C. (1994). A community-based heart disease intervention—predictors of change. *American Journal of Public Health,* 84, 767–772.

Additional Selected Publications by Brenda L. Dervin

Dervin, B. (1976). Strategies for dealing with human information needs: Information or communication? *Journal of Broadcasting,* 20, 325–333.
Dervin, B. (1977). Useful theory for librarianship: Communication, not information. *Drexel Library Quarterly,* 13, 16–32.
Dervin, B. (1980). Communication gaps and inequities: Moving toward a reconceptualization. In B. Dervin & M. J. Voigt (eds.), *Progress in communication sciences: Volume II,* pp. 73–112.
Dervin, B., & Dewdhey, P. (1986). Neutral questioning: A new approach to the reference interview. *Research Quarterly,* 25, 506–513.
Dervin, B., & Nilan, M. (1986). Information needs and uses. *Annual Review of Information Science and Technology,* 21, 3–33.
Huesca, R., & Dervin, B. (1994). Theory and practice in Latin America alternative communication research. *Journal of Communication,* 44, 53–73.
Shields, P., Dervin, B., Richter, C., & Soller, R. (1993). Who needs "POTS-plus" services?: A comparison of residential user needs along the rural-urban continuum. *Telecommunications Policy,* 17, 563–587.
Shields, V. R., & Dervin, B. (1993). Sense-making in feminist social science research: A call to enlarge the methodological options of feminist studies. *Women's Studies International Forum,* 16, 65–81.

NANCY DICKERSON
(1927–   )

Christine L. Ogan

Nancy Dickerson does not fit any general description of a broadcast news reporter of the 1990s, but like all pioneers, she had to carve out her role as the first female correspondent for CBS News, the first woman on television to report from the floor of a national political convention, the first woman in an anchor booth, and the first woman to broadcast from the floor of the Senate. And she did it with style, personal charm, and thorough research on a mission to "save the world."

Ambitious and extremely hard working, Dickerson was also attracted to the social life of Washington, D.C. She made a practice of hobnobbing with politicos from her first job in the city, as staff assistant to the Senate Foreign Relations Committee.

It was this mix of social comings and goings with her work as a television newswoman that led her to be variously labeled in the articles that describe her as Washington gadfly journalist, TV personality, TV newscaster, TV lady, social stalwart, socialite news producer, television doyenne, and journalist extraordinare. Whereas present-day journalists might try harder to separate their social lives from their jobs as political reporters, Dickerson claimed that her contacts never provided her more than an occasional entrée to a source (Gottehrer, 1964). Her detractors claim otherwise, stating that her "social pretensions compromised her credibility as a serious reporter" (Lee, 1982). Dickerson's introduction to Washington politics came partly through her romantic liaisons, which included Henry (Scoop) Jackson, John F. Kennedy, and Jack Brooks. She said she was often asked about whether she had to sleep with anyone to get her position in broadcasting since it was assumed that women couldn't make it any other way— her answer to that question was always "No."

FAMILY BACKGROUND, EDUCATION, AND
EARLY CAREER

Born Nancy Hanschman in Milwaukee in January 1927 to Frederick R. and Florence (Conners) Hanschman, she grew up in Wauwatosa, Wisconsin where she attended the local public high school. Her college education began at a Catholic girls' school, Clarke College in Dubuque, where she majored in piano. She transferred to the University of Wisconsin, Madison, in her junior year with a plan to major in premed. In her autobiography, *Among Those Present,* which she wrote in 1976, she recounted that an admission clerk in the medical school tried to convince her that medical school was not for women, since they were not to take jobs traditionally reserved for men. After deciding that a career in medicine would require too many years of school, she settled on majors in Spanish and Portuguese in the School of Education. She cites as the highlight of those years her selection as a United Nations student delegate to Europe. While on this trip to Europe in the early years following World War II, Dickerson decided that her generation's mission was to change the world. Following the trip, she did brief stints as a model at Nina Ricci in Paris and as a typist at the Economic Cooperation Administration, but was called back to Milwaukee by her parents to fulfill her contractual obligation to teach. But her heart was not in teaching or in Milwaukee; she therefore spent the summers between her teaching as a student in a graduate program in government at Harvard University.

Following an unsuccessful job hunt in New York, she moved to Washington on the advice of a friend. She searched for employment all over D.C., first settling for a job in the registrar's office at Georgetown University and finally securing a position as a secretary with the Senate Foreign Relations Committee. Although she lied about her ability to take dictation, it didn't handicap her; in fact, she was soon asked to edit hearings and assist in speechwriting (Dickerson, 1976, p. 9). She considered her experience on the Committee as a "graduate course in government" (Dickerson, 1976, p. 14). She professed to love every minute of her life and work at the Foreign Relations Committee, but she acknowledged that there was no future for a woman on the Committee. Indeed, because of her gender she was not permitted to make investigative staff trips. Being a woman and not having obtained a doctorate, she realized that she could never be promoted to the chief of staff position. Her wish to change the world was not being enacted fast enough in her low-level job on the Committee, leading her to try her hand at journalism, where she thought she'd have the opportunity to express some of her own opinions. Furthermore, she believed that her training on the Committee well prepared her for such work; she knew how to ask questions and the value of followup questions.

CAREER AT CBS AND NBC

Dickerson's break at CBS came as a direct result of her experience in politics. CBS was looking for a man who was well acquainted with Capitol Hill. In April 1954 she was hired to be a public affairs producer of two radio programs, "The Leading Question" and "Capitol Cloakroom." Both shows required her to ask questions of senators and representatives live on air. Later that year she was made associate producer of "Face the Nation," the competitor to "Meet the Press." She worked as a producer at CBS until 1960. Along the way she was named Edward R. Murrow's assistant and launched her career as a correspondent by convincing her superiors to let her travel to Europe to cover a story on women in the army. While there, she began to cover European reactions to Soviet Premier Nikita Khrushchev's visit to the United States. Once back in the United States, she began to think up stories to cover, being careful not to choose any that would impinge on male correspondents' territory. She said she met resistance from men who were denied opportunities in broadcasting when she appeared on the air. Some people suggested that because she was female and didn't have a family to support she should give up the job. Instead, she kept looking for opportunities that would make her a full-fledged correspondent with the network, which happened following an exclusive interview with then House Speaker Sam Rayburn in 1960. She celebrated her new job at a party thrown for her by Senate Majority Leader Lyndon Baines Johnson (LBJ) and his wife, Lady Bird. The entire Senate and the New York executives from CBS attended. Dickerson says in her book that she marked the occasion with the purchase of a vicuña suit and a Dior coat (which she called her foreign correspondent's coat) from Bergdorf's (Dickerson, 1976, p. 35). Her first assignment was to cover the civil rights movement and Lyndon Johnson; this was a good spot for a reporter in the 1960s.

Dickerson's achievements at CBS were many. She covered both the Democratic and Republican national conventions in 1960, becoming the first woman to file reports from the floor of the convention. Her close relationship with LBJ allowed her to be the correspondent to whom he announced his willingness to run as JFK's vice presidential candidate. She covered Kennedy's inauguration, and her friendship with him led to some exclusive interviews. Later, she accompanied LBJ on a fact-finding mission to Vietnam. Her mentors at CBS were among the very best in journalism—Edward R. Murrow and Eric Severeid. She counts the advice she received from Murrow among the best. "Don't tell everything you know. Just tell them the one thing you want them to know and tell it straight so that they understand. It's not necessary to establish your wide knowledge," he told her in the beginning days of her work as a correspondent (Dickerson, 1976, p. 39). He also advised her on her professional dress. Since he claimed she looked like a "sexy madonna," she should stick to simple clothes on the air (Dickerson, 1976, p. 40). Dickerson was fond of wearing Bill Blass creations over the course of her career.

But as time went on, Dickerson became increasingly annoyed with her status at CBS. She felt that although the network gave her important political assignments, it often relegated her reports to radio or minor television news shows. In the 1960s there was no structure in place for the protection of women in the workforce, and Dickerson had to fight her discrimination battles on her own. Even in the Dickerson profile that appeared in the *Saturday Evening Post,* her work was compared to that of other women reporters, not to all television news men and women. "Nancy Dickerson is seldom beaten. NBC's Pauline Frederick,* the dean of women TV correspondents, may be more scholarly. And ABC's Lisa Howard . . . may be more flamboyant. But Nancy Dickerson is clearly the princess of the industry's press corps" (Gottehrer, October 31, 1964, p. 36).

Her frustrations at CBS led her to move to NBC. She continued to cover LBJ for her new employer. She scooped the other networks when Johnson told her that his choice for a running mate would be Hubert Humphrey. Later, she used her influence with the White House police to be the only woman in the Rotunda when Johnson was inaugurated. NBC fulfilled its promise to her to be given more airtime, and her interviews appeared on important programs—"The Today Show," "The Huntley-Brinkley Report"—and she had her own daily news show. In 1982 when a *Washington Post* reporter asked her if she regretted never becoming an anchor of a major news program, she bristled. "I anchored a show for six years, four times a day, the five-minute news shows. They called them strip shows. It isn't hard work, you know. What you do, you rip the wire, you rewrite the wire, you read the wire. The most exciting thing in television is being on a story live—election night, or a convention, any of those things that you do live . . . but they take a lot of ability" (Lee, 1982, p. D1). She followed that statement with a suggestion of regret—that she hadn't been able to appear regularly the way she might have as a nightly news anchor.

Dickerson worked for NBC until 1970 when she left to become a political commentator for "Inside Washington," a syndicated television program.

MARRIAGES AND PERSONAL LIFE

Nancy Hanschman has been married twice, first to Claude Wyatt Dickerson on February 24, 1962. Dickerson was a Washington real estate investor, a widower with three daughters. The couple's first child was named Michael Wyatt, born on July 11, 1963, the morning after a dinner party at the Johnsons. LBJ thought a more appropriate name for him would have been Lyndon. An extremely busy social schedule matched her hectic work schedule, making it difficult to have time for her children, so they traveled with Nancy on many of her assignments out of the city. Their second child, John Frederich (Nancy's father's name), was born on July 6, 1968. Nancy went back to work, covering the Republican National Convention, three weeks after his birth.

The Dickersons bought the Merrywood estate and the adjacent 50 acres in

McLean, Virginia, in 1963. The estate was the girlhood home of Jacqueline Bouvier Kennedy Onassis. Mr. and Mrs. Hugh Auchincloss, Jackie's mother and stepfather, sold the estate to developers. JFK had written his *Profiles in Courage* from the estate. In 1984, following her divorce from Dickerson, the couple sold the property for a reported $4.25 million.

The Merrywood home was the site of numerous parties that included most of the important political dignitaries in Washington. The social relationships with political officials meant that most senators and Cabinet members referred to her as Nancy or Miss Nancy. She is a member of the prestigious F Street Club, where she admitted to spending a lot of time in her early years in Washington. As to the separation of her social and journalistic lives, Dickerson once said, "I've lived here for fourteen years now and I've always been around these people [political officials]. They know me, and they know they don't have to say 'This or that is off the record' at their parties. The biggest thing is trust" (Gottehrer, 1964, p. 37).

Dickerson remarried in 1989 to John Cunningham Whitehead, an investment executive and then one of Washington's most eligible bachelors. Whitehead had worked with Goldman, Sachs & Co. in New York until 1985 when he joined the State Department. He met Dickerson at a Canadian Embassy dinner. He was a former co-chairman of the Republican National Committee and also a member of the F Street Club.

LATER CAREER

No one can say for sure why Dickerson left NBC in 1970. Frank Jordan, then NBC Washington bureau chief, said, "There was nothing that untoward about it. She had done everything that she could do at NBC News, and that involved breaking down a lot of barriers. People leave. It happens with some frequency" (Lee, 1982, p. D1). In Lee's profile of Dickerson in a 1982 *Washington Post* article, he said that Dickerson was not well liked at NBC. "Too aloof, many said; too impressed with herself, too much the prima donna, the social climber, too hard on her coworkers [staff turnover in her office, former colleagues say, was high, both at CBS and NBC]; too prone to flaunt her jewelry, her designer dresses, her mink coat when working a beat with other, less affluent reporters" (p. D1).

Following her departure from NBC, Dickerson had several different media ventures, none of which particularly advanced her career. She produced a few specials for PBS on single-issue politics, the energy crisis and women in the Arab world. She also did some free-lance work, including an interview with President Reagan, Vice President Bush, and White House officials for an International Communication Agency (now the U.S. Information Agency) film. In the early 1980s she formed the Television Corporation of America, a company reportedly financed by one of her companions, Texas oilman Bill Moss, following the breakup of her first marriage. The television company's major output was a two-hour documentary of a ten-year retrospective of Watergate. The program, which Dickerson said took ten full-time staff more than six months to produce, was picked up by about 60 television stations around the country. Despite the great effort and meticulous research put into "784 Days That Changed America," it was poorly reviewed. The program, nevertheless, won both the Peabody and Silver Gavel awards.

In recent years, Dickerson has appeared on television only infrequently. She has settled into a life spent with her husband between New York and Washington. She continues to work as a member of the board of trustees for Covenant House and the New York Public Library. She is also a member of the White House Endowment Fund and the U.S. Botanic Garden as well as the Central Park Conservancy.

LIFE ACHIEVEMENTS IN PERSPECTIVE

It is easy to judge Nancy Dickerson as a woman who used her social and political connections and perhaps her feminine wiles to climb the broadcast news ladder. But to do so would be to view her career from the perspective of acceptable standards of the 1990s, not the 1960s when she was making her professional way as a lone woman in broadcast news. She had no women mentors, and many men were jealous of her accomplishments, excellent journalistic instincts, and hard work. If she seemed overly concerned about her attire, others were too. Women journalists today would probably respond angrily to a description of themselves like the one that appeared about Dickerson in the 1964 *Saturday Evening Post* article. "Slim (five feet seven and 120 pounds) and social (she is a member of Washington's exclusive F Street Club), chic and charming, she looks and dresses like a fashion model, speaks like a professional actress, and goes about her job like a veteran newsman" (Gottehrer, 1964, p. 36).

Summarizing Nancy Dickerson's contributions to U.S. broadcast journalism is no easy matter. As one of the first television newswomen, she had many successes as well as disappointments. Nevertheless, the women in broadcast journalism who followed Dickerson found in her a role model with dedication to her work and high journalistic standards.

REFERENCES

Dickerson, N. (1976). *Among those present*. New York: Random House.
Gottehrer, B. (1964, October 31). Television's princess of the press corps. *Saturday Evening Post*, 36–37.
Lee, R. (1982, June 16). The "first lady" of network news looks to the future with a retrospective. *Washington Post*, D1.

DOROTHY DIX (ELIZABETH MERIWETHER GILMER) (1861–1951)

Roger D. Haney

Elizabeth M. Gilmer started writing at the age of 33 for the New Orleans *Picayune* to offset her personal depression and earn money to care for her sick husband. By the end of her career 50 years later, she was a millionairess with over 60 million daily readers. She was an attuned listener and a clear, straightforward writer, traits that made her a success both as a trial reporter and as the "mother confessor to millions." She was a gifted writer of sharp prose and common sense and a caring individual who probably affected more lives under her pen name of *Dorothy Dix* than anyone not in the military or government.

Elizabeth Gilmer's first column in the *Picayune* was entitled *Sunday Salad,* a potpourri of essays and sermonettes for which she was initially paid $5 per week. In 1901 she moved to the *New York Journal* where her first assignment was to follow Carrie Nation on a saloon-smashing binge in Nebraska. Then she covered a number of sensational murder trials, including that of Harry Thaw, which led to her being named one of the original *sob sisters* (a woman reporter whose coverage of sensational crimes could bring "a tear" to the reader's eye). At the same time, she wrote a column, *Dorothy Dix Talks,* three times a week.

In 1917 she was able to stop her coverage of sensational murders, which accomplished no purpose other than building circulation in her view, in favor of a daily column written for John Wheeler and the Philadelphia Ledger Syndicate. Not feeling capable of writing a daily essay, required for syndication, she began the practice of publishing letters from her readers along with her *advice-to-the-lovelorn* responses. The format was an extremely successful one, which the advice columnists genre follows to this day.

By the 1930s the column appeared in 300 newspapers. Her income from her syndicated writings was between $70,000 and $80,000 in 1940. On a typical day she received 100,000 letters. Each letter was read and marked by a secretary so that some could be answered directly if warranted and others could be included in her column. In her later years she was able to travel to Europe and Asia a great deal and often wrote of those experiences. She kept up her column until she died in 1951 at the age of 90.

FAMILY BACKGROUND

Elizabeth Meriwether Gilmer was born on November 18, 1861, in Woodstock, Tennessee on the Tennessee–Kentucky border. She was a slight, frail girl who fought illness throughout her early years. But that did not prevent her from living the active life of a tomboy, riding her father's horses, climbing trees, and playing in the woods on her father's farm of over 800 acres and family property of 4,300 acres.

The Meriwether family was of Scottish, Welsh, and English stock that settled in Virginia in the 1680s. A branch of the family moved to Woodstock, Montgomery County, in 1830, and it was here that Elizabeth and her younger sister Mary and brother Ed were born. Ed lost an arm while working in the family factory, and Elizabeth consoled and counseled him through the injury. They remained close throughout their lives to the extent that when Elizabeth finally settled in New Orleans she built a mansion so that Ed and his wife could live in the same house with her. He was her financial adviser and helped make her a millionaire.

The Meriwethers were a distinguished family, descendants of Meriwether Lewis. Elizabeth's family had considerable landholdings but after the Civil War had relatively little cash, most of which went toward farm expenses. Elizabeth's father, Will Meriwether, was a gregarious, industrious follow who tried to augment his income in whatever way he could. A frail man himself, he nevertheless was an active horse-breeder, sometimes augmenting, often decreasing, his inherited wealth with a series of enterprises, including a plow-manufacturing plant, succeeded by a tobacco commission company. His most successful venture was in horse-breeding, a family tradition, and Elizabeth became an excellent horsewoman as a result.

Elizabeth's mother, Maria Winston, died when Elizabeth was still young, and her father soon married Martha Gilmer. Martha proved to be a strict but loving stepmother, although the primary care and education of Elizabeth was undertaken by her Grandmother Barker. She taught Elizabeth a lifelong love of literature and a healthy respect for work. A black house-servant called Mammie taught Elizabeth etiquette with the use of the "hardest and boniest knuckles that any human being ever possessed."

She also learned a great deal informally from her father. They often took long walks together (her father had a protective interest in her which lasted throughout his life because of her early illness), and he shared his interests and opinions with her.

EDUCATION

From an early age, Elizabeth's grandmother had encouraged her to use the extensive family library. By the age of 12, she was a confirmed bookworm. The family had no children's books but did have an extensive collection of the "solid meat of good literature." She became familiar with the works of Shakespeare, Scott, Fielding, Richardson, and Dickens, a lifelong favorite. A family relative staying with the family encouraged her reading and corrected her pronunciation during this period. This interest in reading was a primary source of her education throughout her life.

Her formal education in Woodstock was not as robust.

We were sent to Miss Alice's or Miss Jenny's, not because they were trained or even qualified to teach, but because their fathers had been colonels under Beauregard, or had been killed at Shiloh, and somebody had to help the poor souls along. And so I could climb like a squirrel and ride like a jockey long before I knew a great deal about the three R's.

The family horse-breeding business was doing well, and Will Meriwether moved to Clarksville, Tennessee, so that his children could continue their education at better schools. Elizabeth attended high school at the Female Academy in Clarksville. She learned a smattering of the *ologies* and *isms* and managed to distinguish herself for her writing ability. Her first major composition was entitled *The Pleasures of Anticipation*. By 15, she was putting out her own newspaper, and she enjoyed writing compositions so much that she wrote them for any of her classmates who asked. Upon her graduation at 16, the local paper reported that she was proceeding to Hollins Institute in Virginia where she would no doubt be a bright star due to her brilliant intellect.

The first difficulty Elizabeth encountered at Hollins was that her father had sent her there without knowing that she needed to be accepted first. The second difficulty was that she didn't fit in with the more genteel young ladies of the student body and felt a chill from the experience that lasted her entire life. She did win a medal in a composition contest during her stay there but did not return when the term was over. That experience ended her brief college career. The rest of her education consisted of on-the-job training under the excellent tutelage of Eliza Nicholson, Major Nathaniel Burbank, and Arthur Brisbane. In later years, she also traveled extensively abroad.

MARRIAGE AND CAREER DEVELOPMENT

At 22, Elizabeth married. Her husband was George O. Gilmer, ten years her senior, her second cousin and the brother of her stepmother. He had come for a visit and stayed for a lifetime. It was not a happy lifetime. George was a dashing, exciting man, full of expectations but short of focus. Elizabeth hoped to provide stability, but George turned out to be continually ill and involved in financial ventures that always seemed to require more cash. He did have some worthwhile ideas but had trouble sticking to one job. His longest stay was with the Tennessee Coal and Iron Company. While with them, he got ideas for the distillation of turpentine products; his name is listed in governmental reports as a pioneer in the industry. He raised money to start a plant, and Elizabeth contributed a great deal over the years with money she made as a columnist. All the ventures proved unsuccessful, owing in part to his inability to stick to one task and to get along with others.

It wasn't long after the marriage that it became apparent that George was not well and needed exceptional care. He often became moody and depressed and had trouble keeping a job. His illness grew steadily worse over the 47 years of their marriage until he eventually had to be institutionalized. In spite of his deepening mental illness, Elizabeth never considered a divorce, perhaps in part in deference to her mass audience. "I never once thought of getting a divorce," she wrote. "I felt that I would not be fit to give advice to others unless I could live that advice myself." George died in a sanitarium in 1929. They had no children.

Elizabeth tried her best but had no ready way of making money immediately after the marriage, for she lived in a culture that frowned upon women earning their way. Out of necessity, her interest in writing reasserted itself, and she began sending fictional pieces and stories from her childhood to papers in Nashville and New Orleans. When she was 28 she won a prize of $100 for a Christmas story. The strain of trying to earn enough in this fashion, with inconsistent help from her husband, proved too much for her, however. At the age of 32, Elizabeth suffered a nervous breakdown. Her doctor sent her to Bay Saint Louis, a small resort on the Mississippi coast, for recuperation. This turned out to be the pivotal event in her life.

Eliza Jane Poitevent had begun her journalism career writing poems and as the New Orleans *Daily Picayune* literary editor. She married the 64-year-old publisher, Alva Holbrook, in 1872 at the age of 24 and inherited the paper two years later upon his death. Eliza married her business manager, George Nicholson, in 1878, and together they increased circulation and established the paper as one of the best in the South. They concentrated on making it a family newspaper, avoiding sensationalism and adding a number of features ranging from Sunday comics and increased sports coverage to household hints and society columns. Eliza Holbrook Nicholson was a founder and first president of the Woman's National Press Association, later the Woman's International Press Association. It was she who hired Elizabeth for the *Picayune* in 1894.

Mrs. Nicholson took her vacations in a house next to the one Elizabeth rented for her rest. They got to know and like each other, and Elizabeth submitted a story about a woman who had saved the family silver during the Civil War. Eliza liked the story and paid Elizabeth $3 for it. This was a significant sum when we consider that Elizabeth's brother Ed was making $5 a week. A few months later Elizabeth went to New Orleans and was hired by the paper. She started by reporting births and deaths for the vital statistics column at $6 a week. She improved her writing skill through effort and had the reputation of not forgetting anything she learned. Soon she began to work for Major Nathaniel Burbank, the news editor of the *Picayune.*

The Major was a northern officer during the Civil War who was not immediately appreciated in New Orleans. But he had the full support of Mrs. Nicholson and was a felicitous mentor for Elizabeth. He gave her a variety of assignments ranging from reviews to society notes, taught her an interest in the theater, and honed her writing to a simple, crisp prose that commanded attention. Only a year later Mrs. Nicholson rewarded Elizabeth with her first column, dubbed *Sunday Salad* by the Major.

This weekly sermonette, written for women readers on a variety of topics, was a success from the start. Elizabeth disdained the flowery writing common to the period in favor of a more direct, everyday, colloquial style. The column was to contain "a base of crisp, fresh ideas. Over them a dressing mixed of oil of kindness, vinegar of satire, salt of wit; at the end, a dash of the paprika of doing things," according to the Major. Elizabeth added honesty and openness to the depiction of women, who until that time were only supposed to be mentioned in the paper at the time of their birth, marriage, and death.

In one of these columns, Elizabeth even disdained the advice of *Aunt Margaret* columns as generally "insufficient and unsatisfactory" to the women who asked the questions. The column also covered the traditional areas for women readers of the time: society happenings, recipes, and fashion. It was at this time that Elizabeth took the name *Dorothy Dix.*

Because of the immediate success of the column, the title was soon changed to "Dorothy Dix Talks." Almost from the first, readers wrote letters to the author, which were highly prized because they provided ideas for future columns. Her salary was soon increased from $5 to $15 a week. In 1896, a few months after Elizabeth's column had started, Eliza and George Nicholson died within ten days of each other.

Scouts for the Hearst publications soon discovered her and made an offer to join the New York *Journal.* She at first refused, citing loyalty to Major Burbank. The *Journal* then suggested that she take an assignment to cover the Carrie Nation story, and Elizabeth agreed. The resulting story became a series describing "a vast body of women who see nothing but death and destruction in the wine glass, and are ready to fight to protect their children from it."

As Elizabeth succinctly wrote, "Mrs. Nation is not eloquent, and expresses herself more fluently with a hatchet than by words, but has that strong, invincible, irresistible power that comes to those who are ready to lay down their lives, if needed, for the cause they have espoused." Elizabeth also wrote of the dissension within the ranks when Mrs. Nation refused to go on a midnight raid because she had not yet heard the word of God to do so. The series was a major success, and the *Journal* increased their offer to $5,000 a year, which was more than the governor of Louisiana was making. Moreover, Major Burbank died at this time, removing any remaining objections to taking the job.

Upon arriving at the *Journal,* Elizabeth immediately found that there was little time for debating the approach of a particular story. She was thrust into the beehive of a city newsroom, where crisis was routine, and she responded. Her success with the Carrie Nation series led to her assignment to cover other stories of interest to women in addition to her thrice-weekly column. An early additional assignment was to cover the murder trial of a stepmother accused of killing her 18-month-old child. Authorities did not allow access to the prisoner and would not talk to the press. Elizabeth fortuitously met an earlier boyfriend of the accused who drove her around to relatives who provided valuable insights on the woman and 3-year-old stepchild. She filed a long account that told of a child who cried constantly and who was said to have fallen down the stairs. The defense also argued that arsenic found in the child was from embalming procedures. Elizabeth noted that the stepmother had a child of her own and was expecting another. Elizabeth worried over the length of the story and feared that she would be fired. But the story was a success. She also gained a marriage proposal from the former boyfriend but politely explained that she was married to her work. For the next 15 years she covered major murder trials for the *Journal,* in addition to her column.

The editor of the *Journal* at the time was Arthur Brisbane, a hard-headed, profit-oriented, gruff individual who made great use of Elizabeth's talents and who took an interest in further improving her writing style. Hardly well educated, Brisbane felt that "it would take a young man eleven years to recover from a college education." But he had a good memory and a quick mind, and was an excellent judge of talent. He also had a high regard for his own talents. He wrote an estimated 500,000 words a year and increased his fortune through real estate deals, often using awareness of city projects covered in the paper. He often promoted personal financial interests on the editorial page. His friends included the rich and famous: Bernard F. Gimbel, Henry Ford, the Rockefellers, Gene Fowler, and Gene Tunney.

Elizabeth said that story ideas came to Brisbane in floods and often left the reporter bewildered over which to follow. The key advice he gave Elizabeth was to remember that "a newspaper is read mostly by busy people or very tired people or uneducated people. None of them is going to hunt a dictionary to find out what it means." Elizabeth had a great deal of respect for him and found that with him "the paper was the thing." In turn, Brisbane accepted Elizabeth's work as "good stuff" in a lengthy editorial on her ability in 1902.

MAJOR CONTRIBUTIONS AND ACHIEVEMENTS

Elizabeth was barely five feet tall and became rather stout in her middle and old age. She had the soft-spoken personality of a canary, yet she became the most widely read and discussed columnist of her times. She had little formal education, began her career in her mid-thirties out of domestic despair, lived with an unbalanced husband for 40 years, and had background, experience, gender, and physical stature against her. But she also had sharp, black eyes that could penetrate the truthfulness of a witness during a murder trial and passed for a woman ten years younger in looks and vitality.

To the *Journal* editors, Elizabeth's ability to interview people and win their confidence had far more potential for circulation and profit than her columns. As a result, she was assigned to cover the major murder trials of the time. The bigger the names in the trial, or the gorier the facts, the better the circulation.

Mrs. Lois Bonine was a middle-aged woman accused of killing a young dental student for threatening to break off their affair. Robert Fosburgh was accused of accidentally killing his younger sister while having a violent argument with his wife. The entire family argued that the daughter had been killed by three intruders. Nan Patterson, of Floradora Sextette fame, was accused of killing her well-to-do bookie lover while riding with him in a cab. A mouse of a man who married 36 wives was asked how he did it and replied that it was easy. "All you've got to do is talk to them about themselves." Another case involved a 17-year-old runaway found in a trunk slashed to death. The most famous case of the era, and the one that established Dorothy Dix as one of the *sob sisters*, was that of Evelyn Nesbit, Stanford White, and Harry K. Thaw. Nesbit was a beautiful showgirl, White the middle-aged architect who designed Madison Square Garden, and Thaw a rich playboy who said, "I did it [killed Stanford White] for the purity of the American home." Elizabeth eventually came to say, "I was on speaking terms with every criminal in America." Moreover, she was not averse to publishing her opinions in these cases, with the possible motive of affecting the jury.

It was her column, however, that Elizabeth felt made the greatest contribution to society. The first major personal advice columnist, and the longest lasting feature under single authorship, *Dorothy Dix* had the greatest audience of any man or woman of her time. People turned to her writings for views on dating, marriage, careers, problem-solving, and morals. Her column began in 1896 and continued uninterrupted until her death in 1951. She was popular at the beginning of the century and remained so through two world wars and times that changed so much that "the girls used to write to ask whether, when a young man called on them, it would be proper to help him on with his overcoat as he made ready to leave; now they want to know what I think about going to Atlantic City for a week-end with a man."

Every day Elizabeth received several hundred to sometimes more than a thousand letters addressed to Dorothy Dix from people seeking advice on problems troubling them and many of the readers who had never themselves written. The problems covered a gamut of difficulties:

—An indignant woman tired of her husband's infidelity wrote to ask the merits of pistol vs. poison.

—"I am a fifty-year-old man, in love with a woman who already has a husband. Please suggest the quickest and most humane way of getting rid of same."

—"He has been a perfect gentleman toward me, which I did not expect from a married man."

—A seaman wrote expressing concern over whether various girlfriends around the world were faithful to him.

—A woman wrote, "My husband keeps telling me to go to hell. Can I take the children with me?"

—An engineer wrote that he was forced to marry a pregnant girl, whom he did not know, at gunpoint and asked what could be done about it.

—A boy wrote to ask her help in convincing his parents to allow him a dog. She wrote, "Yes, Bobby, I do think that a boy without a dog is as forlorn as a dog without a boy."

—A woman inquired if she should tell her prospective groom about her false teeth. "Marry him," she advised, "and keep your mouth shut."

People wrote about extravagant wives, interfering mothers-in-law, cruel husbands, how to "pop the question" or wriggle "out of an affair." Her responses were decisive and generally advocated taking control of one's life and working out one's problems by facing them. Generally, she advocated divorce only when children were being harmed; she felt children should obey reasonable parents, lonely people should develop their interests and seek out others, and young men and women should maintain their lofty ideals.

In 1926, when Elizabeth was 65, she was once again called upon to cover a sensational murder trial. Edward Hall, an Episcopal pastor, was murdered with Eleanor Mills, the pretty wife of the church janitor and member of the church choir. She had been shot three times, her tongue slashed, and her abdomen ripped open. Love letters from each of them were spread around the murder scene. Mrs. Hall and her two brothers were charged with the killings. Elizabeth wrote analytically and compassionately of the trial. She argued that the husband, Mr. Mills, was much too sheepish to have committed the crime. She described how Mrs. Hall stoically heard of the love her husband had for another woman and yet never expressed resentment or jealousy but rather described her own love for her husband. Elizabeth also described the jury and how it was unlikely that they would find a verdict of guilty. When Mrs. Hall was acquitted, she broke down in Elizabeth's arms and thanked her.

CRITICAL EVALUATION OF CONTRIBUTION
AND ACHIEVEMENTS

The writings of Elizabeth Gilmer fall into four distinct areas: fictional work that she wrote under her own name; her columns of general interest to women which she wrote during her *Sunday Salad* days; her work covering sensational criminal trials which she did for the New York *Journal;* and her advice column, the work for which she had the largest audience and perhaps did the greatest good. While her fictional work sold well and her first regular column was noted for its even-handed discussion of women's issues, it was clearly her work as a "sob sister" and as "mother confessor to millions" that placed her in the annals of significant reporters and columnists.

Dorothy Dix, along with Winifred Black Bonfils (succeeded by Adela Rogers St. John), Ada Patterson, and Nixola Greeley-Smith, was one of the original sob sisters, a phrase coined by a male reporter. Elizabeth wrote with the view that the individuals she covered in these cases were "not so different from either of us as you think." Female readers were courted by advertisers, and women writers were coming into vogue because of their recognized ability to depict the human quality in hard news. Editors felt that readers would be attracted to coverage of sensational trials in a way that "depicted the human condition in all its variety." She covered the major murder trials of her time and did so in a manner that brought sympathy to victim and accused alike.

Foster Coates, city editor of the *Journal,* said of her that "Everything she sees here is new and wonderful. She sees it with the eyes of a child, but she writes about it with the mature mind of a woman who has gone through a lot." She wrote in everyday words, sometimes included slang, and thus became readable to a far larger audience. She provided advice to those in need in areas that concern us all: how to attract a mate, how to make do on a limited budget, how to improve the quality of a life, how to escape the defeatism in depression, alcohol, or unemployment. Her readers suffered through a Depression and two world wars. The letters were not all cheesecake and romance, and neither were her answers.

Elizabeth had no attraction to the professional "new woman" who called for war on men; men were generally noted as a good thing to have around. She felt that women needed to recognize and be recognized for the contribution they made to the home and family, but she also supported women's ability to support themselves when circumstances required it, although she never spoke of herself publicly in this way.

She had the courage, for the times, to point out that parents were not always infallible, that marital difficulties might be the wife's fault, and that finding a mate might not be the solution to a woman's problems. During the Second World War, she wrote that "yes, a great deal of what's happening today is helping the boys' morale, but it's also ruining the girls' morals." To those contemplating marriage, she suggested that they sit together for three or four hours and see if they enjoyed talking of matters other than love. She composed a list of ten rules for happiness that was often reprinted. The list suggested making up one's mind to be happy, to make the best of one's lot, to not cherish enmities and grudges, and to not borrow trouble. She often suggested that her readers not worry about what they did not know but to focus on what they did.

The ninth and tenth rules were to do something for someone less fortunate and to "keep busy."

Dorothy Dix was eventually published in North, Central, and South America, Australia, England, Europe, and Asia. She was cited in *Middletown,* the sociological study of small-town America (Lynd & Lynd, 1929), as "the most potent single agency of diffusion" of habits and thoughts of marriage from outside the town culture.

INTEGRATION OF PERSONAL AND PROFESSIONAL LIFE

Elizabeth Gilmer's personal life affected her professional life in a number of ways. First, it is clear that her husband's illness led to her pursuing a full-time job to earn money. Teaching, nursing, and writing were the few areas open to women at the time, but fortunately Elizabeth had the writing talent and the willingness to work and learn to sustain her in the journalism field. Second, the financial demands of her husband may have led her to develop her career in New York when she might not have otherwise. Third, her own life experiences, love of reading, and travel no doubt helped her come up with useful suggestions to life's problems. Apparently, she generated answers from within herself. There is no mention of a group of experts that she called upon for guidance in her advice.

Perhaps the most interesting way in which her personal life affected her professional life was in the choice of her professional name. Because male editors felt that women journalists were unlikely to remain in the profession for any length of time, and because any profession for a woman other than teaching, and later nursing, was considered unsavory, female journalists commonly took a pseudonym. At the *Picayune* the practice was to use an alliterative name. Elizabeth liked the name *Dorothy* and so chose that. The last name came from a black servant who was notable in Meriwether lore for having successfully hidden the family silverware from raiders during the Civil War. His name was Dick, but his wife often referred to him as *Mr. Dicks.* The story of this incident of saving the silverware became the basis for the first story that Elizabeth sold to Eliza Nicholson. Elizabeth later learned that *Dorothea Dix* was the name of a woman who crusaded for mental institution and prison reform. By that time, *Dorothy Dix* was well established, however, and Elizabeth was all the more proud to continue using the variation.

Elizabeth was not an outspoken advocate of women's rights, although she did join a number of other women journalists on a 150-mile march to Albany seeking suffrage in 1914. She was ahead of her times in a period when society felt that a woman's happiness was centered on a male and the home. She generally agreed with that notion, often writing that domestic bliss would be enhanced with a new recipe. She herself was an excellent cook and enjoyed entertaining a large number of friends. She did feel that women had worthwhile opinions, however, and should express them, a radical notion for the times.

Elizabeth Gilmer died on December 16, 1951. Perhaps her best epitaph was written by the New Orleans *Item,* when she left the *Picayune* for New York: "She has made nearly all of us laugh and many of us think; and this is a purpose as high and a calling as dignified as any need attempt." The *Dorothy Dix Talks* column was continued by Muriel Nissen until 1959 when she was succeeded by Helen Worden Erskine. Eventually, the market gave way to *Dear Abby* and *Ann Landers.*

REFERENCES

Deutsch, H. B. (1942). *Dorothy Dix talks.* In John E. Drewry (ed.), *Post biographies of famous journalists.* pp. 29–47. Athens: University of Georgia Press.

Gilmer, E. M. (1914). *Mirandy by Dorothy Dix.* New York: Hearst's International Library Co.

Gilmer, E. M. (1924). *My trip around the world by Dorothy Dix.* Philadelphia: Penn Publishing Co.

Gilmer, E. M. (1926, 1937). *Dorothy Dix, her book: Everyday help for everyday people.* New York: Funk & Wagnalls Co.

Gilmer, E. M. (1939). *How to win and hold a husband by Dorothy Dix.* New York: Arno Press.

Gilmer, E. M. (1946, May 5). Mother confessor to millions. New Orleans *Times-Picayune Magazine,* 6–7.

Kane, H. T. with E. B. Arthur. (1952). *Dear Dorothy Dix: The story of a compassionate woman.* New York: Doubleday & Co.

Lynd, R. S., & Lynd, H. M. (1929). *Middletown: A study in American culture.* Princeton, NJ: Princeton University Press.

Schilpp, M. G., and Murphy, S. M. (1983). *Great women of the press.* (pp. 112–120), Carbondale: Southern Illinois Press.

ELAINE GOODALE EASTMAN (1863–1953)

Julia R. Dobrow

Born in an era in which women did not work outside the home, in which single white women were expected to marry white men, and in which the few women who published their writing often elected to write under a pseudonym, Elaine Goodale Eastman was an exception to every rule. Eastman worked as a teacher in boarding schools for Indian children and on the Great Sioux Reservation for ten years of her life. She married a Sioux doctor. Throughout her entire life, she worked as a journalist, dedicating herself to educating the mainstream American population about the problems and issues of Native Americans.

FAMILY BACKGROUND, EDUCATION, AND TRAINING

Elaine Goodale was born in 1863 to Henry Sterling Goodale and Dora Hill Goodale on a farm in Egremont, Massachusetts. She was "fancifully named for Tennyson's lovelorn Elaine" (Eastman, in Graber, 1978, p. 3). Goodale and her sisters were educated at home by their mother. They showed some talent in writing at very early ages, published their poetry in magazines, and had a collection of their poems, *Apple Blossoms: Verses of Two Children,* published in 1879.

Although Goodale won a scholarship to the newly opened Harvard Annex (later Radcliffe College), her parents were financially unable to send her to college. Instead, she accepted an offer to teach at the Hampton Institute, a school for black and Indian children in Virginia. This "novel experiment," as Goodale later called it, posited the philosophy that the best way to assist black and Indian children was to neutralize the differences between them and their white cohorts. The teachers at Hampton attempted to eliminate difference by teaching minority group children to be as much like the dominant group as possible. Reformers of this era "were determined to facilitate closer racial relationships by forcing the abandonment of long-established habits of the red man . . . incorporation of the red man into white society was most frequently defended as an indispensable means of preventing Indian annihilation" (Priest, 1942, p. 145). In this environment, Goodale was trained and flourished. "I caught fire from that irresistible enthusiasm," she wrote, "making bold almost at once to spread the gospel of opportunity for the red man, through impassioned articles in *The Independent* and other leading journals" (Eastman, 1930, p. 22).

Goodale spent much of her time out of the classroom writing articles about the cause of Indian education. Her articles and columns regularly appeared in *The Independent, The Christian Union,* and other newspapers of the era. She realized that her efforts would best be made toward enlightening influential leaders, educators, and politicians "who in those days regularly inveighed against the 'shocking waste' of public funds in a futile attempt to civilize 'a horde of filthy savages' " (Eastman, in Graber, 1978, p. 21). Goodale's articles on Indian education ranged from informational writings about curricular and cultural issues to editorial diatribes urging the "reverend senators and other solemn graybeards" to awaken to the educational reforms being implemented at Hampton and other schools. Twenty-year-old Goodale did not hesitate to write strongly and passionately: "Perhaps on no subject does the average Congressman display a more whole-souled, confiding and self-[con]gratulatory ignorance than upon the Indian question!" (Eastman, in Graber, 1978, p. 21).

Goodale "burned with an intense desire to see the much discussed and little-known Indian country" and discussed this desire with General Samuel Chapman Armstrong, founder of the Hampton Institute. Armstrong arranged a six-week tour of the then-Dakota Territories for Goodale, which she financed by writing travel letters that were published by various Eastern newspapers and magazines. "It was in September of the year 1885 that I had my first glimpse of the 'Great Sioux Reservation,' a straggling concentration camp in the middle of the vast empty spaces of the Dakota Territories," she wrote (Eastman, n.d., p. 1).

Goodale became convinced that the best type of education for Indian children would be to teach them white-oriented skills and trades on the reservations, so that more children could receive the same type of education advocated at the Hampton Institute. Her writings and lectures on this topic earned her a position as the first government day school teacher at the White River Agency, in what was later to become South Dakota. It was these two frontiers—one geographical, the other philosophical—that Elaine Goodale crossed when she left behind her genteel New England upbringing in 1886 to teach on the Great Sioux Reservation. "Standing on life's threshold with a keen appreciation of the pleasures that art, literature, travel and society have to offer, she has deliberately chosen to devote her life to aid in the solution of the Indian problem," reported the *Hartford Courant* (1887). Undaunted by society's admonitions, Goodale set off for her new position, accompanied only by a driver and a "lady missionary."

Goodale wrote of herself,

One young woman came home in spirit, deeply committed to her task as she saw it. She had made up her mind to begin at the beginning in the heart of a newly transplanted, leaderless, bewildered little community. . . . Few, perhaps, would care to blaze a new trail in that obscure corner of a wild land, among recent "enemies" speaking an unintelligible dialect. Behind such considerations lurked, no doubt, a taste for adventure and a distinct bent for pioneering, possibly handed down through a long line of early American forebears. (Eastman, in Graber, 1978, p. 29)

REPORTING FROM "INDIAN COUNTRY"

Goodale's published reports in newspapers included tales of how she began to instruct her pupils with the goal of Americanization and the many difficulties she faced in so doing. For example, while government policy dictated that the language of instruction for Indians should be English, Goodale quickly realized that this method created a major educational stumbling block. She learned the Lakota language so that she could effectively utilize bilingual education, even though her "prim-lipped mentors had gravely advised me not to . . . assuring me that I would often prefer *not* to understand what was being said!" (Eastman, in Graber, 1978, p. 35).

Her many newspaper articles from this time included opinion pieces on the need for bilingual education, the effectiveness of the "industrial day school" in teaching Indian pupils vocational skills for their assimilation into the United States economy, and ardent pleas for greater funding. "Indian educators have direct, definite, practical ends in view," she wrote. "They have not only to develop latent powers, but to develop them in the direction of immediate usefulness. The Indian must learn to do something that needs doing" (Goodale, *New York Evangelist*).

Perhaps Goodale's most important articles of this period were those in which she attempted to explain Indian culture to her white audience. In many pieces published between 1886 and 1889, Goodale attempted to dispel common stereotypes of and prejudices about Indians. "The inference from expressions [such as 'relapse to barbarism' and 'back to the blanket'] is clearly that the general condition of the tribe to which these students return is one of unmitigated wildness and savagery. This is a most amusing and unfortunate error," she wrote, pointing out some "natural" and "acquired" similarities between whites and Indians (Goodale, 1886).

Goodale chose to ignore the advice of "solicitous white friends [who] urged me never to travel with Indians unarmed" and rode around the reservation on horseback to gain further insights into Sioux culture (Eastman, in Graber, 1978, p. 31). An "ardent votary" of dress reform, Goodale often opted for the simple Sioux dress and moccasins, disdaining the fashionable and impractical hoops and whalebone stays. By 1889 she knew the culture so well, and had made such a name for herself through her published work, that the commissioner of Indian Affairs in Washington appointed Goodale the supervisor of the 60-odd schools on the Great Sioux Reservation. She was the first such administrator, and the first—and only—woman to hold a position of such authority in the Bureau of Indian Affairs.

The late 1880s were a difficult time for the Sioux. The U.S. government entered into negotiations with them, attempting to take more of their land. Elaine Goodale attended meetings between federal and tribal officials. When one U.S. government official, suspicious of Goodale's bilingual skills, sternly reminded her that she was on Washington's payroll and demanded to know whether she had encouraged the Sioux to reject the land deal, Goodale replied, "I am here as a representative of the press. The Sioux, in admitting me, have indicated their confidence that I will report them fairly to the American public. I am here solely in what I believe to be the best interest of the Sioux, and the fact of holding a government post would never stand in the way of my honest opinions—if necessary, I could always resign!" (Eastman, n.d., p. 6). In fact, Eastman did not have to resign her post, but her published accounts of these meetings, representing the Sioux point of view on the land negotiations, no doubt met with some disfavor in Washington. "Although this sounds simple and fair to our progressive Eastern friends . . . how one-sided is this great dramatic struggle" (Goodale, 1888).

By 1889 the situation on the Great Sioux Reservation had deteriorated. The Sioux were almost entirely dependent on the U.S. government for inadequate rations of food, their hunting lands had been taken from them, and starvation was rampant. The U.S. government further attempted to assimilate the Sioux by preventing them from practicing their customs and religion, especially the "Ghost Dance." In these desperate conditions, the revival of the Ghost Dance— a return to old Indian ways with a new Christian fundamentalism and Christ imagery—sprang up and spread rapidly throughout the reservation as a means of salvation. Goodale chronicled the progress of the Ghost Dance. She criticized the U.S. government for instituting martial law and for attempting to repress the Ghost Dance as a means of controlling the Sioux:

The practical problem is not the Ghost Dance [but] how to improve these physical conditions surrounding the Indian without hopelessly destroying his already weakened self-respect and power of self-dependence. . . . Give the Indian some measure of independence and freedom, and see his inborn pride and self-respect return in a form compatible with a peaceful civilization! (Goodale, n.d.)

Then, late in 1890, word of the capture and death of the great chief, Sitting Bull, spread throughout the reservation. Goodale, working at the Pine Ridge Agency, noted the tense atmosphere in articles she wrote at the time and in articles she wrote in retrospect.

At this time she met Dr. Charles Alexander Eastman, a Sioux trained at boarding schools, Dartmouth College, and Boston University Medical School. The two fell in love and announced their engagement on Christmas day in 1890.

But their happiness was short lived: the news of a massacre at Wounded Knee devastated them. Goodale and Eastman worked around the clock, attending to the victims. Goodale later wrote a series of impassioned articles about the event, which brought much needed donations of linen, food, and clothing from sympathetic readers. Her articles, which were the only ones to represent the story from the Sioux point of view, were likely influential in launching the first federal investigation of the incident (Dobrow, 1981a). Years later, in her memoirs, Goodale stated, "I think the Sioux story of Wounded Knee is now generally accepted, but at the time it was strongly resented by military authorities, and every effort was made to surpress or discredit it. I was myself censured for putting it into circulation" (Eastman, in Graber, 1978, p. 164).

LIFE AFTER WOUNDED KNEE

Shaken and disheartened by the massacre at Wounded Knee and its aftermath on the Great Sioux Reservation, Charles Eastman and Elaine Goodale decided to pursue their efforts elsewhere. They married in 1891 and moved to St. Paul, Minnesota, and then to Washington, D.C., where they both advocated for Indian rights. Charles Eastman held several different positions, as a physician and as an investigator of Indian claims for the U.S. government and through the YMCA. Both Eastmans also wrote voluminously. Elaine Eastman continued to publish articles in some newspapers, but turned her attention to assisting Charles in the writing of several book-length memoirs. They co-authored two books, *Smoky Day's Wigwam Evenings: Indian Stories Retold* (1910) and *Wigwam Evenings: Sioux Folk Tales Retold* (1919). According to her memoirs, Elaine Eastman had a very heavy hand in helping Charles with his nine other books, published between 1902 and 1919. "For many a year every early drive and ambition was wholly subordinated to helping my talented husband express himself and interpret his people. Whether or not this was wise is perhaps an open question" (Eastman, in Graber, 1978, p. 163). According to Charles Eastman's biographer, Raymond Wilson, Charles "deeply resented the way Elaine would rewrite and change the meaning of his manuscripts. Although Eastman apparently harbored resentment towards his wife's revisions . . . without her editorial assistance he was never able to publish anything" (Wilson, 1983, p. 164).

Elaine Eastman also managed to publish seven books of her own: *Little Brother o' Dreams* (1910); *Yellow Star* (1911); *Indian Legends Retold* (1919); *Luck of the Oldacres* (1928); *The Voice at Eve* (1930); *Hundred Maples* (1935); and *Pratt: The Red Man's Moses* (1935). Several of these books were Indian stories she had written down and edited. *The Voice at Eve* was a semiautobiographical account, and *Pratt,* her longest work, was a biography of a nineteenth-century leader of Indian reform and education.

The Eastmans returned to her native Massachusetts in 1903 and settled in Amherst. They had six children. "From blazing a new path I returned to the old and well-worn road, trodden by women's feet throughout the ages. . . . I was inevitably housebound." She recalled these years as difficult, especially because she was "haunted by a secret sense of frustration. Every woman who has surrendered a congenial task and financial independence will understand. Saving the joys of motherhood, my pleasures must be vicarious ones" (Eastman, in Graber, 1978, p. 173). Charles Eastman spent much time lecturing in the United States and abroad, and served as a federal inspector of Indian reservations throughout the United States. In addition to educating her children at home until they were in mid-elementary school, Elaine Eastman attempted to supplement the family income by running a summer camp. However, the family was plagued by financial difficulties, and tensions mounted between Charles and Elaine. They separated in 1921, although they shrouded this fact in secrecy (Wilson, 1983, p. 164). Charles Eastman died in 1939, living far away from most of his family.

For the remainder of her life, Elaine Eastman continued to write. She never changed her views on the best ways to help Indians; even into the 1930s and 1940s, when such ideas had fallen out of favor, she remained a staunch assimilationist. She often published letters attacking current government policy toward Indians and those who promoted them. To Eastman, the idea of promoting a tribal culture, advocated by liberal government officials, was "frankly appealing, emphasizing as it does their essential human dignity and worth . . . but is it possible? Is there any going back to a child's simplicity in a grown-up world?" (Eastman, 1933). But public opinion rejected Eastman's questions and labeled her a representative of a "lapsed generation." Undeterred, Eastman continued her self-appointed role as a public correspondent of Anglo-conformity well into her eighth decade. She died in Massachusetts on December 22, 1953, at the age of 90.

Although she was widely published in the late nineteenth and early twentieth centuries, and although she defied the conventions of her times, Elaine Goodale Eastman's achievements today go largely unrecognized. However, her roles as a correspondent in newspapers; a woman who, unlike her contemporaries, chose to publish under her own name; a chronicler of significant developments in Indian educational reforms and momentous historical events; and a conveyor of the Indian voice in her articles and books, make her one of the early women of stature in American journalism.

REFERENCES

Collier, J. (1943, January). Letter to the Editor. *Atlantic Monthly.*

Dawes, H. L. (1887, 19 February). Letter to Elaine Goodale Eastman. Northampton, Mass.: Sophia Smith Collection.

Dobrow, J. R. (1981a). Elaine Goodale Eastman: A reformer among the Sioux, 1886–1891. Unpublished thesis. Northampton, Mass.: Smith College.

Dobrow, J. (1981b). Go west, young woman! *The New Current, 6*(3), 9–11, 38–39.

Dobrow, J. (1982). White sister of the Sioux. *The Masterkey, 56*(3), 103–106.

Eastman, C. A. (1916). *From the deep woods to civilization.* Boston: Norwood Press.

Eastman, E. G. (1929, November 27). Our old-new Indian policy. *The Christian Century.*

Eastman, E. G. (1930). *The voice at eve.* Chicago: The Bookfellows.

Eastman, E. G. (1933, 9 September). Under new commissioner, Indian Affairs will be humanized, and aim at self-salvation. *Boston Evening Transcript.*

Eastman, E. G. (1945). The Ghost Dance War and Wounded Knee Massacre of 1890–91. *Nebraska History.*

Eastman, E. G. (n.d.). The Ghost Dance War and Wounded Knee Massacre: One woman's story. Unpublished manuscript. Northampton, Mass.: Sophia Smith Collection.

Goodale, E. (1886, 15 April). The legislator and the Indian. *The Independent.*

Goodale, E. (1888, 20 September). With the Indian—Shall the reservation be opened? *Boston Daily Advertiser.*

Goodale, E. (n. d.). The Indian at work. *New York Evangelist.*

Goodale, E. (n. d.). The Sioux's Madonna. *The World.*

Graber K. (ed.) (1978). *Sister to the Sioux: The memoirs of Elaine Goodale Eastman.* Lincoln: University of Nebraska Press.

Hartford Courant. (1887, 21 January). Elaine Goodale, lady teacher, writer and poet, accepts a new challenge.

Priest, L. B. (1942). *Uncle Sam's stepchildren.* New Brunswick, N.J.: Rutgers University Press.

Wilson, R. (1983). *Ohiyesa: Charles Eastman, Santee Sioux.* Urbana: University of Illinois Press.

MARY ANNE FITZPATRICK
(1949-   )

Beth Haslett

Mary Anne Fitzpatrick has established herself as one of the most influential communication scholars of the last two decades. She has systematically and rigorously explored patterns of marital interaction and, more broadly, family interaction. Her work stands as an outstanding exemplar of the knowledge to be gleaned from a focused, problem-oriented, and multifaceted social science research agenda. Not only has her research contributed substantially to the communication discipline, but also her professional involvement in national organizations and substantial editorial service have advanced the discipline.

FAMILY BACKGROUND

Fitzpatrick is the oldest of ten children from a Philadelphia Irish Catholic family. She was very close to her father, who treated her as an adult, often holding serious conversations with her. Her rapid style of speech was necessary to "wrestle the conversational floor" from other family members. Storytelling was a favorite family activity, and when her extended family gathers over the holidays, storytelling is still an important shared activity. Known as "Doc" to the family, she was always encouraged to accomplish as much as she could and to try new things.

Fitzpatrick is married to Roman Kyweluk, a management information consultant, and they have a daughter, Moira. Moira's name was carefully chosen because "it needed to sound good in both Gaelic and Ukrainian." Fitzpatrick and her husband became parents relatively late in life, and Fitzpatrick was amused to overhear a conversation in which her daughter and her daughter's 20-year-old babysitter were talking about "our dads being the same age."

Achieving balance between family and work is possible with the help of a full-time nanny and a cadre of college babysitters. One-on-one day care has been important to Fitzpatrick because she thinks it is the most beneficial arrangement for children, and allows her daughter lots of older sisters. She and her husband share child-rearing responsibilities and seem quite comfortable searching for jelly-shoes and chaperoning their daughter's play dates. Her husband's European background also makes him very supportive of her career, and she does not experience the career competitiveness that other couples may confront.

EDUCATION

Fitzpatrick credits a private education in Catholic schools for her excellent academic grounding. In addition, she believes that this education fostered a competitive environment in which to achieve because girls were not "holding back because they might be considered unfeminine." Her high school debating experience also contributed to a well-rounded education.

A merit scholar, Fitzpatrick received her Bachelor's degree from Temple University in 1971, with a major in political science. Although Temple had little campus life and was surrounded by a ghetto, Fitzpatrick fondly recalls its "proletarian energy" and the interest and support of her professors. She vividly recollects the day Martin Luther King was assassinated because Temple was closed, as were the subways, and emotions ran high.

It was as a part-time, work study student that Fitzpatrick started her research career. Because she could not type, she got to do more interesting things, such as being a research assistant and working on contract survey research. Fitzpatrick also developed a love of the humanities while at Temple, and a semester abroad at the Tyler School of Art in Rome stimulated a lifelong love of art. In their leisure time and on vacations, she and her husband enjoy touring art museums and galleries.

After graduation from Temple, Fitzpatrick taught social studies at O'Hara High School in Philadelphia for a year and then started her Master's degree at Emerson, where she also served as a junior varsity debate coach. Speech had always been interesting to her, and that blended nicely with her interest in debate. In 1973 she was deciding between graduate school and law school. Financial considerations, as well as being "hooked" on communication theory and cross-cultural communication, prompted her decision to pursue a doctorate in communication. Impressed by the publication output from West Virginia University (WVU) and a persuasive phone call from Michael Burgoon, she chose WVU and enjoyed the energy and commitment of the university's graduate students.

A year later, Fitzpatrick returned to Temple University on a graduate fellowship to complete her doctoral work. Two mentors at Temple helped shape her intellectual growth. Art Bochner gave generously of his time to graduate students and honed her interests in family and marital interaction, whereas Herb Simons served as an important resource and critic.

Fitzpatrick's first position was at the University of Wisconsin at Milwaukee from 1976 to 1978. She subsequently moved to the University of Wisconsin at Madison, received tenure in 1981, and was promoted to full professor in 1985. Since 1993, she has served as chair of the department. During the fall term of 1987, she was a visiting professor at the Department of Psychiatry at George Washington University Medical School, and worked with Dr. David Reiss. During the spring of 1988, she was a visiting professor at the University of California at Santa Barbara.

CAREER DEVELOPMENT

Fitzpatrick's career encompasses multiple roles—teacher, scholar, editor, and administrator. In all areas, her contributions have been impressive. The breadth of courses she has taught is extensive. They include public speaking, business and professional communication, developmental and educational psychology, interpersonal communication, family communication, nonverbal communication, communication theory, and research methodology. In her teaching, Fitzpatrick tries to involve both undergraduates and graduate students in hands-on research because that is the best way to have them appreciate the complexity of communication and the importance of good research. She has served on over 75 dissertation and Master's degree candidate committees. In 1991 and 1992 she won teaching awards from the Panhellenic and Interfraternity Councils at Wisconsin.

As a scholar, Fitzpatrick has published one book and co-edited two others; co-edited three special issue journals; and published 28 book chapters and 36 articles. She has presented 43 invited or competitive papers at national and international conferences. Not only is the volume of her work impressive, but its quality has also been highlighted in several convention panels. In addition, she has given keynote speeeches at numerous symposiums and presented lectures at more than 20 universities both in the United States and abroad. Fitzpatrick has received funding from the National Institute of Mental Health (NIMH) and the University of Wisconsin Alumni Research Fund.

Recognition of Fitzpatrick's scholarly abilities is also reflected in the editorial positions she has held. She has been on the editorial boards of seven communication journals and three journals outside the discipline. She was associate editor for the *Journal of Personal and Social Relationships* in 1984–1985. Fitzpatrick also reviews book manuscripts for Prentice-Hall, W. C. Brown, HarperCollins, Sage, and a number of other presses.

Fitzpatrick has also been committed to the development of the discipline and to its continued growth. She is active in both major professional organizations, the Speech Communication Association (SCA) and the International Communication Association (ICA). Her participation in ICA is particularly noteworthy:

she served as president in 1991–1992 and as president-elect in 1990–1991; she chaired the Interpersonal and Small Group Communication Division from 1981 to 1983; and currently serves on the Board of Directors (1990–1997). She has also organized several major communication conferences. Fitzpatrick is concerned about the future of the discipline, and believes that the discipline needs to be redesigned to reflect the impact of technology and technological change in communication, as well as to integrate journalism and speech communication. She believes a proactive stance is necessary in order to preserve the disciplinary role of communication in higher education.

As departmental chairperson at the University of Wisconsin Madison, Fitzpatrick tries to "protect the reputation of the department internally and to have more external outreach." Her managerial style is one of delegation and group effort, and she works with a fine faculty. Some of her initiatives include working on a departmental newsletter, participating in focus groups at the undergraduate level, restructuring gift funds, and increasing money-raising efforts through the University of Wisconsin Foundation. Fitzpatrick aggressively pursues support and awards for faculty and staff of the department. She also actively represents the department on various university committees and has worked on systemwide university committees as well.

The varied roles Fitzpatrick has played allowed her to contribute in many important ways to the study of human communication and to the discipline itself. Rarely does one find this richness and range of contributions in one individual, particularly when combined with prolific research output.

MAJOR CONTRIBUTIONS AND ACHIEVEMENTS

Fitzpatrick's research explores important communication contexts within interpersonal relationships. She is most reknowned for her research on marital communication, establishing a typology of couple types and correlating these couple types with other marital indices, such as satisfaction, self-disclosure, and patterns of communication and conflict resolution. In addition, she has also published research on family communication, communication on the AIDS issue, and communication with the elderly. In all of these research contexts, she is committed to analyzing interaction on the interpersonal level of analysis.

Family researchers have developed a number of typologies for assessing different family structures or "minicultures." Fitzpatrick's research not only established such a typology, according to David Reiss, a noted family researcher, but also explored the central regulatory principles by which they are established and maintained. Interpersonal communication plays a central role in establishing and maintaining family cultures, and Fitzpatrick's work clearly demonstrates the variety of family minicultures and the communication patterns that sustain them.

Fitzpatrick developed the Relational Dimensions Instrument over a decade ago. Items in this instrument cover ideological beliefs about marriage, interdependence, and conflict. Cluster analysis revealed eight factors on the instru-

ment—two measuring ideological beliefs, four interdependence, and two
conflict. Three different couple types emerge:

The first is the traditional marriage, which supports conventional ideas about marriage
and family life, values interdependence between partners, and favors restricting open
conflicts to serious issues only. The second is the independent marriage, which supports
nonconventional ideas about marriage and family life, values autonomy as well as interdependence between partners, and favors open conflict to resolve major as well as minor
differences. The third is the separate marriage, which supports conventional ideas about
marriage and family life but shows ambivalence about these values. This marriage de-
values interdependence and avoids open conflict. (Fitzpatrick, 1988, p. 84)

Spouses filled out the instrument separately, and on comparing their answers,
couples formed one of several types. Couples were either "pure" traditionals,
"pure" independents, "pure" separates, or mixed. (Mixed couples demonstrated nonagreement on marital type, and the mixed style that is most studied
is the separate/traditional mix.) According to Fitzpatrick's research, about 60
percent of couples are categorized as a "pure" type and 40 percent constitute
a variety of mixed types. These marital types are not correlated with any demographic or intrapersonal characteristics.

Fitzpatrick also places her work in the context of larger social changes, and
suggests that in Western societies, marriage is shifting from an institutional form
(which values its societal role) to a companionate form (which values egalitarianism between spouses and emphasizes the personal, rather than societal, role
of marriage). In the context of her marital typology, this shift reflects movement
toward an independent marital style, and mixed couples reflect the negotiation
of role expectations along a continuum toward increasing egalitarianism.

As Fitzpatrick herself remarks, typologies are of little value, in and of themselves, unless they can be systematically related to other aspects of marital functioning. Once the initial typology was established and validated, her work
explored the connection between marital type and other marital functions, such
as self-disclosure, adjustment, satisfaction, conflict, and power. Her research
program stands as one of the most systematic, long-term investigations of marital
interaction.

The impressive set of findings from her longitudinal research has debunked
some mistaken folklore (like the "inexpressive male") and emphasized the variety of forms marriage may take. As Mark Knapp notes in the foreword to her
book, Fitzpatrick's research shows that " 'being married' means there is an
opportunity for people to negotiate a variety of different types of relationships
. . . and they do."

The depth and breadth of Fitzpatrick's research program is extraordinary, and
the use of multiple methods of inquiry to rule out competing explanations exemplifies how to conduct rigorous, thoughtful social science research. Several
findings help illuminate this depth and breadth of inquiry. One study, for ex-

ample, demonstrated that marital type affects wives' self-attributions of gender-related traits, but not husbands'. Although pure traditionals have the highest marital satisfaction scores among the marital types, other marital types are potentially as well adjusted as traditionals.

A significant marital and relational issue is that of control. Fitzpatrick's research on marital power and control linked the concept of marital type with relational control measures developed by others. As she notes, looking at predominant interaction patterns requires systematic sampling of actors and of their interactional behaviors across different contexts. Marital ideology also plays a role in how conflict is viewed because "the same control patterns observed in interactions will have markedly different meanings for couples in fundamental agreement with one another on a number of family issues versus those couples who fundamentally disagree" (Fitzpatrick, 1988, p. 134). Her findings reveal that traditional couples vary from complementary interactions (when discussion is casual) to symmetrical interaction during conflict. Typically, for traditionals, conflict emerges only on important issues. In contrast, separates maintain complementary patterns of interaction regardless of whether conflict is present or absent. Both independent and mixed couples use competitive symmetry in their patterns of interaction, regardless of whether or not the issue is one of disagreement. Independents are struggling to control how the marriage is defined, whereas mixed couples may disagree but do not "philosophically value such disagreement and dissension" (Fitzpatrick, 1988, p. 134). Such findings underscore the fact that married couples indeed develop different patterns of interaction which carry different meanings for each marital type. These findings also emphasize the richness of Fitzpatrick's analyses and her conceptualization of marital interaction and its consequences.

Other studies have assessed marital type and self-disclosure among spouses. Each marital type has different implicit assumptions about appropriate communication, and these assumptions influence judgments of marital satisfaction. Traditionals value self-disclosure, but the disclosure is typically positive. Traditionals also have high levels of marital satisfaction, in part, Fitzpatrick argues, because both spouses agree on relatively conventional beliefs about their marital roles. Independents also value self-disclosure, but disclose both positive and negative feelings to each other. Although this openness leads to tension and conflict, independents also value closeness to one another, and growth and change. As Fitzpatrick notes, "Open communication and the confrontation of conflict are a sign of relational vitality for these couples although they pay a price in satisfaction for the intensity of the relationship" (Fitzpatrick, 1988, p. 202). In contrast, separates do not self-disclose, generally, and their reserve may create only moderate levels of satisfaction with the marriage.

The findings on self-disclosure and marital satisfaction are particularly noteworthy because of their implications for marriage counseling and various marriage intervention programs. As Fitzpatrick cogently remarks:

The potentially oppressive result for couples seeking help is that "good communication" may require conformity to someone else's idea of what constitutes a satisfying relationship. Within prescriptive communication programs, couples are urged to confront conflicts, self-disclose, and speak in terms that are descriptive, consistent and direct. Indeed, couples regardless of their ideological orientation or levels of interdependence in marriage are urged to become Independents. . . . The Independent relationship is not the only marital type or even necessarily the most satisfying. (Fitzpatrick, 1988, p. 202)

When asked about the application of her marital research to her own marriage, Fitzpatrick jokingly replied that she and her husband's relationship defied social science findings. Rather than validating that similarity and attraction go hand in hand, she and her husband are very dissimilar, and combine the "loud American and quiet European."

In general, when reflecting upon her program of research, Fitzpatrick remains optimistic and hopeful. Two important conclusions based on this research, in her view, are that communication skills can always become better, and that marriage is an interpersonal system with each spouse helping define and maintain that system. Other aspects of her research incorporate communication among the elderly, communication about safe sex, and communication about other health issues in intimate relationships. Family interaction is also a topic of interest, and she is working on a monograph that will report data gathered on family interaction.

Most of Fitzpatrick's research has been done with collaborators. Fitzpatrick enjoys the collaboration with others, as well as the give-and-take and diversity resulting from it. Her research is also interdisciplinary and draws from scholarship in related disciplines.

EVALUATION OF RESEARCH

Any important research usually has its critics, and Fitzpatrick's work is no exception. Criticisms of her work include arguments that, at least initially, it lacked a solid theoretical base. Other criticism centers on the Relational Dimensions Instrument itself, and critics suggest that it lacks reliability. Some subscales appear to be unreliable; some researchers have experienced low test/ retest reliability, and others have found that individual types shift from type to type as a function of the overall sample (e.g., in one sample your scores might make you an independent whereas in a different sample you may be a separate).

Finally, some critics have suggested that the research itself is too complex because it is too contextualized, and have stated that the multiplicity of styles weakens the overall findings. This last criticism seems invalid simply because the general findings in family research and marital communication support increasing diversity in style as well as ideology. Certainly, this is supported by the increasing variety we find for family models, including stepparents and stepchildren, single heads of household, and adoption of children by homosexuals, to name but a few alternatives to the "hypothetical" nuclear family of mother, father, and 2.7 children.

Most scholars praise Fitzpatrick's systematic program of research. The breadth and depth of her marital interaction research program, and the use of different methods of inquiry to probe for subtle differences, add richness and insight to her research findings. The construction of the typology of marital types, and particularly its connection to other aspects of marital functioning, such as self-disclosure, marital satisfaction, and adjustment, make her research valuable and a source of new experimentation.

Fitzpatrick's typology clearly establishes the central role of communication in marital relationships. Reiss notes in the foreword to her 1988 book, *Between Husbands and Wives,* that her findings validate other family research which appears to show the existence of various family systems or minicultures, and illuminates "a whole new array of social regulatory mechanisms that sustain these minicultures." He also notes the importance of both top-down regulatory principles, such as the ideology of beliefs about marriage, and bottom-up regulatory principles, such as interdependence and autonomy, that govern daily activities. Both types of regulatory principles are examined in Fitzpatrick's work.

Finally, Fitzpatrick's consistent exploration of marital interaction over two decades, using a rich array of methodological tools, stands as an outstanding example of social science research and the knowledge that can be acquired through consistently pursuing a problem.

CONCLUSION

Fitzpatrick would most like to be remembered as a consistent problem solver. She views herself as someone who remained interested and involved in a problem, used a broad range of methods to attack that problem, and developed a consistent set of findings that advanced knowledge about it. Her research program clearly demonstrates the excellence with which she succeeded in doing this.

In addition, Fitzgerald views herself as having established a climate in which to help young scholars flourish. The many contributions her graduate students have made to the research literature, and her own collaboration with colleagues, constitute ample evidence that she facilitates the scholarly and personal growth of those with whom she works.

Finally, the sheer volume and quality of her work, achieved roughly at mid-career, is most impressive. Add to this her chairship of the Department of Communication Arts, her involvement in national organizations, her editorial contributions, and her commitment to family life, and it becomes apparent that she is an extraordinarily talented individual who excels in a wide array of activities.

REFERENCES

Books

Fitzpatrick, M. A. (1988). *Between husbands and wives: Communication in marriage.* Newbury Park, Calif.: Sage.
Noller, P., & Fitzpatrick, M.A. (eds.). (1988). *Perspectives on marital interaction.* Clevdon, England: Multilingual Matters.
Edgar, T., Fitzpatrick, M.A., & Freinmuth, V. (eds.). (1992). *AIDS: A communication perspective.* Hillsdale, N.J: Erlbaum.

Book Chapters

Dindia, K., & Fitzpatrick, M.A. (1984). Marital communication: Three approaches compared. In S. Duck and D. Perlman, *Understanding personal relationships: An interdisciplinary approach.* (pp. 137–157). Beverly Hills, Calif.: Sage Publications.
Fitzpatrick, M.A. (1983). Effective interpersonal communication for women of the corporation: Think like a man, talk like a lady. In J. Pilotta (ed.), *Women in organizations: Barriers and breakthroughs.* (pp. 73–84). Prospect Heights, Ill.: Haveland Press.
Fitzpatrick, M.A. (1984). Marital interaction: Recent theory and research. In L. Berkowitz (ed.), *Advances in experimental social psychology.* (pp. 1–47). New York: Academic Press.
Fitzpatrick, M.A. (1986). Self disclosure in marriage. In V. Derlega and J. Berg (eds.), *Self disclosure.* New York: Plenum.
Fitzpatrick, M.A. (1990). A microsocietal approach to marital communication. In B. Dervin (ed.), *Progress in communication science, vol. 10.* (pp. 67–101). Norwood, N.J.: Ablex.
Fitzpatrick, M.A., & Ritchie, D. (1993). Communication theory. In P. Boss, W. Doherty, R. LaRossa, W. Schumm, & S. Steinmetz (eds.), *Sourcebook of family theories and methods: A contextual approach.* (pp. 565–585). New York: Plenum.

Articles

Fitzpatrick, M.A. (1981). Children as audience to the parental relationship. *Journal of Comparative Family Studies, 11,* 81–94.
Fitzpatrick, M.A. (1991). Understanding personal relationships through media portrayals. *Communication Education, 40,* 213–218.
Fitzpatrick, M.A., & Indvik, J. (1982). The instrumental and expressive domains of marital communication. *Human Communication Research, 8,* 195–213.
Williamson, R., & Fitzpatrick, M.A. (1985). Two approaches to marital interaction: Relational control patterns in marital types. *Communication Monographs, 52,* 236–252.
Witteman, H., & Fitzpatrick, M. (1986). A social scientific evaluation of marital enrichment programs. *Journal of Social and Clinical Psychology, 4,* 513–522.

PAULINE FREDERICK
(1908–1990)

Louise Benjamin

During her illustrious broadcast career which spanned four decades, Pauline Frederick was a pioneer, achieving eminence when her field was virtually closed to women. At a time when the United Nations was constantly in the headlines, she was the primary correspondent covering that body for the National Broadcasting Company and was creating her own place in the white male domain of broadcast news. The first broadcast newswoman to receive the coveted Peabody Award for excellence in broadcasting, Frederick fought discrimination and became a role model for untold numbers of women.

FAMILY BACKGROUND AND EDUCATION

The middle of three children of Matthew Frederick and Susan Stanley, Frederick was born on February 13, 1908 in Gallitzin, Pennsylvania. Her father was the town's postmaster and later became a state labor mediator, who encouraged his daughter's interest in foreign affairs.

In part, Pauline's goals were set by her self-confessed feelings of inadequacy. At age 17, she underwent a hysterectomy after two grapefruit-size cysts were discovered on her ovaries. After the surgery, she believed that no man would marry her because she could not have children. She later revealed that she felt like a "freak," and added that "It wasn't until ten years later that I realized that I was just like any other woman, except I couldn't have children."

Her interest in news coverage began early, and as a teenager, she covered society news for the *Harrisburg Telegraph*. Upon graduation, the paper offered her the social editor's position, but she declined in favor of studying political science at American University in Washington, D.C.

Though interested in journalism and political reporting, Frederick received her Master's degree in international law because political reporting was closed to women in the 1930s. At the suggestion of one history professor, Frederick soon combined her interests in journalism and international affairs by interviewing diplomats' wives. Upon graduating in 1931, she sold her first story to the *Washington Times*. She then began a weekly syndicated feature on diplomats' wives offered through the North American Newspaper Alliance. Her break into broadcasting came when NBC's director of women's programs, Margaret Cuthbert, asked her to interview the wife of the Czechoslovakian minister shortly after Germany overran that country in 1939.

CAREER DEVELOPMENT

After this broadcast, Frederick continued her interviews until the beginning of World War II. She also became an assistant to H. R. Baukhauge, an NBC commentator, where she wrote scripts and did research. In 1945 she toured North Africa and Asia with other journalists over his protests that women should not participate in this trip. After two months during which she broadcast from Chungking, China, Frederick quit her job to cover the Nuremberg war crime trials in postwar Germany for ABC radio, the North American Newspaper Alliance, and the Western Newspaper Alliance. She broadcast only once, when Hermann Goering testified, because the male reporter covering testimony was absent.

Although her superiors recognized her superior reporting and writing skills, she could not get a permanent network job because of her gender. ABC radio hired her as a stringer while she looked for a permanent network job. When she applied for a job at CBS, radio legend Edward R. Murrow rejected her application, saying he could not list her name at the top of the women applicants. He added that, while she read well with a pleasing voice, "I would not call her material or manner particularly distinguished."

As an ABC stringer, she was assigned women's stories, such as "How to Get a Husband" and a market rush on nylon hosiery, and she was not allowed on air unless she had exclusives. Her superiors felt that the public would not accept Frederick or any other woman reporter on stories other than those considered "woman's interest," because, as she was told, "a woman's voice just doesn't carry authority."

Frederick break reporting on the United Nations came when she was assigned to a foreign ministers' conference story in an emergency. ABC had two major stories and only one male reporter. He was assigned a truckers' strike, because of the possibility of violence, while Frederick reported the conference. She began covering the U.N., but was still permitted on air only if she had an exclusive. After a few months, she was assigned the U.N. as a regular beat and became an ABC staffer in 1948, specializing in international affairs and politics.

That year, her news director told her she was to cover the first televised Democratic convention, primarily because few ABC staffers volunteered for that assignment. Worried about how she would look on the new medium, she went to Elizabeth Arden to find out how she should make herself up for television. Soon she was doing makeup for all the women appearing at the convention, including Margaret Truman.

After the convention, she continued her hectic schedule, doing six daily radio broadcasts and three weekly television programs, including one non-news show titled "Pauline Frederick's Guest Books." Because she found less gender discrimination in radio and because she believed radio gave more time for analysis, she preferred that medium. In 1981, she noted, "When a man speaks on television, people listen. But when a woman speaks, people look, and if they like her looks, then they listen."

In 1953, because of her growing renown in covering the international political scene, NBC lured her away from ABC to cover the U.N. In 1956 she covered the political conventions, her first and last. Apparently, a few network executives believed she did not ad lib well.

Frederick continued working for NBC until her mandatory retirement at age 65 in 1974. During those two decades she covered many international crises, including the Korean War, Mideast conflicts, the Cuban missile crisis, the Cold War, and the Vietnam War. After "retiring," she began working for National Public Radio. For five years, she was a commentator on international affairs. On October 6, 1976, she realized another "first woman achievement" when she moderated one of the presidential candidate debates between Jimmy Carter and Gerald Ford.

Frederick remained single until she was 61. On March 31, 1969, she married Charles Robbins, former managing editor of the *Wall Street Journal*. She died of a heart attack on May 9, 1990, while visiting relatives in Illinois. Her husband had preceded her in death in August 1989.

INTEGRATION OF PERSONAL AND PROFESSIONAL LIFE

Pauline Frederick believed she would not have achieved excellence in broadcast journalism if she had married young. Of her life, she noted,

My situation is quite different from other women who have children or who have come into their career in an earlier stage in their marriage. I think the kind of career I've had, something would have had to be sacrificed. Because when I have been busy at the United Nations during crises, it has meant working day and night. You can't very well take care of a home when you do something like that, or children.

In many ways, her statement reflects the overall lack of support for women who wanted to integrate family and work during the middle of the twentieth century.

MAJOR CONTRIBUTIONS AND ACHIEVEMENTS

Frederick was the first woman elected president of the United Nations Correspondents Association. Her many honors include the George Foster Peabody Award in 1954 for her coverage of the United Nations and the Paul White Award from the Radio-Television News Directors Association in 1980. In 1975 she was named to the Sigma Delta Chi Hall of Fame. She was also the first woman to receive the Alfred I. duPont Awards' Commentator Award. She also received 23 honorary doctorate degrees in journalism, law, and the humanities.

EVALUATION OF CONTRIBUTIONS AND ACHIEVEMENTS

Pauline Frederick opened the door for many women and became an important role model for newswomen everywhere. Through her work she especially advanced the position of women in broadcast news. Her numerous accomplishments speak for themselves.

REFERENCES

Frederick, P. (1967). *Ten first ladies of the world.* New York: Meredith Press.
Foremost women in communications. (1970). New York: Foremost Americans Publications Corporation.
Gelfman, Judith, (1976). *Women in television news.* New York: Columbia University Press.
Hosley David, & Yamada, Gayle, (1987). *Hard news: Women in broadcast journalism.* Westport, Conn.: Greenwood Press.
Nobile, Philip. (1981, August 10). "TV news and the older woman." *New York.*
"Pauline Frederick." Peabody Awards Collection, University of Georgia Main Library.
Talese, Gay. (1963, January 26). "Perils of Pauline." *Saturday Evening Post.*

ELLEN GOODMAN
(1941–   )

Julia R. Dobrow

A columnist whose articles are syndicated in nearly 500 American newspapers, a journalist who has received many notable prizes and awards, including a Pulitzer Prize, an associate editor of the *Boston Globe,* Ellen Goodman is perhaps one of the most prominent living American journalists. Goodman is recognized by her enormous following of readers for her penetrating, pungent, often humorous, and always lucid observations on contemporary American life. Writing about a wide range of topics, including political and economic issues, profiles of the famous and not-so-famous, reflections on living and dying in the high-tech age, columns revolving around her own life and relationships, social commentaries and beyond, Goodman is arguably best known for her writings on women's issues. Her work has addressed both issues that affect women in public realms—she has written columns on women from Anita Hill to Margaret Sanger, Hillary Rodham Clinton to Madonna—as well as issues that many women (and men) deal with in more private forums—abortion, the work/family dilemma, day care, divorce. Much of Goodman's work connects personal issues to larger public debates. In a review of one of her published collections of essays and columns, *Time* magazine wrote that "Ellen Goodman has firmly established herself as a cool stream of sanity flowing through a minefield of public and private quandaries" (*Time* magazine review, cited in Solberg, 1993).

FAMILY BACKGROUND AND EDUCATION

Ellen Goodman was born on April 11, 1941, in Newton, Massachusetts. The daughter of a prominent attorney, Jackson Jacob Holtz, and Edith Weinstein Holtz, Goodman and her sister, Jane, were raised in an atmosphere that she described as "stimulating and highly politically charged." Her father made unsuccessful runs for the state legislature and Congress when she was young, and according to Goodman, "he was always insistent that we talk about real issues at the dinner table. You had to be able to defend yourself well. My sister and I both had to sharpen our debating skills early on" (November 14, 1994, personal interview with Goodman). Goodman's mother was a "very big influence on us in terms of making us feel competent and good about ourselves as individuals, and as girls" (November 14, 1994, personal interview).

Goodman's early education was at the Buckingham School outside of Boston. In this environment, she recalls, "we had teachers who took us seriously as girls ... there weren't many role models for ambitious young girls in those days" (November 14, 1994, personal interview). She went on to graduate from Brookline High School and then matriculated at Radcliffe College, where she majored in history.

Goodman's undergraduate years were a time during which some of her ideas about the dilemmas faced by women began to percolate. "Much of college was a struggle," she reflected.

We were confident intellectually, but we didn't think of ourselves as professionals. We didn't know what to think. We knew that other women may have to go home and worry about waxy yellow buildup, but Radcliffe women were supposed to write the great American novel while the kids were napping. It was the beginning of the superwoman myth perpetuated in our culture—we were supposed to do it all, somehow, though now we know that you can't. (November 14, 1994, personal interview)

The time during which Goodman was in college was also the beginning of turbulent political events. The early echoes of the civil rights movement and the women's movement were heard on campus, and resonated with Goodman.

She graduated cum laude in 1963, married right out of college, and moved to New York, where her first husband, Anthony Goodman, was in medical school. Goodman recalled that "It was expected that I'd do well in school, go to college, get married. But the idea of having a career was simply not on the charts" (November 14, 1994, personal interview).

CAREER AND FAMILY

Once she was living in New York, Goodman, who had never worked for a high school or college newspaper, applied for a job as a researcher at *Newsweek* magazine, largely because her sister, Jane Holtz Kay, was in journalism, "and because the job sounded good." Goodman arrived at *Newsweek* two months before John F. Kennedy was assassinated, a time she described as "incredibly volatile." She initially worked as a trainee in the television department, assisting Peter Benchley, whom she had known in college, as a researcher. But Goodman was not content to check facts and get coffee for others. She soon began freelancing for the Quincy (Massachusetts) *Patriot Ledger,* the paper where her sister worked, the *Manhattan Weekly,* and other small papers, principally writing arts stories and features. ''I knew that if I wanted to go anywhere in journalism, I had to build up a file of clips'' she said (November 14, 1994, personal interview). Soon Goodman was writing stories for *Newsweek* as well.

After two years at *Newsweek,* Goodman was hired as one of only two women on the news desk at the *Detroit Free Press,* where she worked between 1965 and 1967. Her husband was then a resident at a hospital in Ann Arbor. Goodman wrote mainly news features and general news assignments for the *Free Press.* She said that ''I had never taken a journalism course in my life, and before the *Detroit Free Press,* I'd mostly written features—I'd never really written on deadline before. But I learned how to do it, because I had to'' (November 14, 1994, personal interview).

In mid-1967, Goodman and her husband moved back to Boston. Goodman was hired at the *Boston Globe.* She wrote feature stories and news features. Goodman's work on the *Globe* earned her quick recognition: she was named New England Women's Press Association Woman of the Year in 1968.

In 1971 Goodman approached *Globe* editor Thomas Winship about writing a column. He quickly agreed. Her first columns appeared in the *Globe*'s Living section and were later moved to the paper's Op-Ed pages. Soon she was a full-time columnist, whose work garnered her many awards. Goodman received the Catherine O'Brien Award in 1971; the Commission on the Status of Women Media Award in 1973; the Columnist of the Year Award of the New England Press Association in 1974; the UPI New England Newspapers Award for Columns in 1976; the Mass Media Award of the American Association of University Women in 1977; the American Society of Newspaper Editors Distinguished Writing Award for column writing and the Headliners Best Local Column Award in 1980; and the Hubert Humphrey Civil Rights Award in 1988. She won a Nieman Fellowship at Harvard University in 1973. She has been awarded honorary degrees from Mount Holyoke College, Amherst College, the University of New Hampshire, and the University of Pennsylvania. She was named a trustee of Radcliffe College. And in 1980, she was awarded a Pulitzer Prize for commentary.

Of all her many accolades, Goodman said that the Pulitzer Prize meant the most to her.

I got the Pulitzer for writing about things that other peoj le never wrote about: women, kids, social change, relationships. To be awarded this distinguished prize for my work in these areas meant a lot, personally and professionally. It was an affirmation that the kind of work I do matters to a lot of people, and a recognition in a larger sense that these kind of things are important in our society. (November 14, 1994, personal interview)

Goodman had been affiliated with a group called One Woman's Voice, which marketed articles by and about women to various American newspapers and magazines. But Goodman wanted to do more with her work and achieve a wider readership. She began syndicating her column with the *Washington Post* Writers Group in early 1976. Goodman recalled that "at the time, this group was very small—they only carried the work of a few writers and marketed it to a few papers. It's grown tremendously over the years" (November 14, 1994, personal interview). Goodman's work was offered for both editorial and living pages. According to the *Washington Post* Writers Group, the majority of papers that carry Goodman's "At Large" column have chosen to run it on their editorial pages. In many cases. Goodman was the first woman columnist to appear on the Op-Ed page (*Washington Post* Writers Group, 1994).

Goodman branched out from her columns, and also worked as a radio commentator on Spectrum CBS from 1978 to 1980, on the NBC Radio Network from 1979 to 1980, and was a commentator on the "Today Show" on television between 1979 and 1981. Her published work also appeared in a variety of magazines, including *Life, McCall's, Redbook,* and *Ms.* In 1986 she was named an associate editor at the *Boston Globe.*

INTEGRATION OF PERSONAL LIFE AND CAREER

In the preface to her book, *Turning Points* (1979), Goodman wrote that "When I was a kid, I wanted everything to stay the same. I wanted to live in the same house, go to the same school, keep the same friends . . . forever. When I was ten, I used to tell my mother that I would grow up, get married, have children, but never leave home. The truth was that I didn't have to cope with very much change in my youth. I went from high school to college to marriage to motherhood as if it were all in a contract I'd signed . . . yet in my thirties, my life and the lives of people around me have been in continual process of change" (Goodman, 1979b, p. ix).

Goodman's daughter, Katie, was born in 1968. A couple of years later, Goodman's first marriage ended. Goodman wrote that this "was a time of heightened vulnerability, a time when I was most aware of the weaknesses of my plans and most sensitive about how disruptive change can be" (Goodman, 1979b, p. x).

Goodman reflected that "I was a single mother from the time Katie was 3. The option of whether to stay home or to work was simply out the window. I had to work, and I made the balancing act of working and being a mother a priority" (November 14, 1994, personal interview). Goodman noted that living near her family, having good friends and good child care made this transition somewhat easier. In addition, Goodman stated that "one of the things about being a journalist is getting up and doing it again. Working day by day. Having to do this helped to give my life a sense of stability" (November 14, 1994, personal interview).

The year that Goodman spent as a Nieman fellow (1973–1974) was pivotal for her. In addition to transitions in her personal life, the world around her was changing rapidly. She has written of this time:

On assignment I had met the civil rights movement, the peace movement, and the women's movement . . . and seen the various ways [that people] dealt with the changes these movements brought. . . . I became an observer to, and then a participant in, change, almost against my will . . . I was ready to drop out of my seat at the eye of the hurricane, to see if I could make some sense out of what seemed like chaos. (Goodman, 1979b, p. x)

Goodman spent her year as a Nieman fellow taking courses in law, government, and sociology, reading widely, and studying the dynamics of social change. She said that in this year "I had the luxury of time to think and read." She participated in courses and seminars and made several close friends. "It was," she said, "a time of great reflection and introspection, both personally and professionally. It was a year that was a validation of my work—the stuff I was doing wasn't marginalized" (November 14, 1994, personal interview).

Between 1975 and 1978 Goodman interviewed over 150 women and men, focusing on the changes in their lives that had coincided with the "new perspectives" on sex roles in America. The results of her interviews appeared in many of her published columns and ultimately resulted in the publication of her first book, *Turning Points* (1979).

Since 1979, Goodman has published five other books, all collections of her columns and essays: *Close to Home* (1979); *At Large* (1981); *Keeping in Touch* (1985); *Making Sense* (1989); and *Value Judgments* (1993).

In 1982 Goodman married Robert Levey, a former restaurant critic for the *Globe* and a consultant. She continues to blend family with career by writing often about her changing relationships with her friends and family. "I've gone from being a working mother to being a working daughter," she said. "Now I am helping to take care of my mother. As a woman, you are never without caretaking. The idea that you'll resolve this is a fallacy. And you're always refining and negotiating the balance between your family responsibilities and your career" (November 14, 1994, personal interview).

CAREER ASSESSMENT

In her collection of columns, *At Large* (1981), Goodman wrote that she had been both a beneficiary and a catalyst in effecting change in the world of journalism. The changes, she suggested, had to do with placing the editorial spotlight on issues that affect people in their personal lives, which had not been done before, and with advocating for women's issues. Goodman elaborated on this statement:

It's [been] a double helix of effects. The thing that has most excited my intellect has been issues of social change—that's put a grid over my life, made me really think about what this society is like, or should be like. At the same time, it's validated and helped to explain the things that I was experiencing, personally, or that my friends were. By putting this grid over life, and reflecting on social change as it's happened, I think I've helped to question things, bring them into the light. In this way I've been a beneficiary of the women's movement, and I hope, someone who has helped it. (November 14, 1994, personal interview)

In describing Ellen Goodman's impact, the *Washington Post* Writers Group stated that

What makes Ellen Goodman's column exceptional is that her subjects aren't standard fare. She writes about more than just recent legislation, new taxes, elected officials. Her work touches readers' lives and hearts, as she examines values, relationships, middle age, abortion, condoms, families. Ellen Goodman cracked the domain of male political punditry on editorial and op-ed pages across the country not only with talent, but by expanding the topics considered worthy of editorial comment. (*Washington Post* Writers Group, 1994)

Novelist and journalist Caryl Rivers described Goodman as "perhaps the most prominent American female journalist, and certainly one of the most prominent American journalists, period. [Goodman] has taken on the most controversial issues and has largely succeeded in making sense out of the complications of our life and times" (October 19, 1994, personal interview).

Of her own work, Goodman has written,

It is my job and my predilection to try and put the scattered items from the daily newspaper scrapbook into context. This is one of the challenges of newspaper column writing—to write with some perspective from the middle, always the middle, of a story. I try to chronicle the ambivalence I hear, the mixed feelings and values . . . Most of my columns begin with a question: Why? What's going on here? I write to figure that out for myself and others. (*Washington Post* Writers Group, 1994)

Reflecting on her life and work, Goodman concluded that "One of the most interesting ways to lead life is as a journalist: it's an examined life. If you place a high value on being interested in life, this is a great job. I love what I do. I think—and hope—I've made an impact doing it. I can't imagine a more interesting way to lead life" (November 14, 1994, personal interview).

REFERENCES

Boston Globe. (1980, April 15). The Globe's Pulitzer Prize winners.
Goodman, E. (1979a). *Close to home.* New York: Simon & Schuster.
Goodman, E. (1979b). *Turning points.* New York: Doubleday.
Goodman, E. (1981). *At large.* New York: Simon & Schuster.
Goodman, E. (1985). *Keeping in touch.* New York: Simon & Schuster.
Goodman, E. (1989). *Making sense.* New York: Atlantic Monthly Press.
Goodman, E. (1993). *Value judgments.* New York: Farrar Straus & Giroux.
Goodman, E. (1994, November 14). Personal interview.

ELLEN GOODMAN

161

Los Angeles Times. (1993, November 14). Review of *Value judgments.*
McCarthy, R. (1989, September 23). Columnist sees 90's as a decade of we-ness. *Atlanta Journal Constitution,* 5(4).
New York Times. (1980, April 15). Pulitzer Prize Winners, 1980.
Rivers, C. (1994, October 19). Personal interview.
Solberg, J. (1993). Book review of *Value judgments. Library Journal,* 118(16), 104.
Washington Post Writers Group. (1994). Ellen Goodman biography. Washington, D.C.
Who's Who of American Women. 18th ed. (1993–1994). New York: Marquis.

DORIS APPEL GRABER
(1923–   )

Douglas M. McLeod

Doris Appel Graber is a luminary in both communication and political science. Undoubtedly one of the foremost figures in the area of political communication research, she has addressed fundamental questions about the role of the media in political processes. Ultimately, her work has helped to establish an agenda for political communication research. As a result, she has frequently been called upon to assess the status of current knowledge in political communication. When *Political Communication*, a journal co-sponsored by the American Political Science Association and the International Communication Association, was inaugurated in 1992, Graber was a natural choice to be the first editor, a position she currently holds. She has also been elected president of the Midwest Political Science Association and the Midwest Association for Public Opinion Research (MAPOR). She was recognized as a MAPOR fellow in 1988 and received awards from the American Political Science Association, including the Mentor Award in 1991 and the Edelman Career Award in 1992. Doris Graber's voluminous accomplishments place her among the giants in both communication and political science.

FAMILY BACKGROUND

Graber's family played an important role in shaping her formative years. When Graber was young, her family nurtured her intellectual development by providing a loving and supportive environment. The family stressed both intellectual and physical activities and emphasized a family tradition of scientific, arts, and public service contributions. Graber says that "Our home was full of books and paintings, even when the icebox was near-empty."

Since then, her family has provided a source of support and enjoyment. Graber married her husband Tom during graduate school. They have four sons and one daughter. All of her children—Lee, Tom, Jack, Jim, and Susan—received advanced degrees in health professions or social sciences.

EDUCATION

Graber received a Ph.D. in international law and relations from Columbia University. Both her M.A. and B.A. degrees were in political science from Washington University in St. Louis.

Graber says that even as far back as grade school, she was fascinated by learning new things. When the pace of grade school lagged, she would "sneak crossword puzzles onto my desk and work on them secretly and earn reprimands from several teachers and from my mother who thought that good-conduct marks were the most important achievement for girls." Graber describes herself as a tomboy who often played with the boys in athletic activities. The grade school friendships that she developed with both boys and girls contributed to a happy childhood and helped her to develop self-confidence.

As a high school freshman, Graber felt that her schoolwork was not challenging enough, so she took and passed the high school admission test to Washington University in St. Louis. Not only was she one of the youngest students on campus, but also she finished her coursework in less than four years and graduated second in her class. She majored in political science with a minor in economics, although she took courses in a wide variety of subjects. To this day, she continues to be interested in all areas of scientific inquiry, especially the life sciences. She graduated with honors and a Phi Beta Kappa key. In the midst of all this success, she actually failed one course—tap dancing.

While in college, Graber participated in a variety of extracurricular activities including water and winter sports, photography, and social clubs. She financed her undergraduate studies by reporting for local newspapers, dabbling in portrait photography, and babysitting. Ultimately, her career goal was to combine her studies of political science and international law and relations with her professional experience as a newspaper reporter so that she could become a foreign correspondent.

Graber says that she owes a great debt to her major adviser, Professor Arnold J. Lien:

He taught me that politics was life written large—much more than the sterile study of institutions and written rules. He also taught me the importance of thorough, detailed knowledge of the legal aspects of the field. Above all, his intolerance of anything that was even remotely slip-shod taught me that scholarship means striving for perfection as much as possible and insisting on absolute integrity. Dr. Lien's picture hangs in my office to this day. His message is needed more than ever.

The Ph.D. dissertation stage of Graber's career provided the toughest test of her academic resolve. Originally, her doctoral adviser at Columbia University was Professor Charles Cheney Hyde, a leading authority on international law. Under his direction, Graber prepared a dissertation on the legal aspects of war crimes trials. Sadly, Professor Hyde died before the completed dissertation was defended. A political scientist with no expertise in international law was assigned to advise Graber. He argued that her dissertation was a work of ''legal fiction,'' and voted not to accept it on the dubious grounds that war trials were political events devoid of substantial legal issues. Because the University required a unanimous committee, Graber had to return to the drawing board to draft a new dissertation. Ultimately, the second dissertation was published as a book, *The Development of the Law of Belligerent Occupation* (1968). After the end of World War II, military officers serving occupation duty used this book as a legal ''bible.'' Graber's doctoral experience serves as an inspirational lesson on the value of perseverance.

CAREER DEVELOPMENT

Graber describes her career as a ''multi-colored braid.'' She says that ''different strands came into prominence depending on the opportunities of the moment, on the need to balance marriage demands and children's upbringing with career demands, and on my eagerness to meet new and different challenges.'' In addition to her family roles as wife, mother, and homemaker, Graber says she has five other career strands—the journalist, the researcher, the teacher, the editor, and the officer for professional associations.

Graber's career as a journalist began as a feature writer at the *St. Louis County Observer* while she was an undergraduate. She covered issues related to the St. Louis County juvenile court system, local media ethics, and occupational hazards in the construction industry. She also worked for a weekly newspaper, the *University City Tribune*. Early in her career, she learned at first hand about the kinds of problems that journalists can cause when they make mistakes; one time she printed the incorrect dates for garbage collection causing a ''mini-disaster.''

Graber's journalistic career continued after she finished her Ph.D. coursework. She worked for the Commerce Clearing House of Chicago in charge of two publications, the *U.S. Supreme Court Digest* and the *Legal Periodical Digest*. As part of her responsibilities, she wrote summaries of U.S. Supreme Court decisions and cases from North American law reviews.

As a researcher, Graber has written 11 books, edited 2 others, and published 25 book chapters and 35 journal articles. Since 1970, she has presented 93 conference papers and has made 89 colloquium presentations on five different continents. In the process, she has played a major role in surveying the past and charting the future of political communication research. Graber has written five reviews of the current state of research in political communication. Her book, *Mass Media and American Politics* (about to come out in its fifth edition), provides an important compendium of current knowledge.

Graber also served as a research associate at the Center for the Study of

American Foreign and Military Policy at the University of Chicago. It was here that she did the work for *Public Opinion, the President and Foreign Policy* (1968).

Graber has taught at Northwestern University, the University of Chicago, North Park College, and the University of Illinois at Chicago, where she has been a full professor of political science since 1970. She once taught international politics at a Texas military base.

Her political science courses have focused on international law and relations, U.S. foreign policy, the politics of national development, Latin American politics, American government, regulatory policy, the relationship between government and religious institutions, and globalism and nationalism. She has also taught political communication courses on mass media and politics, public opinion, propaganda, and communication in public sector organizations.

Graber has had extensive experience as an editor, beginning with the *U.S. Supreme Court Digest* and *Legal Periodical Digest*. She has edited two books: *Media Power in Politics* (1994) and *The President and the Public* (1982).

For eight years, she served as Harper and Row's social science college textbook editor. This job gave her the opportunity to read in a variety of fields such as anthropology, social psychology, sociology, economics, history, and political science. Through this reading and her interactions with the authors, Graber came to fully appreciate the interrelations of the social sciences and the more complete understanding provided by an awareness of the unique contributions of different disciplinary approaches to similar phenomena. For instance, knowledge of presidential politics is enhanced by examination of the political culture, the social psychological reactions of the public, the "driving force" of economics, the historical context, candidates' rhetorical strategies, and so on.

Most recently, Graber has edited *Political Communication*. As this journal's first editor, she has played an important role in establishing its editorial policy, which stresses not only mainstream political communication research, but also interdisciplinary, nontraditional, and policy-oriented research.

Graber's involvement in professional service was initially motivated by the need to redress the absence of women in the leadership positions of professional organizations. As female leadership became more common, Graber began to devote more attention to research, her primary professional interest. In the past, she served as president of academic organizations, including the Midwest Association for Public Opinion Research, the Midwest Political Science Association, and the Illinois chapter of Phi Beta Kappa. She will also serve as the president of the International Society for Political Psychology. She is a past vice president of the American Political Science Association and has been the head of both the Political Communication section of the American Political Science Association and the Political Communication division of the International Communication Association. She has been on the editorial board of eight social science journals and served as an officer or committee member for numerous other professional organizations and associations.

Throughout her career, Graber has confronted and overcome several obstacles stemming from stereotyping. She is firmly committed to combatting discrimination on the basis of gender, race, ethnicity, religion, class, and the like. Her fight against stereotyping began early. As she later learned, her father expressed disappointment when she was born because, as a girl, she would not be able to carry on the family name or to have a successful career.

It wasn't long before Graber discovered a pattern of gender discrimination. The most glaring episode occurred when she graduated from college. In order to encourage her graduate studies, she was presented with a fellowship for "promising young scholars." However, this fellowship was rescinded because her marital engagement was seen as disqualifying her as a promising scholar. If outraged faculty members had not been able to arrange alternative sources of funding, she would not have been able to attend graduate school.

Graber also faced gender discrimination when she was writing legal digests for the Commerce Clearing House of Chicago. Her employers were concerned that their clients, who were mostly male lawyers, would be skeptical of summaries written by women. As a result, inquiries from clients were always handled by a male employee.

When Graber approached one publisher about turning her dissertation into a book, he "laughed in my face" at the prospect of a "cute, young girl" writing about such serious matters. The book was eventually published by Columbia University Press and later by a commercial publisher.

Graber has also had to deal with age discrimination. Because she was so young when she graduated from college, potential employers did not take her seriously. Ultimately, Graber was only able to secure employment after removing references to her gender and age from her résumé. In retrospect, Graber's career provides a model for how to address stereotyping head on.

MAJOR CONTRIBUTIONS AND ACHIEVEMENTS

In surveying Graber's research, we are immediately struck by the volume and breadth of her contributions. Her work has been eclectic and interdisciplinary in its approach to theory construction. Graber has addressed many of the major questions in the field of political communication. In order to provide more complete answers to these questions, she often employs multiple methodological procedures including panel surveys, in-depth interviews, content analyses, computer-based textual analyses, and experiments.

Graber describes her current research in political communication as including

Multi-faceted investigation of the audio-visual content of television newscasts and their impact on audiences. Experimental research on mass media information processing. Continuing research on the effects of mass media information on political learning, public opinion, election politics, political institutions and public policy. Analyses of organizational communication in the public sector, especially in administrative agencies.

Mass Media and American Politics (1993) is one of Graber's most influential books and provides a sense of the variety of questions that Graber tackles. This book, a comprehensive analysis of research on the media's role in American politics, serves the dual function of introducing political scientists to media studies and bringing a political science focus to communication scholars. It begins with a discussion of media–government relations, including regulatory, First Amendment, and other policy issues. She then takes a closer look at media organizations by examining the newsmaking and gatekeeping processes. Other chapters look at how the media cover crises, the court system, local politics, and foreign policy. One of the most impressive features of this book is that it tackles important issues from micro-level questions about the impact of mass media on audience attitudes, knowledge, and behaviors to macro-level questions about the impact of modern media on the course of electoral politics. Ultimately, this book is a roadmap to political communication research and should be considered compulsory reading for scholars interested in media and politics.

In *Media Power in Politics* (1994), Graber has compiled and edited a collection of articles designed as a companion to *Mass Media and American Politics* (1993). In its third edition, this book presents a diverse set of readings in political communication representing a variety of theoretical perspectives.

Although Graber has dealt with both micro and macro issues of political communication, she is most well known for her micro-level research on information processing. In 1984 she published *Processing the News: How People Tame the Information Tide,* which has been subsequently updated with new editions in 1988 and 1994. This book reports on landmark research on how members of the public choose, interpret, and retain information from the news media. Graber utilized both content analysis and in-depth interviews with panel respondents to investigate the process by which people extract information from the news in order to maintain a minimum level of democratic participation. Graber draws heavily on schema theory to explain information processing. She argues that individuals evaluate new information according to their preexisting belief structures (cognitive schema). People attend to and retain information according to their individual worldviews, personal preferences, gratifications sought, and perceived utility of that information.

Graber argues that schema are relatively stable and somewhat insulated from mass media influence. However, she does note that the influence of the media is greater for individuals with less developed schema, those without direct personal experience, and those with limited access to information.

Graber takes an optimistic stance toward individuals' ability to "tame the information tide." Through the application of schema-based processing, people weed out and ignore all but a small portion of the news that they are exposed to through various forms of mass media. Yet, they still seem to find the information they need to perform as responsible democratic citizens. Despite Graber's optimism at the individual level, she clearly acknowledges macro-level issues about information equity and the problems posed by knowledge gaps between rich and poor that reduce social mobility.

In conjunction with David Weaver, Maxwell McCombs, and Chaim Eyal, Graber contributed to one of the most systematic investigations of the agenda-setting functions of mass media. The results of this study were published as the book, *Media Agenda Setting in a Presidential Election* (1993). The research in this book breaks down agenda setting into three types: issue agenda patterns, image agenda patterns, and interest patterns. The issue agenda-setting power of the media was shown to be strongest at the beginning of the presidential campaign. Over the course of the campaign, the newspaper agenda was relatively stable, whereas the television news agenda shifted to be more like the newspaper agenda, leading the authors to posit a "two-step flow" of agenda setting. Voters' perceptions of issue importance tended to follow the television agenda, which in turn followed the newspaper agenda. Media were also shown to have an effect on public perceptions of candidate image salience. Finally, the media were shown to influence interest in the campaign, particularly in the pre-primary and primary stages of the presidential campaign.

In *The President and the Public* (1982), which Graber edited and to which she contributed two chapters, she explores the concept of "linkage." She argues that the mass media help to provide a linkage between public officials and the public. The provision of linkage is essential to the efficient functioning of a representative democracy. Political leaders, the president in particular, are dependent on mass media to reach the public with information; they tend to view the media as a tool to achieve policy objectives. Members of the media, on the other hand, recognize their informational and surveillance roles, but are also bound by the drive to maximize audience to generate revenue. While the often countervailing profit pressure causes mass media to deemphasize or even abandon the coverage of important political stories, Graber argues that audience members routinely ignore much of this type of information anyway.

When Graber (1976b) examined television and newspaper coverage of the 1968 and 1972 presidential campaigns, she found that the coverage devoted considerable attention to the candidates' personalities and to campaign events. By contrast, there was very little discussion of either the candidates' qualifications or their stands on campaign issues.

Graber's research has not been confined strictly to political coverage. In *Crime News and the Public* (1980), she examined why the media seem to focus so intently on crime coverage, particularly violent and sensational crimes. The focus of this book has become even more relevant in the decade and a half since its publication in 1980. Graber conducted a detailed content analysis of a year's worth of midwestern newspapers and local and national television news to document how the media present crime news. She also utilized panel surveys to reveal how the public uses and interprets news information. In addition to the content and survey data, Graber presented actual crime statistics to show how vastly different they are from media depictions and audience perceptions of crime. Audience misperceptions of crime were in part a function of media-use patterns; however, she also found differences between media accounts and audience images of crime. For instance, audience members are more likely than mass media to stereotype criminals as poor and as minorities.

Graber (1979) maintains that, despite public concern about the large amount of coverage that the media devote to crimes, especially violent crimes, her surveys show that audiences pay more attention to crime news. She also asserts that coverage of crime news does not force other important stories off the media agenda. Crime news is typically used as filler in the sense that the time allotted to crime news varies depending on the importance of other stories on the news agenda.

Graber's analyses of media content have contributed not only to our understanding of content, but also to the method used to study content. In the process, Graber has addressed an important methodological issue that mass communication researchers have long neglected. Mass communication researchers have customarily treated the content of television news like print coverage by ignoring the significance of the auditory component, the visual component including graphics and film, as well as the interaction between the various components of the televised message. Graber (1985) has pioneered content analytic techniques specifically designed for studying the entire message of television news.

Graber (1990) has also investigated the impact of the visual component of television news. In order to isolate the visual contribution, she conducted an experiment in which subjects watched television news stories, some of which had their visual track removed. Subjects had greater recall for visual than for verbal themes.

Some of the other interesting topics that Graber's research has addressed include horse-race campaign coverage (1983), "flashlight" media coverage (1989), media framing (1987a), incumbency effects on presidential news coverage (1976a), and the role of the media in opinion formation (1976b).

CRITICAL EVALUATION OF CONTRIBUTIONS AND ACHIEVEMENTS

As is typical of scholars who adopt an eclectic, interdisciplinary approach to theory building, Graber has been criticized for "embracing too many different theories." Graber argues that this type of approach is a strength rather than a weakness. She considers truth to be a "plural noun," and as such she prefers to benefit from the insights garnered from multiple theoretical perspectives. As a result, she has rejected pressures to confine her inquiry to the boundaries of a particular discipline or theoretical perspective.

Research in political communication is complicated by the rapid pace of change in media technology, the proliferation of sources of news and entertainment, and the rapidly changing face of American politics. Knowledge and supporting examples become dated very quickly. Even more significantly, Graber has tended to develop middle-range theoretical explanations rather than attempting to test more formal, grand theories. It can be argued that this type of scholarship tends to fade more quickly. However, Graber has worked very hard to update her books on a regular basis; thus, she has maintained their utility in the wake of the rapidly evolving mass media system and the transitory environment of American politics.

One of the great dilemmas for social scientists is the tension between theory and praxis. Often, what draws researchers to politics and political communication is a deep concern for the great social, moral, and political issues of the time. This can create problems for the social scientist who is, on the one hand, trying to maintain objectivity and, on the other, trying to have an impact on society.

Graber has dealt with this issue by making a clear distinction between her role as a social scientist and her role as an advocate. While recognizing that complete objectivity is never possible, she strives to address controversial issues "even-handedly, presenting all major arguments fairly and dispassionately." She feels that it is extremely important for political scientists to present research findings and interpretations without being influenced by political predispositions. However, there are some issues, such as press freedom, privacy rights, and the defense of human dignity, on which she finds it necessary to take a definitive stand. In such cases, she clearly labels where her personal views begin and end.

One limitation of Graber's work is that she tends to focus on news media and thus to ignore the importance of entertainment media. For instance, her study of media coverage of crime news and its impact on the public images of crime seems somewhat incomplete by failing to deal with the impact of entertainment media.

While Graber has contributed scholarship in a variety of formats, she prefers writing books to journal articles and book chapters because books provide an opportunity to develop subject matter with greater breadth and depth. Of course, the drawback to books is that they are often subjected to a lower level of scrutiny in terms of peer review. However, books often reach a wider audience. Graber stresses the importance of producing research that has an impact beyond academic circles. For this reason, she is most proud of her "most useful" books, *The Development of the Law of Belligerent Occupation* (1968) and *Mass Media and American Politics* (1993). But she considers *Verbal Behavior and Politics* (1976) and *Processing the News* (1988) to be her "most important" books because they contribute the most new knowledge.

Graber's research contributions have been recognized in a variety of ways, including the American Political Science Association's Edelman Award and her selection as the first MAPOR fellow. The Midwest Political Science Association devoted an entire panel at the 1993 conference to her research contributions. Graber is particularly proud of the mentoring award that she received from the Women's Caucus of APSA.

INTEGRATION OF PERSONAL AND PROFESSIONAL LIFE

Graber has done an admirable job of integrating her personal and professional life. In fact, she feels that the two facets of her life have complemented each other:

When professional life has been tense and exhausting, home has been a bastion of support. When household chores, childcare, and social responsibilities seemed overpowering, retreating to a quiet office has been a god-send. The ups and downs of daily personal and professional life can be borne easily when there is love and companionship to share the joys as well as the burdens.

Graber has not let her busy professional schedule stand in the way of an active life outside of academia. She has traveled throughout the globe, quite literally from the Antarctic to the North Pole. In her travels, she has "hiked in Tibet, dived on the Great Barrier Reef, canoed the Amazon River, traveled on a barge in China, and camped throughout Europe and parts of Asia." Her diverse interests have led her to engage in such activities as flying a single-engine airplane and monitoring city council activities for the League of Women Voters. She is an avid fan of theatrical and musical performances, and is a frequent visitor to art museums and archaeological sites. She also participates in several hobbies, including gardening, raising pets, and photography.

Graber and her husband managed to balance their careers and parenting obligations through "teamwork" and "careful time management." Having two professional parents brought Graber's children unique opportunities to travel and to meet interesting people. Be it by nature or nurture, all of Graber's children have gone on to their own professional careers. As an outstanding academician and successful parent, Graber is an excellent role model and proof that a career and a family are not mutually exclusive.

REFERENCES

Graber, D. A. (1968). *The Development of the law of belligerent occupation from 1863–1914: A historical survey.* New York: AMS Press.

Graber, D. A. (1968). *Public opinion, the president and foreign policy: Four case studies from the formative years.* New York: Holt.

Graber, D. A. (1976a). Effect of incumbency patterns in the 1972 presidential campaign. *Journalism Quarterly, 53,* 499–508.

Graber, D. A. (1976b). Press and television as opinion resources in presidential campaigns. *Public Opinion Quarterly, 40,* 285–303.

Graber, D. A. (1976c). *Verbal behavior and politics.* Urbana, Ill.: University of Illinois Press.

Graber, D. A. (1978). Agenda-setting: Are there women's perspectives? In L. K. Epstein (ed.), *Women and the news.* (pp. 15–37). New York: Hastings.

Graber, D. A. (1979). Is crime news coverage excessive? *Journal of Communication, 29,* 81–92.

Graber, D. A. (1980). *Crime news and the public.* New York: Praeger.

Graber, D. A. (1982a). The impact of media research on public opinion studies. In D. C. Whitney, E. Wartella, & S. Windahl (eds.), *Mass communication review yearbook, 3,* 555–564.

Graber, D. A. (ed.) (1982b). *The president and the public.* Philadelphia: Institute for the Study of Human Issues.

Graber, D. A. (1983). Hoopla and horse-race in 1980 campaign coverage: A closer look. In W. Schulz et al. (eds.), *Mass media and elections in democratic societies.* München: Ölschlager.

Graber, D. A. (1985). Approaches to content analysis of television news programs. *Communications,* 11, 25–36.

Graber, D. A. (1986). Mass media and political images in elections. In S. L. Long (ed.), *Research in micropolitics.* Vol. 1. (pp. 127–159). Greenwich, Conn.: JAI Press.

Graber, D. A. (1987a). Framing election news broadcasts: News context and its impact on the 1984 presidential election. *Social Science Quarterly,* 68: 552–568.

Graber, D. A. (1987b). Kind pictures and harsh words: How television presents the candidates. In K. L. Schlozman (ed.), *Elections in America.* (pp. 115–141). Boston: Allen & Unwin.

Graber, D. A. (1987c). Researching the mass media/elections interface: A political science perspective. *Mass Communication Review,* 14, 3–19.

Graber, D. A. (1987d). Television news without pictures? *Critical Studies in Mass Communication,* 4, 74–78.

Graber, D. A. (1988). *Processing the news: How people tame the information tide.* 2nd ed. New York: Longman.

Graber, D. A. (1989). Flashlight coverage: State news on national broadcasts. *American Politics Quarterly,* 17, 277–290.

Graber, D. A. (1990). Seeing is remembering: How visuals contribute to learning from television news. *Journal of Communication,* 40, 134–155.

Graber, D. A. (1991). Media in politics. In W. J. Crotty (ed.), *Political science: Looking into the future.* (pp. 91–124). Evanston, Ill.: Northwestern University Press.

Graber, D. A. (1993a). Failures in news transmission: Reasons and remedies. In P. Gaunt (ed.), *Beyond agendas: New directions in communication research.* (pp. 75–89). Westport, Conn.: Greenwood Press.

Graber, D. A. (1993b). Making campaign news user-friendly: The lessons of 1992 and beyond. *American Behavioral Scientist,* 37, 328–336.

Graber, D. A. (1993c). *Mass media and American politics.* 4th ed. Washington, D.C.: Congressional Quarterly Press.

Graber, D. A. (1993d). Media impact on the political status quo: What is the evidence? In R. J. Spitzer (ed.), *Media and public policy.* (pp. 19–29). Westport, Conn.: Praeger.

Graber, D. A. (1993e). Political communication: Scope, progress, promise. In A. Finifter (ed.), *The state of the discipline II.* (pp. 305–332). Washington, D.C.: American Political Science Association.

Graber, D. A. (1994a). Do the media inform? In G. L. Rose (ed.), *Controversial issues in presidential selection.* (pp. 107–117). Albany, N.Y.: University of New York Press.

Graber, D. A. (ed.) (1994b). *Media power in politics.* 3rd ed. Washington, D.C.: Congressional Quarterly Press.

Weaver, D., Graber, D. A., McCombs, M., & Eyal, C. (1993). *Media agenda setting in a presidential election: Issues, images and interest.* New York: Praeger.

KATHARINE GRAHAM
(1917–   )

Candace Lewis

Katharine Graham is something of a modern legend. In the 1970s and 1980s, she was routinely referred to as one of the most, if not the most, powerful women in the country. Her mythical stature arose in the early 1970s when, as publisher of the *Washington Post,* she approved printing the Watergate exposé that heralded President Richard Nixon's undoing and ultimate resignation. She was also responsible for the *Post*'s publication of the Pentagon Papers, the U.S. Defense Department's classified history of the Vietnam War, despite court injunctions against their publication. Exercising First Amendment rights in the face of immense political pressure and adversity, these two editorial decisions established Katharine Graham as the strongest and most courageous publisher in recent history.

In addition to these brave publishing decisions, Katharine is also legendary for her corporate accomplishments at the Washington Post Company: being only one of three female chief executive officers at a Fortune 500 company; making the Post company one of the most profitable Fortune 500 companies in the 1970s and 1980s; and being inducted into the National Business Hall of Fame in 1989 (Nulty, 1993; *Publisher's Weekly,* 1989; Sherrid, 1984). Katharine's biography is evidence, however, that legends are not necessarily born as such. Although she was an heiress of the *Post* and although her parents were examples of politically influential people, her upbringing and marriage prepared her to be little more than the wife of an important publisher. Thus, when she succeeded her deceased husband as the Post company president in 1963, and as the *Post* newspaper's publisher in 1969, the society wife and mother of four lacked formidable business and publishing experience. Her life story must be considered in order to appreciate her achievement, and, as her son later admitted, "It's the most amazing damn story" (Thompson, 1985, p. 83).

THE MEYER FAMILY

The legend of Katharine Meyer Graham originates in her father's exceptional influence in matters of world finances, her mother's standing in cultural affairs, and both her parents' presence in national politics. Her father, Eugene Isaac Meyer, Jr., was born into a cultured mercantile family of Jewish heritage in 1875 pioneer California. Educated at Yale, he began his own Wall Street brokerage house in 1903. While small, the company was prominent and enabled Eugene to be a capital investor in both the Allied Chemical Company and Anaconda Copper, which were essential to the nation during both world wars (Davis, 1991; Sherrid, 1984). In addition to profits, the two companies also brought Eugene international recognition as a financier. Such recognition led to his first government post during World War I as the head of the War Finance Corporation (WFC).

Director of the WFC until 1925, Eugene continued his public service career as a member of the Farm Loan Board until 1929 when he returned to investment banking. His return to private finance was brief, however, because in 1931, President Herbert Hoover asked Meyer to draft legislation for a Reconstruction Finance Corporation (RFC) that would lend money to companies in order to jump start the depressed economy. Eugene modeled the RFC after the WFC, and his draft was enacted in January 1932. It continued to be expanded throughout President Franklin D. Roosevelt's New Deal as a means of stimulating economic activity during the Depression (Felsenthal, 1993). In 1933 Eugene resigned from his work as a Federal Reserve Board governor and promptly purchased the moribund *Washington Post* for $825,000 at a bankruptcy auction on the front steps of the newspaper's building. The purchase was made with politics—not profits—in mind: Eugene wanted to remain a powerful, politically independent voice in the nation's affairs after retiring. Although the paper initially served as his means of remaining in public life, Eugene's "hobby" became a valuable property as Washington, D.C. became a boom town and the *Post*'s competitors fell to the wayside.

When Eugene purchased the *Post* in 1933, Katharine, then 16, had already begun preparation for a career in journalism having been on her grammar and high school papers' editorial boards. Born in New York City on June 16, 1917, she was the Meyers' fourth child. Although the Meyers' were one of the most important, influential couples in Manhattan, they were also becoming influential in Washington, D.C. because of Eugene's public service. Shortly after her birth, Katharine's father made a permanent move to D.C. Her first three years were spent with very little contact with him and almost as little with her mother, Agnes.

Born in 1877, Agnes Elizabeth Ernst was a svelte and intelligent young woman of German descent who had paid her way through Barnard College— after losing a scholarship for "insolent" behavior—by tutoring high school students in math and by managing a Baptist school in Hell's Kitchen. Following graduation at age 21, she was one of the first women employed as a reporter for the *New York Sun*. As a student and lover of modern art, Agnes associated with members of the avant garde in Paris and New York to the extent that she was considered a member of the "291 Club" whose roster of artists included Alfred Stieglitz, Georgia O'Keeffe, and Edward Steichen. A successful and cruel flirt with men, Agnes attracted the attention of many admirers—most notably August Rodin—and later Eugene Meyer who, despite being a consummate businessman, preferred the company of liberal intellectuals like Agnes. Their marriage on February 12, 1910, afforded Agnes the opportunity to pursue her intellectual pursuits, including her published studies of Chinese language and translations of the German author Thomas Mann, a personal friend.

Following her husband to Washington, Agnes, too, became involved in political affairs, campaigning against overcrowded schools and racial discrimination, and working for health and welfare community facilities. Her efforts to establish a Department of Health, Education, and Welfare even caused President Harry Truman to quip, "There's hardly a day I don't get a letter from that Meyer woman or from Eleanor Roosevelt* telling me how to run this job" (Beasley & Gibbons, 1993, p. 161). Because both parents were engaged with political work or with their individual financial and cultural interest, the business of child care was left to the children's governess who raised Kay—as Katharine was called—and her older siblings Florence, Eugene the third (known as "Bill" in the family), and Elizabeth, as well as their younger sister, Ruth. Their nanny was one of the full staff of 12 available to the children at their palatial mansion winter home in D.C. Summers were spent at the family's opulent Westchester County, New York, home which housed a Turkish bath, a bowling alley, as well as indoor and outdoor pools.

Although Kay grew up amidst extraordinary wealth and power, she would later comment that she felt like an orphan as a child because her parents were so distracted from their family life (Felsenthal, 1993, p. 36). In addition to such isolated feelings, Kay also had to contend with her mother's contemptuous and self-centered nature, which was very distinct from Kay's serious and deep demeanor. Later describing her mother as something of a Viking, young Kay had to "develop an armor, albeit wobbly, to protect herself from Agnes" (Felsenthal, 1993, p. 38). Furthermore, in light of her namesake, Katharine Rhoades—a renowned beauty, talented painter, and early feminist who was Agnes' dear friend from the 291 Club—the ever-practical and retiring Kay could not measure up to her mother's expectations. Agnes often displayed her daughters Florence and Elizabeth as beauties and little Ruth as a sensitive artist. Kay, however, was largely ignored, to the extent that later she would recall feeling like "the plodding peasant walking around brilliant people" (Felsenthal, 1993, p. 37).

Her father, however, saw Kay quite differently. Eugene was largely bored by his children's pastimes in sports or social rituals, choosing instead to base his relationships with his children on their intellect. Family dinners thus became political debates in which the children were encouraged to argue competitively among themselves. Although Kay impressed her father, his approval was hardly ever explicit. According to her sister Elizabeth's recollection years later, Eugene had come to see Kay as most like himself. "You watch my little Kay," he told a friend when she was only 5, "no matter how many times she's knocked down, she'll always come up straight" (Davis, 1991, p. 50). He also told Alice Roosevelt Longworth that Kay "has got a hard mind. She'd make a great businessman" (Felsenthal, 1993, p. 68).

EMERGING FROM THE FAMILY MYTH

Eugene favored Kay because he realized as she progressed through school that she had a seriousness and direction that were absent in his other children. Kay attended a Montessori school in Washington for nursery and kindergarten classes, the Potomac Elementary School, and later the Madeira School, America's oldest, finest, and most elite girls' preparatory school. There, she undertook rigorous training in languages, economics, science, and philosophy. She excelled not only academically but also athletically and extracurricularly—playing field hockey and lacrosse, working as a hospital assistant as well as a congressional messenger, and serving as class president, student body head, and editor of the school newspaper.

In September 1934, Kay began at Vassar College, in Poughkeepsie, New York. There, she continued to develop her fledgling interest in journalism; she was a regular editorial staff member of the college's paper, the *Miscellany News,* by her sophomore year. She focused her studies on literature and economics, and was very active in student politics. In the fall of her sophomore year, she was elected to the national board of the American Student Union (ASU), a liberal student organization that organized political activities on major U.S. campuses. The ASU was left-leaning, preaching such progressive politics as solidarity with labor unions; Eugene and Agnes, however, were successful in encouraging Kay to be moderate. Originally perceived by many classmates as shy, retiring, and self-apologetic, Kay was recognized as an outspoken advocate of student political activism and was one of the most prominent young women on campus by her second year at Vassar (Felsenthal, 1993). Eugene, continuing to recognize his daughter's studious nature, agreed with Kay that she had exhausted Vassar's worth and should proceed to more challenging studies.

Thus, in September 1936 Kay continued her education at the University of Chicago, a hotbed of radicalism and intellectual debate. The university, for example, was a proponent of the then-radical idea that women should have the same educational opportunities as men. It was also a sanctuary for European political refugees. There, Kay lived in the International House and became immersed in the intensely intellectual and electric political debate exchanged among her worldly housemates. She pursued her political activism through her studies as well as pragmatic displays of her labor sympathy at strike demonstrations. The University of Chicago chapter of the ASU, however, was more militant than Vassar's had been, and Kay became weary and disenchanted with political battles by her senior year. She now limited her ASU participation to the publication of a weekly organizational bulletin she had founded, and increased her attention to her study of European history and such classics of the Western world as Homer, Machiavelli, Dante, and St. Augustine.

By the time of her graduation in 1938, Kay had assumed the distinct style of the University of Chicago woman who would express her political opinion with a stridency offensive to most men of the time—particularly those working in her hometown of Washington, D.C.—and to women who believed in being demure rather than intelligent (Davis, 1991). Because she had risen to the intellectual challenges of her studies and Chicago peers and because she was separated by a greater distance from Agnes, she began to show more self-confidence than ever before (Felsenthal, 1993). Unfortunately, however, Agnes' demeaning manner still affected her daughter: on Kay's graduation day, for example, Agnes did not show up, instead sending a note from her secretary who misspelled Katharine's name. Kay was said to have read it and burst into tears (Davis, 1991; Felsenthal, 1993; Rowland, 1989).

After she graduated, Katharine's father arranged for her to begin work as a reporter for the *San Francisco Daily News.* Kay had displayed an interest in reporting and publishing throughout her college experience and had also spent the summer of 1937 working as a copygirl at the *Post,* and the next summer at the Mount Vernon, New York, *Argus.* At the *Daily,* she promptly began paying union dues to the recently formed American Newspaper Guild, and began to cover dockworkers' strikes. Initially, she was not happy at the *Daily;* she complained that male reporters ridiculed her, treated her in an off-handed and demeaning manner, and did not take her education seriously. Such treatment was typical of the trenchant sexist attitudes that marked journalism of the time, particularly with its noisy, pressurized, hard-drinking, and rough-talking aura. Indeed, a group of journalists addressing a forum of female journalism students in 1940 warned that "women don't have any more chance for jobs on newspapers than Jews have of surviving in Germany" (Beasley & Gibbons, 1993, p. 14).

Despite such adversity to her gender, Kay, at her father's suggestion, remained at the *Daily.* He soon regretted encouraging her. After receiving some professional recognition for her work as well as a better beat (the Treasure Island navy base), Kay began to enjoy San Francisco so much that she did not want to return to her D.C. home. Eugene, however, wanted her for his *Washington Post,* and, after some discussion, Kay returned home in 1939 to work for her father's paper. Eugene wanted her to learn about the various workings of the *Post* because he intended that she would someday be part of maintaining the family's paper. Thus, Kay wrote articles, edited letters to the editor, sat in on conferences that determined editorial policy, worked in the advertising and circulation departments, and did page layout and headline writing (Davis, 1991;

Felsenthal, 1993; Rowland, 1989; Stroud, 1974). Regardless of this preparation, Kay's role maintaining the Meyer empire was not as Eugene's successor.

ENSURING THE MEYERS' *POST* LEGACY

"I worked on the [*Post*] when I was young," Kay would later explain, "but there was never any idea of my going on it permanently" (Davis, 1991, p. 63). Indeed, it was difficult for a man of her father's generation and background to imagine that a woman could be a worthy successor—particularly a daughter just a year out of college and 22 years of age. Kay therefore planned to do graduate work in American history at Harvard or in economics at the London School of Economics. These plans changed, however, after her sister Ruth's Christmastime debutante ball in 1939. There, Kay met an intense, young Supreme Court law clerk whom she would marry less than six months later. With her June 5, 1940, marriage to Philip L. Graham, the *Post* legacy would soon unfold; Kay's story became her husband's for the next 23 years.

THE *POST*'S PUBLISHER AND HIS WIFE

Philip Leslie Graham, born on July 18, 1915, was something of a country boy from rural Florida. His father, Ernest Graham, had been a Michigan drifter of Scottish heritage who settled down upon marrying Florence Morris, a Black Hills, South Dakota, school teacher. After serving in World War I, Ernest found work as the resident manager of a sugar farm in the Florida Everglades. Phil's father eventually prospered in dairy farming and later won a seat in the state senate. Phil's mother encouraged his intellectual pursuits, and on her deathbed demanded that Phil be sent to Harvard law school after he completed his work at the University of Florida (Felsenthal, 1993, p. 83). Thus, in September of 1936, Phil was admitted to Harvard where he proceeded to earn some of the highest grades in the law school's history; to be elected as the much-coveted *Harvard Law Review*'s president; to be selected as one of Supreme Court Justice Felix Frankfurter's few protégés; and—because of his connection with Frankfurter—to become a Supreme Court law clerk (Davis, 1991; Felsenthal, 1993).

Like many of his contemporaries, Phil arrived in Washington, D.C., as one of the passionate New Dealers who soon lost their altruistic intentions as the town was swept up in preparations for war. In 1942 Phil left for officer candidates school, with new wife Katharine in tow. When he was shipped overseas to the Pacific for intelligence work that earned him the Legion of Merit, Kay busied herself writing at the *Post,* preparing for a family (their first child was stillborn in 1942), and volunteering for her mother's Committee on the Reorganization of Community Services and her father's refugee committee (Davis, 1991). When Phil was discharged from the Army as a major in the fall of 1945, Katharine and he had a daughter, Elizabeth—called Lallie, born in early 1944, and a son, Donald, born in April 1945.

With a family to support and the glory of war fading, Phil suggested to Katharine that they move to his native Florida where he could practice law and perhaps run for Congress. Katharine, however, was still very much tied to her parents and their newspaper. Thus, in January of 1946—after anxiously mulling over his career options with Harvard chums during the Christmas holidays— Phil accepted a $30,000-a-year position as associate publisher of the *Post.* Within a short time he brilliantly mastered the newspaper, and his father-in-law transferred ownership to Philip and Katharine in August 1948.

Now steering the Meyers' *Post,* Phil set the newspaper's course to success and acquisition. He firmly established the paper's liberal editorial leanings and was determined to make the *Post* the dominant voice of Washington. To this end, he purchased the newspaper's morning competition in 1954, effectively creating a monopoly on that critical daily news slot. He also purchased 55 percent of WTOP, Washington's CBS radio station, and in 1961 added *Newsweek* newsmagazine to the *Post*'s growing publishing empire. Phil was a determined and enigmatic young man who believed that if history did not mold men, then men could mold history (Davis, 1991, p. 119). He was a pragmatic man who linked his intellectual ideas with action, and who was aware that politics were sustained on two levels: what they appeared to be for his readers, and what they really were in Washington inside circles. With such insider knowledge, he expanded the *Post* and appeared comfortable in his role as publisher, his "feet on the desk, chain-smoking Parliaments, running the *Post* with little money but enormous charm" (Davis, 1991, p. 119).

His charm was noted throughout his career, from Harvard to the Supreme Court to the *Post.* Although he was a gossip who gave the impression of being very open—a lady's man who loved to talk about feelings and personalities as well as ideas—it seemed he rarely said anything of substance about himself. He was also nervous and high-strung—frenetic and moody to the point of being volatile—and was perceived as being arrogant and self-centered (Felsenthal, 1993, p. 118). As his work at the *Post* and his Washington life developed, he became increasingly frustrated that his status was attained through marriage, and that the Meyers expected his accomplishment and brilliance to further their publishing empire. Unfortunately, Kay became the target of his frustrations and his self-doubt.

For her part, Kay accepted the role of Phil's stooge or fall-guy, becoming the butt of his jokes about her intelligence and appearance. Sources later reported that Phil considered Kay dowdy, overweight, and boring (Rowland, 1989), and that he was bothered by people's insinuations that he had married her because of her family's exalted place in D.C.'s political echelon (Felsenthal, 1993). While Phil was rising as an influential Washington figure and publisher, Kay was ensconced in her role as a dutiful Washington wife who permitted herself to be excluded from the men's parlor talk, who left politics and matters of substance to men, and who aspired to be charming, accepting, deferential, and feminine. As her four children grew—two more boys, William and Stephen, were born in 1948 and 1953, respectively—Kay was perceived as just "another frumpy housewife, often seen bundled up in the bleachers at school" (Thompson, 1985, p. 80). In a telling comment from one of Kay's friends, she was seen less as a wife than as a prince's attendant (Rowland, 1989).

In 1961 Phil was at the height of his influence in publishing and politics as one of President John Kennedy's elite group of reporters. Simultaneously, however, his adultery, drinking, and bouts of depression became more intense. Diagnosed as a manic depressive in 1952, Phil had periodically withdrawn from work over the years in order to endure his depressions. Because manic depressives were described during the 1940s and 1950s as faking those social qualities they lacked (notably wit, conversation, and social aggression), Phil was plagued from the time of his diagnosis by the "fear that everything he did, every political involvement, every judgment, was somehow a fraud" (Davis, 1991, p. 137).

In 1962 Phil began a passionate affair which he carried on flagrantly, inviting family friends who knew Kay and even his own teenage daughter to parties he hosted with his mistress. Although he requested a divorce from Kay, the legal process was never begun because Kay was fearful of publicly accusing her husband of being mentally incompetent and also because she was still in love with him. "She was loyal—long-suffering," recalled a family friend (Felsenthal, 1991, p. 206). Her loyalty extended beyond his affair, when Phil voluntarily committed himself to a private psychiatric hospital in Maryland. Convincing his doctors that he was well enough to visit Kay at their farm in Glen Welby, Virginia, he killed himself there with a self-inflicted gunshot to the head on August 3, 1963. Kay and two servants were the only other people in the house.

SUCCEEDING PHILIP GRAHAM AS POST PRESIDENT

On the day of Phil's funeral, Kay assured associates of the Washington Post Company that "there is another generation coming, and we intend to turn the paper over to them" (Thompson, 1985, p. 82). That generation was, namely, Donny, Kay and Phil's first son. When Phil had bought out the Post's morning competition in 1954 to establish a monopoly on Washington's morning news, Eugene Meyer said, "The significance of the event is that it makes the paper safe for Donny" (Thompson, 1985, p. 82). Thus, in order to maintain the paper for Donny (18 years old at the time of his father's suicide), Kay assumed the position of the Post company's president in 1963 and, six years later, assumed the title of the newspaper's publisher. In so doing, Kay continued a tradition among women publishers and editors who, as widows, acted to carry out family responsibilities and to ensure family legacies but not to seek independent careers (Beasley & Gibbons, 1993, p. 8). Katharine Graham, however, would stray far from this tradition and develop quite an impressive career of her own.

Initially, Kay's transition from caretaker to decision maker was difficult because she did not see her work as the beginning of a career. "I was very much in the old world of women. I didn't view myself as coming in to run things"

(Rowland, 1989, p. 118). The dominantly male staff and board of the *Post* also shared this view; many believed Kay did not merit the position and appropriately treated her with condescending, arrogant, and patronizing attitudes (Davis, 1991, p. 178). The *Post* men, however, were not her only formidable obstacle; her own lack of belief in her abilities and intellect—after more than 20 years of being shadowed by Phil's figure—compounded her initial years at the newspaper. She began her work at the company "with a clean slate of ignorance," she said. "I didn't know anything about business, or running a newspaper" (Nelson, 1991, p. 52). But understanding it was up to her to protect the family's company, she endeavored to study and learn every aspect of the business operation, often depending on loyal male executives to be her "mentors." Following a tendency of successful women journalists to identify with male figures as professional mentors (Beasley & Gibbons, 1993, p. 14), Kay had no pretense in her early days about needing help from reliable and trustworthy male executives and editors.

Although as president and later publisher, Kay always assumed ultimate responsibility for the *Post*'s actions, the contributions of such male executives and editors cannot be overlooked. For example, Kay developed an unlikely but outstanding publisher relationship with Ben Bradlee. Formerly *Newsweek*'s Washington bureau chief and another of President Kennedy's elite group of reporters, Bradlee knew torrid details about Phil's philandering and had even once encouraged Phil to divorce Kay. After Kay chose him to be the *Post*'s managing editor in 1964, Ben promptly infused the parochial paper with style and irreverence, and he began to earn Kay's trust and support (Davis, 1991; Felsenthal, 1993; Rowland, 1989; Thompson, 1985). Such trust was necessary, for Kay was very occupied "learning by doing"—the "Montessori school of business" she called it—how to run the Washington Post company, and thus left Ben and his editors to themselves. "In day-to-day operations," she later said, "I believe strongly in department autonomy. My department heads give me knowledge and I give them policy and, beyond that, I leave them pretty much alone. . . . Professional people work best in an atmosphere of freedom, whether it is in a news or business department" (Hill, 1975, p. 42).

Kay gained such knowledge through her initial years at the *Post*. Gradually, as her early years as president and then publisher passed, several characteristics emerged in the once under-thumb Washington wife. She began to develop a management style that was distinctly her own and deliberately not Phil's. Whereas he was intuitive, she was logical; whereas he was sporadic and inspired, she was methodical. She managed with more rigidity but also with more principles (Davis, 1991, p. 161). The goals she set for the *Post* were financial profit and editorial excellence (Slater, 1974). Her own goal was to be a good manager—a goal many believed unattainable because of Kay's "off-with-their-heads" approach to dealing with executives (Davis, 1991; Diamond, 1993; Felsenthal, 1993; Sherrid, 1984; *Time,* 1977). Indeed, the Post company became infamous within the media industry for its executive turnover rate, inciting Kay to quip, "If people say I murder and use arsenic, I still won't comment" (*Time,* 1977).

A sense of self dormant since the University of Chicago was also rising in Kay as her *Post* education continued. She became authentically assertive and hard-minded, with a capacity for action and boldness (Davis, 1991). Gone, however, were the altruistic and political interests she had pursued while in college. Kay was now interested in money, power, and position, for these were the raw materials of her new corporate role as president of the Post company. In Katharine Graham, as she was now signing her name, a toughness and a hardness were emerging—qualities she would essentially need in the early 1970s when, as publisher, she faced two of the most important editorial decisions known to modern journalism.

WRITING HISTORY AS THE *POST'S* PUBLISHER

In June 1971, the *New York Times* was restrained by court injunctions from continuing publication of the Pentagon Papers, secret Defense Department reports that indicated the Vietnam War was not proceeding as well as officials claimed it was. The *Post* quickly obtained its own set of the papers and—convening reporters and editors at Ben Bradlee's home—began to prepare stories for publication. As the deadline approached, however, Bradlee and his editors could not convince the *Post*'s legal and businesspeople that the stories should go to press; they phoned Katharine in order to make a decision. Both business and legal executives advised against publication. The business executives claimed that publication might have financial repercussions because the Post company's stock had gone public only several days earlier; the legal executives cited the grave risks that would be incurred by disregarding the court-ordered restraints placed on the *Times* that very morning. The editorial side, however, argued that to back off would seem cowardly and would violate the people's right to know. It would also put the *Post* on the government's side and would fail to put the *Post* on top of their competitor, the *Times*. Although the *Times* had had more than three months to make their decision to publish the Papers, Katharine had only a matter of minutes to decide for the *Post*.

"The decision had to be made quickly," she later recalled. "The story was written and ready to go; it was valid; there had never before been prior restraint of the press. Weighing all factors, it seemed like the right thing to do. And I still feel the same" (Slater, 1974, p. 192). Calling it the most difficult news-oriented decision she ever had to make, Katharine was supported by Ben who fully credited her with the decision. "The decision was hers alone," Ben said, "and it was the most important editorial decision of the last 25 years. She did it against the popular wisdom of all her colleagues except the news side. It was a very dramatic moment" (Rowland, 1989, p. 118). When the Nixon administration sued to restrain further *Post* publication of the Papers, the Supreme Court ruled in favor of the newspapers, inspiring Justice Hugo Black to note, "The

Washington Post and other newspapers should be commended for serving the purpose that the Founding Fathers saw so clearly'' (Davis, 1991, p. 246).

The Pentagon Papers was not the first incident in which President Richard Nixon had tangled with a Graham; in 1948, when Nixon was a congressman, he accused the *Post* of being a communist newspaper after Phil Graham had editorially spoken in favor of Alger Hiss, a fellow Harvard graduate accused of spying. While Nixon's accusation was meant to discredit—albeit unsuccessfully—Phil's *Post,* ironically it would be Katharine's *Post* whose accusation of Nixon would be successful—beyond all imagination—in discrediting the president.

With Katharine's approval, encouragement, and financing, *Post* reporters Bob Woodward and Carl Bernstein conducted an investigative exposé of a break-in at the Democratic National Committee headquarters in mid-June of 1972. What became known as the Watergate scandal began when the five men arrested during the break-in were found to be carrying wiretapping equipment. Upon further investigation, the *Post* reporters developed and published stories linking high-ranking Republicans in Nixon's administration to a secret Republican fund to gather dirt on Democrats. In the course of the investigation, the Nixon administration threatened Katharine by challenging the federal licenses held by the Post company's television stations, whose legal defense cost the company over $1 million.

Besides resisting the Nixon administration's tactics, Kay stalwartly supported her reporters' right to keep their sources anonymous, agreeing that she would rather go to jail than comply with a court subpoena for her reporters' notes (Felsenthal, 1993, p. 315). Her encouragement and approval of the story was also notable, for the *Post* was the sole newspaper reporting on Watergate for months and months. ''Being alone had its chilling moments,'' Katharine later recalled. ''You thought, 'If this is such a hell of a wonderful story, where is everybody else?' '' (Rowland, 1989, p. 118). But Katharine continued to publish the exposé, and thus brought the *Post* national recognition and ultimately spurred Nixon's resignation. As legend has it, history might very well have turned out differently had Katharine not been so tough. As she told it, however, ''The image of me as someone who likes or can deal with a fight is wrong. Some people enjoy competition and dustups and I wish I did, but I don't. But once you have started down a path, then I think you have to move forward. You can't give up'' (Rowland, 1989, p. 118).

MANAGING LABOR AND WOMEN'S ISSUES AS THE COMPANY'S CHAIRPERSON AND CEO

If the 1970s proved anything about Katharine Graham, it was that she did not give up. In late 1975, yet another test of her mettle arose when the *Post*'s pressmen responsible for printing the newspaper began a bitter strike that would last into 1976. Katharine, having been appointed as the chairman of the Post company's board and as the company's CEO in 1973, was infuriated by Wall

Street's perception of her as a publisher soft on unions—like a "little lady" on the board who was afraid to tangle with labor. In addition to that perception, a recession and severe difficulties motivated Katharine to hire a tough professional labor negotiator in order to hold a hard line on the pressmen's demands regarding their contract renewal, and so shoot for a high rise in yearly profits (Rowland, 1989; Thompson, 1985).

Earlier in the year she had promised Wall Street investors this profit gain by maintaining her labor costs; following the promise, Post company stock had promptly risen. Maintaining that one-third of the pressmen's $5-million a year wages came from overtime, Katharine had to play tough with the union when the contracts came up for renewal and thus make good on her promise to Wall Street (*Time,* 1975). On October 1, some of the pressmen walking off their jobs vandalized the paper's nine presses by crippling and burning them. While seven other unions' members followed them, the paper's 843-member newspaper guild—representing editorial and clerical workers—did not.

Working under siege conditions, these workers and Katharine managed to get the paper out. When the strike began, 200 of the guild members started living in the picketed building—cots were set up in offices, the building's executive dining room served as an all-night diner, and piles of dirty laundry began to accrue as workers put in all-day shifts writing the paper and all-night shifts printing it (*Time,* 1975). Outside the building, Katharine was hung in effigy and a placard was displayed that read, "Phil shot the wrong Graham." After Katharine announced she would hire scab press workers by offering rates higher than the industry standard, the union acquiesced to negotiations; Katharine Graham had broken the union (Davis, 1991; Felsenthal, 1993; Rowland, 1989; Thompson, 1985). Her company had never been healthier (*Time,* 1977).

Critics, however, found Kay's hard line with unions to be an incongruity and a hypocrisy; the paper—while liberal in pages—was not practicing its preaching in relation to unions, women, and minorities. In 1972, 46 women at the Post-owned *Newsweek* filed a sex discrimination complaint with the Equal Employment Opportunity Commission (EEOC). They described their relegation to researcher roles while men were reporters and writers. They timed their complaint to coincide with a *Newsweek* edition about "Women's Liberation," which featured a cover article by a woman not even employed at *Newsweek.* Encouraged by these women, female employees at other news organizations—including the *Washington Post*—soon began to file sex discrimination complaints themselves (Beasley & Gibbons, 1993, pp. 25–26).

Although the *Post* had covered such women's issues as abortion rights, alimony, and child care seriously since the late 1960s, in 1974 the EEOC called for the *Post* to improve its hiring, promotion, and salary practices for women (Beasley & Silver, 1977, pp. 138–141). In 1980 *Post* female employees sued the company for not keeping promises made in response to the 1974 EEOC findings (Felsenthal, 1993, p. 286). For her part, Katharine was not too sympathetic with the women's movement. Her goal was to be accepted and respected in a man's world, and she attributed her early difficulties as the Post company's president to her lack of confidence rather than sexist attitudes (Felsenthal, 1993; Slater, 1974).

Inadvertently, however, Katharine helped women through her election as the first woman to the traditionally chauvinist Associated Press board of directors (Stroud, 1974, p. 192), and her invitation in 1972 to attend dinner at the Gridiron Club, which refused to admit women to its roster of prominent newsmen until 1975—the first year Katharine accepted their invitation (Felsenthal, 1993, p. 288). Her capital investment of $20,000 in Gloria Steinem's* *Ms.* magazine, however, elevated her to superstatus according to many women's groups, though any reputation attributed to her as a feminist was largely undeserved (Felsenthal, 1993). In addition, her role as the highest ranking female CEO, and her high visibility as a woman making crucial editorial decisions during the Pentagon Papers and Watergate controversies contributed to women's advances in corporate and media spheres, despite the fact that Katharine's unique biography had positioned her in such positions of power.

BEING SUCCEEDED BY DONNY

Although her birthright availed her power and prestige, Katharine Graham exceeded any expectations of the widow who was simply protecting her son's inheritance and her family's fortune until he could succeed her. As her friend, columnist Art Buchwald, explains, "She had the burden of an entire enterprise on her shoulders. It could have all gone down the drain. She was in a war and she won" (Davis, 1991, p. 193). Katharine took hold of a loosely structured family business and—by educating herself in business and editorial matters— built an immensely profitable and professional publicly held company. She guided the Post company through the shrewd acquisitions of cable properties and cellular phone operations, making the Post the nation's fifth largest publishing company (Sherrid, 1984), earning the company a rank of 16 among *Fortune* magazine's most profitable Fortune 500 companies between 1978 and 1988 (Rowland, 1989, p. 126), and raising the value of the company's stock from $6.50 in 1971 to over $230 in 1993 (Nulty, 1993).

With strength and quiet determination as a publisher, Katharine also transformed a very good Washington, D.C., newspaper into a national institution, establishing it as a symbol of journalistic integrity and courage. In so doing, her political power rose directly and distinctly within the capital city. Katharine became an undeniable political force and actor (Davis, 1991; Felsenthal, 1993; Stroud, 1974; *Time,* 1977). Sit-down dinners for 40 to 50 guests at her Georgetown home would summon the crowned heads of journalism and government, and her seventieth birthday celebration would bring together 600 national and international media figures including President Ronald Reagan, nearly his entire Cabinet, Supreme Court justices, foreign prime ministers and ambassadors, the heads of such corporations as Sony, IBM, Ford, General Motors, and General

Electric, and such publishing magnates as Rupert Murdoch, Malcolm Forbes, and Clare Boothe Luce (Felsenthal, 1993, p. 426).

After her son, Donny, returned from the Vietnam War and completed work as a D.C. police officer, he began an eight-year apprenticeship at the *Post* in 1971 that took him through every department of the newspaper and *Newsweek*. Katharine, he found, was no longer a frumpy housewife waiting for him to take over. Rather, she was something of his rival, keeping the position of publisher until 1979, and the titles of CEO and chairman of the board until 1991 when he succeeded her. From 1991 to date, she has been the chairman of the Post company's executive committee. She also holds titles as a board co-chair of the International Herald Tribune; as a board member of Reuters Founders Share Company, the Urban Institute, and the Federal City Council; as a life-trustee of the University of Chicago and an honorary trustee of George Washington University; as a fellow of the American Academy of Arts and Sciences; and as a member of the National Business Hall of Fame, the American Society of Newspaper Editors, the National Press Club, the Council on Foreign Relations, the Overseas Development Council, the Metropolitan Club, and the 1925 F Street Club.

REFERENCES

Beasley, M., & Gibbons, S. (1993). *Taking their place: A documentary history of women and journalism.* Washington, D.C.: American University Press.

Beasley, M., & Silver, S. (1977). *Women in media: A documentary sourcebook.* Washington, D.C.: American University Press.

Davis, D. (1991). *Katharine the great: Katharine Graham and her* Washington Post *empire.* New York: Sheridan Square Press.

Diamond, E. (1993, February 22). Oh Kay. *New York, 26,* 12–13.

Felsenthal, C. (1993). *Power, privilege, and the Post: The Katharine Graham story.* New York: Putnam's Sons.

Hill, I. W. (1975, April). Interviewer senses publisher's success formula. *Editor & Publisher, 108,* 42.

Nelson, W. F. (1991, July). Katharine Graham. *Washingtonian, 26,* 52.

Nulty, P. (1993, April). The national business hall of fame. *Fortune, 127,* 109–110.

Publisher's Weekly. (1989, November 3). Katharine Graham memoirs go to Knopf. 55.

Rowland, M. (1989, November). The mastermind of a media empire. *Working Woman, 14,* 114–115.

Sherrid, P. (1984, April). Embarrassment of riches. *Forbes, 133,* 15–16.

Slater, C. (1974). Publisher Kay Graham: The woman. In *Authors in the news.* Vol. 1. (p. 192). Detroit: Gale Research Co.

Stroud, K. (1974). The private and public wars of Katharine Graham. In *Authors in the news.* Vol. 1. (pp. 193–194). Detroit: Gale Research Co.

Thompson, T. (1985, April). Prince Donny. *Esquire, 103,* 79–83.

Time (1975, December 29). The right to manage, 106, 66.
Time (1977, February 7). Krusty Kay tightens her grip, 109, 70.
The Washington Post Company. (1994). *Annual Report*. Washington, D.C.: Washington
    Post Co.

SARAH JOSEPHA BUELL HALE (1788–1879)

Diane Zimmerman Umble

In December 1877 Sarah Josepha Hale wrote her farewell editorial for *Godey's Ladies Book:*

And now, having reached my ninetieth year, I must bid farewell to my countrywomen, with the hope that this work of half a century may be blessed to the furtherance of their happiness and usefulness in their Divinely appointed sphere. New avenues for higher culture and for good works are opening before them, which fifty years ago were unknown. That they may improve these opportunities, and be faithful to their high vocation, is my heartfelt prayer. (Finley, 1931, pp. 312–313)

With these words, Sarah J. Hale concluded 50 years of editorial advocacy for women's causes through the pages of two of the earliest American women's magazines. Her priority was education for women, but she lent the considerable influence of her editorial voice to fights for property rights for women, medical education for women, the hiring of women educators, the formation of kindergartens, and public policies protecting children and promoting sanitation. She spearheaded efforts to address the needs of women and children through the formation of the Seaman's Aid Society. She demonstrated the considerable power of women to raise funds through her efforts to complete the Bunker Hill Memorial and acquire Mount Vernon as a national museum. She tirelessly advocated the designation of Thanksgiving as a national holiday until she succeeded in 1863. In addition, she diligently published and promoted the work of American writers, particularly women writers. In the process, the "Widow Hale" raised and educated her five children, published her own poetry and fiction, and edited numerous anthologies and gift books.

Her determination to improve opportunities for women was based on her conviction that women were the moral guardians of society. A woman's destiny, in Sarah Hale's words, was "to carry onward and upward the spirit of moral and intellectual excellence in our own sex, till their influence shall bless as well as beautify civil society" (Martin, 1928, p. 70). The base of that influence was in the home, the foundation of society. "Hers . . ." one commentator suggests, "was a conservative mind animated by a radical spirit" (Martin 1928, p. 62).

FAMILY BACKGROUND AND EDUCATION

Martha Whittlesey Buell, Sarah's mother, was born in Saybrook, Connecticut, in 1751. At the close of the Revolution, Martha Whittlesey married a soldier, Gordon Buell of Killingsworth, and settled with him on a 400-acre tract of uncleared land near Newport, New Hampshire. Martha Buell bore four children. The eldest, Charles Whittlesey, born on September 27, 1784, was lost at sea. The youngest, Martha Maria, born on April 19, 1793, died of consumption. The second son, Horatio Gates, was born on January 13, 1787, and was named after the Revolutionary general under whom his father served. Sarah Josepha was the third child, born on October 24, 1788.

The Buell children received their early education from their mother. Sarah credits her "predilection for literary pursuits" to her mother. Sarah's reading included the Bible, *Pilgrim's Progress,* Milton, Addison, Pope, Johnson, Cowper, Burns, and Shakespeare. Later, her brother Horatio entered Dartmouth College. On his vacations, Horatio and Sarah kept regular hours of study as he tutored her in college studies. "To my brother . . ." she wrote, "I owe what knowledge I have of Latin, of higher branches of mathematics, and of mental philosophy. He often regretted that I could not, like himself, have the privilege of a college education" (Finley, 1931, p. 29). By the time Horatio was graduated from Dartmouth, his sister, too, had acquired the equivalent of a college education.

At 18 years of age, Sarah opened a small private school and began teaching boys and girls. Her biographer reports: "The girls were not taught sewing, but to write well and read intelligently for their own pleasure and profit, and each was made mistress of more mathematics than was known by all their fathers and mothers put together" (Finley, 1931, p. 30). Hale's commitment to intellectual training for women was rooted in her own seven years of teaching experience.

The day before her twenty-fifth birthday, October 23, 1813, Sarah married David Hale, a young attorney from a neighboring village. A member of a distinguished New Hampshire family, the promising young attorney was remembered as handsome, kind, and sociable. The couple set up housekeeping in the town of Newport. Their first child, David Emerson, was born on February 19, 1815. A second son, Horatio Emmons, was born on May 3, two years later. On March 20, 1819, a daughter, Frances Ann, was born. And on December 4, 1820, Sarah Josepha was born. Despite their busy lives, Sarah wrote:

We commenced, soon after our marriage, a system of study and reading, which we pursued while he lived. The hours allotted were from eight o'clock until ten—two hours in twenty-four. How I enjoyed those hours! In this manner we studied French, Botany . . . and obtained some knowledge of Mineralogy, Geology, etc., besides pursuing a long and instructive course of readings. In all our mental pursuits, it seemed the aim of my husband to enlighten my reason, strengthen my judgment, and give me confidence in my own powers of mind, which he estimated more highly than I did. (Finley, 1931, pp. 35–36)

David also encouraged her to write, critiqued her prose, and persuaded her to pursue publication.

In the fall of 1822, David Hale developed pneumonia and died. Sarah delivered her fifth child, William George, shortly thereafter. After nine years of marriage, Sarah Hale was faced with the challenge of supporting herself and five children. She wrote,

My husband's business had been large for the country, but he had hardly reached the age when men of his profession begin to lay up property. . . . We had lived in comfort, but I was left poor. For myself the change added not one particle to my grief, but for my children I was deeply distressed. . . . I cared not that they should inherit wealth, but to be deprived of the advantages of education was to make them "poor indeed." (Finley, 1931, p. 37)

Sarah set out to support her family, first by entering the millinery business with her sister-in-law, Hannah Hale. But, as one biographer reports, "The millinery business . . . did not engage Sarah's attention sufficiently to crowd out of her mind the poems and pieces she had formerly set down for the entertainment of the family" (Entrikin, 1946, p. 9). In 1823 Masonic friends of her late husband helped her to publish a small volume of her poems, *The Genius of Oblivion.* That year she had poems accepted for publication in *The Minerva,* and the following year, her poetry appeared in *The American Monthly Magazine.* By 1826 she was also published in the *U.S. Literary Gazette* in the company of Bryant and Longfellow (Entrikin, 1946, p. 10).

In January of 1826, the editor of the *Boston Spectator and Ladies' Album* announced a competition for the best poem. Sarah entered a poem "Hymn to Charity" and was awarded the $20 first prize for her efforts. That year the *Boston Spectator* published her first prose, the story called "The Lottery Ticket." The story won a prize (a volume of Cowper's poems) as the best original piece of prose contributed to the magazine. In 1826 Sarah, using the names "H.," "Cornelia," "Sarah," and "S.J.H.," had published 17 poems, 2 short stories, 1 critical review, and a long extract from her forthcoming novel—all in the *Spectator.* "S.J.H." had become one of the magazine's principal contributors.

During 1826, Sarah was also writing her first novel, *Northwood,* "with a baby in my arms" (Entrikin, 1946, p. 14). The novel, one biographer argues, was the "first American novel of consequence written by a woman . . . the first novel—by either man or woman—to deal with the question of slavery . . . the most accurate and detailed picture of the domestic habits, customs and manners of the post-Colonial period contemporaneously recorded" (Finley, 1931, p. 266). In the preface of a later edition, Sarah wrote that the novel was undertaken "not . . . to win fame, but a support for my little children" (Entrikin, 1946, p. 14). The novel was well received and began her transformation from an obscure New England milliner-widow to a literary personage.

"THE LADY EDITOR"

After the 1827 release of her novel, Sarah Hale received a letter from the Reverend John L. Baker of Boston. She wrote:

[I]n less than a month after the book appeared I had received many letters . . . among those letters was one, from a publishing firm . . . proposing to establish a periodical for Ladies, and offering me the editorship. . . . this was not only unsolicited, but entirely unexpected. . . . A magazine edited by a woman for women had never been conducted, so far as I know, either in the old World or the New; and it seemed, at first, impossible for me to accept. . . . Yet . . . this change seemed to me to be the ordering of Divine Providence. (Entrikin, 1946, p. 14)

Magazines of the day were risky business. Many publishing ventures failed within a few years. American publications were imitations of their British counterparts in both format and content. Poetry, fiction, and illustrations were borrowed freely from British publications and reprinted, often without citation, in American magazines. While most of them had pages devoted to women readers, early attempts at publication strictly for women had not succeeded. "It must be considered a sign of great character," a biographer writes, ". . . at forty, with five children and no promise of assured income, this woman could embark upon a career, uncertain for the most accomplished and talented men, and unpromising in the extreme for a women. . . . in the writing world her place was unknown, subject to criticism and actual condemnation" (Entrikin, 1946, p. 16). Nevertheless, the public accepted the new "Lady Editor," in part because of her literary reputation and in part because she was a widow with children to support instead of a mother "deserting" her family (Riley, 1970, p. 211).

Sarah launched her editorial career with the *Ladies' Magazine* in late 1827 from her home in Newport. But by April 1828, long-distance editing proved unsatisfactory, and she moved to Boston. Her goal was clearly articulated from the start. "The work will be national . . . , American . . ." she wrote in the first issue, "a miscellany which, although devoted to general literature, is more expressly designed to mark the progress of female improvement" (Finley, 1931, p. 40). Over the next decade, Sarah built both the reputation and the circulation of the *Ladies' Magazine*. She introduced a new approach to the literary land-

scape by publishing the writings of American authors and by addressing issues
of importance to American middle-class women. She refused to underestimate
the intellectual and moral potential of her readers and resisted the introduction
of the frivolous into her magazine. Each issue emphasized the moral influence
of women, the value of education for women, and the importance of employing
women as teachers.

From the beginning "the Lady Editor" had intellectual priorities. Unlike other
popular magazines, in its early years the *Ladies' Magazine* did not publish popular music, patterns for embroidery, or fashion plates. Hale wrote: "There is no
part of our duty as editor of a ladies Journal which we feel so reluctant to
perform, as to quote, or exhibit the fashions of dress" (Martin, 1928, p. 53).
Nevertheless, her readers and her competition forced her to compromise. She
published fashion plates in November 1830. The plate featured a low-cut, ornate
evening gown and an intricate headdress of European design. The editorial on
the opposite page declares how shameful it is that "we have no *American fashions* to *exhibit*" and challenges "elegant and intelligent ladies" to invent their
own fashion instead of blindly following the standards of others (Martin, 1928,
p. 54). In the months following the introduction of fashion plates, Sarah Hale
continued to make them serve as "moral" cartoons (Martin, 1928, p. 55). In
September 1831, she commented:

the servile imitation of European extravagances, and works, we cannot think creditable
to the taste, and character of our intelligent, and refined, moral community. We would
do nothing to increase this mania of fashion, but much, were it in our power, to diminish
it—and it is, therefore, that we endeavor to make our *plate of fashion* teach a lesson to
the heart, as well as the vanity of our fair readers. (Martin, 1928, p. 55)

In addition to calling for American fashion, Sarah Hale also promoted the
work of American writers. Her magazine was unique in its commitment to original material. In 1834 she acknowledged the "gifted writers" who had contributed to the magazine: Sigourney, Sedgwick, Gilman, Embury, Smith, Child,
Gould, Wells, Willard, Phelps, Locke. Her list includes the names of women
writers who constituted the female literary renaissance in the decades preceding
the Civil War. In some cases, their reputations had been established before their
publication in the *Ladies' Magazine;* in other cases, publication in the *Ladies'
Magazine* made their reputations.

Hale's tenure in the Boston publishing world was the context for another
innovation—the mobilization of women to raise funds for public service through
editorial advocacy. The power of women to address social issues was compell-
ingly demonstrated by the founding of the Seaman's Aid Society and the successful completion of the Bunker Hill Monument.

Hale conceived and organized the Seaman's Aid Society in early 1833. She
reflected on its beginnings: "we assembled monthly, while a work basket containing our stock of goods, was carried to our place of meeting. . . . There we

passed the afternoon . . . making garments to be given to the poor when the greatest need of most of them was . . . employment'' (Finley, 1931, p. 73). The shipping and fishing industries were second only to agriculture in the 1830s. "The lot of the sailor's wife is of extreme hardship,'' Hale wrote (Finley, 1931, p. 75). Sailors were often gone months or even years at a time, leaving wives and families with little support. "The only means of earning money for women who cannot go out to service in families or take in washing, is needlework,'' Hale wrote. By 1836, the Society opened a clothing store, selling clothing made by seamen's wives who were paid fair wages. Soon the Society opened a trade school for girls, a day nursery for working mothers, and a free library. It was through her experiences with the Seaman's Aid Society that Hale began public advocacy for better housing and for property rights for married women. Finley (1931) writes: "A sailor's wife, who with her children had been rescued from abject poverty and who for the first time in her life was enjoying the comfort of a decent wage earned at the Store, had suffered legal confiscation of her earnings, in the mid winter of 1836 by a creditor of her husband. . . . The creditors were within the law; all property of a wife, including her earnings, belonged to her husband. Her wages were subject to seizure for his debts'' (p. 80). This situation and others like it launched Hale's decades of editorial campaigning for women's property rights.

Hale's experiences with the Seaman's Aid Society honed organizational and advocacy skills that culminated in a personal triumph. The cornerstone for a monument commemorating the battle of Bunker Hill was laid on June 17, 1825. However, the association of prominent men was $23,000 in debt and unable to complete its construction. For 20 years, the unfinished monument was Boston's eyesore and embarrassment. Sarah Hale thought her readers could help. Reluctantly, the men of the monument association agreed to her proposal to collect money from her readers, and she began an editorial campaign in 1830. Money came in, but more was needed. So in June of 1840, Sarah Hale proposed a woman's fair. That summer, readers from New England and as far as the Carolinas and Ohio donated needle work, preserves, and cash for the fair. For seven days in September 1840, thousands of people visited the largest hall in Boston to attend the Woman's Fair. In the process, $30,000 was raised for the completion of the Bunker Hill Monument. Women had demonstrated to men and to themselves their latent power of organization and cooperation.

By 1840 Hale had already served as the editor of *Godey's Lady's Book* for three years, editing the publication from Boston. Louis A. Godey was a Philadelphia publisher who had launched his own women's magazine in 1830, the *Lady's Book*. Although the content of his early issues was borrowed heavily from foreign publications, Godey shared Sarah Hale's perspective on "American periodicals.'' He, too, announced his intention to engage "native writers.'' And he paid them a "liberal price'' for their work (Finley, 1931, p. 44). Godey admired and respected Sarah Hale. As his own publication grew, he looked to his able competitor for competent editorial services.

Godey's offer was attractive. After nine years as the editor of *Ladies' Magazine,* Hale acknowledged the difficulties of sustaining her magazine "without funds, pledged assistants, or other support than annual subscriptions" (Entrikin, 1946, p. 57). Louis Godey visited Hale in Boston to negotiate the purchase of her magazine in exchange for her editorial services on a new combined publication. In December 1836 she announced the consolidation of the two magazines. Hale assumed the editorial duties, and Godey managed the business side of the operation.

In her first editorial in the new *Godey's Lady's Book,* Hale again states her intentions "to carry onward and upward the spirit of moral and intellectual excellence in our sex" (Entrikin, 1946, p. 59). The new publication combined Godey's emphasis on fiction and departments (hand-colored fashion plates, recipes, his own column—"The Arm Chair") with Hale's interests in education, "discipline of the mind necessary for every female," reviews, and poetry. She wrote, "We must carry out our plan of the beautiful and appropriate in dress, in poetry, in fiction, in education, till all shall meet like the rays of a star . . . in the sacred beauty of the Christian character" (Martin, 1928, p. 70).

For her first four years, Hale insisted on editing the *Lady's Book* from Boston, because her youngest son William was finishing his education at Harvard. As a young adult, William moved south and was later admitted to the Virginia bar. In 1846 he moved to Galveston and became famous for his handling of old Spanish claims after the separation of Texas from Mexico.

David, Hale's eldest son, was 13 when she began her educational career in Boston. Later, he received an appointment to West Point and was commissioned lieutenant and stationed in South Carolina. In January 1839, David was assigned to the Canadian line. The exposure to the intense cold induced hemorrhages, and he died in April at the age of 25.

Horatio, her second son, graduated from Harvard in 1837 and joined the United States Exploring Expedition as a philologist. Horatio traveled in South America, Samoa, and Antarctica, as well as the American West. His first monograph, "Ethnography and Philology," was hailed by scientists around the world. His later research documented the languages and dialects of Native Americans.

Sarah educated both of her daughters at Emma Willard's Female Seminary in New York, then the most intellectually challenging girls' school in the country. Sarah Josepha, the younger, trained as a teacher. After a sojourn teaching in a private school in Georgia, Josepha opened her own Boarding and Day School for Young Ladies in 1826 in Philadelphia. She died at her desk in 1863, a dedicated teacher.

Frances Ann, the eldest daughter, accompanied her mother to Philadelphia in 1841. Three years later, Frances married naval surgeon, Lewis Boudinot Hunter, and settled near her mother's Philadelphia home. Frances Ann's six children were regular visitors to their grandmother's study during the 38 years Sarah Hale lived and worked nearby.

Having educated her children, Sarah Hale devoted her life in Philadelphia to editing and publishing. Her partnership with Godey met with success. When she began as editor in 1837, Godey boasted a circulation of 10,000 subscribers to his *Lady's Book*. By June 1849, circulation was 40,000. The magazine had expanded from 48 pages in 1837 to 100 pages by December of 1849 (Entrikin, 1946, p. 99). In 1861 circulation reached 61,000, twice that of any competitor. At its peak, the *Lady's Book* had a circulation of 150,000. "It was commonly said," Tarbell* (1910) writes, "that no lady would think her drawing-room table furnished without it" (p. 668). By the beginning of the Civil War, Hale and Godey had garnered a nationwide audience for the magazine.

Each issue of "the Book," as Godey referred to the magazine, contained departments of cooking, interior decorating, etiquette, and fashion. The magazine was famous for its hand-colored and black-and-white fashion plates and engravings. Over the years, music, house plans of model cottages, drawing lessons, handwork patterns, a children's department, a health department, and a department on chemistry for the young were added to its pages. Nevertheless, consistently half of the magazine's content was literary in nature. Poetry, fiction, and nonfiction remained at the center of Hale's editorial attention. Publication in "the Book" built the reputations of men and women writers of the day. Hale published the early work of Edgar Allan Poe and Harriet Beecher Stowe. She fostered the work of many women writers of the day, including Lydia H. Sigourney, Lydia M. Child, Catherine Sedgwick, and Eliza Leslie. She garnered contributions from Irving, Longfellow, Lowell, Holmes, Emerson, Bryant, and Whittier.

Additional pages of each issue were given to book reviews, publication notices, and Hale's own column, the "Editor's Table." The column was her platform for advocacy. Here she made appeals for funds. During the 1850s, for example, she used the "Editor's Table" to report the fund-raising efforts of the Mount Vernon Ladies' Association to raise money to purchase Washington's home. She preached the need for hospitals for women and children and was instrumental in the founding of the first Female Medical College of Philadelphia in 1850. She advocated the education of women as medical missionaries, founding the Ladies Medical Missionary Society of Philadelphia in 1851. She applauded Matthew Vassar's plans for a women's college and goaded him into hiring women faculty and adding "Domestic Science" to the curriculum. But she campaigned against the name "Vassar *Female* College." "Female!" she wrote to Vassar, "What female do you mean? Not a female donkey? Must not your reply be, 'I mean a female woman'? Then . . . why degrade the feminine sex to the level of animals . . . I write thus earnestly because I wish to have Vassar College take the lead in this great improvement in our language. . . . I plead for the good of Vassar College, for the honor of womanhood and the glory of God" (Finley, 1931, pp. 206–207). Hale won the battle. The word "female" was stricken from the state charter and removed from the facade of the main college building at Vassar.

Hale's "Book Table" was another regular feature. Here she reviewed a wide array of literature of her day, articulating her critical standards for poetry, prose, and nonfiction and popular music. She found "a thousand matters of interest" in Darwin's *Origin of Species*. In response to Elizabeth Barrett Browning, Hale called her "*poet,* not *poetess* because we wish to number among the stars of which she is queen, not only women, but men" (italics in the original; Finley, 1931, p. 122). She praised quality when she saw it, deplored "perversion of moral sentiments" in certain silly novels, and insisted that the poetry of women express the greatest human truths. Through this column, she not only commented on the writing of the day, but she also recommended reading lists for the intellectual development of her readers. In successive issues in 1847, she began with the Bible and proceeded through an extensive list of books on Jewish and Christian history, ancient history, American histories, biographies, European history from the Middle Ages to modern Europe, poetry, philosophy, and ethics. The September issues rounded out the list with a supplement on famous women from ancient to modern times.

Despite Hale's strong opinions, Godey's policy prohibited the publication of opinions on sectarian religion and partisan politics. At the celebration of the magazine's fiftieth volume, Godey publicly boasted: "I allow no man's religion to be attacked or sneered at, or the subject of politics to be mentioned in my magazine. The first is obnoxious to myself and to the latter the ladies object; and it is my business to please them, for to them—God bless the fairest portion of his creation—am I indebted for my success." (Finley, 1931, pp. 176–177). The policy was imposed to the extreme during the Civil War. The pages of "the Book" provide little hint that the conflict existed, and Hale's potential to mobilize women for good causes was effectively muzzled. Hale believed that education and time would have solved the problems of slavery without war. Although she did not believe in slavery and deplored the war, her position was not articulated in the magazine. Her biographer argues that "neutrality" was a mistake. As a result, Finley (1931) concludes, the Book "lost step with its times . . . its readers looked in vain for the advice and encouragement they had been wanting to receive so lavishly from its pages. Soon it was no longer the arbiter of the nation's parlors, no longer the last word or authority in every home" (pp. 193–194).

Louis Godey brought his sons into his organization in 1877 and retired in August 1877, after 48 years as publisher. On the evening of November 29, 1878, he died peacefully in his favorite chair at the age of 75. Sarah Hale also retired in 1877 at the age of 90, after 50 years of editing magazines for women. Hers was also a short retirement; she died on April 30, 1879, just five months after her partner. Under new leadership, the magazine lived on as *Godey's Lady's Book and Magazine,* without the voices from "The Arm Chair" and "The Editor's Table."

THE AUTHOR

Although Sarah Josepha Hale is remembered as "the Lady Editor," she also wrote and edited numerous volumes of poetry, prose, and plays. Hale was a regular contributor to at least 18 gift-books which were so popular in the 1830s–1850s. These collections of literature featured detailed engravings and beautiful covers. Hale offered her own gift-books in 1845, 1848, and 1849. *Flora's Interpreter* (1832) was both popular and profitable, going to 14 editions. It combined botanical entries about each flower and its meaning with accompanying poetry. *The Opal* and *The Crocus* (1849) were gift-books aimed primarily at young people.

One of her most ambitious projects was the *Woman's Record* (1853), a 900-page universal bibliographical dictionary with over 2,500 sketches of noteworthy women. "My object," she wrote, "was to prepare a comprehensive and accurate record of what women have accomplished, in spite of the disadvantages of their position, and to illustrate the great truth that woman's mission is to educate and ameliorate humanity. . . . I have aimed to render it the most thorough and trustworthy of feminine biographies" (Sewell, 1988, pp. 165–166).

Hale's collections of poetry by women were motivated by her effort to debunk her contemporaries' opinions that women's poetry was feminine in style, and by implication inferior. Instead, she argued that because women were morally gifted, their poetry was superior. She published collections of the works of English and American woman poets to prove her point. The first collection, *The Ladies' Wreath,* was published in 1837. *The Poet's Offering* (later published as *A Complete Dictionary of Poetical Quotations* in 1850) was hailed as the first effort to publish an anthology of poetry by women and was the most complete work of its kind.

Hale also published her own short fiction. Compiling collections of previously published stories, she published *Sketches of American Character* (1829) and *Traits of American Life* (1835) that told moral tales in the American context. Her dramatic novelettes were designed to promote the importance of the domestic role and to instruct young women in the management of their households. She published *Keeping House and House Keeping* in 1845 and *"Boarding Out": A Tale of Domestic Life* in 1846.

Hale's early experiences in the classroom prompted her to take an active and long-term interest in publishing books for children. She edited a ten-volume series promoted as the Little Boy's and Girl's Library. *Poems for Our Children* (1830) was written in response to a request from Lowell Mason for verses appealing to children to be used in teaching music in school. (Mason is remembered for introducing music into the public school curriculum.) He popularized Hale's children's poems by including eight of her catchy poems in his *Juvenile Lyre* (1832). One of the poems, "Mary's Lamb," became an American classic when McGuffey published it without attribution in his popular series of readers.

Although the authorship of "Mary's Lamb" was contested by Mary Sawyer Tyler in 1879, Hale defended herself in a letter dictated four days before her death. Despite Hale's declaration, the controversy was continued in the popular press for decades.

In addition to poetry and music, Hale also wrote and edited collections of fiction for young readers and pioneered the publication of children's magazines with the launching of *Juvenile Miscellany* in the 1830s. Although the effort eventually failed, Hale's concern for young readers continued for the remainder of her career. One of her later books, *Manners; or, Happy Homes and Good Society All the Year Round* (1869), was dedicated to young people. Based on a collection of articles Hale had written for a family newspaper, the *Home Weekly*, the book contains sections on parties, advice on domestic etiquette, a plea for "Happy Sundays for Children," a justification for the rights of women, and a diatribe against the barbarous use of the term *female.*

Although Hale enjoyed a considerable literary reputation during her lifetime, her conventional morality and sentimental style went out of fashion with the passing of the Victorian sensibilities. She also parted company with some of her contemporaries in her later years, when she refused to embrace the cause of women's suffrage. From the "Editor's Table" Hale wrote:

"I control seven votes: why should I desire to cast one myself" said a lady who, if women went to the polls would be acknowledged as a leader. This lady is a devoted, beloved wife, a faithful, tender mother; she has six sons. She *knows* her influence is paramount over the minds she has carefully trained. She *feels* her interests are safe. . . . She *trusts* her country will be nobly served by those whom her example has taught to believe in goodness, therefore she is proud to vote by her proxies. This is the way American women should vote, namely, by influencing rightly the votes of men. (*Godey's Lady's Book,* vol. 44: pp. 1852, 293)

MAJOR CONTRIBUTIONS AND ACHIEVEMENTS

After her death, the Seaman's Aid Society passed a resolution praising Hale's 75 years of "noble industry." The resolution celebrated her contributions to the character of American women: "while guarding with jealous care women's real rights and highest culture she so mingled in her daily life and writings the spirit of progress with true conservatism that she never compromised true womanly nature." Sarah Josepha Hale reflected the values of many of her contemporaries. She saw herself first as a mother. She argued that women had to be educated because they were God's moral agents. Their power lay in the moral and intellectual elevation of the members of their households. To detract for this high calling was to weaken—rather than strengthen—their power.

Some twentieth-century interpreters of Sarah Hale's life and work cast her as a retrograde force who impeded women's progress through her views on separate spheres. Others characterize the content of *Godey's Lady's Book* as "mawkish, moralistic fiction'' and ''doubly mawkish, moralistic poetry'' (Bulsterbaum, 1946, p. 144). Recent scholarly analysis, however, has attempted to assess the influence of Hale and the ''Book'' on American middle-class culture by analyzing the music (Koza, 1988), the domestic rhetoric (Lawrence, 1989), the domestic arts (Winkler, 1988), and the literature (Hoffman, 1990) articulated through the pages of *Godey's Lady's Book.*

Okker (1990) argues that Hale redefined literary culture in a way that elevated the status of the ''woman writer.'' Okker challenges the notion that Hale promoted a circumscribed poetic aesthetic and concludes that Hale used her magazine to ''expand and glorify other woman's poetic achievements'' (1993, p. 33). In contrast, Hale declared women to be the superior poets and ''insisted upon women's strength, poetic achievement and public authority'' (Okker, 1990, p. 40). In a careful analysis of Hale's *Woman's Record,* Baym (1990) argues that ''the work attempts nothing less than to reconstitute world history around the figure of a woman, to restructure world history *as* the history of women'' (p. 252). Hale's selection of women from across time and nation is a testimony to the ''diversity, difference, endurance, and adaptability of specific and imperfect earthly women'' (p. 369).

In her own biographical sketch in the *Women's Record,* Hale defines herself as a ''Chronicler of my own sex.'' She chronicled the development of women's organizations for social and public service, she tirelessly promoted the education of women, and she published and promoted the work of women writers. Hale used domestic ideology to increase women's intellectual and literary opportunities. In doing so, she accomplished her desire to ''promote the reputation of my own sex.'' The Lady Editor worked to educate her own children. She educated her readers as well.

REFERENCES

Baym, N. (1990, July). Onward, Christian women: Sarah J. Hale's history of the world. *New England Quarterly,* 63, 249–270.

Bulsterbaum, A. (1986). Godey's Lady's Book. In E. E. Chielens (ed.), *American literary magazines: The eighteenth and nineteenth centuries.* (pp. 144–150). New York: Greenwood Press.

Entrikin, I. W. (1946). *Sarah Josepha Hale and Godey's Lady's Book.* Philadelphia: University of Pennsylvania.

Finley, R. (1931). *The Lady of Godey's: Sarah Josepha Hale.* Philadelphia: Lippincott.

Hoffman N. T. (1990). Scribbling, writing, author(iz)ing: Nineteenth century women writers. Ph.D. diss., University of Utah.

Koza, J. E. (1988). Music and references to music in ''Godey's Lady's Book,'' 1830–77. Ph.D. diss., University of Minnesota. 1185 pp.

Lawrence, K. A. (1989). The domestic idiom: The rhetorical appeals of four influential women in nineteenth century America. Ph.D. diss., Indiana University.

Martin, L. (1928, January). The genesis of *Godey's Lady's Book. New England Quarterly,* 1, 41–70.

Okker, P. A. (1990). Feminizing the voice of literary authority: Sarah J. Hale's editorship of the "Ladies' Magazine" and "Godey's Lady's Book." Ph.D. diss., University of Illinois at Urbana-Champaign.

Okker, P. A. (1993). The poetic tradition in two nineteenth century women's magazines. *American periodicals: A journal of history, criticism, and bibliography*. Denton, Tex.: Journals Division of the University of North Texas Press, 3, 32–42.

Riley, G. G. (1970, February). The subtle subversion: Changes in the traditionalist image of the American woman. *Historian, 32*, 210–227.

Sewell, E. N., Jr. (1988). "Sarah Josepha Hale." *Dictionary of Literary Biography, 73*, 159–167.

Smedman, M. S. (1981). "Sarah Josepha Hale." *Dictionary of Literary Biography 42*, 207–217.

Tarbell, I. M. (1910, March). The American woman: Those who did not fight. *American Magazine, 69*, 656–669.

Winkler, G. C. (1988). Influence of "Godey's Lady's Book" on the American woman and her home: Contributions to a national culture (1830–1877). Ph.D. diss., University of Wisconsin–Madison.

Representative Publications by Sarah Josepha Buell Hale

The genius of oblivion; and other original poems. (1823). Concord, N.H.: Jacob A. Moore.

Northwood: A tale of New England, 2 vols. (1827). Boston: Bowles & Deardorn: republished as *Sidney Romelee: A tale of New England*. (1827). London: Newman.

Sketches of American character. (1829). Boston: Putnam & Hunt/Carter & Hendee.

Poems for our children. (1830). Boston: Marsh, Capen, & Lyon.

Traits of American life. (1835). Philadelphia: Carey & Hart.

The good housekeeper; or, the way to live well and be well while we live. (1839). Boston: Weeks, Jordan.

Keeping house and house keeping. (1845). New York: Harper.

"Boarding out." A tale of domestic life. (1846). New York: Harper.

Liberia; or, Mr. Peyton's experiments. (1853). New York: Harper.

Manners; or happy homes and good society all the year round. (1868). Boston: Tilton.

Flora's interpreter: or, The American book of flowers and sentiments. (1832). Edited, with contributions, by Hale. Boston: Marsh, Capen & Lyon; republished as *Flora's interpreter, and Fortuna Flora*. (1849). Boston: Mussey; revised and enlarged (1856). Boston: Sanborn, Carter & Bazin/Portland: Sanborn & Carter; revised again (1860). Boston: Chase, Nichols & Hill.

The ladies' wreath; A selection from the female poetic writers of England and America. (1839). Edited, with contributions, by Hale. Boston: Marsh, Capen, Lyon & Webb.

The school song book. (1834). Edited by Hale and Lowell Mason. Boston: Allen & Ticknor; republished as *My little songbook*. (1841). Boston: Allen & Ticknor.

Good little boy's book. (ca. 1842). Edited by Hale. New York: Edward Dunigan.

Good little girl's book. (ca. 1842). Edited by Hale. New York: Edward Dunigan.

The three baskets; or how Henry, Richard, and Charles were occupied while Papa was away. (ca. 1842). Edited by Hale. New York: Edward Dunigan.

The opal: A pure gift for the holy days. MDCCCXLV. (1845). Edited, with contributions, by Hale. New York: Riker.

The opal: A pure gift for the holy days. MDCCCXLVIII. (1848). Edited, with contributions, by Hale. New York: Riker.

The opal: A pure gift for all seasons. (1849). Edited, with contributions, by Hale. New York: Riker.

The crocus: A fresh flower for the holidays. (1849). Edited by Hale. New York: Edward Dunigan.

The poets' offering: For 1850. (1850). Edited by Hale. Philadelphia: Grigg, Elliot; republished as *A complete dictionary of poetical quotations.* (1850). Philadelphia: Lippincott, Grambo; republished again as *The poets' offering: For 1851.* (1851). Philadelphia: Lippincott, Grambo.

The ladies' new book of cookery: A practical system for private families in town and country. (1852). Edited by Hale. New York: Long; republished as *Modern household cookery.* (1863). London: Nelson; enlarged as *Mrs. Hale's new cookbook.* (1857). Philadelphia: Peterson.

Woman's record; or sketches of all distinguished women, from "The Beginning" till A.D. 1850. (1853). Edited by Hale. New York: Harper; (1863). London: Low; revised and enlarged. (1855). New York: Harper; revised and enlarged again. (1870). New York: Harper.

HERTA HERZOG
(1910–   )

Elizabeth M. Perse

Herta Herzog's career has spanned the entire history of modern mass communication research. She was part of the first Office of Radio Research where she conducted pilot studies and interviews with the audiences of popular radio programs. Her work on listeners of radio serials, in particular, was an important influence in the development of uses and gratifications research. After moving to market research, Herzog had considered concentrating on the study of the individual and began training in psychoanalysis, but she soon discovered that she was a social psychologist.

FAMILY BACKGROUND

Herta Herzog was born in Vienna, Austria, in August 1910. Although her father's heart condition rendered him ineligible for the front during World War I, he volunteered for service anyway, motivated by his family's tradition of strong patriotic sentiments. Herzog remembers her father leaving the family estate where they spent their summer vacations and her mother, along with other women, preparing bandages and knitting for the soldiers on the front. Although she was too young to grasp its full meaning, Herzog remembers that all her family's savings were converted into war bonds (*Kriegsanleihen*) that were worthless by the end of the war.

Herzog's clearest memory of the war years was the scarcity of food. A kind of turnip, *wrucken,* became the mainstay of their diet when most other foods were severely rationed. There was a black market and people went to the farms around the city to barter for food, but her family did not resort to this. She and her younger sister survived thanks to the United States' distribution of food in the public schools. She remembers that most of the meals consisted of beans, except for Fridays, when the children were given cake and cocoa.

The real war victim in her family was Herzog's much-loved mother, a handsome, strong woman. She contracted a bronchial infection in a train returning from the front and being undernourished she was unable to shake it off. It developed into tuberculosis, and she lingered for seven years. Her mother's illness and death was the key experience of Herzog's teenage years. She attributes her later work habits and her desire to excel to these early years when she sought to please her mother by bringing home good school reports.

Herzog was consistently first in her class, due mainly to her attention to work in school rather than time spent on homework. She and her sister tutored schoolmates several hours after school each day, using their pay as pocket money. Herzog's father, a graduate of the Law School of Vienna University, had just begun his career in government, and her mother's illness was expensive. Although the children received a stipend in school, little money was available for extracurricular activities. Herzog especially valued her violin lessons, taught by a violinist of the Vienna Philharmonic. She loved playing duets with her father, a fine pianist. This was one of the activities she would miss the most after she was afflicted with polio.

EDUCATION

After four years in elementary school (she skipped the final year), Herzog attended a humanistic *gymnasium* for eight years. This private school was the only all-female school in the area with a strict humanistic curriculum: Latin daily for all eight years and Greek daily for five years. Her teacher for these subjects was superb, teaching not only the language, but also providing insights into the lives of the ancient Romans and Greeks described in the literature. Herzog believes that this positive experience was responsible for her initial focus on Latin, Greek, and archaeology (with a secondary interest in German) when she entered the University of Vienna in 1928.

After a year of these studies, Herzog began to explore other subjects, notably philosophy, German literature, and some courses in the law school. She also attended a class given by Professor Karl Bühler, a psychologist, and at last found the area she wanted to work in: translating the life of antiquity to modern humans.

In 1923 Charlotte and Karl Bühler were appointed to the University to establish an Institute (department) of Psychology. Karl Bühler was an experimental psychologist who had made important contributions to the psychology of thinking, whereas Charlotte had recently published the first edition of her work, *Das Seelenben des Jugendlishen,* an extensive discussion of child development related to a sociocultural context.

The Institute of Psychology was staffed with several brilliant assistants: Egon Brunswick, who worked mainly in perception; Else Frenkel, who worked with

Charlotte Bühler on her studies of children and later on development along the life span (*Lebensläufe*); Käte Wolf, who worked with Karl Bühler on his theory of language; and Paul Lazarsfeld, a mathematician who taught statistics and studied social-psychological problems.

The stimulating intellectual climate of the Institute was reflected in the interaction among colleagues. The Bühlers initiated the *Psychologische Praktikum,* a Wednesday evening seminar consisting either of a report presented by a senior student detailing his or her work or the talk of a well-known scientist, followed by discussion. After the seminar, guests and senior students ate together at a nearby restaurant. These meetings gave students the opportunity to talk with renowned scholars and experts. Herzog remembers meeting Jean Piaget and Konrad Lorenz, among others.

In her dissertation, Herzog decided to study a social-psychological problem that was of current importance. Radio was then a new and exciting medium, and the Institute had been involved in an large survey of listener tastes for Austrian radio. Lazarsfeld suggested that she replicate an earlier study completed by T. H. Pear in England which focused on the effects of the "physiognomics" of the human voice, or voice and personality as they came over on the radio. The topic, based on Bühler's theory of language that viewed expression (*Ausdruck*) as one function of language, was of great interest to Herzog.

Her study, the first large field experiment in Austria, was designed to explore the social and personality characteristics that the audience would derive from voice and diction. Six speakers, who differed in sex, age, physical type, and occupation, read the same text over the radio on subsequent days of the same week. Listeners were invited to fill out questionnaires and add any personal observations on the six speakers. The questionnaires were distributed in the popular tobacco shops throughout the city and a total of 2,700 listeners participated. Her dissertation, *Stimme und Persönlichkeit,* was completed in 1933 under Lazarsfeld's supervision.

Analyzing the huge amount of data would have been a major problem had Herzog not contracted poliomyelitis toward the end of the summer vacation. (Hers was the first case recorded in Austria, and so there was no treatment for the disease.) Herzog survived but was paralyzed to the waist for six months; her right arm remained lame permanently. Herzog's dissertation eased her situation greatly, providing immensely interesting and distracting work for her. She also trained herself to use her left hand.

CAREER DEVELOPMENT

Herzog credits Paul Lazarsfeld as the first and one of her main intellectual influences. He was not only a brilliant scientist but also a great teacher. He joined the Institute because of his interest in social psychology and impressed Charlotte Bühler with his statistical abilities. In order to support himself financially and obtain the funding needed to establish a division of social psychology at the Institute, Lazarsfeld created an independent social science research center: *Wirtschaftspsychologische Forschungsstelle* (the Research Center for Economic Psychology).

The *Forschungsstelle* was independent of the Institute, but many of the Institute's students worked there and wrote their dissertations based on data collected at the *Forschungsstelle*. The primary focus of the Research Center was on the application of psychology to social and economic problems. Of the several works produced by this group, *Die Arbeitslosen von Marienthal (Marienthal: The Sociography of an Unemployed Community,* Jahoda, Lazarsfeld, & Zeisel, 1933) became the best known.

The second focus of the *Forschungsstelle* was market research, which had not been practiced in Austria. This commercial work not only funded the theoretical work of the *Forschungsstelle* and the Institute's division of social psychology, but also fit in with Lazarsfeld's early interest in decision making, such as voting choice. During those years when the Nazi party first assumed power, analyzing consumer products provided a more manageable and politically safer way to study the process of choice in Austria.

The *Forschungsstelle* also developed new methods to study consumer preferences. In *Die Krise der Psychologie,* Karl Bühler had pointed out three sources of psychological knowledge: the observation of behavior, the interpretation of cultural products, and introspection. Lazarsfeld believed that through proper questioning, introspection could be obtained from ordinary people (Lazarsfeld, 1935). One questioning method, the open-ended question, or "depth interview," was a qualitative research approach that Herzog developed and continued to use throughout her career in both individual interviews and focus groups.

After completing her Ph.D., Herzog became an assistant professor in 1933 at the Psychological Institute of the University of Vienna, taking over Lazarsfeld's classes and Ph.D. students. Lazarsfeld, a Jew and therefore unable to expect a university career, obtained a Rockefeller fellowship and moved to the United States in 1933.

Herzog left Vienna in 1935 to marry Lazarsfeld and work in the United States. She began as a research assistant to Robert Lynd, whose functional study of a Midwest community (*Middletown: A Study in American Culture,* Lynd & Lynd, 1929) became a classic. Herzog also worked with Lynd conducting interviews of well-to-do suburbanites in New Jersey which examined how they were handling the Depression. This work gave Herzog her first insight into contemporary aspects of U.S. life as well as an introduction to the English language, which at the time she knew only moderately well.

When the Radio Research Project was created at Princeton in 1937 (it moved to Columbia two years later and was eventually renamed the Bureau of Applied Social Research), Herzog was offered a research position. Originally, the Project had been funded by the Rockefeller Foundation and headed by Lazarsfeld and his co-directors Hadley Cantril of Princeton and Frank Stanton, research director at CBS. Research in these early years focused on aspects of communication, radio in particular. Herzog comments that the Bureau never ran out of research ideas worth investigating.

Herzog remembers a pioneer-like atmosphere of involvement and enthusiasm during the Bureau's early years (she left in 1943). Lazarsfeld had a good deal to do with the feeling that they were working on worthwhile projects. He helped each of the staff members on his or her specific projects and was instrumental in attracting interesting scholars from a variety of disciplines to contribute ideas and help with the various projects. (See Barton, 1982, for summaries of funding, personnel, and publications of the Bureau.) Some of them (e.g., Arnheim, Adorno) worked temporarily at the Bureau on their own projects. While Herzog was there, Robert Merton became director of the Bureau and conducted government research. Over 30 researchers contributed to the first three Bureau publications, *Radio and the Printed Page* (Lazarsfeld, 1940), *Radio Research 1941* (Lazarsfeld & Stanton, 1941), and *Radio Research 1942–43* (Lazarsfeld & Stanton, 1944).

While the researchers did not share their work, they all exchanged advice, calling on each other's specialties. For example, Hazel Gaudet handled statistical matters, and Ed Suchman was a particularly good organizer. Rose Kohn, a very competent junior secretary, was well liked for her quick wit. Herzog especially remembers Professor Sam Stouffer of Chicago, who became a close friend. Her strongest recollections are of colleagues whom she knew both professionally and socially, such as Rena Batos, Helen Kaufmann, Ilse Zeisel, and Hedy Ullmann.

Herzog continued the type of work she had done at the *Forschungsstelle* in Vienna; thus, she was called upon for "qualitative" pilot studies and for "applied research." (Like the *Forschungsstelle,* the Bureau received some of its funding from market research to supplement private and government grants.) One such research study was done for Alexis Somaripa, the creative head of the Fabric Division of E. I. Dupont de Nemours, who was interested in predicting trends in consumer fabric preferences and responses to the new synthetic fibers. So, Herzog conducted "wear tests." Herzog also worked on projects for various government agencies, among her projects, she pretested Office of War Information (OWI) pamphlets and later did some work on the film *This Is War.*

The Bureau also initiated an audience-centered approach to studying mass communication, focusing on the functions radio served for people, why people paid attention to certain programs, and the gratifications they derived from listening. Herzog contributed heavily to this line of inquiry. Her research strategy differed from the current "effects" model by pioneering a "gratifications" approach; specifically, she asked listeners how they used a popular quiz show and radio serials and what the programs meant to them (Herzog, 1940, 1941, 1944). Herzog also recalls with pleasure her contributions to Orson Welles' *The Invasion from Mars* (Cantril, Gaudet, & Herzog, 1940). The day after the CBS broadcast, she initiated qualitative interviews to find out why some listeners had been frightened. These early interviews were published in a memo to Frank Stanton and became the basis for the interview schedule for the larger study.

In 1943 Marion Harper, who was the head of copy research at the McCann-Erickson advertising agency, asked Herzog to join his department to initiate motivation research and direct the qualitative aspects of radio research on programs and commercials. Intrigued by the notion of putting the methodologies developed in the "Ivory Tower" setting to the tough test of performance in the competitive marketplace, she accepted the offer. She never regretted the move, although it meant a radical change from academic life.

The methodological challenges of her new position turned out to be as exciting as her responsibilities, which broadened quickly. Under Harper's presidency, McCann-Erickson had become one of the largest advertising agencies in the country and encompassed sales promotion and public relations. As director of research at the home office, Herzog worked on and applied various experimental tools such as the Lazarsfeld-Stanton Program Analyzer, to which McCann-Erickson had acquired exclusive commercial rights. Lazarsfeld had invented the device in Vienna to record listeners' emotional responses to music. Stanton later added technical improvements. The Analyzer was used at the Bureau in various research projects (e.g., Hollinquist & Suchman, 1944) and by the military (e.g., Hovland, Lumsdaine, & Sheffield, 1949). Herzog used it as a prelude to focus group interviews.

Later, Herzog used a pupil-dilation recorder, the "Eye Camera," developed by ecologist E. H. Hess of the University of Chicago, for research with visual materials. She also introduced and frequently used a projective approach, building on ideas developed in the Marienthal project. Respondents were asked, for example, to draw products, products in use, or brands, and to tell a story about the drawing. She also initiated the use of relatively easily administered personality tests, such as the Figure Drawing test (created by Karin Machover) to gain some insight into the types of people holding certain notions or attitudes. The basic concept of this approach, psychological environment, was stressed by Bühler and is now in general use. Herzog introduced this phenomenological notion into market research under the name of "Image."

When the agency's research operation was set up as a separate market and public relations research company, Herzog was named chairperson of Marplan, the new affiliate. Her duties expanded to include the organization and training of employees abroad. In 1959, for example, she spent a year in Germany, training and consulting with German clients.

After returning from abroad, Herzog began the last phase of her market research career. Interpublic, a set of companies put together by Harper, included a think-tank, the first of its kind in this field: Jack Tinker and Partners. The group was designed to work on major client problems of top management, such as new product introductions and major changes in marketing strategy. The group was small, consisting of four partners each with one assistant and a clerical staff. Herzog was the partner in charge of research. The group produced some very successful work and also received a good deal of attention in advertising work (for the Alka Seltzer commercials). Herzog found that work particularly rewarding because the partnership entailed the integration of research findings and marketing and creative implementation. She retired prematurely in 1970 to spend time with her second husband, Paul Massing, during his illness. Massing, a political scientist at Rutgers who had written on Hitler and anti-Semitism in Germany, was suffering from Parkinsonism, an incurable and progressive disease.

After her husband's death in Europe in 1979, Herzog decided to remain there. After trying to finish his book on the recent history of the village in which he was born and failing to do so because it was in too early a stage, she decided to return to some professional activities. It seemed natural to her to return to her early academic interests which had broadened over the years through her commercial research experience.

Herzog began with a series of lectures on U.S. television and television research at the University of Tübingen in Germany (*Institut für Empirische Kulturwissenschaft*, with Professor Bausinger). Later, she repeated these lectures at the University of Vienna (*Institut für Kommunikationswissenschaft*, with Professor Langenbucher). Herzog also directed several qualitative pilot studies, using the methodology she had perfected during her market research years.

The first pilot study centered on audience reactions to "Dallas" and "Denver Clan (Dynasty)," two U.S. programs that were popular worldwide. She was interested primarily in how the German viewers received by the U.S. programs (Massing, 1986, 1990). When the problem of hostility toward foreigners (*Ausländerfeindlichkeit*) became pressing in Austria, she completed a study with the Vienna Institute of Communications Research. More recently, Herzog has been working on problems of anti-Semitism (e.g., Massing, 1994). This role of communication in sociopolitical problems is her main research focus at this stage of her career.

HERZOG'S WORK AND ACHIEVEMENTS

Herzog's 60-year career has had three distinct phases: study of the gratifications of radio listeners, which she began in the Radio Research Bureau; study of the advertising audience as a market researcher in private industry; and study of the audience "decoding" of various media messages, begun after her retirement. The methodology she learned in Vienna, the in-depth interview, and the focus on motivation are consistent themes of her work.

Herzog's Bureau research is her best known and most widely cited work. Her early interviews regarding the *War of the Worlds* broadcast became the basis for the interview schedule for the larger project (Cantril, Gaudet, and Herzog, 1940). She is also credited with the initial analysis of the reality checks listeners made and with conducting the in-depth case studies reported in Chapter 8. (Lazarsfeld recognized her contribution to the project and wrote that he had originally hoped that Herzog would receive major credit for "her imaginative work on that study" [1969, p. 313]).

Herzog's research on radio serial listeners (1944), which built on early Bureau studies concerned with the effects of radio, is her best known work and has served as a major impetus to the uses and gratifications perspective. It continues to be widely cited and has been called a "milestone in mass communication research" (Lowery & DeFleur, 1995). Her analyses of data collected from four separate studies revealed the value in focusing on active audience members who selected media content consistent with their interests and abilities. Her work also made it clear that people derive a number of less obvious gratifications from the media.

Her radio research was a springboard for several subsequent qualitative and quantitative studies and research programs that focus on the uses and gratifications of other mass media. But Herzog herself notes three limitations of her work. First, it took an unsophisticated approach to the social origins of the needs the audience brought to the programs. Second, because the research was grounded in a functional approach, it was not critical of the programs, nor did it explore possible dysfunctions for the listeners or for society. Third, the research was so greatly oriented toward the diversity of audience uses (the major innovation of the project) that she failed to pay much attention to the constraints of the content. Herzog believes that this third limitation was the most serious and that studying audience "decoding" is a more productive research approach. Decoding involves the social, cultural, and personal notions brought to the "negotiation" with the text. This approach also holds that media texts do not necessarily constrain a predominant reading. Herzog's later study on the decoding of "Dallas" and "Denver Clan" among German viewers documents the readings in this specific non-U.S. sociocultural context (Massing, 1990).

After she joined McCann-Erickson in 1943, most of Herzog's work was client-sponsored and, therefore, not published. She did, however, publish a summary of radio developments and an analysis of letters to Voice of America written during those years (Herzog, 1946, 1952). While in industry, she chaired a group on motivation research for the Advertising Research Foundation. In 1986 she was selected as "Hall of Fame Honoree" of the Market Research Council.

INTEGRATION OF PERSONAL AND PROFESSIONAL LIFE

Herzog admits that she was unable to integrate her personal and professional life, focusing on one or the other separately. (The camaraderie and enthusiasm of the Bureau days, however, suggests that the lines may sometimes have merged.) Lazarsfeld's daughter, Lotte (Bailyn), joined the couple in New York only when she began grammar school. Real family life, according to Herzog, occurred mainly over the weekends and during long vacations in New Hampshire where Lotte learned to swim and ski. But Herzog feels that Lotte herself deserves the credit for her personal and professional achievements.

Herzog's second marriage, to Paul Massing in 1954, was childless. During the week, both spent most of their time working, with only an occasional time-out for some concerts or plays. Weekends became their time for social life and recreation. During these days the Massings—and their guests—worked hard renovating a large but rundown farm in the Jersey hills until it was in "beautiful shape." During the evenings, they conversed leisurely around a big open fireplace. The farm had to be sold when Massing's illness progressed, and they spent his few remaining years traveling and visiting their families in Germany and Austria.

Since Massing's death, Herzog has directed funded pilot studies conducted by local interviewers whom she herself trains. This gives her the freedom to do work that interests her. At the same time, she is able to enjoy the mountains of Tirol where she lives near her sister's large family. She derives a good deal of satisfaction looking back at a professional career that has been rich in change and challenges, and she expects to continue her professional work as long as her health permits.

NOTE

I have relied heavily on material Dr. Herzog graciously provided about her life. I am grateful for her help with this project. I have also drawn background material about the days of the *Wirtschaftspsychologische Forschungsstelle* and the Radio Research Project from Lazarsfeld (1969), Rogers (1994), and Sills (1987).

REFERENCES

Barton, A. H. (1982). Paul Lazarsfeld and the invention of the University Institute for Applied Social Research. In B. Holzner & J. Nehnevajsa (eds.), *Organizing for social research.* (pp. 17–83). Cambridge, Mass.: Schenkman.

Cantril, H., Gaudet, H., & Herzog, H. (1940). *The invasion from Mars: A study in the psychology of panic.* Princeton, N.J.: Princeton University Press.

Herzog, H. (1940). Professor Quiz: A gratification study. In P. F. Lazarsfeld (ed.), *Radio and the printed page.* (pp. 64–93). New York: Duell, Sloan & Pearce.

Herzog, H. (1941). On borrowed experience: An analysis of listening to daytime sketches. *Studies in Philosophy and Social Science,* 9, 65–95.

Herzog, H. (1944). What do we really know about daytime serial listeners? In P. F. Lazarsfeld & F. N. Stanton (eds.), *Radio research 1942–1943.* (pp. 3–33). New York: Duell, Sloan & Pearce.

Herzog, H. (1946). Radio—The first post-war year. *Public Opinion Quarter,* 10, 297–313.

Herzog, H. (1952). Listener mail to the Voice of America. *Public Opinion Quarterly,* 16, 607–611.

Hollinquist, T., & Suchman, E. A. (1944). Listening to the listener: Experiments with the Lazarsfeld-Stanton Program Analyzer. In P. F. Lazarsfeld & F. N. Stanton (eds.), *Radio research 1942–1943*. (pp. 265–334). New York: Duell, Sloan & Pearce.

Hovland, C. I., Lumsdaine, A. A., & Sheffield, F. D. (1949). *Experiments on mass communication*. Princeton, N.J.: Princeton University Press.

Jahoda, M., Lazarsfeld, P. F., & Ziesel, H. (1933/1971). *Marienthal: The sociography of an unemployed community*. Chicago: Aldine-Atherton. (First published as *Die arbeitslosen von Marienthal: Ein soziographischer*. Leipzig: Hirzl.)

Lazarsfeld, P. F. (1935). The art of asking why. *National Market Review*, 1, 32–43.

Lazarsfeld, P. F. (ed.). (1940). *Radio and the printed page*. New York: Duell, Sloan & Pearce.

Lazarsfeld, P. F. (1969). An episode in the history of social research: A memoir. In D. Fleming & B. Bailyn (eds.), *The intellectual migration: Europe and America, 1930–1960*. (pp. 270–337). Cambridge, Mass.: Harvard University Press.

Lazarsfeld, P. F. & Stanton, F. N. (eds.). (1941). *Radio research, 1941*. New York: Duell, Sloan, & Pearce.

Lazarsfeld, P. F., & Stanton, F. N. (eds.). (1944). *Radio research 1942–1943*. New York: Duell, Sloan & Pearce.

Lowery, S. A., & DeFleur, M. E. (1995). *Milestones in mass communication research*. 3rd ed. White Plains, N.Y.: Longman.

Lynd, R. S., & Lynd, H. M. (1929). *Middletown: A study in American culture*. Princeton, N.J.: Princeton University Press.

Massing, H. H. (1986, November/December). Decoding "Dallas." *Society*, 74–77.

Massing, H. H. (1990). Der stich ins böse: Dallas un Denver Clan, garantiert anders als der Alltag. *Medien Journal, Öst. Ges. Komm. Fragen*.

Massing, H. H. (1994). On communicative aspects of antisemitism. (A pilot study in Austria). *Acta, SISCA*. Jerusalem: Hebrew University of Jerusalem.

Rogers, E. M. (1994). *History of communication study: A biographical approach*. New York: Free Press.

Sills, D. L. (1987). Paul Lazarsfeld: 1901–1976. In National Academy of Sciences (ed.), *Biographical memoirs*. Vol. 56. (pp. 251–282). Washington, D.C.: National Academy Press.

MARGUERITE HIGGINS
(1920–1966)

Jessica Staples

Marguerite Higgins' career was dedicated to covering world crises (Higgins, 1955). Her calling in life was to be a newspaper reporter, a profession for which she would be highly acknowledged. She was instrumental in the 1945 liberation of the Nazi concentration camp at Dachau, and her coverage of the Korean War led to her being the first woman to receive a Pulitzer Prize for foreign correspondence.

Through her hard work Higgins overcame what she believed to be the biggest disadvantage of being a foreign correspondent: being both young and a woman (Higgins, 1955). Her contributions have helped pave the way for all women reporters.

FAMILY BACKGROUND AND EDUCATION

Marguerite Higgins was born on September 3, 1920, in Hong Kong, China. She was the only child of Lawrence Daniel Higgins, an Irish American, and Marguerite de Godard, a Frenchwoman. Most of her childhood was spent in Oakland, California, after the family moved there in 1923.

In one of her books, *News Is a Singular Thing* (1955), Higgins recalls her father's fondness for war. He participated in both world wars as an aviator. Her mother lived for crisis, always making the family the talk of the neighborhood (Higgins, 1955).

Higgins' father worked as a freight manager of a steamship company while her mother taught French lessons to earn extra money, some of which paid for Marguerite's education at the Anna Head School in Berkeley, California. After enrolling, she received an academic scholarship. As she says, "It was at Anna

Head's that getting good marks, excelling at sports, and generally justifying my free education became a real business'' (p. 39).

Higgins attended the University of California at Berkeley where she graduated cum laude with a degree in French. In 1941 she moved throughout the West, Midwest, and finally reached New York. While in New York, she received her M.S. in journalism at Columbia University.

In 1942 Higgins married her first husband, Stanley Moore; their relationship ended in divorce six years later. Her second husband was Lieutenant General William E. Hall who, at the time, was the director for U.S. intelligence in Berlin. In 1953 the couple had their first child, Sharon Lee, a premature baby girl who lived only five days. In 1955 Higgins and her husband moved to Washington D.C. It is here that she had two children, Lawrence O'Higgins born in 1958 and Linda Marguerite born in 1959.

CAREER DEVELOPMENT, MAJOR CONTRIBUTIONS, AND ACHIEVEMENTS

Higgins' first taste for reporting came when she still lived in California. While there she worked on the *Tahoe Tattler,* the *Daily Californian,* and the *Vallejo Times-Herald.* After graduating, she searched for a job throughout the West and Midwest, and to her dismay she found that having a college education was a disadvantage. But even when she didn't mention her degree to potential employers, she still could not find a newspaper that would hire her (Higgins, 1955). New York was her last chance because, as she writes, "On graduation from the University of California I had given myself just one year in which to land a newspaper job'' (p. 16).

Her first effort to get a job in New York landed her in the newsroom of the *New York Herald Tribune.* Her contact was with L. L. Engelking, the city editor of the paper, who told her to come back in a month. It was not until a classmate at Columbia University quit his job as the Columbia University correspondent of the *Herald Tribune* that she got her chance.

In 1944 Higgins received her first overseas assignment, at the *Herald Tribune*'s London office, but did not obtain the position until she went directly to the publisher with her request. Her next position landed her in France, and in 1945 she was transferred to Berlin as the paper's bureau chief. It was here that she made many a front page of the newspaper with articles covering the capture of Munich and Berchtesgaden and the release of inmates at Dachau and Buchenwald.

In 1950 Higgins moved to Tokyo, becoming the Far East Bureau chief, and then to Korea to cover the Korean conflict. While there Lieutenant General Walton H. Walker, who was convinced that women did not belong in a war setting, ordered all women, including Higgins, transferred to Tokyo. A determined Higgins confronted General Douglas MacArthur to request that she be allowed back to Korea. Her petition was granted, and she returned to do what she did best, reporting on the war. In 1963 Higgins left the *Herald Tribune* for *Newsday*. During this time she covered many international meetings and presidential trips. In addition, she wrote a thrice weekly column that was syndicated in 92 other newspapers. She kept up this pace until the week before she died.

Higgins interviewed some of the most important figures of her time, including Taiwan's Madame Chiang Kai-Shek, Soviet Premier Nikita Khrushchev, Generalissimo Francisco Franco of Spain, and Shah Reza Pahlavi of Iran. She also covered the Nuremberg war trials, the treason trial of Marshal Henri Pétain, and the Berlin Blockade.

She received awards early in her career, notably the 1951 Woman of the Year Award from the Associated Press, the Overseas Press Club's George Polk Memorial, the New York Newspaper Women's Club Award, the Marine Corps Reserve Officer Award, the Veterans of Foreign Wars Gold Metal, the Distinguished Service Award from the National Federation of Business and Professional Woman, the Long Island University Polk Award, and the Theta Sigma Phi Award.

While working for the *Tribune,* Higgins wrote for *Reader's Digest, Mademoiselle,* and numerous other magazines. She penned a juvenile book named *Jessie Benton Tremont* and many real-world books including *War in Korea: Report of a Woman Combat Respondent* (1951), *News Is a Singular Thing* (1955), *Red Plush and Black Bread* (1955) about her time in Russia, *Overtime in Heaven: Adventures in the Foreign Service* (1964) with fellow reporter Peter Lisagor, and *Our Vietnam Nightmare* (1965).

Sadly, her career was cut short when, during a tour of Vietnam, India, and Pakistan, she contracted a tropical infection, Leishmaniasis, from a sand fly bite. On January 3, 1966, she died of complications of the disease in a Washington, D.C., hospital. In her 45 years, Marguerite Higgins accomplished many of the things people only dream about. Her hard work, dedication, and passion for reporting the news are reflected in every one of her writings.

REFERENCES

Downs, R. B., & Downs, J. B. (1991). *Journalists of the United States: Biographical sketches of print and broadcast news shapers from the late 17th century to present.* Jefferson, N.C.: McFarland & Co. Publishers.

Findling, J. E. (1989). *Dictionary of American diplomatic history.* 2nd ed., Westport, Conn.: Greenwood Press.

Higgins, M. (1955). *News is a singular thing.* Garden City, N.Y.: Doubleday & Co.

Marzolf, M. (1977). *Up from the footnote.* New York: Hasting House Publishers.

McKerns, J. P. (1989). *Biographical dictionary of American journalism.* Westport, Conn.: Greenwood Press.

Schilpp, M. G., & Murphy, S. M. (1983). *Great women of the press.* Carbondale: Southern Illinois University Press.

Sicherman, B., Green, C. H., Kantrov, I., & Walker, H. (eds.). (1980). Notable American

women, the modern period: A biographical dictionary. Cambridge, Mass. and London, England: Belknap Press of Harvard University Press.
Sloane, Wm. D., Hedgepeth, J. K., Place, P. C., & Stoker, K. (1992). *The great reporters: An anthology of news writing at its best.* Newport, Ala.: Vision Press.

HILDE HIMMELWEIT
(1918–1989)

Scott E. Caplan

Throughout her nearly 40 years in academics, Hilde Himmelweit achieved international recognition for her work in social psychology and communication research. She is best remembered for her ground-breaking work on the effects of television during the 1950s which culminated in her book *Television and the Child* (1958, with Oppenheim & Vince). With the success of this work, Dr. Himmelweit went on to become one of the most respected scholars of communication and psychology.

Born in Berlin on February 20, 1918, Hilde Himmelweit came from a long line of scholars and academics. In 1859 her great-grandfather, Robert Remack, a celebrated neurologist, was the first Jew to be allowed to become a professor in Prussia. In addition, several other of her close relatives held positions at Berlin University (one of whom was murdered in a Nazi concentration camp). In an effort to escape the oppression of Nazi Germany, Hilde Himmelweit was sent to school in England in 1939.

In 1940 she married Fred Himmelweit, with whom she eventually had her daughter, Susan. By 1942 Hilde Himmelweit had completed two Master's degrees in modern languages (1940) and psychology (1942) at Cambridge. Shortly thereafter, she was awarded a doctorate in psychology from London University (1945). In a brief break from academics, she took a position as a clinical and educational psychologist at the Maudsley Hospital in England from 1945 to 1948.

In a return to academics, Dr. Himmelweit joined the London School of Economics in 1949 and became a reader in social psychology in 1954. Eventually, in 1964, she became a professor of social psychology. Her early research focused on a variety of areas concerning children, adolescents, and learning and achievement. Several of her early publications examined student selection, intelligence, student achievement, social class differentials, the outlooks of adolescents, and the attitudes of teachers.

Although much of her early work focused on psychology, her research into television and children is of particular interest to communication scholars. The work that brought her the most recognition was her research into the still new medium of television. As director of the Nuffield Foundation Television Enquiry from 1954 to 1958, Professor Himmelweit conducted one of the most extensive studies that had ever been carried out into the impact of television on children. Over a four-year period, she and her associates interviewed over 4,000 children in five different cities, along with their parents and teachers. The results of this study were published in what was to become her best known work, *Television and the Child* (1958, with Oppenheim & Vince).

This project attempted to provide a comprehensive evaluation of television's impact on all aspects of children's lives and families. Included in the study were attempts to measure how children were actually using the new medium. For example, she investigated the amount of television that children viewed, factors that reduced their interest in television, and whether or not children watched many programs designed for adults. In addition, this project focused on children's tastes for mass media, including television. Himmelweit explored whether or not children's tastes in television reflected their tastes in other media, how taste is affected by access to more than one television channel, and what actually constituted television's appeal for children.

With regard to these research topics, Himmelweit found evidence suggesting that children spent more time watching television than on any other leisure activity. In terms of factors influencing viewing habits, the single most important factor was intelligence; the higher a child's intelligence, the less television he or she watched. In addition, she found that most children regularly watched programs designed for adults. In fact, three-quarters of children voted adult programs as being their favorites. Finally, her results suggested that television is so appealing to children because of its easy availability and value as a "time filler" (Himmelweit, Oppenheim, & Vince, 1958, p. 15).

A second major focus of the Nuffield Foundation Television Enquiry dealt with the effects of television on children's values, anxieties, and education. For example, the study explored what views of life and of the adult world television offers children, to what extent children's outlooks are influenced by what they see on television, how television frightens children, whether or not television improves children's knowledge and school work, and whether or not children's lives are dominated by television.

With regard to these research areas, Himmelweit and her associates found that television had a "solid and consistent" impact on children's lives (Himmelweit, Oppenheim, & Vince, 1958, p. 245). Overall, their results showed that television presented children with an adult view of the world—more specifically, depictions of violence—for which they may not have been ready.

Himmelweit came to believe that it was the duty of parents and teachers to protect children from the "risks" of television. She believed that adults were to a large extent responsible for directing children toward quality programming. She argued that children needed to be supervised in their programming choices and encouraged to make the distinction between the make-believe world of television and reality.

With the publication of *Television and the Child* in 1958, Hilde Himmelweit became internationally recognized as one of the most important scholars to study the still new medium. Her expertise was sought by numerous committees and organizations: she was a research consultant for the Israeli Instructional Television Trust (1965–1968) and director of the Communication and Attitude Change Research Unit at the London School of Economics (1970–1974). In addition, she was awarded fellowships from the Center for Advanced Study in Behavioral Sciences at Stanford (1967 and 1983), the Van Leer Foundation in Jerusalem (1978–1979), and the Gannet Center for Media Studies at Columbia University (1987).

Aside from all of her awards, Hilde Himmelweit's academic career was filled with numerous professional appointments. She was instrumental in planning the Open University (1968–1969) and served as both a member and chair of the Academic Advisory Committee (1969–1983). Her professional appointments also reflected her stature in the area of television research. From 1973 to 1979 Himmelweit was a member of the Committee on Television and Social Behavior of the United States Social Science Research Council. At the same time, she served as a trustee of the International Institute of Communications and as a member of the Annan Committee on the Future of Broadcasting. In addition, in the late 1980s, she served as president of the International Television Studies Conference and as a member of the Advisory Committee of the Center for Communication and Information Studies.

Himmelweit was also active in both psychology and communication. She was awarded several visiting professorships and participated as a member of the editorial boards of several scholarly journals. Aside from teaching psychology at the London School of Economics, she was a visiting professor in the Department of Psychology at the University of California, Berkeley, in 1959. She also taught communication as a visiting professor in the Communication Department at both the Hebrew University in Jerusalem (1974) and Stanford University in California (1975). She served as a member of the editorial boards for several important journals, including the *Journal of Communication*; *European Journal of Communication*; *Media, Culture, and Society*; and *Applied Social Psychology Annual*.

Although a large portion of her career was devoted to television and mass media research, Hilde Himmelweit also began to explore voting and decision making in elections. Toward the end of her career, she published two more books, *How Voters Decide* (1981, with Humphreys, Jaeger, & Katz), and a revised and updated edition of *How Voters Decide* in 1985.

When she announced her retirement from the London School of Economics in 1983, Dr. Himmelweit was named emeritus professor of social psychology at the University of London. Shortly afterward, she began a battle with cancer which eventually took her life on March 15, 1989. During this time, her colleague Dr. George Gaskell notes that she worked on the manuscript of her final book almost to the day she died. This last book, *Societal Psychology* (1990, with Gaskell), was published posthumously.

REFERENCES

Himmelweit, H. T., & Gaskell, G. (eds.). (1990). *Societal psychology.* Newbury Park, Calif.: Sage Publications.

Himmelweit, H. T., Humphreys, P., Jaeger, M. J., & Katz, M. (1981). *How voters decide.* New York: Academic Press.

Himmelweit, H. T., Humphreys, P., Jaeger, M. J., & Katz, M. (1985). *How voters decide.* Revised and updated. New York: Academic Press.

Himmelweit, H. T., Oppenhiem, A. N., & Vince, P. (1958). *Television and the child.* New York: Oxford University Press.

ALETHA C. HUSTON
(1939–   )

John P. Murray

The tapestry of Aletha Huston's life is woven with threads pulled from personal and professional experiences of her early childhood in Illinois; her later childhood, youth, and undergraduate work in California; her graduate study in Minnesota; and professional appointments in New York, Pennsylvania, and Kansas. The sequential ''geography'' of these experiences is mentioned here because these locales are not independent of the intellectual and social influences that have shaped Huston's contribution to the field of communication. As she moved through these particular points on a map, at particular points in time, she encountered several individuals who have had a lasting influence on her career and daily life.

FAMILY BACKGROUND

Aletha was an only child, born in Urbana, Illinois, to Alfred D. and Hazel F. Huston, on May 16, 1939. Her father was an attorney in Urbana and a strong New Deal Democrat who was twice a candidate for Congress. Unfortunately, he was killed in World War II when she was about 5 years old. Her mother was a teacher, school psychologist, and university professor in special education. Hazel Huston never remarried following the death of Alfred, on September 24, 1944. Aletha and her mother moved to California when Aletha was about 8 years old, and her mother took a position as a school psychologist in the Long Beach public schools. Aletha recalls that her mother served as an important role model for her during her youth because she was a very competent single parent and an effective professional woman.

Aletha is married to John C. Wright, a colleague and co-author of many publications, whom she initially met in the late 1950s when she was an undergraduate at Stanford and he was a graduate teaching assistant. Previously, she was married to Harry H. Stein, whom she married in 1961 while they were both graduate students at the University of Minnesota. They have one child, Serena Lynne Stein, who was born in 1972. She divorced Harry Stein in 1975, when Serena was about 3, and Aletha was a faculty member at Penn State. In 1976 she became a professor at the University of Kansas and married John Wright. In this marriage, she has four stepchildren (Beth, Jennifer, Melanie, and Kennedy Wright) and four grandchildren.

EDUCATION

Aletha entered Stanford University in 1956. In her sophomore year, she was assigned to Albert Bandura, a young faculty member who was interested in studying the development of imitation in young children. Bandura urged Aletha to apply for admission to the Psychology Honors program and develop an honors thesis topic. Aletha was accepted in the honors program and searched for a thesis topic until she took an honors seminar offered by a graduate teaching assistant, John Wright. In the course of the seminar, they reviewed research on "incidental" imitation, that is, learning peripheral components in modeled behavior, and eventually Aletha worked with Bandura on his proposal for a laboratory study of "nurturance" in the imitation of modeled behavior. The resulting project became one of Bandura's first laboratory studies in imitation (Bandura & Huston, 1961) and launched Aletha Huston's career interest in this area.

During the summer of 1960, following Huston's graduation from Stanford and before she was to start graduate studies at the University of Minnesota, Bandura asked her to stay at Stanford to work as an assistant on a followup study to their initial report. This followup was to focus on imitation and aggression, but Aletha was still interested in the issues of nurturance and incidental learning and felt the need to move on to Minnesota. Hence, the job as an assistant was offered to Dorothea and Sheila Ross, and they became identified with Bandura's first studies of TV violence (Bandura, Ross, & Ross, 1961, 1963).

Aletha enrolled in the psychology program at the University of Minnesota, intending to specialize in the clinical child psychology program. However, she encountered John Wright, the former graduate teaching assistant at Stanford, who was now a new faculty member in the Institute of Child Development at Minnesota, and continued her interest in imitation but not necessarily television (e.g., Stein & Wright, 1964). At this point, her research focused on the effects of sex-typing on children's achievement motivation, and that set the stage for a series of studies in the mid- to late-1960s (e.g., Stein, 1969).

CAREER AND IMPACT

Following the completion of her doctoral program, with a major in psychology and a minor in child development at the University of Minnesota, Huston accepted an appointment as an assistant professor in the Department of Child Development and Family Relationships at Cornell University. During her tenure at Cornell from 1965 to 1968, she continued her work on sex-typing in an attempt to move beyond the issues of mere identification with the parent as the basis for sex-role behavior and gender identity. She began work on children's concepts of sex roles and the ways in which children perceive these roles as differentially available to boys and girls. The work on sex-typing was greatly influenced by Virginia Crandall and her colleagues at the Fels Institute in Yellow Springs, Ohio, especially the work on achievement motivation and gender as it was being studied in the Fels longitudinal investigation of children and adults. During this period, Huston was joined by Lynette Friedrich, a new Ph.D., working on a research project on women's achievement, who shared Aletha's interest in sex-typing and imitation. In 1967 Friedrich would move from Cornell to Penn State as an assistant professor where she would alert Aletha and her husband, Harry Stein, about an opening in the History Department for Harry and a position in the Department of Individual and Family Studies for Aletha. The Steins moved to Penn State in 1968.

Aletha remained at Penn State from 1968 to 1976 serving as assistant (1968–1971), associate (1971–1975), and professor (1975–1976). It was during this period at Penn State that Aletha's interests in television and children emerged in full flower from the earlier interests in imitation and her work with Albert Bandura as an undergraduate student at Stanford. In 1969 a new government study of television violence was announced, the Surgeon General's Scientific Advisory Committee on Television and Social Behavior at the National Institute of Mental Health (NIMH). This three-year study of the impact of TV violence on children was just getting underway, and the Surgeon General's Committee (a 12-member panel of experts appointed by the surgeon general to review the research evidence) was asked to suggest the names of researchers who could be contacted about their current and proposed research. One of the Committee members, Alberta E. Siegel, who was a professor at Stanford University, mentioned that one of her former students, Lynette Friedrich, and a former student of Albert Bandura, Aletha Huston-Stein, had just moved to Penn State and were developing a research program on children and social learning. (Alberta Siegel and her late husband, Sidney Siegel—of nonparametric statistics fame—had been faculty members and had kept in contact with the Penn State community.)

In my role as research coordinator for the surgeon general's program, I called both Aletha Huston-Stein and Lynette Friedrich to arrange a visit to Penn State to discuss their current research and possible future directions. In particular, the Committee was interested in research that would evaluate the impact of TV violence in a naturalistic setting, using more realistic representations of television programming than had heretofore been employed in experimental studies. The meeting proved fruitful as Aletha and Lynette sketched out the rudimentary design of a naturalistic study while we sat in an observation room watching preschool children in the laboratory nursery school at Penn State. Further discussions helped to elaborate the design of what was to become a "classic" study of TV violence and preschoolers. The team of Huston-Stein and Friedrich was invited to submit a proposal to the surgeon general's program for competitive peer review by NIMH. The proposal to study the impact of a diet of Batman and Superman cartoons versus "Mister Rogers' Neighborhood" on the aggressive and prosocial behavior of 100 preschool children was approved by NIMH, and the study began in the summer of 1970. The results of that study were published in the final report of the Surgeon General's Committee (Stein & Friedrich, 1972) and elaborated in a Monograph of the Society for Research in Child Development (Friedrich & Stein, 1973).

Looking back on those years, and the vast volume of research on the issue of television violence, Aletha summarized her views on the research question: "There is ample evidence to suggest a 'probable cause' relationship of television violence to children's aggressive behavior. The shoe is on the other foot for the skeptics to prove that TV violence does *not* cause aggressive behavior" (Huston, personal communication/interview, June 1994). However, Aletha Huston and her colleagues moved far beyond the issue of television violence—and even beyond television—in the ensuing years. The surgeon general's study included a comparison of violent cartoons with the impact of Mister Rogers and found that, indeed, youngsters who viewed Mister Rogers displayed more "prosocial" behavior (e.g., sharing toys, helping the teacher, playing cooperatively, and expressing concern about their classmates' feelings and moods), while those who watched the Batman and Superman cartoons were more active and engaged in more aggressive activities. This research led to another set of studies (see Friedrich & Stein, 1975; Friedrich-Cofer, Huston-Stein, Kipnis, Susman, & Clewett, 1979) on prosocial or helping behavior. In like manner, these studies raised questions about the nature of the transmission of these rather complex issues that Mister Rogers and Sesame Street address, and this led to an ambitious program of research on the "noncontent" features of television programming.

And so, a new research path opened in the mid-1970s but one that was rooted in the previous paths with their origins traceable from Stanford and Albert Bandura, to Minnesota and John Wright, to Cornell and Virginia Crandall, to Penn State and Lynette Friedrich/Alberta Siegel/Albert Bandura/the Surgeon General, and now to the University of Kansas and John Wright and the Kansas students and colleagues. Throughout the period from 1961, including the Bandura/Huston article on incidental learning and identification and the Stein/Friedrich work on aggression and prosocial behavior, there were recurring excursions into the study of the transmission of complex behaviors, attitudes, and values through live or symbolic models. These inquiries included reviews and studies on the socialization of achievement orientation in females (Stein & Bailey, 1973), the effects of maternal employment on the sex-typed attributes of college females (Stein, 1973), and analysis of sex-role cues in children's TV commercials (Welch, Huston-Stein, Wright, & Plehal, 1979). Now, the stage was set to bring it all home in a new set of studies on the impact of form versus content in children's television and some broad-ranging inquiries undertaken by Aletha Huston, John Wright, and their students and colleagues at the University of Kansas.

The move to Kansas in 1976 included not only a professional move but also a personal reorientation. Aletha left Penn State to become a professor in the departments of Psychology and Human Development and Family Life at the University of Kansas. In addition, she married John Wright, already a professor at Kansas. Several circles were closing now, and the intellectual amalgam at Kansas led to the establishment of a new research center and a new line of inquiry. The research center, in which Aletha Huston and John Wright are the co-directors, is the Center for Research on the Influence of Television on Children, or CRITC, the productivity of the center and its staff has been substantial. Since the founding in 1978, CRITC and Aletha have obtained substantial grants from the Spencer Foundation, the Federal Trade Commission, the National Institute of Mental Health, the National Institute of Child Health and Human Development, the Markle Foundation, and the Children's Television Workshop. The publications that have emerged from this collaborative venture have included studies of the "formal features" of television (Fitch, Huston, & Wright, 1993; Huston, 1994; Huston-Stein & Wright, 1979; Huston, Wright, Wartella, Rice, Watkins, Campbell, & Potts, 1981; Wright & Huston, 1984); nutritional information and commercials (Ross, Campbell, Huston-Stein, & Wright, 1981); attention and comprehension of television messages (Calvert, Huston, Watkins, & Wright, 1982; Huston, Greer, Wright, Welch, & Ross, 1984; Potts, Huston, & Wright, 1986); along with studies of gender issues (Alvarez, Huston, Wright, & Kerkman, 1988; Huston, 1987); and perceptions of television reality (Wright, Huston, Reitz, & Piemyat, 1994).

Despite the focus of CRITC on children and television, Aletha Huston has maintained a continuing interest in related issues concerning gender and socialization and broad policy issues relating to the well-being of children and families (see Huston, 1991; Huston, Donnerstein, Fairchild, Feshbach, et al., 1992). Aletha has remained true to an integrated school of intellectual inquiry that spans almost four decades. Her accomplishments are many and her legacy is great. There is a coherence and a completeness in her life that makes the reader sense a clear purpose in this intellectual odyssey. The "past is prologue" is a commonplace observation in studies of human development, and Aletha Huston's past has been prologue for her current accomplishments and will continue to foreshadow achievements in the distant future.

NOTE

Unless otherwise referenced, personal material and reflections are derived from an interview conducted with Aletha Huston on June 3, 1994.

REFERENCES

Alvarez, M., Huston, A. C., Wright, J. C., & Kerkman, D. (1988). Gender differences in visual attention to television form and content. *Journal of Applied Development Psychology,* 9, 459–475.

Bandura, A., & Huston, A. C. (1961). Identification as a process of incidental learning. *Journal of Abnormal and Social Psychology* 63, 311–318.

Bandura, A., Ross, D., & Ross, S. A. (1961). Transmission of aggression through imitation of aggressive models. *Journal of Abnormal and Social Psychology,* 63, 575–582.

Bandura, A., Ross, D., & Ross, S. A. (1963). Imitation of film-mediated aggressive models. *Journal of Abnormal and Social Psychology,* 66(1), 2–11.

Calvert, S. L., Huston, A. C., Watkins, B. A., & Wright, J. C. (1982). The effects of selective attention to television form on children's comprehension of content. *Child Development,* 53, 601–610.

Calvert, S. L., Huston, A. C., & Wright, J. C. (1987). Effects of visual and verbal televised preplays on children's attention and comprehension. *Journal of Applied Developmental Psychology,* 8, 329–342.

Fitch, M., Huston, A. C., & Wright, J. C. (1993). The forms of television and the process of learning from television. In G. Berry & J. K. Asamen (eds.), *Children and television in a changing socio-cultural world.* (pp. 38–52). Newbury Park, Calif.: Sage.

Friedrich, L. K., & Stein, A. H. (1973). Aggressive and prosocial television programs and the natural behavior of preschool children. *Monographs of the Society for Research in Child Development,* 38(4), Serial No. 151.

Friedrich, L. K., & Stein, A. H. (1975). Prosocial television and young children's behavior: The effect of verbal labeling and role playing training. *Child Development,* 46, 27–38.

Friedrich-Cofer, L. K., Huston-Stein, A., Kipnis, D. M., Susman, E. J., & Clewett, A. S. (1979). Environmental enhancement of prosocial television content: Effects on interpersonal behavior, imaginative play, and self-regulation in a natural setting. *Developmental Psychology,* 15, 637–646.

Greer, D., Pott, R., Wright, J. C., & Huston-Stein, A. (1982). The effects of television commercial form and commercial placement on children's attention and social behavior. *Child Development,* 53, 611–619.

Huston, A. C. (1987). Gender, socialization, and the transmission of culture. In S. Brehm (ed.), *Seeing female: Social roles and personal lives.* (pp. 7–19). Westport, Conn.: Greenwood Press.

Huston, A. C. (1994). Educating children with television: The forms of the medium. In D. Zillmann, J. Bryant, & A. C. Huston (eds.), *Media, family, and children: Social scientific, psychodynamic, and clinical perspectives.* Hillsdale, N.J.: Erlbaum.

Huston, A. C., & Alvarez, M. M. (1990). The socialization context of gender role development in early adolescence. In R. Montemayor (ed.), *Transitions form childhood to adolescence.* Vol. 1. (pp. 156–179). Newbury Park, Calif.: Sage.

Huston, A. C., Donnerstein, E., Fairchild, H., Feshbach, N. D., Katz, P. A., Murray, J. P., Rubinstein, E. A., Wilcox, B. L., & Zuckerman, D. (1992). *Big world, small screen: The role of television in American society.* Lincoln: University of Nebraska Press.

Huston, A. C., Greer, D., Wright, J. C., Welch, R., & Ross, R. (1984). Children's comprehension of television forms with masculine and feminine connotations. *Developmental Psychology*, 20, 707–716.

Huston, A. C., & Wright, J. C. (1983). Children's processing of television: The informative functions of formal features. In J. Bryant & D. R. Anderson (eds.), *Children's understanding of television: Research on attention and comprehension.* (pp. 37–68). New York: Academic Press.

Huston, A. C., Wright, J. C., Wartella, E., Rice, M. L., Watkins, B. A., Campbell, T., & Potts, R. (1981). Communicating more than content: Formal features of children's television programs. *Journal of Communication,* 31 (3), 32–48.

Huston-Stein, A., Friedrich-Cofer, L. K., & Susman, E. J. (1977). The relation of classroom structure to social behavior, imaginative play, and self regulation of economically disadvantaged children. *Child Development,* 48, 908–916.

Huston-Stein, A., & Welch, R. L. (1979). Sex role development and the adolescent. In J. Adams (ed.), *Understanding adolescence.* 4th ed. Boston: Allyn & Bacon.

Huston-Stein, A., & Wright, J. C. (1979). Children and television: Effects of the medium, its content and its form. *Journal of Research and Development in Education,* 13, 20–31.

Murray, J. P. (1983). Mickey Mouse: A brief psychohistory. *Television & Children,* 6 (3), 30–34.

Potts, C. R., Huston, A. C., & Wright, J. C. (1986). Effects of television form and violent content on children's attention and social behavior. *Journal of Experimental Child Psychology,* 41, 1–17.

Rice, M. L., Huston, A. C., Truglio, R. T., & Wright, J. C. (1990). Words from *Sesame Street:* Learning vocabulary while viewing. *Developmental Psychology,* 26, 421–428.

Rice, M. L., Huston, A. C., & Wright, J. C. (1982). The forms and codes of television: Effects on children's attention, comprehension, and social behavior. In D. Pearl, L. Bouthilet, & J. B. Lazar (eds.), *Television and behavior:* Vol. 2. *Ten years of scientific progress and implications for the 80s.* (pp. 24–38). Washington, D.C.: Government Printing Office.

Ross, R. P., Campbell, T., Huston-Stein, A., & Wright, J. C. (1981). Nutritional misinformation of children: A developmental and experimental analysis of the effects of televised food commercials. *Journal of Applied Developmental Psychology,* 1, 329–345.

Stein, A. H. (1969). The influence of social reinforcement on the achievement behavior of fourth-grade boys and girls. *Child Development,* 40, 727–736.

Stein, A. H. (1973). The effects of maternal employment and educational attainment on the sex-typed attributes of college females. *Social Behavior and Personality,* 1, 111–114.

Stein, A. H., & Bailey, M. M. (1973). The socialization of achievement orientation in females. *Psychological Bulletin,* 80, 345–366.

Stein, A. H., & Friedrich, L. K. (1972). Television content and young children's behavior. In J. P. Murray, E. A. Rubinstein, & G. A. Comstock (eds.), *Television and social behavior.* Vol. 2. *Television and social learning.* Washington, D.C.: Government Printing Office.

Stein, A. H., & Wright, J. C. (1964). Imitative learning under conditions of nurturance and nurturance withdrawal. *Child Development,* 35, 927–938.

Welch, R. L., Huston-Stein, S., Wright, J. C., & Plehal, R. (1979). Subtle sex-role cues in children's commercials. *Journal of Communication,* 29, 202–209.

Wright, J. C., & Huston, A. C. (1984). The potentials of television for young viewers. In J. P. Murray & G. Salomon (eds.), *The future of children's television: Results of the Markle Foundation/Boys Town Conference.* (pp. 65–80). Boys Town, Nebr.: Boys Town.

Wright, J. C., Huston, A. C., Reitz, A. L., & Piemyat, S. (1994). Children's perceptions of television reality: Determinants and developmental differences. *Developmental Psychology,* 30, 229–239.

KATHLEEN HALL JAMIESON
(1946–   )

David S. Birdsell

Since publication of the first edition of *Packaging the Presidency* in 1984, Kathleen Hall Jamieson has been widely acknowledged as one of the nation's leading authorities on political communication. A rhetorical scholar by training, Jamieson has contributed to media studies, political history, and contemporary feminist thought. The quality, consistency, and sheer volume of her work has earned a wide, interdisciplinary audience. She finds frequent voice in the media as a source for journalists working on campaign communication and as a guest on television news programs. She has testified before the Congress on communication issues and advises organizations funding studies in communication. While maintaining an active research program, since 1989 she has been dean of The Annenberg School for Communication at the University of Pennsylvania.

FAMILY BACKGROUND AND EDUCATION

Kathleen M. Hall, the oldest of five children, grew up in the small town of Waconia, Minnesota, where her parents ran a gas station. She learned early that women could take strong roles in the family and the community. Her mother kept the books for the gas station, and her grandmother, Myra Zabel, was a Montana homesteader who later became a nurse practitioner. Jamieson says, "My grandmother saw no limits and set no limits. She got up every morning and remade the world" (Dribben, 1994).

Educated in Catholic schools, Jamieson became active in interscholastic debate at the insistence of Sister Anne Rose while she was a student at St. Benedict's, an all-girls high school in St. Joseph. Graduating as the class valedictorian, she accepted a full scholarship to Marquette University, where she continued to debate. She completed her undergraduate degree in rhetoric and public address in 1967.

She went on immediately to graduate school, again at the urging of Sister Anne Rose. Her doctoral studies at the University of Wisconsin, Madison, led to a dissertation on *Humanae Vitae,* the 1968 papal encyclical on birth control, which won her the Speech Communication Association's Award for Outstanding Doctoral Dissertation in 1972.

While a student at Marquette, she met Robert Jamieson, an engineer, whom she married in 1968. The Jamiesons have two children, Robert, who works in advertising, and Patrick, who is completing college.

CAREER DEVELOPMENT

Before defending her dissertation, Jamieson accepted a position as assistant professor at the University of Maryland, College Park. She taught in the Department of Speech Communication from 1970 to 1986 where she was promoted to associate and then full professor. Her tenure at Maryland was punctuated with grants from Lilly (1976), Fulbright (1980), and Mellon (1982), as well as an East-West Center fellowship (1985).

She also took on the role of director of communication for the House Committee on Aging from 1977 to 1978, an experience that required her to become deeply familiar with the nitty-gritty of political communication in the nation's capital. Her ability to combine theories derived from the academy with a thorough understanding of professional practice honed in application to real political problems would come to characterize much of her research and teaching throughout her career. She was instrumental in establishing Maryland's interdisciplinary doctoral program in communication and pioneered an exceptionally popular series of courses for graduate and undergraduate students in which they met regularly with political consultants to get the professionals' views of campaign communication. She continued teaching courses modeled along much the same lines at her subsequent postings.

Jamieson's early scholarship focused on the study of a genre that she first launched in her dissertation. In 1976 she co-chaired with Karlyn Kohrs Campbell a conference entitled " 'Significant Form' in Rhetorical Criticism" at the University of Kansas. The conference marked the beginning of a long and rewarding series of collaborations with Campbell that has to date resulted in three books, including *Form and Genre* (1978) and *Interplay of Influence* (1983), a textbook on media studies. Subsequently, her work shifted toward more directly political issues. Political communication occupied most of her scholarly attention during her last years at Maryland, during which time she released *Packaging the Presidency* (1984).

Jamieson left the University of Maryland in 1986 to become the G. B. Dealey Regents Professor of Communication and Chair of the Speech Communication Department at the University of Texas, Austin, a position she occupied until

1989. During this period, she also served on the Twentieth Century Fund's Task Force on Presidential Debates. Her research in political communication continued, marked by publication of *Eloquence in an Electronic Age* (1988), a revision of *Interplay of Influence* (2nd ed., 1988), and *Presidential Debates* (1988), co-authored with David S. Birdsell.

In 1989 Jamieson became dean of The Annenberg School for Communication at the University of Pennsylvania. She has continued to conduct research and teach during her tenure as dean, releasing over the last six years *Deeds Done in Words* (1990) co-authored with Karlyn Kohrs Campbell, *Dirty Politics* (1992), and *Beyond the Double Bind* (1995), as well as revised editions of *Packaging the Presidency* (2nd ed., 1992) and *Interplay of Influence* (3rd ed., 1992).

A frequent commentator on issues in political communication for print and broadcast outlets since the release of *Packaging* in 1984, Jamieson became a regular guest on Bill Moyers' "Listening to America" in 1992. Her commentary on that year's presidential campaign provided the PBS audience with a sustained, academically grounded critique of political communication. She continued her appearances on other programs as well, serving so frequently as a media commentator that she has been dubbed "Queen of Quotes" by several publications.

MAJOR CONTRIBUTIONS AND ACHIEVEMENTS

Jamieson's most important contributions fall into three broad and closely related areas: (1) developing rhetorical theory relating to institutions and genre, (2) advancing the field's understanding of the nature and influence of political media, particularly of the possible relationships among media, and (3) developing programs for improving public discourse. Each category ties to the other across her teaching, research, and public activities and has extended—with varying degrees of emphasis—throughout her career.

In her dissertation, "A Rhetorical-Critical Analysis of the Conflict over *Humanae Vitae*" (which has yet to be published in book form), Jamieson examined the power of generic form. As she once told an interviewer, "What I wanted to understand is how a document, written in a third-century language, based on arguments that have no relevance to the modern world, could have been so consequential" (Dribben, 1994). Her work extended an approach to rhetoric, which heavily focused on situational issues and closely identified with Lloyd Bitzer (1968). As she summarized her position in "Generic Constraints and the Rhetorical Situation" (1973), one of several articles drawn from her dissertation, "I do not wish to deny Bitzer's contention that rhetorical forms are prompted by comparable responses to comparable situations. What I do wish to suggest is that perception of the proper response to an unprecedented rhetorical situation grows *not merely from the situation* but also from antecedent rhetorical forms" (p. 163, emphasis in the original). Sometimes, those antecedent forms become sufficiently regular and recognizable to constitute a genre, which is "a complex of elements—a constellation of substantive, stylistic and situational character-istics'' (Campbell & Jamieson, 1978, p. 17).

Jamieson extended this work together with Karlyn Kohrs Campbell in the jointly edited *Form and Genre* (1978). Built from a core of papers delivered at the 1976 University of Kansas conference on genre, the book was an important impetus to a surge of generic criticism in the 1970s and 1980s. The lead essay established practices of generic criticism that still serve as a benchmark almost 20 years later. In 1978 Campbell and Jamieson jointly authored another book, *Deeds Done in Words* (1990), which dealt with presidential rhetoric in terms of the principal genres of presidential speechmaking. Campbell and Jamieson cover inaugural addresses, special inaugurals, State of the Union addresses, veto messages, war rhetoric, rhetoric to forestall impeachment, impeachment, pardons, and farewells. Jamieson and co-author Birdsell also dealt with debates as a genre in American politics in *Presidential Debates* (1988).

Jamieson's rhetorical background surfaces throughout her work in political communication. In addition to her theoretical work per se, her extensive under-standing of the history of public address and its role in governance lends to her work a depth lacking in less historically sensitive treatments of political dis-course. *Packaging the Presidency* (1984), an encyclopedic analysis of presiden-tial advertising in the television age, begins with a very quick review of the more common techniques of campaigning in the nineteenth and early twentieth centuries. The point of this introductory chapter is not to cover campaigning thoroughly, or even to inventory the state of the art prior to television, but to show in what ways television advertising was continuous with earlier modes of presidential campaigning. By extension, she is better able to point to the differ-ences fostered by television advertising in the context of campaign communi-cation as a whole. As with genre *tout court,* she develops in her study of political advertising a sense of the ''constellation of substantive, stylistic and situational characteristics'' involved in assessing advertising in the aggregate, as well as the peculiarities of individual advertisements.

Eloquence in an Electronic Age asks what it means to be eloquent in the context of modern political discourse. As was the case with the role of adver-tising, her understanding of eloquence is established in a historical review of the concept, which is then applied to contemporary politics. Drawing on Kenneth Burke's work on eloquence, Jamieson builds a definition of the term that ac-counts for the radically different tastes and standards at work in different his-torical periods. Her work explains how different ages can anoint such disparate practitioners as Daniel Webster and Ronald Reagan as exemplars of ''eloquent'' speech. She further argues that even as our criteria for eloquence change, those deemed eloquent still command attention and respect in ways that bear directly on the practice of political communication, and by extension, the aggregation of power.

Beginning with the study of media interrelationships that begat *Interplay of Influence* (1983), Jamieson has been concerned with the different ''logics'' represented in various media forms and their respective implications for sound campaign practice. Her most extensive analysis of the associative and often elided reasoning that takes place in political advertising, and is sometimes abetted on the evening news, can be found in *Dirty Politics* (1992). The book examines the relationships among advertising, speeches, debates, and other forms of campaign discourse in the context of news coverage of campaigns. She finds that political coverage on television, even coverage explicitly devoted to uncovering deceptive practices in campaigning, often reinforces precisely the messages it seeks to examine.

The kind of work reported in *Dirty Politics* has direct implications for the practice of political communication, particularly of campaign coverage by news organizations. In one of her most significant efforts to improve the quality of public discourse, these are implications Jamieson is determined to bring to the attention of journalists, and where possible, the voting public. She briefed news organizations prior to the 1992 campaign to encourage use of a "visual grammar" developed in a series of studies at The Annenberg School for Communication with a grant from the MacArthur Foundation. Interested in viewer responses to critiques of advertising on television news programs, she and her colleagues found that if an advertisement were simply shown on television while a verbal critique ran before, after, or during the spot, viewers would tend to have the message of the advertising reinforced, regardless of how negative the commentary might be. To offset this tendency, a series of recommendations regarding placement and duration of the images, superimposition of written, verbal materials, and scheduling of broadcasts was assembled and discussed with reporters. Several organizations adopted the adwatch guidelines for at least a portion of their advertising analyses in 1992. In a subsequent study of voter responses during that campaign, she and Joseph Cappella recommended some refinements in the technique (Cappella & Jamieson, 1994).

Beyond the Double Bind, released in 1995, moves away from political campaign discourse and into the discursive practices that snare women in "double binds," or catch-22 situations that trap them rhetorically. She takes to task feminists who argue that there has been no progress in women's rights or that whatever progress has been made has been effectively reversed since roughly the time of Ronald Reagan's election to the presidency in 1980. She is particularly critical of Susan Faludi's *Backlash* (1991) for its neglect of what she feels to be very real gains that have not been seriously compromised over the last decade. Jamieson does not claim that feminism has achieved all of its goals. Working directly from texts and case studies, she shows both the continuing influence of the double binds (Womb/Brain; Silence/Shame; Sameness/Difference; Femininity/Competence; Aging/Invisibility) and where appropriate, the rhetorical responses to escape them.

For Jamieson, countering the "backlash" theory is more than a matter of interpreting recent history for the benefit of scholars. She argues that the backlash thesis is needlessly discouraging to women who can and should take heart from the examples of women who have triumphed over institutions that opposed their interests. This recognition and the implicit invitation to action is a form of empowerment effectively denied by those who argue that all rights erode in the tide of reaction. As she notes at the outset, "Although subtle and overt forms of sex discrimination persist, there are now forms of redress, some institutional, some rhetorical, available not just to the educated and well-to-do. I chart them in the book" (p. viii). In large part an examination of the condition of women in the America of the 1990s, *Beyond the Double Bind* is also an effort to improve the public debate on gender equity.

CRITICAL EVALUATION OF CONTRIBUTIONS AND ACHIEVEMENTS

Jamieson's books have been widely reviewed in popular and academic venues. Her notices are overwhelmingly favorable, although there are, of course, reviewers who disagree with her positions. Published reviews, sympathetic and hostile alike, call attention to her prodigious scholarship, her exacting attention to detail, and her theoretical consistency. She is sometimes taken to task for feeling that public discourse can be made more reasonable through the guidance of those who study it, the careful attention of its practitioners, and persistent pressures from the voting public. For the most part, this criticism is misplaced. Jamieson has never argued that politicians can be expected voluntarily to accede to standards that compromise their electoral effectiveness. Nor has she said that the public consciously hungers for satisfying discourse, far less the preferred argumentative models of an academic elite. Instead, her work argues for a broad project in public education, a prospect admittedly limited in the face of burgeoning technology, innovations that outpace analysis, and limited attention to political discourse in basic education. Though significant barriers to change, none of these is a reason to abandon projects in either discourse studies or public decision making.

Jamieson's public activities evidence at the very least a nonacademic audience for her ideas. Her success in getting networks first to listen to and then to adopt the results of the adwatch studies credentials the practicality of attempts to shape discourse in the public sphere. Her ability to take complex ideas and distill them into a palatable form for television makes publicly available exactly the kind of sustained, careful analysis that she has championed in her academic writing. Her testimony before the Congress and her work on the Twentieth Century Task-forces on political communication (*Presidential Debates,* 1983 and 1986; Press Coverage of Campaigns, 1992–1993) has given her a voice in the elite policy processes that influence the trajectory of public discourse. In this way, her arguments for incremental change have achieved wide circulation and affected a number of audiences among professional practitioners and lay consumers of political communication.

Jamieson has also come under attack for failing to "prove" her interpretations empirically, that is, showing, through surveys, or some other such instrument, that average viewers are able to coax the rich complexities from political language that she does herself. This is a fairly common complaint about the practical value of rhetorical criticism in the academy, a criticism often amplified in the popular press. Jamieson does not, of course, argue that mass publics "see" what trained rhetorical critics see, but that critics can chart the interpretive paths available to audiences operating out of a given cultural and temporal milieu. In the past several years, she has begun to test her qualitative analysis with a great deal more empirical work based on her criticism. The work reported in *Dirty Politics* and the analysis of "Broadcast Adwatch Effects" (1994) are good examples of empirical extensions of her critical projects.

The academy has consistently rewarded her with her field's top honors. After winning the Speech Communication Association's dissertation award in 1972, she received the Zeta Phi Eta Award for outstanding contributions to communication by a woman (1979); the Golden Anniversary Book Award (for *Packaging the Presidency, 1985*); the Winans-Wichelns Award for Distinguished Scholarship in Rhetoric and Public Address (for *Eloquence in an Electronic Age, 1989*); the Douglas Ehninger Distinguished Rhetorical Scholar Award (1990); and the Distinguished Scholar Award (1992). The John F. Kennedy School's Joan Shorenstein Barone Center awarded her its Goldsmith Award for contributions to Press and Public Policy in 1992. In 1995 she was honored with the American Political Science Association's Murray Edelman Distinguished Career Award for lifetime contributions to the study of political communication.

REFERENCES

Campbell, K. K., & Jamieson, K. H. (1978). Form and genre in rhetorical criticism: An introduction. In K. K. Campbell and K. H. Jamieson (eds.), *Form and genre: Shaping rhetorical action*. Annandale, Va.: Speech Communication Association.

Campbell, K. K., & Jamieson, K. H. (1978). *Form and genre: Shaping rhetorical action*. Annandale, Va.: Speech Communication Association.

Campbell, K. K., & Jamieson, K. H. (1990). *Deeds done in words: Presidential rhetoric and the genres of governance*. Chicago: University of Chicago Press.

Cappella, J. N., & Jamieson, K. H. (1994). Broadcast adwatch effects. *Communication Research, 21*, 342–365.

Jamieson, K. H. (1972). A Rhetorical-Critical Analysis of the Conflict over *Humanae Vitae*. Unpublished Ph.D. diss., University of Wisconsin.

Jamieson, K. H. (1973). Generic constraints and the rhetorical situation. *Philosophy and Rhetoric, 6*, 162–170.

Jamieson, K. H. (1973). Natural law as warrant. *Philosophy and Rhetoric, 6*, 235–246.

Jamieson, K. H. (1974). Interpretation of natural law in the conflict over *Humanae Vitae*. *Quarterly Journal of Speech, 60*, 201–211.

Jamieson, K. H. (1975). Antecedent genre as rhetorical constraint. *Quarterly Journal of Speech, 62*, 406–415.

Jamieson, K. H. (1984). *Packaging the presidency: A history and criticism of presidential campaign advertising*. New York: Oxford University Press. (Second edition published 1992).

Jamieson, K. H. (1988). *Eloquence in an electronic age: The transformation of political speechmaking*. New York: Oxford University Press.

Jamieson, K. H. (1992). *Dirty politics: Deception, distraction and democracy*. New York: Oxford University Press.

Jamieson, K. H. (1995). *Beyond the double bind: Women and leadership*. New York: Oxford University Press.

Jamieson, K. H., & Birdsell, D. S. (1988). *Presidential debates: The challenge of creating an informed electorate*. New York: Oxford University Press.

Jamieson, K. H., & Campbell, K. K. (1983). *Interplay of influence: Mass media and their publics in news, advertising, politics*. Belmont, Calif.: Wadsworth. (Second edition published 1988; third edition 1992.)

Additional References

Bitzer, L. (1968). The rhetorical situation. *Philosophy and Rhetoric*, 1, 1–14.

Dribben, M. (1994, November 20) B.W.O.C.: The prominent and powerful women of Penn. *Philadelphia Inquirer*.

Faludi, S. (1991). *Backlash: The undeclared war against American women*. New York: Crown.

JEAN KILBOURNE
(1943–   )

Juliet Dee

Media analyst Jean Kilbourne was recently featured in the *New York Times Magazine* as one of the three most popular lecturers on college campuses (''Who's Hot on Campus,'' 1994). Probably best known for her 1979 film ''Killing Us Softly,'' Kilbourne has raised public consciousness about social issues that affect young women in particular. She has done extensive research on advertising's images of women, alcoholism, nicotine addiction, and eating disorders, for example, in order to create videos and slide shows designed to help her audience become critical consumers of advertising.

FAMILY BACKGROUND

Jean Kilbourne was born in Kansas in 1943. Her parents were New Yorkers, although her father, W. Wallace Kilbourne, a lieutenant colonel in the cavalry, was stationed at Fort Riley in Junction City, Kansas, during World War II. When he left for the front lines, her mother, Lillian Brazier Kilbourne, brought Jean and her three brothers back to New York. Her father returned in 1945, and the family moved to Hingham, a small seacoast town south of Boston, where Jean grew up and attended public schools, graduating from Hingham High School in 1960.

Neither her father nor her mother attended college. Her mother went to private school and chose a trip to Europe instead of college, not an uncommon choice in those days. Her father, an excellent student, was unable to attend college because of the Depression. Following the war, he remained in the Army reserves and had a career as an executive with Curtis Publishing Company, which published *The Saturday Evening Post* among many other magazines. Her mother was a homemaker. Jean was the third of four children; she has two older brothers, Frederick (Rick) and Donald (Don) and one younger brother, James (Jim). All of her brothers now live in Southern California.

Jean's mother died of cancer when Jean was only 9 years old. It is a loss that still haunts her, more than any other in her life. She recently participated in "Once Upon a Loss," a film by Carolyn Stonewell about women who lost their mothers when they were young. After her mother died, she grew up in a predominantly male environment with her father and three brothers. Her father traveled a great deal and was often absent. As a result, she considers herself to be "somewhat less socialized than most women of that time" (Kilbourne, November 18, 1994). This had the positive benefit of allowing her to remain more independent than most women and to become more objective about the culture she lived in. However, her mother's death also left her depressed for many years and with what she describes, in the words of the poet Cesar Vallejo, as "my silver wound, my eternal loss."

As an adult, Kilbourne is still very close to her three brothers:

It's lucky for me that I have three brothers. It has helped me be more empathic with men, to be sympathetic and take a broader view than I might have taken otherwise.

I come from a very right-wing family—my father, everyone—I'm a real deviant in my family! My three brothers are right-wing also, even the one who is gay. However, they are also charming, funny, extremely bright and very compassionate as individuals (although somehow that doesn't translate into public policy, something that has surprised me about a lot of conservatives I know).

Even though I was brought up in a conservative family, I've always had a real sympathy for the underdog and a kind of identification with the oppressed. Like many people of my generation, I was really changed by the Vietnam War. I'm very much a child of the sixties. I entered the sixties coming from a conservative Republican family in a mostly white suburb of Boston, and left the sixties a radical feminist and an activist. (Kilbourne, November 25, 1994)

EDUCATION

Jean Kilbourne was an acting star in high school, voted "Best Actress" in her class. She was also an outstanding student with a straight-A record and the first person in her high school to get a perfect score on the verbal SAT. She received a full scholarship to Wellesley College. She was most influenced there by writer May Sarton and psychologist Thelma Alper, two women who encouraged Kilbourne to think both critically and creatively. "There was no explicit feminist consciousness at Wellesley then, nor much emphasis on women having careers. Still, I had no desire to get married right away. I wanted to see the world" (Kahn, 1994, p. 3). She received her Bachelor of Arts degree in English from Wellesley College in 1964.

After working in Europe and the United States for some years, Kilbourne received a Master's degree in education from Boston University in 1972. She earned her doctorate in education (in humanistic and behavioral studies) from Boston University in 1980.

CAREER DEVELOPMENT

In her senior year at Wellesley, Jean won a fellowship that enabled her to live in London for a year, with a secretarial job at the British Broadcasting Corporation. Part of winning this award involved writing an essay on why she wanted to work for the BBC. She wrote that she was interested in observing commercial-free television, foreshadowing the interest that was to become her life's work.

Kilbourne went to Paris and spent a year working for a French film company and then returned to London and became heavily involved in the antiwar movement. Her friend Harry Pincus got her involved in guerrilla theater. "Once I even dressed up as Miss America and marched on [Prime Minister] Harold Wilson's house." But Kilbourne concluded that the best way she could change the world, even a little, was to become a teacher (Kahn, 1994, p. 3).

When she returned to the United States, she got a Master's degree in education and eventually began teaching high school. During the first two years that she was back in the United States, however, she had several jobs. One was placing ads in *The Lancet,* a medical journal. One ad for a birth control pill caught her attention. It portrayed a woman associating each weekday with a specific chore such as laundry or shopping: "Works the way a woman thinks," read the copy. Kilbourne was not amused. "Basically it was saying women are too stupid to remember their own menstrual cycles. I don't know why, but that one leapt up at me" (Kahn, 1994, p. 4). She cut out the ad and put it on her refrigerator. Her fridge was soon plastered with other ads with similar stereotypes.

Kilbourne made slides from her collection and created a lecture to go with them; she called her slide presentation "The Naked Truth: Advertising's Image of Women." She first showed it in her classes at Norwell High School and then again to her classes at Emerson College (where she taught in an interdisciplinary program from 1972 to 1975). Her presentation proved so popular that friends urged her to get a booking agent and hit the lecture circuit full time. Success came incrementally thereafter. In 1979 she turned her slide presentation into the film "Killing Us Softly: Advertising's Image of Women." In 1987 she made the video "Still Killing Softly"; both of these award-winning programs are shown throughout the world. "Killing Us Softly" is perhaps the most popular feminist film of all time.

Kilbourne has been a visiting scholar at Wellesley College since 1984 and has done extensive research on alcoholism, alcohol-related problems and policies, nicotine addiction, and alcohol and cigarette advertising. She is especially concerned about the effect of addictions on women, minorities, and young people. Her focus is on prevention, education, and public policy.

Kilbourne's concern about ads for alcohol and cigarettes is reflected in her videos "Pack of Lies: The Advertising of Tobacco" (1992), and "Calling the Shots: Advertising Alcohol" (1982, updated 1991). In 1993 she participated with Dr. George Gerbner in the video "The Killing Screens: Media and the Culture of Violence." She has developed slide presentations dealing not only with alcohol and tobacco addictions but also with eating disorders as well. Some of her slide presentations are "Deadly Persuasion: Advertising and Addiction" (1991), "Eating Our Hearts Out: The Obsession with Thinness" (1991), "Marketing Misery: Selling Addictions to Women" (1989), "You've Come the Wrong Way, Baby: Women and Smoking" (1987), and "Under the Influence: The Pushing of Alcohol via Advertising" (1979).

Kilbourne has published many scholarly and popular articles on all of these topics in publications ranging from *Media & Values* and the *Journal of the American Medical Women's Association* to the *New York Times* and *USA Today*. She has been interviewed by *Time, Newsweek, Business Week, Family Circle,* the *Christian Science Monitor, The Wall Street Journal,* the *Globe and Mail,* the *New York Times,* and many other publications. She has also been a guest on many radio and television programs including the "Today Show," "20/20," the "Oprah Winfrey Show," and "PrimeTime Live."

Kilbourne has given several thousand lectures, workshops, and seminars. In 1994 she was featured in the *New York Times Magazine* as one of the most popular speakers on college campuses today. She has spoken at over 1,000 college campuses, including Harvard, Princeton, Wesleyan, Duke, Queen's University, and the universities of Michigan, Pennsylvania, California, and almost every other state. In 1992 she was the keynote speaker for an All Court Conference on gender bias for over 300 judges in Massachusetts. She has also lectured in 49 states and several foreign countries, including Canada, England, France, Italy, and Brazil.

In 1992 she was appointed by Louis Sullivan, the U.S. secretary of Health and Human Services, to the National Advisory Council on Alcoholism and Alcohol Abuse. Surgeons General C. Everett Koop and Antonia Novello (with whom she appeared at a press conference on college students and alcohol in 1991) both asked her to serve as an adviser to them. In 1986 and 1990 she testified before Congress on behalf of the National Council on Alcoholism and Drug Dependence.

Kilbourne is on the Board of Directors of the Marin Institute for the Prevention of Alcohol and Other Drug Problems and the National Council on Alcoholism and Drug Dependence, and is on the Board of Advisers of the Greater Boston Council on Alcoholism. She currently serves on the National Advisory Boards of the Women's Action Alliance, the Media Education Foundation, and the Center for the Study of Commercialism. She has recently served on the Board of Directors of STAT (Stop Teenage Addiction to Tobacco) and was chair of the Council on Alcohol Policy of the National Association for Public Health Policy. She also served on the National Advisory Committee of the Alcohol Education Project of the Junior League.

MAJOR CONTRIBUTIONS AND ACHIEVEMENTS

Jean Kilbourne has received numerous awards, including a Leadership in Action Award, a grant from the Educational Foundation of America for a study of gender stereotyping in television commercials, an Award of Merit from the Non-Smokers' Rights Association of Canada, and an award from the Women's Action Alliance. She has twice received the Lecturer of the Year Award (1988 and 1989) from the National Association for Campus Activities (NACA) (for which she has been a finalist nine times). The Boston Chapter of the National Organization for Women elected her Woman of the Year in 1982.

CRITICAL EVALUATION OF CONTRIBUTIONS AND ACHIEVEMENTS

Jean Kilbourne's loudest critics are spokespersons for the Tobacco and Beer Institutes, as might be expected. However, some advertisers have responded positively. Charles Jackson wrote in an editorial for ADWEEK, "After listening to Jean Kilbourne, I would never doubt her intellectual honesty. While she bills herself as a critic of advertising, she is more akin to a prophet calling out in the wilderness for fundamental change in the way we communicate publicly with one another."

People in government have responded positively as well. The director of the U.S. Consumer Product Safety Commission wrote to her, "Your presentation was a smashing success! . . . provocative, skillfully designed and molded by your superb commentary . . . a first-rate educational experience." Scott Harshbarger, the attorney general of Massachusetts, said, "You were superb! Everyone was both very impressed and very much enlightened and educated by your presentation." Carole Beebe Tarantelli, a member of the Italian Parliament, said, "Hearing Jean Kilbourne is a profound experience. Audiences leave her feeling that they have heard much more than another lecture, for she teaches them to see themselves and their world differently."

A spokesperson for the International Women's Year said, "Having Jean Kilbourne to keynote a program is catalytic. Once she's on stage, everything else pauses as if suspended in time. Having experienced her presentation, no one is ever the same person . . . for throughout the experience, growing happens."

The students who listen to Kilbourne's lectures praise both her sense of humor and her sense of moral outrage. Reactions from the academic community have been overwhelmingly positive. A spokesperson for the University of Michigan wrote to her, "Very few speakers have made an impact as great as yours on our student body." One from Presbyterian College in South Carolina wrote, "You really made an impression upon your hearers, not only for your content but because of your intense, sincere, and warmly human way of presenting your message. It will be some time, if ever, before we forget you."

When asked what she herself was most proud of accomplishing, Kilbourne commented:

Enormous numbers of women come up to me and say that "Killing Us Softly" changed their lives—often that they became feminists as a result of it or changed their career direction. That's very rewarding. This is an issue that almost all women can relate to, and so in a way it made feminism acceptable to someone who might not readily have been a feminist.

I was a pioneer in this field, both in terms of the image of women in advertising, and alcohol and tobacco advertising. There's been a tremendous change in consciousness about this issue since I started looking at it 20-odd years ago. I feel that I've been a part of that increased awareness of the impact of advertising on our lives and some of the public policy changes that have come about as a result. I feel very good about that.

It's always bothered me when people say that feminists have no sense of humor, so it's been important to me to counteract that myth. Humor was a major way that my brothers and I coped when we were growing up. My brothers are very funny, and we're very good at one-liners—a little too good sometimes. It's always been our chief defense, and as defenses go, I think it's not a bad one. I think that one of the reasons that "Killing Us Softly" has been successful is that it's not what people expect; it's not a polemic, it's funny, and that gives people permission to feel that they can be feminists without having to be grim—that they can be serious without having to be depressed, and I think that that's important, too. I also think it's therapeutic for people to laugh at Madison Avenue, to ridicule the ads and to ridicule these moronic images. (Kilbourne, November 25, 1994)

INTEGRATION OF PERSONAL AND PROFESSIONAL LIFE

An unexpected event during Kilbourne's year in London occurred when she attended a party at director Roman Polanski's flat. She met a man there whom she assumed was a Ringo Starr lookalike. " 'Hullo,' the man said. 'I'm Ringo Starr.' 'Right,' Kilbourne replied. 'And I'm Jackie Kennedy.' " But it turned out that it really was Ringo Starr (Kilbourne once dabbled in modeling and does look a bit like the late Jackie Kennedy) (Kahn, 1994, p. 3). She went out with Ringo Starr a few times: "It was fun. It was at the height of the Beatles' fame, and I do love the Beatles" (Kilbourne, November 25, 1994).

Upon returning to the United States, Kilbourne had serious long-term relationships with writer Jerzy Kosinski and psychologist Louis Sass, but she remained unmarried until she was 40. In 1980 her 16-year-old niece Julia Kilbourne came across the country from Los Angeles to live with her. Julia went to Brookline High School while living with Jean. She then went to Sarah Lawrence College in New York, spent two years in the Peace Corps in Honduras, and launched a career in international public health. She lives in Washington, D.C. and the two remain close.

In 1983 Jean married poet Thomas Lux, who teaches at Sarah Lawrence

College. Their daughter Claudia Kilbourne Lux was born in 1987 when Kilbourne was 44. Kilbourne divorced in 1994.

Asked how she manages to balance her career with raising her daughter Claudia, Kilbourne explained:

When my daughter was a baby, I took her with me on the road. She went everywhere. The first year of her life, I did 80 lectures and I took her with me to almost all of them. I still take her with me sometimes, although now it's more difficult because of her school. I try to be away from home no more than two nights a week. I'm able to arrange my schedule so that I'm home the rest of the time. I'm also home a great deal in the summer and around the holidays. I'm in a much better position than if I had a regular job, for two main reasons: one is that I'm my own boss so I have very flexible hours, and the other is that I make quite a lot of money. That's probably the most important thing, because it means that I can hire extremely good help.

I've had the same nanny/assistant for six years. Her name is Tisha Gomes. She lives in her own apartment in my home. She came here from Brazil when she 21, speaking no English. She got a job as a hotel maid and as a nanny for a couple years and then we met. It was immediately clear to me that she is very, very smart, so I encouraged her to go to school, to take some courses at a community college. She did very well. Then I told her about Wellesley College's Davis Scholar program for women returning to college. She is now a Davis Scholar, halfway to her Wellesley degree. I went to Wellesley, too, of course, so it's really been a magical story for both of us. So my immediate family now consists of Tisha and Claudia and me. We all live in an old Queen Anne Victorian house, which needs constant work but has wonderful turrets and towers.

I have tremendous sympathy for working women. I have full-time help and a good income and flexible hours, and it's still difficult and stressful for me. How people do it when they don't have any help or support or money or resources is beyond my comprehension. I've been blessed to find someone as wonderful as Tisha who's stayed on for the long course. She's a major part of what makes my life work. (Kilbourne, November 25, 1994)

If Jean Kilbourne has indirectly forced Madison Avenue to improve its portrayals of women, it will probably never admit it. But one thing is self-evident: she has raised consciousness about the effects of advertising among thousands of women—and men—on college campuses, in high schools, and in community and professional groups across the country. Because of her work, our young people are better equipped to respond to advertising with critical awareness rather than with mesmerized acceptance. Because she has touched so many with her lectures, films, and videos, she has had a profound impact not only on public policy but also on consumers, transforming them from credulous into critical thinkers.

REFERENCES

Kahn, J. P. (1994, May 3). The terror of Madison Avenue: Jean Kilbourne becomes a superstar on the college circuit by taking ads to task. *Boston Globe*.

Kilbourne, J. (1994, November 18). Telephone interview.

Kilbourne, J. (1994, November 25). Telephone interview.

DOROTHY MAE KILGALLEN (1913–1965)

Sheila Clough Crifasi

These days, those who remember Dorothy Kilgallen from the 1950s and 1960s tend to identify her as a panelist on one of that era's most popular television game shows, "What's My Line?" Although she was a productive print journalist for most of her professional life and had gained national celebrity as a gossip columnist for Hearst papers in New York (and briefly in Hollywood), Kilgallen imprinted her image on the American psyche by venturing into broadcasting—first in 1941 with weekly radio readings of her "Voice of Broadway" column, next with another radio program, "Breakfast with Dorothy and Dick," from 1945 to 1963, and then into television as a regular "Line" panelist from 1959 to 1965.

The image was one of a glamorous life among the movers and shakers of her world. Early morning radio chats with husband Dick Kollmar included references to a daily routine that included dinners at exotic restaurants, Broadway openings, travels abroad, fancy dress parties in their 22-room home, and nightly visits to the Stork Club, "21," and El Morocco. On television, Kilgallen sat among and exchanged quips with panelists Arlene Francis, Bennett Cerf, and Steve Allen, and appeared to be on a first-name basis with the program's many guests, usually famous people from entertainment, government, and other fields.

In a somewhat less public way, she continued to ply her trade as a reporter, covering controversial trials and, during her last years, digging into the events surrounding the assassination of President John F. Kennedy. In the latter case, she was able to arrange and carry out the only interview conducted with Jack Ruby, killer of Lee Harvey Oswald. She never discussed or wrote about what she learned in the conversation, and her mysterious and sudden death from an overdose of alcohol and barbiturates in 1965 only added to the speculations that the deaths of Kennedy, Oswald, Ruby, and the many other major and minor figures involved in the assassination were the result of a conspiracy and coverup.

FAMILY BACKGROUND AND EDUCATION

Dorothy Mae Kilgallen, born on July 3, 1913, was the daughter of Mary Jane ("Mae") Ahern Kilgallen and James Lawrence ("Jim") Kilgallen, a news reporter in Chicago. Solidly Irish Catholic, the Kilgallens reared their two daughters—Eleanor joined the family when Dorothy was 6—in a firm moral religious environment. According to Lee Israel in *Kilgallen* (1979), that environment included a tradition that avoided dealing with emotions, especially anger. In an interview about her early married life, Kilgallen said that she never argued with her husband; any type of argument, she believed, was "selfish" (Israel, 1979).

Her mother, Mae, introduced the element of social awareness and aspiration that stayed with Dorothy all of her life. Mae's influence can also be seen in Dorothy's love of beautiful clothes and ultra femininity, which was probably supported by her father, who adored her. He, of course, had the major impact on his eldest daughter. Her growing-up years were filled with her father's newspapering exploits. Away a good deal of the time, he wrote dispatches that read like letters. Dorothy even learned journalist language, such as "your father got a good play today" (Israel, 1979).

During the years that Dorothy was growing up, the family moved from Illinois to Wyoming to Indiana and finally to New York as Jim moved from job to job. As exciting as her father's world might have seemed and although she worshiped him, she had no intention of becoming a journalist herself. She planned to become a school teacher when she graduated from Erasmus Hall High School in Brooklyn and enrolled at the College of New Rochelle. She retained that goal as she completed her freshman year and set out to find a summer job.

This was the summer of 1931, in the middle of the Depression, and jobs were scarce. Dorothy was discouraged until she remembered a comment made by Amster Spiro, city editor of the New York *Evening Journal,* at a party she had attended with her parents. According to John Jakes in *Great Women Reporters* (1969), Spiro had said to Jim Kilgallen, "I suppose you're going to make a reporter out of her." Jim said he'd rather not do that, and Spiro replied, "Well, if you decide to put her to work, I'll give her a job." And he did. He hired her as a cub reporter at $20 a week, and Dorothy, at 17, began her career with the Hearst empire. She never returned to New Rochelle. "Unquestionably she got the job because she was Jim Kilgallen's daughter," Jakes writes, "but that was the last time her father's influence was needed. From there on she made her way on her own ability."

CAREER DEVELOPMENT

Isabel Ross in *Ladies of the Press* (1974) describes Kilgallen's first days at the *Journal.*

She looked the part of the sweet girl graduate as she stepped out on her first assignment. Her professional ducking was swift and thorough. For the first summer she practically lived in police stations, court houses, hospitals and the morgue. It wasn't easy. Newspaper work was exciting enough, but more of a struggle than she thought. But she stuck it out and became an excellent reporter. (p. 242)

Ross includes an anecdote about an assistant editor who when he found out that Dorothy had never seen a dead body, gave her repeated assignments at the morgue. "She wrote a succession of stories about unidentified suicides, described their clothes and urged their relatives to come forward and claim them. She interviewed every sort of freak and celebrity," he points out.

Kilgallen wrote with color and human interest, including all the minute details of every scene she observed. As the years went by, she covered many of the major criminal trials that dominated the Hearst papers, using her youthful innocent appearance to win interviews with even the most reluctant people and scooping more experienced reporters—even, on some occasions, her father.

In a few years, she had become well known to the readers of the *Evening Journal* and was soon to make her leap to a national audience. She accomplished this by competing with two reporters from other papers to see who could travel around the world in the shortest time using regularly scheduled transportation. Kilgallen made the trip in 24 days, 12 hours, and 52 minutes, coming in second but providing moment-by-moment reports of her exploits to readers of Hearst papers throughout the country. The series was later published as a book, *Girl Around the World* (1936) and served as the basis for a movie, *Fly Away Baby*. While in Hollywood to advise on the film, she took a screen test that resulted in a bit part as a reporter in *Sinner Take All*.

When she went to Hollywood in 1936, the *Evening Journal* decided that since Dorothy was there, she should become its Hollywood columnist. "Hollywood Scene as Seen by Dorothy Kilgallen" was short-lived, however, because Louella Parsons already had the Hollywood scene covered for Hearst and found this interloper from New York an annoying competitor. Parsons was a favorite of William Randolph Hearst, so it wasn't long before Kilgallen's column was eliminated.

Her brief stint in Hollywood earned Kilgallen the following description in *Who's Who in Hollywood 1900–1976*—and reduced her career to one brief sentence: "Famed gossip columnist and television panelist (What's My Line); played a young reporter in Bruce Cabot's *Sinner Take All*."

Kilgallen returned to New York and headed in a new direction by dropping her focus on crime. She now specialized in the social arena. She covered the wedding of Franklin Delano Roosevelt, Jr., to Ethel DuPont and wrote a feature about debutantes and their diets. She also was able to get an interview with Helen Wills (tennis champion) (Israel, 1979). She went to London to cover the coronation of George VI and sat for a coronation portrait that appeared next to those of the duke and duchess of Kent on page two of the *Evening Journal*.

She was making the scene in New York, mingling with Cafe Society and reveling in her contacts with the glamorous and wealthy. She was a natural to take over the "Voice of Broadway" column for the *Journal,* and did in 1938. This marked a change in many ways, not the least of which was a new circle of friends. No longer was she escorted by friendly newspapermen—they couldn't afford to make the rounds of nightclubs and cafes where Dorothy sought material for her column. Now she traveled with debutantes, movie stars, and other rich and famous companions.

It was in this milieu that Dorothy met Richard Tomkins Kollmar, an actor about whom she had written a number of items in her column. They were married in April 1940.

Kilgallen added radio to her outlets in 1941 with a "Voice of Broadway" chat show that aired on CBS on Saturday mornings. Four years later, she and Kollmar began their "Breakfast with Dorothy and Dick" series on WOR. "Breakfast" was another chat format, broadcast initially from the Kollmars' 16-room apartment at Park Avenue and 66th Street and later from the East 68th Street townhouse. The program was larded with commercials and, as the Kollmar children came along, included them in the conversation. They actually did eat breakfast as they talked.

In a *New Yorker* piece on breakfast talk shows in 1946 (August 10), the writer described a visit to the Kollmar apartment to meet the Kollmars and see them do the show. The butler answered the doorbell and led the writer down a long marble hallway to be greeted by Dorothy, garbed in a full-length white hostess gown. She suggested the writer listen to the program in the living room and talk to them later. "I was ushered into a square room with black walls, black ceiling, and a green carpet. Near the door stood a cigar-store Indian, and at the center of the room was a carrousel gondola, newly upholstered in red velvet."

The program consisted of a warm introduction—

"Good morning, Sweetie!"

"Good morning, Darling! It's time for Dorothy and Dick. My, my, this is good orange juice." Glasses tinkled and a canary chirped in the background.

"It's Juicy Gem. Would you like some toast?"

A 10-minute chat about food and theater was followed by a few lisping comments from the Kollmar children, who soon left to enable their parents to swap observations about soaps and polishes.

When the program ended, Dorothy joined the writer to crow with delight about the services provided to listeners (e.g., weather reports), but pointed out, "Doing this program is not easy. We must rise at 7:30, and often after a busy night at the clubs."

Making the club rounds was a reminder of her column, which appeared daily in spite of the added demands of her broadcasts. In a 1950 *Coronet* article, Carol Hughes called Kilgallen "amazing. . . . One of the best-liked and most respected of the lady news hawks, she is also one of the most talented and prolific. Dorothy turns out six long columns a week for 45 newspapers in the King Features Syndicate. She writes features, fiction and chitchat for many national magazines. She ad libs a 45-minute radio program six days a week over station WOR.''

Hughes continues with a recitation of other activities that include handling servants, planning menus, shopping, doing and giving interviews, reading six newspapers a day, giving parties, walking in the park with her children, attending the opera, and reminding her husband to get a haircut. "And yet," Hughes adds, "she remains as placid and calm as a Trappist monk." Obviously an admirer, Hughes asserts that Dorothy "is one celebrity who has not been corrupted by fame. She is seldom biting or critical" (June 1950).

These observations would be strongly challenged by those who felt the sting of Kilgallen's words when she disagreed with or disapproved of someone. The Voice of Broadway column

was declarative, name-naming, hard-core gossip about marriage, divorce, nose bobs, public drunkenness, pregnancy, brouhahas, comebacks, broken kneecaps, hairline fractures, lost dogs, nervous breakdowns, gambling losses, political shenanigans, hiring, firing, trysting, fisting, overnight success, and terminal self-destruction among the famous and the notorious. (Israel, 1979)

Israel (1979) notes that her language was clever. The romance between a Mexican politico and a socialite was described as "most Caliente." Blossoming romances were called "Heart Toddys." Her copy was seldom touched by her editors except when Carl Helms, the Hearst lawyer, would excise something from her column for fear of libel.

Israel (1979) points out that her negativity and nastiness increased through the years. "The public Dorothy Kilgallen—about whom Cole Porter would say, with reference to a missed appearance on 'What's My Line,' 'I'm sorry. I shall miss hating her this week'—had not fully formed."

Formation was nearly complete in 1959 when Kilgallen caused an uproar here and abroad with comments about Soviet Premier Nikita Khrushchev's wife, Nina, a woman whose "avoirdupois" and lack of style were grist for the Kilgallen mill (Israel, 1979). The Khrushchevs arrived in New York for a nine-day state visit which Dorothy was assigned to cover. On the second day, she wrote about Mrs. Khrushchev, "It would be difficult to find clothes comparable to hers in the waiting room of a New York employment agency for domestic help; in this decadent capitalistic republic, applicants for jobs as laundresses, chambermaids and cooks usually are far more a la mode than Russia's first lady." She added that Nina's suit was "like a home-made slip cover on a sofa."

Hostile mail from outraged readers poured into the newspaper when the column appeared, and editors were appalled that they had let such a gaffe slip by them. Bill Hearst and Frank Conniff, his aide, admitted for publication (and for perhaps the first time in Hearst history) that they allowed a member of the staff to overstep the limits of good taste (Israel, 1979).

Kilgallen was shocked at the response of readers and of the paper, which had always supported her in previous offenses. The *New York Times* even mentioned her reaction in Kilgallen's obituary, quoting a friend, ''It was the first time I've ever seen her crushed—and she's taken plenty of kicks in the teeth'' (November 9, 1965).

Ten years before the Khrushchev incident, Kilgallen began her stint with ''What's My Line?'' Wherever she traveled in connection with her column and with her continuing coverage of major news stories, she returned to New York on weekends to do the program. She joined a distinguished and popular group— Bennett Cerf, Arlene Francis, and Steve Allen—at the table facing the various guests whose occupation or name they were to determine through questioning.

In a book about the show, producer Gil Fates (1978) describes Kilgallen's role on the panel. ''Dorothy was consumed by a fierce determination to win. She cared about our game. Cared so much that Bennett told about finding her in tears backstage one night after the show. He was concerned that she was ill. 'I feel so stupid,' she said in explanation, 'I haven't guessed one occupation in three weeks.' ''

One assignment that had Kilgallen commuting to New York for the show was covering the Sheppard murder trial in 1954. Although her fellow panelists did not approve of her Voice of Broadway column, they were impressed with the quality of her coverage of the trial. They were eager to hear what she thought about the Sheppard murder (Israel, 1979).

Kilgallen was assigned to cover the trial of Dr. Samuel Holmes Sheppard of Bay Village, Ohio, who was accused of beating his wife to death. Before she arrived in Cleveland, Dorothy thought he must be guilty, but once in the courtroom, she changed her mind. Her sympathy was clear in her stories. Israel writes about the visit Sam Sheppard and the jurors made to Sheppard's home. Only one reporter was allowed to accompany them and bring back information to others in the pool. Kilgallen made the most of the secondhand information. Although all the reporters wrote that Dr. Sheppard broke down when he saw reminders of his 7-year-old son Chip (who had slept through his mother's murder), none gave the osteopath such tragic stature. Kilgallen wrote,

On the dresser sat a furry teddy bear, and the sight of this was too much for Dr. Sheppard to take with his usual immobility. His face crumpled like a child's; he made no sound or movement, but the color of his eyes deepened and glittered, and the tears flowed down his cheeks. (Israel, 1979)

At the beginning of the trial, when Kilgallen was about to take a seat in the press section, a bailiff approached her and asked her to come to the judge's chambers. Judge Edward Blythin wanted to say hello. During the brief encounter, the judge said that the case was open and shut. Startled, Dorothy asked him why. ''He's guilty as hell,'' the judge said. ''There's no question about it.'' Although she recognized the statement as an indication of prejudice, she tucked it in the back of her mind and went out to cover the trial. She told no one about it and wrote nothing about it in her stories. It wasn't until ten years later, long after Sheppard had been convicted and sent to jail, that she finally revealed the information. Dorothy was part of a panel discussion at the Overseas Press Club and was asked to comment on a libel case, and, to draw a parallel, she said, "Sam Sheppard should collect fifty million dollars because he had the worst trial I ever saw." She described her interview with Judge Blythin. When an incredulous reporter asked why she hadn't written about the conversation, pointing out that she could have changed the venue and complexion of the case, Dorothy replied, "Things said to a reporter in confidence should be kept in confidence" (Israel, 1979).

In 1964 Dorothy traveled to Dallas to cover the trial of Jack Ruby, charged with murdering Lee Harvey Oswald. Once she had arrived and began digging for information in earnest, she began to doubt the federal government's commitment to revealing all the facts of the case. She wrote a story that prodded the attorney general to give all the reports and evidence accumulated by the Warren Commission to the defense team. (J. Edgar Hoover and the commission counsel refused to pass along any information.) In response, Jack Ruby asked to see her, and she met with him briefly. Later in the trial, she asked to see Ruby again, telling the defense lawyer that she had a message for Ruby from "a mutual friend." She was able to spend eight minutes with him; no one else was present and the room where they met was small and private. No one overheard the conversation. It was not recorded. Dorothy never told her friends about the conversation, nor did she refer to the private interview in any of her prolific published writings. Whatever notes she took during her time alone with Jack Ruby in the small office off the judge's bench were included in a file she began to assemble on the assassination of John F. Kennedy (Israel, 1979).

She continued to assert in her writings that the government was not telling the entire truth. Few if any other journalists were posing questions. "Dorothy was open-minded, accessible, and fearless. In this regard, she was almost unique among heavyweight establishment journalists in the United States. What she was publishing has been made tepid by time, but doubting the official version then verged on apostasy" (Israel, 1979).

In August 1964 Kilgallen obtained and published Jack Ruby's testimony before the Warren Commission, material that had not been revealed to the press. The *New York Times* reported, "Officials of the Warren Commission expressed distress today at the publication of testimony supposedly held for the group's forthcoming report on the assassination of President Kennedy" (August 19, 1964). Although no new or revealing information emerged from the transcript, government officials conducted an investigation to discover who gave it to Kilgallen. They never found the culprit, and Dorothy never spoke about it.

Kilgallen died reportedly of an overdose of alcohol and barbiturates on November 8, 1965, leaving many unanswered questions. She was remembered by *Newsweek* (November 22, 1965) as the "Newsman in a $500 Dress." *Time* (November 19, 1965) said she remained a triple threat in the communications world—"She wrote a daily gossip column, 'The Voice of Broadway,' which was syndicated in 146 papers; she appeared as a panelist with a waspish will to win on the TV show 'What's My Line?'; and she covered occasional front-page events for the Hearst papers with a flair rarely equaled by the competition."

BOOKS AND OTHER ACCOMPLISHMENTS

Only two books were published under Dorothy Kilgallen's byline, *Girl Around the World* (1936) and *Murder One* (1967)—the second after her death. According to Gil Fates (1978), "Her fellow panelist, Bennett Cerf, gave Dorothy a ten thousand dollar advance on a book he wanted her to write on the famous murder trials she had covered. She only got to write part of it. It was finished after her death by her father, Jim."

Dorothy never received the Pulitzer or any other prize for journalism, but she earned the respect of her peers who admired her even when they didn't like her. Carol Hughes claims in the *Coronet* (June 1950) piece,

Her talents as an ace reporter have won her the admiration of every hard-boiled male in her profession. Surely it was no sweet, gentle little girl who won the plaudits of the great Damon Runyon. He wrote: "Dorothy Kilgallen is one of the best women journalists in all the history of the game." Louis Sobol wrote: "If you want a gal who can write a fast-breaking story on any subject along the beat, Dorothy Kilgallen is your *man*." (June 1950)

In that era, when recognition for a woman doing anything well was to say she did it "like a man," these assertions were high praise indeed. For her work in radio, Kilgallen was the joint recipient, with her husband, Dick Kollmar, of the 1950 award of the National Conference of Christians and Jews.

MARRIAGE AND FAMILY

All of her life, Kilgallen was close to her mother, father, and sister. She lived at home in Brooklyn until she married, and she had the family move into Manhattan to be nearby when she and Kollmar established their household. While it seems a contradiction to say she led a sheltered life as a young woman while traveling into dangerous parts of town and covering sordid criminal proceedings, it is nevertheless true. Her mother accompanied her when she traveled any distance, but early in her career she was protected by her appearance of innocence and youth. Of course, she recognized this and used it to her advantage to gain access to important witnesses in trials.

She apparently never felt that she needed to cut loose from her immediate family; and they never seemed to intrude, only to support and enable her to do what she wanted. She was certainly independent, forging her own career and willingly jumping into challenging situations such as the trip around the world.

Her aggressive approach to her work, and her willingness to criticize the world around her, belied a deeply romantic nature. She fell in love with Dick Kollmar and during the early years of their marriage apparently enjoyed a companiable as well as passionate relationship with him.

Current Biography 1952 describes their life together as if it were a movie.

Husband and wife dine out together about three times a week, attending all first nights and regularly covering several night clubs; they return home about 3 a.m. The Kollmars are alike in their religion (Catholic) and politics (independent). Slim, with dark brown hair, fair complexion, and blue-gray eyes, Dorothy is called "Dresden-dollish." The gowns she wears before the TV camera are described as "gorgeous." Kollmar is five feet eleven inches tall, is of medium weight, and has brown eyes and brown hair. The Kollmar home has been called one of the show places of New York—"a mixture of our mutual tastes, brainstorms, whims and caprices" is her comment.

She had three children—Richard Tomkins Kollmar II, born in 1941; Jill, born in 1943; and Kerry, born in 1953. According to Israel (1979), she spent as much time as she could with them, holding them and singing lullabies to them at bedtime. In 1954, when she was covering the Sheppard trial, someone asked her how she made time for her family. She answered, "My husband and three children are more important to me than anything. I wouldn't miss their school plays or any other school meeting that was important to them" (Israel, 1979).

But while her children were important to her, at that point in their marriage, her husband probably was not. This knight in shining armor had become tarnished. According to Israel (1979), "Richard had always been a heavy drinker. Now, in his middle years, his face began to bloat, making his teeth appear shrunken. He was never totally sober. . . . He was experiencing the malaise and torpor associated with advancing alcoholism. Dorothy, on the other hand, was in her prime—healthy, successful, perilously energized."

For a number of years, Richard had found reassurance in the arms of other women. Now Dorothy looked elsewhere for the passion and romance she had lost in her marriage, and found singer Johnnie Ray, an unlikely Sir Galahad for this poised, worldly woman. Ray was younger than she, and lacking in sophistication. Her friends were appalled and told her so, but she was so very much in love with Johnnie (Israel, 1979). The affair lasted several years during which the nightclub circuit and fast pace of her life began to take its toll. Dorothy drank heavily and took a number of drugs as well. As a result, she was often ill and unable to carry out her commitments. She and Dick remained together, but both were on a downhill slide that ended in death—for her in 1965 and for him in 1971.

Israel (1979) raises a number of questions about Dorothy's death. In her research she found several different stories about the time when Kilgallen's body was found and about who found it. She also found some contradictory statements from police and medical people about the cause of death. She tried to ask family members if they could shed light on these inconsistencies, but only Kerry would talk to her and he had little information to share. He was only 12 when his mother died and had not been privy to what the adults in the house were doing.

There are also the questions about Kilgallen's investigation of the Kennedy assassination, her interview with Ruby, and her refusal to discuss or write about what she had learned. Israel (1979) asked Richard Kollmar about Dorothy's notes and the file she was building about the assassination, and he simply said he had destroyed them. He didn't explain why.

Many of those who have studied the assassination propound a conspiracy theory that includes the mysterious deaths of many people who were on the periphery of the event. Was Kilgallen's one of those mysterious deaths?

That question will probably never be answered, but whether accidental or intentional, Dorothy's death brought an early and abrupt end to a woman who had scratched the surface of her potential as a journalist, but never went beyond. Perhaps if she had forgone the Broadway beat and the role of the celebrity to focus on being a reporter, she would have produced many important stories—including the Ruby interview—and today she would likely rank among the great women journalists.

REFERENCES

Alcohol and a drug traced as causes of Kilgallen death. (1965, November 16). *New York Times*, 41.

Current Biography 1952. (1953). (pp. 303–305). New York: H. W. Wilson Co.

Dorothy Kilgallen, 52, columnist and TV panelist, dies in sleep. (1965, November 9). *New York Times*, 43.

Fates, G. (1978). *What's My Line? TV's most famous panel show*. (pp. 32–35, 108, 109). Englewood Cliffs, N.J.: Prentice-Hall.

Featherston, J. S. (1989). Kilgallen, Dorothy Mae. In J. P. McKern (ed.), *Biographical dictionary of American journalism*. (pp. 384–386). Westport, Conn.: Greenwood Press.

Hughes, C. (1950). Dorothy Kilgallen: Star reporter. *Coronet*, 28, 53–57.

Israel, L. (1979). *Kilgallen*. New York: Delacorte Press.

Jakes, J. (1969). *Great women reporters*. (pp. 159–181). New York: G. P. Putnam's Sons.

Lambsy & Chopsy. (1961). *Time*, 78, 40.

Locher, F. (ed.). (1980). *Contemporary authors, Volumes 89–92*. (p. 292). Detroit: Gale Research Co.

Newsman in a $500 dress. (1965). *Newsweek*, 66, 68.

Onward and upward with the arts; The All-American breakfast. (1946). *The New Yorker*, 22, 50–52.

Ragain, D. (1976). *Who's Who in Hollywood 1900–1976*. (p. 671). New Rochelle, N.Y.: Arlington House Publishers.

Reports on Ruby distress inquiry. (1964, August 19). *New York Times*, 38.

Ross, I. (1974). *Ladies of the press*. (pp. 240–245). New York: Arno Press.

The triple threat. (1965). *Time*, 86, 70.

Who's Who in America Vol. IV 1961–1968. (1968). (p. 527). Chicago: Marquis-Who's
    Who Inc.

Books by Dorothy Kilgallen

Kilgallen, D. (1936). *Girl around the world.* Philadelphia: David McKay Co.
Kilgallen, D. (1967). *Murder one.* New York: Random House.

GLADYS ENGEL LANG
(1919–   )

William P. Eveland, Jr.

As a researcher and scholar, Gladys Engel Lang is a pioneer in the field of mass communication. As a woman in a field dominated by men, she is all the more a pioneer. Throughout much of her career, she faced discrimination in hiring and promotion, but she persevered and succeeded, serving as an inspiration to the women who have followed in her footsteps. Many of Lang's landmark publications in the field of mass communication utilize critical events analysis methodology, an approach for which she has become famous. Currently professor emeritus at the University of Washington conducting research on artistic reputation, she has received, among other honors, the Edward L. Bernays Award of the American Sociological Society (1952, jointly with her husband and research partner Kurt Lang) and the American Association for Public Opinion Research's Award for Exceptionally Distinguished Achievement (1991). Her research interests have been exceptionally diverse, and she has made significant contributions to the study of mass communication and public opinion, as well as to the areas of collective behavior, the sociology of the arts, and human ecology.

FAMILY BACKGROUND

Gladys Engel was born in Atlantic City, New Jersey, on August 7, 1919. Her father, Matthew, held many jobs in order to care for his family, including positions as a boxing manager and stage hand. Her mother, born Jenny (but who preferred to be called Jean), did not work outside the home. Engel has only one sibling, an older sister named Violetta.

Neither of Engel's parents finished high school, and they were married at a young age. When it came to their children, however, they insisted that both

Engel and her sister pursue higher education. She remembers that the atmosphere in her home was so politically oriented that there were heated discussions at the dinner table nightly. Her father was an active union man who was a member of the AFL and strongly opposed the incorporation of the CIO. These factors may have contributed to some of Engel's political interests, which came to the forefront later in her life.

Engel remembers Atlantic City as much different now than it was when she lived there as a child. At that time it was a place where real people actually lived (as opposed to a gambling mecca), and resident children had fun playing on the beach during the summer. She recalls that in the 1920s and 1930s, Atlantic City was a stopping point for Broadway plays, many of which she saw as a child. She described it as "a world of mass entertainment." One of the major influences on her life was a movie she saw as a child in which the heroine was a lawyer. (Interestingly, she has attempted to identify what movie this was, but has yet to discover it.) From that point until her sophomore year as an undergraduate, she wanted to become a lawyer and emulate her heroine. Even as a child, she says she wanted more than to be just another "frustrated housewife."

EDUCATION

Engel attended what she termed a "rough" elementary school in Atlantic City populated primarily by working-class Italian and Irish children. Admitted to school at a younger age than the other children, she considered herself a good and popular student who was more likely to be a leader than a follower. Even at that young age, she consistently fought for her rights and the rights of others, and she now considers herself at that age "a premature woman's liberate." Even though it was a rough environment, she felt that both the students and teachers were protective and supportive.

Her years in junior and senior high school were similar to her elementary school experience, except that the students were from more diversified backgrounds. Although she describes herself as "very feminine," Lang says that she had closer relationships with the boys in her classes than the girls, possibly because she didn't enjoy discussing the cooking and sewing that the girls were taking. During this time in her education, Lang's favorite classes were American government, English (she loved to write), Latin, and algebra. With regard to extracurricular activities, Lang says she was involved in "everything." Her activities included being a member of student government, writing for the school magazine, editing the yearbook, and acting in plays. Although she was a good student, Lang notes that she was also frequently involved in "private conversations" while her teachers attempted to quiet down the class.

For her bachelor's degree, Engel enrolled in the University of Michigan in 1936. Probably the most important turning point in Engel's education came during her sophomore year. Although she was still planning to be a lawyer, she

was required to take breadth courses, including an introductory course in sociology taught by Charles Horton Cooley's nephew, Robert Angel. It was this
course which ignited the fire for sociological study in Engel. She changed her
major to sociology, deciding that her goal was to understand the means by which
society is held together. Engel received her B. A. with distinction and honors
in sociology from the University of Michigan in 1940. Her education was not
over, though; she was determined to go on for her Master's and doctoral degrees.

Assistantships for graduate students were few and far between at the time,
but Engel was able to get funding to continue her study of sociology at the
University of Washington the following year. When she had only partially completed her work for the Master's degree, World War II broke out and she was
offered a vacated teaching position at Indiana University. She turned down the
position because "if the people I knew were having to go off and fight, it wasn't
exactly what I wanted to do to be able to simply step into their shoes and make
my way up while they were off fighting." Instead, she completed her Master's
degree in 1942 and moved to Washington, D.C., to utilize the skills she had
learned in school to aid the war effort.

After working for the government for seven years in several different positions (first for the Office of War Information and later with the Office of Strategic Services), Engel returned to school to get her Ph.D. The impetus came on
a trip across the country with her mother. She made a stop in Chicago to visit
friends, and there she met with Herbert Blumer and some other faculty members
at the University of Chicago. These conversations ultimately led her to decide
that she would continue her education in Chicago instead of returning to Washington, D.C., and her job at the Office of Strategic Services. During her time
working for the government she had begun to study communication. Her work
toward her doctorate focused on this area, for she realized that communication
was "one of the major factors that hold society together."

Engel's time at the University of Chicago was some of her most productive
in terms of academic research. After meeting and marrying fellow doctoral student Kurt Lang in 1950, the couple collaborated on several research projects
which have become classics in the field of mass communication. This work
included a study of MacArthur Day in 1951 (which they devised during a course
in crowd behavior taught by Tom Shibutani) and her doctoral dissertation (under
Don Horton) on the televised political conventions in 1952. Both of these works
were ground-breaking in the nascent study of television, and resulted in several
publications (as well as the Edward L. Bernays Award for the MacArthur Day
paper) for the couple. Lang says that most of her learning and support at the
University of Chicago came from other graduate students because at that time,
the department was "falling apart" and because the study of television was so
new that no one really knew much about it.

While at the University of Chicago, Gladys Engel, now Gladys Lang, also
become one of the first women to be awarded a predoctoral fellowship from the
Social Science Research Council (SSRC). Although this was a great honor, it

turned sour for Lang after the SSRC attempted to revoke the award when they learned that she was pregnant. The SSRC reasoned that she could not be working on her dissertation if she was going to have to care for an infant. Although Lang was able to keep the award, she considers this one of the most disappointing events in her career. It was just part of a pattern of roadblocks she faced as a woman in academia. Lang received her Ph.D. from the University of Chicago in 1954.

CAREER DEVELOPMENT

Lang's career development progressed through two primary stages, the first when she worked as a researcher for the U.S. government after she received her M.A. at the University of Washington, and the second when she entered academia after completing her doctoral dissertation at the University of Chicago. Specifically, her professional career began in 1942 at the Office of War Information (OWI) in Washington, D.C., where she served as information analyst and acting chief of the Radio Section of the Bureau of Intelligence. There she conducted research on the usage and effectiveness of internal propaganda messages that were embedded in daytime radio soap operas and were designed to help the war effort.

In 1943 she accepted a position with the Office of Strategic Services (OSS) as a research analyst in the Research and Analysis Branch. This position took her from Washington, D.C., to London, where her research projects included such diverse topics as the assessment of food consumption in occupied Europe, the planning of psychological warfare, and the observation of postwar feminist movements. Later, she was transferred to Italy and then to China to engage in political and press analysis. This phase of her career ended in 1949 when she decided to return to school and work toward her doctorate degree at the University of Chicago.

The prospects for women in academia were not bright when Lang graduated with her Ph.D. in the mid-1950s and entered the second phase of her career. There were few job openings in academia at the time, and even fewer for female candidates. Realizing this, she and her husband decided that they would try to find a good job for him at a place where she could possibly locate work as a lecturer. Lang admits that watching her husband get the first shot at job openings was difficult for her to endure, and that "it hurt."

The Langs' first solid opportunity came in the form of a job offer from the University of Miami for Kurt Lang. Although Lang did not want to live in the South, the couple decided he should accept the position. Lang obtained a job as an instructor at the Fort Lauderdale campus of the University of Miami in the spring of 1954, but the couple quickly realized that the prospects at the University of Miami were not as good as they had expected. They spent that year in Florida attempting to make their mark by publishing as much as possible from their dissertations and building their academic reputations. After their first year at Miami, they decided it was time to move on. They both resigned from their positions and left without any other offers awaiting them.

Lang took a position as sessional lecturer in sociology at Carleton College (now Carleton University) in Ottawa, Canada, in 1955, after her husband was hired as the first research sociologist for the Canadian Broadcasting Corporation (CBC). While at Carleton College, Lang assisted her husband with some research for CBC designed to examine the before-and-after effects of television's introduction in Nova Scotia. However, she was restricted from training interviewers for the project because she was pregnant with her second child. Again, Lang was disturbed by the discrimination she experienced in the workplace. The Langs never completed the second phase of the study, and later another researcher conducted the second wave of data collection independent of them.

Because of her husband's desire to return to teaching, the Langs moved to New York in 1957 so that Kurt could assume a position at Queens College. Meanwhile, Lang took a position as lecturer of anthropology and sociology at Brooklyn College. In 1959 she, too, moved to Queens College to become a lecturer in sociology and anthropology, a position she held until 1965. She was unable to advance to a full-time permanent-line appointment with faculty rank owing to the antinepotism rules in place at the time. Lang describes this period of teaching at Brooklyn College and Queens College as difficult because of horribly bureaucratic systems that did not allow advancement at a reasonable rate, either for herself or her husband.

At this point in her career, Lang chose to take a position outside of academia with the Center for Urban Education (CUE) in New York City. At the same time, however, she had made a commitment to a one-year term as visiting associate professor at Rutgers University, from which she was unable to extricate herself. To accommodate her desire to work at the CUE as well as fulfill her contractual obligations, Lang caught a train after work at the CUE from New York to New Jersey one evening each week to deliver her lecture at Rutgers. Lang continued her work at the Center for Urban Education until 1969, studying school integration as senior research sociologist and director of the Field Research Unit from 1965 through 1967, and as the assistant director of the CUE in charge of research on mass media reporting of educational news, the education of children from low-income families, and parental involvement in school affairs from 1967 through 1969.

While working at the CUE, Lang was also a lecturer on the graduate faculty in the Department of Sociology at Columbia University from 1967 through 1970. She became a senior research associate and member of the Executive Board of the Bureau of Applied Social Research (again at Columbia University) in 1969 and remained at this post through 1971.

Throughout the 1970s and early 1980s, Lang taught at the State University of New York's Stony Brook campus along with her husband. During her time there, she served as the chair of the Interdisciplinary Program on Communication in Society (1972–1979), as a visiting professor, then professor of sociology and communication (1972–1984), and professor of political science (1980–1984). Several events during this point in her career illustrate the problems of discrimination against women which Lang felt in academia. First, she recalled the first time she was invited to a scholarly meeting without "& Kurt Lang" attached. To that point, all offers were either for Kurt alone or for the couple together. She considers this first solo invitation to a meeting at Syracuse University as a turning point in her career—a time when the discrimination she had felt throughout her career finally began to subside.

There was yet another indication of women's difficulty advancing in academia: after having built a distinguished career in governmental research for nearly a decade, a quarter-century teaching at universities across the country, and a very substantial list of publications and awards, Lang's first sabbatical did not come until the 1980s! She feels that it took all those years because, due to hiring practices and antinepotism rules, she had to take lecturer positions while her husband took the faculty posts wherever they went.

In 1984 the Langs were offered positions at Lang's alma mater, the University of Washington. Although when the position was offered, they were no longer actively looking to change universities, Lang jumped at the opportunity to return to Seattle, which she considered one of the most beautiful areas of the country. At the University of Washington she was professor of communications, political science, and sociology, and finally became professor emeritus in 1991.

MAJOR CONTRIBUTIONS AND ACHIEVEMENTS

The Langs' primary communication research may be remembered by most as "firehouse" research. That is, the research team of Lang and Lang is renowned for conducting critical events research, which, according to Lang, is a strategy used to study the impact of media coverage of major events and crises that are typically accompanied by shifts in public opinion. Included in the long list of events they have analyzed are the 1951 MacArthur Day celebration in Chicago (Lang & Lang, 1953), the 1952 Democratic convention (Lang & Lang, 1955, 1956a, 1956b, 1956–1957), the 1960 televised presidential debates (Lang & Lang, 1961, 1962), the 1976 televised presidential debates (Lang & Lang, 1978a, 1978b, 1979), and the Watergate scandal (Lang & Lang, 1980, 1983) among others.

The Langs have a knack for constructing an instrument and getting it into the field in relatively short order; their success has been proven through their many articles based on this form of research. In fact, the Langs published a book chapter on the topic of critical events analysis, drawing on their vast experience using this form of research (Kraus et al., 1975). Lang admits, however, that she is not necessarily very good at working up a detailed research proposal long in advance of the actual research (a requirement for grants from organizations such as the National Science Foundation). Instead, her approach is to find a topic of interest and simply determine the best way to answer whatever questions she may have formulated. Several times in her career she recalls being involved in research projects where so much time and money were devoted to preparation and planning that the research itself was either never conducted or never completed (including the study of the introduction of television in Nova Scotia for the CBC). The critical event research she has conducted has provided answers to many important questions that could not have even been asked by researchers following a more traditional route.

Lang considers the concept of *refraction* (first advanced in the paper that won her the Edward L. Bernays Award) to be her major theoretical contribution to the field of communication, primarily because it came so early in the study of electronic media in general and television in particular. The concept refers to the way the medium affects what is disseminated and understood by the audience—that is, the idea that the experience of watching, hearing, or reading media depictions of an event is not the same as being there. This idea was quite innovative at the time it was introduced, for many considered the medium of television to be analogous to a mode of transportation to an event without any change in effective content. One illustration of refraction is what Lang refers to as ''reciprocal effects,'' a term that describes how, for instance, a television camera makes people act differently simply by virtue of its presence (Lang & Lang, 1953).

Lang also believes that her work for the U.S. government during World War II helped in some way toward the war effort. She considers this work important because of the high stakes and practical application of the work she did for the OWI and OSS. By contrast, Lang feels that some of the work in academia (both her own and others') has been so mired in endless debate (such as the ever-present question ''Do media *really* have effects?'') that it has not been utilized in a meaningful manner.

Lang has done little research that focuses on women in particular or that might be of particular benefit to women. (For one example, however, see Lang, 1978.) One of Lang's major contributions to women might not have been any particular research or concept, but simply the fact that she was one of the first women social scientists to succeed in academia. She faced discrimination in hiring and promotion for at least the first 20 years of her career, and the fact that she was still able to make a significant contribution to several fields has been an inspiration to generations of women researchers. This inspiration may have in fact been her greatest contribution because it has spawned further research by female scholars who have followed in her footsteps.

CRITICAL EVALUATION OF CONTRIBUTIONS AND ACHIEVEMENTS

Although there has been little harsh criticism of her work, Lang feels that her research has also not made the impact that it might have made. As an example, she points out that her analysis in ''Mass Media and Voting'' (1959) has been acknowledged by McCombs and Shaw (1972) as an important essay leading to the agenda-setting hypothesis. However, when agenda setting is referred to, few go further back than to the paper by McCombs and Shaw. In addition, the Langs' book on public opinion and the Watergate affair (Lang & Lang, 1983) included a critique of the contemporary form of agenda-setting theory and worked toward a conception of "agenda building," which has received little attention in the field thus far. In her opinion these important contributions, as well as some others, have not been utilized by the field as a whole and have since fallen into disuse. Lang feels that, over the past 15 years, her research has simply not been quoted, partially because she was not schooled in and did not teach at a university with a large and prestigious communication program. Therefore, she did not have the ties to graduate students who might have furthered her work in the area of mass communication.

Lang believes that this trend may also be related to one of her shortcomings as a researcher: her apparent inability to formulate long-lasting concepts and devise catchy names for them. Also, she laments that she is simply one of those people who are "not apt to be quoted."

INTEGRATION OF PERSONAL AND PROFESSIONAL LIFE

For the most part, Lang has noticed few conflicts between her personal and professional life. The one major conflict related to her career, however, ended in a divorce. She married her first husband, a journalist, the year she graduated with her B.A. from Michigan. The marriage did not work out, however, primarily because of the competitive nature of the relationship, which she described as similar to a rivalry.

Since that time, however, Lang has felt that she experienced little—if any—dilemma when trying to coordinate her family and professional responsibilities. She met and married Kurt Lang while in her doctoral program and has worked closely with him as a research partner on a majority of her research. In this second marriage Lang found the mutually supportive relationship that she did not have in her first marriage.

The Langs had their first child, Glenna, in 1951 while both were still at the University of Chicago, and their second, Kevin, in 1955 after they had graduated and were working in Canada. Lang believes that she was a better mother because she was happy, and that it seemed to her to be a very natural way of life. She recalls bringing her young daughter to a conference and not seeing her for quite some time. Later, she met several people she was interested in talking to through her daughter's interactions with them! In addition, both children contributed to her research, with her son Kevin doing coding for some of her research projects at only 9 years of age.

Lang is also confident that she has been able to keep her personal feelings and her research separate. She feels that by approaching political issues from an academic perspective, she has been able to become an unbiased observer.

This was especially important for her doctoral dissertation on the 1952 political conventions, because she was a fervent supporter of Adlai Stevenson, the Democratic party nominee at that convention, and was personally involved in the events she studied. Considering her future work in critical events analysis, her cool and disinterested perspective was a distinct advantage.

Lang's life is replete with examples of seizing the moment. Her decisions to work toward the war effort for the government and to conduct research from a critical events analysis approach are a few examples of this approach. Lang has also not shied away from taking all that life has to offer, from having a successful marriage and raising children to having a hugely successful career in a time-demanding profession simultaneously without feeling that she was doing anything unnatural. Beginning in the 1940s, Gladys Engel Lang blazed a trail through academia for women, and now she rightfully takes her place as a pioneer in the field of mass communication.

NOTE

All quotations and biographical information not otherwise referenced are drawn from interviews with Gladys Engel Lang conducted by the author on August 2 and August 16, 1994.

REFERENCES

Kraus, S., Davis, D., Lang, G. E., & Lang, K. (1975). Critical events analysis. In S. Chaffee (ed.), *Political communication: Issues and strategies for research.* (pp. 95–216). Beverly Hills, Calif.: Sage.

Lang, G. E. (1978). The most admired woman: Image-making in the news. In G. Tuchman, A. K. Daniels, & J. Benet (eds.), *Hearth and home: Images of women in the mass media.* (pp. 147–160). New York: Oxford University Press.

Lang, G. E., & Lang, K. (1955). The inferential structure of political communications: A study in unwitting bias. *Public Opinion Quarterly, 19,* 168–183.

Lang, G. E., & Lang, K. (1978a). Immediate and delayed responses to a Carter-Ford debate: Assessing public opinion. *Public Opinion Quarterly, 42,* 322–341.

Lang, G. E., & Lang, K. (1978b). The first debate and the coverage gap. *Journal of Communication, 28*(4), 93–98.

Lang, G. E., & Lang, K. (1979). Making the least of it? Television coverage of the audio gap. In S. Kraus (ed.), *The great debates: Carter vs. Ford.* (pp. 158–174). Bloomington: Indiana University Press.

Lang, G. E., & Lang, K. (1980). Polling on Watergate: The battle for public opinion. *Public Opinion Quarterly, 44,* 530–547.

Lang, G. E., & Lang, K. (1983). *The battle for public opinion: The president, the press, and the polls during Watergate.* New York: Columbia University Press.

Lang, K., & Lang, G. E. (1953). The unique perspective of television and its effect: A pilot study. *American Sociological Review, 18,* 3–12.

Lang, K., & Lang, G. E. (1956a). Political participation and the television perspective. *Social Problems, 4,* 107–116.

Lang, K., & Lang, G. E. (1956b). The television personality in politics: Some consid-
erations. *Public Opinion Quarterly, 20,* 103–112.
Lang, K., & Lang, G. E. (1956–1957). Television and the intimate view of politics.
Journal of Broadcasting, 47–54.
Lang, K., & Lang, G. E. (1961). Ordeal by debate: Viewer reactions. *Public Opinion
Quarterly, 25,* 277–288.
Lang, K., & Lang, G. E. (1962). Reactions of viewers. In S. Kraus (ed.), *The great
debates.* (pp. 313–330). Bloomington: Indiana University Press.
McCombs, M. F., & Shaw, D. L. (1972). The agenda-setting function of mass media.
Public Opinion Quarterly, 176–187.

Additional Representative Communication Publications

Lang, G. E. (1987). Still seeking answers. *Critical Studies in Mass Communication,* 4,
211–214.
Lang, G. E., & Lang, K. (1984). *Politics and television reviewed.* Beverly Hills, Calif.:
Sage.
Lang, K., & Lang, G. E. (1968). *Politics and television.* Chicago: Quadrangle.
Lang, K., & Lang, G. E. (1968). *Voting and nonvoting: Implications of broadcasting
returns before polls are closed.* Waltham, Mass.: Blaisdell.
Lang, K., & Lang, G. E. (1983). The "new rhetoric" of mass communication research:
A longer view. *Journal of Communication,* 33(3), 128–140.
Lang, K., & Lang, G. E. (1984). The impact of polls on public opinion. *Annals, AAPSS,*
472, 129–142.
Lang, K., & Lang, G. E. (1988). Collective memory and the news. *Communication,* 11,
123–139.

Representative Noncommunication Publications

Lang, G. E. (1943). Some neglected temporal aspects of human ecology. *Social Forces,*
22, 43–47.
Lang, G. E. & Lang, K. (1990). *Etched in memory: The building and survival of artistic
reputation.* Chapel Hill: University of North Carolina Press.
Lang, K., & Lang, G. E. (1961). *Collective dynamics.* New York: Thomas Y. Crowell.
Lang, K., & Lang, G. E. (1965). Resistance to school desegregation: A case study of
backlash among Jews. *Sociological Inquiry,* 35, 54–106.

MARY MARGARET McBRIDE (1889–1976)

Sheila Clough Crifasi

Mary Margaret McBride started her career as a newspaper reporter but early on turned to magazines and became one of the highest paid magazine writers of the 1930s. She had the potential to achieve greater glory in the print media of her day, but instead she launched a new career in radio and turned herself into what *Forbes* magazine called one of "America's Twelve Master Salesmen" (Forbes, 1952) and into the first female talk show host in broadcasting. Combining journalistic techniques with a natural gift for chitchat, McBride adhered to stringent standards in selecting, researching, and interviewing guests, but she obscured her professionalism with an on-air persona that was over-the-back-fence folksy, ingenuous, and often somewhat dithery. Her vast, predominantly female audience adored her and purchased in huge quantities any product she recommended; they were still anchored to her program when the network took it off the air to replace it with a soap opera in 1954. She then left New York City to retire in the Catskills where she wrote several books and hosted a local radio program in Kingston, New York, three times a week. She died of cancer in 1976.

FAMILY BACKGROUND AND EDUCATION

Born in Paris, Missouri, on November 16, 1899, Mary Margaret McBride was the eldest of four children and the only daughter of Thomas Walker and Elizabeth Craig McBride. Bright and impressionable as a child, she was much influenced by her two grandfathers. Her maternal grandfather, a Baptist minister, taught her the Bible, saw that she attended church regularly (beginning when she was 4 years old), and was, no doubt, the one who inspired her to take the pledge against the evils of liquor when she was 8. Her McBride grandfather brought a totally different but apparently not incompatible perspective to the youthful Mary Margaret. He was a scholar who urged her to read Latin and Greek poetry, and he fostered her love for the classics and the written word. At a time when a female child—especially one reared in a Midwestern Baptist farm family—was expected to dedicate herself to learning domestic skills, Mary Margaret was encouraged by her grandfather to write.

She did write, but she also learned her domestic skills as she looked to her mother, a paragon of homemaking, as a role model. Elizabeth Craig McBride was the long-suffering wife of a man who enjoyed buying rundown farms, fixing them up, and, when they were repaired and operating smoothly, selling them and moving on to repeat the process. Elizabeth's way of smoothing out the lives of her children during these periodic upheavals was to whip the ramshackle kitchen into shape and immediately create a warm delicious center where they could eat her bountiful meals and feel at home. Mary Margaret never lost her appreciation for her mother and her homemaking abilities, nor for the rich foods that meant security, pleasure, and constancy during her early years.

When she was 6, McBride was enrolled at William Woods College, a private boarding school endowed by her Great Aunt Albina, whose dream it was to see her niece become headmistress of the institution. To that end, she paid for Mary Margaret's schooling from 1906 until 1916 when the girl entered the University of Missouri. But Mary Margaret had never given up her dream of becoming a writer and informed her aunt that she intended to major in journalism. With indignation at such a change in her plans, Great Aunt Albina thereupon ceased to be Mary Margaret's benefactor. As Bennett Cerf wrote in *The Saturday Review*, "when her horrified aunt heard that [Mary Margaret's plans] included writing, she not only withdrew all financial support, but hid the family silver" (March 1, 1947).

By cutting off the funds, Great Aunt Albina served as the impetus for her niece's first job on a newspaper. In order to pay her tuition, McBride became part-time reporter, copy boy, and society editor on the *Columbia Times* for $10 a week, and in spite of the demands of job and courses, she managed to complete her degree in two and a half years.

CAREER DEVELOPMENT

After graduation, Mary Margaret left Missouri to go to Washington, D.C., where she worked in the U.S. Senate briefly. Then, with the help of a college chum, she landed a job as cub reporter with the *Cleveland Press* and moved to Ohio. As a writer, she had a particular talent for finding and exploring the human interest elements in a story. This, in turn, led to many feature assignments, and before long she returned to Washington for a year as a special correspondent. McBride was happy with her work at the *Press*, but longed to go to New York; in 1920 she jumped at the chance to move there as assistant to the publicity director for the Interchurch World Movement. Although the job was short-lived, through it she met Stella Karn, who became her roommate in a Greenwich Village apartment and ultimately her business manager and closest friend.

McBride left this post when she applied for and got a job as reporter for the *New York Mail* at $40 a week. She soon hit her stride as a writer, selling features to the *Saturday Evening Post* and other popular magazines. When the *Mail* closed in 1924, she devoted all her time to magazine articles for top publications that paid her the astronomical sum of $1,000 and later $2,000 for each assignment. She collaborated with Paul Whiteman on a series on jazz for the *Saturday Evening Post*. The pieces were compiled into a book published by Sears. Now McBride entered the world of books and soon even had a best-seller with *Paris Is a Woman's Town,* written with Helen Josephy.

By 1929 McBride was well established professionally and, along with thousands of other rising stars, began to dabble in the stock market. When the crash came, she lost everything, including most of the outlets for her articles as magazine after magazine folded. She had to start all over again.

THE WONDERFUL WORLD OF RADIO

To McBride, looking for a job meant scouring the city for openings in print media, but someone told her a local radio station was looking for a woman to do an afternoon program and, with strong encouragement from Stella Karn, she decided to try out for it. She auditioned but quickly put it out of her mind because she thought the producers would find her Missouri twang inappropriate for giving household hints to the sophisticated women of New York City. Much to her surprise, she got the job and went on the air as Martha Deane, the helpful grandmother who could offer advice and encouragement to her grateful listeners.

She immediately left her mark on the role, according to an account written in 1941.

After three venerable days she unceremoniously amputated a couple of generations and came out under her true colors. The household hints soon went the way of Grandmother. Fascinated by the antics of a trained flea on Forty-Second Street, Mary Margaret told her audience about him the next day. Demands for more such tales came pouring in, and presently she was simply rattling on about whatever struck her fancy. (*Current Biography 1941*)

McBride would follow this pattern throughout her broadcast career, even after she added interviews with guests to the mix of recipes, homemaking tips, and chitchat that was the original format—and even when she went on network radio to a national audience. She was one of the first broadcasters to ad-lib anecdotes and observations, but her off-the-cuff remarks and exclamations about the glories of her sponsors' products did not come without preparation. McBride spent most evenings and long into the nights reading and preparing for the next day's program. She also had a staff of researchers and aides to arm her with all the background information she would need for her interviews, commercials, and chatter. She worked from scribbled notes on scraps of paper, and if she misplaced them, listeners from coast to coast would hear her scrambling through papers and mumbling to herself until she found what she was looking for.

McBride's aides also helped her test products to make sure they lived up to a potential sponsor's claims, because, as Grandpa Craig had taught her, McBride would not tell a lie. When she marveled at the taste of a new canned food or the effectiveness of a laundry soap, she could speak with gusto (and did) because she had found out the taste and the effectiveness for herself. Often she would eat while on the air, smacking her lips and sighing ecstatically over each yummy morsel.

Grandpa Craig's influence was also evident in her strict policy against doing commercials for cigarettes or liquor. That wasn't a problem for her listeners, however. First regionally, and then nationally when she moved from WOR to the NBC network in 1940, she had an audience who followed her every recommendation. Both her natural honesty and her careful preparation contributed to her effectiveness as a salesperson. Her approach might have appeared scatterbrained to some, but Bennett Cerf observed, "The products of the sponsors creep unobtrusively into the conversation. Mary Margaret's thoughts, it develops, are about as scattered as a Times Square crowd on a New Year's Eve, her approach as vague as a pay-off punch by Joe Louis" (March 1, 1947).

Throughout the 1940s, the Mary Margaret phenomenon fascinated the press. *Time* observed, "She is easily the number one salesman on the air. Her five to ten million women listeners buy any product she plugs," and pointed out that sales of a soft drink that was advertised only on her show rose 900 percent (December 2, 1946). Collie Small, writing in *Collier's*, compared McBride to the charismatic evangelist preacher Aimee Temple McPherson in her ability to generate passionate devotion from followers (December 11, 1948).

Also the subject of commentary was Mary Margaret's interviewing skill. Grandpa McBride's influence is clear in her choice of guests. As Bennett Cerf asserted, "She frankly prefers authors as her guest stars—and what a job she does with them! ... The authors are so at ease they frequently forget they're broadcasting." Cerf recounted a time when writer Jesse Stuart told Mary Margaret some racy stories about his "grandpaw in the Kentucky hills, then drawled, 'We goin' on the air soon?' " They had been on the air for 35 minutes, he was told. " 'Hell, ma'am,' he exclaimed, 'I never would have talked that way about old Grandpaw. I was so comfortable, I thought we were rehearsin!' " (March 1, 1947).

Publishers' Weekly reported McBride's comment that she couldn't remember how she first happened to have authors on her show, but estimated that about 20,000 had appeared through the years (December 12, 1960). During these interviews, authors were often astonished to hear McBride reel off long passages from their books verbatim. She could do this, *Newsweek* explained, because she read from one to three books a day "with a photographic eye." The magazine quoted Robert E. Sherwood, the playwright, author, and Pulitzer Prize winner, who gushed, "I absolutely love her. She makes [the broadcast] a lot of fun. It's most painless; you forget the microphone and really enjoy yourself. . . . She simply has a phenomenal mind." *Newsweek* also credited Mary Margaret's as the "only worth-while talk show on radio" (May 30, 1949).

Allen Churchill in *The American Mercury* presented some other comments on her interview techniques. " 'It's the damnedest thing the way she makes people give,' a studio official muttered after hearing her lead Sally Rand through a touching account of an Ozark childhood. Mary Margaret's seemingly aimless technique is really a rich mixture of experience and skill. 'You have to be a professional to realize the terrific genius behind that careless informality,' a rival once said." Churchill pointed out that McBride selected her guests carefully, and when she asked people to be interviewed, they rarely refused. "After his triumphant return from Europe, General Omar Bradley rejected other offers for radio appearances but accepted with alacrity when Mary Margaret reached him. His reply, on that occasion, sums up the married man's reaction to her program. 'Maybe my wife will appreciate me at last' " (January 1949).

BOOKS AND OTHER ACCOMPLISHMENTS

McBride's innovations in radio were recognized and studied by international broadcasters. According to *Current Biography 1954*, "She flew to the opening of Norway's government radio station in 1948 upon that country's invitation and received from King Haakon a medal for notable broadcasts." And after leaving NBC to join the American Broadcasting Company in 1950, "The 'first lady of radio' broadcast the coronation of Queen Elizabeth II from London's BBC station, where British radio engineers came in to study her expert handling of commercials" (*Current Biography 1954*).

The Haitian government recognized Mary Margaret with its National Order of Honor and Merit. She also received the One World Award, was cited for special recognition by the Virgin Islands, and was awarded a special medal of honor from the city of Vienna in the early 1950s. A member of Kappa Alpha Theta and Theta Sigma Phi journalism honor societies, Mary Margaret also belonged to the Women's City Club, the Authors' League, New York Newspaper Women's Club, Query, and Heterodoxy.

In reporting that Mary Margaret had been honored by the Society of Audubon Artists for making "the most notable contribution to radio in the past year," *Time* magazine said that her radio awards come "by the baker's dozen" (December 2, 1946). Even the State of Missouri got into the act when it dedicated November 22, 1939, as Mary Margaret McBride Day. Later, in 1943, a rose was named for her.

An even more telling consequence of her impact on listeners was the number of people who joined her for her various anniversaries in radio. "Her first five years in radio were marked by emotional ceremonies which packed the commodious Grand Central Palace in New York. Her tenth anniversary was held in the vastly larger Madison Square Garden, into which 20,000 of her followers crowded after 125,000 had requested tickets," reported *The American Mercury* (January 1949). So many were turned away during the Garden ceremony that fifteenth-anniversary festivities were held at Yankee Stadium—and it was filled to capacity.

During all these years in radio, McBride continued to write. She was editor of the women's page for the Newspaper Enterprise Association of New York City in 1934 and 1935. And for a number of years in the 1950s, the Associated Press syndicate was the outlet for "Mary Margaret McBride Says," a daily newspaper column. In addition to the book on jazz with Paul Whiteman, she collaborated with others to write histories, biographies, travel guides, commentaries (some autobiographical), cookbooks, and even a children's story. She worked with Prince Christopher of Greece on a history of his family, as she had with Alexander Williams on *Charm* earlier (1927), and with Helen Josephy on three more travel books—*London Is a Man's Town* (1930), *New York Is Everybody's Town* (1931), and *Beer and Skittles* (1932). She also wrote *The Story of Dwight Morrow* (1930); *Here's Martha Deane* (1936); *How Dear to My Heart* (1940); *America for Me* (1941); *Tune in for Elizabeth* (1945); *Harvest of American Cooking* (1957); *Encyclopedia of American Cooking* (1959); *A Long Way from Missouri* (1959); *Out of the Air* (1960); and *The Growing up of Mary Elizabeth* (1966). In addition, she edited *How to Be a Successful Advertising Woman* (1948).

CONTRIBUTIONS AND ACHIEVEMENTS

Because accounts of Mary Margaret McBride's radio years tend to emphasize sales over substance, it is easy to forget that she played an important role in the history of broadcasting. Even in 1949, Allen Churchill wrote,

Today, when women's programs glut the air, it is difficult to believe that in 1934, when Mary Margaret's agent steered her to a mass audition at WOR, there were no such programs. The one visualized by WOR, conducted by a lone woman, was a daring experiment. No one knew what to do on such a program, or what to expect. (January 1949)

Mary Margaret showed them how to do it. She established the pattern not only for women's programs, but also for all talk shows.

Considering the uneven quality of some of the television shows that have evolved from the earlier radio models, this might seem a dubious contribution to journalism. But McBride's pattern of mixing the mundane with larger issues and personalities of her day served to enlighten an audience that normally would never have had exposure to them. At a time when the "little woman" was expected to devote herself to cooking, cleaning, and children and leave it to her man to think about the really important things, Mary Margaret had housewives by the thousands listening to the observations of Jesse Stuart, Robert E. Sherwood, General Omar Bradley, Eleanor Roosevelt,* Harry S Truman, and many other leaders from a variety of fields. Among the hundreds of letters she received each week were those "from husbands, who thanked her for giving their wives something to talk about at dinner" (Churchill, January 1949).

Like John Reith, the first director-general of the British Broadcasting Corporation, McBride used the power of radio to educate. But while Reith felt he should elevate the tastes and broaden the outlooks of his listeners through BBC programs (Head, 1985), McBride wanted to share interesting people and ideas with the friends who tuned into her show every day. She looked at potential guests with the journalist's eye, always seeking out those with stories to tell, those who embodied timeliness, uniqueness, human interest, and the other qualities intrinsic in news. She would never gear her offerings to the lowest common denominator, a concept that would appall her as much as it would Reith. She was able to hook her audience because she brought her guests to them as new neighbors in the comfortable world that she created with her chatter about food and other homey subjects (and even those were thoroughly researched and prepared).

In observing what she did and how she did it, one is reminded again of the triumvirate whose influence made her the person she was both on and off the air—because she truly was the embodiment of the domesticity of her mother, the high moral standards and no-nonsense approach of one grandfather, and the love for knowledge and the written word of another grandfather.

Perhaps because of some of the contradictory messages she received as a child, McBride became a capable professional who often doubted her own ability. According to Anne S. Bittker (1981),

Though, on the one hand, M.'s work was characterized by deep-seated religious and moral convictions, plus sincere and un-self-conscious sentimentality, she was at the same time a tough and searching reporter. And though she struggled against and never conquered deep feelings of guilt and insecurity, she numbered among her close friends heads of state and celebrities in diverse fields in the U.S. and abroad. (pp. 62–63)

Although she had warm relationships with many, she had little time in her life for others. Allen Churchill wrote in *The Mercury* (January 1949):

Friends of Mary Margaret complain that she devotes more time to her listeners than to the people she really knows. This is true. She seems perfectly content to sleep only five hours a night and to give nearly every waking moment to work—broadcasting, reading three or four books a day, answering hundreds of letters.

Her closest friend was her manager, Stella Karn, who handled all her business dealings. "Miss Karn, a small woman with snapping black eyes and a firm chin, supplies the qualities Mary Margaret lacks that are necessary to success in commercial radio," observed Barbara Heggie in *The New Yorker* (December 19, 1942). Karn's death in 1954 coincided with Mary Margaret's forced retirement from NBC and probably was the deciding factor in her move to West Shokan in the Catskills in 1960. Her brief encounter with the new world of television during those years was neither successful nor particularly inviting for her without her partner there to support and encourage her.

Typically for McBride, she did not totally retire. Her thrice weekly program on local station WGHQ occupied her later years, and even when she was dying of cancer, she went on broadcasting from her hospital bed.

When she died in 1976, she ended an active productive career and put her dreams of being a great writer to rest. As she herself observed, "I've enjoyed my life and don't regret any of it. But I can see that, taken altogether it is faintly, sometimes even blatantly ridiculous. I wanted to be a great writer, and now I never shall be" (Bittker, 1981, pp. 62–63).

REFERENCES

America's 12 master salesmen. (1952). *Forbes*, 107–119.

Bittker, A. S. (1981). Mary Margaret McBride. In L. Mainiero (ed.), *American women writers*. (pp. 61–63). New York: Frederick Ungar.

Cerf, B. (1947). Here comes McBride. *The Saturday Review*, 30, 4–6.

Churchill, A. (1949). Mary Margaret McBride. *The American Mercury*, 68, 7–14.

Current Biography 1941 (1941). (pp. 540–542).

Current Biography 1954 (1954). (pp. 420–422).

Deaths (1976). *Newsweek*, 87, 55.

Deaths (1976). *Time*, 107, 97.

Exit Mary Margaret (1957). *Newsweek*, 69, 52.

Goodness! (1946). *Time*, 48, 80–81.

Head, S. W. (1985). *World broadcasting systems*. (pp. 74–75). Belmont, Calif.: Wadsworth Publishing Co.

Heggie, B. (1942). The forty-five-minute tempo. *The New Yorker*, 18, 27–30, 32, 34.

Krebs, A. (1976, April 8). Mary Margaret McBride of radio talk show dies. *New York Times*, 40.

Mary Margaret McBride reviews her career on radio. (1960). *Publishers' Weekly*, 178, 15.

Ross, Ishbel. (1974). *Ladies of the press*. (pp. 254–256). New York: Arno Press.

Small, C. (1948). The private life of a Pied Piper. *Collier's*, 122, 28, 36, 39.

The McBride phenomenon. (1949). *Newsweek*, 33, 50.

Books by Mary Margaret McBride

McBride, M. M. (1930). *The story of Dwight Morrow*. New York: Farrar & Rinehart.

McBride, M. M. (1932). *The life story of Clark Gable*. New York: Star Library.

McBride, M. M. (1932). *The life story of Constance Bennett*. New York: Star Library.
McBride, M. M. (1932). *The life story of Greta Garbo*. New York: Star Library.
McBride, M. M. (1936). *Here's Martha Deane*. Garden City, N.Y.: Garden City Publishing.
McBride, M. M. (1940). *How dear to my heart*. New York: Macmillan Co.
McBride, M. M. (1941). *America for me*. New York: Macmillan Co.
McBride, M. M. (1945). *Tune in for Elizabeth*. New York: Dodd, Mead & Co.
McBride, M. M. (ed.). (1948). *How to be a successful advertising woman*. New York: Whittlehouse.
McBride, M. M. (1957). *Harvest of American cooking*. New York: Putnam.
McBride, M. M. (1959). *Encyclopedia of American cooking*. Evanston, Ill.: Homemaker Research Institute.
McBride, M. M. (1959). *A long way from Missouri*. New York: Putnam.
McBride, M. M. (1960). *Out of the air*. Garden City, N.Y.: Doubleday.
McBride, M. M. (1966). *The growing up of Mary Elizabeth*. New York: Dodd, Mead & Co.
McBride, M. M., & Josephy, H. (1929). *Paris is a woman's town*. New York: Coward-McCann.
McBride, M. M., & Josephy, H. (1930). *London is a man's town*. New York: Coward-McCann.
McBride, M. M., & Josephy, H. (1931). *New York is everybody's town*. New York: Putnam.
McBride, M. M., & Josephy, H. (1932). *Beer and skittles*. New York: Putnam.
McBride, M. M., & Whiteman, P. (1926). *Jazz*. New York: Sears.
McBride, M. M., & Williams, A. (1927). *Charm*. New York: Rae D. Henkle.

ANNE O'HARE McCORMICK (1880–1954)

Margot Hardenbergh

Anne O'Hare McCormick was one of the foremost foreign correspondents who reported and interpreted world events for Americans from 1920 through 1954, years rich with events, dictators, wars, and transformations. She was known for her interviews with world leaders and their peoples and for her ability to place them in the larger context of history. Midway through her career as a correspondent she won the Pulitzer Prize, the first woman to do so in her own name only. Although she had no formal schooling in the field, her first job was in journalism and she led a life in pursuit of excellence as a reporter, a profession she held in the highest regard. Anne O'Hare McCormick was amply rewarded for her efforts with popularity among her readers and her sources. In her lifetime she received as many honors as could be bestowed on one person.

FAMILY BACKGROUND AND EDUCATION

Anne O'Hare McCormick was born Anna Elizabeth O'Hare on May 16, 1880 in Wakefield, Yorkshire, England, of American parents, Thomas and Teresa Beatrice Berry O'Hare. Shortly after her birth and her Roman Catholic baptism, the family moved to the United States and settled in Columbus, Ohio.

Anne was the eldest of three daughters and attended St. Mary's of the Spring Academy in Columbus, Ohio, for convent high school. St. Mary's was her only formal educational experience, but it gave her an excellent grounding in Latin and religious studies, areas that would prove beneficial to her coverage of events in Europe, particularly in Italy. Although Anne never went to college, when St. Mary's became a four-year college she was asked to speak at its first commencement in 1928.

Anne's father was a regional manager for the Home Life Insurance Company but ran into business problems and left the family when Anne was 14. He was never heard from again. To earn a living, her mother ran a dry goods store and sold, door-to-door, a book of her poetry, *Songs at Twilight* (1898). After Anne's graduation from high school, the mother and three daughters moved to Cleveland, Ohio. Anne's mother took a publishing job and began writing a column and editing the woman's section of the weekly *Catholic Universe Bulletin*. Anne joined her mother and became the *Bulletin*'s associate editor. She worked there for ten years. At the age of 30, on September 14, 1910, Anne married Dayton businessman Francis J. McCormick.

CAREER DEVELOPMENT

McCormick moved with her husband to Dayton, Ohio, and kept active in journalism by writing articles for the *Catholic World Reader Magazine* and the *New York Times Magazine*. She wrote poetry for *Smart Set* and *Bookman* and also wrote a history of her former parish church titled *St. Agnes Church, Cleveland, Ohio: An Interpretation* (1920).

Francis McCormick had taken over his father's business, the manufacturing, importing, and selling of plumbing supplies in Dayton, Ohio. His job demanded that he travel to Europe many months every year, and Anne O'Hare McCormick accompanied him. While on the trips she observed the habits and politics of all the countries she visited and developed her reporting and interviewing skills. She talked with everyone she could, leaders and tradespeople, Catholic bishops and hotel porters. She made friends and on return visits was sure to maintain contact and make new friends.

Before one visit to Europe in 1921, realizing the political activity she would be in the midst of, she tentatively sent a note to Carr Van Anda, managing editor of the *New York Times*, offering to send back articles based on her reporting. Van Anda responded by saying "Try It." She did and from then on filed articles to the *Times* until her death. McCormick became a regular contributor to the *Times* in 1922, wrote articles for the *Times* and *Atlantic Monthly,* and then exclusively for the *Times* after 1925 except for a series of articles for *Ladies' Home Journal* and a book based on her *Times* articles.

McCormick prepared assiduously for every interview through research in complex issues and conversations with any people she could meet, turning off the main avenues to strike up conversations in the small alleys and shops. By the time she reached the interview, she would be well versed in the factual background and public opinion of the issue and person. Because of her knowledge and personality, people were as interested in talking with McCormick as she was with them. The preparation was appreciated especially by the many leaders she interviewed, including Prime Minister of Ireland Eamon De Valera; Adolph Hitler; Joseph Stalin; Greek Premier Eleutherios Venizelos; Austrian Chancellors Engelbert Dollfuss and Kurt von Schuschnigg; German statesman and winner of the Nobel Peace Prize Gustav Stresemann; and U. S. Presidents

Franklin D. Roosevelt, Harry S Truman, and Dwight D. Eisenhower. But it was her initial response to Italy's fascist leader, Benito Mussolini, that brought her success with the *Times*.

McCormick was one of the first reporters to recognize Mussolini as a powerful force. Her colleagues knew Mussolini as a fellow reporter covering news events for his newspaper, *Il Populo d'Italia,* and paid no attention to him. But while covering an address of King Victor Emmanuel II in the Italian Chamber of Deputies on June 21, 1921, McCormick heard Mussolini give a speech and reported it to be one of the best political speeches she had heard, "a little swaggering, but caustic, powerful and telling." Perhaps because of her religious training, or her study of Latin, she could predict the hold he would have over the Italians. Over the next decades she interviewed him many times and as with many other important figures came to be seen as a serious reporter who would help explain events.

In 1927, accompanied by her husband, she set off for a trip through Russia for a series of articles on the first ten years after the Russian Revolution. She was granted a private audience with Stalin, when no other American journalist was granted such an interview. She was able to keep him answering questions for six hours. Her only book, *The Hammer and the Scythe* (1928), is based on the series of articles she wrote for the *Times*.

McCormick continued to write articles for the *Times* based on her travels on the Continent, but she also wrote while she was in the United States. She wrote articles based on lengthy interviews with presidential candidate Franklin D. Roosevelt, articles on the early days of the New Deal and the American scene, as well as a series about the South. Despite all this output, she was unable to get a full-time position at the *Times* until there was a change in publishers. Adolph S. Ochs, publisher of the *Times* from 1896 to 1934, was a Southern conservative who worked diligently to keep women out of the newsroom.

One of Arthur Hays Sulzberger's first appointments as president and publisher of the *New York Times,* in late 1935, was to ask McCormick to join the editorial board. He told her she was to be the voice for freedom, "to shout whenever freedom is interfered with in any part of the world." McCormick had been an ardent supporter of the League of Nations and later the United Nations, hoping for "individual freedom to be safeguarded by universal law." McCormick was the first woman to write for the editorial page, and for the next 18 years she wrote a column three times a week; on the other days when she was in the country she contributed unsigned editorials. Her column was first entitled "In Europe" and then "Abroad."

In 1937 she won the Pulitzer Prize for her correspondence. She was the second woman to receive a Pulitzer, the first to receive it on her own, and the only woman to receive it for her work as a whole, rather than just one article. In that year the Pulitzer Prize in correspondence included both national and foreign correspondence.

Winning the Pulitzer Prize was not the culminating event for her days as a foreign correspondent; rather, it was the first step in public recognition. She covered the buildup to U.S. involvement in the Second World War, the North Atlantic Treaty Organization, the Korean War, the United Nations, U.S.-European relations, as well as U.S.-Asian relations.

MAJOR CONTRIBUTIONS AND ACHIEVEMENTS

Curious, modest, friendly, proud to be a reporter are all terms used to describe Anne O'Hare McCormick, the first woman to serve as a regular contributor to the editorial page of the *New York Times* and the first woman to win a Pulitzer Prize in her name alone. McCormick wrote only one book, *The Hammer and the Scythe,* because she found reporting to be more important to the reader. She said the reader tended to pay attention to the news only when some great event commanded their attention. Thus, she found the best use of her time to be covering the events and the people's roles in those events, people both notable and obscure. After numerous articles written as a free lancer from 1910 through 1936, McCormick wrote a column for the *New York Times* three times a week and many unsigned editorials from 1937 until her death on May 29, 1954. There are two collections of her articles edited by Marion Turner Sheehan published posthumously, *A Vatican Journal* (1956) and *The World at Home* (1956). There are also copies of the many speeches she was asked to give.

Anne O'Hare McCormick was respected by both men and women, and they showered her with recognition. In 1941 she was listed as being one of four people who had received the greatest number of honorary degrees (Columbia, Fordham, Ohio State, Dayton, and New York universities, Elmira, Manhattan, Middlebury, Villanova, Lafayette, Smith, Wellesley, Mount St. Vincent, Wilson, and Rollins colleges and the New Jersey College for Women). She received the *New York Evening Post* Medal (1934); the New York Newspaper Women's Club prize for best feature article; a gold watch for best interpretation of foreign affairs from the Overseas Press Club; the Woman of the Year by the National Federation of Business and Professional Women's Clubs, the American Woman's Association Medal (1939); the Theodore Roosevelt Memorial Medal of the Women's Roosevelt Memorial Association (1941); and the Gold Medal of the National Institute of Social Science (1942). Other honors included the Siena Medal of Theta Phi Alpha (1944); the University of Notre Dame Laetare Medal (1944); the International Altrusa Distinguished Service Award (1945); the Women's National Press Club Achievement Award (1945); the Chi Omega National Achievement Award (1946); the Theodore Roosevelt Distinguished Service Medal (1950); and the William the Silent Award for journalism (1952). She held membership in the National Institute of Arts and Letters. She was a Chevalier of the French Legion of Honor. McCormick was a delegate to the United Nation's Educational, Scientific and Cultural Organization Conferences in 1946 and 1948. At her death she received tributes from journalists and world leaders, including President Dwight D. Eisenhower, British Foreign Secretary Anthony Eden, and many ambassadors. She was offered a mass at the American College in Rome by Cardinal Francis Joseph Spellman.

CRITICAL EVALUATION OF CONTRIBUTIONS AND ACHIEVEMENTS

McCormick learned the skills of reporting and writing as her career developed, but she brought to her profession a passion to understand people both famous and hidden. She was always a thorough researcher, a compassionate interviewer, and a writer interested in style.

McCormick's first interview with Mussolini reveals how industrious a reporter she was. He considered the interview with her as yet another confrontation. When she started asking him his opinion of a new book, *The Law of Corporations,* a voluminous legal volume about law for a corporate state, he asked her if she had read the book. She responded that she had, and he congratulated her, saying they were probably the only two people who had. From then on she never had trouble arranging an interview with him—access that would be very helpful to the *Times* in its coverage of fascism. Later McCormick would often comment on Mussolini's affableness in the interviews in contrast to his arrogance at the podium.

McCormick never took notes during interviews, for she felt they hampered the exchange, making people too cautious. Instead, she listened carefully, absorbed facts and figures, and drank in the mood of persons and places. And invariably her interviews resulted in more interviews. She treated important figures as human beings, and they admired and respected her for her understanding of world politics and people. Her experience offered the American public a way to compare its leaders with other leaders throughout the world. And she synthesized the leaders' views with the people's for the benefit of all her readers.

The title of her book, *The Hammer and the Scythe,* is indicative of McCormick's concern with detail and her observations. Rather than use the term *sickle* as used in the communist emblem, she used the term *scythe* because it was the scythe that she saw being used throughout the country. Her keen observation always dominated her work.

The broad scope of *The Hammer and the Scythe* also demonstrates McCormick's thoroughness as a reporter. The 14 chapters cover Russia's geography, ethnic groups, major cities, bureaucracy, past royalty, peasants, river Volga, role of women, new Soviet generation, religious images or *ikons,* the way the workers spent their leisure time, the arts, the Russians' view of the rest of the world, and a comparison of Moscow, Rome, and New York. This extensive, encompassing approach to covering foreign affairs won her the interviews, the space in a major newspaper, and the devoted readership and popularity that she gained as she continued writing.

McCormick was also known for her acceptance of editing by her editors. In the beginning of her work for the *Times,* her longwindedness gave her the nickname Verbose Annie. Her editors would cut her articles down, but she never complained. Soon she wrote seamless, smooth articles that went to press unedited.

Her writing was fresh, full of wisdom, and prophetic. She was intrigued by the influence that news events would have on people's lives, their characters and values. Instead of the "he said, . . . she said" often found in interviews, her articles uncovered the characters and the setting. Some referred to her as a poet with a sense of style about everything she did.

McCormick also was sure of herself as a woman. Her colleagues referred to her as a deeply feminine person who would not be otherwise. All of her reporting included women's concerns, family issues, and social issues.

She maintained her style of reporting by speaking to as many people as possible. Danger did not warn her away. She always wanted to be where the news was, whether interviewing American General George S. Patton at the front when the Allied forces invaded France or covering the guerrilla war in Greece. Her compassion led her to cover the horrors of war as she grieved for those who were hurt the most—the individuals, the families, the young and the old.

INTEGRATION OF PERSONAL AND PROFESSIONAL LIFE

It is difficult for anyone to find fault with McCormick. Modesty may have been her greatest fault. She claimed her success came simply because she happened to bump into the crises as they were happening.

Some say her love of hats was her greatest vice. Although innocent enough for a small woman of 5'2", her hats did lead to a problem on at least one occasion. In June 1944, while in Washington trying to get an interview with President Roosevelt, McCormick attended a press conference held by Eleanor Roosevelt.* The president had time available for an interview and sent his assistant to look for her in the conference. Although she was at the press conference, the assistant was unable to find her under her hat and she missed the opportunity for the interview.

Throughout her career as a journalist, Anne O'Hare McCormick had the benefit of a unique marriage that lasted through her career, with her husband serving as a very devoted companion, sounding board, and debater. There were no children. Francis J. McCormick was always with her, discussing her work. At first their travels were dictated by his business needs, but as she grew in stature and the *Times* sent her abroad, he retired from his business and accompanied her. In the later years, Anne was always sure to have him by her side in spite of his failing health.

McCormick was known as a friendly, cheerful, and a talkative person with a sense of humor. As good as she was at taking editors' requests for rewrites, she could look at the situation humorously. One time after Lester Markel, the Sunday editor, asked for three or four rewrites, which she graciously submitted, she resubmitted her first draft which Markel accepted without question. When covering the 1952 Republican convention she wore a silk dress covered with little Democratic donkeys, and when covering that year's Democratic convention her silk dress was covered with little Republican elephants.

Robert Duffus' tribute to McCormick on May 31, 1954 in her "Abroad" column is a fine summary of Anne O'Hare McCormick's life as a reporter:

She was a reporter and gloried in the title. She could not understand how anyone could be satisfied with less than the personal observation on the spot. . . . She shrank in horror from much that went on, but her heart was associated with a keen and logical mind. She would never have said, and never did say, that because the strife for justice was costly we must admit to injustice. She knew that there are eternal truths and eternal principles for which sacrifices must be made. She felt and showed in her writing the great pulses of history and did not deceive herself. (p. 12)

REFERENCES

Beasley, M. H., & Gibbons, S. J. (1993). *Taking their place: A documentary history of women and journalism*. Washington, D.C.: American University Press, in cooperation with the Women's Institute for Freedom of the Press.

Belford, B. (1986). *Brilliant bylines: A biographical anthology of notable newspaperwomen in America*. New York: Columbia University Press.

Davis, K. S. (1993). *FDR into the Storm, 1937–40*. New York: Random House.

Edwards, J. (1988). *Women of the world. The great foreign correspondents*. Boston: Houghton Mifflin Co.

Letter of Eleanor Roosevelt to Lorena Hickok, April 3, 1933, Box 1, Lorena Hickok Papers, Franklin D. Roosevelt Library, Hyde Park, New York.

Marzolf, M. T. (1977). *Up from the footnote, A history of women journalists*. New York: Hastings House.

Memoranda of Franklin D. Roosevelt. (1944). President's Personal File #675, June 1944. Franklin D. Roosevelt Library, Hyde Park, New York.

New York Times. (1954, May 30). Anne O'Hare McCormick is dead . . . 1 & 44.

New York Times. (1954, May 31). Abroad, A tribute to Anne O'Hare McCormick.

New York Times. (1954, May 31). Mass for Anne O'Hare McCormick.

Reston, J. B. (1956). Introduction to *The world at home, selections from the writings of Anne O'Hare McCormick*. Marion Turner Shannon, ed. New York: Alfred A. Knopf.

Robertson, N. (1992). *The girls in the balcony: Women, men and the New York Times*. New York: Random House.

Roosevelt, Eleanor. (1949) *This I remember*. New York: Harper & Brothers.

Ross, I. (1974). *Ladies of the press*. (pp. 360, 366–368). New York: Arno Press.

Representative Works Available

McCormick, Anne O'Hare. (1928). *The hammer & the scythe: Communist Russia enters the second decade*. New York: Alfred A. Knopf, (2nd printing 1928, 3rd, November 1929.)

McCormick, Anne O'Hare. (1932, September 11). Roosevelt's view of the big job. *New York Times Magazine.*

McCormick, Anne O'Hare. (1934, July 8). Roosevelt surveys his course. *New York Times Magazine.*

McCormick, Anne O'Hare. (1941, May 14) "Ourselves and Europe." The second lecture on the Helen Kenyon Lectureship at Vassar College.

Sheehan, M. T. (ed.). (1956). *The Vatican journal, Selections from the writings of Anne O'Hare McCormick.* New York: Alfred A. Knopf.

Sheehan, M. T. (ed.). (1956). *The world at home, Selections from the writings of Anne O'Hare McCormick.* New York: Alfred A. Knopf.

SARA MILLER McCUNE
(1941–   )

Candace Lewis

Sara Miller McCune has had only one job interview in her life—a 1961 interview that landed her a job at Macmillan, Inc. in Manhattan. No further interviews were necessary for this confident, young professional. In 1966, one month before her twenty-fourth birthday, Sara founded Sage Publications, Inc., and proceeded to establish her company as a premier publishing house of social scientific books and journals. Within the communication field, Sage disseminates serials such as *Communication Abstracts, Communication Research, American Behavioral Scientist,* and *The European Journal of Communication.* Over its history, Sage has "gone global," establishing affiliates in London and New Delhi, distribution relations in Sydney and Tokyo, and co-publishing relations in Singapore. As the knowledge of future scholars is informed and shaped by the information Sage publishes, the work both she and her late husband George McCune dedicated to the social scientific community and disciplines is irrefutable.

FAMILY BACKGROUND AND EDUCATION

Sara Miller was born to Rose Blass Miller and Nathan M. Miller on February 2, 1941, in Manhattan's New York Hospital. Her parents were both natives of the New York metropolitan area, and raised Sara and Abraham—her younger brother by five years—in the Bronx and later Queens boroughs of New York City. Because of the Depression, neither Rose nor Nathan attended college after they graduated from New York City's public school system. Sara describes her father as an independent, small-business owner, and says her mother was something of a frustrated actress who encouraged Abraham and her to pursue dramatic efforts like singing, dancing, and acting lessons throughout grade school and high school.

Having learned to read at age 4, Sara describes her young self as "a great reader," a good student, and a curious child. "Growing up in a Jewish family," she says, "education was highly valued. The expectation was that you'd do well in school and go as far in school as you could." Sara did so well, in fact, that she was advanced a grade in junior high school, enabling her to graduate from high school at age 16 in 1957. She remembers English and drama teachers as being influential during her schooling, although her own extracurricular experiences as president of a neighborhood B'nai B'rith youth organization was also extremely formative. Between ages 16 and 19, Sara's leadership role enabled her to travel around the United States and Canada in order to deliver speeches and raise funds for B'nai B'rith causes. "Maybe I was just cocky because I was always the youngest to be doing this or doing that," she says. "However, between the leadership experience of the "B'nai B'rith youth organization, and [later] being active on newspapers and the yearbook in college, I just assumed that I could turn my hand to many different things and be good at them."

Sara also attributes her sense of self-esteem and confidence to her family's support and encouragement—especially that of her paternal grandmother. "No one in my family ever said or implied that I couldn't do anything because I was a girl," she explains. "I guess no one in my family would have *dared* to say I couldn't do something—either because of my grandmother's influence or just because I was who I was," she laughs. She says that as a young woman her disposition very much reflected her grandmother. "Around the family, I got the reputation for being a bit like my grandmother—tough and determined, shrewd and hard working," she says. "I was seen as a chip off the old block."

As such, her grandmother had expectations that she would become a lawyer—hoping, Sara thinks, to live out her own ambitions through her granddaughter and to have a lawyer in each generation of Millers. (One of Sara's uncles was a lawyer.) "Her hope was pinned on me," she says, "and I disappointed her. She was okay with it after a while—although she doesn't take disappointment lightly," she adds with a laugh. Sara's mother, on the other hand, continued to encourage theatrical pursuits. Prompted by her mother, Sara performed in volunteer shows for local USO and VA hospitals throughout high school. Upon graduation, however, she received a New York State Regent's Scholarship and qualified as a semifinalist in the National Merit competition; therefore, she informed her mother that she did not intend to pursue theater professionally. "Either there was a part of me that said, 'You're not good enough,' or, 'You're not enjoying it enough," Sara says of her performing. "There was a certain kind of urge to perfection in me that wasn't satisfied by doing all that [performing] so I just kept looking."

Her search for a satisfying career path continued at the City University of New York's (CUNY) Queens College, where she began by majoring in English and later switched to political science. While a college student, Sara continued some work with B'nai B'rith, was active on college newspapers and the college yearbook (of which she became editor-in-chief), and campaigned for John F. Kennedy even though she was not yet old enough to vote. Despite her studies and activities, she says she was still "totally undirected" in her consideration of career paths as she approached the end of her college years. Her mother, no longer pressing dramatic pursuits, attempted to convince her to become a radio or television broadcaster, while her grandmother continued to encourage her to become a lawyer. She laughs that by this time, she had dated enough lawyers in college to know that being a lawyer was one occupation she did *not* want to pursue.

Outside of career expectations, cultural expectations about marriage also surrounded Sara throughout college and her early career days. "In those days," she recalls, "it was assumed that nice Jewish girls were going to get married and have nice Jewish grandchildren—none of which I did." Sara describes herself as "quietly determined" not to marry merely in order to be married or to have children. "If I met someone that I cared about deeply," she says, "and whom I could feel committed to and who was committed to me, [that would be] well and good. If that didn't happen, that was well and good, too." Single and graduating from college in 1961, Sara says she remembers taking a variety of vocational guidance tests in order to determine what career path to follow. "Since [the test results] said I could do almost anything except be an engineer or a plumber," she says, "it wasn't very helpful. I always knew I could do anything I wanted [to do]. The problem was how to focus."

CAREER DEVELOPMENT

A summer publishing job after her graduation would provide that focus as well as lifelong direction. Deciding not to join the Peace Corps and postponing travel in Europe with a friend until the fall, Sara sought summer employment through a career placement agency in New York City. "The agent who interviewed me gave me this large, forced grin and asked, 'And what would you like to do?' I said, 'I don't know. I thought that's what *you're* suppose to tell me.' " After examining her newspaper and yearbook experience as well as her responses to an agency questionnaire, the placement agent decided Sara was "clearly destined for a career in publishing."

"I didn't argue when she sent me on these three interviews," she continues. "I just went and the first one was at Macmillan. They offered me the position so [the agent] canceled the others and that's how I got started in publishing. I guess I've only been on one interview," she concludes with a laugh. She had not intended that the position would launch her career in publishing; it was meant only to occupy her until the fall trip to Europe. However, the "interesting and fast-paced" nature of publishing as well as its "deadlines, bright people characters, and [amount] to read" caused her to cancel her intended travel, apologetically explaining to her friend that she loved her summer job too much to leave.

At the time, Macmillan had been recently absorbed by Crowell Collier, and the company was ripe with "great chaos, turmoil, and opportunity," Sara says. She liked walking into "Macmillan's lobby and seeing the autographed pictures of famous authors on the wall"; she also enjoyed her work as research assistant to the marketing consultant of Macmillan's new president. "I loved the fact that people were willing to answer just about any question I might ask." One of those people was George D. McCune, whom she met in the course of her first year of research. When she was permitted to explore and move to another position within Macmillan after her first year, it was George's offer she accepted.

During his stay at Macmillan, George acted as the assistant director of the College Division, vice president, and later director of sales, director of the Free Press, and founding president of Glencoe Press, Macmillan's junior college division. At the time he offered Sara Miller a job, George worked for Jeremiah Kaplan. Sara considers Kaplan an early role model in her career, citing his "quick-thinking and insight," his work with the social sciences, his founding of the Free Press and Meridian Books, and his "unparalleled experience and invaluable publishing expertise." (Kaplan was president of Macmillan and Simon & Schuster, Inc. as well as managing director of a division of Macmillan.) "I got to know Jerry later on [as a friend]," she adds, "and the more I knew, the more I respected and admired him." It was George, however, who acted more as her mentor during her employment at Macmillan.

After two and a half years with the company, Sara worked for a year in Oxford, England, for Pergamon Press Ltd. Upon her return to the states in 1964, she considered leaving the publishing industry, having become "disenchanted with large-scale publishing houses" (McCune, 1993). Her disenchantment lay in her frustration with the bureaucracy of such houses as Macmillan and Pergamon, both of which employed over a thousand employees at the time. "It wasn't just the 'small is beautiful' thing; it was a desire for control," she explains. 'It was a feeling that I kept seeing things that were being done in ways that seemed to me to be wrong. I wanted to avoid making those mistakes and felt all along that if I was going to make mistakes, I'd rather they be my own than someone else's."

Besides her desire to have control over her own work, Sara also cites the existence of a "glass ceiling" for women in publishing as an indicator that she needed to branch away from large bureaucracies. "In those days," she explains, "it had become pretty obvious that there was what has become known as a 'glass ceiling' in publishing. It's changing now [but] in the early sixties, there *really* was a limit. It didn't seem like I'd have a clear shot at the top." At age 23 then, Sara Miller was primed for George McCune's suggestion to start her own publishing company.

The idea of owning a business was nothing extraordinary to Sara because her father and uncles were small-business owners. It seemed only natural that people ran their own businesses and were their own boss. "It didn't come as any great shock or surprise to think of having a business of one's own," she says. "In that sense my family background was influential." Owning her own business, however, was not merely a situation in which Sara was following family example; it was also a situation of expressing her own self. "There's always been some part of me," she says, "that [believed] if I'm going to do something, I ultimately want to run it. That seems to be part of my nature. And if I wasn't running it, then I certainly wanted to be in the inside circle and very influential. [I wanted to be] making policy, not carrying out other people's policies."

Furthermore, launching her own business venture before 24 years of age was a matter of George's endless support and encouragement. "I think George in this case was living out a fantasy of his own," Sara says. "He always wanted a publishing company of his own but due to financial and family commitments from prior marriages, he saw no clear way of doing that. And here I was—footloose, fancy-free, hard-working, young, and energetic. It seemed to him that if he were in my position, [starting a company] was what he'd do, so I thought, Why not?!''

THE FOUNDING OF SAGE PUBLICATIONS, INC.

With "nothing to risk and everything to gain" (McCune, 1993), Sara set up a corporation with $500 startup capital—half of which was generated from the sale of a used air-conditioner. Having only a "precarious" income from some independent consulting she did for three small New York City publishers, she recognized the need for a positive cash flow from Sage's onset. Starting a social science journal and publishing a booklist around the journal seemed the most effective means of doing so. Thus, the evening her corporation's charter had been granted, she offered to publish *Urban Affairs Quarterly* (*UAQ*), an idea that came from Marilyn Gittell, a City University of New York political science professor.

Still retaining her independent consulting at least three days a week, Sara worked as Sage's sole employee in her every spare moment. "Publishing itself is more than a business," she explains. "For the people who really love it and adore it, publishing is a way of life. Having your own publishing company is just that [way of life] to an exponential degree. It's very special but it's very all-consuming." Indeed, it was "all-consuming" as Sara did all the copy editing and proofreading, often working 80 to 100 hours per week. Ultimately, her dedication paid off and she had the pleasure of "[watching] the type-setting forms being locked up, and [smelling] the ink as the first issue of *UAQ* rolled off the presses in September, 1965. Just like producing a baby, it took nine months to 'birth' Sage's first issue," she recalls (McCune, 1993).

During those nine months, Sara had also been busy combing the United States to gather a mailing list of 3,600 urban affairs specialists to target for subscriptions to *UAQ*. In the process, she also introduced herself to many social scientists and sought potential periodical materials for publication in disciplines such as sociology and political science. Having successfully launched *UAQ*, she closed 1965 with the imminent publication of an annual companion series to the journal, the *Urban Affairs Annual Reviews* series, as well as the acquisition of a second journal, *American Behavioral Scientist* (*ABS*), Sage's "flagship journal."

FAMILY AND STEPPARENTING

Throughout this year of Sage's birth, growth, and success, George McCune had been a "behind-the scenes brainstorming presence" (McCune, 1993) while continuing his work at Macmillan. Like Sara, however, by 1966 he had had enough of Macmillan's bureaucratic structure and his lack of control over company policies. He was also tired of New York and had made the decision to file for his second divorce. Having convinced her to move the publishing company to Southern California in July 1966, George also convinced Sara to marry him. In October 1966, after what Sara describes as a somewhat "stormy courtship," they were married.

Marrying George, she became a stepmother to his four children, two from each of his previous marriages. She says that being a stepmother "was very, very hard," but she does not attribute the difficulty of the role to her career in publishing. "While stepparenting has certainly been tricky, difficult and at times very tension-producing, I think it probably would have been under any career circumstances given the particulars of our family situation." In fact, she thinks her work in publishing actually afforded her the rewarding opportunity to travel with immediate family members more than other business careers would have. Looking back at her own experience as a stepmother, Sara states there is a "constant struggle to strike a balance" between parental and career demands for any working woman. "I don't think it's possible to strike a balance," she says. "I think that all you can do is juggle and run very hard." Today, George's children—Kathy and David from his first marriage, Keith and Susan from his second—are adults. While she may not be "running very hard" for them these days, Sara is certainly willing to do so for their children. "I'd like to be remembered as a good friend to my family and friends, as well as one of the world's greatest grandmothers."

SAGE'S GROWTH AND CONTRIBUTION TO COMMUNICATION

In its 30-year history, Sage Publications has adapted to changes within the publishing industry, the academy, and the social sciences. Sara's initial commitment to quality scholarly publishing from Sage's presses is one aspect of the company that has not changed. "Once Sage was started," she says,

I wanted it to be the very best it could be. That meant I wanted it to grow, to be very good at disseminating the information that we publish, and therefore to be very good at marketing. I wanted [Sage] to perform a service but I also wanted it to make money so it could continue to grow. I wanted it [to grow] to be global . . . and international just the way the social sciences are.

Working to achieve these goals, Sara put more than 100 percent of herself into her work, partly, she says, because of her inclination toward perfectionism. "I've always been 150 percent for whatever I did," she says. "It just doesn't matter [what it is], it's got to be the best it can be if it's going to have my name on it." Although she has become "a little more mellow" over time, she says she was "a terrible perfectionist" in her younger years. "I'm one of those people that for too long believed that if you wanted something done right, you would do it yourself. I had a hard time delegating [work]—it was very difficult for way too long." She says she would "rescue [herself] from burnout" by reinventing and tailoring her responsibilities as Sage's president. Working with her husband also served to inspire her. "Part of the joy of going to work used to be that we were working at building something together. While sometimes that led to tensions, it also led to many, *many* great satisfactions."

One early satisfaction was the increase in Sage sales from $12,000 during the company's first fiscal year (1965) to nearly $100,000 after its first full fiscal year in California (1967). By then, the company was staffed by four employees other than Sara and George and was branching into several more periodicals as well as a book publishing program. As the 1960s closed, Sara and George not only sought capital to expand the company, but also brought the company's services to other disciplines, including communication. The field, Sara remembers, was one with which she and George were extremely taken. "There was an extraordinary amount of intellectual excitement amongst people in the field in the late 1960s and early 1970s when we first began to talk with people in this area," she says. "George attended our first International Communication Association meeting and came back with his eyes just absolutely glowing. Those early years, as we began building our publishing program in communication, were just [full] of this incredible feeling George used to call 'perspective.' There were people who—because of what they were studying and the way they were approaching it—had a less narrow focus than many of the other social sciences that we were dealing with."

Both Sara and George believed that the communication discipline presented an opportunity to impart extremely meaningful considerations about a variety of social interactions and social problems as well as about media effects on society and culture. She adds, however, that after ten or so years of publishing communication literature, George became greatly disappointed to see that the field did not escape the "fragmentation and overspecialization so common in the social sciences in the 1970s and 1980s." Sara herself, however, was reluctant to recognize the trend because of the many personal friendships she had developed with communication scholars. "In the field of communication, there are many very special friendships that stand out to me," she says. "I really do feel that my life has been immeasurably enriched both intellectually and also in terms of friendships by people I've met [in academic disciplines] and by particular authors rather than fellow publishers."

Despite the disappointment that overspecialization seemed to leave fewer communication scholars "asking the grand questions or seeking the grand answers," Sara says she views the study of communication as an all-encompassing, all-pervasive discipline. She sees it as a field that, ironically enough, sets about studying the very nature of the business she and her husband established: the dissemination of information. Thus, Sage's contribution to communication studies has been to assist communication between scholars and larger audiences. As a publisher of the discipline's scholarly work, Sara observes that Sage has facilitated discourse

not only amongst academics, but also amongst the present generation of scholars and future generations of scholars. I think we made it possible for many scholars to communicate with one another and to influence subsequent generations of communication scholars. We probably existed as a sort of a shaping voice, if you will, throughout certain strains or themes being articulated [within the communication discipline].

SAGE TODAY

Sage has been this "shaping voice" within the communication field as well as within the educational publishing industry. "Our most important contribution to publishing," she says, "was the role that we played in building a major independent and global publishing house for the dissemination of the social sciences." The company began to expand into international markets when it first established a London affiliate in 1971 and later one in New Delhi in 1981. "We've worked to be international," Sara says. "If you do your job as publisher well, you facilitate communication amongst the international community of scholars [besides U.S. scholars] and make sure that your products are marketed effectively overseas." Sage also manages distribution relations in Sydney, Australia, and Tokyo, Japan; co-publishing relations in Singapore; and since 1990, three subsidiary companies: Corwin Press, Pine Forge Press, and Baskerville Communications Corporation.

Sara now presides over Sage's subsidiaries and foreign affiliates as a director on the company's board of directors. Having served, from its inception, as the president of Sage Publications, Inc. since 1984, she has been its chairperson. George's death in May 1990 closed a publishing career that spanned four decades; the position of president was transferred to his son, David McCune. David, Sara says, was not pressured into or specifically led to the publishing business by his father or stepmother. "There certainly was no pressure," she laughs. "A McCune male is not susceptible to pressure—they are definitely going to march to the tune of their own different drummer."

McCUNE'S ROLE AS A WOMAN IN PUBLISHING

As her company continues to change and prosper, Sara has experienced immense changes in her own life as she adapts to her widowhood. Losing George signified the passing of both her marital and business partner, and both were "very, very difficult transitions." As she notes, "you're living with a different sort of reality—not only has the fabric of your life been torn but the fabric of your work has been torn, too." In 1993 she moved to Santa Barbara, California, and currently occupies her time with work at Sage as well as with a variety of nonprofit, voluntary endeavors. She is a member of the boards of trustees at the University of California, Santa Barbara (UCSB); the Fielding Institute; the American Academy of Political and Social Science; and the Center for Media Literacy. Referring to her work in the nonprofit sector, Sara comments that she is inspired by a "feeling that it's time to give something back, especially to higher education and the social sciences."

Sara is also president of the McCune Foundation that was incorporated to benefit higher education in March 1990 through George's effort and planning. The foundation is currently involved in a three-year micro-development project at the village level in India, and awards dissertation fellowships to urban studies students at CUNY's Graduate Center and UCSB communication studies students. Book scholarships for social science undergraduates and graduates at selected universities within the United States, Great Britain, and India have also been established under the McCune Foundation's direction.

In 1988 Sara was awarded the American Evaluation Association's Special Award for Distinguished Contributions to the Field of Evaluation in recognition of Sage Publications' influential role in institutionalizing the evaluation. In 1992 a "Best Paper Award" was named in honor of Sara and George McCune by the Sage journal, *Group & Organization Management,* for published papers that increase the "responsiveness and humanity of organizations to their employees"—a spirit with which the journal's editor believes Sage was founded (Kavanagh, 1992). The Knowledge Utilization Society also recognized Sara for her "Outstanding International Service" in 1993.

In retrospect, Sara is unsure whether her experiences as a woman in publishing "are directly comparable" to women's experiences in the industry now. "There could have been obstacles there [because I was a woman]," she says, "that I was just naturally blind to—it just never would have occurred to me that anybody would have dreamed of putting an obstacle in my way. [I never even considered] why anybody would want to do that." Today, she views her contribution to women in publishing as fourfold, involving her position as a role model to women in the industry, her roles as both a mentor and friend to women at Sage, and her ability to help women network in the publishing profession. Her advice to women in publishing today is "generic advice for doing anything. Work hard. Ask lots of questions. Learn as much as you can. And— if you think you've got it in you—start your own."

Sara McCune hopes to be remembered as a builder of an institution—perhaps multiple institution—who gave much to the publication of social science information because she herself was receiving so much in return. In her eyes, one of the greatest of those returns lies modestly in an achievement others may be quick to dismiss. "What I consider a great achievement," she enthusiastically tells, "is holding the first of anything that comes off the press. I love the smell of a book and the feel of a new journal! I love browsing in something new with the Sage imprint on it."

As the Sage imprint continues to roll off its presses in the United States as well as around the globe, Sara Miller McCune's modest sense of satisfaction and achievement will continually return to her. Of equal significance, each Sage publication that goes to press reinforces Sage's contribution to the growth of scholarly information. "There was a poem I used to quote when I traveled around making speeches for B'nai B'rith," she recollects. "The verse I liked the most said, 'in vain you build the world, unless the builder also grows.' I've tried to live my life like this." Having given so much to the growth of social science information, Sara Miller McCune—builder of Sage Publications, Inc.— does continue to grow. Her work has not been in vain, for Sage's scholarly publications contribute a wealth of knowledge and information necessary for tomorrow's scholars.

REFERENCES

Kavanagh, M. (1992, June). Transitions: The Sara and George McCune best paper award. *Group & Organization Management,* 17(2), 115–116.
McCune, S. M. (1993, Fall). In the beginning. *Sage Thymes* (Sage Publications Inc., in-house newsletter), 3(3).

MARGARET L. McLAUGHLIN (1943–   )

Wendy Samter

With over 45 publications to her credit, Margaret McLaughlin is one of the communication field's most productive scholars. But even more importantly, McLaughlin's research has brought to light many key issues for students of interpersonal communication. For example, her systematic study of persuasive episodes illumines for us the importance of considering situational features when analyzing any communicative episode. Her rigorous study of accounts teaches us many lessons about the strategies through which actors seek to manage communicative failures and the effects these strategies have on social evaluations. Her work on conversation synthesizes disparate bodies of literature and provides a clear and detailed picture of the mechanisms that organize everyday conversation.

Remarkably, McLaughlin's contribution to the field does not end with her scholarship. She has been elected to several offices in national and international organizations and is editing (or has edited) a number of prestigious journals. In these capacities, she has shaped the body of knowledge we have accrued as a discipline as well as the direction in which we are currently heading.

FAMILY BACKGROUND

Margaret McLaughlin was born on December 26, 1943 at Georgetown Hospital in Washington, D.C. At the time, her father, Dr. Edward Savage, was a lieutenant commander in naval intelligence assigned to decipher the Japanese code. After her birth, the family moved—first to Cornell and then to the University of Mississippi where Savage worked as a professor of English until his death in 1972. Although McLaughlin's mother, Mary Johnston Savage, earned several credits toward a Master's degree and briefly taught high school history, she chose to work inside the home for most of her adult life. McLaughlin does not have any living siblings; her only sister, Katherine, was born with Down's Syndrome and died when she was 18 months old.

In many ways, it was inevitable that McLaughlin became a college professor. During her childhood, the university was her second home; she spent many hours on campus taking classes, going to the library, and "hanging out" in her father's office. Everyone in the family was an avid reader, and, according to McLaughlin, it was not uncommon to find the three of them huddled together each with "noses stuck in a separate book." In addition, McLaughlin's parents came from families that emphasized education; of four grandparents, three were college graduates. Her mother's family were bankers and businessmen. Her father was the first in several generations not to enter the ministry.

McLaughlin dedicated her first book, *Conversation: How Talk Is Organized* (1984), to the memory of her father who was a prolific scholar of Elizabethan and Jacobean drama. During his career, Savage edited a journal called *Studies in English* and published several articles, although he did not write his first book until he was well into his sixties. As McLaughlin explains in her acknowledgments of *Conversation*, "When I asked him why he had waited so long to write a book, his reply was that up until then, he hadn't known enough to fill up that many pages." Savage was awarded several grants and fellowships that took the family to what McLaughlin recalls seemed like exotic and glamorous places to a "small town girl." The family spent one summer in London where her father had won a grant to research a book at the British Museum and another in Los Angeles when he was named a fellow at the Huntingdon Library. Savage's scholarship also earned him a coveted appointment to the Committee on the 400th Anniversary of Shakespeare's Birth. When invited to attend a reception at the White House, Savage refused because he disagreed with Lyndon Johnson's politics. As McLaughlin lovingly notes, "I'm not sure mother ever forgave him for that."

The value her family placed on education, the comfort and familiarity she felt with the university setting, the vicarious excitement she experienced because of her father's research, and her love of reading made higher education an obvious choice for McLaughlin. Both McLaughlin and her parents always expected her to attend college, although everyone was somewhat surprised when she did not settle into a "more conventional lifestyle" after earning her Bachelor's degree.

PRIMARY, SECONDARY, AND UNDERGRADUATE EDUCATION

McLaughlin attended public schools and state universities. She does not remember much about elementary school "except for recess and throwing food in the lunchroom." As for her years in junior high school, she recalls being somewhat less than a model child. "In seventh grade, I was expelled for writing on the walls of the girl's room with lipstick. I cut class quite a bit and didn't study very hard.'' While formal education may not have been McLaughlin's strong suit throughout childhood, it was during this time that her love of reading developed. The family lived on the edge of town, so McLaughlin had few opportunities to play with other children. Thus, books and short stories were her after-school companions for much of childhood. By the time she began high school, however, McLaughlin's social side blossomed. She became active in several clubs, played in the band, and discovered boys.

It was not until she entered the University of Mississippi that McLaughlin felt at all inspired or challenged by formal academic pursuits. She ultimately graduated cum laude but had some ''memorable'' semesters along the way. In one semester, she obtained five A's and an F in psychology; she made C's and D's in math courses, and excelled in physical education classes, earning A's in archery and bait and fly casting.

McLaughlin soon discovered that she loved making speeches and working at the university's radio station. She also loved literature. So, instead of loading up on electives, McLaughlin took a triple major to accommodate her interests in French, English literature, and speech. Throughout her college career, McLaughlin earned many honors including an award from the French government for her work in the department and a trip to the National Association of Broadcasting Conference in New York where Pauline Frederick* was the keynote speaker. In addition, she was Phi Kappa Phi, Mortar Board, president of her sorority, and very involved in campus life.

Although her college days were filled mostly with socializing and studying, ''real life'' did impinge in one very significant way. McLaughlin was in her sophomore year when the University of Mississippi was integrated with the admission of James Meredith. As she remembers,

The rioting and the murder, which was committed right behind my dormitory, had a very sobering effect on all of us. Some of the students did not return. Those of us who stayed went back to classes still filled with the stinging fumes of tear gas. The Federal Troops who were there for weeks were in effect an occupying army; my mother still has a copy of the ''pass'' for travel around campus that she was issued. I still have the pictures, taken by a military photographer, of a dinner with the troops which I attended as a student government officer.

McLaughlin maintains that the events surrounding the desegregation did not radically alter her political views, mostly because she did not have any to speak of at that time. They did, however, bring to the surface for her the ugliest aspects of racism, a phenomenon with which she had had little previous experience.

In her senior year, McLaughlin applied to graduate programs in French and speech. She received assistantships in both areas, but ultimately chose to accept an offer from the University of Illinois in speech.

I accepted one of the offers in Speech for what in retrospect was not a very good reason— I didn't think my French was good enough for me to handle a class in it. I would like to say I was forward-looking enough at the age of 21 to realize that foreign languages would enter a period of decline, and communication a period of growth. But that wasn't it.

GRADUATE EDUCATION

In the summer of 1965, McLaughlin moved to Champaign-Urbana where she remained for the next two years. After obtaining a Master's degree emphasizing rhetoric, McLaughlin took a two-year hiatus from graduate studies and moved to New York. There she worked as a "Girl Friday" for Radio News International and an instructor at Hunter College. In 1967 she returned to Illinois to resume work on her doctorate. By that time, Karl Wallace, who was, in her words, "a brilliant rhetorician and kindly mentor," had left the university and McLaughlin found herself most excited by courses she took from Tom Scheidel and Ruth Anne Clark—both of whom were considered "of the empirical persuasion as it was called back then." As McLaughlin explains, "I took their classes and felt right at home—perhaps because I discovered I could do well in things like social science and statistics, in which I had performed so poorly as an undergraduate."

McLaughlin's dissertation, directed by Roger Nebergall (who studied with the famous Sherifs), was a multidimensional scaling analysis of a popular social judgment instrument. She claims that even her professors thought it was "unutterably boring"; yet it did demonstrate that the claims of intervality made by the authors of the scale were invalid. McLaughlin obtained her Ph.D. in 1972, officially majoring in speech and minoring in psychology and communication.

For McLaughlin, the most rewarding part of graduate school was the intellectual excitement generated by the "wonderful library, computer center, and stimulating faculty" she encountered at the University of Illinois. McLaughlin lived in "a constant state of intellectual euphoria," staying up to all hours of the night writing what she then regarded as "unspeakably brilliant papers."

CAREER DEVELOPMENT

In spite of excellent letters of recommendation, a high grade point average, and a single-authored paper in the field's leading journal, McLaughlin could not find a job her first year on the market. Unfortunately, universities were just one of many contexts in which sexist attitudes predominated during the early 1970s, and McLaughlin encountered several instances of discrimination.

In one interview, the first question posed to her was, "What does your husband do?" Similarly, in response to a letter of recommendation Nebergall had written on McLaughlin's behalf, the chair of a department advertising four assistant professorships wrote, "If we should need a good woman this year, we'll be sure to take a look at her." On another occasion, McLaughlin learned she had not been offered a position because "any woman who would apply for a job without her husband's having one first had to be emotionally unstable." At the time, McLaughlin and her husband had a 2-year-old son to support. In desperation, she sought employment at a social service agency. Her interviewer, a woman, refused to consider her for the position because, in her experience, "women with children could not be counted on in the workplace."

"If my undergraduate career had led me to believe that there was nothing I couldn't do," recalls McLaughlin, "then my years in graduate school, and my experience trying to get a job, led me to wonder what I would be allowed to do." Finally, she and her husband were offered positions at Texas Tech University (TTU). In 1976 she received tenure and was promoted to associate professor. McLaughlin remembers TTU as an "ideal first position" where she had wonderful colleagues, free run of the library, a good computer center, and elaborate research facilities. During her employment there, one survey ranked the department as having the most prolific publishers per capita of any graduate program in communication.

In 1982 McLaughlin accepted an offer from The Annenberg School of Communication at the University of Southern California (USC), where she is presently a full professor. The decision to move to USC was difficult because of the affinity McLaughlin had developed for her colleagues at Texas Tech and because the "big city" of Los Angeles loomed as a large and scary place for someone who had spent most of her adult life in small towns.

MAJOR CONTRIBUTIONS AND ACHIEVEMENTS

McLaughlin's contributions to the field of communication are manifold. Although she has published on a variety of topics, she is perhaps best known for two lines of research: her work on situational influences in compliance-gaining contexts and her studies of accounts.

Throughout the 1980s, McLaughlin and co-author Michael Cody conducted a series of investigations designed to examine the structure underlying perceptions of persuasive episodes (e.g., Cody & McLaughlin, 1980, 1985a; Cody, McLaughlin, & Schneider, 1981; McLaughlin, Cody, & Robey 1980). Across these studies, subjects' ratings of common compliance-gaining situations (e.g., persuading a boy/girlfriend to confide in you more, persuading a professor that an answer on a test is incorrect) indicated that different dimensions did, in fact, underlie different situations. In other words, McLaughlin and Cody found that "the who" and "what" components of settings for behavior influence perceptions of situations (Cody & McLaughlin, 1985a, p. 287). This line of work highlighted the need for researchers to pay careful attention to the multiple dimensions actors use when forming impressions of and responding to persuasive episodes.

McLaughlin and Cody were also among the first in the field to study the accounts people employ when attempting to manage communicative failures (or potential failures). McLaughlin initially became interested in accounts after she read Scott and Lyman's (1968) landmark piece in which they drew an important distinction between excuses (where actors admit failure but deny responsibility) and justifications (where actors accept responsibility but maintain it was not untoward). Since that time, she and Cody have engaged in a systematic and rigorous research program exploring how accounts are offered and judged.

For example, they have examined the level of credibility associated with different types of accounts (e.g., Cody & McLaughlin, 1988), the sequencing of account episodes (e.g., Cody & McLaughlin, 1985b; McLaughlin, Cody, & Rosenstein, 1983), the affective reciprocity of accounts (e.g., McLaughlin, Cody, & O'Hair, 1983), contextual determinants of accounting events (McLaughlin, Cody, & O'Hair, 1983) impressions of moral responsibility as a function of the type of account given (McLaughlin, Cody, & Rosenstein, 1983, McLaughlin, Cody, & O'Hair, 1983), the effectiveness of accounts (McLaughlin, Cody, & French, 1990), and the accounts people offer when they fail to follow another's advice (e.g., McLaughlin, Cody, Dickson, & Manusov, 1992). Their research has investigated the use of accounts across a variety of populations (e.g., college students, "real-world" people) and contexts (e.g., interpersonal settings, traffic courts). This body of work has not only served to highlight the important and complex nature of the "verbal devices" individuals use to "neutralize negative evaluations" (Cody & McLaughlin, 1990, p. 230), but has also stimulated interest in communicative failures, a topic that is now one of the most highly researched in the field.

In addition to these lines of research, McLaughlin is also the author of *Conversation: How Talk Is Organized* (1984). The book was among the first to provide a cogent synthesis of conversational studies conducted by scholars in a wide variety of academic disciplines. As such, it represents a significant step in our understanding of the mechanisms through which conversations are organized. The book addresses many questions, including how and why simultaneous talk occurs, the rules we use in conversation, ways of signaling topic change, and the sequencing of conversational openings and closings. As Mark Knapp (1984, p. 10) commented in his foreword to the book,

In my opinion, *Conversation: How Talk Is Organized* is a useful, timely, and important book. It brings together a wide variety of scientific materials, provides an assessment of what we know and don't know, and suggests guidelines for future research. While we have all been practitioners of conversation, this book should go far toward making us all students of conversation.

McLaughlin's current research interests are moving in two directions: electronic publishing and the delivery of art galleries and museum services over the Internet. She and Sheizaf Rafaeli (Hebrew University of Jerusalem) are co-editors of *The Journal of Computer-Mediated Communication*. Delivered over electronic media, the journal seeks to make information more accessible and affordable, to emphasize global involvement, and to underscore the dynamic nature of research by encouraging reader-editor-reviewer-author interaction. Along with Rafaeli and Fay Sudweeks, McLaughlin has also contracted with

MIT Press to co-author a book, *Network and Netplay: Virtual Groups on the Internet*. Finally, she is presently involved in a project designed to develop a tele-interactive virtual art museum on the World Wide Web.

In addition to her scholarly contributions, McLaughlin has given a remarkable amount of service to the discipline. In 1989 she was elected president of the International Communication Association (ICA). As president, she was responsible for planning the 1990 ICA conference in Dublin, an activity she claims gave her the "most satisfaction" of any academic endeavor. She has also been active in the Speech Communication Association (SCA), chairing the Interpersonal and Small Group Interaction Division in 1982 and 1983.

Since the mid-1980s, McLaughlin has held two prestigious editorships: *Communication Monographs* (1986 through 1989) and *Communication Yearbook Volumes 9 and 10* (1986 and 1987). She is presently serving (or has served) on nine editorial boards, including *Human Communication Research*; *Progress in Communication Sciences*; *Text*; *Communication, Mass Media and Journalism*; *The Quarterly Journal of Speech*; and *The International and Intercultural Communication Annual*.

INTEGRATION OF PERSONAL AND PROFESSIONAL LIFE

Throughout much of her adult life, McLaughlin's professional and personal involvements have overlapped. She is married to Jim Buckalew, a professor of journalism at San Diego State University and a news anchor for KSDO, the top-rated AM radio station in San Diego. They met through a mutual friend who, along with Buckalew and two other partners, owns a thoroughbred named "Academic Farms." The couple's educational backgrounds are remarkably similar. Both hail from Big Ten institutions; Buckalew attended the University of Iowa while McLaughlin was enrolled at the University of Illinois. Because of their common interest in communication, they "talk a lot about their work." But marriage has influenced McLaughlin's career in another, more significant way. After marrying Buckalew, she decided to relocate to San Diego. As a result of her move, she now makes the 250-mile roundtrip commute to USC two to three times a week. While the long drive gives her plenty of time to think, it has also forced her to rely heavily on electronic media as a way of communicating with students and colleagues. McLaughlin sees this as a "blessing in disguise." What might have seemed like a burdensome aspect of her living arrangements has led to McLaughlin's current research interest in computer-mediated communication and the Internet—an area she finds "totally absorbing."

McLaughlin is the mother of two children and the stepmother of five. For McLaughlin, the key to balancing work and family is having a mate who is supportive of career decisions and willing to assume a fair share of the responsibilities associated with home and childrearing. She feels extremely fortunate, "having always been over-benefited rather under-benefited in that regard." Still, McLaughlin admits to having assigned different priorities to professional and personal demands at different stages of life. There are times when she does little more than teach class, attend meetings, and advise students. When "the muse disappears" and McLaughlin has nothing to say, she does not write. At other times, however, she writes for 12 to 16 hours a day, "bounding out of bed at four or five in the morning to power up the computer." Family members complain about her during these times, while colleagues complain about her during the other phase. In general, she tries to strike a balance between putting out fires and tackling long-range professional projects. As McLaughlin notes, however, she isn't always successful. "There are days when [my daughter] Julia can't find any clean socks for school or I have forgotten to turn in my book order form."

Given the extent of her professional and personal commitments, it is surprising that McLaughlin finds time for community service. However, within the last few years alone she has volunteered for a number of noteworthy organizations. For example, she was on the board of directors of Haven House, a shelter for victims of domestic violence. She has taught Sunday School for St. Edmund's Episcopal Parish and served as a member of their Outreach Commission, a group working on the problems of homelessness in the San Gabriel valley. McLaughlin also edited a newsletter and served as secretary for the Elizabethan Guild, a support group for Hillsides Home for Children, a residential facility for abused and neglected children.

In many ways, McLaughlin can be regarded as a pioneer. Her scholarship has shaped current thinking on situational features in communicative episodes, the use of accounts in everyday interaction, and the mechanisms through which conversation is organized. By overcoming sexual discrimination and going on to preside over some of the field's most prestigious organizations and scholarly outlets, McLaughlin paved the way for other women to hold positions of influence and responsibility. But regardless of gender, as long as people are students of human communication, they are indebted to McLaughlin for the contributions she has made.

REFERENCES

Cody, M. J., & McLaughlin, M. L. (1980). Perceptions of compliance-gaining situations: A dimensional analysis. *Communication Monographs, 47,* 132–148.

Cody, M. J., & McLaughlin, M. L. (1985a). The situation as a construct in interpersonal communication research. In M. L. Knapp & G. R. Miller (eds.), *Handbook of interpersonal communication.* (pp. 263–312). Beverly Hills, Calif.: Sage.

Cody, M. J., & McLaughlin, M. L. (1985b). Models for the sequential construction of accounting episodes: Situational and interactional constraints on message selection and evaluation. In R. L. Street & J. N. Cappella (eds.), *Sequence and pattern in communicative behavior.* (pp. 50–69). London: Arnold.

Cody, M. J., & McLaughlin, M. L. (1988). Accounts on trial: Oral arguments in traffic courts. In C. Antaki (ed.), *Analysing everyday explanation: A casebook of methods.* (pp. 113–126). London: Sage.

Cody, M. J., & McLaughlin, M. L. (1990). Interpersonal accounting. In H. Giles & W. P. Robinson (eds.), *Handbook of language and social psychology.* (pp. 227–255). New York: Wiley.

Cody, M. J., McLaughlin, M. L., & Schneider, M. J. (1981). The impact of intimacy and relational consequences on the selection of interpersonal persuasion strategies: A reanalysis. *Communication Quarterly,* 29, 91–106.

McLaughlin, M. L. (1984). *Conversation: How talk is organized.* Beverly Hills, Calif.: Sage.

McLaughlin, M. L., Cody, M. J., Dickson, R., & Manusov, V. (1992). Accounting for failure to follow advice: Real reasons versus good explanations. In M. L. McLaughlin, M. J. Cody, & S. J. Read (eds.), *Explaining one's self to others: Reason-giving in a social context.* (pp. 281–294). Hillsdale, N.J.: Erlbaum.

McLaughlin, M. L., Cody, M. J., & French, K. (1990). Account-giving and the attribution of responsibility: Impressions of traffic offenders. In M. J. Cody & M. L. McLaughlin (eds.), *The psychology of tactical communication.* (pp. 244–267). Clevedon: Multilingual Matters.

McLaughlin, M. L., Cody, M. J., & O'Hair, H. D. (1983). The management of failure events: Some contextual determinants of accounting behavior. *Human Communication Research,* 9, 208–224.

McLaughlin, M. L., Cody, M. J., & Robey, C. S. (1980). Situational influences on the selection of strategies to resist compliance-gaining attempts. *Human Communication Research,* 7, 14–36.

McLaughlin, M. L., Cody, M. J., & Rosenstein, N. E. (1983). Account sequences in conversations between strangers. *Communication Monographs,* 50, 102–125.

Rafaeli, S. R., McLaughlin, M. L., & Sudweeks, F. (in press). *Network and netplay: Virtual groups on the Internet.* AAAI/MIT Press.

Scott, M. B., & Lyman, S. M. (1968). Accounts. *American Sociological Review,* 33, 46–62.

ELISABETH NOELLE-NEUMANN (1916–)

K. Viswanath

Elisabeth Noelle-Neumann's contributions to the study of public opinion have generated considerable interest among scholars and practitioners on both sides of the Atlantic. Drawing from the work of several classical Western philosophers and psychologists such as Solomon Asch and Stanley Milgram, Noelle-Neumann offers a dynamic model of public opinion integrating the role of the news media with the public opinion process. She contributed to the return of the notion of the ''powerful effects'' of mass media at a time when the conventional wisdom was that the media had limited effects. Her theory of public opinion has implications for media studies, political science, and sociology as well as for the political arena. She co-founded and continues to direct the first public opinion institute in Germany. Because of the implications of her scholarly work and her very visible role as a social critic, political analyst, public opinion pollster, and adviser to German politicians, Noelle-Neumann's work has attracted wide attention and made her one of the more visible and controversial media scholars of our times.

FAMILY BACKGROUND

Elisabeth Noelle was born in Berlin, Germany, on December 19, 1916 to Dr. Ernst Noelle and Eva Schaper. She was the second child, with an older sister and two younger brothers. She hails from a distinguished Berlin family. Her father, Ernst Noelle, earned a law degree (''Doctor of Law'') and ran an Iron and Steel construction company founded by her grandfather. He subsequently sold the firm, but continued to be engaged as a banker and adviser to several companies. Elisabeth's mother, Eva, also was born in Berlin to a well-known sculptor and professor of art, Fritz Schaper. Eva Noelle's grandfather was a noted German poet, Emil Ritterhaus. While Eva was not a professional, she did attend the gymnasium, which was unusual for women at the time.

By her own account, Elisabeth Noelle had a privileged childhood. She grew up in a large house with a family that often took vacations and cultural trips. Her mother "trained" her in art and the "love of beauty," and taught her "how to keep a well-cared for house." From the time she was ten years old, Elisabeth Noelle's father set aside time each week to discuss "serious" matters. At age 19, she traveled alone to the Balkans, Scandinavia, France, and Italy.

Her father's training as a lawyer and a businessman, her mother's interest in art and aesthetics, and the fact that a great aunt was a teacher at the University of Zurich, combined with the childhood of privilege, strong tradition, and freedom, appeared to have had a long-lasting influence on her life and career and to explain her interest in politics and art.

EDUCATION

Elisabeth Noelle's childhood education was mostly in private schools. She was a sickly child, suffering from illness and undergoing five operations by age 10! She kept mostly to herself. "I liked being alone and had a fine time by myself," says Noelle.

For junior high and high school, she attended a public school in Berlin and subsequently went to private boarding schools. Noelle was curious and active and enjoyed solitude. She felt she was different from other girls of her age; she said that she felt like a "green sparrow." She spent her time reading, writing, painting, corresponding, and working on her school projects.

In her junior and senior years in high school, she founded a student paper, which was banned by her school after only six issues. This experience influenced her decision to become a journalist. While at school, she attended lectures at the University of Göttingen and Berlin. In 1934, while attending a course in journalism with Emil Dovifat, she decided to get a "doctorate in journalism," with him as her adviser. But she was not admitted to the university after graduation from high school because she was the "only member of her class not to have joined a national socialist organization." Instead, she started to train as a painter and graphic artist.

Noelle eventually gained admission to the University of Berlin in "newspaper science," and also studied history, philosophy, and American studies. In addition, she studied at Konigsberg and the University of Munich and gathered material for her dissertation while on a fellowship at the School of Journalism at the University of Missouri. While studying in the United States, she traveled throughout America and Mexico, and then in Asia.

In 1939 Noelle returned to Germany and resumed studies for her doctorate. After the war broke out, however, she almost gave up her studies. Urged to continue, she wrote her dissertation, at the age of 23, on American public opinion research between September and December 1939. In March 1940, she took her orals for the doctorate and passed with a "good grade."

CAREER DEVELOPMENT

The early stages of Noelle's career were controversial and bumpy. Between 1940 and 1945, she worked for several different newspapers, including *Deutsche Allgemeine Zeitung, Das Reich,* and the *Frankfurter Zeitung.* She was tried before the press court in 1941, fired from the *Reich,* and was threatened with denial of permission to work by the Ministry of Propaganda, a denial which, she says, was subsequently rescinded as a result of intervention by the editors of *Frankfurter Zeitung.*

A different version of the events in her life during the late 1930s and early 1940s has also come to light. Leo Bogart and others have argued that her actions during this time, particularly her writings, were more supportive than critical of the Nazi party and even reflected anti-Semitism. Noelle-Neumann denies these allegations and explains that the time and place, particularly the climate of the authoritarian system in which she did her writings, must be kept in mind. Several others have defended Noelle-Neumann. This part of her life remains a source of some controversy.

In 1947 Noelle co-founded, with her first husband, Erich Neumann (whom she married in 1946), the Allensbach Institute (*Institut für Demoskopie Allensbach*) and became its first director. This was the first German survey research institute of its kind. She has directed the Allensbach public opinion polls and media research since 1947. At about this time, Theodore Adorno and Max Horkheimer, the well-known "Frankfurt School" theorists, invited her to teach and do research at the University of Frankfurt/Mainz, but she declined because she wanted to manage the Allensbach Institute.

In 1961 she began to lecture in communication research at the Free University of Berlin. She moved to the University of Mainz in 1964 as an associate professor and became a full professor in 1967. In 1966 she founded the *Institut fur Kommunikationsforschung* at the University of Mainz and was its director until 1983.

From 1972 through 1991 Noelle was a visiting professor in the Department of Political Science at the University of Chicago, and in 1993–1994 she was the Eric Voegelin visiting professor in the Department of Communications at the University of Munich. She has also worked as a journalist and as a public opinion analyst for *Frankfurter Allgemeine Zeitung.*

Looking back at those early career days, Noelle-Neumann says that her only role model then was one of her great aunts who taught at the University of Zurich. Noelle-Neumann's goal at that time was to "develop" the survey research method and work "on important problems in social sciences." To this end, she found it important to start her own institute, but received little financial support for this endeavor.

MAJOR CONTRIBUTIONS AND ACHIEVEMENTS

Noelle-Neumann offers a framework relating public opinion and mass media. As Salmon and Kline (1985) point out, her concepts of opinion climate, the spiral of silence, and the role of media in the creation of opinion climate were not new. What was new in her work was the integration of these concepts into a comprehensive theory of public opinion. In addition, by observing that the media tend to have a pronounced role in shaping the climate of opinion around individuals, she contributed to the return of the paradigm of powerful effects of mass media.

Noelle-Neumann has also made a unique contribution in her creative use of multiple methods to address her research questions. She remains one of the few scholars in the field who has tackled research problems using different approaches.

Noelle-Neumann also contributed to the study of public opinion by founding the first German survey research institute—the Allensbach Institute—and by participating in organizations devoted to the study of public opinion. As the founding director of the institute, she has co-edited the series *Allensbacher Jahrbucher der Demoskopie* since 1956; nine volumes have been published to date. These works present, in thematically organized chapters, all of the Allensbach findings that are of interest to either the public or historians.

Noelle-Neumann considers *Fischer Lexikon fur Publizistik—Massenkommunikation,* which she initiated with her colleague Winfried Schulz in 1971, her most influential work. A third revised edition appeared in November 1994, with Winfried Schulz and Jurgen Wilke as co-editors. According to Noelle-Neumann, the *Fischer Lexikon* is the most widely used compilation of information on the current state of communication research and the German media system and has sold over 120,000 copies in Germany.

Noelle-Neumann's *The Spiral of Silence* (1984) has been published or is soon to be published in seven languages: German (1991), English (2nd ed., 1993), Japanese (1988), and Korean (1990). The Russian, Spanish, and Chinese translation should be published in 1995.

Noelle-Neumann is very active in professional organizations that study public opinion such as the World Association for Public Opinion Research (WAPOR). She served as its president from 1978 to 1980 and was awarded its Helen Dinerman Award for her contributions. In addition, she has trained many of the important communication scholars in Germany today.

She is still active, directing the Allensbach Institute with its 90 full-time staff members and teaching at the Mainz's Institute for Communications Research, which has about 1,200 students and 700 majors and awards about 165 degrees a year.

THE SPIRAL OF SILENCE

In her introduction to the American edition of her book, *The Spiral of Silence: Public Opinion—Our Social Skin,* Noelle-Neumann zeroes in on the individual need to be part of society and on their fear of isolation. She focuses on social integration and argues that the social nature of humans is to be in the mainstream and that humans fear isolation more than anything else. This fear of isolation forms a crucial component of her hypothesis regarding a spiral of silence.

This hypothesis was the product of her attempt to resolve a puzzle in the 1960s: the difference in how people responded about their intention to vote and their expectation of which party would win an election. Noelle-Neumann and her colleagues discovered that even when respondents in public opinion surveys stated that they intended to vote for a particular party, they thought that the other party would win the election.

The hypothesis posits that those who feel that a majority share their views on a given issue are more likely to express it openly. On the other hand, those who feel that they are in the minority are reticent to do the same. The reluctance of the perceived minority to speak out and the enthusiasm of the perceived majority to speak out results in a spiral where one opinion remains ascendant over the other in the public sphere, while the second may even disappear from the public realm. This causes, she says, the "spiral of silence."

Noelle-Neumann found a "precise description" of the spiral of silence in Tocqueville's history of the French Revolution, particularly in his comments on the silence of the French church. She also draws from the works of political philosophers Jean-Jacques Rousseau, David Hume, John Locke, Martin Luther, Machiavelli, and John Hus, among others (1993, p. 7).

The hypothesis makes several assumptions:

1. People observe the opinion environment around them.

2. They not only observe, but also are perceptive enough to realize which opinion is in the ascendance and which is not.

3. They fear isolation from society.

4. They are either reluctant or willing to express an opinion based on such a perception.

Noelle-Neumann suggests that only when the spiral is complete will people either speak out or stay silent; it does not happen in the case of open or unsettled controversies.

CONTRIBUTION TO MEDIA EFFECTS

Noelle-Neumann's thesis marks the return to the notion of powerful media effects. Media effects, she argues, are cumulative, unconscious, and indirect (1983; 1993, pp. 168–169). The limited effects model, Noelle-Neumann states, evolved partly because of researchers' reluctance to antagonize the media companies. In addition, media companies are more comfortable with limited effects, since they invite "less control" of media content and activities (Noelle-Neumann, 1983).

In her major contribution, the spiral of silence theory, Noelle-Neumann posits that public opinion is nurtured by two sources: direct observation by the public and indirect observation through the mass media. Noelle-Neumann also argues that journalists' political preferences, which differ from those of the general population, influence the way the media cover events such as elections, which in turn, influence the climate of opinion. Journalists have a liberal bias that affects their reporting; this, in turn, influences public opinion on issues leading to a spiral of silence. This argument is somewhat akin to the conservative criticism of the media in this country.

Another of her contributions, though insightful, has received little attention. Noelle-Neumann states that the media serve an "articulation function." That is, they provide (formulate) the arguments for the majority on a given issue. By implication, this function is more likely to be beneficial to the minority than to the majority point of view, and the majority in the absence of "articulation" by the media are ill served by it (Noelle-Neumann, 1993, pp. 172–173). It is conceivable, she maintains, that the majority are silent because the media have not developed or "formulated" the arguments they need to articulate! This point is closer, if not related, to the recent argument that the media "frame" issues for the public. Her book provides limited evidence to buttress this thesis, though subsequent work in this area in the United States has shown that the media do frame the issues for the public (Entman, 1993; Gamson, 1992; Gitlin, 1980; Iyengar, 1991; Pan & Kosicki, 1993). One can say that Noelle-Neumann anticipated the notion of media framing by a few years.

METHODOLOGICAL CONTRIBUTION

Noelle-Neumann has used several different methods to assess the climate of opinion, voting intention, fear of isolation, and people's willingness (or unwillingness) to offer an opinion. At one time or other, she and her colleagues used cross-sectional surveys, panel studies, surveys of journalists, and analyses of media content.

Noelle-Neumann and her colleagues measure the perception of the opinion climate in creative ways (see, for example, Chapter 2 of her book, especially pp. 8–16). In her approach, situations are simulated where responses have to be made in public. The nature of the method is crucial to the definition of public opinion: expression of an opinion on a controversial topic in public (as opposed to in private). For example, survey respondents are given a scenario in which they face a fellow traveler on a train who has an opposing view on an issue or a subject. Respondents are then asked about their willingness to disagree with that person. According to the hypothesis, the "camp" that was willing to vocalize their disagreement was the one whose opinion was likely to dominate the public space.

CRITICAL EVALUATIONS OF CONTRIBUTIONS AND ACHIEVEMENTS

Noelle-Neumann's work can be evaluated on theoretical and methodological grounds.

Theoretical

Salmon and Kline (1985) observed that the spiral of silence theory fails to take into consideration the role of primary groups in opinion formation and change, and so they offered alternative explanations. For example, Noelle-Neumann, using the work of Asch (1965), argued that people are likely to conform to the majority opinion either by speaking openly or by remaining silent since they fear isolation. Salmon and Kline's reinterpretation of the Asch data led them to suggest that the pressure to conform is situation specific and that Asch's studies seldom found total conformity. Glynn and McLeod (1985) made a similar argument, failing to find that the "minority" in their sample were silent. Glynn and McLeod (1985) also argued that the conditions under which Asch's experiments were conducted were different from the conditions under which people may or may not hold opinions: (1) Asch's stimuli were "unambiguous," unlike people's judgments of other people's opinions; (2) the Asch experiments did not allow interpersonal interaction, which was not possible in the conditions under which Noelle-Neumann collected her data; and (3) Asch studied short-term immediate effects, where Noelle-Neumann speaks of long-term effects. Finally, Glynn and McLeod suggest that the spiral of silence theory could be refined by taking into account the work of Sherif (1966) and his colleagues.

Noelle-Neumann argues that the Asch experiments were cited only to show that the individual's social nature "tends toward conformity." What is more important, she says, is the fact that "a spiral of silence is only possible in connection with morally loaded subjects," and the topics in Asch's experiments "have no moral dimension whatsoever. The spiral of silence, on the other hand, can *only* be set in motion by the moral component of a subject." Noelle-Neumann's contention is that the spiral of silence cannot be "triggered" by small changes in the distribution of opinion and that only "massive pressure" over the long term on topics that are controversial and that have a moral dimension are subject to the spiral of silence. In sum, the stimuli precipitating a spiral of silence have to be strong to observe any effects. She has thus set an important boundary condition to the hypothesis.

Noelle-Neumann's thesis on media effects was a significant departure from the accepted notion of the 1960s and 1970s that the media have "limited effects." She argues that media effects are cumulative, indirect, and unconscious because the media are ubiquitous and media messages are "consonant." This proposition regarding consonance in messages can be challenged, however. Several scholars have argued that the media are a subsystem of a total community system and that media content and media behavior are subject to the characteristics of community (Tichenor, Donohue, & Olien, 1980). The media are more likely to support the more powerful groups with authority in the system, particularly in homogeneous communities where power is more centralized (see Paletz & Entman, 1981; Tichenor, Donohue, & Olien, 1980). In contrast, in pluralistic systems there could very well be diversity in media content reflecting the diversity in the interest groups (Olien, Donohue & Tichenor, 1978). Thus, with few exceptions, pluralistic environments could provide the kind of content diversity that would allow different groups to be exposed to different kinds of content. Noelle-Neumann's argument about the media's articulation function, whereby they provide arguments for people, may still be served in more pluralistic environments.

In summary, her theory of society draws from the mass society model, which assumes that the media have powerful effects on the mass audience who are considered to be isolated individuals (Katz, 1981; also see Beniger, 1987). As such, her theory shares some of the limitations of the mass society theory. That is, people are not isolated, undifferentiated masses, but are members of primary and secondary groups, which along with community organizations could mediate the impact of mass media (Glynn & McLeod, 1985).

Noelle-Neumann (1991) counters this argument by writing that the fear of isolation is based on the "very ability . . . of arriving at common assessment." In fact, "rather than feeling atomized . . . the individual feels embedded in solidarity." A more "fundamental aspect" of the theory, however, is that the spiral of silence has explained the hitherto unexplained phenomenon of when and under what conditions people are willing to speak out. That is, the theory adds to our existing understanding of public opinion, which other explanations do not.

Methodological

Noelle-Neumann's design has also come under some criticism. For example, Salmon and Kline (1985) maintain that the direction of causality, relating voting intentions to perception of change in opinion climate, is unclear since she does not provide individual level data. Nonetheless, in her 1984 publication, data from panel studies are provided. Critics also say that the data do not make it clear whether those on the ascendant side do so out of fear of negative sanctions as Noelle-Neumann argues, or out of more positive incentives (wanting to be on the winning side). Moreover, her media content data have been criticized because they are too short term to permit definitive conclusions.

There is also some concern about survey questions that ask respondents whether they know what other people are thinking about an issue. For example, one question asks, "Now regardless of your opinion, what do you think: are most people for or against. . . ." Noelle-Neumann finds that people typically have no hesitation about answering this question. One may ask, however, whether this approach could be used in other cultures and countries where people are reluctant to offer opinions for cultural reasons. Verification in a cross-cultural context could add considerably to the viability of her theoretical framework (see Glynn & McLeod, 1985). The concern here is not that the method is flawed, but that its applicability is limited to certain contexts and structures.

In conclusion, Noelle-Neumann's theory has generated not only great interest, but also some controversy because it draws attention to her politics of past and present. Some have argued that the implications of the theory could lead one to support a more conservative, even an antidemocratic ideology. This is a clear and remarkable example of the risk involved in working in social science where values, motives, and ideology are close to the surface. Values and ideology influence the kind of questions researchers ask. By the very nature of our enterprise, as social scientists, we leave ourselves open to criticisms.

INTEGRATION OF PERSONAL AND PROFESSIONAL LIFE

Although she had many friends as a young woman, Noelle-Neumann speaks of the "perennial problem" of being different from others her own age. She enjoyed solitude and devoted herself to literature and arts and school projects. At a young age, she decided to become a journalist and devote herself to her career. In 1940, after receiving her doctorate in journalism, she worked for a "conservative newspaper," *Deutsche Allgemeine Zeitung.* Eric Peter Neumann was one of the editors and her supervisor. They were married in 1946 at the end of the war, and from the beginning, the marriage appeared to be an equal partnership. They co-founded the now well-known Allensbach Institute, the first opinion research institute in Germany. Noelle-Neumann credits Erich Neumann for introducing opinion research to German politics.

Erich Peter Neumann died in 1973, and in 1979 Noelle-Neumann married Heinz Maier Leibnitz, a distinguished physicist and one-time president of *Deutsche Forschungsgemeinschaft* (the German equivalent of the National Science Foundation) whom she had known from her high school days.

From the beginning, Elisabeth Noelle-Neumann says, her career came first, and both her husbands understood that. In fact, she and her second husband married in 1979, after he had completed his term as the president of the German science foundation, because she "had no time for the lifestyle required by his status." She has no children, for the Allensbach Institute and her work took "precedence" over everything else. Having devoted herself to her goal of linking "applied research with journalism," she has more or less subordinated her personal life to her career.

Because of her gender, Noelle-Neumann encountered her share of professional problems from both colleagues and people in the survey research business. She was also a target of student unrest in the early 1970s, which she felt might have been "especially vehement" because she was a woman. However, the issue of gender was "never important" to her.

Noelle-Neumann's contributions to public opinion polling and communication research in Germany are legendary. Even at age 78, she is still active commenting about German politics and public opinion in the press and acting as an adviser to German politicians. She has lived a life that has achieved much of what she set out to do.

REFERENCES

Asch, S. E. (1965). Effect of group pressure upon modification and distortion of judgements. In J. H. Campbell & H. Hepler (eds.), *Dimension in communication*. Belmont, Calif.: Wadsworth Publishing.

Becker, L. B., McCombs, M. E., & McLeod, J. M. (1975). The development of political cognitions. In S. H. Chaffee (ed.), *Political communication: Issues and strategies for research*. Beverly Hills, Calif.: Sage.

Beniger, J. R. (1987). Toward an old new paradigm: The half-century flirtation with mass society. *Public Opinion Quarterly*, 51, s46–s66.

Bogart, L. (1991). The pollster and the Nazis. *Commentary*, 47–49.

Chaffee, S. H., & Hochheimer, J. L. (1985). The beginnings of political communication research in the United States: origins of the "limited effects" model. In E. M. Rogers & F. Balle (eds.), *The media revolution in America and Western Europe*. Norwood, N.J.: Ablex.

Commentary. (1992, January). Letters from readers, 9–19.

Commentary. (1992, April). Letters from readers, 11–13.

Entman, R. M. (1993). "Framing: Toward clarification of a fractured paradigm." *Journal of Communication*, 43(4), 51–58.

Gamson, W. A. (1992). *Talking politics*. New York: Cambridge University Press.

Gitlin, T. (1978). Media sociology: The dominant paradigm. *Theory and Society*, 6, 205–253.

Gitlin, T. (1980). *The whole world is watching: The mass media in the making and unmaking of the New Left*. (Chapters 1, 10, & 11, pp. 21–31, 250–292). Berkeley: University of California Press.

Glynn, C. J., & McLeod, J. M. (1985). Implications of the spiral of silence theory for communications and public opinion research. In K. R. Sanders, L. L. Kaid, & D. Nimmo (eds.), *Political communication yearbook. 1984*. (pp. 43–65). Carbondale: Southern Illinois University Press.

Iyengar, S. (1991). *Is anyone responsible? How television frames political issues*. Chicago: University of Chicago Press.

Katz, E. (1981). Publicity and pluralistic ignorance: Notes on the 'the spiral of silence.'
    In H. Baier, H. M. Kepplinger, & K. Reumann (eds.), *Offentliche Meinung und
    sozialer wandel/Public opinion and social change.* (pp. 28–38). Festschrift for
    Elisabeth Noelle-Neumann. Opladen, Germany: Westdeutscher Verlag.
Klapper, J. T. (1960). *The effects of mass communication.* New York: Free Press.
Noelle-Neumann, E. (1993). *The spiral of silence—Public opinion: Our social skin.* (2nd
    ed.). Chicago and London: University of Chicago Press.
Noelle-Neumann, E. (1983). The effects of media on media effects research. *Journal of
    Communication, 33*(3), 157–165.
Olien, C. N., Donohue, G. A., & Tichenor, P. J. (1978). Community structure and media
    use. *Journalism Quarterly, 55,* 445–455.
Paletz, D. L., & Entman, R. M. (1981). *Media, power, politics,* New York: Free Press.
Pan, Z., & Kosicki, G. M. (1993). Framing analysis: An approach to news discourse.
    Political Communication, 10 (1), 55–75.
Salmon, C. T., & Kline, F. G. (1985). The spiral of silence: Ten years later. In K. R.
    Sanders, L. L. Kaid, & D. Nimmo (eds.), *Political communication yearbook.
    1984.* (pp. 3–30). Carbondale: Southern Illinois University Press.
Sherif, M. (1966). *The psychology of social norms.* New York: Harper & Row.
Tichenor, P. J., Donohue, G. A., & Olien, C. N. (1980). *Community Conflict and the
    Press.* Beverly Hills, Calif.: Sage.

Selective List of Publications by Noelle-Neumann

Professor Noelle-Neumann's publications are extensive, and she is published in several
languages. Her list of publications runs to almost 23 pages. Given below is a very
selective list of her published work.

Noelle-Neumann, E. (1963). *Umfragen in der Massengesellschaft. Einfuhrung in die
    Methoden der Demoskopie.* Reinbek.
Noelle-Neumann, E. (1973). Return to the concept of powerful mass media. *Studies in
    Broadcasting, 9,* 67–112.
Noelle-Neumann, E. (1979). Experiments in the measurement of readership. *Journal of
    the Market Research Society, 21,* 251–267.
Noelle-Neumann, E. (1979). Public opinion and the classical tradition. *Public Opinion
    Quarterly, 43,* 143–156.
Noelle-Neumann, E. (1984). International opinion research: How to phrase your ques-
    tions. *European Research, 12* (3), 124–131.
Noelle-Neumann, E. (1984). *The spiral of silence—Public opinion: Our social skin.* 1st
    ed. Chicago and London: University of Chicago Press.
Noelle-Neumann, E. (1984). The theory of public opinion: The concept of the spiral of
    silence. In J. Anderson (ed.), *Communication Yearbook 14.* (pp. 256–287). New-
    bury Park, Calif.: Sage.
Noelle-Neumann, E. (1987). Federal Republic of Germany: Election forecasts and the
    public. *European Research, 15,* 162–165.
Noelle-Neumann, E. (1987). Identifying opinion leaders. *European Research, 13* (4), 18–
    23.
Noelle-Neumann, E. (1989). Advances in spiral of silence research. *Keio Communica-
    tions Review, 10,* 30–34.

Noelle-Neumann, E. (1989). The public as prophet: Findings from continuous survey research and their importance for early diagnosis of economic growth. *International Journal of Public Opinion Research,* 1 (2), 136–150.

Noelle-Neumann, E. (1991). The German revolution. The historic experiment of the division and unification of a nation as reflected in survey research findings. *International Journal of Public Opinion Research,* 3, 238–259.

Noelle-Neumann, E., & Kocher, R. (eds.). (1993). *Allensbacher Jahrbuch der Demoskopie, 1984–1992.* Vol. 9. Munich & New York: K. G. Saur.

Noelle-Neumann, E., & Mathes, R. (1987). The ''event as event'' and the ''event as news'': The significance of consonance for media effects research. *European Journal of Communication,* 2, 391–414.

HELEN ROGERS REID
(1882–1970)

Elizabeth V. Burt

During a period spanning more than four decades, Helen Rogers Reid was a forceful presence at one of New York City's largest metropolitan dailies in a time when women were still struggling to enter and win recognition in the journalism profession. Although Reid entered journalism perhaps unintentionally as the result of her marriage to the heir of the New York *Tribune,* she soon became a newspaper personality in her own right, encouraging the paper's acquisition of and merger with the New York *Herald,* directing its advertising department, participating in major editorial decisions, and eventually becoming president of the New York *Herald Tribune* corporation. In her various roles as wife, manager, and president, she used the newspaper as a springboard for civic and social projects and established forums and foundations that reached all levels of society from the city's poor children to the nation's most influential citizens. A feminist, she was active in the campaign to win votes for women and later encouraged and supported women to go to college and enter the workforce on an equal basis with men. As a result of her work, she was recognized by a wide range of professional and academic organizations, received honorary degrees from more than a dozen colleges and universities, and was remembered as a vital force in New York's civic and professional community.

FAMILY BACKGROUND AND EDUCATION

Helen Miles Rogers was born on November 23, 1882 in Appleton, Wisconsin, the youngest of 11 children of Benjamin Talbot Rogers and Sarah Louise Johnson Rogers. Her father, a former store owner who had sold his business to invest in a hotel in Appleton where he could send his children to nearby Lawrence College, failed in the venture and died when Helen was 3. Although the family was not poverty-stricken, the older children were obliged to contribute to the family's finances, and those still in school worked to cover their expenses. Helen attended public school until the age of 11 and then enrolled in Grafton Hall, the college preparatory boarding school where her brother, the Reverend Talbot Rogers, was headmaster. She supported her tuition at Grafton Hall with odd jobs and, after graduating in 1899, entered Barnard College in New York.

At Barnard, Helen also worked her way through school, juggling jobs in the bursar's office, as dormitory manager, and as a tutor. She first chose to major in Greek and Latin and later switched to zoology, most likely with the idea of becoming a teacher, one of the few guaranteed professions open to women in those years. When she received her B.A. in 1903, however, rather than pursuing a teaching career, she applied for an opening as social secretary to Mrs. Whitelaw Reid, a prominent socialite, civic leader, suffragist, and wife of the wealthy publisher of the New York *Tribune*.

MARRIAGE AND CAREER

The sumptuous Manhattan home of the Whitelaw Reids was a world away from the modest Rogers family home in Appleton. Mrs. Reid, the daughter of the wealthy financier, Darius Ogden Mills, was accustomed to the most sophisticated forms of social entertainment. The Reid family's Florentine mansion on Madison Avenue across from St. Patrick's Cathedral had a dinner table seating 80 people, and the table often was graced by the company of the city's wealthiest, most powerful, and most illustrious citizens as well as members of the European nobility and intelligentsia. As Mrs. Reid's social secretary, Helen came into contact with some of society's most influential people, an experience she later put to good use when she herself became a member of the New York elite. When Whitelaw Reid was appointed ambassador to the Court of St. James in 1905, the Reid family divided its time between England and the United States and Helen traveled between the two countries on a regular basis, soon becoming an accepted member of the international social and diplomatic set.

In 1911 Helen became engaged to the Reid's only son, Ogden Mills Reid, who, after his graduation from Yale Law School in 1910, had joined his father in London to become the ambassador's private secretary. After a short engagement, the couple married in March 1911 and returned to Manhattan to set up house. When Whitelaw Reid died within the year, Ogden inherited the *Tribune* and became its president and editor. As his bride, Helen at first found her life filled with the details of managing their home and entertaining, and she patterned her life in many respects after that of her mother-in-law, who in addition to her role as *materfamilias* maintained the position of grande dame in the city's civic and social life and was a prominent suffrage leader. During the first six years of her marriage, Helen had little visible involvement in the newspaper, devoting herself instead to the final thrust of the woman's suffrage movement. Here, she was able to use the contacts she had made through her association with the Reid family and her new position as wife of one of the city's most powerful men. She helped raise $500,000 for the final thrust of the movement in New York, where, in 1917, women finally won the vote.

But domestic life (she eventually had three children, Whitelaw, Elisabeth—who died in childhood—and Ogden) and her social and civic activities proved inadequate for the ambitious Helen. "When I was at Barnard working my way through," she said later, "the necessity for complete independence of women was borne in on me." Thus, in 1918 she became an advertising solicitor for the *Tribune* and within two months had become its advertising manager. This step, which was encouraged by her husband, was revolutionary in the Reid's social and economic class, for while it was quite acceptable for wealthy women to volunteer their time to social and civic causes, to assist their husbands in the pursuit of their careers, and even to dabble in writing and other artistic pursuits, it was unheard of for them actually to take a professional *job*. Helen, however, took her new job quite seriously, working as hard if not harder than her staff, so that her salesmen were fiercely loyal to her and eager to win her praise. As for her style with clients, she blended her sales pitch with a mixture of hard fact, banter, and flattery and often included an invitation to luncheon with her request for a business meeting. Within five years, the *Tribune,* which had been struggling to survive throughout the war years, doubled its advertising revenue. By 1923 its daily circulation had increased to more than 133,000, and it was considered a worthy competitor to the city's three leading morning dailies, the *New York Times,* the *World,* and the *American.*

In 1924 the Reids resisted a buyout attempt by publishing mogul Frank Munsey, the owner of more than a dozen publications, including the New York *Herald,* the New York *Sun,* the New York *Evening Telegram, Munsey's,* and *Argosy.* At Helen's prompting, the Reids instead acquired the *Herald* and its Paris edition for $5 million. They merged the two papers, and the New York *Herald Tribune* became the only morning Republican paper in the city. Helen became vice president of the corporation and assumed the major responsibilities of the publisher's office, while Ogden focused on the editorial side. But despite the clear distinction between their formal positions, the two clearly collaborated in their efforts, and Helen provided regular input at editorial board meetings. This influence apparently became known among the couple's social circle, for Helen often received letters from friends complaining about the way the newspaper had covered a particular issue or event. In 1937, for example, her friend, the wealthy socialite Eleanor Robson Belmont, complained about the paper's treatment of a mutual acquaintance. Reid replied that, although she was not happy with the paper's editorial on the subject, she had been "unavoidably prevented from seeing it in advance," implying that if she had seen it, she would have stopped it. One notable exception to her influence on editorial policy was in the case of Prohibition. Helen, who supported the reform, failed to convince her husband to make the paper dry.

After the merger with the *Herald,* Helen played a key role in the newspaper's expansion of its coverage to include and appeal to the suburban middle class, especially the women of this untapped market. She introduced a new section on gardening designed to appeal to these readers and established the "Home Institute," an experimental kitchen where chefs employed by the newspaper could develop new recipes that were then published in the newspaper. She also introduced a literary section, "Books," as well as a Sunday supplement featuring fiction and articles, "This Week," both of which were designed to expand readership and provide a challenge to the competition.

Reid used advertisements and promotional devices targeted at this new audience to increase readership and then touted the increase in female readership to attract new advertisers. These ads also revealed some of her faith in the power and competence of women. One such full-page advertisement directed toward advertisers in 1933, for example, showed a well-dressed woman reading a book to a child on her lap. "SHE holds your success in her capable hands," the advertisement proclaimed. "Reach her well through the newspaper she *prefers*. Who is 'she?' She is simply a New York housewife . . . but she represents the greatest concentration of buying power in the world . . . tell her your sales story through the pages of the New York Herald Tribune. She reads the Herald Tribune . . . conscientiously . . . every day and Sunday too." Reid, in fact, credited women readers with a profound influence on the nature of the press, saying in 1932 that it was the "force of women on public opinion that has changed the pattern of the newspaper of today, making the news more human and more interesting than ever before."

As her influence at the *Herald Tribune* expanded into the editorial department, Helen Rogers Reid sought new and stimulating writers and succeeded in attracting prominent syndicated columnists such as Walter Lippmann, Mark Sullivan, and Joseph Alsop. In 1936 she was instrumental in breaking the male monopoly on column writing when she convinced her husband to hire the fiery and often emotional Dorothy Thompson* to write an international column, "On the Record." Sometimes, however, Reid's strongly Republican views interfered with the "objectivity" of her editorial and managerial decisions. Thus in the early 1940s when Thompson went against the *Herald Tribune*'s position and used her column to endorse Franklin D. Roosevelt for a third term, she was dropped abruptly from the newspaper.

Reid remained vice president of the *Herald Tribune* until the death of her husband in 1947, when she inherited his control of the newspaper and succeeded him as president of the corporation. She remained in this role until 1953, when she stepped down for her son, Ogden R. Reid, who became president, publisher, and editor. Helen acted as chairman of the board of directors until 1955, when she retired at the age of 77. The paper, which had been failing in circulation and advertising ever since the early 1950s was sold in 1958 to millionaire John Hay Whitney. It continued under his editorship until 1967 when it was merged with Hearst's *Journal-American* and Scripps-Howard's *World Telegram and Sun* to become the *World Journal Tribune*.

CONTRIBUTIONS TO WOMEN IN COMMUNICATION

Always supportive of women in the professions, Helen Rogers Reid was especially encouraging to women in advertising and journalism. She often used the occasion of her public appearances to speak on the need for women to reach for the best they could accomplish. In 1932, for example, she told the women at a conference of the Women's Intercollegiate News Association that they must go after the top jobs in their fields, even if they had to work twice as hard to get the same recognition as men. And at the height of the Depression in 1939, she told the graduating class of a women's private school that, despite the nation's high unemployment, women should continue to pursue their own careers, not only for economic reasons but for the sake of their own happiness and to save themselves from the "intellectual snobbery" of men.

Reid not only strove for her own professional success, but also acted as a mentor to other women. At the paper, she promoted women to editorial positions and went to bat for them in getting significant reporting assignments. She named two women, for example, to head the sections she had created: Irita Van Doren as editor of "Books," and Mrs. William Brown Meloney, as editor of "This Week." She followed the same policy of promoting women reporters, often sending letters to the newspaper's editors and bureau chiefs to recommend a particular female candidate for a position as correspondent. Emma Bugbee, Ishbel Ross, Fay Wells, Tanya Long, Janet Owen, Ann Cottrell, and Marguerite Higgins* were just a few of the women reporters hired at the paper after Helen's marriage into the Reid family and assent to power.

During World War II, Reid distinguished the paper by promoting the war's first female war correspondent, Sonia Tomara. Reid backed Tomara in her bid to cover the war in Asia, despite a War Department policy restraining women from going overseas and the *Herald Tribune*'s own reluctance to assign female correspondents to the war zone. When the War Department refused to issue Tomara accreditation, Reid pulled the necessary strings and in one hour in Washington obtained Tomara's travel documents. In a similar vein, when the newspaper's editors refused to send staff reporter Marguerite Higgins* overseas, Reid backed the reporter's bid to be assigned to the European theater. With Reid's blessing, Higgins traveled to London in August 1944 and then to the continent where she covered the wind-down of the war. Higgins went on to cover the Korean conflict for the *Herald Tribune,* and in 1950 Reid intervened for her once again when the military ordered the journalist, along with all other American women except nurses, out of Korea. Reid appealed the decision to the commanding general, Douglas MacArthur, and the ban on women reporters was lifted immediately. Reid's intervention was paid off with the quality of Higgins' first-page stories on the conflict; the reporter was later awarded the Pulitzer Prize for her stories on the war.[1]

OTHER ACCOMPLISHMENTS

Apart from her role as advertising director and vice president and then president of the *Herald Tribune,* Reid played an important political and cultural role as the organizer of the newspaper's annual Forum on Current Problems. Established in 1930 and continued until 1955, the forum was initially a promotional device aimed at clubwomen and succeeded in attracting more than 3,000 by its sixth anniversary in 1935. The forum met with such great success, in fact, that it was later expanded to include the general public and became an early multimedia event, with some speakers who could not attend in person addressing the audience by radio broadcast. Topics such as "America Faces a Changing World," and "America's Role in the European Conflict" attracted a wide range of speakers over the years, including national and international political leaders, academics, journalists, and economists representing all viewpoints. Reid presided over the meetings, all of which were held at the posh Waldorf-Astoria, and published the proceedings in a special supplement to the *Herald Tribune* for high school and college students.

Reid also frequently appeared as a speaker at important conferences and events and used these occasions to promote her favorite topics: freedom of the press; the necessity of advertising in the American press; and equality for women in work. Either because these events were newsworthy in their own right or because they became newsworthy because the prominent Mrs. Reid was the speaker, they were usually covered by the press. Reid thus succeeded in placing her ideas before a far larger audience than that which attended the event. In a speech at a Barnard College graduation in 1943, for example, she aired a typical publisher's complaint about the delay in receiving war news from the War Department, pointing out that both American newspapers and the American people were cooperative with the government but needed to know the facts to function as free citizens in a democratic society.

Reid professed political impartiality on the news pages of the *Herald Tribune* but was a supporter of moderate Republicanism. She backed Thomas E. Dewey for the presidency in 1948 and became a strong supporter of Dwight D. Eisenhower in 1952. Although the *Herald Tribune* endorsed the Republican candidates on its editorial pages, Reid was adamant about giving impartial coverage to all political candidates. She clearly viewed only the candidates of the two dominant parties as legitimate contenders, however, and, like so many other newspaper publishers at the time, she shared the national phobia about communism. Thus, she told an audience of 200 at a lecture at City College of New York in 1951 that in covering a political campaign, a responsible newspaper would cover news developments equally for both sides and would expect its reporters to act fairly and professionally. "A good editor today does not care and seldom knows whether his staff are Republicans or Democrats. He merely tries to make sure that they are not Communists as no one holding their views could be trusted to tell the truth.''

Reid was a leader in civic affairs. She created the newspaper's Fresh Air Fund, which raised public contributions to send needy children to summer camps and homes in the country. She also served nine years as chairman of the board of trustees of Barnard College, and in the early 1960s she helped raise funds to build a dormitory that was later named for her. She was also a trustee of the Metropolitan Museum of Art and often appeared as a speaker at fund-raising functions for the museum. She was a longtime member and officer of the New York Newspaper Women's Club, where she often spoke on freedom of the press, the role of women in journalism, and the need for a healthy advertising revenue in maintaining a newspaper's political independence. After the death of Ogden Reid in 1947, she became the president of the Reid Foundation, established by her husband in 1946 to award fellowships to journalists for study and travel abroad. By 1955, 36 journalists, all of them from news organizations other than the *Herald Tribune,* had received the one-year fellowship. In 1951 the Department of Defense recognized Reid's frequent campaigns for equal opportunity for women in the military by appointing her, along with 47 other prominent women, to a Women's Advisory Committee. The committee's mission was to assist the military in its efforts to recruit women and to provide them with positive job opportunities and career possibilities.

AWARDS AND RECOGNITION

Reid was amply recognized for her accomplishments during her lifetime, receiving honorary degrees from more than a dozen colleges and universities, including Columbia, Yale, and the New School for Social Research. In addition, she received numerous awards for her civic and professional contributions, including the Medal of Award in 1935 from the American Women's Association on Freedom of the Press for ''professional achievement, public service and personality.'' In 1946 the Hundred Year Association of New York awarded her a gold medal ''in recognition of outstanding achievement for the advancement of New York,'' a ceremony that the association repeated when it gave her a second gold medal 14 years later in 1960. Several awards were made to her for her progressive role in civil rights issues, and she received the Zionist Award and the New York Jewish Philanthropic Award in 1949, the 1949–1950 seal of the Council Against Intolerance for her ''outstanding service in the cause of tolerance and equality,'' a B'nai B'rith award in 1954 for her contributions to the civil rights cause, and, in 1955 a citation from Hadassah for her humanitarian services to the citizens of New York. In 1957, two years after her resignation as chairman of the board of the *Herald Tribune,* she received the Fairbanks Award from the American College Public Relations Association.

On several occasions Reid was named as one of the outstanding women in the country. In 1935, for example, suffrage veteran Carrie Chapman Catt named her as one of the first ten women in the nation. The others included such illustrious figures as Eleanor Roosevelt* (who was number one on the list), Dr. Florence Sabin, Secretary of Labor Frances Perkins, and aviator Amelia Earhart. In 1950 Reid was one of four women elected fellows of the American Academy of Arts and Sciences, and in 1951 she was listed among ten notable women in industry, communication, labor, and the professions in New York State.

Helen Rogers Reid faded from the public eye after she released her hold on the *Herald Tribune,* first with her resignation from the presidency in 1953 and then from the chairmanship of the board in 1955, and finally with the Reid family's sale of the paper to Whitney in 1958. Yet when she died in 1970 at the age of 87, her funeral was attended by 300 people, including national and international political figures, newspaper associates, and admirers. She was hailed on the editorial page of her former competitor, the *New York Times,* as "a vital and constructive figure in the life of New York and the nation" and as a "born journalist"—"tiny, spirited, thoroughly feminine and every inch a newspaperman."

Although Reid was perhaps one of the most influential women in New York for more than four decades, little is written about her in history books, and she is barely mentioned in journalism histories. When she is mentioned, more often than not her name is linked with the names of women such as columnist Dorothy Thompson* and war correspondent Marguerite Higgins.* It is ironic that it is these women, who were mentored by Reid and perhaps achieved their fame as "firsts" among women because of her sponsorship, who have captured the interest and attention of scholars and historians.

NOTE

1. Whether it was Helen Rogers Reid or Marguerite Higgins who confronted General MacArthur remains in question. Higgins' biographers say she did, whereas those writing about Reid say that Reid was responsible for having the ban lifted.

REFERENCES

Correspondence of Helen Rogers Reid in the Rare Book and Manuscript Library, Columbia University, New York.

Downes, Robert B. (1991). Helen Rogers Reid. *Journalists of the United States.* Jefferson, N.C.: McFarland.

Edwards, Julia. (1988). *Women of the world: The great foreign correspondents.* Boston.

New York Times
    (1911, February 14). Ogden Reid to wed Helen Miles Rogers.
    (1924, March 18). Reid buys *Herald* from Munsey.
    (1932, December 11). Urges girls to aim for top jobs.
    (1935, February 10). Fields for women seen as widening.

(1935, September 8). 40 will speak at women's meeting here.

(1935, December 10). Mrs. Catt names ten "first women."

(1939, June 3). Todhunter girls urged to seek careers to foil men's "intellectual snobbery."

(1943, February 13). Military seeking Barnard College.

(1951, May 18). Duty of press defined.

(1958, August 29). Control of the *Herald Tribune* passes from Reid family to Ambassador Whitney.

(1970, July 28). Mrs. Ogden Reid dies at 87.

(1970, July 29). Mrs. Reid of the *Tribune.*

COKIE ROBERTS
(1943–)

Juliet Dee

FAMILY BACKGROUND

Cokie Roberts, whose full name is Mary Martha Corinne Morrison Claiborne Boggs Roberts, was born on December 27, 1943, in New Orleans, Louisiana. (Her brother Tommy gave her the nickname Cokie because "Corinne" was too difficult to say.) Cokie's parents were Thomas Hale Boggs and Corinne Morrison Claiborne Boggs, known as Lindy Boggs. Her father Hale Boggs graduated Phi Beta Kappa from Tulane University. He was elected to the U.S. House of Representatives and served from 1941 to 1943 and then from 1947 to 1972. He was majority whip in the House from 1961 to 1971 and was then elected majority leader of the House.

In 1972 congressman Nick Begich begged Hale Boggs to go to Alaska and help him campaign. Although Boggs did not want to take this trip, he went because he had promised to help Begich. His plane, however, never arrived in Juneau. Cokie was about 27 (with 2 small children) when her father's plane disappeared. When she arrived in Washington her mother said,

"We're going to Alaska." I said, "Are you crazy? What are we going to do in Alaska? Here we are surrounded by friends and family and support." And she said, "If *we* were in Alaska and lost, he'd come look for us." So we went. . . . It was on Air Force 2— President Nixon was very nice about that. (Gross, 1993, p. 9)

Majority Leader Boggs, Begich, and two others had taken off from Anchorage on October 16, 1972, in a twin-engine craft for the 550-mile flight to Juneau.

The plane lost radio contact with the ground and disappeared. After a 39-day search, Hale Boggs and the three other men were never found.

A former schoolteacher, Lindy Boggs had managed 12 of her husband's re-election campaigns as well as his congressional office, and she later coordinated the inaugural celebrations of Presidents John Kennedy and Lyndon Johnson. "Mamma gave us the role model of someone who knew how to juggle," Roberts has said. "She was always there, and yet she was always working. We thought she was the most beautiful woman alive" (*Current Biography*, 1994, p. 41). Lindy Boggs was elected to her husband's seat in the House of Representatives after his death in 1972. She served until she retired in 1990. Thus, Roberts' parents together served in Congress for nearly 50 years (with the exception of 1943–1947). At age 78 Lindy Boggs is still known as the loveliest, most gracious person in Washington.

Roberts is the youngest of three children; her older sister Barbara Boggs Sigmund was mayor of Princeton, New Jersey, for six years until her death from cancer in 1990 at age 51. Her brother Thomas Hale Boggs, Jr., is a partner in the Washington law firm of Patton, Boggs.

EDUCATION

As a child, Cokie Roberts spent part of each year in the Garden District of New Orleans and the rest of the year in Bethesda, Maryland, where the family lived while Congress was in session. She attended Catholic schools taught by Sacred Heart nuns in both Washington, D.C., and Louisiana. In an early indication of her talent for journalism, Roberts edited the student newspaper at her Catholic high school.

Roberts no doubt learned as much in her home as she did at school: Lyndon Johnson and Speaker of the House Sam Rayburn (and later, Speaker of the House Tip O'Neill) often came for dinner. Cokie, Tommy, and Barbara also had spirited arguments with their parents about civil rights and Vietnam. Roberts knew that as a child whose father was a Congressman, she had to careful and more well behaved in public than her friends. When she was older, during the civil rights battles, she realized that she and her family were on one side while the rest of New Orleans was on the other. She found that even though people would say hurtful things that she was limited in the degree to which she could fight back (Gross, 1993). Roberts majored in political science, graduating from Wellesley College in 1964 at age 20. More recently, she received three honorary doctorates in 1993 and three more in 1994.

CAREER DEVELOPMENT

At age 21, Roberts was an anchor of "Meeting of Minds," a midday public affairs program for WRC-TV in Washington, D.C., but left when she married her husband Steve who was already working for the *New York Times* in New

York City. Even though she had been making more money than her husband, she did not find it difficult to quit her job: "Growing up, our expectation was to do what our mother did. We thought we would graduate from college, have an interesting job for a year or two, get married, have babies, and contribute to the community" (*Current Biography*, 1994, p. 41). Once she was settled in New York, however, Roberts decided to continue working in journalism. She spent eight months looking for work with various New York magazines and television stations, but wherever she went she was asked how many words she could type. Eventually she found work as a reporter and editor for Cowles Communications in 1967 and as a producer at WNEW-TV in 1968.

In an interview with Terry Gross on NPR's "Fresh Air," Gross asked Roberts about her early career:

Gross: Were you turned down for jobs that you thought you should have gotten?

Roberts: Absolutely.

Gross: Were you told point blank that it was because you were a woman?

Roberts: Point blank. "We don't hire women to do that. Their voices lack authority," or "We don't hire women writers because men have to work for the writers and obviously men can't work for women," or "You'll leave because you'll get pregnant." And it was all straight out loud. . . .

Gross: Did you ever challenge it?

Roberts: No. It was 1966, and it was in New York. By then it was against the law and I could have gone around suing people—and never worked for the rest of my life. (Gross, 1993, p. 11)

Roberts later commented: "One other thing: While these men were saying we couldn't have the jobs, their hands were on our knees" (Dreifus, 1994, p. 6:3).

When her children were born, Roberts put their needs over her own journalistic aspirations. In 1969 she moved with her husband to Los Angeles, where she worked as a producer with Altman Productions until 1972. She then spent two years as a producer at KNBC-TV, winning an award for excellence in local programming. In 1974, with two small children in tow, she went with Steve on his overseas assignments. "But that's what I wanted to do," Roberts says. "We had little kids. My career came second—in both my husband's and my mind."

The *New York Times* stationed her husband, Steve, in Athens, Greece, and Cokie began working as a stringer for CBS News radio. When a coup toppled the ruling military junta, Cokie Roberts found herself in a bad place at the right time: she was riding by the presidential palace when the junta fell. Roberts gave such a vivid eyewitness account of the pandemonium that it became the voice-over for the lead story on Walter Cronkite's "The CBS Evening News" that night. Despite such recognition, Roberts has acknowledged that her commitment to journalism as a career was still casual at that time: "We kept moving around the country . . . and it was by far the easiest thing to do—go out and report a story and come back and write it—because that is portable. That is how [my career] evolved" (*Current Biography,* 1994, p. 41).

When Roberts and her family returned to the United States in 1977, Nina Totenberg, who was already working at National Public Radio (NPR) with Linda Wertheimer, a fellow Wellesley alumna, recruited Roberts to fill a third reporter's spot. "When I came in for an interview, Linda and Nina were there, greeting me and encouraging me. And it just made all the difference in the world. NPR was a place where I wanted to work because they were there" (Dreifus, 1994, p. 3). Roberts thus began covering Congress for NPR in 1977 and still works as a senior news analyst for NPR, whose 14.7 million listeners can hear her on "Morning Edition." Along with Linda Wertheimer and Nina Totenberg, Roberts is known as one of the "Three Musketeers" of NPR. The three are close friends, sharing vacations, theater subscriptions, and general emotional support.

In addition to her work at NPR, from 1981 to 1984 Roberts co-hosted "The Lawmakers," a weekly public television program on Congress and the first collaboration between public radio and public television. "The Lawmakers" covered House and Senate committee hearings and floor debates and profiled members of Congress.

As the regular congressional correspondent for PBS' "MacNeil/Lehrer Newshour," on which she appeared from 1984 to 1987, Roberts attracted national attention in her final year on the job, when she joined Elizabeth Drew and Judy Woodruff in their coverage of the Iran/Contra hearings for PBS.

In 1988 ABC took the unprecedented step of offering Roberts a contract that allowed her to be the network's Washington correspondent for ABC News and a regular panelist on "This Week with David Brinkley," the top-rated of the three Sunday morning network news programs, while continuing her work for NPR. Roberts was a floor reporter at the 1992 Democratic National Convention in New York as well as at the Republican National Convention in Houston, Texas. When Sam Donaldson was unable to attend the Houston convention, she served as a political analyst as well. In 1993 she became a full-time panelist on "This Week with David Brinkley." She has even hosted the program in Brinkley's absence. She often substitutes as anchor on "Nightline" when Ted Koppel is away, and she is a correspondent for "World News Tonight with Peter Jennings."

MAJOR CONTRIBUTIONS AND ACHIEVEMENTS

As the congressional correspondent for National Public Radio, Cokie Roberts has won the Edward R. Murrow Award, which is the highest award in public radio. She was also the first broadcast journalist to win the highly prestigious Everett McKinley Dirksen Award for coverage of Congress. In 1987 her coverage of the Iran/Contra scandal for the "MacNeil/Lehrer Newshour" won her

the Weintal Award, and in 1985 she received a Distinguished Alumnae Achievement Award from Wellesley College "in recognition of excellence and distinction in professional pursuits." Roberts is also a former president of the Radio
and Television Correspondents Association.

Considered one of the country's foremost experts on Congress, Roberts is
also known for her coverage of politics and particularly the role of women in
politics. Her op-ed columns have appeared in the *New York Times* and the
Washington Post; she has also written for the *New York Times Magazine* and
The Atlantic. She and her husband now have a weekly newspaper column, syndicated by United Media.

CRITICAL EVALUATION OF CONTRIBUTIONS
AND ACHIEVEMENTS

In addition to winning the Weintal Award for her coverage of the Iran/Contra
scandal in 1987, Roberts takes quiet pride in her role in urging Congress to take
a stand on the Persian Gulf War:

I was certainly not the only voice, but I was one of the first and loudest voices insisting
that the Congress debate and vote on the Persian Gulf War. They were trying desperately
to duck it; they were not in session when Iraq invaded Kuwait, and all the UN resolutions
occurred when Congress was not in session. There was a great desire on Congress' part
to just let that cup pass from them, and to those of us who have an institutional concern,
it was our view that if Congress did that, fine, but then don't ever go whining again
about Congress' right to declare war, because they would have abrogated it. So I think
that because of people who had an institutional concern—this had nothing to do with
policy or partisanship or anything like that—it had to do with the Constitution, and I
think that there were a number of people who wrote and broadcast from that perspective,
and in the end, combined with people inside Congress who had the same view, it combined to push Congress to have that debate, and it turned out to be a wonderful thing
for them. On that particular subject perhaps we in the media functioned as watchdogs.
(Roberts, 1994)

Asked about the effects of her coverage of women in Congress, Roberts responds with great modesty:

I doubt that my stories on women in Congress have helped women get elected, but I
certainly have spent a lot of time talking about women in politics because it's clearly a
subject that interests me. To the degree that people listen and say, "Hmm, that might
be a good reason to elect a woman," it might have had a small effect, but all I've done
on that subject is to just put it out there. There's been a lot of very interesting stuff to
report on, both on women in office and women as voters. It's just information that's
always fascinated me, and therefore to the degree that I've reported on it and people
have listened, it might have made some difference. (Roberts, 1994)

Indeed, Roberts is more likely to give the public rather than the media credit for setting the agenda on local and national issues, although she credits the media with setting the agenda on international issues:

By and large what we do is report the news that is obvious to anybody. To the degree that we go outside what is patently obvious, which is not often, it is generally because the public has already set the agenda for us, so that we slowly catch on that they are interested in X, Y, or Z. I think we're much slower on the draw than we are given credit for.

But there are certainly times when the media set the agenda, either consciously or unconsciously. In the case of Rwanda—you know Rwanda is many miles away; it is not on most Americans' radar screens, or at least it wasn't—but by committing the resources which were very difficult to commit (I mean, it was an extremely expensive story), and by committing the airtime that we gave to that story, it clearly put it on the agenda in a way that it would not be just by the nature of things. Then we ask the question "Why?" and I really think in that story the answer is because it was the right thing to do. When you have hundreds of thousands of people dying, even if it is halfway around the world, that is a story. (Roberts, 1994)

INTEGRATION OF PERSONAL AND PROFESSIONAL LIFE

In her junior year of college, Roberts attended a midwestern student conference where she met Steve Roberts, who was an editor of the *Harvard Crimson*. Steve Roberts was Jewish, whereas the Boggs were devout Catholics. But after four years of dating, they were married in 1966 under an apple tree in the garden of her family's home in Bethesda, Maryland. Cokie's uncle, a Jesuit priest, performed the ceremony. Arthur Goldberg, the United States ambassador to the United Nations, read Hebrew prayers. President Lyndon Johnson, his wife Lady Bird, and most of Congress were among the 1,500 guests at the wedding. Cokie and Steve Roberts have kept their faiths. Every Sunday after she appears on "This Week with David Brinkley," she dashes over to Mass at the Little Flower Catholic Church. And she recently prepared a Passover seder for Steve and 30 other people just after finishing an NPR broadcast. Cokie and Steve brought their children up with both traditions. She says: "We have celebrated everything, and enjoyed it greatly. It means you cook a lot and buy a lot of presents" (Roberts, 1994).

Steve Roberts is now a senior writer for *U.S. News & World Report* and appears as a news commentator on PBS' "Washington Week in Review." Steve and Cokie Roberts have been married for 28 years and have two children. Their daughter Rebecca graduated from Princeton in 1992 and works at a political consulting firm in Philadelphia. Their son Lee graduated from Duke and from Georgetown Law School. He now practices law in Washington, D.C.

Roberts was named one of *Glamour* magazine's "Ten Outstanding Women of 1991," *M* magazine named her a "Powerbroker of 1991," and the National

Mother's Day Committee honored her as "Outstanding Mother of the Year" for 1991.

In an interview with Terry Gross (1993), Roberts revealed that she believed that she had been able to achieve a much better balance between career and family than most other women. She counsels young women to remember that they'll be in the workforce for a long time and not to try to do everything at once. The time to have a family and the time that your children will be young is short, especially in relation to the number of years you will be in the workforce. Roberts especially believes that her family should come first and has turned down a number of very good positions because they were not appropriate for her family at that particular time.

Roberts also put family first when her beloved older sister Barbara Boggs Sigmund developed cancer a second time. Cokie would camp out on a cot near Barbara's bed. Then she would dash back to Washington, D.C., for her NPR and ABC broadcasts. What held Cokie together during this difficult time was the support from her husband Steve and her two children. Their mother Lindy Boggs announced her retirement from Congress in order to help care for Barbara, but Barbara died before the congressional term ended.

Her husband Steve calls himself "her greatest fan," and Roberts says, "I am married to the world's most wonderful human being. He is a wonderful man who's totally centered in his own self: he has done nothing but push me."

In the last few years Cokie Roberts has appeared on both Jay Leno and David Letterman's programs, and she has also been in "Entertainment Weekly." Her family may have to make some adjustments to her recent celebrity status, but in view of the Gibraltar-foundation of her family relationships, any adjustments will be no more than fine tuning.

REFERENCES

Current Biography. (1994, May). Roberts, Cokie. 40–43.

Dreifus, C. (1994, January 2). Cokie Roberts, Nina Totenberg and Linda Wertheimer. *New York Times Magazine,* Section 6, 1.

Gross, T. (1993, September). The politicians' daughter. *Applause,* 9–12.

Lynch, L. (1993, June 18–20). The prime of Cokie Roberts. *USA Weekend Magazine,* 2–3.

Roberts, C. (1994, August 15). Telephone interview.

L. EDNA ROGERS
(1933–   )

Carol Wilder

Edna Rogers' lifelong enchantment with an ecological metaphor for communication and interaction is grounded quite literally in the Iowa soil of her childhood farm. Rogers is a leading scholar of her generation in the development of a view of interpersonal communication based on systems theory, one that is operational in the research domain while maintaining the integrity of cybernetic epistemology. Her work has been recognized with many awards, including the Speech Communication Association Woolbert Research Award, the Michigan State University Teacher-Scholar Award, the Cleveland State University Distinguished Faculty Award, and numerous "top paper" awards. In 1987 she garnered one of the field's highest honors by being elected president of the International Communication Association. A warm and ebullient person, Rogers currently labors happily at the University of Utah, far from her childhood home but in an equally splendid ecological context. It could be said that Iowa farm life gave Rogers roots and systems theory gave her wings.

FAMILY BACKGROUND

The second of four children, and the only girl born to Esther and Berle Needham, Edna entered the world on the front porch of the family home near Greene, Iowa, on a warm June night in 1933. "My folks moved their bedroom out onto the enclosed porch for the summer. When we would celebrate my birthday we could light the candles right on the porch. My older brother now farms the home place, so for most of my life I literally could go home again."

Until age 12, Roger's dream was to be a cowboy and live on a ranch. She could ride a pony almost before she could walk and even rode her pony to grade school. She could also run a tractor. "My dad said I could drive the tractor when I was strong enough to push in the clutch pedal. It took all the strength I had at nine years old, but at nine I started driving that tractor.''

While Rogers has never been identified as a feminist scholar per se, her consciousness was raised early. ''There was no question in my mind that men were allowed more freedom than women and that always puzzled me, but rarely interfered with my climbing trees, playing football, and breaking horses.'' Housework never held much interest for Rogers, who preferred to be outdoors doing farmwork or riding horses with her brother. Television has never held much interest for Rogers either, perhaps because she ''lived a pre-television life, with free time filled with playing games, social and family gatherings, and church on Sunday.''

Rogers recalls that in a sense she had two mothers: her mother and her grandmother. ''Both were influential in shaping my views, especially my mom's active and involved approach to life.'' Rogers' family stressed the values of education, family, hard work, and doing your best at whatever you did. Though a child of the Great Depression, her family gave her ''the richest gifts of all: competence, inclusion, and liking of self.''

EDUCATION

Rogers was a good student but never considered herself academically talented because she couldn't spell well in an era when spelling was considered a main measure of intelligence. Although she tested as gifted, the spelling problem, which she identified only many years later as a mild dyslexia, was always there.

In first grade I couldn't even spell my first name—Lilian. Most of the letters looked the same, and so I became L. Edna. It wasn't until I taught English to Spanish-speaking students in Colombia in 1963 at Universidad de Los Andes and took a linguistics course that I realized if I had been a Spanish speaking person I probably could have spelled just fine. It was then I realized my native language was part of the problem. That sat well with me, especially when I read Margaret Mead's quote that spelling is such a trivial thing. ''My kind of woman,'' I thought.

It was always expected that Rogers would obtain a college degree, and in the fall of 1950 she went to Iowa State University. ''If you were a farm kid you went to Iowa State, and if you were a girl you majored in Home Economics.'' Rogers made female dorm friends from Cedar Rapids—the ''big city''—who majored in such exotic fields as psychology and history, which intrigued her. ''I had clearly bought into the cultural givens. In retrospect, it is still amazing how enraptured we can become in culture driven role definitions.''

Still, Rogers specialized in the most technical/scientific area of home economics—household equipment—under the tutelage of Dr. Louise Peets, and got the basic education of a ''lady engineer.'' Steeped in math, statistics, physics, and chemistry, her undergraduate education served her well and, although not anticipating her future direction, provided a firm research foundation for later work in graduate school. Still, at Iowa State the idea of being a college professor was not a career goal or even within the realm of imagination.

In 1951 Edna Needham met a young agricultural student, a senior named Everett Rogers. Three years later they married, and with the 1957 completion of his Ph.D., they moved to Columbus, Ohio. There Edna entered the M.A. program in sociology and anthropology at Ohio State University (OSU). At OSU she worked with some "very fine scholars" like her adviser, social psychologist Melvin Seeman, anthropologist John Bennett, and social theorist Kurt Wolff who at that time was translating Georg Simmel and discussing these translations in his social theory class. Rogers' experience at Ohio State marked a major period of intellectual growth, a honing of research skills. She engaged in discussions of the research process and realized these processes rarely unfold as neatly as it sounds in the text books. It was also at OSU that Rogers first entered the classroom as a teacher, not knowing that this somewhat intimidating experience would blossom into a lifelong love affair. Since that time teaching has been a top priority for Rogers.

The M.A. research Rogers completed in 1958 was part of a major Systems Research Group patient care project funded by the National Institutes of Health that cut across disciplines from philosophy to economics to engineering and beyond. Rogers' thesis research aimed to identify the stratification system within a hospital by having nurses describe doctors' behavior, and to try to come up with measures on three status dimensions: power difference (the extent that doctors kept decision making in their own hands), social distance, and prestige distinctions (see Seeman, Evans, & Rogers, 1960). Rogers characterizes the M.A. work as "at least a middle step, moving in the direction of trying to describe interaction, process and pattern."

CAREER DEVELOPMENT

After a decade as a faculty wife and mother with teaching and research simmering on the back burner, Rogers found herself again "trying to figure out a way to behaviorally index social interaction," this time as a Ph.D. student in communication at Michigan State University. Son David had joined the Rogers family in 1962, but like many women of her generation, Edna Rogers subsequently found herself a single parent wondering where the health insurance and a livable income were going to come from. "Getting a Ph.D. so you won't be poor isn't a very scholarly approach, but since I wanted to stay in university teaching that was an underlying motive."

In her search for ways to code interaction, Rogers turned to many sources, but in particular to Mead's (1954) symbolic interaction notions and to Bales' (1950) individual-based "interaction" categories. Then Rogers came upon a reference to Paul Watzlawick's *Anthology of Human Communication* text and tape (1964), and persuaded her adviser David Berlo to order it for the Communication Department.

Watzlawick's slender but highly original teaching text led Rogers to Watzlawick, Beavin, and Jackson's *Pragmatics of Human Communication* (1967), and then to Sluzki and Beavin's seminal 1965 "Simetria y Complementaridad: Una definicion operacionaly y una tipologia de parejas." Rogers translated the piece into English, and the rest, one might say, is history. Rogers had found the systems framework for interaction she had long been seeking. Sluzki and Beavin's work on symmetry and complementarity, grounded conceptually in the rich work of Gregory Bateson and in the *Pragmatics* text, provided the inspiration for Rogers' dissertation wherein she developed the interactional coding scheme that put her work, as well as the concepts it operationalized, on the map.

From Roger's description, the Michigan State years were vitalizing ones. In general, it was a time of social revolution, but in particular, communication was a newly established academic arena, cybernetic and system thinking held the promise to reformulate afresh the study of interactive processes, "and my son, a centering part of my life, was starting school."

Following completion of her Ph.D. in 1972, Rogers remained at Michigan State until 1976, attaining the rank of associate professor in the departments of Social Science and Communication. From 1976 (the year of her second marriage) to 1987 she was associate professor and then professor of communication at Cleveland State University, punctuated by visiting professorships at Kent State University (1985) and the University of Wyoming (1985).

The Cleveland State years were fruitful ones for Rogers, resulting in nearly two dozen major publications and dozens more formal presentations, often in collaboration with colleagues like John Courtright, Jan Beavin Bavelas, and Frank Millar. In 1987 Rogers made what she intends to be a permanent move to the University of Utah, an environment she found stimulating both intellectually and environmentally. Still, Rogers is in demand across the country and has completed visiting professorships at the University of Delaware (1988), the University of Miami (1989), and the University of Washington (1990).

MAJOR CONTRIBUTIONS AND ACHIEVEMENTS

Edna Rogers is best known generally in the field of communication as one of the few researchers (Janet Beavin Bavelas* is a notable other) who has attempted to operationalize constructs from interactional systems theory. She is best known specifically for the interactional coding scheme first developed during her dissertation research and subsequently widely used and imitated.

Rogers muses tongue-in-cheek about the possible numerological significance of her June 9, 1933 birthdate, but whatever the case there is a certain conceptual "threeness" to her thinking from the M.A. stratification work on power, social distance, and prestige, through the transactional patterns of symmetry, complementarity, and transitory, to the relational distance regulation dimensions of control, trust, and intimacy.

Of these, it is Rogers' work on symmetry and complementarity that is best known and most distinctive. Rogers herself provides the best overview of the constructs and early research in "Symmetry and Complementarity: Evolution and Evaluation of an Idea" (1982). The ideas of symmetry and complementarity were formulated during the 1930s by Gregory Bateson (1937) in his anthropological observations of the Iatmul in New Guinea. In Bateson's words, "a relationship between two individuals (or two groups) is said to be symmetrical if each responds to the other with the same kind of behavior, e.g., if each meets the other with assertiveness" (p. 311). It is said to be "chiefly complementary if most of the behaviour of the one individual is culturally regarded as of one sort (e.g., assertive) while most of the behaviour of the other, when he replies, is culturally regarded as of a sort complementary to this (e.g., submissive)" (p. 308).

The significance of these ideas goes far beyond the patterns they describe in that they are among the first (and still few) ideas that describe patterns of interaction rather than features of monadic behavior. The epistemological importance of this shift from the individual to the interaction cannot be overstated. Yet from the interactional perspective, research becomes exponentially complex because behavior from a systems view is nonsummative—that is, the whole is more than the sum of its parts. With the goal of analyzing larger, sequentially ordered patterns and their consequences, the limits of conventional research and statistical design can be reached rather quickly.

In developing the interactional coding scheme to identify communication-based patterns of symmetry and complementary, Rogers, following in the footsteps of Sluzki and Beavin (1965), went where many fear to tread, because the epistemological big thinkers and the detail-tolerant nuts-and-bolts researchers seldom meet in one person. Rogers, with her facility in both theoretical and practical thinking, with both the broad view and the skills to execute painstaking research, played a central role in the creation of a model for the operationalization of interactional constructs that holds up well even today.

In the relational communication control coding system (Rogers, 1972), three steps lead to the creation of a "musical score" of control dynamics. First, each message in an interaction is assigned a code to indicate the speaker, the grammatical form, and the response mode relative to the previous message. Next, these three-digit codes are translated into control directions of one-up (messages attempting to assert definitional rights), one-down (requests or acceptance of the other's definition of the relationship), and one-across (messages that are nondemanding, nonaccepting, or leveling). Finally, the control directions of each pair of sequentially ordered messages are combined to form the different types of symmetry, complementarity, and transitory transactions, with the object of sketching a "pattern of connectness" of the interaction.

Rogers estimates that the coding protocol has been used in well over 100 studies since her pioneering work. More than 20 years later she is still receiving requests for the coding manual and related writings. Rogers' work has been important in establishing the notion that patterns of self-correcting fluidity typically "work for us," while patterns of nonadapability and rigidity typically "work against us." This is the one most consistent findings across empirical studies and across contexts.

While relational dynamics play out with different nuances in different contexts, some patterns have emerged from the findings of a wide range of studies. For instance, a consistent finding in a series of studies of marital couples (Rogers-Millar & Millar, 1979; Courtright, Millar, & Rogers-Millar, 1979; Millar, Rogers, & Courtright, 1979; Escudero, Rogers, Gutierrez, & Caceres, in press) is the negative relationship between high levels of wife one-up control messages and various indices of marital and communication satisfaction on the part of both spouses. In contrast, flexible patterns of complementarity, with relatively equal sharing of assertions (one-up) and accepting (one-down) by the two spouses, were positively related to measures of satisfaction. Conversely, with more rigid, dominant forms of complementarity, with one spouse consistently deferring to the other's one-up messages, the level of satisfaction and dyadic understanding significantly declined. As expected, the more dominant partner had lower levels of understanding of their spouse than the less dominant partner.

The studies of clinical couples of different levels of marital adjustment (Escudero, Rogers, Gutierrez, & Caceres, in press), and clinical and nonclinical couple comparisons (Escudero, Rogers, & Gutierrez, in press) are especially poignant in demonstrating the dark side of redundancy, with patterns of communication rigidity clearly associated with high levels of distress. Rogers and her colleagues found that highly distressed couples suffered from a "double redundancy"; that is, they specialized in a small set of redundant interaction patterns which offered limited potential for problem exploration and resolution. Clinical couples with more flexible patterns indicated less distress and offered quite a different, more hopeful, picture for intervention success.

In 1976 Rogers first articulated with Millar a broad conceptualization of a communication-based model of interpersonal relationships. This three-dimensional model is grounded in the communication patterns that form the central interactive bonds of relational systems. Basic to the model is the spatial metaphor of interpersonal distance (or closeness) that represents how connected or separate the relational members are to one another along three generic dimensions of control, intimacy, and trust that can be said to characterize all relationships. Control here refers to patterns of constraint that emerge from the negotiation of system members' relational rights; intimacy or affect refers to patterns of sentiment, expressing emotional closeness; and trust indexes patterns of commitment and predictability. In combination, these three dimensions allow the mapping of relationship into a three-dimensional social space.

This model has served as a guide to research and as a framework for distinguishing different types of relationships; thus, it permits the meaningful comparison of empirical research. The dimension of control is clearly the most developed and researched aspect of the model, but Rogers' current work, especially with Spanish relational communication researchers and family therapists Escudero and Gutierrez, is exploring the combination of control and interactional measures of nonverbal affect.

The path of Rogers' work over the past several decades has been clear, consistent, and evolutionary, with concerns for the original coding scheme now subsumed into a broader view of the process of detecting multidimensional patterns of interpersonal relationships. In a variety of ways the nuances of managing or mismanaging relational issues come into light with the inclusion of more aspects of the Rogers and Millar model, ever moving to sketch the outlines of interpersonal dynamics. One is reminded here of William Blake's thought, often quoted by Gregory Bateson, that "Wise men draw outlines because they see them."

CRITICAL EVALUATION OF CONTRIBUTIONS

Rogers' role in bringing systems theory ideas into the communication research realm has been widely acknowledged. At the same time, her contributions have received their share of criticism. This criticism is largely on the basis of epistemological views that "stand outside" the assumptions of the systemic-cybernetic epistemology.

The critical debates that followed the early work on relational communication were part of the widespread polemics and metatheoretical debates of the late 1970s and early 1980s. The relational perspective represented a clear contrast with more entrenched psychological, cognitive, or interpretive models of communication which privileged the individual, internal meanings, intentions, motives, and so on. The relational model offered what Bateson called a "new order of communication," one that focused on the interaction rather than the individual, including but not replacing monadic models.

Rogers has long argued that the primary goal of the relational communication perspective was not to replace cognitive approaches, but to offer a different perspective based on a shift to relational variables that "do not lie within the individual interactors, but rather exist between them" at the dyadic or system level (Rogers & Farace, 1975, p. 222). Furthermore, she has maintained that both individual and interactional analyses are necessary for a comprehensive theory of interpersonal relations.

Many of the criticisms that find relational communication research wanting for its lack of attention to individual qualities ask questions that the relational approach was not designed to answer. These criticisms have ranged from dismissal, such as Heyman and Shaw's remark that this approach studies relationships by analyzing "mere behavior" (1978, p. 231), to simply asking the wrong questions such as "who is in control?," or using inappropriate procedures by assigning control codes to singular noncontextualized messages, or equating measures of dominance only to the frequency of a speaker's one-up messages.

Rogers' work has also been scrutinized in terms of the representational validity of the coding system. The issues of debate were whether the control codes represented the perceptions of the interactors being observed (Folger & Poole, 1982), and whether these perceptions represented the appropriate criteria for judging the validity of the regulative function of relational codes (Rogers & Millar, 1982). These debates were constructive in clarifying perspective differences and related validity issues. In terms of the relational system, evidence of construct validity has been supported (Heatherington, 1988; Henry & Villaume, 1991). This is in addition to the consistently strong predictive validity and reliability of the coding procedures.

Another criticism of Rogers' coding procedures notes their lack of attention to the nonverbal, analogic implications of the message exchange process (Parks & Dindia-Webb, 1978). As desirable as this inclusion would be, it is a daunting task, although progress is slowly being made—for instance, in Rogers' current work, which combines control codes with nonverbal affect codes.

In light of the attention that the relational perspective has attracted over the years, Rogers indicates that she "must have been doing something right." Trivial research or research solidly nested within the prevailing paradigm rarely receives much notice. The establishment of programmatic lines of research in other fields and other cultures is further evidence of Rogers' impact. Most notable is her receipt of the Speech Communication Association 1988 Woolbert Research Award, an honor bestowed on those whose research continues to have a significant impact on the field more than 15 years after its original publication.

INTEGRATION OF PERSONAL AND PROFESSIONAL LIFE

Edna Rogers' thinking is never far afield from her rural roots. "I am very much of the earth and the influences of that grounding. It's difficult not to think ecologically when you're raised on the land where being in temporal sync with the rhythmical cycles of the seasons is a way of life. My early family life is one I count as a central richness in my experience." Iowa farm life was a universe apart from the aristocratic English world of Gregory Bateson's childhood, but perhaps only a short step apart epistemologically for those like Bateson and Rogers who honor the lessons of the natural world.

"Ecological wisdom"—an awareness of connectedness, a knowledge of larger interactive systems—is the Bateson idea that strikes Rogers most profoundly. "The notion of ecological connectedness is a very freeing and thus very powerful idea. It allows us to both respect yet go beyond the individual by taking into account the contextualization of the larger connecting system," Rogers observes. "We are bounded as to how far we can reach, but I think the dream of expanding these constructs is a worthy one."

The aesthetics and even spirituality of the ecological approach "makes one's research, one's teaching, life itself more hopeful. It bumps against traditional linear thinking and provides a more holistic, enriching view." Rogers is passionate about the idea that "the systems view of relationships has such a healing aspect by recognizing the intertwining nature of relationships and at the same time recognizing the influence of each member on the direction and shape of the relationship as it is jointly created. Rogers joins those who believe that relational systems are of our own making, move in various ways, and are thus malleable and changeable. "Individually we make a difference; together we *are* the difference," she states. Rogers feels strongly about what she sees as the humanistic aspects of this way of thinking. "I can live that epistemology. I can live it in my teaching. I can live it in my research."

In "Why Do Things Have Outlines?," one of Gregory Bateson's deep and delightful "metalogues"—quasi-imaginary father/daughter recursive dialogues—father asserts that "the point is that our conversations do have an outline, somehow—if only we could see it clearly" (1972, p. 29). The work of Edna Rogers has measurably improved our ability to draw those conversational outlines, and her life bears witness to the humanism and hope that lie on the path to ecological wisdom.

NOTE

All quotations and biographical information not otherwise referenced are drawn from conversations between Edna Rogers and the author which took place May 13–15, 1994, in San Francisco.

REFERENCES

Bales, R. F. (1950). *Interaction process analysis.* Cambridge, Mass.: Addison-Wesley.

Barbatsis, G. S., Wong, M. R., & Herek, G. M. (1983). A struggle for dominance: Relational communication patterns in television drama. *Communication Quarterly, 31,* 148–155.

Bateson, G. (1937). *Naven.* Cambridge: Cambridge University Press.

Bateson, G. (1972). *Steps to an ecology of mind.* New York: Ballantine.

Courtright, J. A., Millar, F. E., & Rogers-Millar, L. E. (1979). Domineeringness and dominance: Replication and expansion. *Communication Monographs, 46,* 179–192.

Escudero, V., Rogers, L. E., & Gutierrez, E. (in press). Patterns of relational control and nonverbal affect in clinic and nonclinic couples. *Journal of Social and Personal Relationships.*

Escudero, V., Rogers, L. E., Gutierrez, E., & Caceres, J. (in press). Relational control and nonverbal affect in marital conflict: An exploratory study. *Journal of Family Therapy.*

Folger, J. P. & Poole, M. S. (1982). Relational coding schemes: Question of validity. In M. Burgoon (ed.), *Communication Yearbook 5.* (pp. 235–237). New Brunswick, N.J.: Transaction.

Heatherington, L. (1988). Coding relational communication control in counseling. *Journal of Counseling Psychology, 35,* 41–46.

Henry, D. M., & Villaume, W. A. (1991). Validating the Rogers-Farace relational coding scheme using content and relational listening ability. Paper presented at the Speech Communication Association, Atlanta, Georgia.

Heyman, R., & Shaw, M. (1978). Constructs of relationships. *Journal for the Theory of Social Behavior, 8,* 231–262.

Mead, G. H. (1954). *Mind, self and society.* Chicago: University of Chicago Press.

Millar, F. E., Rogers, L. E., & Courtright, J. A. (1979). Relational control and dyadic understanding: An exploratory predictive regression model. In D. Nimmo (ed.), *Communication Yearbook 3.* (pp. 213–224). New Brunswick, N.J.: Transaction.

Parks, M. R., & Dindia-Webb, K. (1978). Recent developments in relational communication research. Paper presented at the International Communication Association, Philadelphia.

Rogers, L. E. (1972). Dyadic systems and transactional communication in a family context. Ph.D. diss., Michigan State University.

Rogers, L. E. (1982). Symmetry and complementarity: Evolution and evaluation of an idea. In C. Wilder & J. H. Weakland (eds.), *Rigor and imagination: Essays from the legacy of Gregory Bateson.* New York: Praeger.

Rogers, L. E., & Farace, R. V. (1975). Analysis of relational communication in dyads: New measurement procedures. *Human Communication Research, 1,* 222–239.

Rogers, L. E., & Millar, F. E. (1982). The question of validity: A pragmatic response. In M. Burgoon (ed.), *Communication Yearbook 5.* (pp. 249–257). New Brunswick, N.J.: Transaction.

Rogers-Millar, L. E., & Millar, F. E. (1979). Domineeringness and dominance: A transactional view. *Human Communication Research, 5,* 239–245.

Seeman, M., Evans, J., & Rogers, L. E. (1960). A measurement of stratification in formal organizations. *Human Organizations, 19,* 90–96.

Sluzki, C. E., & Beavin, J. (1965). Simetria y complementaridad: Una definicion operacional y una tipologia de parejas. *Acta Psiquiatrica y Psicologica de America Latina, 11,* 321–330.

Watzlawick, P. (1964). *An anthology of human communication.* Palo Alto, Calif.: Science & Behavior Books.

Watzlawick, P., Beavin, J., & Jackson, D. (1967). *Pragmatics of human communication.* New York: W. W. Norton.

Watzlawick, P., Weakland, J., & Fisch, R. (1974). *Change: Principles of problem formation and problem resolution.* New York: W. W. Norton.

Additional Representative Publications

Brown, J. R., & Rogers, L. E. (1991). "Miscommunication" and problematic talk. In N. Coupland, H. Giles, & J. Wiemann (eds.), *Openness, uncertainty, and intimacy: An epistemological reformulation.* (pp. 146–165). Newbury Park, Calif.: Sage.

Millar, F. E., & Rogers, L. E. (1987). Relational dimensions of interpersonal dynamics. In M. Roloff & G. Miller (eds.), *Interpersonal processes: New directions in communication research.* (pp. 117–139). Newbury Park, Calif.: Sage.

Rogers, L. E. (1989). Relational communication processes and patterns. In B. Dervin, L. Grossbert, B. O'Keefe, & E. Wartella (eds.), *Rethinking comunicacion: Paradigm exemplars.* (pp. 280–290). Newbury Park, Calif.: Sage.

Rogers, L. E. (1993). The concept of social relationship from an interactional pragmatic view. *Personal Relationship Issues,* 1, 20–21.

Rogers, L. E. (1993). El enfoque pragmatico y la investigacion sobre comunicacion relacional: Influencia y reflexiones. *Cuadernos de Terapia Familiar,* 23–24, 45–58.

Rogers, L. E., & Bagarozzi, D. (1983). An overview of relational communication and implications for therapy. In D. Bagarozzi, A. Junch, & R. Jackson (eds.), *Marital and family therapy: New perspectives in theory, research, and practice.* (pp. 48–78). New York: Human Science Press.

Rogers, L. E., & Millar, F. E. (1988). Relational communication. In S. Duck (ed.), *Handbook of personal relationships.* (pp. 289–305). Chichester: Wiley.

Rogers, L. E., Millar, F. E., & Bavelas, J. B. (1985). Methods for analyzing marital conflict discourse: Implications of a systems approach. *Family Process,* 24, 175–187.

ANNA ELEANOR ROOSEVELT (1884–1962)

Maurine H. Beasley

Eleanor Roosevelt stands out as the single most visible and important woman of the middle twentieth century in the United States (Chafe, 1980). She achieved this distinction by taking full advantage of her opportunities as first lady to communicate with the public, particularly other women. During her 12-year residency in the White House, from 1933 to 1945, she occupied a public platform that gave her access to the media both as a news source herself and as a news commentator. As the wife of President Franklin D. Roosevelt, Eleanor Roosevelt garbed her public appearances and activities in the political philosophy of the New Deal and was portrayed as a wife helping her husband lead the nation through the trying days of the Depression and World War II. Nevertheless, she lectured and traveled widely and used a variety of media channels to reach the public as an individual in her own right. She held weekly press conferences for women reporters only, wrote a daily syndicated newspaper column, gave sponsored radio broadcasts, contributed articles to women's magazines, and published books. She supported causes that transcended racial and economic barriers, encouraged individual women to take part in politics in their communities, and displayed more sympathy for civil rights than her husband. Although the subject of vicious criticism by segregationists and others opposed to her liberal views, Eleanor Roosevelt also drew an immense amount of admiration and praise.

In 1939, for example, she was featured on the cover of *Time* magazine and described as "the world's foremost female political force" due to her hold "on public opinion" (*Time,* April 17, 1939). During World War II, she helped unify the nation's women behind the war effort. After the death of Franklin D. Roosevelt, Eleanor Roosevelt identified herself as a newspaperwoman and continued to play a public role (Roosevelt, 1945). Freed from the restriction of being a president's wife, she spoke out on issues of international peace and morality. In the early days of television, she was one of the relatively few women to appear on "Meet the Press" and other programs dealing with current affairs topics.

Appointed a delegate from the United States to the United Nations, she served from 1946 to 1952, leading the movement for creating the Universal Declaration of Human Rights in 1948. Surmounting accusations that she was "soft" on communism, Eleanor Roosevelt became increasingly revered on the world stage. In 1961, the same year that President Kennedy chose her to head his Commission on the Status of Women, the Gallup poll found her America's "most admired woman," a distinction that she received for years after leaving the White House (*New York Times,* 1962). When she died, she was eulogized as the First Lady of the World. From the standpoint of public communication, she represents a case study of a woman who understood the importance of the media in expanding the dimensions of her own and other women's lives.

FAMILY BACKGROUND AND EDUCATION

Anna Eleanor Roosevelt, the daughter of Anna Hall and Elliott Roosevelt, was born on October 11, 1884, in New York City, the oldest child of a family that represented the city's inner circle of society. Her parents, both descendants of prominent colonial families who had made fortunes in commerce and supported the American Revolution, epitomized wealth, style, and good looks. Her mother was 19, and her father, 23 and already a world traveler at the time of their wedding, which was described as one of the most brilliant of the 1883 New York social season. Anna Hall, a renowned beauty who put great stress on personal appearance and social success, apparently rejected the daughter who arrived ten months after the wedding. Describing herself in her autobiography, Eleanor Roosevelt wrote sadly that she was "a more wrinkled and less attractive baby than the average" (Roosevelt, 1937, p. 5). Although the mother bestowed affection on Eleanor's two younger brothers, she viewed little Eleanor as a homely, shy child who never smiled and behaved like a mirthless grownup.

By contrast, the dashing, debonair Elliott Roosevelt, younger brother of Theodore Roosevelt (who served as president of the United States from 1901 to 1908), adored his little girl. "He dominated my life as long as he lived, and was the love of my life for many years after he died. With my father I was perfectly happy," Eleanor Roosevelt recalled in her autobiography (Roosevelt, 1937, p. 6). Yet the charming Elliott, prone to bouts of mental illness, could not be relied on to take care of his children. An alcoholic, he once left Eleanor outside his club in New York while he went in for a drink. The child waited patiently for hours, holding his dogs on a leash, until she saw him carried out unconscious. Finally a doorman took her home.

Eleanor Roosevelt's early childhood was dominated by the family's effort to deal with the father's increasing instability (Cook, 1992). When she was two and one-half, her parents set off with her to Europe in hopes that a trip abroad would cure Elliott. At the start of their voyage, the passengers had to abandon ship when another steamer ran into their vessel. A crewman threw the screaming Eleanor into her father's arms as he stood in a lifeboat, an experience that left her with lifelong fears of being abandoned. Her fears intensified when her parents embarked for Europe without her, leaving her with Elliot's family at Oyster Bay. Although this trip failed to end Elliott's erratic behavior, which intensified after the return home, Eleanor's parents returned to Europe in 1890, this time taking her with them.

Eleanor Roosevelt's limited formal education began in 1891. She was placed in a convent in France ostensibly to learn French but also to remove her from the family, then living near Paris, while her mother coped with the arrival of a third child and Elliott sought treatment in a sanitarium. Describing the convent experience as "a very unhappy one," Eleanor Roosevelt remembered herself totally isolated from the other pupils (Roosevelt, 1937, p. 11). Her mother took her home in disgrace after she sought attention from the nuns by making up a story that she had swallowed a penny. She then attended a French day school briefly. Disturbed by fresh reports of Elliott's philandering and bizarre behavior, Theodore Roosevelt insisted that his brother be institutionalized. Anna and the children returned to the United States without him and moved into a new home in New York City. When Eleanor's great-aunt, Elizabeth Ludlow, discovered that Eleanor, then six and one-half, could not read or sew, she insisted that more provision be made for the child's education. A schoolroom was set up in the home, and teachers were hired for Eleanor and several children of family friends who joined in the lessons.

The estrangement between her parents continued when Elliott returned to the United States and sought to rehabilitate himself in Abingdon, Virginia, following additional treatment for alcoholism. Even though Anna became fatally stricken with diphtheria after an operation, she refused to let her husband see her. She died on December 7, 1892. To eight-year-old Eleanor, who received the news from a cousin, "death meant nothing" (Roosevelt, 1937, p. 19). Instead she looked forward to a reunion with her father, who had written glowing letters of his devotion during their long separation. This fantasy of making a home with Elliott, who was in no position to look after his children, did not materialize. Eleanor and her brothers went to live with their maternal grandmother, Mary Livingston Ludlow Hall, a strict individual who stayed in New York in the winter and spent the summer at Tivoli, her mansion on the Hudson River. She arranged for governesses and private classes to educate Eleanor.

The family faced another loss in 1893 when Eleanor's brother, Elliott Jr., not yet 4, died of scarlet fever and diphtheria. Eleanor continued to dream that she and her father would someday live together, a vision fed by his letters to her. Painfully insecure, she made occasional visits to the home of Theodore Roosevelt and his family, but she was overshadowed by her witty and sophisticated cousin, Theodore's daughter, Alice. When Elliott died in 1894 after convulsions stemming from drinking, Eleanor, not yet 10 years old, refused to believe the news of his death. Years later, in her autobiography and in her magazine articles, she alluded repeatedly to the sad circumstances of her childhood, perhaps because she believed it had given her compassion for others who faced loneliness and a lack of love.

The happiest years of Eleanor Roosevelt's girlhood came when she was sent, at the age of 15, to Allenswood, a girls' school outside of London headed by Marie Souvestre, a Frenchwoman who embraced liberal intellectual causes. Eleanor Roosevelt flowered during her three years there, becoming a favorite with both Souvestre, who stimulated her interest in helping the unfortunate, and other students. After she returned to the United States in 1902, she made the conventional debut into society expected for a young woman of her social class. Yet she also wanted to carry out the teachings of Souvestre, who urged her students to think seriously about improving the world. Consequently, Eleanor Roosevelt threw herself into settlement house work and joined the National Consumers' League, which sought safer working conditions for women. But she had no interest in woman suffrage or radical causes.

MARRIAGE AND CAREER

In the midst of the debutante season, Eleanor Roosevelt, described as willowy and elegant in appearance, found herself drawn to her fifth cousin once removed, Franklin D. Roosevelt, a student at Harvard University, who sought her company at parties. They became secretly engaged in the fall of 1903. The news stunned Franklin's domineering mother, Sara Delano Roosevelt. She insisted that the couple wait at least a year before making an announcement and made it plain that she intended to continue to play a central role in Franklin's life.

Surmounting her objections, Eleanor and Franklin were married on March 17, 1905 with the bride escorted down the aisle by her uncle, President Theodore Roosevelt. She was 20, two years younger than her husband, then studying law at Columbia University. During the early years of her marriage, Eleanor Roosevelt immersed herself in motherhood, giving birth to six children in ten years: Anna (1906); James (1907); Franklin (1909), who died seven months later; Elliott (1910); Franklin, Jr. (1914), and John (1916). She had little time or energy for public activities. Sara Roosevelt objected to her settlement house work, so Eleanor Roosevelt discontinued it. She devoted herself to Franklin as he pursued a legal career. Experiencing feelings of inadequacy about her abilities as a wife and mother, Eleanor Roosevelt allowed her mother-in-law to take command of the household.

When her husband entered politics and was elected to the New York legislature in 1910, Eleanor initially was repelled by political advisers like Louis M. Howe, a cynical newspaperman, who irritated her with his chain-smoking of cigarettes. After Franklin was appointed assistant secretary of the navy in 1913, she was confronted with fulfilling the social obligations expected of political wives in Washington as well as overseeing family moves from the capital to

Hyde Park and Campobello in New Brunswick (the Roosevelts' summer home) and back again. The patriotic fervor of World War I, however, allowed her to escape from social rituals and to pursue more fulfilling pursuits. She helped at a canteen for soldiers on their way to camps, participated in Red Cross activities, and visited mental patients at St. Elizabeth's Hospital.

By chance, in 1918 Eleanor learned that her husband had been carrying on a long-standing affair with her beautiful social secretary, Lucy Mercer. Eleanor Roosevelt offered to give him a divorce, but he ended the relationship, and the Roosevelts decided to remain together because of their children and his political career. Although the couple maintained affection and some emotional intimacy, the Roosevelts apparently did not resume a sexual relationship and the marriage turned into one of convenience. After Eleanor Roosevelt helped her husband campaign for his unsuccessful bid for the vice presidency in 1920, she gradually ventured on her own into the political arena.

Even before Franklin Roosevelt was paralyzed by polio in 1921, Eleanor had become involved in the League of Women Voters in New York State. Although the public was led to believe that she entered politics only to keep the name of Roosevelt before the public while Franklin Roosevelt struggled to rehabilitate himself, her league activity shows that she had moved outside the domestic realm before his illness (Watrous, 1984). Guided by Howe, who became her political mentor as well as her husband's, she wrote on current issues for the league's weekly newspaper. She also became active in the Democratic party and the Women's Trade Union League, which worked for maximum hour and minimum wage laws for women.

By 1928, when Franklin Roosevelt was elected governor of New York, Eleanor Roosevelt had become a political leader herself, writing, speaking, and acting as an advocate for social reform and women's issues. Among her activities was editorship of the *Women's Democratic News,* a magazine that presented the ideas of social feminists who sought greater opportunities for women without changing traditional family roles. Developing self-confidence, she broke away from the influence of her mother-in-law and located herself within a support network of professional women who lived and worked with other women. In addition, she sought a career in education, teaching history, current events, and literature at the exclusive Todhunter School for Girls in Manhattan.

At the same time, she looked for opportunities to communicate with a national audience. During the four years that her husband was governor, Eleanor Roosevelt wrote some 20 articles for mass periodicals, mainly women's magazines. These often contained autobiographical fragments designed to offer inspiration and advice drawn from her own experiences. In one article she wrote that the test of marital companionship lay in a wife's ability to contribute to her husband's success (Roosevelt, 1931). Years later she referred to this philosophy by writing of her husband, "I was one of those who served his purposes" (Roosevelt, 1949, p. 349). One could argue, however, that the marriage also served her purposes. Eleanor Roosevelt's magazine articles probably would not have been published if it had not been for Franklin Roosevelt's position. Yet she viewed the money they brought her as a tangible symbol of achievement and independence, the "necessary evidence that she could go it alone," according to her son Elliott (Roosevelt & Brough, 1973, p. 281).

When Franklin Roosevelt was elected president in 1932, Eleanor feared that her role would be limited to the social rituals expected of a first lady. She confided her apprehensions to Lorena A. Hickok, an Associated Press reporter assigned to cover her during the campaign. Hickok suggested one approach to activism—the holding of press conferences (Lash, 1971). White House appointment calendars show that 348 of these conferences were held while Eleanor Roosevelt was in the White House. These weekly gatherings enabled her both to voice her own ideas and present to reporters prominent women in the New Deal, many of whom owed their positions to her influence. They were restricted to women, giving them access to news that men could not get during the Depression when women reporters were in danger of losing their jobs. The conferences were intended to serve as communications links for women throughout the country. At the first gathering, Eleanor Roosevelt told reporters that their role should be "to try to tell the women throughout the country what you think they should know." Their job, she said, should be "leading the women in the country to form a general attitude of mind and thought" (Furman, 1933, p. 7).

By today's standards, the conferences seem sedate affairs. Eleanor Roosevelt announced White House social events, described her schedule, and answered various personal questions. Some reporters complained that she avoided direct comment on pending legislation and spoke only in general about controversial subjects such as housing, the right of married women to work, and world peace (Black, 1934). Nevertheless, political issues frequently provided a backdrop for discussion. For example, she argued against the proposed Equal Rights Amendment on the grounds that it would interfere with protective legislation for women workers.

Her willingness to confer with the press broke new ground for first ladies who traditionally had stayed aloof from reporters (Beasley, 1987). The conferences provided a focus for friendships with reporters who pictured her as the first activist first lady devoted to humanitarian causes (Ross, 1936).

Not content with her press conference as the sole way to reach the public, as first lady Eleanor Roosevelt also undertook a paid career as a journalist, broadcaster, and lecturer, using her White House position to campaign for greater public empathy with the unfortunate. In 1936 she began writing a syndicated newspaper column, a diary of her activities called "My Day." It chronicled her repeated travels, including trips to coal mines and relief sites, to gain first-hand knowledge of the plight of citizens during the Depression. At the same time, it offered a somewhat fragmented portrayal of Roosevelt family life in the White House.

Even more than the press conferences, "My Day" served to showcase the accomplishments of women. Eleanor Roosevelt made it a stage for women of achievement whose names paraded through its paragraphs. She also used it to urge women to become more involved in their communities. While critics sneered at the column's unsophisticated prose and apparent lack of depth, "My Day" reached hundreds of thousands of readers. By 1938 it ran in 62 newspapers with a total circulation of more than 4 million.

Over the years it became an oblique source of information on administration policy. Eleanor Roosevelt used the column to announce her resignation from the Daughters of the American Revolution when the organization refused to let an African American, Marian Anderson, sing in its hall (Roosevelt, 1939). The resignation, which generated tremendous controversy, signaled the New Deal position on civil rights. Although the column's circulation and influence dwindled after she left the White House, Eleanor Roosevelt continued to write "My Day" until shortly before her death in 1962. She made it a voice for liberal Democratic politics and international understanding.

In her magazine articles Eleanor Roosevelt continued to offer advice to women. During her 12 years as first lady, she published more than 60 articles in national magazines, gearing the subjects to changing times. In a monthly column for *The Woman's Home Companion* from 1933 to 1935, she appealed to readers to "write me" (Roosevelt, 1933). They did, many presenting tales of Depression-era distress. She occasionally responded with small sums of money, but usually she transmitted their requests to relief agencies. During World War II she emphasized women's role in the war. In 1941 she inaugurated a monthly question-and-answer column in the *Ladies' Home Journal* with a proposal that women be drafted for compulsory government service (Roosevelt, 1941). The idea, viewed as a plan to remove women from their protected status in society, drew almost no support. In 1949 the column, which at that point dealt mainly with topics like etiquette and advice to parents, moved to *McCall's*.

As a paid radio broadcaster, Eleanor Roosevelt drew on similar themes. Shortly after her husband was elected president, she delivered a dozen commentaries dealing with childrearing and family relationships sponsored by a cold-cream manufacturer. On subsequent broadcasts she described her travels as first lady and offered noncontroversial, first-person vignettes on White House life for various sponsors, including a mattress company and a shoe manufacturer. At the time the United States entered World War II, Eleanor Roosevelt had a $28,000 contract with the Pan-American Coffee Bureau for a total of 28 Sunday evening broadcasts. She used these programs to urge American women to support the war. As a broadcaster, she sometimes received criticism for her high-pitched voice, but admirers praised its warmth and earnestness (Beasley & Belgrade, 1984).

MAJOR CONTRIBUTIONS AND ACHIEVEMENTS

As a communicator, Eleanor Roosevelt's strengths lay in what some saw as her weaknesses. Political detractors and others who did not approve of her nontraditional ways as first lady scorned her speeches and writings as vapid and trite, void of either originality or distinction in expression. Yet these were the characteristics that appealed to a somewhat unsophisticated audience. When Eleanor Roosevelt entered the White House, the vast majority of American women were isolated within their homes where they served as unpaid domestics (Ware, 1982). The 25 percent who held paid employment were concentrated in rigidly sex-typed, low-status occupations (Milkman, 1979). The commonplace quality of Eleanor Roosevelt's observations allowed ordinary individuals to identify with her.

Unlike any woman before her, Eleanor Roosevelt gave visibility to women through her own presence in the media. Although the circumstances of her life were far different from those of most women, she worked to elevate the stature of women in general. Not only did she provide herself as a role model, but she also called attention to other noteworthy women. Since most columnists of the day were male, women found Eleanor Roosevelt one of their few representatives in a male-dominated media world.

As she pursued a public role, she insisted that she had the right to receive money for her lectures, writings, and broadcasts. Opponents denounced her as profiting from her husband's position, but she defused the criticism by donating most of her earnings to charity. Still, she upheld the right of all women, married or not, to engage in careers even if they did not need the money. This represented one of the most significant stands that Eleanor Roosevelt took in her career as a communicator.

To understand Eleanor Roosevelt's influence, one should remember that women were relatively new to political participation in her era. When Franklin D. Roosevelt was elected president in 1932, women had voted in only three previous presidential elections. Eleanor Roosevelt's message of involvement in community and political activity appealed to women who wanted to expand their horizons beyond the home but did not seek to challenge conventional gender relationships. In upholding the concept of conventional marriage and family life as important entities, Eleanor Roosevelt communicated a philosophy of respect for women's traditional roles.

Her work implied that women were linked in sisterhood by a culture separate from men's—an assumption that ran through ''My Day'' in such comments as ''There are practical little things in housekeeping which no man really understands'' (Roosevelt, December 4, 1937). Through her public communication Eleanor Roosevelt served to make her own life meaningful, to transform her own suffering as an orphaned child and a wronged wife into a personal testimony of spiritual growth and caring for others. Although she kept many facets of her experiences private, she conveyed to the public the sense that she had retained her feminine nature while stepping into a man's world of political power that she tried to utilize for social gain. She can be seen as a transitional figure in the history of American women—an individual who played a key part in the modernization of women's roles. She demonstrated that a woman could still be womanly even though she moved beyond her traditional sphere.

REFERENCES

Beasley, M. (1987). *Eleanor Roosevelt and the media: A public quest for self-fulfillment.* (pp. 38–50). Urbana: University of Illinois.

Beasley, M., & Belgrade, P. (1984). Eleanor Roosevelt: First lady as radio pioneer. *Journalism History,* 11, 42–45.

Black, R. (1934, February 10). "New Deal" for news women in capital. *Editor & Publisher,* 11.

Chafe, W. (1980). Anna Eleanor Roosevelt. *Notable American women: The modern period.* (pp. 595–601). Cambridge, Mass.: Belknap Press. [Provides single best brief biographical sketch of Eleanor Roosevelt's life.]

Cook, B. (1992). *Eleanor Roosevelt: 1884–1933.* (pp. 39–155). New York: Viking Press.

Furman, B. (1933, March 6). Typescript of Eleanor Roosevelt's first press conference. In M. Beasley (ed.), *The White House press conferences of Eleanor Roosevelt* (1983). New York: Garland Publishing.

Lash, J. (1971). *Eleanor and Franklin.* (pp. 361–364). New York: W. W. Norton.

Milkman, R. (1979). Woman's Work and the Economic Crisis. In N. Cott & E. Pleck (eds.), *A heritage of her own.* (pp. 511–515). New York: Simon & Schuster.

New York Times (1962, November 8). Mrs. Roosevelt, first lady 12 Years, often voted "world's most admired woman." A1.

Roosevelt, E. (1931, December). Ten rules for success in marriage. *Pictorial Review,* 33, 4.

Roosevelt, E. (1933, August). Mrs. Franklin D. Roosevelt's page. *Woman's Home Companion,* 60, 4.

Roosevelt, E. (1937). *This is my story.* New York: Harper & Brothers.

Roosevelt, E. (1937, December 4). My day.

Roosevelt, E. (1939, February 27). My day. [Complete file of the columns as distributed to newspapers by United Features Syndicate is available at the Franklin D. Roosevelt Library, Hyde Park, New York.]

Roosevelt, E. (1941, May). Defense and girls. If you ask me column. *Ladies' Home Journal,* 58, 25, 54.

Roosevelt, E. (1945, April 18). My day.

Roosevelt, E. (1949). *This I remember.* New York: Harper & Brothers.

Roosevelt, E. [Elliott], & Brough, J. (1973). *The Roosevelts of Hyde Park: An untold story.* New York: Putnam.

Ross, I. (1936). *Ladies of the press.* (pp. 309–322). New York: Harper & Brothers.

Time. (1939, April 17). Oracle, 22.

Ware, S. (1982). *Holding their own: American women in the 1930s.* (p. 24). Boston: Twayne.

Watrous, H. (1984). *In league with Eleanor: Eleanor Roosevelt and the League of Women Voters, 1921–1962.* (p. 3). New York: Foundation for Citizen Education.

Additional Books by Eleanor Roosevelt

Roosevelt, E. (1938). *My days.* New York: Dodge Publishing.

Roosevelt, E. (1954). *It seems to me.* New York: W. W. Norton.

Roosevelt, E. (1958). *On my own.* New York: Curtis Publishing Co.

Roosevelt, E. (1963). *Tomorrow is now.* New York: Harper & Row.

Roosevelt, E., & Ferris, H. (1961). *Your teens and mine.* Garden City, N.Y.: Doubleday.

Roosevelt, E., & Hickok, L. (1954). *Ladies of courage.* New York: Putnam.

ANNE NEWPORT ROYALL (1769–1854)

Carol Sue Humphrey

A myth about Anne Royall provides much insight into her reputation, both during her life and in the years since her death. The most repeated story about Anne Royall describes her as getting a personal interview with President John Quincy Adams by sitting on his clothes while he swam in the Potomac River. He had to grant the interview before Royall would leave and thus allow him to exit the river. This story has no basis in fact, but it has often been repeated. Its popularity indicates something about Anne Royall's strong personality, and reactions to her have never been mild. Described as "a pioneer traveling pamphleteer" (Whitton, 1954, p. 60), "a shrew of a newspaperwoman" (Beasley, 1990, p. 32), and "the grandma of the muckrakers" (Blankenhorn, 1927, p. 87), she was all of these things and much more. Driven by financial necessity, Anne Newport Royall became one of America's first female travel writers and America's first crusading female editor.

Born on June 11, 1769, near Baltimore, Maryland, Anne Newport was the eldest daughter of Mary and William Newport. Rumored to be an illegitimate relative of the Calvert family, Anne's father was ostracized by his neighbors because of his support for the British during the Revolution. No longer comfortable in Maryland, Newport moved his family to Westmoreland County in western Pennsylvania, seeking a new chance and the cheap land available west of the Appalachian Mountains. Anne was 3 at the time of the move west, and she and her family lived in Pennsylvania until she was 15. Sometime prior to 1775, while Anne was still a young child, her father died, possibly in an Indian massacre. Her mother soon married a man named Butler, but her second husband also died, probably in another Indian attack in July 1782. At this time, broken financially and physically, Mary Newport Butler decided to seek aid in Virginia. Anne walked east with her mother, assuming that life could not get any worse.

Mary Butler happily took a job as a household servant in Staunton, Virginia, but her daughter was proud and resented having to sit with the indentured servants during Sunday church services. In 1785, however, Mary and Anne moved to Sweet Springs, Virginia, a move that would change Anne's life forever.

When they moved to Sweet Springs, Mary Butler became the housekeeper for Captain William Royall. A gentleman farmer, Royall was the wealthiest citizen of Monroe County. During the Revolutionary War, he had raised and financed Virginia's first company of militia. He served with Lafayette, considered George Washington a friend, and referred to Thomas Jefferson as "cousin." Royall had received the land at Sweet Springs as payment for his military service. Considered very eccentric by many people, Royall was tolerated by his neighbors because of his wealth and social position in the community. He freed most of his slaves and refused to have "unnatural" animals such as geldings and steers on his plantation. Royall was fanatically devoted to Freemasonry and the democratic ideals of Paine and Voltaire. His library, full of books by democratic authors and French philosophers, was considered radical by most people who knew what it contained. For Anne Newport, however, Royall's library became the door to a wider world.

Anne was fascinated by Royall's library and by his ideas. Finding Anne an eager student, Royall tutored her, providing her with an education that easily surpassed that available to most women in the late 1700s. Royall considered himself a deist and introduced Anne to the writings of other deists, particularly Voltaire, Thomas Paine, and Thomas Jefferson. Royall emphasized history and literature primarily, but he also instilled in Anne a belief in the ideas of Freemasonry. As a member of the Masonic Order, Royall believed the ideas of Freemasonry came closer to reflecting the true meaning of Christ's teachings than did the doctrines and dogmas of organized religion. In later years, Anne would translate this early training in the ideas of Freemasonry into a rabid support for the Masonic Order as it came under attack from outsiders.

Slowly over the years, the friendship between William Royall and Anne Newport grew into something more, and, on November 18, 1797, they were married by a circuit-riding minister. At the time, Anne was 28 and Royall 20 years her senior. The marriage seemed to be a happy one and lasted 16 years. During this time, Anne managed Royall's business affairs and kept the plantation running as her husband increasingly drank more and more. They had no children. Royall died on December 12, 1812, apparently from natural causes aggravated by his drinking. He left the bulk of his estate to his wife, including 7,000 acres of land, seven slaves, and a sizable amount of livestock.

Royall's family had always been scandalized by his marriage to a woman 20 years his junior, and a servant to boot. They quickly sought to break the will. They charged that Anne Royall had forged the will, had lived immorally with Royall prior to their marriage, had forced Royall to marry her, and had abused him after their marriage. Anne denied all of these charges except the accusation of cohabitation prior to marriage. The case took seven years to settle, but, in the end, the servant girl who had married above her station lost her inheritance. Anne Newport Royall was once more penniless and in need of some means to make a living.

Anne Royall's first answer to the question of how to earn some money had already been brought to her attention even before the final settlement of her husband's will. Shortly after William Royall's death, she decided to travel. Having spent all of her adult life in western Virginia, Anne Royall was ready to see the rest of the country. She traveled first to Charleston, West Virginia, and then on to the new State of Alabama. While traveling, she wrote a series of letters about her trip to her lawyer and good friend, Matthew Dunbar. In the process of describing her journey to Dunbar, Royall discovered that she had a talent for talking to people, observing her surroundings, and describing all of this in a very readable prose. As a result of this natural ability, Anne Royall quickly turned to travel writing as a means of financial survival following the loss of her inheritance.

From 1819 until 1830, Anne Royall roamed across the United States, keeping detailed notes of everything she saw and everyone she met. Travel books were very popular in the early nineteenth century, and Royall hoped to take advantage of this situation. Her first book, *Sketches of History, Life, and Manners in the United States by a Traveller,* appeared in 1826. Full of details about people and places and the conditions Anne Royall saw on her journey, the book produced wide comment and sold well. The *Boston Commercial* carried the most balanced review of Royall's first writing efforts: "Sometimes she lets fall more truths than the interested reader would wish to hear, and at others overwhelms her friends with a flattery still more appalling. At any rate, hit or miss, the sentiments she gives are undoubtedly her own; nor will it be denied that she has given some very good outlines of character. Her book is more amusing than any novel we have read for years" (Wallace, 1957, p. 254).

Anne Royall filled all of her travel books with detailed descriptions of everything she saw, and she did not spare her readers her opinions, positive and negative, of the places she visited. Baltimore, Maryland, was "illiterate, proud and ignorant," and, in Virginia, the "roads were as bad as its schools." Charleston, South Carolina, was "the receptacle for the refuse of all nations on earth— the only reputable people were the Jews." But Royall's strongest criticism fell on Philadelphia, the "most unfeeling, inhospitable and uncharitable toward strangers" (Wallace, 1957, p. 257; Whitton, 1954, p. 62)

Anne Royall also commented frequently on the people she met while traveling. She described a Pennsylvania hostess as "a savage in petticoats," while a Virginia widow was "ignorant and proud as Lucifer." In New Orleans, she found women "of every shade from snowy white to sooty." Her biggest complaint concerning the women she met was that they were uneducated and ignorant. Among the men she encountered, the problem was drink: "There is too much whiskey everywhere" (Whitton, 1954, pp. 61–62).

Besides describing her surroundings and the people in general on her travels,

Anne Royall also sought to include in her books sketches of the celebrated people of the regions where she traveled. As a result, she sought interviews with a vengeance. In New York, she met Governor Dewitt Clinton, describing him as silent, but also ''a man of great size, great soul, great mind and a great heart.'' Royall walked some distance in order to meet Dolly Madison, someone she quickly liked: ''Her face is not handsome nor does it ever appear to have been so. It is suffused with a slight tinge of red and is rather wide in the middle. But her power to please—the irresistable grace of her every movement—sheds such a charm over all she says and does that it is impossible not to admire her'' (Wallace, 1957, p. 258).

Traveling from New Orleans to Canada, Anne Royall published ten books between 1826 and 1831. Traveling by horseback, stagecoach, boat, and foot, she tried to see it all. She visited the lunatics in a Maine asylum and smoked a peace pipe with the Cherokee Indians. She investigated the boilers on a steamer and searched for Jefferson relics at Monticello. She visited schools, iron mines, and bar-rooms, all in an effort to gather as much specific information as possible for her readers. Her books were packed full of facts, figures, and names. Ultimately, Anne Royall became a ''tramp reporter,'' long before that term would be applied to roving journalists such as Bret Harte and Mark Twain. Her travel books provide an interesting and provocative view of the young nation during the 1820s, containing ''vivid and valuable portraits of the personalities and social customs of the times'' (Fleener, 1985, p. 404)

Anne Royall also published one novel during this period, *The Tennessean, a Novel Founded on Facts.* Published in 1827, it describes the adventures of Burlington, a Princeton student who has a hard life because his father had lost everything through fraud. After many ups and downs, the hero settles down to peace and prosperity. A literary and financial failure, the book was described by one critic as being ''in plot, execution and characters . . . one of the worst ever written in America'' (Dodd & Williams, 1976, p. 35). Royall probably rushed the book into print in order to take advantage of the success of *Sketches,* her first travel book. Thankfully, she returned to travel books and left fiction writing to others.

Although generally detailed and relatively objective in her descriptions of her travels, Anne Royall also exhibited several personal biases in her writings. John Quincy Adams, writing in his diary, described how Royall's own sense of justice affected how others viewed her:

Mrs. Royall continues to make herself vexious to many persons, tolerated by some and feared by others, by her deportment and books; treating all with a familiarity which often passes for impudence, insulting those who treat her with civility, and then lampooning them in her books. Stripped of all her sex's delicacy, but unable to forfeit its privilege of gentle treatment from the other, she goes about like a virago in enchanged armor, and redeems herself from the cravings of indigence by the notoriety of her eccentricities and the forced currency they give to her publications. (Schilpp & Murphy, 1983, p. 31)

Two groups in particular were recipients of abuse from Anne Royall's pen: the anti-Masons and evangelical Protestants. Writing at a time when the Anti-Masonic party was at the zenith of its power and influence, Royall struck back, praising both the beliefs and the work of the Masons. Her attacks against the anti-Masons incensed many people, and, while traveling in Vermont, a man pushed her down a flight of stairs for her efforts. Royall fractured her leg and walked with a limp for the rest of her life.

Her attacks on evangelical Protestants produced even more trouble. She described male church members as "Hallelujah Holdforths" and women members as "Miss Dismals." Royall feared that organized religion sought to influence the government too much and urged her readers to work against their efforts. Her diatribes created many enemies, and clergymen everywhere sought to silence her if at all possible. When traveling in Ohio, a Cincinnati pastor complained that his church, enjoying "a glorious harvest, a fest of love," was distracted by her presence in the city. Royall responded with laughter at the thought of a city being intimidated by

a single old woman, who was raised in the woods among the Indians. I am a heathen and have come to your door. From the heathen I learned nothing but virtue and independence. When introduced among civilized people the Bible was put into my hands. But before I looked into it I watched the conduct of those who read it, and I found they committed murder, they got drunk, they betrayed their friends, and were guilty of all kinds of abominations, and I was afraid to read the Bible lest I might do so too. (Dodd & Williams, 1976, p. 36)

It was this low opinion of organized religion which finally produced the public spectacle that ruined Royall's career as a travel writer.

Since 1824, Anne Royall had used Washington as her base of operations. The capital city was convenient because it was centrally located and her occasional returns there gave her the opportunity to push her claim for a pension as the widow of a soldier of the Revolutionary War. Initially denied her request because the pension law applied only to widows married before 1794, she finally received a small pension in 1848. In 1829, while home for a brief rest from her travels, Anne Newport Royall stood trial in the District of Columbia, charged with being a common scold. The case received attention throughout the nation and made Anne Royall infamous, cementing her public reputation as a strange and eccentric woman.

The charge resulted from her conflict with the evangelicals. A group of Presbyterians worshiped in an engine house near Royall's home, and she and the church soon came into conflict. When children of the congregation threw stones at her house, Royall lost her temper and yelled at them. The church's response was to begin prayer services for Royall's soul underneath her window. These prayer vigils were led by John Coyle, a church member who Anne Royall accused of fathering her servant girl's baby. She publicly berated Coyle for being "a damned old bald-headed son of a bitch" and castigated the rest of the church members as well. Outraged at her attacks, the Presbyterians sought to silence Royall by having her tried on the outdated charge of being a "common scold" (a woman addicted to abusive speech).

The trial opened in the summer of 1829, with the chief justice of the District of Columbia, William Cranch, presiding. The court was crowded, as people came to see this unusual trial. The charge of common scold, a holdover from English common law, had never been tried in the United States before. The prosecution presented ten witnesses, most of them church members and neighbors, who testified that Anne Royall always spoke with "torrents of the most coarse, vulgar and obscene language." They all concluded that Royall had verbally abused them and that, clearly, she had made a general nuisance of herself.

Royall, testifying in her own defense, strongly denied all the charges. She also asserted that a conviction would be an attack on the freedom of speech. *The New York Commercial Advertiser* described her plea for protection of this basic right:

Advancing her wrinkled visage, she proceeded to obtest and objure them, as they loved liberty and their country, not to sacrifice both in her person. They stood not only for the present age, but were the guardians of posterity. . . . If [the prosecution] were to succeed, nothing would be safe—bigotry and all the horrors of the Inquisition would overwhelm the land; nothing would be left of all for which her husband and other worthies of the Revolution had shed their blood. (Beasley, 1976–1977, p. 100)

Royall's testimony was followed by a series of character witnesses, including Secretary of War John H. Eaton of Tennessee, who stated that Mrs. Royall had always acted like a lady when she came to his office. Others who testified in Royall's behalf included her companion and assistant, Sally Stack, the wife of the publisher of Royall's travel books, and John Underwood, owner of Washington's first water system. Providing support by his presence at Royall's side throughout the trial was James Gordon Bennett, Washington correspondent for the New York *Courier and Enquirer*. Bennett supported Royall's case because he saw the charges against her as an assault against the freedom of the press that resulted from her attacks on the evangelicals in her travel books.

All of this support was to no avail, for the jury quickly convicted Anne Royall. The traditional punishment for conviction as a common scold was a dunking stool, and the Navy Yard had actually built one in Alexandria. The judge, however, decided that Anne Royall's age precluded such a punishment. He fined her $10 and ordered her to post a $100 bond as security to ensure her future good behavior. Two reporters for the *National Intelligencer* paid the fine and posted the bond. A newspaper in Pennsylvania declared that the reporters had supplied the needed money because they "stood up for the honor of the press and the gallantry of the profession" (Beasley, 1976–1977, p. 100).

Anne Royall expressed disappointment at the outcome of the trial, but she briefly benefited from it. For a short time, her notoriety boosted the sales of her books. She even embarked on a new series of journeys to take advantage of the trial's publicity. This benefit, however, was fleeting in duration, and Royall's eccentric reputation slowly undermined her book sales. With her health also becoming more precarious, Anne Royall decided to end her travels and settle down in Washington. Without the small income she received from her books, she needed a new way to make money. This necessity forced her to embark on a new career, that of newspaper editor and publisher.

In 1831, at the age of 61, Anne Royall began publishing the weekly *Paul Pry,* perhaps taking the name from an English play that exposed the alliance between church and state. With few funds to invest in the business, Royall published the newspaper in the kitchen of her home on an old press. Also working on the publication were a tramp printer, two orphan boys serving as printer's devils, and Royall's friend Sally Stack, who delivered the newspapers after they were printed. Although not the best produced publication in the country, Royall sought to use her newspaper as a vehicle to protect the nation her husband had helped to create. In her initial editorial of December 3, 1831, she declared: ''The welfare and happiness of our country are our politics. We shall expose all and every species of political evil, and religious fraud, without fear or affection. We shall patronize merit of whatsoever country, sect, or politics. We shall advocate the liberty of the press, the liberty of speech, and the liberty of conscience'' (Beasley, 1976–1977, p. 100).

In an age of partisanship in the media, Anne Royall remained an independent voice, always expressing her own strong feelings for and against various concerns or issues. Seeking to expose corruption and incompetence wherever she found it, Royall became the country's first muckraking editor. She protested the high price of flannel and blamed the cholera epidemic in Washington in 1832 on the city government for its failure to put in sewers and drain the marshes in the area. She supported internal improvements, the trade labor movement, and the abolition of the Bank of the United States. Of particular interest to Anne Royall were issues related to individual liberties, such as the separation of church and state, freedom of the press, and the need for justice for the Indians. But, above all, she fought for honesty in government, attacking any government official who abused the powers of office or used the public's money for personal profit.

Royall continued her dislike of organized religion, decrying its failure to truly deal with the concerns of the less fortunate in American society. In response to a criticism from one editor of a religious paper, Royall wrote:

If he calls robbing the poor and ignorant of vast sums of money Christianity, we are opposed to it! If he calls leaving the poor to die in our streets Christianity, we are opposed to it. If he calls Sunday Schools, Sunday mail, tract Bible, rag-bag, mite, missionary and temperance societies Christianity, we are opposed to it! We believe in no God who cannot govern the world without money (which is the end of all those). . . . Alarmed at the progress of Christianity? We see none to be alarmed at. (Blankenhorn, 1927, p. 91)

Although volatile, provocative, and clearly one of the liveliest newspapers being published at the time, *Paul Pry* failed financially. It struggled on for five years but barely made enough money for Royall to survive. She constantly appealed to subscribers to pay up, declaring that her personal survival depended on it. With money tight, Royall tried to write a comic drama, *The Cabinet or Large Parties in Washington.* The play ran for two performances in 1833, but failed to meet Royall's financial needs. On one occasion, President Andrew Jackson invited her to lunch at the White House after glimpsing the bony partridge which Royall was carrying home for her own sparse meal.

Finally, in 1836, Anne Royall ended *Paul Pry,* hoping that a fresh start would bring more success. Two weeks after the demise of *Paul Pry, The Huntress* began publication. Although announcing that she would continue in her search for corruption and fraud in government, she also decided to broaden the appeal of her newspaper by including literary selections from time to time. In the first issue, Royall stated that "the name is not inappropriate as we have often followed the chase in our younger days. My stand will be precisely where it always has been—on the side of the PEOPLE. . . . The only difference between *The Huntress* and *Paul Pry* will be the introduction of amusing tales, dialogues and essays upon general subjects" (Beasley, 1976–1977, p. 101).

As was true of *Paul Pry, The Huntress* failed to be a well-printed and well-designed newspaper. However, it continued publication for 18 years, and throughout its history, its editor continued to seek out corruption in government and to defend the rights of individuals which she cherished so strongly. She opposed women's suffrage and attacked the abolitionists because of their ties to organized religion, even though she herself opposed slavery. She strongly opposed those who sought to eliminate Catholic immigration, blaming their goals on misguided patriotism: "A Catholic foreigner discovered America, Catholic foreigners first settled it. . . . When the colonies were about to be enslaved, foreigners rescued it. . . . At present, we verily believe, that the liberty of this country is in more danger from this native combination than from foreigners" (Wallace, 1957, p. 265).

Anne Royall refused to allow circumstances to stand in her way when pursuing stories for her newspaper. She regularly visited the Capitol and cornered senators and representatives, seeking news items and subscribers. Isaac Bassett, Senate doorkeeper for 60 years, described her and her actions in his diary. He called her "homely in person, careless in dress, poor in purse—and vulgar in manners," but "she had much shrewdness, and respectable talents" (Beasley, 1990, p. 35). Bassett went on to say that he often saw senators get up and leave the Senate chamber when they saw Anne Royall coming.

Anne Royall represented a dying breed: editors who stamped their newspapers with their own personality. The era of personal journalism was waning in the United States, and Anne Royall was one of its last practitioners. She ranted and raved whenever she felt the occasion called for it. Typical of her attitude was this "correction": "Speaking of Attorney General B. F. Butler, we were made

to call him a 'detestable reptile.' It ought to have read 'detestable hypocrite' "
(Beasley, 1990, p. 35). She continued her campaigns against groups she considered dangerous to the welfare of the nation, particularly the evangelicals. Seeing too strong a connection between organized religion and the Free Soil party, she bitterly attacked the latter: "There are two dangerous parties in our country: Church and state, alias Free Soilers, and the Demagogues, alias office-seekers. The Free Soil men are doing their utmost to annihilate the constitution and put an end to freedom" (Beasley, 1976–1977, p. 101).

But Anne Royall's health did not allow her to keep up the fight. As she aged, she filled the columns of her newspapers with more and more reprinted material. She particularly liked the works of Charles Dickens, readily available because of the lack of international copyright laws. Eventually, her health forced her to cease publication altogether. But even though she was unable to write as she had done previously in her life, Anne Royall continued to express concern for the future of her country. In the final issue of the *The Huntress,* published just three months before Royall's death, she articulated her personal hope that "the union of these states may be eternal" (Beasley, 1976–1977, p. 101). Luckily, she did not live to see her hope dashed in the bloody battles of the Civil War.

Anne Newport Royall died in Washington, D. C., on October 1, 1854, at the age of 85. Having an estate of only 31 cents, she was buried in an unmarked pauper's grave in the Congressional Cemetery. In its obituary, the Washington *Evening Star* declared that "to the hour of her death, she preserved all the peculiarities of thought, temper, and manners, which at one time rendered her so famous throughout the land." Furthermore, "she was a woman of considerable literary attainments and benevolence, and of strict integrity" (Beasley, 1990, p. 35; Wallace, 1957, p. 266).

In many ways, history has not been fair to Anne Royall. Her first biographer, Sarah H. Porter, blamed the problem on contemporary male journalists:

It was unfortunate for Mrs. Royall's posthumous reputation that, along toward the close of her life, special correspondents began pouring into Washington. The funny little old woman, trotting through the corridors of the Capital, made amusing copy when news was scarce. Anne Royall's bitterly poor old age has contributed a facetious paragraph to nearly every book that has been written about early Washington. The tradition of her trial as a common scold gave the key-note. Her quick tongue did the rest. (Beasley, 1976–1977, pp. 101–102)

The survival of the myth about the river interview with President John Quincy Adams supports this assessment.

But Anne Newport Royall was much more than an eccentric woman who haunted the nightmares of congressmen. Her travel writings alone should give her a place in history, for their production made her one of America's first roving correspondents and their wealth of detailed information provide valuable insights concerning the society and culture of the early United States. Frank Luther Mott labeled her the forerunner of the modern gossip columnist because of the tone of her publications. She became the first American woman to establish herself as a journalist (without inheriting the business from a relative). She was the first woman to report on Congress and the first woman to edit and publish a newspaper in Washington, D.C. She interviewed every president from John Quincy Adams to Franklin Pierce. As "grandma of the muckrakers," she was one of the first investigative reporters, and, in doing this work, she set a standard of zeal and vigilance for future crusading journalists. Finally, she was simply an amazing woman. Time and time again, she refused to give in when facing defeat. On more than one occasion, she carved herself a niche in a male-dominated world in order to ensure her personal survival. Such tenacity deserves to be remembered and respected.

REFERENCES

Avery, D. R. (1989). "Royall, Anne Newport." In J. P. McKerns (ed.), *Biographical dictionary of American journalism.* (pp. 609–611). Westport, Conn.: Greenwood Press.

Beasley, M. (1976–1977). The curious career of Anne Royall. *Journalism History,* 3, 98–102, 136.

Beasley, M. (1990, May). Anne Royall, huntress with a quill. *The Quill,* 78, 32–35.

Blankenhorn, H. (1927, September). The grandma of the muckrakers. *The American Mercury,* 87–93.

Dodd, D., & Williams, B. (1976, January). "A common scold": Anne Royall. *American History Illustrated,* 10, 32–38.

Fleener, N. (1985). Anne Royall in *Dictionary of literary biography.* vol. 43. pp. 402–44. Detroit: Gale Research Co.

Schilpp, M. G., & Murphy, S. M. (1983). Anne Newport Royall. *Great Women of the Press.* (pp. 21–36). Carbondale: Southern Illinois Press.

Wallace, I. (1957). *Square pegs.* (pp. 243–266). New York: Alfred Knopf.

Whitton, M. O., (1954). *These were the women USA 1776–1860.* (pp. 60–66). New York: Hastings House.

Publications by Anne Newport Royall

Sketches of history, life, and manners in the United States. By a traveller. (1826). New Haven, Conn.: Printed for the Author.

The Tennessean: a novel founded on facts. (1827). New Haven, Conn.: Printed for the Author.

The black book; or, A continuation of travels in the United States. (1828–1829). 3 vols. Washington, D.C.: Printed for the Author.

Mrs. Royall's Pennsylvania; or, travels continued in the United States. (1829). 2 vols. Washington, D.C.: Printed for the Author.

Letters from Alabama on various subjects; to which is added, an appendix containing

    remarks on sundry members of the 20th & 21st Congress and other high char-
    acters &c. &c. at the seat of government. (1830). Washington, D.C.
Mrs. Royall's Southern tour or second series of the black book. (1830–1831). 3 vols.
    Washington, D.C.

REBECCA BORING RUBIN
(1948–   )

Elizabeth E. Graham

Rebecca Boring Rubin has published numerous journal articles, books, grants, and assessment instruments. Indeed, she was recently identified as the fourth most prolific female scholar in the nation (Hickson, Stacks, & Amsbary, 1992).

FAMILY BACKGROUND

Rebecca Boring was born in York, Pennsylvania, on December 11, 1948. Her father, Byron, was a furniture factory owner and operator; her mother, Sybilla, primarily a homemaker, did some drafting work and, after her children were born, was self-employed in the sweater industry. Of English, German, and Scotch-Irish descent, and a direct descendant of both Daniel Boone and Milton Hershey, Rubin describes her family as middle class. She has one sister, Barbara, three years her senior. Rebecca grew up in an extended family; her grandmother, a tailor, lived with them. Consistently named to her high school honor roll, Rebecca was editor of her high school yearbook. In fact, this was the first book of many that she would edit. She has produced many works, despite the lack of support from a high school English teacher who once suggested she didn't have any writing ability.

Although neither parent was a college graduate, they recognized the value of a college education, especially for women. Her mother was a particular source of support and encouragement.

EDUCATION

Rebecca entered Pennsylvania State University in 1966 and earned a Bachelor of Arts degree in speech (with her major emphasis in speech education and broadcasting) in 1970. Although she would have preferred a career in television production, she knew employment opportunities were limited for women in that industry at that time. She therefore shifted course and pursued high school teaching. However, after a brief stint as a student teacher, she realized she wasn't challenged. So, although a self-described "border-line high apprehensive," Rubin continued at Penn State in communication and received her Master of Arts degree in 1971. Completed in record time, her thesis (directed by David E. Butt), "A Study to Determine Factors Which Contribute to Student Exemption of a Beginning College Speech Course," was indicative of an early interest in speech education.

Rebecca Boring took an instructor position at Messiah College from 1971 to 1972. She taught numerous courses (including art, music, literature, and religion), because it was a small college. Teaching such diverse subjects required that she engage in intensive study in the evenings in order to keep up with the class. Rubin was not happy living at home and being employed at a college that required church attendance and had a dress code; she therefore began applying to graduate schools. In the fall of 1972 Rubin entered the speech communication program at the University of Illinois at Urbana–Champaign. It was here that her interests in cognitive development began. Because much of what was known about interpersonal communication at that time was based on psychology, her advisor, Dr. Jesse G. Delia, encouraged her to consider the role of cognitive processes in interpersonal interactions. Her dissertation, "Cognitive Complexity, Context of Anticipated Interaction, and Information Seeking Processes in Impression Formation," was an outgrowth of this early experience.

It was at the University of Illinois that Rebecca met Alan Rubin, also a Ph.D. student in speech communication. They were married in 1975 and credit their similar interests as a major contributor to their happy and successful marriage. Today, they are the proud "parents" of two cats: Rocky, a short-haired domestic tiger, and Michelle, a short-haired domestic calico. True to her belief in leading a balanced life, Rebecca can be found playing golf, reading mystery novels, painting with water colors, and traveling. Although her 30s were spent primarily at the keyboard of her computer, she says that her 40s have been a time to "create" and "explore" untapped talents and interests. "The decade of the 80's was a decade of work—work hard and do nothing else."

CAREER DEVELOPMENT

In 1975, at the age of 26, Rebecca Rubin received her Ph.D. from the University of Illinois and assumed a part-time assistant professor position at Georgia Southern College (now Georgia Southern University), teaching speech fundamentals and public relations. Eager to succeed, she started publishing articles from her dissertation. Her husband Alan, also embarking on a new career as an assistant professor, was employed full time at Georgia Southern College. The following year Rebecca accepted a full-time one-year appointment at the University of North Carolina at Greensboro. It was here that she met colleague Ethel Glenn, who was very influential and had a significant impact on Rebecca's professional development. During the late 1970s mentoring was not a recognized activity, especially for women by women. Rubin described Glenn as "a someone with a purpose—she was strong and outspoken and knew where she was going." It was this early experience that would mold Rubin's later handling of new students and faculty.

Although the Rubins were excelling in their respective positions, they were also living apart, which was an unusual arrangement for this time, predating most dual-career long-distance relationships by about a decade. Consistent with their egalitarian marriage, Rebecca explained that "Alan got the new car since he did most of the commuting and I got the apartment." Finding jobs for both of them was particularly difficult. So when they were offered two full-time faculty positions at the University of Wisconsin at Parkside, they accepted. During this time, Rebecca took on administrative duties serving as coordinator of the communication discipline.

After four years in Wisconsin, both Alan and Rebecca Rubin were recruited by the Communication Department at Cleveland State University. Their stay at Cleveland State was brief because they were vigorously pursued by Kent State University. In 1982 the Rubins joined the communication faculty at Kent State. Rebecca was promoted to full professor in 1988, meeting her goal of attaining this rank by age 40. She had numerous administrative duties at Kent: she served as director of the Communication Research Center as well as director of graduate studies. Her administrative activities strongly influenced the future direction of the school.

It was at Kent State during the 1980s that Rebecca Rubin's research flourished. She describes her work ethic as "doing the most you can do while you can do it." She managed to accomplish an incredible amount of writing as well as to fulfill a childhood goal of being a teacher. It was at Kent that she first began to work closely with graduate students. Contrary to academic tradition, she does not require her students to study only her research interests; rather, they are encouraged to find their own way. As a result of this open-mindedness, a variety of research lines have emanated from Kent State.

Rubin describes her teaching philosophy as akin to being a tour guide—she points out important sites/cites along the way, encouraging understanding and allowing travelers to get to their destination the best and fastest way they can. Ultimately, Rubin mused, "to be well known would be good, but not necessary. We all live on in our students—an unbroken chain—our ideas will be all that will be left."

MAJOR CONTRIBUTIONS AND ACHIEVEMENTS

Rebecca Rubin's research interests can be categorized into four content areas: competence, interpersonal communication, interpersonal/mediated communication, and measurement.

She was one of the first to incorporate uncertainty reduction theory (the most formally articulated relationship development theory, Sunnafrank, 1986) and consider the role of context in initial interactions (Rubin, 1977, 1979). As initial research made clear, context would be a cornerstone in her research repertoire for some time to come. This is particularly unusual given the strong dispositional leanings of the field at that time.

During this time, she and Alan Rubin were embarking on a series of articles concerning contextual age (A. Rubin & R. Rubin, 1981, 1982a, 1982b; R. Rubin & A. Rubin, 1982). Having received a grant from the American Broadcasting Corporation, she and Alan proposed to detail contextual age as an alternative life-position concept to chronological age. This research helped end many of the stereotypes of the elderly, particularly in regard to media use. In addition to uncovering and providing a viable alternative for measuring and conceptualizing age, this early work foreshadowed her later efforts to interface personal and mediated communication. Although it was a decade later, Alan and Rebecca Rubin initiated a line of research whose influence is still coming to fruition.

Rubin is best known for her competence research. Her theoretical, conceptual, and methodological contributions to the study of competence helped unravel many of the complexities surrounding skill development research in the 1970s and early 1980s. While the field of communication was grappling with the definition of competence, Rubin held on to a rather purist approach to the definition of competence: speaking and listening skills. She felt that these skills were fundamental to relational success and survival. Furthermore, her work made explicit the central assumption underlying skill development. For instance, she questioned: Does instruction actually make a difference? Can skills be taught?

Aside from an academic interest in competence, Rubin's writing and research efforts in skill development underscore her genuine interest in the well-being of students and their academic performance. A proponent of the belief that there is an implied relationship between interpersonal competence and overall mental health, Rubin contends that skill development is of paramount importance for students.Thus, she found it necessary to identify students experiencing speaking and listening difficulties.

This interest and concern for students prompted Rubin to develop an instrument to measure speaking and listening competence. This assessment tool, the Communication Competency Assessment Instrument (CCAI), was introduced in 1982 and consists of three sections. The first part asks the student to present a three-minute extemporaneous speech on a topic of his or her choice. During this procedure, six judgments about the student's speaking ability are made (pronunciation, facial expression/tone of voice, speech clarity, persuasiveness, clarity of ideas, and ability to express and defend a point of view). Second, the student views a videotaped presentation of a class lecture. The material on the videotape provides the criteria for assessing the ability to differentiate between fact and opinion, understand suggestions, identify work necessary to complete an assignment, and summarize. Finally, participants are asked to respond in various ways to statements about their experiences in an educational environment. These items permit an assessment of ability to perform a social ritual, ask and answer questions, express feelings, use topical order, give accurate directions, describe another's point of view, and explain differences in opinion.

Rubin and associates (Rubin & Graham, 1988; Rubin, Graham, & Mignerey, 1990) engaged in longitudinal research in order to determine factors that contribute to the development of students' speaking and listening competence over their college career. The results were provocative and unsettling. It appears that communication courses do not have a singular or an immediate effect on communication skill development. However, students do develop interpersonal competence by being exposed to, and participating in, extracurricular communication activities (e.g., participation in student government, social and professional organizations and events). Rubin was an early proponent of incorporating outside communication activities into classroom learning and encouraging participation in nonclassroom communication events so that students could have an additional means of developing their skills.

In addition to determining student (high school and college) needs, the CCAI has been very useful in the assessment of student teacher communication competence. The primary assumption guiding this line of research was as follows: successful teaching is a matter of effective communication (Norton, 1977; Rubin & Feezel, 1986; Scott & Nussbaum, 1981). Citing recent societal concerns about improving instruction, Rubin and associates detailed the need for school districts and state agencies to assess the skills of teachers (and teachers in training) and to identify qualities and skills that influence cognitive learning. Rubin's work provided an impetus to train teachers *throughout* their careers rather than solely at the beginning.

In retrospect, Rubin admits that she never intended to become a leading figure in competence research; her entrance into this area was serendipitous. During the late 1970s while teaching at the University of Wisconsin at Parkside, there was a nationwide movement to measure student skill development. Because there was no speech skills test, Rubin acquired a grant and developed a measure of student speaking and listening skills. Surprisingly, this turn of events would ultimately define her career.

In addition to contributing to the instructional literature, Rubin has also been a consistent voice in the interpersonal communication field. Recently, Rubin and associates (Rubin, Perse, & Barbato, 1988) proposed a model and measure of Interpersonal Communication Motives. Recognizing that people have different reasons for communicating, the model identifies six motives individuals have for talking to others: pleasure, affection, inclusion, escape, relaxation, and control. Consistent with the uses and gratifications perspective, motives research suggests that people are discriminating and mindful of their communication choices.

Rubin has also been involved in "popular culture" research which explored the ideal traits and terms of address for male and female college professors

(Rubin, 1981). She also engaged a group of graduate students to conduct one of the first empirical studies of MTV (Rubin, Rubin, Perse, et al., 1986). One of her more unusual writing projects resulted in a book entitled *The Road Trip, An Interpersonal Adventure* (1988). With the assistance of her advanced undergraduate interpersonal communication class, Rubin and Nevins (1988) developed a reader to accompany introductory interpersonal texts. The text details the exploits and experiences of five college students in order to "provide a method by which you can read and talk about elements in interpersonal communication competence" (p. vii).

Rubin's writing emphasizes measurement. Although she does not consider herself a methodologist, she has developed and co-developed four measurement scales (Contextual Age Index, Interpersonal Communication Motives Measure, Communicator Flexibility Scale, and Interpersonal Communication Competence Scale) and one assessment instrument (Communication Competency Assessment Instrument); she has written a research text (*Communication Research: Strategies and Sources*); and published book chapters concerning evaluation of interpersonal measures. She considers good research to be methodologically solid, complemented by error-free analysis and, of course, a sound conceptual base. It is not surprising, then, that these qualities best describe her writing and research. Rubin is quick to point out that, in order to sustain a level of inquiry, it is necessary to be truly interested in the topic and to move on once that interest is gone.

Rebecca Rubin has also demonstrated a research and service interest in the national and international communication associations. She has been elected chair of the Instructional Division and of the Committee on Testing and Assessment, and elected to the Legislative Council of the Speech Communication Association (SCA). In addition to receiving recognition for numerous "top paper" awards, Rubin consistently submits her work to conferences for feedback from colleagues.

CRITICAL EVALUATION OF CONTRIBUTIONS AND ACHIEVEMENTS

Although most competence research is characteristically applied, Rubin and others (Rubin, 1983; Spitzberg, 1983) posited a perceptual model of competence. Loosely based on Bloom's Taxonomy of Learning, the proposed model suggests that skill development is a function of knowledge, motivation, and skill. One must know what is effective and appropriate, be motivated to enact these behaviors, and also be capable of carrying out these goals. Although a conceptually sound model, there were measurement problems, particularly with the motivation construct, that detracted from the usefulness of the model. Rubin points to knowledge, learning, and cognitive theories as providing useful perspectives to consider competence, and she admits that there is still a lack of a conceptual base that characterizes competence research.

When asked what she would do differently, Rubin responded that she wished she was more of a leader in the field of interpersonal communication. A competence focus has tended to drive her research, and she has had little time to devote to "pure interpersonal communication" research topics.

INTEGRATION OF PERSONAL AND PROFESSIONAL LIFE

Rubin's professional life clearly permeates her personal life. Given that her husband Alan is in the same discipline and department, as well as her consistent collaborator, it is not surprising that work or talk of work is with them all the time. Over the years they have learned how to be each other's best fan and critic—a delicate balance to achieve. She credits the success of the relationship to "knowing what each other needs." She points out that it is difficult for women to be good spouses, good scholars, and good parents, and claims it was fortuitous that she and Alan chose not to have children.

Although Rebecca and Alan Rubin have collaborated on a number of writing projects, it was not until they introduced their model of the interface of personal and mediated communication (Rubin & Rubin, 1985) that the marriage of ideas and people was truly captured. Working from a uses and gratification perspective, they set out to illustrate how mediated and interpersonal channels are equal alternatives to one another for the fulfillment of social and psychological needs. Although it is too soon to forecast or report on the ultimate impact of the interface perspective, it is clear that their writing will prompt others to consider the rich potential for interfacing multiple and seemingly disparate perspectives.

With regard to the role of the communication discipline in society, Rubin states that "society will generate enough problems on its own and communication skills will certainly be necessary for problem-solving and conflict-management." Although it is far too soon to assess her overall contribution to academia and society, it is clear that her research will continue to advance knowledge of communication.

NOTE

All quotations and biographical information not otherwise referenced are drawn from an interview with Rebecca Rubin conducted by the author on June 29, 1994 in Kent, Ohio.

REFERENCES

Hickson, M., Stacks, D. W., & Amsbary, J. H. (1992). Active prolific scholars in communication studies: Analysis of research productivity, II. *Communication Quarterly, 40*, 350–356.

Norton, R. (1977). Teacher effectiveness as a function of communicator style. *Communication Yearbook 1*, 525–542.

Rubin, A. M., & Rubin, R. (1981). Age, context and television use. *Journal of Broadcasting, 25,* 1–13.

Rubin, A. M., & Rubin, R. B. (1982a). Contextual age and television use. *Human Communication Research, 8,* 228–244.

Rubin, A. M., & Rubin, R. B. (1982b). Older person's TV viewing patterns and motivations. *Communication Research, 9,* 287–313.

Rubin, A. M., & Rubin, R. B. (1985). The interface of personal and mediated communication: A research agenda. *Critical Studies in Mass Communication, 2,* 36–53.

Rubin, R. B. (1977). The role of context in information seeking and impression formation. *Communication Monographs, 44,* 81–90.

Rubin, R. B. (1979). The effect of context on information seeking across the span of initial interactions. *Communication Quarterly, 27,* 13–20.

Rubin, R. B. (1981). Ideal traits and terms of address for male and female college professors. *Journal of Personality and Social Psychology, 41,* 966–974.

Rubin, R. B. (1982). Assessing speaking and listening competence at the college level: The Communication Competence Assessment Instrument. *Communication Education, 31,* 19–32.

Rubin, R. B. (ed.). (1983). *Improving speaking and listening skills.* San Francisco: Jossey-Bass.

Rubin, R. B., & Feezel, J. D. (1986). Elements of teacher communication competence. *Communication Education, 35,* 254–268.

Rubin, R. B., & Graham, E. E. (1988). Communication correlates of college success: An exploratory investigation. *Communication Education, 37,* 14–27.

Rubin, R. B., Graham, E. E., & Mignerey, J. T. (1990). A longitudinal study of college students' communication competence. *Communication Education, 38,* 1–14.

Rubin, R. B., & Nevins, R. J. (1988). *The road trip: An interpersonal adventure.* Prospect Heights, Ill.: Waveland.

Rubin, R. B., Perse, E. M., & Barbato, C. A. (1988). Conceptualization and measurement of interpersonal communication motives. *Human Communication Research, 14,* 602–628.

Rubin, R. B., & Rubin, A. M. (1982). Contextual age and television use: Reexamining a life-position indicator. *Communication Yearbook 6,* 583–604.

Rubin, R. B., Rubin, A. M., Perse, E. M., Armstrong, C., McHugh, M., & Faix, N. (1986). Media use and meaning of music video. *Journalism Quarterly, 63* (2), 353–359.

Scott, M. D., & Nussbaum, J. F. (1981). Student perceptions of instructor communication behaviors and their relationship to student evaluation. *Communication Education, 30,* 44–53.

Spitzberg, B. H. (1983). Communication competence as knowledge, skill, and impression. *Communication Education, 32,* 323–329.

Sunnafrank, M. (1986). Predicted outcome value during initial interactions: A reformulation of uncertainty reduction theory. *Human Communication Research, 13,* 3–33.

Additional Representative Publications

Rubin, R. B. (1985). Validity of the Communication Competency Assessment Instrument. *Communication Monographs,* 52, 173–185.

Rubin, R. B. (1989). Communication competence. In G. M. Phillips & J. T. Wood (eds.), *Studies in honor of the 75th anniversary of the Speech Communication Association.* (pp. 94–129). Carbondale: Southern Illinois University Press.

Rubin, R. B., Fernandez-Collado, C., & Hernandez-Sampieri, R. (1992). A cross-cultural examination of interpersonal communication motives in Mexico and the United States. *International Journal of Intercultural Relations,* 16, 145–157.

Rubin, R. B., Palmgreen, P., & Sypher, H. (eds.). (1994). *Communication research measures: A sourcebook.* New York: Guilford.

JESSICA SAVITCH
(1947–1983)

Sue Lawrence

On October 23, 1983, Jessica Savitch and Martin Fischbein, a *New York Post* executive, died when their car drove into the Delaware Canal in New Hope, Pennsylvania, flipped over, and fell 12 feet into several feet of water and mud. Jessica Savitch was 36. The freak accident ended Savitch's six-year career as anchorwoman and reporter at NBC.

FAMILY BACKGROUND AND EDUCATION

Jessica Savitch's grandfather, Ben Savitch, a Jewish emigrant from southwest Russia, moved to Kennett Square, Pennsylvania, in the early 1930s. He was successful in the clothing business and eventually owned several stores. Jessica's father, David (known as Buddy), was born in Coatesville on November 19, 1925. During World War II he was a pharmacist's mate in the Navy. When he was hospitalized in the service with the early stages of an incurable kidney problem, he met a navy nurse, Florence (Spadoni) Goldberger, a Catholic from South Philadelphia. They married on September 6, 1945, in California, and the couple moved to Kennett Square. Florence gave up nursing and became a house-wife; Buddy managed Benny's, his father's men's store. The couple had three daughters. Jessica Beth was born on February 1, 1947, in Wilmington, Delaware; Stephanie and Lori were born in 1948 and 1956, respectively.

Jessica was only 12 years old when David Savitch died on May 11, 1959, of uremic pericarditis at the age of 33. Following this tragic event, the family moved to Margate, New Jersey, near Atlantic City, to be closer to Florence's parents, and Florence resumed her nursing career. Only four months after the family moved, Florence's father, Edward Goldberger, a Hungarian emigrant, was found dead in his garage of carbon monoxide poisoning, an apparent suicide. So it was that Florence's mother moved in with the family.

When the family moved to Margate, halfway through her freshman year, Savitch transferred to Atlantic City High School. After graduation in 1964, she enrolled at Ithaca College in New York where she majored in communications; she graduated in the spring of 1968. Later in her career, Ithaca College asked her to return to teach a course as visiting professor, which she did in 1975, 1976, and 1978.

CAREER DEVELOPMENT

Savitch's broadcasting career began in high school. When she was a sophomore, she dated a senior who worked part-time at WOND-AM, a 1,000-watt ABC-affiliated Top 40 station in Pleasantville, New Jersey. Soon after he introduced her to the station, she became a regular co-host of "Teen Corner," a Saturday morning show that reported on local events for teens. Eventually, she became the first female disc jockey in the area, broadcasting from 12:00 to 8:00 P.M. on Sunday afternoons under the name Jesse James. She got some experience covering the news with a report on the assassination of President John F. Kennedy as well as President Lyndon Johnson's speech to the United Auto Workers in March 1964 and the Democratic National Convention in Atlantic City in August. For the teenage Savitch, the radio station became the center of her life. "At last I felt as though I belonged" (Savitch, 1982, p. 19).

At Ithaca College, Savitch found women a minority in the communications major. She thought her high school experience at WOND would assure her a disc jockey shift on WICB, the college-owned AM station, but, to her disappointment, it did not. She eventually accepted a rip-n-read news shift at WICB after complaining to faculty about the station's discriminatory policies favoring male students. She also worked on "Town Talk," a daily AM show run by the women students in communications, and in November 1964 she made her first television appearance during election night coverage on ICB-TV, the college cable channel. But Savitch wanted an AM disc jockey shift, and when she could not get the type of broadcasting experience she desired at school, she made a name for herself in Rochester, a two-hour drive from Ithaca. There she found production jobs and did on-camera and voice-over commercial work, including television ads for a Dodge dealership. In 1966 she got a weekend air shift at WBBF, the leading Top 40 AM station in Rochester, as their first female disc jockey. Known as Honeybee, she became a local celebrity, broadcasting live remotes from a van called the Beemobile.

After graduation from college in 1968, Savitch returned to her job at WBBF for the summer and then moved to New York City in the fall. There she met the woman she acknowledged as her mentor, Joan Showalter, personnel director for CBS, who hired her, in spite of her lack of typing or dictation skills, as a floating administrative assistant. By late 1969, she was working for the news director of WCBS-AM Radio (NewsRadio 88) as an administrative assistant. While WCBS would not hire Savitch to report news because she had no professional experience, she did get writing tips from Charles Osgood, who was then anchoring morning drive-time news. She also met Ed Bradley, then a WCBS radio reporter, whom she dated. During her time at CBS, Savitch took some college courses and continued free-lance production work—she was line producer for the Miss Black America Pageant at New York's Felt Forum in 1970. She also used the WCBS facilities to make an audition tape to help in her job search. Savitch took herself very seriously even at this stage of her career. She later wrote in *Anchorwoman* about this time at WCBS: "I tried not to take my job as a personal insult. I kept reminding myself that I was only biding time, strengthening my experience and thus my resume. On the other hand, it was dispiriting to have to put up with people who thought I was just a starry-eyed little girl" (Savitch, 1982, p. 49).

In June 1971, at the age of 24, with no professional news-reporting experience, Savitch was hired for an on-air reporting job with KHOU-TV, Channel 11, a CBS affiliate in Houston. Three months after her arrival, she became the first woman television anchor in the South when she successfully auditioned for a weekend shift. The fact that KHOU was nonunion gave Savitch on-the-job training in every aspect of news production. She did not have a regular news beat but preferred to compete with other reporters for breaking stories. Her work gained national exposure when "CBS Evening News with Walter Cronkite" broadcast her report on a fire caused by a train derailment.

Even this early in her career, Savitch sometimes overshadowed the events she covered as a reporter. Twice, while working for KHOU, she made the news when she was detained for striking police officers. First, she hit a deputy sheriff on the arm with her microphone in Abilene. Then, in July 1972, she kicked a police officer while she was covering a story of a plane hijacking.

In November 1972, Savitch moved on to a job as general assignment reporter and weekend anchor at KYW, Channel 3, a Westinghouse station in Philadelphia. Houston was the fifteenth largest market in the country; KYW was the fourth largest market, covering southeastern Pennsylvania, Delaware, and part of New Jersey. Unlike Houston, KYW was a union shop, which meant she was hired to read news. She signed a five-year contract starting at $16,000, but Savitch thought she had a verbal understanding that she could leave earlier if a better opportunity arose. In early 1973 Savitch became weekend anchor with newscasts at 6:00 and 11:00 P.M.

CBS offered Savitch a job in New York after she had been in Philadelphia a year. Savitch wanted to leave, but KYW refused to release her from her contract. She had to stay but wrote, "Their choice was to aid me in my development, live up to the law of the land that called for equal pay for equal work—or fire me" (Savitch, 1982, p. 105). The station increased her salary and made her a weeknight anchor. In August 1974 Savitch was paired with Mort Crim on

"Newswatch 5:30." And in 1976 the station named Savitch tri-anchor of the 11:00 news with Mort Crim and Vince Leonard.

Savitch had several other duties at the station. She co-anchored the noon news for a time and, in 1975, became solo anchor. Savitch also hosted "Meeting-house" with Matt Quinn, a live one-hour weekly prime-time public issue forum featuring a panel of experts and a studio audience. She also reported for a number of heavily promoted multipart series ranging in subject matter from rape to abortion to famous Philadelphians in Hollywood.

Savitch wanted to leave local television for a network assignment, and her opportunity came when the audio line blew during the nationally televised debate between President Gerald Ford and Democratic nominee, Jimmy Carter, on September 23, 1976. Savitch was reporting from the Walnut Street Theatre, where the debate was being held, and her ability to cover the 27 minutes the presidential candidates silently waited for the line to be fixed impressed an NBC executive. The network offered her a three-year contract starting in September 1977 as a Washington correspondent, with some anchor work, at $115,000 the first year, $125,000 the second year, and $140,000 the third year. Savitch did her last 5:30 newscast in Philadelphia on August 19, 1977.

After KYW had held her to the terms of her contract, Savitch's days in Philadelphia were difficult. Gwenda Blair writes: "Savitch's once-pleasant relations with a number of producers and directors headed downhill and never went back up. Always a perfectionist on the set, she became a humorless prima donna, frequently lashing out at the hapless crew" (Blair, 1988, p. 182). For example, during her last weeks at the station Savitch, arriving at the last minute for the 5:30 news, discovered on-air that either the pages in her script or on the teleprompter were out of order. During the two-minute commercial break, she threw a temper tantrum that was recorded without sound on videotape. Station employees set her performance to Aram Khachaturian's "Sabre Dance," and the tape did not help her reputation when it wound up in NBC affiliate newsrooms all over the country.

Savitch spent the last years of her life under contract to NBC. She began her career there full of hope of becoming a network weekday anchor. Her first assignment was to cover the Senate in Washington, a job previously held in 1971 and 1972 by a woman, Cassie Macklin. Savitch did not have any background for the job, but the position was highly visible. Alanna Nash writes: "The idea of putting Jessica on the Senate beat was a calculated move to establish her credentials as a journalist to validate her as an anchor," (Nash, 1988, p. 206). Her assignments included covering Vice President Walter Mondale on a fence-mending tour through the West and Northwest, the funeral of Hubert Humphrey, and some of the 1978 election Senate campaigns. She considered the Panama Canal debate the most important story she reported. But in early 1979, less than two years after she started covering the Senate, NBC demoted her; Tom Pettit replaced her on the Senate beat, and Savitch was put on general assignment. Carl Stern, NBC Supreme Court reporter, remembers her days covering the Senate:

The entire time she was up there, I don't recall one story that she dug up. I don't recall her going around talking to people, I don't recall crossing her tracks on the Hill, and I never heard a word from anybody reacting to a meeting or an on-air piece that she did. It was as though she wasn't here. She left no footprints in the sand. (Nash, 1988, p. 218)

Starting on November 6, 1977, besides covering the Senate, Savitch began commuting to New York on weekends to anchor the Sunday news. On November 20, 1977, only two months after she started at NBC, she co-anchored a special one-hour Sunday newscast from New York with John Chancellor in Jerusalem and David Brinkley in Washington. Savitch had various other duties at the network for six years. She delivered several one-minute prime-time news updates a week. She occasionally appeared on "Meet the Press" and contributed for a time to "Segment 3," an in-depth report on "Nightly News." But, once again, Savitch ran into problems. To showcase her as a reporter, the network assigned Savitch to cover the Canadian elections of May 1979, replacing the correspondent who regularly covered Canada. But there were so many problems with the story she filed that NBC producers banned her from reporting for weekday "NBC Nightly News." One witness at the network says, "I remember watching and going, oh, my God. I was embarrassed to be part of the program that aired the spot" (Nash, 1988, p. 224).

Between October 1979 and June 1980, Savitch worked on the magazine show "Prime Time Sunday" (later "Prime Time Saturday"), both in the studio with Tom Snyder and as a reporter—an assignment she found frustrating. And she occasionally filled in on the "Tomorrow Show" for Snyder. In 1980 the network put her in the highly visible position of podium correspondent at the Republican and Democratic National Conventions, but she was not allowed to complete the assignment. While she did scoop an interview at the Republican convention from Senator Paul Laxalt denying the possibility of a co-presidency between Ronald Reagan and Gerald Ford, she was replaced by Tom Pettit on the podium at the Democratic convention right before the final address by President Carter.

Savitch occasionally substituted for Jane Pauley on "Today" and, in the fall of 1981, when Tom Brokaw went to "Nightly News," she and Pauley co-anchored "Today" for several weeks. She also provided commentary for NBC Radio Network and worked on a television documentary, "Spies Among Us," about Russian spies in the United States. Beginning on July 5, 1982, Savitch also became the principal correspondent for A-News Capsules to NBC affiliates. In the fall of 1982, her autobiography, *Anchorwoman,* written at the age of 34, came out to mixed reviews.

In 1982 producer David Fanning asked Savitch to work on the $6 million

"Frontline" series for PBS. Between November 1982 and January 1983, she was on leave from some of her duties at NBC (while keeping the Saturday edition of "Nightly News") so she could narrate and sometimes conduct brief studio interviews for the series from Boston. "Frontline" debuted with "An Unauthorized History of the NFL."

By this point, Savitch was concerned about her future at the network. In early 1983, she was offered but passed up a new NBC show, "Sunrise." In May, NBC announced that Connie Chung would replace her as Saturday anchor of "Nightly News." Her last contract, issued in August, implied that NBC was phasing her out. The new contract contained a commitment to restore her to anchor of the Sunday evening news beginning in January 1984, and also mentioned a significant assignment at the 1984 conventions. For the first four months she would do a minimum of three evening updates a week. However, while the pay was $315,000, the contract, unlike her two previous three-year contracts, was for only one year. Simultaneously, the producers of "Frontline" decided to decrease her role in the second season of the program. Her death in October, of course, ended speculation about her career.

MAJOR CONTRIBUTIONS AND ACHIEVEMENTS

Savitch was extremely popular with the public and the press. In 1979 *Newsweek* dubbed her "NBC's Golden Girl." A poll conducted in 1982 named her and Dan Rather as the sexiest anchors; another named her as the fourth most trustworthy anchor on the networks. She was in great demand on the lecture circuit. In fact, in 1980 she was one of the 12 most popular speakers in the country.

Savitch achieved critical acclaim for some of her longer work in Philadelphia. One five-part series that followed a young couple through natural childbirth and showed the actual birth was a first for local television and "launched Jessica as Philadelphia's first true female news star" (Nash, 1988, p. 152) Her five-part report, "Rape . . . the Ultimate Violation," featured Savitch walking alone down a dark deserted street and won the Clarion Award from Women in Communications, Inc., in 1974. The series was credited with prompting changes in rape legislation. "Lady Law," a 1976 program about women police recruits, won the Broadcast Media Conference Award and a second award from Women in Communications.

Her work on the weekend Sunday night newscasts on NBC, though less prestigious an assignment than the weeknight newscast, was usually well received. In November 1978 she felt she earned herself a small measure of respect for her on-air ad-lib narration of the unpreviewed footage from Jonestown, Guyana, of the ambush of Congressman Leo Ryan and two NBC employees in Jonestown, Guyana. "Before I could stop myself I said 'Unbelievable' . . ." (Savitch, 1982, p. 143) Herb Dudnick, executive producer on "Sunday Nightly News" called that job "her finest hour at NBC" (Nash, 1988, p. 217).

By all accounts, Savitch had a charismatic presence on camera as a newsreader that was magnetically striking and unusual. She said she centered herself at a spot between the bridge of her nose and the back of her head where ''she would focus all her energy. She would then take that spot and project it through her eyes to a point about a foot and a half on the other side of the lens—that is, to the viewer'' (Blair, 1988, p. 308). She worked extremely hard on perfecting her delivery—taping her casts for critique and working with voice coach Lilyan Wilder to remove a lisp. Early in her career, she had developed a technique of recording stories on cassette, then playing them back through a concealed earphone as she repeated them on-air so she could concentrate on the camera.

While she never achieved her goal of anchoring the weekday ''NBC Nightly News'' (beyond substituting for the regular anchors), Savitch made inroads into the male bastion of television news. She only missed by a few months achieving her goal of becoming a network correspondent by the age of 30. And, at a time when women were underrepresented on the air, Savitch served as an inspiration for countless women. Conversely, she was undoubtedly helped by the women's movement. Early in the 1970s, the Federal Communications Commission had issued a ruling prohibiting discrimination in hiring and promoting women in the broadcasting industry, and right after Savitch arrived at KYW, the Philadelphia chapter of the National Organization of Women actively pressed the media to present more stories covered by women and about women on the local news. More specifically, it pressed KYW to hire anchorwomen. In 1977, right before Savitch arrived at NBC, 16 women had won a $2 million lawsuit charging the network with sexual bias. NBC had to give 1,000 women backpay and pursue affirmative action more aggressively.

CRITICAL EVALUATION OF CONTRIBUTIONS AND ACHIEVEMENTS

While extremely popular with the public, Savitch faced problems with her colleagues. Co-workers perceived her as a broadcasting star, hired for her looks and ability to present the news, rather than as a working journalist. She did not have an education in journalism, and she had only a modest amount of journalistic experience before NBC hired her and put her into highly visible assignments, including anchor. According to Nash, ''she was perceived as local talent who hadn't worked her way up through the usual ranks'' (Nash, 1988, p. 206). Savitch addressed her resentment of this perception in her autobiography. ''Thus, though I'd worked in broadcasting since age fifteen, I was categorized as a beginner, pigeonholed as a glossy blond news reader hired to dress the set and fill out the minority hiring quotas'' (Savitch, 1982, p. 126). Savitch did not ever quite seem to understand the concept of paying the journalistic dues her colleagues at the network expected. In her autobiography, she wrote that nothing she had ever done on-air was tougher than the 60-second updates she read (Savitch, 1982, p. 157).

Savitch found herself caught in several no-win situations. Because NBC treated her like a star, she could not ask for help from colleagues as she had done in Houston and in Philadelphia in the early days. Fighting the perception that she had been hired partly on the basis of her looks and her reading ability, she wrote, "I have my own theory that attractive people in the industry are considered bad journalists; average looking reporters are automatically given more credence" (Savitch, 1982, p. 73). NBC hired her over women already at the network and promoted her over men for plum assignments. In her contract negotiations she asked for and received perks, such as a hairdresser and limousine, that many reporters at the network did not have. Linda Ellerbee recounts an incident in which Tom Pettit and Senator Bob Mathias stood in front of the rotunda in the pouring rain waiting to go on the air, listening in their headsets to Savitch complaining about her hairdresser (Ellerbee, 1986, p. 113).

Savitch worked at NBC under four different news presidents during a time when the network was seriously slipping in the ratings. There is speculation that NBC could have nurtured her talents and utilized her strengths more effectively. Tom Brokaw said: "The people who brought her in here abandoned her. They used her for their own purposes, to attract audiences and so on, but they never really cared about her career beyond that, never really worked very hard at figuring out where do we go from here" (Blair, 1988, p. 319). For example, NBC asked her to cover the U.S. Senate on a part-time basis, keeping her busy with other assignments and speaking engagements at affiliate meetings, knowing that nothing in her local news background had prepared her sufficiently for the complexities of the assignment. Paul Duke, NBC's congressional correspondent from 1969 to 1974, says: "She had no real background in Washington politics, much less how Congress operated. NBC obviously wanted her glamour more than her reporting" (Nash, 1988, p. 207).

From her early days in broadcasting, Savitch wanted to become the first national woman anchor at a network. But in 1976 Barbara Walters* moved to ABC to co-anchor "Evening News with Harry Reasoner" for a salary of $1 million while Savitch was still under contract to local television in Philadelphia. At NBC, Savitch hoped eventually to replace John Chancellor. But her performance covering the Senate and problems reporting for "NBC Nightly News" led to her downfall. Even though she pulled off a bit of a coup by being the only journalist to get an interview with Carter as he left the podium at the Democratic convention in 1980, Savitch was humiliated when Tom Pettit replaced her on the podium. She wrote, "One does not argue in tight, competitive field situations. Pettit was, after all, the senior correspondent. Logic like that didn't help. I was devastated" (Savitch, 1982, p. 146).

Savitch fought health problems all her life and was hospitalized several times. There was speculation that she had been anorexic since high school and also that some of her miscarriages were abortions. Rumors she was a lesbian followed her throughout her career, and she allegedly tried to commit suicide several times. But the most damaging rumors involved her drug addiction.

According to many sources, Savitch used marijuana in Houston, and by Philadelphia was using amphetamines and cocaine for energy. At the network the cocaine problem apparently became even more serious, although the management at NBC could not prove these rumors and never took any action. But on October 3, 1983, millions of viewers watched her self-destruct on air during the 8:58 news capsule. According to Nash,

Her performance would be described in several ways: as excessive, woozy, slurring; as serious, massive brain fade; as merely simple faltering. But at NBC most people saw it as the final, tangible evidence of the ravages of cocaine addiction. She slurred her words so wildly that even the most inattentive viewer realized something was dreadfully wrong. (Nash, 1988, p. 325)

Blair writes, "In a single Digest, 43 seconds of live television, she destroyed what was left of her career" (Blair, 1988, p. 322). And she would be dead within three weeks.

INTEGRATION OF PERSONAL AND PROFESSIONAL LIFE

Savitch had a lifelong relationship with a man she met in 1972 in Houston but never married. Ron Kershaw left his job as a reporter at KTRK-TV in Houston to follow her to Philadelphia in the hopes of getting a job with WPVI. However, when the station found out he was engaged to a member of the competition's news team, WPVI refused to hire him. He eventually took a job at WBAL in Baltimore where he became news director. Savitch and Kershaw allegedly had a stormy relationship, complete with physical fighting.

Despite her lifelong connection to Kershaw, Savitch married twice. Her first marriage lasted ten months before her husband filed for divorce. She married Melvin Robert Korn, president of the advertising agency J. M. Korn & Sons, on Sunday January 6, 1980. Korn had arranged to meet Jessica in 1975 after reading an article about her in the *Philadelphia Inquirer,* and spent the next five years advising her about everything from her on-air look to her health to her career moves and contract negotiations. But Blair writes: "The sole unresolved item in Korn's and Savitch's meticulous planning for their marriage had been their future together" (Blair, 1988, p. 256). Even after the wedding, they maintained separate residences, with Savitch in Washington and Korn in Philadelphia. The marriage started disintegrating almost immediately, despite occasional weekends together in New York. Right after the wedding, Korn faced financial trouble when he lost two of his largest accounts and was slapped by his second ex-wife with an emergency support summons. Savitch, meanwhile, was busy with Campaign '80 and resumed her affair with Kershaw. But in September she met Donald Rollie Payne, a Washington, D.C., gynecologist and obstetrician, when she went to his office for a professional visit. By the time her divorce was final on March 9, Savitch was pregnant with Payne's child. She and Payne married on March 21 in Washington. Again, there were serious problems in the marriage and Savitch lost the child. Payne was bisexual, and within three months of the wedding he was hospitalized in White Plains, New York, for substance abuse. He was released in July, and on August 2 Savitch returned to her Washington townhouse after reading the news in New York on Saturday to find he had hanged himself in the basement with her dog's leash. Three weeks later, on August 22, Savitch was back at NBC doing the weekend "Nightly News."

SELECTED BIBLIOGRAPHY

Blair, Gwenda. (1988). *Almost golden: Jessica Savitch and the selling of television news.* New York: Simon & Schuster.

Buckley, W. F. (1982, September 17). Stick 'em up, NBC. *National Review,* 34, 1140+.

Ellerbee, Linda. (1986). *And so it goes: Adventures in television.* New York: G. P. Putnam's Sons.

Hennessee, Judith Adler. (1979, August). "What it takes to anchor the news: Has Jessica Savitch finally beaten TV's catch 22—an attractive woman with credibility?" *Ms.,* 8, 84+.

Krupp, C. (1988, August). Blonde ambition: The short, tragic life of anchorwoman Jessica Savitch. *Glamour,* 200+.

Nash, Alanna. (1988). *Golden girl: The story of Jessica Savitch.* New York: E. P. Dutton.

Powers, R. (1988, August). Broadcasting ooze. *Gentleman's Quarterly,* 58, 119.

Sanders, Marlene, & Rock, Marcia. (1988). *Waiting for prime time: The women of TV news.* Urbana and Chicago: University of Illinois Press.

Savitch, Jessica. (1982). *Anchorwoman.* New York: G. P. Putnam's Sons.

Waters, H. F. (1988, June 13). Flameout of a golden girl. *Newsweek,* 111, 70.

Zuckerman, L. (1988, June 27). TV News' fallen star. *Time,* 131, 58.

DOROTHY G. SINGER
(1927–   )

Robert Miller

> Above all, I'd like to be remembered as a good teacher. It is very rewarding to feel that I have been able to influence a few young minds over the years . . . and be a good mother to my own children as well.

FAMILY BACKGROUND

Dorothy Singer was born in the Bronx on February 4, 1927. Her father completed a degree in chemistry but made a living in real estate as the owner and manager of several New York properties. Her mother, trained as a teacher, opted to stay at home and care for her growing children. She later adopted the life of a "professional volunteer" as the champion of a number of civic and charitable organizations.

The family lived in Riverdale, a suburb of New York City on the banks of the Hudson River. Singer readily recalled her neighborhood as very countrylike with an abundance of trees and grass and noted that she and her friends used to run to and from school barefoot in the spring and fall until the weather mandated shoes. She longingly remembers lazy afternoons spent with her closest friends "Janet" and "Claire," playing in and around a trellis and greenhouse on the Phelps Dodge estate which bordered the Hudson River near her home. "We did a lot of pretending," Singer remembers, "the rocks were castles and houses and pirate ships, and the whole Dodge estate was like a big fairy tale to us."

a   The roots of what would later become Singer's professional fascination with children's fantasy play can be traced even farther back, to her maternal grandmother, Ida Katz, who lived in the family home. Singer recalled that her grandmother was always taking her to different places around town, and she fondly remembers standing beside her wrapped in her white apron while she would make candy and breads and cakes in the kitchen. The family matriarch even assigned young Singer her own area of the family kitchen for imaginary play and to hang up her artwork. Indeed, Singer credited her grandmother as one of the most important influences in her early life.

EDUCATION

At the local public elementary school she attended, Singer remembers very strict teachers and could still talk of several by name and their respective quirks. She was a very good student and loved school, anxiously awaiting the first day of each new academic year with a fresh clipboard notebook and a new case full of sharpened pencils. Taught to read at a young age with the assistance of her doting parents and grandmother, Singer suggests that another defining snapshot of her childhood would be one of her snuggled up in the family's big leather chair with a book and an apple. "I did a lot of reading when I was young. I think that was very important," she recalled.

Upon graduating from grammar school, Singer continued her education, accompanied by best friends Janet and Claire, at Walton, an all-girls high school which Singer noted was a four-mile walk each way from her home. At Walton, no doubt guided by her mother's influence, Singer began what would become a lifelong commitment to social service, spending afternoons reading to the elderly at the Baptist Home and Saturdays taking blind children from the Lighthouse for the Blind on outings in New York City. "It was also sometime around then," Singer recalls with an impish grin, "that we all became interested in boys and dating . . . but those stories are too embarrassing to publish."

After high school, Singer went to Hunter College. There, she found a faculty mentor who awakened in her an interest in classics and inspired her to pursue a humanities major. She would later win a fellowship to study archaeology at the Institute of Fine Arts in New York, although one of life's more magical moments would prevent her from ever embarking on that pursuit.

After graduating with a degree in humanities in 1948, Singer spent the summer working in an advertising agency in New York City. There, on a particularly hot afternoon, she ventured into the Liberty Music Store on Madison Avenue, which, Singer recalls, was one of the most popular summer hangouts in the city because the store had air-conditioned listening booths where patrons could sit and listen to popular selections. Little did Singer know that her trip to the Liberty that afternoon would provide the introduction to her husband Jerome (Jerry) and change the course of her life.

CAREER DEVELOPMENT

Singer reminisces that she was sitting in a booth listening to Bach's Coffee Cantata when she saw a "nice-looking young gentleman" also with a Bach selection pacing back and forth waiting for a booth. Singer invited him into her booth and the two talked a bit; then they exchanged phone numbers and agreed to a picnic date on the weekend. Each brought a friend—Singer took her childhood friend Claire, while Jerry brought his best friend Bernard. The date had all the makings of a fairy tale, as Singer recalls Jerry chasing her through the forest as he played his recorder, while Bernard and Claire sat in the grass spellbound with each other. Bernard and Claire fell in love and were engaged shortly thereafter, but Jerry and Dorothy lost touch until the following spring when, after a second chance meeting, Jerry proposed. They were married in September 1949, and the two couples remain best friends to this day.

After their marriage, the Singers moved to Philadelphia where Jerry continued to pursue his Ph.D. in psychology at the University of Pennsylvania and Dorothy worked at an advertising agency and took additional courses at Temple University. While studying at Temple, she was fascinated by the work of the renowned psychologist Kurt Lewin and fell in love with psychology. When Jerry finished work on his Ph.D. that spring and took a job at the VA Hospital in New York City, Singer decided to pursue her newfound interest in psychology and after relinquishing her fellowship in archaeology, began part-time work on a Master's degree in psychology at New York University. She took a clinical internship in 1951 at the Westchester County Mental Hygiene Clinic and gave birth to Jon, the first of her three sons, just after completing her Master's in May 1952.

For the next several years, Singer postponed her academic pursuits in order to raise her firstborn son, but when Jon (now a science fiction writer) was in nursery school, she returned to the clinical world on a part-time basis with the Jewish Child Care Association and the Pleasantville Cottage School working with disturbed children. "It worked out very well," Singer recalled, "because I could be mom and still keep my hands in psychology." She would later give birth to two other sons, Bruce (now a successful Hollywood screenwriter) in December 1954, and Jeff (a professor of psychology at Connecticut College) in 1958.

After her youngest son Jeff went to kindergarten, Singer enrolled at Columbia University's Teachers' College earning her doctorate in school psychology (Ed.D.) in 1966. She took a research associate's position at the Child Welfare League of America where she designed experiments in foster child care, helped to design test batteries for the AFL-CIO, and provided counseling and job retraining for unemployed youths.

TEACHING EXPERIENCE

In 1968 Singer accepted an invitation to teach at Manhattanville College, a small liberal arts college in Purchase, New York, where she provided instruction in psychology and consulted at the Donald Reed Speech Center in Tarrytown, New York, testing children with language difficulties. She rose to the department chairmanship in 1972, but left at the end of that academic year to accept a joint appointment in Connecticut in the departments of psychology at the University of Bridgeport and Yale University, where husband Jerry had just accepted a professorship.

"I enjoyed my years teaching at Bridgeport," Singer remembers, "because many of those students were the first in their families to ever go to college. Many of them were very excited about their studies, and it was always a thrill to find a diamond in the rough that I could work with. There were a number of them over the years, and several of them have gone on to get Ph.D.s and now teach or practice all over the country."

While at Bridgeport, Singer continued to push back educational boundaries, encouraging an interdisciplinary approach to teaching by offering psychology courses at the University of Bridgeport Law School and creating and team-teaching courses with professors in other departments. "The Twilight of the Gods" (psychology and philosophy), "Psychology and Literature" (with a professor of English), and "The Search for Identity" (biology, philosophy, psychology, art, engineering, and English) were several of Singer's creative course offerings at Bridgeport in the late 1960s.

"It was a thrilling time," Singer recalls. "We taught literature courses by examining the psychological underpinnings of the novels we read, or examining the characters in the novels from various psychological perspectives. The students really seemed to enjoy this approach."

Meanwhile, at the University of Bridgeport, Singer became the William Benton Professor of Psychology and rose to the department chairmanship until leaving in 1990 to channel more of her energies into her work at the Yale Family Television Research and Consultation Center.

While Singer's teaching schedule at Yale is currently limited by the demands of her research and her extensive schedule of national and international lectures, she currently maintains an interdisciplinary seminar, "Television and Human Behavior" which remains one of the most popular and most demanding undergraduate seminars at Yale. She has also taught "Psychology and Law" and "Psychology through Children's Literature" at Yale.

MAJOR CONTRIBUTIONS

In 1975 Singer and her husband Jerry co-founded within the Psychology Department the Yale University Family Television Research and Consultation Center, which, for the past 19 years, has conducted some of the most definitive studies of children and television in the psychological literature, including investigations of links between television and aggression, and television's effects on learning in children of various ages. In 1992 the Center was commissioned to prepare a report on the effects of television on children for the United States Congress, an indication of the respect accorded to the institution that Singer has built over the past two decades with the partnership of her husband.

During the years she has been affiliated with the Center, Singer has published over 100 articles in a variety of professional journals in the fields of psychology, media, and communication. She has served on the editorial boards of *The Journal of Early Adolescence,* and *The Journal of Communication,* and she has authored or co-authored 13 books, most of which have confronted the issue of television and its effects on children. In addition to her written contributions, Singer has consulted for dozens of corporations and groups ranging from the HBO and Nickelodeon Cable Networks to the Walt Disney Company and media delegations from Puerto Rico, France, and the People's Republic of China. Over the years, Singer has shown particular consulting interests in work related to the roles of the media in inspiring children's play and imagination ("Fraggle Rock," "Brain Games") and also in the media's role in the social education of teenagers ("Life Lessons").

Singer's most memorable and most famous research echoes many of these same themes. She cites books co-authored with her husband, the recently completed congressional report, "A Role for Television in the Enhancement of Children's Readiness to Learn," "The House of Make Believe" which draws together all the available research on imagination from childhood through adulthood, and her two most recent research projects on the effects of television (investigating the potential positive roles of two PBS series, *Degrassi Junior High* and *Barney & Friends*) as examples of her work in both television and imagination.

Play therapy with children is another aspect of Singer's work. "It is difficult to work with kids and important for the family to play an active role in the healthy development of the child. Helping to restore a life, helping to give a kid a chance to develop more fully and not be afraid anymore, and to feel loved and cared for have been my goals in play therapy." A recent book, *Playing for Their Lives: Helping Troubled Children through Play Therapy,* describes her work with six different children and the various techniques she used.

Singer also has a special place in her heart for the big purple dinosaur after having recently completed a national study in five cities on the effects of *Barney & Friends* on its audience. With a twinkle in her eye she admits,

at first, I couldn't stand his silly laugh, and I thought to myself, that laugh is going to drive me crazy by the end of this project . . . but there is no question that the show is good for three and four year olds. *Barney* is slow paced and nurturing, which is exactly what children of that age need. There's plenty of time for them to become exposed to the harsher realities of the world. The *Barney* bashers just aren't looking closely enough at the positive messages this program provides.

While Singer's early research on television violence may be her most famous and admittedly "probably the most important," her work on imagination and fantasy are dearer to her. In fact, despite being one of the most recognizable names in the field of television research, Singer laments that researchers seem to have reached an impasse with the television industry, advertisers, and the American public on the subject of television and television violence.

We've probably done all we can with television—we've developed curricula for families and for students in kindergarten through high school; we've done a lot of outreach programs, but often it seems like we're beating our heads against a wall. People don't really see the problems in allowing their kids to watch too much television, nor do they pay much attention to what their kids are watching. They don't seem to be taking our findings very seriously. That's frustrating. It seems that every day, another letter comes in about another conference on television violence, or asking us to edit or review a new book on violence, or asking us what we think about the subject . . . but the real question is, "Hasn't anyone been listening?" "Why do some parents still allow their kids to watch violent television programs knowing that long term exposure to such shows can harm their children? That's what's frustrating.

Surprisingly, when asked to recall the biggest challenge and most memorable moments of her long and distinguished career, Singer did not reflect on a particularly arduous research project, or a book that was difficult to write. Instead, the answer came to her immediately and was the same for both questions.

The biggest challenge was raising three children and maintaining good relationships with each of them. The career was secondary until they were grown, and the most important thing about trying to do both was having a supportive and loving husband. I think it's hard for women to have a successful career and spend enough time with their children. It can be done, but you really need to remember that it's more important to worry about whether your children are happy and healthy than whether or not your house is spotless. . . . Getting tenure at Manhattanville and teaching there was a great beginning, and getting my first book published was memorable, but nothing will ever compare to the important moments I've shared with my family.

Still, Dorothy Singer's impact on the worlds of psychology, television, and education is indisputable. She has left a legacy of elegant research that has helped the world better understand the effects of television on children, and she has left an indelible impression on countless students across four decades. Many of her former students have acquired Ph.D.s of their own and gone on to professorships and research positions across the country. Others continue to line up to staff the Yale Family Television Research and Consultation Center with hopes of getting an invitation to join Singer on her latest project or acquiring her assistance as their senior essay adviser.

Since Dorothy Singer prides herself most as an educator, perhaps it is appropriate to sum up her career with the words of a former student and co-worker in his 1992 nomination of Singer for Yale's most prestigious undergraduate teaching award:

During the course of a four-year education at Yale, a student has the privilege of meeting and working with many excellent educators; some famous for their knowledge of a particular field or discipline, and others famous for the interest they take in the lives of their individual students. Once or twice in a lifetime, however, a student has the great fortune of meeting a professor who exemplifies both of these qualities simultaneously, who makes an indelible impact and forever alters that student's life and the course of his study and interests . . . and this is Dorothy Singer.

Truer words were never spoken. I know. I wrote them.

REFERENCES

Books

Singer, D. G. (1993). *Playing for their lives: Helping troubled children through play therapy.* New York: The Free Press.

Singer, D. G., & Revenson, T. (1978). *A Piaget primer: How a child thinks.* New York: International Universities Press and New American Library. (New edition, July 1996, Penguin Books.)

Singer, D. G., & Singer, J. L. (1990). *The house of make believe: Children's play and the developing imagination.* Cambridge, Mass.: Harvard University Press.

Singer, D. G., Singer, J. L., & Zuckerman, D. M. (1990). *The parent's guide: Use TV to your child's advantage.* Reston, Va.: Acropolis Books.

Publications

Singer, D. G. (1982). Television and the developing imagination of the child. In D. Pearl, L. Bouthilet, & J. Lazar (eds.), *Television and behavior: Ten years of scientific progress and implications for the eighties.* Vol. 2. (pp. 39–52). Washington, D.C.: National Institute of Mental Health.

Singer, D. G. (1986). The development of imagination in early childhood: Foundations of play therapy. In R. Van der Kooij & J. Hellendoorn (eds.), *Play, play therapy, play research: proceedings of the International Symposium Amsterdam.* (pp. 89–99). The Netherlands: Swets & Zeitlinger.

Singer, D. G. (1993). Creativity of children in a television world. In G. L. Berry & J. K. Asamen (eds.), *Children & television: Images in a changing sociocultural world.* (pp. 73–88). Newbury Park, Calif.: Sage Publications.

Singer, D. G. (1993). Fantasy and visualization. In C. E. Schaefer (ed.), *The therapeutic powers of play.* (pp. 189–221). Northvale, N.J.: Jason Aronson Inc.

Singer, D. G., Cohen, P., & Tower, R. (1978). A developmental study of animistic thinking: Preschoolers through the elderly. In R. Weitzmann, R. Brown, P. J. Levinson, & P. A. Taylor (eds.), *Piagetian Theory and the Helping Professions, Seventh Annual Conference.* Los Angeles: U.S.C.

Singer, D. G., & Singer, J. L. (1992). Television influences. In L. R. Williams & D. P. Fromberg (eds.), *Encyclopedia of early childhood education.* (pp. 374–377). New York: Garland.

Singer, D. G. & Singer, J. L. (1994). Evaluating the classroom viewing of a television series: "Degrassi Junior High." In D. Zillmann, J. Bryant, & A. C. Huston (eds.), *Media, children and the family.* (pp. 97–115). Hillsdale, N.J.: Lawrence Erlbaum Associates Publishers.

Magazine Columns and Television Film Productions

Singer, D. G., & Singer, J. L. (1981). "Getting the most out of television" Videotapes. Eugene, OR: New Dimension Films, 85895 Lorane Highway, 97405.

Singer D. G., & Singer, J. L. (1994–1995). *Barney Family Magazine.* Columns for parents about child development. New York City: Welsh Publishing Group, Inc.

GLORIA M. STEINEM
(1934–   )

Johnna M. Moyer

The name Gloria Steinem is synonymous with many different roles: daughter; feminist; accomplished public speaker; prolific publisher; and writer. The roles she has played and continues to play have shaped not only her own life but also the lives of women and men who have read her work or have heard her speak. Her convictions concerning equality have forever changed the landscape on which both men and women work and live.

FAMILY BACKGROUND

Gloria Steinem was born in Toledo, Ohio, on March 25, 1934. Her paternal grandmother, Pauline, headed a women's suffrage group and also acted as a representative at the 1908 International Council of Women. Her father, Leo Steinem, ran his summer resort during the summer months and, during the off-season, traveled the roads, selling antiques from his car. Her mother, Ruth Nuneviller Steinem, worked as a reporter. Gloria has one sister, Susanne Steinem Patch, 9 years her senior, who is both a gemologist and a lawyer. Susanne has one daughter and five sons.

Gloria's parents were very different from each other. Her father, Leo, although from a middle-class family, never finished college. He prided himself on his self-employment which, unfortunately, did not bring in enough money to take care of his family or his household. Described by Gloria as "cavalier," he did not worry about money or the bills getting paid, always hiding from possible bill collectors. Her father died in 1962.

In comparison, Ruth's upbringing made her insecure about money. Her family worked the railroad, which did not provide a lot of income. As a result, Gloria remembers her mother being constantly worried about money. She would squirrel away every bit of change she could, keeping it in empty ketchup and mustard jars. Ruth's upbringing also informed her belief about the importance of education. Her mother saved to send her and her sister to college; Ruth herself graduated from Oberlin College and also obtained a teaching certificate. Ruth honored her mother's tradition in raising her own two daughters by either saving or using money from the sale of real estate to send them to college.

When Gloria turned 10, her parents separated, and in 1945 they divorced. Gloria and her mother first moved to Massachusetts to be with her sister, Susanne, while she finished college. They then moved to Ruth's hometown, East Toledo. During this period, Ruth became increasingly withdrawn. Family members feared that she was again "sick," having spent some time in a sanitorium when Gloria was first born. Her mental illness increased, which eventually landed her in a Baltimore hospital where she could receive the help that she needed. Gloria's mother eventually died in 1981, just shy of her eighty-second birthday.

EDUCATION

As a result of Leo's "gypsy" lifestyle, Gloria did not attend elementary school on a full-time basis until she reached the sixth grade. She considers herself lucky in that respect, because the school system did not have the opportunity to "brainwash" her. In the interim, her education lay in books—any book she could get her hands on. Her father and mother fed her hunger for books—young girl novels, adult novels, feminist novels, political novels—by buying them at auctions. Gloria escaped into these books, which she described as being a much better fate than being stuck at school. For example, she recounts an incident where a teacher's disbelief about Gloria's writing ability put an end to her poetry. These types of experiences, however, could not extinguish her love for books.

After graduating from Western High School in 1952, Gloria set her sights on Smith College, majoring in government. According to Gloria, she accomplished every child's goal: attending college was the only way to escape the "working-class neighborhood" which served as her home. While in college, she traveled extensively. During her junior year, she visited Geneva and also spent a summer in Oxford. Gloria also satisfied her love for dance by dancing in college shows. She graduated from Smith in 1956 with many honors: Phi Beta Kappa; magna cum laude; and a Chester Bowles Fellowship to India.

CAREER DEVELOPMENT

Gloria's life experiences provided her a foundation from which she wrote and spoke. Her trip to India gave her a sense of the stark differences in lifestyles and made her realize that India's, not the United States', lifestyle was more representative of those throughout the rest of the world. Posing as a Playboy Bunny gave her the sense of outrage against people's views of women. She was continuously turned down for writing assignments that had any meaning for her and, instead was assigned to what her editors considered topics more fitting a woman writer. For example, Gloria wrote about various celebrities, such as Paul Newman and Joanne Woodward, but was asked to change the slant on that article when she dared to suggest that Joanne Woodward had power in the relationship. The lowest point of her writing career, however, came in the form of an article espousing the virtues of textured stockings. When *Show* magazine published her exposé on Playboy Bunnies, Gloria could only see its negative effects: it overshadowed an *Esquire* article covering the contraceptive revolution; she lost an opportunity to investigate the United States Information Agency to uncover its misrepresentations to other countries about the United States; finally, someone suggested she go undercover as a call girl and then write an article on prostitution. It wasn't until the pervasiveness of feminism that Gloria viewed the article as a vehicle to inform the public about the glamorous myth of the Playboy Club and its "exploitative employment" practices.

In 1968 Gloria's personal interest combined with her writing as a contributing editor of *New York* magazine. She wrote about a myriad of subjects, such as Martin Luther King, Jr.'s assassination, politicians' trips to other countries, and Vietnam veterans. Gloria concludes that, finally, "[she] wasn't writing about one thing, while caring about something else."

These experiences fueled her passion for the subject of reproductive issues, among others, that signaled her interest in feminism and politics. Her newfound interest, however, did not win her the support of her male counterparts. Rather, she became all the more aware about the unfairness of being the only woman reporter among men. From all this was born her sense of feminism. When avenues to write about feminism were blocked, she turned to public speaking, which was not easy for her. She joined forces with Dorothy Pitman, Florence Kennedy, and Margaret Sloan, all of whom helped her lose her fear of public speaking. She recalls one of her mentors, Florence Kennedy, telling her during one speech: "If you're lying in the ditch with a truck on your ankle, you don't send someone to the library to find out how much it weighs. You get it off."

Gloria persevered and eventually worked through this fear. As a result, she learned three lessons about public speaking: "(1) you don't die; (2) there's no right way to speak, only your way; and (3) it's worth it. A mutual understanding can come from being in a room together, and a sense of character and intention can come through the television screen that could never happen on a printed page." This realization, however, did not prevent Gloria from expressing her views on the printed page, as evidenced by both her own numerous books and her various magazine articles.

MAJOR CONTRIBUTIONS AND ACHIEVEMENTS

Although Steinem wrote extensively in the 1950s and early 1960s, it wasn't until her 1963 article, "I Was a Playboy Bunny," published by *Show* magazine, that she earned a public identity as a writer. This article focused on the discrimination and humiliation heaped on women. It was not until 1968, however, with the founding of *New York* magazine, that Gloria's penchant for writing and personal interest in feminism combined. As one of its editors and political columnists, she had access to more meaningful writing assignments, such as covering the assassination of Martin Luther King, Jr.

A turning point in Gloria's career came when she covered an abortion hearing for *New York*. Hearing women testify about the indignities they suffered while seeking an abortion pushed her to examine her own experience with this matter on a more social, macro level. In her words: "Why should each of us be made to feel criminal and alone? How much power would we ever have if we had no power over the fate of our own bodies?" These questions led Gloria to publish an article in 1969 entitled "After Black Power, Women's Liberation," which won her the Penney-Missouri Journalism Award in 1970.

Steinem's feminist writing led to sporadic, limited opportunities to publish similar works, such as an article exploring the possibility of a woman president for *Look* magazine. These limited publishing opportunities, coupled with her growing public speaking career and negative reaction from colleagues regarding the abortion article, led to the birth of *Ms.* magazine in 1972. This magazine "for, by, and about women" catered to women's definition of feminism: "the equality and full humanity of women and men."

Despite these achievements, Gloria points to the 1977 National Women's Conference to assist in the writing of a resolution concerning women and their issues as the high point of her writing career. As she looked out over the sea of faces representing every minority, color, and nationality, acting in concert to accept one representative resolution, a pride welled within her which equaled the pride she feels when she sees her own viewpoints in print. And print she did. Her books *Outrageous Acts and Everyday Rebellions* (1983, 1995), *Revolution from Within: A Book of Self-Esteem* (1992), and *Moving Beyond Words* (1994) chronicle her public and private journeys as a feminist and have earned her acclaim throughout the world.

Her writing did not interfere with her public speaking, and the exposure she received as a result of her achievements opened the door to various speaking engagements. Traveling the country with Dorothy Pitman, Florence Kennedy, and Margaret Sloan afforded her a platform on which she could espouse those ideas reflected in her writing and hear other women's and men's views on various subjects that affected them. For example, Gloria remembers a train conductor denying Dorothy access to a certain train car because of her skin color. She also recalls Margaret blocking a man who attempted to storm the platform in protest of their message of equality. She also remembers auditoriums filled to capacity with both men and women clapping and laughing at the ridiculousness of sexual politics. Gloria continues to pursue her writing and speaking, traveling sometimes alone, sometimes with others, always with a goal of self-discovery or helping others to discover their full potential by knocking down those barriers that block their, and her own, success.

CRITICAL EVALUATION OF CONTRIBUTIONS AND ACHIEVEMENTS

Through the years, there have been as many reviews of Gloria's work as there are critics. Her first book, *Outrageous Acts and Everyday Rebellions* (1983, 1995), a collection of essays, received mixed reviews. Angela Carter of the *Washington Post* for example, wonders about Gloria's purpose. In speaking about Steinem's article "I Was a Playboy Bunny," Carter questions why she would "regret" having written such a piece laden with feminist consciousness. These types of pieces, Carter argues, more thoroughly represent feminism than other, less worthy articles published by *Ms.* magazine. Says Carter, "[Steinem writes] 'Now, we are becoming the men we wanted to marry.' Speak for yourself, Gloria. I'd hope to do better than that!" Carter also opines that the collection of essays lacks a precise focus on women's history and the economic factors that affected and continue to affect them.

Leah Fritz, in her December 1983 review of the same book, has a different interpretation. To her, its message is clear: "How far we have come—and how much further we need to go—is the central message" (Matuz, 1991). She understands Steinem's desire to make feminism more popular and more accessible through her essays, but, in doing so, Fritz notes that her tendency to "tidy images" may accomplish this goal only in the short run. She senses that Steinem's "cautiousness" arises from her political viewpoints. Fritz feels Steinem should think about a more long-term view: accentuating women's divorce from ladylike "norms" may make them stronger to withstand possible future hostile reactions. This, however, does not prevent Steinem's work from being an effective statement on feminism. Fritz applauds her attacks on religion, the right-wing view of the family, and the romantic view of marriage. Fritz comments, however, that it will take another book to make more clear the path to follow to become as effective a feminist as Steinem.

That second book came with *Revolution from Within: A Book of Self-Esteem* (1992), and it elicited the same wary comments that critics voiced to *Outrageous Acts*. For instance, Deirdre English of the *New York Times* notes in her February 1992 review that while an inner journey for self-esteem is important, she wonders whether Gloria's journey will bring her back out to rejoin her feminist cause. English concedes that self-help techniques, such as meditation, may help a woman to become stronger to stand against a male-dominated world. "What is disturbing is to see the empowering therapy supplant the cause. . . . It isn't that Ms. Steinem has forgotten about sexism, but strangely, she has forgotten to get angry about it." This practice, English cautions, presents a new problem: women now have one more barrier, a lack of self-esteem, to knock down in order to pursue their dreams.

Susan Lee (1992) expresses no doubts concerning her feelings about the book in her March 1992 review. She writes, "as bad as Ms. Steinem's best-selling book is, it is hard not to feel some admiration, even fondness for the author."

At the same time, however, she chides Steinem for seemingly practicing "pop psychology" in its pages. She criticizes Steinem's pages of private stories and confessions that aided her voyage to self-discovery. The driving force behind Lee's criticism seems to be her belief that whatever is private should remain so.

The title of Gloria's most recent book, *Moving Beyond Words* (1994), echoes a sentiment placed on the pages of an article she wrote in 1972: "I have met brave women who are exploring the outer edge of human possibility, with no history to guide them, and with a courage to make themselves vulnerable that I find moving beyond the words to express it." Maureen Corrigan (1994) writes that these most recent essays "demystify" what appears to be natural and shows it for what it is: "social construction." As evidence for this thesis, she points to "What if Freud were Phyllis?" in which Steinem reverses Sigmund Freud's sex and makes commentary from a woman's viewpoint. Corrigan commends Gloria's denunciation of Freud's comments on female sexuality, but criticizes the essay for its lack of "nuance." It seems that Corrigan finds the other essays a bit lacking. For example, she criticizes Steinem's choice of a subject for "The Strongest Woman in the World" as too "idiosyncratic . . . to bear the weight of the stereotype-defying symbolism [she] wants to place on her." Despite her criticism, Corrigan does find a message in this most recent book: "women should grow less willing to conform to the 'tyrannies of the social expectation.' "

Although there are many opinions concerning Gloria Steinem's books, the importance of her work to furthering the feminist movement cannot be denied. She brought to the forefront the idea and the word of feminism and made them less frightening to a public that seemed ready to embrace its ideology. She did not, however, stop there. Sharing her own personal struggles both as a feminist and a woman in her work added a humanistic element and let the public know that the struggle existed on both a macro and micro level.

INTEGRATION OF PERSONAL AND PROFESSIONAL LIFE

If anything can be said about Gloria Steinem, it is that her professional life is her personal life. Every step she took along her path to awareness or every lesson that she learned along that path became a lesson or step that she shares through her writing and her public speaking with those who wished to listen. She realizes, however, that these lessons are not learned, nor are these steps taken in a vacuum. Through her travels and her writing, she has been not only the teacher but also the student. She learns from all the different experiences the of all the different women whom she meets, and these experiences help to make ever clear the next step to take or the next lesson to be learned. "The odd thing about these deep and personal connections of women is that they often ignore barriers of age, economics, worldly experience, race, culture—all the barriers that, in male or mixed society, had seemed so difficult to cross."

REFERENCES

Buck, C. (1992). *The Bloomsbury guide to women's literature*. New York: Prentice-Hall General Reference.

Corrigan, M. (1994, May 22). I, Gloria: Essays on feminism by an icon of the women's movement. *New York Times Book Review*.

English, D. (1992, February 2). She's her weakness now. *New York Times Book Review*.

Lee, S. (1992, March 6). Feminist leader offers true confessions. *The Wall Street Journal*.

Matuz, R. (ed.). (1991). *Contemporary literary criticism*. Vol. 63. Detroit: Gale Research.

May, H., and Lesniak, G. (eds.). (1990). *Contemporary authors*. Vol. 28. Detroit: Gale Research.

McPhee, C., and FitzGerald, A. (1979). *Feminist quotations: Voices of rebels, reformers, and visionaries*. New York: Thomas Y. Crowell.

Silbert, P. (1993, March 17). Transcript of Tape Oral History Project. New York.

Steinem, G. (1983). *Outrageous Acts and Everyday Rebellions*. New York: Holt, Rinehart, & Winston; 2d ed. (1995), H. Holt.

Steinem, G. (1992). *Revolution from within: A book of self-esteem*. Boston: Little, Brown & Co.

Steinem, G. (1994). *Moving beyond words*. New York: Simon & Schuster.

IDA MINERVA TARBELL (1857–1944)

Amy Sarch

Ida Minerva Tarbell, journalist, editor, and historian, is best known as a "muckraker" through her articles on political and corporate corruption published in *McClure's* magazine. While other women of her generation chained themselves to the White House fence fighting for women's suffrage, Tarbell immersed herself in the traditional male world of business and politics. She developed a reputation as an expert on industrial tariffs and established mutual working relationships with Presidents Grover Cleveland, Woodrow Wilson, and Herbert Hoover. Although male leaders and editors valued Tarbell's contributions, Florence Kelly, Jane Addams, and other feminist pioneers accused Tarbell of betraying the cause of women. She became president of The Pen and Brush, a club composed of female artists and writers, but generally felt that women's groups, as well as women's fight for suffrage, were a waste of time. Indeed, Tarbell's career and lifestyle appear paradoxical—she was a single, powerful, progressive career woman who overtly believed that women belonged in their traditional role as mother, wife, and homemaker. Tarbell does not fit neatly into any category; she is classified as muckraker but not as a feminist. Both "muckraker" and "feminist" defy neat definitions, and Tarbell's reputation suffers as a result. Ida Minerva Tarbell's professional accomplishments challenge semantic borders and point to a woman who dared the expectations of her profession and her gender.

FAMILY BACKGROUND AND EDUCATION

In 1857 President James Buchanan gave his inaugural address, the Supreme Court handed down the Dred Scott decision, and young couples like Franklin and Esther Tarbell planned a life out west with land and a house of their own.

Franklin, a teacher, farmer, river pilot, and carpenter, left for Iowa in the spring of 1857 and arranged for his wife to join him after he secured land. The Panic of 1857 halted the construction of the railway, dried up Iowa's money supply, and prevented Franklin from seeing his first child, Ida, born on November 5, 1857 in Erie County, Pennsylvania. Franklin walked from Iowa to Pennsylvania and reunited with his wife and child 18 months later. The Tarbells still planned to move west, but freshly tapped oil wells of Northwestern, Pennsylvania, lured Franklin into the oil business. The oil market held many promises for a profitable future and became the mainstay of the Tarbell family's life.

Ida was the oldest of four children, but lost her youngest brother to scarlet fever when she was 11. Most of her childhood revolved around her father's independent oil business and her mother's active interest in the women's rights movement. She sympathized deeply with her father's struggles against a growing monopoly in the oil business and helped her mother receive women's rights activists Mary Livermore and Frances Willard into their home. At 15 years of age, Ida felt more sympathy for the independent oil producer's crusade than for the women's fight for suffrage. She noted that the visiting male lecturers talked to her as "a person," while the women treated her as merely a possible member of a society they were promoting.

Both the fight for women's rights and the fight against an oil monopoly convinced Ida that independence was invaluable. Franklin and Esther's struggles gave Ida the tools and courage to believe that she deserved a right to an education and a right to earn her own living. She considered marriage an obstacle to freedom and graduated from high school determined never to marry. "I didn't quite know what freedom meant," she explained, "certainly I was far from realizing that it exists only in the spirit, never in human relations, never in human activities—that the road to it is as often as not what men call bondage. But above all I must be free; and to be free I must be a spinster" (Tarbell, 1939, p. 36). Ida believed that a married woman belonged at home with her family, so the only way for a woman to remain free was to remain single. Marriage and a career were two separate paths, and Ida felt that a woman should choose one or the other but never combine them.

Ida was part of the first generation of women to attend college and entered Allegheny College in Meadville, Pennsylvania, in the fall of 1876. She was the only female in her class and in the beginning felt she was an "invader" to the college's "spirit of masculinity" (Tarbell, 1939, p. 40). Ida compared her feelings to the emotions Virginia Woolf expressed in *A Room of One's Own* when she was barred from the college green at Oxbridge. "It was not so simple to find a spot where you could go and be comfortable," Ida remarked (Tarbell, 1939, pp. 40–41). The isolation she felt during her first year yielded under the increasing number of women attending Allegheny. The class of 1880 elected a woman president, and half of its officers were female. When Ida graduated in the spring of 1880, the early masculine prohibitions were a thing of the past.

CAREER DEVELOPMENT

Like most college women of her generation, Ida's first job out of college was as a teacher. She received a two-year appointment as preceptress of the Poland Union Seminary in August 1880 at an annual salary of $500. She taught geology, botany, geometry, trigonometry, as well as two classes in each of four languages—Greek, Latin, French, and German. Ida found the work unrewarding, and she left when her contract ended in 1882. She returned home and was offered a job as an annotator for *The Chautauquan,* a monthly magazine established as part of a popular correspondence program run by Chautauqua Literary and Scientific Circle. The program offered an equivalent to four years of college, and the magazine, *The Chautauquan,* provided contact between students and course leaders. It is here that Ida learned writing and editing skills which served as a basis for her later career as an editor of *McClure's* and *The American Magazine.*

Tarbell began her investigative reporting career at *The Chautauquan* with an inquiry into the number of women who had obtained patents since the Patent Office in Washington opened in 1802. In "Women and Inventors" (March 1887), she used detailed facts to counter the "calculated belittling" of women's achievements by suffragists (Tarbell, 1939, p. 75). Suffragists highlighted an article published in *The Chautauquan* that reported women had taken out only 300 patents in order to make their point that men excluded women from the public arena. Tarbell argued that suffragists discounted women's past advances to arouse action for their cause and found that the number of women who obtained patents was misreported. She discovered that 1,935 patents were issued to women since the year the Patent Office opened and most were for household appliances. Ida considered the making of a home to be the "most delicate, complex, and essential of creative tasks" (Tarbell, 1939, p. 75); her definition of creativity differed from that of militant feminists whose central issue was equality in the male domain. Ida maintained that "man-made world or not, if a woman had a good idea and the gumption to seek a patent she had the same chance as a man to get one" (Tarbell, 1939, pp. 75–76).

Tarbell espoused the view that a woman's place was at home; yet she never married and she lived her life through her career. At 32 years of age, Ida left for Paris to pursue a free-lance journalism career and conduct research on the life of Madame Roland, a French Revolutionary heroine. Despite the friends who bid her farewell with warnings like, "Remember you are past thirty. Women don't make new places for themselves after thirty" (Tarbell, 1939, p. 85), Ida Tarbell established herself as a journalist and biographer.

Tarbell continually questioned women's role in society throughout her career and conducted research on Madame Roland's life to clarify her own belief that women play important placating roles in public life, particularly in times of stress. She hoped to find that Madame Roland was "no party to violence." Instead, she discovered that "this woman had been one of the steadiest influ-

ences to violence, willing, even eager, to use this terrible revolutionary force"
(Tarbell, 1939, p. 143). Ida concluded that Madame Roland was motivated by
her love of two powerful men and generalized that it was "eternal and necessary
natural law that a woman backs up her man" (Tarbell, 1939, p. 143). Fifteen
years after publication, she admitted that she may have been too harsh on her
subject: "You see I started out thinking I had an impeccable heroine and I
found *qu'une pauvre femme* ['only a poor woman'] and I fear I took it out on
her rather stiffly" (quoted in Brady, 1984, p. 78).

Ida's biography of Madame Roland was not published until after she began
her successful business relationship with Sam McClure. McClure had read an
article Ida sent through McClure's newspaper syndicate and made a special
detour in Paris to meet her. Ida declined the job he offered, but agreed to work
as a freelancer while remaining in Paris. Two months after Ida left Paris in the
summer of 1894, she received an urgent letter from McClure requesting that she
write a biography of Napoleon Bonaparte.

MAJOR CONTRIBUTIONS AND ACHIEVEMENTS

From 1895 to 1897 *McClure's* magazine received more advertising patronage
than any magazine in the world, and Ida's series on Napoleon produced and
secured *McClure's* lead. Sam McClure published a magazine that was comparable to class magazines, like the *Century,* but that sold for the same price as
lower quality magazines, such as *Munsey's Magazine.* Printing technology was
rapidly changing, and innovations in illustration reproduction and the development of cheap glazed paper made low production costs possible and price competition feasible. After Ida's first article on Napoleon debuted in November
1894, *McClure's* circulation rose from 24,500 to 65,000. Magazine readership
increased to 100,000 by the time the Napoleon series ended in April 1895, and
almost every issue sold out. *McClure's* was the first magazine to set firm advertising rates, and by the late 1890s, Sam McClure guaranteed advertisers a
circulation of at least a quarter million.

The Napoleon series gave *McClure's* the circulation boost it needed, and it
established Ida Tarbell as an accomplished writer. The series received critical
acclaim from a small group of Bonaparte scholars and newspaper reviewers.
The *Boston Globe* stated that Tarbell's Napoleon biography "recognized the
scientific spirit of modern historical criticism, and is firsthand and attractive in
style" (quoted in Brady, 1984, p. 91). *McClure's* published a book edition of
The Short Life of Napoleon that immediately followed the series' conclusion in
the magazine. Ida later added a short biography of Josephine Bonaparte and
included it in the book's second edition. Over 40 years after the biography first
appeared in book form, Ida expressed surprise that she still received an annual
royalty check. The biography provided her with financial stability as well as a
"sense of vitality, of adventure, of excitement . . . of being admitted on terms

of equality and good comradeship into the McClure crowd'' (Tarbell, 1939, p. 153).

Tarbell considered herself an "unusually lucky woman" to be accepted as a member of *McClure's* staff and found the place "so warmly and often ridiculously human" (Tarbell, 1939, p. 159, 160). A *McClure's* staffer recalled her obedience to Sam McClure's demands:

One little thing that I marveled at in those days was that she could mobilize just as swiftly as any lad in the place—could accept a decision at noon to start for Chicago that night without turning a hair. I suppose there have been other females like that . . . but she is the only one I ever saw keep it right along; thereby in her case wiping out one good ground for paying women less than men. (Quoted in Brady, 1984, p. 95)

Tarbell's career was only beginning, and her gender never prevented her success. McClure recognized Ida's notoriety with the magazine's readers and further exercised Ida's talents to ensure the magazine's continuing popularity.

The Napoleon biography built an auspicious reputation for Ida that convinced Charles Scribner to consider publishing Madame Roland's biography—a subject that lacked popular appeal. Scribner, believing that the Tarbell signature would attract readers, published *Madame Roland* in 1895. Although today's critics claim that Madame Roland is "superior in depth and complexity" to Napoleon, it never received the same following as Tarbell's other works. Ida remarked that her reward for writing it came form her interest in doing it and certainly not in the royalties (Tarbell, 1939, p. 153; Tomkins, 1974, p. 37).

Ida was fascinated by French history and so dreaded her next assignment: a biography of Abraham Lincoln. American history did not interest her, but she enjoyed the economic security that *McClure's Magazine* offered and therefore chose security over creative freedom. *McClure's* followed the lead of *Century Magazine,* which published an abridged version of *Abraham Lincoln: A History* by John G. Nicolay and John Hay. *Century* completed the series in 1890, but McClure envisioned a wider market for Lincoln's legend; established Lincoln scholars did not share McClure's vision. John Nicolay viewed Tarbell as an invader too young to enter his field and believed that allowing a "girl" to write a Lincoln biography was absurd (Tomkins, 1974, p. 44). Tarbell plowed ahead undaunted and became the first of a new generation to interpret Lincoln's life. Previous biographers knew Lincoln or lived adult lives during his presidency, and their bias for or against Lincoln distorted their works.

Tarbell's series on the *Life of Lincoln* detailed Lincoln's life through his election as president and ran in *McClure's* from November 1895 to November 1896. The series proved extremely popular and prompted a second one which followed Lincoln's presidency through his assassination and ran from December 1898 through September 1899. Lincoln's son, Robert, donated his father's papers to the Library of Congress with the condition that they not to be opened until 21 years after Robert's death. He died in 1926 and so the papers were not available until 1947. Despite this handicap, Tarbell found over 300 previously uncollected documents and an unpublished daguerreotype of Lincoln that shattered a widely accepted tradition of Lincoln's shabby appearance. Ida found documents that proved prevalent legends false and commented, "a biographer who tries to break down a belittling legend meets with far less sympathy than he who strengthens or creates one" (Tarbell, 1939, p. 174). The Lincoln biography shattered some standard tales but replaced them with the myth of the Anglo-American frontiersman who was born to save the American Union (Tomkins, 1974, p. 46). *The Life of Abraham Lincoln* was published in two volumes in 1900 and received high critical acclaim. A review in *The Nation* stated that the new facts and Tarbell's interpretation added a fresh dimension to Lincoln studies (in Tomkins, 1974, p. 49). The editor of the *New York Sun* heralded *The Life of Abraham Lincoln* as one of the ten foremost books for Americans to read (Brady, 1984, p. 106).

IDA TARBELL—MUCKRAKER

Tarbell's reputation as a biographer and editor of *McClure's Magazine* was firmly established before the term *muckraker* was introduced into the English language. Tarbell and the other members of the *McClure's* writing staff, Lincoln Steffens and Ray Standard Baker, initiated changes in the magazine that reflected and criticized the country's changes at the turn of the century. The Spanish-American War provided *McClure's* with a steady stream of articles that kept the magazine part of active, public life. "Having tasted blood," Ida remarked, "[*McClure's*] could no longer be content with being merely attractive and readable" (Tarbell, 1939, p. 196). President Theodore Roosevelt labeled this bloody approach "muckraking."

Roosevelt first used the term in 1906 during a speech directed at an organization of reporters that sought to encourage cooperation between public officials and the press. Frustrated and disgusted by the scandalous newspapers of William Randolph Hearst, Roosevelt condemned crusading journalists for encouraging the public to believe that all crimes were connected with business and politics. Roosevelt's public speech made no distinction between Hearst's tabloid journalism and *McClure's* investigative reporting, though privately he admitted that his speech only referred to Hearst. Nevertheless, newspapers and magazines carried Roosevelt's speech and linked Steffens, Baker, and Tarbell to Roosevelt's label. The speech compared reporters to the man with a "muckrake" in John Bunyan's *Pilgrim's Progress* who concentrated so hard on the dirt at his feet that he lost sight of the "celestial crown." "There are beautiful things around him," Roosevelt stated, "and if they gradually grow to feel like their whole world is nothing but muck, their power of usefulness is gone" (quoted in Brady, 1984, p. 175). Despite Roosevelt's intentions, the public and the press interpreted the meaning of the term *muckraker* as a condemnation of *McClure's* journalists.

Tarbell, Steffens, and Baker led a new school of journalism that thrived in the Progressive Era: the time period between the turn of the century and World War I when reformers advocated that the government should protect its citizens from corrupt private business. They published a flood of articles that exposed dirty political and corporate practices and challenged American democratic optimism. An abundance of monopolistic trusts arose after the Spanish-American War ended, which appeared to threaten the democratic philosophy of free opportunity and free competition. Roosevelt agreed that the abuses of the trusts needed serious attention, but he feared that if journalists encouraged the public to hate business, quality of life would only get worse. Sam McClure noted that Americans felt threatened by trusts, yet they knew little about them. The idea to write a story of a typical trust grew, and Ida Tarbell brought the *History of the Standard Oil Company* (1925) to life.

THE HISTORY OF THE STANDARD OIL COMPANY

In early 1872 oil profits declined when the railroads raised shipping rates 100 percent. Independent oil producers, like Ida's father, Franklin Tarbell, learned that the South Improvement Company obtained illegal rebates from the railroads, while making the independents pay extraordinary fees. John D. Rockefeller of the Standard Oil Company manipulated the South Improvement scheme and strategically swallowed his independent competitors. Ida stated that she began her investigation with an open mind, not sure that Rockefeller broke the law. However, she personally lived through the effects Rockefeller had on her family—Standard's oil monopoly forced Franklin Tarbell to mortgage his home in 1893—and her moral outrage is apparent in her historical account. *The History of the Standard Oil Company* is certainly well documented; she includes over 300 pages of official documents and transcripts of court testimony. The conflict between independent oil producers and the Standard Oil Company reads as a moral struggle that reeks of privilege and unfair corruption. Tarbell concluded that the Standard Oil Company unfairly dominated the oil industry by illegally controlling oil transportation: Standard received illegal rebates and drawbacks from the railroad that allowed them to monopolize the oil business. "As I saw it," Ida stated in her autobiography, "it was not capitalism but an open disregard of decent ethical business practices" (Tarbell, 1939, p. 206).

The History of the Standard Oil Company first appeared in a 17-article series in *McClure's*. The series began in November 1902 and ended in October 1904. The book was published soon after the last article appeared in the series, and it became Ida Tarbell's legacy. Reviewers called *The History of the Standard Oil Company* "the most remarkable book of its kind ever written in this country" (quoted in Brady, 1984, p. 152). The *New York Times* said, "as readable as any 'story' with rather more romance than the usual business novel . . . honest the writer has tried to be to both sides of the controversies" (quoted in Brady, 1984,

p. 152). Newspapers across the country printed glowing reviews, along with Tarbell's picture and a short biography.

Tarbell's *History of the Standard Oil Company* had long-ranging effects apart from its reputation among fellow journalists. The government filed a petition against Standard Oil in 1906 that charged the company with conspiring to monopolize trade by securing rebates from railroads and a range of other illegal activity Tarbell documented in her book. The case reached the Supreme Court in 1911, and the Standard Oil Company was dissolved.

Tarbell and her fellow "muckrakers" stirred public opinion and moral outrage that dictated many government reforms during Theodore Roosevelt's administration. The Hepburn Act of 1906, for example, gave the government more efficient control over railroad rates. But once reforms came into effect, readers became saturated with the political and corporate dirt that reporters continually uncovered. The muckraking tradition continued and flourished in novels like Upton Sinclair's *The Jungle* (1926), but monthly exposés lacked their initial shock value and magazines like *McClure's* lost circulation.

IDA TARBELL—MUCKRAKER?

Tarbell, Steffens, and Baker brought *McClure's* to the height of its popularity, but a rift with Sam McClure led them to purchase *The American Magazine* in 1906 and compete against their former employer. The atmosphere at *The American* never quite resembled *McClure's* ground-breaking spirit. The *American* staff still investigated corruption, but they also tried to concentrate on the more positive aspects of private business. Ida stated that the magazine had "a large and fighting interest in fair play . . . but it sought to present things as they were, not as somebody thought they should be" (Tarbell, 1939, p. 281). The "muckraking" label did not represent the type of journalism in which Tarbell and the others believed. "We were classed as muckrakers," Ida stated, "and the school had been so commercialized that the public was beginning to suspect it. The truth of the matter was that . . . the muckraking school . . . had lost the passion for facts in a passion for subscriptions" (Tarbell, 1939, pp. 298–299). Although Ida distinguished between her investigative reporting and tabloid journalism, her reading public never made that distinction.

History books, encyclopedias, and dictionaries categorize Ida Tarbell as a muckraker, and *History of the Standard Oil Company* is the only work they mention (see Davis, 1990, a *New York Times* best-seller). *The American Heritage Dictionary* (3rd ed.), for instance, defines Ida Tarbell as "American muckraking writer and editor remembered for her investigations of industry, including *History of the Standard Oil Company*." Ida feared that her classification as a "muckraker" diminished the legitimacy and quality of her historical research. Upon discussing the work that earned her muckraking title, Ida stated that she preferred to label herself as an historian and a journalist "intent on discovering what had gone into the making of this most perfect of all monopolies" (Tarbell 1939, p. 206).

Ida published numerous articles and books after Standard Oil, which included investigative work on tariffs (*The Tariff of Our Times*, 1911) and biographies of two powerful industrialists, Elbert H. Gary and Owen D. Young. President Wilson considered Tarbell a tariff expert and invited her to be a member of a tariff commission that he formed in 1916. Ida refused—"I was an observer and reporter," she said, "not a negotiator. I am not a good fighter in a group; I forget my duty in watching the contestants" (Tarbell, 1939, p. 278). Jane Addams begged Ida to accept the position "for the sake of women," but Ida stated that she "did not feel that women were served merely by an appointment to office. . . . I believed that harm is done all around by undertaking technical jobs without proper scientific training. The cause of women is not to be advanced by putting them into positions for which they are untrained" (Tarbell, 1939, p. 279).

IDA TARBELL—FEMINIST?

Tarbell did not support women's suffrage, and her outspoken views continually roused militant feminists. She was not convinced that women were superior to men and that women's vote would automatically strip the country of corruption and injustice. She viewed democracy as a spiritual faith and not something that could be achieved through laws alone. The spirit must be nurtured, deepened, and broadened along with laws and systems. Ida feared that women would substitute the law for the spirit. Part of women's work at home was to instill that spirit in their children and to keep the spirit of democracy alive. She believed that suffragists belittled women's work at home to further their cause and thereby threatened the essence of democracy.

Tarbell wrote a series of articles on women's nature for *The American Magazine* that culminated in the book, *The Business of Being a Woman* (1913), in which she passionately argued for the value and power of the homemaker. Women reformers interpreted Tarbell's insistence that women belong at home as antifeminist and ridiculed Tarbell behind her back. Jane Addams remarked that "there is some limitation to Ida Tarbell's mind," and Helen Keller, a militant suffragist, exclaimed that Ida was growing too old to understand the changing world (Brady, 1984, p. 203). Ida accepted a position as a member of the Woman's Committee of the Council of National Defense during World War I where she joined suffragists Anna Howard Shaw and Carrie Chapman Catt. Shaw led the Council and told Tarbell quite frankly that she resented Ida's activities.

The suffrage cause united women at the turn of the century—a cause that Tarbell rejected. Suffragists themselves were torn between the belief in distinct, separate spheres for men and women and demands for equality between the sexes, but the struggle to obtain women's vote outweighed fundamental differences. These differences surfaced in the fight for an Equal Rights Amendment in the 1920s. Many of the views Ida Tarbell expressed were similar to those voiced by reformers like Florence Kelley and Mary Anderson who believed that women were naturally weaker than men and that society should compensate for this inequality by passing laws that protected women. The major difference between Ida Tarbell and those considered feminists, like Florence Kelly, is that Ida Tarbell was never a reformer; she considered herself an observer, not an advocate of a cause or a system.

Ida supported a separate sphere for women, yet she spent most of her career investigating the political values associated with men. She strongly believed that men were responsible for politics and the public work of business, while women should develop their own separate, domestic sphere. The history of feminism is a history of ideological conflicts that Ida Tarbell's life brings to the surface— the conflict between those who believe women ought to have the *same opportunities* as men against the notion that society should enable women to be *different* from men. Can one woman espouse opposing beliefs? The answer, of course, is yes, but the question then becomes, can we label that one woman a feminist?

Marie Jenny Howe, reformer and suffragist, spoke at the first feminist mass meeting in 1914 at the Heterodoxy Club in Greenwich Village and posed the question, "What is feminism?" The answer, she asserted, was women's effort to gain entry into civilization and to experience the full range of activities that men enjoyed. Ida Tarbell certainly fits the definition of feminism that Howe offered, yet two years earlier Charlotte Perkins-Gilman rallied at the Metropolitan Temple in New York specifically against the views Ida expressed in her article, "Making a Man of Herself" (1912).

IDA TARBELL—AN EXERCISE IN SEMANTICS

Ida Tarbell's classification as a muckraker and feminist is an issue of great importance to communication scholars. Both labels encompass such a wide array of opinions that it is difficult to locate where or with whom the "true" label belongs. The term *muckraking* applied to the exposés published in Hearst's New York *Journal* and Tarbell's Standard Oil series. Can two opposing schools of journalism be included under one category, "muckraking"? Ida Tarbell lived the life traditionally associated with men in an era when such opportunities were not readily available to women—a life economically independent of a spouse and children and dictated by a career. Is that enough to earn her a feminist label? What does the label mean? How do we judge when the label fits? By what an individual says or does—which is more important? Tarbell's biographer, Kathleen Brady, summarizes Ida in terms of women's advancement as a "weather vane, not an engine of change" (Brady, 1984, p. 6). Can a woman be labeled a feminist without advocating for change?

Definitive answers are less important than the discussion that such questions raise. A review of Tarbell's life is an exercise in semantics where meanings of the terms *feminist* and *muckraker* come into question. The term *muckraker* is commonly applied to Ida Tarbell; in fact, her name is often used under the term's definition. Can we assert that the word is the person? Introductory Semantics textbooks suggest otherwise, that the word is not the thing. It is best to apply basic semantics to Ida Tarbell's biography and examine the *relationship* between Ida Tarbell's career and the words used to classify her achievements. The underlying assumption is that the categories "muckraker" and "feminist" cannot accurately represent Tarbell's achievements, nor can her achievements truly account for the complexity of these terms' meanings. We should examine the language that critics, historians, and journalists use when highlighting Ida Tarbell's accomplishments to tap into the process by which a cultural leader is constructed. This is not to deny or undermine the value of Ida Tarbell's contributions, but to indicate that the categories we apply to her work both reflect and direct Ida Tarbell's meaning and significance. Ida Minerva Tarbell was an investigative journalist who succeeded in a man's world—call her what you will.

REFERENCES

Brady, K. (1984). *Ida Tarbell: Portrait of a muckraker.* New York: Seaview/Putnam.
Chafe, W. H. (1991). *The paradox of change: American women in the 20th century.* New York: Oxford University Press.
Cott, N. (1990). Historical perspectives: The Equal Rights Amendment conflict in the 1920s. In M. Hirsch & E. F. Keller (eds.), *Conflicts in feminism.* (pp. 44–59). New York: Routledge.
Cott, N. F. (1987). *The grounding of modern feminism.* New Haven, Conn.: Yale University Press.
Davis, K. C. (1990). *Don't know much about history: Everything you need to know about American history but never learned.* New York: Avon Books.
Degler, C. (1980). *At Odds: Women and the family in America from the revolution to the present.* New York: Oxford University Press.
Dubois, E. C. (1978). *Feminism and suffrage: The emergence of an independent women's movement, 1848–1869.* Ithaca, N.Y.: Cornell University Press.
Rosenberg, R. (1992). *Divided lives: American women in the twentieth century.* New York: Hill & Wang.
Rothman, S. (1978). *Woman's proper place: A history of changing ideals and practices, 1870 to the present.* New York: Basic Books.
Sinclair, U. (1926). *The Jungle.* New York: Vanguard Press.
Tarbell, I. (March 1887). Women as inventors. *The Chautauquan,* 355–357.
Tarbell, I. (1895). *A short life of Napolean Bonaparte.* New York: S. S. McClure.
Tarbell, I. (1896). *Madame Roland: A biographical study.* New York: Scribner's.
Tarbell, I. (1900). *The life of Abraham Lincoln.* 2 vols. New York: S. S. McClure, 1904. Reissued in a one-volume edition including both volumes of the original edition. Gloucester, Mass.: Peter Smith, 1963.
Tarbell, I. (1911). *The tariff in our times.* New York: Macmillan.
Tarbell, I. (1912, Feb.). Making a man of herself. *The American magazine,* p. 430.

Tarbell, I. (1913). *The business of being a woman* New York: Macmillan.

Tarbell, I. (1915). *Ways of woman.* New York: Macmillan.

Tarbell, I. (1925). *The History of the Standard Oil Company.* New York: Macmillan.

Tarbell, I. (1925). *Life of Elbert H. Gary: The story of steel.* New York: Appleton.

Tarbell, I. (1932). *Owen D. Young: A new type of industrial leader.* New York: Macmillan.

Tarbell, I. (1939). *All in the day's work: An autobiography.* New York: Macmillan.

Tomkins, M. (1974). *Ida M. Tarbell.* New York: Twayne Publishers.

Weinberg, A., & Weinberg, L. (1961). *The muckrakers.* New York: Simon & Schuster.

Wilson, H. S. (1970). *McClure's magazine and the muckrakers.* Princeton, N.J.: Princeton University Press.

DOROTHY THOMPSON
(1893–1961)

James W. Tankard, Jr.

Dorothy Thompson was an American newspaper columnist who achieved celebrity status during the 1930s and 1940s. She was perhaps the major voice in the United States during the late 1930s speaking out against the threat from Nazi Germany.

Thompson became noted in 1934 when she was thrown out of Berlin for having written articles that criticized Hitler. While working as a correspondent in Europe, she had shown a knack for being at the right place at the right time to get the big stories. She returned to the United States and began writing a newspaper column that was read by millions of Americans. She wrote numerous columns trying to get the United States to wake up to the Nazi threat. She also became a popular NBC radio commentator. During the late 1930s, she is said to have been the second most influential woman in America—second only to Eleanor Roosevelt.* She was so well known that she was the subject of cartoons in *The New Yorker* and other popular publications. One biographer said she was possibly the greatest journalist America has known "since the first batch, Hamilton and Jefferson and Madison" (Sheean, 1963, p. 281).

FAMILY BACKGROUND AND EDUCATION

Dorothy Thompson, the daughter of the Reverend Peter Thompson and Margaret Grierson, was born on July 9, 1893, in Lancaster, New York. She had two younger siblings: a brother, Peter Willard, and a sister, Margaret May. Her father was a Methodist minister. As punishment for wrongdoings, Thompson was sometimes required to memorize passages from her father's extensive library. As a child, she was known for her intelligence and her memory. Schoolmates said she was very bright.

Thompson's mother died when she was 7, and she was forced to take on some of the duties of being a mother to her younger brother and sister. The year after her mother died, Thompson discovered the joy of reading. She read everything she could get her hands on—even theological tracts.

Two years after his wife died, the Reverend Thompson married Eliza Maria Abbott, the church pianist. The relationship between Dorothy Thompson and Eliza became a difficult one. When she was 14, Thompson was sent to Chicago to live with two aunts, Margaret Heming and Hetty Thompson. She was enrolled in the Lewis Institute, an innovative school that combined high school and junior college. At the Institute, she came under the wing of Edwin Herbert Lewis, who taught English literature. Lewis took a personal interest in Thompson and corresponded with her much of her life. In one class, he admonished the girls for missing the magic of poetry and said all they would ever be good for was rustling pots and pans. Thompson is reported to have said to herself, "No, I won't."

After graduating from the Lewis Institute, Thompson began study at Syracuse University, which she was able to attend on a Methodist scholarship. It was here that her lifelong habit of monopolizing conversations began to appear. A common story told later around the university was that a date with Dorothy Thompson meant a walk in the moonlight and a talk about Hegel. One of the teachers who influenced her at Syracuse was Jean Marie Richards, the dean of women. She and Thompson spent many afternoons together drinking tea and talking. During this time at Syracuse, Thompson decided she wanted to be a writer. Because she had attended junior college at the Lewis Institute, Thompson graduated from Syracuse in two years.

MARRIAGES AND CAREER

After graduating, Thompson took a job stuffing envelopes at the Buffalo headquarters of the New York Woman Suffrage party. She worked with the suffragettes for three years, becoming a successful organizer and traveling around the state delivering public speeches.

When the Nineteenth Amendment was passed in New York, the suffrage campaign there was over. Thompson went to New York City and shared an apartment with people she knew from the suffrage movement. She began to work for the Social Unit, an early version of a social work program, and to do some writing. She fell in love with the program's creator, Wilbur Phillips, who was married—her first love affair. Phillips abandoned Dorothy when his wife became pregnant, and so Thompson decided to go abroad. She and a friend from the suffrage movement, Barbara De Porte, sailed for Europe to become journalists.

The ship to Europe was filled with Zionists going to an international conference; this was a fortuitous event that Thompson was able to turn to her journalistic advantage. She spent much of the 12-day cruise talking to the Zionists, learning about their cause. When she arrived in London, she persuaded Earl Reeves, the bureau chief of the International News Service, to let her cover the Zionist conference. Her articles on the conference were so well done that she was offered a job as a reporter with the Jewish Correspondence Bureau, but she did not take it. She did other reporting for Reeves, including a "scoop" interview in Ireland with leaders of the Sinn Fein rebellion. In this early reporting, she began to show the qualities that Kurth (1990) said distinguished her from other young women aspiring to be journalists: a passion for detail, an eagerness to go to any lengths for a story, and a willingness to invest any amount of time and effort in writing a piece.

Thompson and De Porte left England and began traveling on the continent, ostensibly to make their way to Vienna to do some reporting for Reeves. On the way, they stopped in Paris and wrote publicity materials for the American Red Cross. They traveled to Italy, where metalworkers were threatening to strike. Thompson realized that she had come to Europe at a time of crisis. In Italy, she began to learn about labor movements, unions, and political ideology. After De Porte left to get married, Thompson tried to continue writing alone in Paris. She became friends with Rose Wilder Lane, a writer and the daughter of Laura Ingalls Wilder, the author of the *Little House on the Prairie* books. The two women went on a three-day walking tour of France and became lifelong friends. Eventually, Dorothy talked Wythe Williams, the head of the European bureau of the *Philadelphia Public Ledger,* into letting her be the *Public Ledger*'s correspondent in Vienna on a piece-rate basis.

In Vienna, Thompson began to interview world leaders and showed an ability to see stories that were not stories to more experienced correspondents. She emulated Floyd Gibbons, a correspondent for the *Chicago Tribune,* whose notion of journalism was to be wherever anything was likely to happen and dramatize the occurrence to the hilt (Kurth, 1990). She met Marcel W. Fodor, the correspondent in Vienna and Budapest for the *Manchester Guardian,* who became a friend and journalistic mentor. In 1921 she was offered the position of the *Public Ledger*'s salaried correspondent in Vienna. She became the first woman to head a foreign news bureau of importance. Fodor introduced her to Joseph Bard, a Hungarian who was an occasional correspondent for Reuters and the Associated Press. After a courtship of two years, the two were married.

In her new position, Thompson was responsible for covering nine countries. She essentially worked alone, and, like other foreign correspondents of the time, she was dependent on "her own quick thinking, her swift feet, and a variety of floating stringers and tipsters" (Kurth, 1990, p. 83).

In 1925 she was transferred to Berlin as the *Public Ledger*'s permanent correspondent in that city. She began to socialize with prominent people in Berlin, including the writer Rebecca West, who would become a longtime friend. Thompson's reputation and influence grew to the point that it was said that no American journalist had ever interviewed Sigmund Freud without Thompson's permission.

Bard was not happy in Berlin and was reported to be seeing other women. In 1927, he and Thompson were divorced. In the same year, Thompson met the American novelist Sinclair Lewis, who was in Berlin. Lewis was so impressed by Thompson that he immediately proposed marriage, even though he was still legally married to Grace Hegger. Lewis was the author of *Main Street* and *Babbitt,* and when he met Thompson, *Elmer Gantry* had just been published. People who knew Lewis warned Thompson that he was an alcoholic. In November 1927, the *New York Evening Post* sent Thompson to Russia to cover the tenth anniversary of the Bolshevik Revolution. She worked hard on her stories, but everywhere she went people asked her about Lewis. They were married on May 14, 1928, in London.

Thompson and Lewis returned to the United States later that year and bought a country home in Vermont. The property included two houses and was called Twin Farms. They weren't back in the states long before Thompson became embroiled in a dispute with the writer Theodore Dreiser. Dreiser's book, *Dreiser Looks at Russia,* which had just been published, had a number of passages that were identical to parts of Thompson's *New Russia.* Thompson finally decided not to sue when it appeared likely that the passages had been copied by Dreiser's assistant without his knowledge.

The marriage between Thompson and Lewis was a difficult one. At dinner parties, Thompson would dominate the conversation with her favorite topic of international politics, and Lewis would drink too much and behave outrageously. The couple had a son, Michael Lewis, who was born on June 20, 1930.

In November 1930, Lewis received word that he had won the Nobel Prize for Literature. Thompson traveled to Stockholm with him in December to receive the award. Afterward, she visited Berlin and for the first time heard Minister of Propaganda Joseph Goebbels. She returned to New York and, during 1931, began to build a reputation on the basis of her lectures and articles in national magazines. She revisited Berlin in November and, taking advantage of the Nazis' desire for international publicity, interviewed Hitler. The resulting article and later book, *I Saw Hitler,* presented the German leader as a weak and insignificant figure.

Thompson and Lewis were spending the winter of 1932–1933 in the mountains in Austria when Thompson became involved in a relationship with Christa Winsloe, a German writer and sculptor. For a while, the two women were inseparable. At this point, Thompson and Lewis were often apart for long periods of time. Winsloe shared a house for six weeks with Thompson, Thompson's son, and the son's nurse at Portofino, on the Italian Riviera. She also traveled to the United States with Thompson and lived at Twin Farms for a while. Winsloe returned to Europe in 1934.

Thompson went back to Europe in the summer of 1934 to report on an unsuccessful Nazi coup in Vienna. She went to Berlin and on August 25, was presented with an order expelling her from the country. The reason given was that she had written numerous anti-German publications, but it was apparent that the highest levels of the Nazi movement had objected to her earlier critical pieces on Hitler. Being thrown out by the Nazis was an international incident and the start of Thompson's rise to fame. When the boat taking her back to the United States arrived in New York, she was met by a crowd of reporters.

Back in the states, Thompson went on an 18-month lecture tour in which she spoke primarily on Hitler and the Nazis. Her lectures were attended by 2,000 to 3,000 people a night.

She was then offered the opportunity to write a column three times a week for the New York *Herald Tribune*. The offer came from Helen Rogers Reid,* the vice president of the newspaper's board and the wife of the publisher. Reid was responsible for bringing some liberal writers to the largely conservative newspaper and for hiring numerous women staffers.

Thompson's column began in March 1936, and she wrote a thrice weekly newspaper column for the next 22 years—at first for the *Herald Tribune* and, later, for other newspapers. She became, along with Walter Lippmann and a few other writers, something new in American journalism—a celebrity columnist. During the peak of her popularity, her column was read by 8 to 10 million people a day.

The column—"On the Record"—ran on the *Herald Tribune*'s editorial page next to Lippmann's column. Thompson's column dealt primarily with politics but also ranged over many other topics. She once wrote a column listing the guests for the perfect dinner party. Some of her most popular columns reported breakfast conversations with "the Grouse," a figure based on Sinclair Lewis. Her columns contained a "blend of solid reporting and naked emotion" that had not been seen before in a syndicated column (Kurth, 1990, p. 220). In the years before World War II, she used the column to become the loudest American voice opposing Nazism. Sanders (1973) has suggested that Thompson felt like a lover betrayed by the changes in Germany, and that this feeling charged her columns.

She was known for the verbal knockout. For example, when President Franklin Roosevelt said "this generation of Americans has a rendezvous with destiny," Thompson replied in her column that "this generation had better not make any blind dates." Secretary of the Interior Harold Ickes gave her the nickname of Cassandra, after the Greek figure whose warnings of misfortune were disregarded.

Thompson's attacks on aviator and popular hero Charles Lindbergh, who flirted with Nazism, were especially venomous. She called him a "somber cretin" with "a notion to be the American Fuehrer" (Kurth, 1993, p. 11).

Thompson demanded a separate office at the *Herald Tribune,* but in fact she seldom worked there. She would often compose her columns while still at home in bed, having her morning coffee and surrounded by newspapers, books, cablegrams, and letters. She would recite the columns aloud, working on getting the words right, and, when ready, dictate them to one of her secretaries.

Branching out from newspaper writing, Thompson attended the national political conventions in 1936 as a reporter for NBC. In the spring of 1937 she also began writing a column for the *Ladies Home Journal,* an assignment she kept up until the end of her life.

Lewis, struggling with alcoholism and the ups and downs of being a famous writer, had a fear of being known as Mr. Dorothy Thompson. He separated from Thompson in April of 1937. During that summer, she took on a regular position in radio broadcasting and became a weekly news commentator for the "Hour of Charm" on NBC.

Thompson once again became a newsmaker herself in 1939 when she attended a Nazi rally in Madison Square Garden. She took a seat in the press gallery and began heckling the speakers by laughing loudly at them. People began shouting to have her removed, and she was finally escorted out by security.

She ran into trouble with her newspaper in 1940 when she wrote a column supporting Roosevelt for reelection. The *Herald Tribune* had endorsed Wendell Willkie. Thompson became actively involved in helping Roosevelt with his campaign. One apocryphal story quotes Lewis as saying a certain speech by Roosevelt was a good one, and has Thompson replying, "I know. I wrote it."

As a result of her stand for Roosevelt, her column was not renewed. The last one for the *Herald Tribune* appeared in March of 1941. Her popularity was such, however, that she was given the opportunity to continue her column with the *New York Post,* again at three times a week. Her column was also picked up by the Bell Syndicate, with the net result that her readership increased.

In 1941 a movie appeared with a character obviously based on Thompson. It was *Woman of the Year,* starring Katherine Hepburn. Thompson objected to the way the character was portrayed but, on the advice of a lawyer, decided not to sue.

Once the United States entered World War II, Thompson lost her crusader's cause of waking people up to the Nazi threat. She turned to helping in the war effort by making some propaganda broadcasts that were transmitted to Germany by shortwave radio. These messages were anti-Nazi speeches delivered in German to a hypothetical friend named Hans. Later they were collected in a book titled *Listen, Hans* (1942).

Thompson and Lewis had been spending less and less time together, and they were divorced on January 2, 1942. During the following summer, an artist named Maxim Kopf came to Twin Farms to paint Thompson's portrait. The two fell in love and, after Kopf obtained a divorce from his wife, were married on June 16, 1943. Thompson said Kopf was the man she should have married all along.

Around this time, Thompson took the position in her column that Germany alone was not responsible for the war and that the German people should still be thought of as human beings. This message, which was out of step for the times, resulted in her being called a turncoat.

After the war, she opposed the Jewish effort to create a nation in the Middle East, arguing that a separate Jewish state would lead to years of tension with neighboring states. As a result, she lost favor with many American Jews. The *New York Post* dropped her column at the beginning of 1947, but she still had her contract with the Bell Syndicate and was appearing in 150 newspapers. She continued to write her column, but her popularity and influence were declining.

Thompson's husband had a heart attack in May 1958, and then died from a second one in July. She gave up her column in August 1958. She spent the following winter at Hanover, New Hampshire, where she wanted to use the Dartmouth library and mix with students. She was shocked to find that most of them did not know who she was.

On July 17, 1959, she suffered a heart attack while lunching in Woodstock, Vermont, but she recovered. She was experiencing some tough times that year with her son Michael, who was drinking excessively and having marital difficulties. Her old friend Rebecca West, whose own son, Anthony West, had criticized her in a book, advised Thompson not to feel guilty, but Thompson found this difficult to do.

Thompson traveled to Portugal in December 1960 to visit her grandsons and daughter-in-law. She had a second heart attack and died there on January 30, 1961.

MAJOR CONTRIBUTIONS AND ACHIEVEMENTS

Dorothy Thompson was the first woman to write a regular national column dealing with serious issues. During her day, she was treated on an equal footing with Walter Lippmann, who shared the same editorial page in the New York *Herald Tribune*. Her columns were penetrating in their analysis, but they also conveyed emotion that was lacking in the columns of most of her male colleagues. She was passionate about the issues that concerned her, and that passion came through in her columns.

Thompson was also the strongest voice rallying the United States against the Nazis prior to U.S. entry into World War II. More than half of her "On the Record" columns from 1938 to 1942 dealt with the increasingly disturbing situation in Europe. Thompson spoke out more strongly about the Nazi danger than President Roosevelt, who was hampered before the war by the official policy of U.S. neutrality.

Her writings sometimes inspired world leaders to concrete action. She wrote a piece in *Foreign Affairs* in 1938 pointing out the problem faced by refugees forced to leave Germany but who were not being welcomed by other countries. Shortly thereafter, Roosevelt called an international conference at Evian-les-Bains, France, to discuss the refugee problem.

In the days prior to television, Thompson and some of the other celebrity columnists such as Lippmann had an influence over public opinion that may never again be equaled by individual journalists. In 1939 *Time* magazine proclaimed her the second most influential woman in the United States—second only to Eleanor Roosevelt.

Thompson became a role model for later women newspaper columnists. Two Pulitzer Prize winners in the commentary category, *Washington Post* columnist Mary McGrory and *New York Times* columnist Anna Quindlen, have said Thompson opened doors for them. Quindlen has said she was inspired by Thompson's ability to "write about the Third Reich one day and her nasturtiums the next" (Quindlen, 1993, p. xxvii).

CRITICAL EVALUATION OF CONTRIBUTIONS AND ACHIEVEMENTS

Thompson did something in her newspaper columns that had not been done before by either a man or a woman—she combined intellectual analysis with passionate commitment. Her prose was not elegant, but blunt and to the point. The columns were often similar to her speeches in being outspoken and emotional. In reviewing the book *Let the Record Speak* (1939), Lewis Gannett praised the emotion in Thompson's writing. "Where the intellectualized columns of her colleagues fade when pressed between the leaves of a book," he wrote, "these columns still ring." (Kurth, 1990, p. 265).

Her writing was also the target of criticism. "If all the speeches she has made in the past twelve months were laid end to end," said rival columnist Heywood Broun, "they would constitute a bridge of platitudes sufficient to reach . . . the cold caverns of the moon" (Kurth, 1990, p. 234).

Thompson was also courageous in her writing, expressing her opinions freely and strongly, whether or not they were popular. She switched her allegiance from Willkie to Roosevelt even when her newspaper was a leading booster of Willkie. She showed compassion for the German people during World War II when such action earned her the label of "turncoat." And she spoke out against the formation of the state of Israel when her column had many Jewish readers.

Thompson is largely unknown today, particularly by young people. Her chief biographer, Peter Kurth, said he thinks this is because she was a woman and journalism is regarded as a male institution (Griffith, 1990). If she had been a man, he implied, her name would be as familiar as those of male journalists of the time such as Walter Lippmann, William Shirer, and John Gunther.

INTEGRATION OF PERSONAL AND PROFESSIONAL LIFE

Like many successful people, Thompson struggled all her life for the proper balance between her personal and professional lives. Her dinner parties, in which she obtained column material from an informal "brain trust" of intellectuals and experts, showed a useful joining of her personal and professional lives. But even these parties came at some cost to her personal life, with husband Sinclair Lewis becoming more and more alienated by them.

Her single-minded devotion to her profession came at the cost of those involved with her personally, particularly members of her family. Her first two marriages were not happy, although her third, which occurred after her major fame, was more satisfactory. She and Sinclair Lewis had a rocky relationship. During the early years of the marriage, they helped each other by critiquing each other's work, and they each wrote things based on or inspired by the other. But they also became professional rivals, with Lewis, as noted earlier, having a fear of becoming known as "Mr. Dorothy Thompson."

Her relationship with her son was a tortuous one. When he was young, she left him often in the care of nannies. This was not unusual for well-to-do people at the time, but Thompson, with her travels, may have done it more than others.

Some of Thompson's steadiest relationships were with other women. She had lifelong friendships with Rose Wilder Lane and Rebecca West, and at least one lesbian love affair, with writer and sculptor Christa Winsloe.

CONCLUSION

Dorothy Thompson was one of the best-known people in the United States during the late 1930s and early 1940s. She was a journalistic pioneer in writing a nationally distributed column that combined intellectual analysis of major political issues with a passionate voice. She used that voice to warn the United States of the international dangers from Nazi Germany at a time when few others, in either journalism or politics, were sounding that alarm. In sounding that alarm, she was more than a celebrity; she was a hero of her time.

REFERENCES

Griffith, T. (1990, July 29). The woman who interviewed Hitler. *New York Times,* Sec. 7, 12.
Kurth, P. (1990). *American Cassandra: The life of Dorothy Thompson.* Boston: Little, Brown.
Kurth, P. (1993, January 31). When the cheering stopped. *The Washington Post Book World,* 11.
Quindlen, A. (1993). *Thinking out loud: On the personal, the political, the public and the private.* New York: Random House.
Sanders, M. (1973). *Dorothy Thompson: A legend in her own time.* Boston: Houghton Mifflin.
Sheean, V. (1963). *Dorothy and Red.* Boston: Houghton Mifflin.
Thompson, D. (1939). *Let the record speak.* Boston: Houghton Mifflin.
Thompson, D. (1942). *Listen, Hans.* Boston: Houghton Mifflin.

JUDITH CARY WALLER
(1889–1973)

Louise Benjamin

Women had just voted for the first time in a presidential election, flappers were all the rage, and radio was beginning to sweep the country. A phone call from an old friend in 1922 began the distinguished broadcasting career of Judith Cary Waller, manager of WMAQ (Chicago) and later public affairs/educational director for NBC. Waller was a true pioneer, one of the first women to enter the growing field of broadcasting.

FAMILY BACKGROUND AND EDUCATION

Born on February 19, 1889, to physician John Waller and Katherine Short, Waller was the oldest of their four daughters. After graduation from high school in 1908, Waller embarked with relatives and friends on the traditional tour of Europe. An aunt, Mrs. William Johnston, was a personal friend of Mrs. Victor Lawson, founder and publisher of the Chicago *Daily News*. Her husband's secretary, a young man named Walter Strong, soon became a close friend of Judith's. Almost 14 years later Strong, then business manager of the Chicago *Daily News,* called Waller to ask her to manage a radio station the paper had just started. Waller had misgivings about her competence in running something she had never heard of, and she told him so. But Strong convinced her to take the job when he said no one really knew what a radio station was and explained that everyone in radio was a pioneer. So, in February 1922, Waller became a manager of station WMAQ, Chicago.

CAREER DEVELOPMENT, MAJOR CONTRIBUTIONS, AND ACHIEVEMENTS

In many ways, Waller's career parallels radio broadcasting's evolution. During her life, she was devoted to programming excellence. When WMAQ went on the air in April 1922, jazz and popular music were programming mainstays. The first program she carried, however, was a live performance by opera diva Sophie Braslau. A few years later she received permission from Cubs owner, William Wrigley, Jr., to carry the Cubs' games, and WMAQ became the first radio station to carry baseball play by play from a home ballpark. That same year, WMAQ began broadcasting the home football games of the University of Chicago and Northwestern University.

Waller contributed yet again to programming history when Charles Correll and Freeman Gosden came to her during their dispute with another Chicago station, WGN, over permission to record their show, "Sam 'n' Henry," for sale to other stations. They wanted WMAQ to pick up their program, but their price was $25,000—one year's operating budget for WMAQ. She took the problem to Strong and other newspaper department heads at the *Daily News*. They agreed to pay the sum, but the show's name would have to be changed because WGN held copyright to "Sam 'n' Henry." So, Correll and Gosden moved to WMAQ and the show became "Amos 'n' Andy." With *Daily News'* publicity efforts, including a new blackface comic strip—the first of its kind in a daily newspaper—the program soared in popularity and aired six nights a week, another first in radio. When she tried to sell the program and the concept of stripping it daily Monday through Friday to CBS, then WMAQ's network, she was all but laughed out of a network executive's office and told she knew nothing about radio. Subsequently, she sold the program to NBC, and "Amos 'n' Andy" was a network success for more than 20 years.

Waller also aided the development of broadcast news. Because WMAQ was associated with the *Daily News,* she had ready access to its pages and correspondents. After listeners' interest in news and current events was piqued with broadcasts of the 1924 conventions and elections, she supplemented local news and feature reports over WMAQ with foreign correspondents' stories.

Waller attended all four radio conferences called by Secretary of Commerce Herbert Hoover during the 1920s. She was a member of several committees, including those investigating program sponsorship and program censorship.

Waller believed that radio stations needed to include educational material in their programming, and she began "Radio Photo Log" in 1924. The show featured explorers, scientists, and travelers on international and national subjects and was tied to the *Daily News* Sunday photogravure section. A few years later, CBS president William Paley asked her to come to New York to organize the same program for the network. She also created adult educational programs through both the University of Chicago and Northwestern University. One series of lectures, from the University of Chicago, became "The University of Chicago Round Table." After WMAQ became an NBC-owned and operated station in November 1931, that network carried the Round Table nationwide. It was a model for other such programs and remained on the air for more than 20 years.

When NBC purchased the station, Waller resigned, but NBC's management refused to accept it. She became the public service director for the network's

Central Division. She also continued her work in educational broadcasting, serving on the Federal Radio Education Committee, a congressionally appointed council. In the mid-1940s she wrote a textbook for use in college and university broadcast courses, *Radio, the Fifth Estate* (1946).

With the advent of television, Waller continued her public service and educational work. She was directly responsible for the development of the 1950s preschool favorite, "Ding-Dong School" with "Miss Frances," Dr. Frances Horwich, dean of the School of Education at Roosevelt University in Chicago. It ran locally in Chicago for several years and won the prestigious George Foster Peabody Award. In the fall of 1953 NBC put the program on the network, where it again earned extensive recognition.

Waller officially retired from NBC in 1957 and soon after became head of airborne workshops headquartered at Purdue University. Teachers in a six-state area prepared courses for television transmission from a plane flying 5,000 feet over northern Indiana. She also lectured at Northwestern's School of Speech and was on the board of the Interlochen Music Camp. MacMurray College and Northwestern University awarded her honorary doctorates. In 1951 she received the Northwestern University Centennial Award, and in 1955, the Chicago Council on Foreign Relations World Understanding Award. The Judith Waller Award was established in 1947 at Washington State College, now Washington State University. She never married. She died of a heart attack on October 28, 1973, at the age of 84 in Evansville, Illinois.

EVALUATION OF CONTRIBUTIONS AND ACHIEVEMENTS

Waller's many lifelong achievements rank her high among broadcasters. Perhaps her life's contributions are best summed up by two of her contemporaries, cited in an article in *Journalism History* by Mary Williamson in 1976–1977. A former NBC vice president, Sydney Eiges, said in 1974, "She had a beguiling, enchanting smile, which concealed a streak of tenacity and a restless mind." In 1975 Betty Ross West, assistant director of public affairs for WMAQ-TV, called Waller her mentor and described her as "dynamic, vital, determined, sincere and realistic. She was unique in her time because she was the person she was." West concluded that Waller "had spirit, strength, foresight and she reacted quickly and was usually right. She was also a woman of great class and dignity, a real lady."

REFERENCES

"Ding-Dong School." Peabody Awards Collection, University of Georgia Main Library.
Foremost women in communications. (1970). New York: Foremost Americans Publications Corporation.
Judith Cary Waller Papers. Broadcast Pioneers Library. Washington, D.C.
Knight, Ruth Adams. (1939). *Stand by for the ladies!*

McKerns, Joseph (1989). *Biographical dictionary of American journalism.* Westport, Conn.: Greenwood Press.

Obituary. (1973, October 29). *Chicago Tribune.*

Waller, Judith Cary. (1946). *Radio, the fifth estate.* Boston: Houghton Mifflin. Second edition published in 1950.

Williamson, Mary. (1976–1977 Winter). Judith Cary Waller: Chicago broadcasting pioneer. *Journalism History.*

BARBARA WALTERS
(1931–   )

Suzanne Marcus

In 1976 ABC-TV offered Barbara Walters over a million dollars to become the first woman to anchor a prime-time network newscast. At this time, no other journalist, male or female, earned this much money. The shy girl from Brookline, Massachusetts, with a funny accent and slight lisp had come a long way. Today, photographs line the walls of her New York apartment—Barbara and Richard Nixon; Barbara, Menachem Begin, and Anwar Sadat; Barbara and Castro, Arafat, Quaddafi (Reed, 1992, p. 223)—all a tribute to Walters' hard work and perseverance, even in the face of discrimination and adversity.

Before Barbara, no news organization would have dreamed of sending a woman to interview a world leader; female reporters usually covered women's issues, light features, or the weather. In a business where a woman's appearance would often determine whether she got a chance to appear on-camera, Barbara proved that diligence and determination are the keys to on-air success. Currently, Barbara co-hosts the popular newsmagazine "20/20" and produces her celebrity interview specials, which continue to draw large ratings. She has been awarded four Emmys and named one of the most admired women in America by the Gallup polls. Her intimate interviewing style and her commitment to asking the questions her viewers want answered have redefined the television interview. Barbara Walters has left her mark on broadcast journalism.

Barbara was born in Boston, Massachusetts, on September 25, 1931, to Louis Edward Walters and Dena Sletsky Walters. A few years earlier, Barbara's older brother Burton contracted lobar pneumonia and died shortly after his first birthday. Her older sister, Jackie, was born retarded. By the time Barbara was born, her mother had pledged to devote her life to Jackie, and her father had lost himself in his work (Oppenheimer, 1990, p. 5). Lou Walters founded a thriving booking agency; he scouted for talent acts and booked them into vaudeville houses and theaters. Lou made a lot of money, but what he had, he spent. There were lavish gifts for Dena and the family, hours of card games and gambling, and stocks and bonds on margin. When the stock market crashed in 1929, Lou lost heavily; by the time Barbara was 4, he was broke (Oppenheimer, 1990, p. 16).

Lou was determined to bounce back. In 1937 he leased a dilapidated church, cleaned it up, and turned it into his first nightclub, the "Latin Quarter." It was a wild success. "The Latin Quarter caught on a week after Lou opened because he had a line of beautiful girls," said Eddie Davis, a friend and competitor of Lou's. "Lou brought Parisian-style entertainment to Boston" (Oppenheimer, 1990, p. 21). The Walters were well-off again and Barbara saw even less of her father. Sometimes, after school, Barbara and her sister would sit in the lighting booth and watch the performances. "To this day," she says, "if I have three glasses of wine I can do Milton Berle and Sophie Tucker and Willie Howard" (Reed, 1992, p. 222). However, Barbara didn't think the nightclubs were glamorous. She often wished her father was an accountant or a doctor (Reed, 1992, p. 222).

Walters has said that her sister Jackie was "the most influential part" of her life: "It had more effect than anything else. When you have a sister or brother who dies, or if you have one who is handicapped, there's part of you that says, 'Why am I so lucky?' " (Reed, 1992, p. 222). Barbara rarely spoke about her sister, but she was very protective of her. "Barbara couldn't do ordinary things like other girls," her cousin Shirley Budd said. "Barbara did not have a birthday party, or have girlfriends over, because Jackie didn't. When Barbara wanted to go out with friends Jackie would get excited and say, 'Me, too! Me, too.' So Barbara would stay home, or read a book. When she got older Barbara didn't learn to drive a car because Jackie wasn't capable of driving" (Oppenheimer, 1990, p. 6).

When Barbara was 11, her father opened another Latin Quarter in Miami and the family moved to Florida. Two years later, when Lou opened a club in New York City, Barbara moved again. At 15, she was back in Miami, and at 16, she returned to Manhattan. Lou was down on his luck again, many of his business ventures had failed and he actually lost his Boston Latin Quarter in a gin rummy game. The constant roller coaster the Walters family rode deeply affected Barbara. They moved so often she couldn't develop lasting friendships: "The insecurities of show business permeated my life, so that I knew: A, I had to work. B, I had to be self supporting. No matter how much money there was, it was always going to finish. The curtain was going to come down. We would not all go the the seashore on Sunday" (Probst, 1975, p. 138).

After graduating from Sarah Lawrence College, Barbara tapped her father's network of connections and landed her first job in the publicity department at WNBT television in New York (Oppenheimer, 1990, p. 66). She wrote press releases for programs that aired on this WNBC-owned and operated station. A year later, in 1953, Barbara became the producer of a daily 15-minute live children's program "Ask the Camera." She would sort through questions children sent in and narrow them down to those that could be answered using stock footage from the station's film library. After a year the show was canceled.

In April of 1955, Barbara became engaged to Robert Henry Katz, a businessman whom she had begun dating only two months earlier. In mid-April, Barbara had second thoughts and called off the engagement, but the couple reconciled a few weeks later and were married in a lavish ceremony at the Plaza Hotel on June 21.

Late in 1955, Barbara again sought work and found a job at the CBS "Morning Show" with Dick Van Dyke. This was CBS's attempt to steal ratings from the popular "Today" show on NBC. Barbara's job was to book guests, and like her father, she had an eye for talent. Charlie Andrews, her producer, said, "If you put 20 girls in a room, Barbara would be one of the two smartest girls there. She could think things out. She was street-smart certainly, logical, not afraid to work. . . . Sooner or later, Barbara would float to the top" (Oppenheimer, 1990, p. 85).

When the "Morning Show" with Dick Van Dyke was canceled in 1956, Barbara was hired to work on its replacement, "Good Morning with Will Rogers, Jr." Her job remained the same—booking guests and generating story ideas. "All you would say was, 'Barbara have you got any ideas?' and she'd say, 'Well, I'd like to do a fashion show,' " said Mike Sklar, the show's producer. "And she'd go out and organize the whole thing. She'd bring in a package" (Oppenheimer, 1990, p. 89). Eventually, "Good Morning" was also canceled, and Barbara once again found herself unemployed.

Around the same time, Barbara's father decided to sell off his interest in the Latin Quarter clubs, due to years of conflict with his financial backer, Elias Loew. Lou wanted to start up his own clubs and soon opened the Cafe de Paris in Miami. Unfortunately, it never enjoyed the same success as the Latin Quarter and closed after only one season. Lou Walters' next venture, a Cafe de Paris in Manhattan, also went bankrupt. He lost most of his money in these two bad investments and in the middle of June 1958 suffered a heart attack. To further add to Barbara's misery, her marriage had failed. She and Katz were granted a divorce on May 21, 1958—one month short of their three-year anniversary.

While her father was recovering in Miami, Barbara hunted down another job, at Tex McCrary Inc., a New York public relations firm. She was hired by Bill Safire who would later gain fame as a speechwriter for President Nixon and as a columnist for the *New York Times*. Barbara now found herself on the other side of the fence—pitching guests to producers and trying to create favorable publicity for the McCrary clients.

In the spring of 1961 Barbara finally got her foot in the door at the "Today Show" when she was hired as a free-lance writer. Dave Garroway hosted the show, and Beryl Pfizer was the "Today Girl," whose job it was to report lighter stories with feminine appeal, such as fashion and cooking. Barbara was assigned to write for Anita Colby, a former model who prepared a daily feature. Barbara made cameo appearances several times in her stories, once receiving a makeover in an exclusive salon, another time appearing in the crowd at a fashion show (Oppenheimer, 1990, p. 113). She never hid the fact that she dreamed of one day being on-air talent.

Garroway and Pfizer were eventually replaced by John Chancellor and Robbin Bain, and producer Fred Freed left to produce documentaries. Shad Northshield, former producer of the CBS "Morning Show" where Barbara had begun her television career, replaced Freed. Northshield promoted Barbara to the position of full-time writer. Her first big story was covering the Dior and Maxime fashion shows in Paris. Normally, the script she prepared would have been read by the Today Girl, but Barbara thought it would be more credible if she presented the story herself, since after all, she was the one who had gone to Paris (Oppenheimer, 1990, p. 119). Her producer agreed, and Barbara reported on air for the first time.

A year after she joined the "Today" staff, Barbara was selected to be part of the press corps accompanying Jackie Kennedy on her 27-day visit to India. Jackie Kennedy wasn't giving interviews; she was content to pose for photographs and make short statements. Barbara was not dissuaded; she remained determined to come home with an interview. To this end, she used all of her connections and persuasiveness in order to score a coup—a short interview with the first lady herself. Barbara returned home triumphant, and her producer enthused, "It was a very important milestone in her career" (Oppenheimer, 1990, p. 134).

Things change rapidly in the television business. When news rolled in that ratings were down and the "Today Show" had lost money, Northshield and Chancellor were let go. Al Morgan was brought in as the new producer with Hugh Downs as the new host. Despite the shakeup, Barbara kept on doing what she did best—writing and reporting stories. When she heard Al Morgan was searching for a new Today Girl she suggested herself, but Morgan chose Pat Fontaine, a former weather girl. Although he hadn't wanted to put her on air daily, Morgan recognized Barbara's talent and assigned her more and more feature stories. Barbara remained determined to succeed. A production assistant, Gail Rock, recalls, "Barbara was thorough, worked longer hours than anybody, really did her homework. . . . She was smart and ambitious because she wanted them to put her on the air" (Oppenheimer, 1990, p. 145).

Years later Barbara would offer this advice to other young professionals, "Don't quit. Do so well you become valuable, and then you can name what you want. You're not going to get it by quitting, because there's someone there to take your place. Just become so good you're important to the show" (Reed, 1992, p. 222).

When John Kennedy was assassinated, Barbara handled most of the coverage. "I found myself using her more and more," said Morgan, her producer. "Pat [Fontaine, the Today Girl] didn't have the background for it" (Oppenheimer, 1990, p. 150). Barbara reported naturally and skillfully. However, when it was decided Fontaine would have to be replaced, Maureen O'Sullivan, a Broadway actress, was chosen. Morgan was worried about Barbara's lisp, which affected the way she pronounced her R's and L's. It wasn't until after O'Sullivan was fired that Barbara finally got the break she was waiting for. "They hired me for [a] 13 week [trial period]," she says, "over everybody's dead body in the sales department" (Shalit, 1975, p. 172).

On December 8, 1963, Barbara married a second time. Her new husband, Lee Guber, was a successful producer and partner in a chain of tent theaters and wanted to try his hand producing on Broadway. Barbara and Lee attempted to have children, but Barbara suffered several miscarriages and the couple realized they would have to adopt. Lou Walters declared bankruptcy in 1966, and Barbara's worry that she would eventually have to support her entire family was now realized. Despite this turn for the worse, things began looking up again in June of 1968, when the Gubers adopted a baby girl, Jacqueline Dena, named for Barbara's mother and sister. Barbara adored her new daughter, but didn't give up her career for motherhood. Instead, she hired a nanny and a cook and worked hard to balance both sides of her life.

Barbara nabbed her first major political scoop in 1969 when she landed an interview with Secretary of State Dean Rusk after his resignation. Rusk had once written her a letter stating "If any NBC Vice President ever bothers you, show them this letter and others like it and tell them to leave you alone" (Reed, 1992, p. 222). Barbara conducted a hard-hitting interview and gained the respect as well as jealousy of her Washington peers.

Later that year, Barbara produced a segment on "The New Sexuality" for the decade-ender "From Here to the Seventies" produced by Shad Northshield. Participating as one of the 18 correspondents gave Barbara even more credibility as a journalist.

With all her newfound respect and popularity, it wasn't surprising that Doubleday publishers approached Barbara in 1970 about a book deal. Barbara had previously written a short magazine article that dealt with the art of conversation. Editor Ken McCormick suspected her article could be expanded into a bestseller, and he proved correct (Oppenheimer, 1990, p. 197). Controversy arose in 1977 when *Variety* and *People* magazine published articles stating that a ghostwriter, June Callwood, had written the book after conducting a series of interviews with Barbara (Oppenheimer, 1990, p. 201). Barbara claimed sole authorship, but McCormick affirmed that it was Callwood who actually penned the book (Helmbreck, 1990, p. 1D).

Barbara's contract allowed her to work on other projects besides "The Today Show," and the ever-alert reporter began seeking them out. When Aline Saarinson, host of a morning talk show titled "For Women Only" was promoted, Barbara jumped at the chance to become her replacement. The show's name was changed to "Not For Women Only" and featured feminine themes such as relationships and sex. "I was an expert on premature ejaculation," joked Barbara (Reed, 1992, p. 222). The show was a forerunner of today's talk show format popularized by Oprah Winfrey and Phil Donohue. It soon became such a success that it was syndicated nationally. Barbara continued her trademark of seeking hard-to-get interviews and produced a five-day special in which she interviewed the wives of Nixon's Cabinet members. This generated huge publicity for the show and its host.

Barbara's next milestone was landing an interview with the president himself. On March 11, 1971, Barbara interviewed Richard Nixon in the White House Blue Room, asking him, among other things, if he thought he had an image problem. The president again honored Barbara when he invited her to be part of the press corps accompanying him on his trip to the People's Republic of China in February 1972.

In 1972 word hit the press that the Gubers had separated. Barbara was now working longer hours than ever before and rarely had free time to spend with her family. Their divorce became final in 1976.

In April 1974 Frank McGee, host of "The Today Show," lost his battle with bone cancer. It was in Barbara's contract that should McGee ever leave the show, Barbara would be promoted to co-host. "Today" then became "the only TV network news or public affairs program to have a female cohost" (Oppenheimer, 1990, p. 236).

Barbara became the most controversial woman on television in 1976 when ABC offered her a million dollars to co-anchor their evening news and produce four entertainment specials. Barbara jumped at the opportunity. NBC matched ABC's proposed salary, but the network wasn't ready to move Walters to the prime-time anchor desk. They preferred that she remain on "The Today Show." Barbara accepted ABC's offer, switched networks, and ended her 15 years at "The Today Show."

Barbara's salary raised eyebrows among the public and drew resentment from other reporters who felt Barbara was a celebrity and not a professional journalist. In an interview with Ben-David from the *Jerusalem Post* she indicated that she, along with rock stars and movie stars, probably are overpaid. But, she went on to explain that her salary (and that of others in similar roles) is due to the fact that she is popular and her program receives high ratings. Consequently, it attracts the kind of audience desired by the networks, whose goal is to be able to sell its commercial time at as high a price as possible.

It was rumored that Harry Reasoner was very upset at the thought of gaining Barbara as his co-host. Reasoner didn't want to share his anchor desk with anyone. As an incentive, the network mentioned the possibility of expanding the nightly news to an hour. A longer newscast would give Reasoner and Walters more time to do their own stories and features. This temporarily appeased Harry, and he and Barbara began meeting secretly to get to know each other better and resolve their differences. Barbara didn't want to accept the job if Harry remained hostile toward her. She'd been through that before with former "Today" host, Frank McGee, who had made no secret of his dislike for her. She knew what it was like to deal with daily tension on the set and didn't want to have to endure a similar situation. Finally, during one of his newscasts, Reasoner announced, "I welcome Barbara with no reservation" (Hosley & Yamada, 1987, p. 130).

Unfortunately, Harry and Barbara's attempt to forge a relationship didn't work. As time passed, the two even stopped speaking to each other. At the inaugural party for President Carter, ABC's executive producer for Special Events Coverage, Walter Pfister, had to hold two separate meetings, one with Harry and another with Barbara, in order to go over the format of the coverage (Oppenheimer, 1990, p. 270). Ratings for the "ABC Nightly News" never increased significantly; the network remained in third place, and affiliate station objections dashed any hope of expanding the news to an hour.

After a year and a half, Reasoner departed to CBS, and ABC did away with the "anchor" position. Their news now consisted of reports from three desks; foreign news from London, national news from Chicago, and a third desk in Washington that tied everything together. Barbara was now free to report stories, chase big interviews, and, of course, devote more time to her specials.

Barbara's first special, unlike her newscasts, was a ratings success. It featured interviews with Barbra Streisand, Jimmy and Rosalyn Carter, and a tour of Walters' Manhattan apartment. It captured a 36 percent share of the viewing audience, even though many critics panned it (Oppenheimer, 1990, p. 281). Barbara's specials continue to be ratings successes. She has interviewed the big names—Tom Cruise, Whoopi Goldberg, Katherine Hepburn, Audrey Hepburn, Clint Eastwood, Sharon Stone; she tries to get the stars while they're hot. Originally, Barbara conceived of the shows featuring a mix of celebrities and politicians. However, it soon became apparent that the ratings for the newsmaker interviews always dropped (Smith, 1994, p. 16). As a result, celebrities became the sole focus of her specials.

Walters has developed an intimate style of interviewing that has been both praised and criticized. She generally interviews a star in their home, or where they feel comfortable and can forget about the camera. Her in-depth questions encourage her guests to open up, reveal their emotions on air, and yes, sometimes even cry. "If one more person cries on my special," Barbara threatens, "I'm going to throw a pie in their face" (Castro, 1990, p. 160). Barbara says she doesn't intend to make her guests weepy and that sometimes seemingly innocuous questions elicit tears. "I did an interview with Roseanne Barr in which she talked about having been in a mental institution for eight months, and she didn't cry. Then I asked her about her sister, and she started to cry" (Chase, 1990, p. 358).

Walters points out that it isn't always easy for her to land the big-name stars. "We can work years trying to get someone. We don't like to do someone just because they're plugging a movie" (Chase, 1990, p. 358). Stars, she states, appear on her show when they want to "explain themselves, promote projects, clear up misimpressions or maybe they are flattered to be asked" (Smith, 1994, p. 18). "They know they'll be on by themselves, we interview only them, we don't go back and interview their ex-husband or their manager" (Chase, 1990,

p. 358). Barbara believes that the purpose of her specials is to discover "what makes the stars tick, and what their personalities are" (Smith, 1994, p. 16). When asked what she is proudest of, she responds: "That our audiences feel satisfied with our interviews; that they feel they've learned something; they've gotten to know these stars without our going for the jugular" (Smith, 1994, p. 16).

Barbara's most historic interview for ABC News was the one she conducted with Israeli Prime Minister Menachem Begin and Egypt's president, Anwar el-Sadat. Sadat was flying to Israel for the first time to discuss peace in the Middle East with Begin. Barbara wanted to be the first to conduct a joint interview with the two leaders, and once again she attained her goal—beating both Walter Cronkite and John Chancellor to the scoop. This interview restored Barbara's tarnished image in the eyes of the public. She hadn't succeeded as an anchorwoman, but when it came to her skill and persistence as a reporter, Barbara had what it takes.

Barbara joined the newsmagazine "20/20" because she was looking for a permanent forum in which to present her interviews and to reach the public. Barbara was reteamed with Hugh Downs, former host of "Today." At first, Hugh was upset; he wanted to remain the sole anchor. When Barbara joined the staff, it wasn't as Down's co-host. Her job "was to discuss various pieces with the correspondents, make some observations, and converse with Downs at the end of the show" (Oppenheimer, 1990, p. 298). However, this new format was awkward, and after Downs reconsidered, Barbara became his co-host. Barbara remains at "20/20," still obtaining those hard-to-get interviews and working as diligently as ever.

Barbara Walters was the first woman to break into the all-male world of reporting, on their level. While she says she never minded "doing the so-called female things—the fashion shows, cooking spots, whatever" (Rovin, 1990, p. 280), she didn't want to be limited to soft features. "I was not allowed to write anything for the men. I couldn't write anything that supposedly was hard news, or that had to do with science, or that had to do with economics" (Remington, 1992, p. F2). "It *did* bother me that I wasn't allowed to participate in a Washington interview, a Dean Rusk or a Bobby Kennedy one-on-one," she says of "The Today Show." "That's why I started going out and getting my own stories" (Rovin, 1990, p. 280). Had she brought her guests into the studio, one of the men would have gotten the interview (Reed, 1992, p. 221). It was even written into host Frank McGee's contract that Barbara wasn't allowed to question any political guest until he had asked at least three questions (Reed, 1992, p. 221).

Barbara knew she could report just as well as her male counterparts, and she dedicated herself to her work with extraordinary drive and persistence. Barbara recently mentioned, to her male colleagues' astonishment, that she had dealt with sexual discrimination throughout most of her career. But at the time, she says, "It was taken for granted. We didn't think we were being sexually discriminated against" (Reed, 1992, p. 221).

In essence, Barbara opened up the world of broadcast journalism to women, but she says she never intended to pave any roads. "There are many women on television today, but it isn't because of me," she asserts. "My contributions were relatively small. Because I was able to go off and interview a head of state and do a serious, good job, people could no longer say, 'Only a man can do that, because the head of state won't take it seriously.' " Walters credits the whole women's movement, Gloria Steinem,* and Betty Friedan for the increased career opportunities opened up to women (Rovin, 1990, p. 199).

After years of living the single life, Barbara married Merv Adelson, chairman of Lorimar Production Company, in May of 1986. Like Barbara, Adelson had been married twice before. He had three children from a previous marriage. This time, Barbara seemed sure it would last. "I think when you have an independent life and can support yourself, your reason for marriage becomes different," she said. "You really want to be with this person, and you don't get married for security or position. You just want to be with that person" ("Barbara to Marry," p. C 30). It took the pair a while to commit, but after an 11-month engagement they "made up [their] minds on a Wednesday and were married on a Saturday," says Walters (Sutherland, 1986, p. 160). During the wedding reception, following Merv's toast, Barbara predicted, "This is the way it will always be: Merv will always say the perfect thing, and I'll always get the last word" ("Those East-West," p. 93). Although Merv's career required him to live in California and Barbara was based in New York, the couple was confident that they could make a bicoastal marriage work. The challenge turned out to be more difficult than they expected—in 1992 the couple filed for divorce.

Barbara has often stated that "to have a really superb career, a wonderful marriage, terrific kids and all that goes into it is very, very hard" (Sutherland, p. 157). She does believe women can have all three, "but not necessarily at the same time" (Smith, p. 21). Walters knows—her personal life has often suffered at the expense of her career. When she was married to Lee Guber and still working for "The Today Show," she would often be asleep by nine, in order to be up early and on the set by five. When she had a few hours of free time on the weekend, she would often spend them catching up on her sleep. As a result, she and Lee rarely had time to spend together. Her relationship with her daughter also suffered. While Barbara adored Jackie, her hectic schedule didn't allow the two much time alone together. A young Jackie once summed up Barbara in these words, "Mummy doesn't drive; Mummy doesn't play games; Mummy burns the meatloaf; all Mummy can do is television!" (Carter, 1992, p. 55). Barbara admits "children grow out of those feet-pajamas, and you're not just dealing with a cute little baby. My daughter and I went through some very tough times during her adolescence. Working mothers so often feel guilty because we're not there enough, or when we *are* there we have work to do or else it's all we can do at night to get our clothes off and fall into bed" (Rovin, 1990,

p. 281). Yet it's almost as if Barbara is lost without her work. When she accepted an anchor position at ABC, she could not begin right away, because NBC claimed she still had a contractual obligation to them. Barbara found herself with her first summer off in years, yet she was unable to enjoy it. "One of the *problems* with my life, probably the only problem," she admits, "is that I feel guilty doing *anything* just for *pleasure*" (Shalit, 1975, p. 174).

Barbara has faced her share of criticism throughout the years. She's too soft, she's too tough, she's too pushy and aggressive, she's intimate. "I'm damned if I do, damned if I don't," Walters says. "I think what people don't understand is that I do different kinds of interviews. I talk to world leaders, politicians, people suddenly in the news. Those are much harder-hitting. They are more journalistic and investigative and inquiring. But on the specials we are intent on . . . trying to discover what makes stars tick" (Smith, 1994, p. 16). In the face of constant criticism, it would have been very easy for Walters to have become discouraged and given up, especially after she was passed over twice for the position of Today Girl. But Barbara had confidence in herself and the intense effort she channeled into her work. In the world of broadcast journalism, where the odds were heavily stacked against a female with an accent and a lisp, Barbara still rose to the top, eventually commanding the highest salary in the field. Barbara Walters is a model of persistence and versatility, proving time and again that she can rise to any occasion.

REFERENCES

Barbara Walters to marry. (1985, June 14). *New York Times,* C 30.

Ben-David, Calev. (1990, April 13). Barbara Walters: Interviewer interviewed. *Jerusalem Post*, Features.

Carter, Bill. (1992, August 23). "Tender trap." *New York Times Magazine*, 22–55.

Castro, Peter. (1990, November 5). Barbara Walters' sob story. *People*, 160.

Chase, Chris. (1990, May). Special on Barbara Walters. *Cosmopolitan*, 356–359.

Helmbreck, Valerie. (1990, March 9). Barbara Walters; An unscripted look: New bio goes beyond her '20/20' vision. *USA Today*, 1D.

Hosley, David H., and Yamada, Gayle K. (1987). *Hard news: Women in broadcast journalism*. Westport, Conn.: Greenwood Press.

Oppenheimer, Jerry. (1990). *Barbara Walters*. New York: St. Martin's Press.

Probst, Leonard. (1975). *Off camera: Leveling about themselves*. New York: Stein & Day.

Reed, Julia. (1992, February). Woman in the news. *Vogue*, 218–223.

Remington, Bob. (1992, February 9). 'Baba Wawa' gets last laugh. *Edmonton Journal*. Entertainment: Showcase, F2.

Rovin, Jeff. (1990, November). Barbara Walters: Media mover. *Ladies Home Journal*, 199–281.

Shalit, Gene. (1975, November). The woman you never see on TV. *Ladies Home Journal*, 99–175.

Smith, Liz. (1994, March 19). The Barbara Walters interview. *TV Guide*, 12–21.

Sutherland, Christine. (1988, March). TV's superwomen: Barbara Walters. *Ladies Home Journal,* 124–166.

Those east-west power brokers: Barbara Walters and Merv Adelson wed after an 11-month engagement. (1986, May 26). *People,* 93.

ELLEN WARTELLA
(1949-   )

Alison Alexander

Ellen Wartella is a scholar, administrator, and advocate. Her work with a developmental perspective on children and television, particularly advertising, has helped shape the way children and the media are studied. She has been a public advocate for children, and her advocacy for the place of communication within the university and society has made her a visible spokesperson at the forefront of contemporary public debate. Her enthusiasm for new ideas and the challenge of integrating her intellectual understandings have continually produced forward-looking scholarship. Now as her career takes a turn toward administration, her impact on the profession and on the public cannot be underestimated.

FAMILY BACKGROUND

Ellen Wartella was born on October 16, 1949, in a small industrial city in northeastern Pennsylvania. Her family, father Nicholas and mother Margaret, were entrepreneurs in Wilkes-Barre, Pennsylvania, owning an apartment building and a grocery store. The youngest of her family, she has an older sister, Marie, and two older brothers, Nicholas and Michael. It was a strong family, and Ellen particularly remembers the strength of her mother, who virtually managed the apartment building on her own.

She was not only the youngest of her family, but also the youngest of her cousins within a close extended family with a strong education ethic that resulted in an entire generation of doctors, lawyers, businesspeople, and entrepreneurs. Protected, even coddled, it was apparent that Wartella would be doing something different from everyone else. Although it was always clear she would go to college—she was after all the "smart one"—the ultimate decision to become a university professor came as a surprise to her extended family, who never were quite clear on what academic life entailed. Even now she notes that she cannot account for herself to this group. "Now what is it that you do?" they ask, still finding the academic life unfathomable. Other old attitudes still lingered. One aunt remarked at Ellen's traditional Russian Orthodox wedding to her colleague, Chuck Whitney, "How nice. She's marrying a doctor. Now she won't have to work."

EDUCATION

The seeds of her defection from traditional norms were sown early. In the wake of Sputnik, an educational innovation swept her into an "extra work" school program with 12 other sixth-grade students that would last through high school. For Wartella it was a defining experience. Pulled from the normal classroom, these students were challenged to excel in enriched classrooms with the system's best teachers. As a group they read, talked about ideas, became socially conscious—she had to hold her own from the beginning. It was okay to be smart, but it was also a competitive environment in which pressure to excel was intense—so intense that Wartella developed an ulcer at age 14.

The themes of activism and concern with social issues were played out in college. At the University of Pittsburgh, from which she graduated with honors in 1971, Wartella became a student activist involved in the women's movement and student politics. She helped found Pittsburgh's Women's Liberation organization, but perhaps her greatest success was as a student activist. Through her efforts to create an alternative curriculum for the university, she had an opportunity to see the politics of a university in action as an undergraduate. She was appointed student assistant to the dean of Arts and Sciences where she sat in on the faculty senate and assisted the dean in curricular decisions. In 1970 she made the national news when she chastised the university for its failure to comply with affirmative action goals while giving an honorary degree to Elliott Richardson during commencement. Combining her economics major, a self-designed major in communication and technology issues with a love of sociology and history, Wartella decided to become a community organizer like Saul Alinsky.

A three-year National Defense Education Act (NDEA) fellowship seemed the perfect place to learn about the media in order to have the background to know how the media can work to help in community organizing. Yet, early on she became intrigued with children and the media. When Dan Wackman asked her to join with him on an HEW grant on children and television, she readily accepted. Dan was an important mentor, valuing her insights and engaging her in intellectual debate. Minnesota provided her with a fine education in quantitative methods and the effects of television on children. Perhaps most importantly for her career, at a time when graduate students routinely worked for little recognition, Dan Wackman and his co-author Scott Ward acknowledged her contributions by including her as a co-author on publications. Thus, recognition for several publications, a book contract, and a National Science Foundation grant on children and advertising were crucial in launching her career. She received her Ph.D. in 1977, at the age of 27. However, she never published anything from her dissertation, which was an attention study.

If Dan Wackman was her advisor and mentor, Gerald Kline, then of Michigan, was her academic and publishing mentor. After working with her on several publication projects, Gerry Kline introduced her within the discipline and worked with her on her publications. And it was during graduate school that she met her husband to be, Chuck Whitney, also a Ph.D. student in journalism and mass communication at Minnesota.

CAREER DEVELOPMENT

Wartella's first job, at the Ohio State University as an assistant professor in the Department of Communication, lasted from 1976 to 1979. Going there helped produce a broader sense of communication study: she learned about speech communication and was introduced to rhetoric. Previous ties to the Association for Education in Journalism and Mass Communication (AEJMC) and the International Communication Association (ICA) were broadened with her introduction to the Speech Communication Association (SCA). The years at Ohio State were fun; she particularly enjoyed the great arguments she had with suite mates Tom McCain and Norm Elliott. Coming in with a grant established her credibility. During that time she published her first book, an edited collection entitled *How Children Learn to Buy* (1977) with Ward and Wackman, and made her first appearance (in 1979) before a federal commission in her testimony to the Federal Trade Commission on children's television advertising. Suddenly, she was in the public arena with a public agenda of her own.

From Ohio State Wartella moved to the Institute for Communication Research at the University of Illinois where she remained from 1979 until 1993. The early 1980s were a time of unprecedented personal, intellectual, and career growth. The diversity of perspectives at the Institute forced her to directly engage concepts of ideology and cultural studies. With colleagues such as Larry Grossberg, Jim Carey, Cliff Christians, and, of course, Chuck, she plunged into these debates with her usual enthusiasm, even sitting in on courses and, as always, enjoying the great arguments these ideas engendered. From those ongoing discussions, a number of conferences and books were formed, particularly with Chuck Whitney and Larry Grossberg. The cross fertilization of ideas continued as she was awarded a number of research fellowships. She completed a NIMH Post-Doc at the Center for Research on the Influences of Television on Children (CRITC) at the University of Kansas in 1980–1981 and during 1985–1986 was a fellow for the Gannett Center for Media Stuides at Columbia University. During her time at Illinois, a number of Ph.D. students who have now begun to take their place in the discipline worked with her. One point of pride is that every student who worked with her made a conference presentation or a publication from the experience. Not surprisingly, she became involved in working with larger issues within the university. She chaired many important departmental and universitywide committees, developing the administrative expertise that would be so important in her present position.

Her most recent position is as dean and Walter Cronkite Regents Chair of the College of Communication at the University of Texas at Austin. Administering one of the largest and most prestigious of communication colleges has not halted her scholarly activities. She is involved in a major violence-monitoring project, and by the end of her first year she had called a disciplinewide conference to discuss threats to the communication discipline. The administrative aspects of the position are demanding, yet it is too soon to predict the ways in which she will change Texas or Texas will change her.

MAJOR CONTRIBUTIONS AND ACHIEVEMENTS

Since the 1970s children and television have been Ellen Wartella's primary research focus. The shift to cognitive and interpretive perspectives in the study of children and television has been so complete that it may help to remind the reader that the literature of the 1960s centered almost exclusively on behavior and its linkage to televised violence. She, along with a very few others, was crucial in fostering a developmental perspective on children and the media, particularly children and advertising. Wartella still takes a developmental approach and talks to children of different ages. However, recently she has been influenced, as has the field of developmental psychology, by activity theory, particularly the work of Russian theorist Lev S. Vgotsky. This approach attempts to meld cultural/social issues with developmental issues as a way of understanding the changes and influences of culture and society on development. Rather than the Piagetian approach in which stages unfold in an inevitable progression, activity theory examines how environment influences development.

A related area of endeavor has been her work on the state of the field, which she fears may become only historical artifacts, but which have been important attempts to historically situate the intellectual and public policy issues of the discipline. Together with friend and colleague Byron Reeves she has published analyses of the social issues and political concerns that have historically guided public debate and public funds for the study of children and television. The ongoing series of discussions with Reeves has been significant to her continuing efforts to understand the intersection of the academic and public arenas.

But Wartella's greatest contribution has been as a public advocate for children and the media and for the field of communication. As the respect for "academic intellectuals" in public discourse wanes and the cost of such efforts to the individual rises, the willingness of individuals such as Wartella to link research and policy in a public forum is vital. From her initial testimony before the FTC in 1979 to ongoing submissions to the FCC and her appearance at many national and international symposiums designed to discuss issues of children and television, Ellen Wartella has become a visible, politically savvy, and respected spokesperson for the interests of children in the media environment.

This activism has been a common thread in her life. Because of her own social consciousness and a belief in public debate and discourse, Wartella sees herself as obligated to be part of public life. Scholarship is public and should be addressing public issues. In the same way, a public university has to be connected to the larger culture. This does not mean that the university has to be researching the "questions of the week," but it does mean for her that concerns with public issues are part of the role of a public institution.

Although early in her career she "cut her teeth" on children and media agenda issues, her interest in the public agenda has broadened considerably. Her current agenda for public debate now includes an interest in the place of the university and the communication field within the university. In an era in which the public perception of the university is changing and higher education is being called to account for itself, Wartella feels that the need to confront this issue is compelling. In this era, the university and discipline must defend itself and show its relevance and importance to the academy, to society, and to the questions of the day.

Unfortunately, a lot of lip-service in the field of communication does not translate into scholars actually engaging in public debate. As Wartella argues, most agree that communication issues are among the most important ones of our era. Few, however, believe that communication scholars are the ones to address these issues. Those in the field need to publicly demonstrate that they have answers to help the larger public sort through communication questions. Yet, this is not on the disciplinary agenda. Members of the discipline are too focused internally; they don't see linkages, nor do they craft arguments for the public agenda. This lack of attention may cost them dearly in public perceptions of efficacy and rigor. As one example, Wartella asserts, there is a huge body of literature on audiences and media effects that they are too timid to share, fearing that they don't have enough and so do not even venture into these discussions.

The juxtaposition of research and the public agenda is amply demonstrated in Wartella's current independent television monitoring project. Coordinated by Mediascope, this ambitious project seeks to monitor violence on cable among 14 researchers at four universities. This $3.5 million contract is designed to help develop a contextualized code for violence. Researchers at the University of Texas will be coding violence in reality programming and will be involved in the development of this contextualized code.

CRITICISMS

Wartella's various endeavors have not been extensively criticized. Certainly, the overthrow of the Piagetian paradigm for a more environmentally cognizant perspective has targeted works such as hers. Wartella, however, has been in the vanguard of those advocating such an overthrow.

Perhaps the most important criticism has come as part of the global debate engendered by the introduction of critical/cultural studies into the theoretical formulations of mass communication research within the United States. Wartella's training had been in mainstream U.S. theory and methodology. Yet her years at Illinois, the preeminent institution for cultural studies at that time, forced her to confront issues of ideology and hegemony. Integrating the critiques offered by her cultural studies colleagues at Illinois was a monumental challenge. Yet this previous student activist was already politically aware, and she soon found that the concerns of critical/cultural theorists about structures of power and the economic and political forces that influence public communication began to inform her commentaries on the history of the field and the public agenda for children and television. Wartella described this as a time of intellectual ferment, which has been crucial in providing a larger social context within which to frame research questions and issues for public debate.

Nonetheless, one does not become a public advocate without detractors. The issues at the center of public debate concerning children and television are inherently controversial. When one advocates for the interests of children in public forums, the resulting outcry can be extreme. As an example, to return to early concerns about children and television advertising, some of the questions debated in 1979 are still being discussed today: Should children's advertising be banned? What is deceptive to children? How do children understand the selling intent or persuasive nature of advertising? Can they defend against persuasive techniques? What are the consequences of children's lack of understanding or their inability to defend themselves against advertising persuasiveness? And, most importantly, what is the solution? What would be the components of an ethical advertising policy? What would be the policy and business implications?

These are only representative questions of those that public policy must address in one arena. Between the apocalyptic visions of the doomsayers who see the media as destroying society in general and childhood in particular and the rosy visions of those who are sure that the next technology will miraculously transform our society, nuanced discussions of the practical, the possible, and the desirable are hard to achieve. Nonetheless, that is Ellen Wartella's goal.

Wartella has amassed a number of awards and elected offices. She was president of the International Communication Association (ICA) in 1992–1993 and has served as chair of the Mass Communication Division of every major communication association in the United States. The task forces, executive boards, visiting lectures, and committees are too many to enumerate. But this service to the profession and her strong program of research have been recognized in an number of awards: ICA fellow; Association for Education in Journalism and Mass Communication (AEJMC) Young Scholar Award; and University Scholar at the University of Illinois.

INTEGRATION OF PERSONAL AND PROFESSIONAL LIVES

The single most important person in Ellen Wartella's life is her husband, D. Charles Whitney (Chuck). Married on August 1, 1976, they initially met in graduate school at Minnesota. They have been collaborators throughout their careers, with a number of published books and articles as testimony to their joint efforts. Ellen Wartella considers her husband to be her friend and colleague. Their discussions are literally endless, and both acknowledge the important influence of the other on their thinking and research endeavors.

Chuck Whitney works in the area of public opinion, media industries, and media theory. He has recently been selected editor of *Critical Studies in Mass Communication*. His most recent book is an edited volume with James Ettema entitled *Audiencemaking: How the Media Create the Industry* (1994). Their children are David Charles Whitney, Jr. and Stephen Wright Whitney.

Ellen Wartella frames the discussion of family and work not as conflictual, but as integrated. She notes, "I lecture and talk about kids. I'm a whole person and have always tried to be a whole person in classrooms. Let students see models of women who are whole people: scholars, wives, mothers, researchers. They need to see examples of a woman with marriage, family, and friends who is also a researcher, teacher, as well as a dean." (She has even noticed a few student double takes as they realize that the new dean is a woman.) Yet her family and marriage are very important to her, and she doesn't separate them from her work. Particularly as a dean, the time demands are extreme and handling them is sometimes rough, but "a wonderful husband and good child care" make it possible.

Yet her success in life has not been the result of a grand plan. It seems to her more of an unfolding, with changes coming at the right time and opportunities seized when she felt ready to meet those challenges. Not that there haven't been times when the challenges seemed too great and the resources to accomplish her aims too small.

The zest for argument has been crucial to Ellen Wartella's achievements. Incontestably, she is skilled in public debate. In addition, in her work in the public agenda she has developed an impressive ability to articulate the relevance and importance of research in a persuasive manner. Scholar, administrator, advocate, Ellen Wartella fills all these roles, and the field of communication is richer because of her contributions.

REFERENCES

Dervin, B., Grossberg, L., Wartella, E., & O'Keefe, B. (1989). *Rethinking communication: Paradigm dialogues*. Newbury Park, Calif.: Sage Publications.

Ettema, J. S. & Whitney, D.C. (1994). *Audiencemaking: How the media create the audience*. Thousand Oaks, Calif.: Sage.

Huston, A., Wright, J., Wartella, E., Rice, M., Watkins, B., Potts, R., & Campbell, T. (1981). Communicating more than content: The formal features of children's television. *Journal of Communication,* 21(3), 32–48.

Ward, S., Wackman, D. B., & Wartella, E. (1977). *How children learn to buy: The development of consumer information-processing skills.* Beverly Hills, Calif.: Sage Publications.

Wartella, E. (1981). Individual differences in children's responses to television advertising. In E. Palmer & A. Dorr (eds.), *Children and the faces of television: Teaching, violence, selling.* New York: Academic Press.

Wartella, E. (1987). Television, cognition, and learning. In M. Manley-Casimir & C. Luke (eds.), *Children and television.* New York: Praeger.

Wartella, E. (1993). Communication research on children and public policy. In P. Gaunt (ed.), *Beyond agendas: New directions in communication research.* Westport, Conn.: Greenwood Press.

Wartella, E. (1994). Challenge to the profession. *Communication Education,* 43, 54–62.

Wartella, E. (1994). Producing children's television programs. In J. Ettema & C. Whitney (eds.), *Audiencemaking: How media create the industry.* Beverly Hills, Calif.: Sage.

Wartella, E. (ed.). (1979). *Children communicating: Media and development of thought, speech, understanding.* Beverly Hills, Calif.: Sage Publications.

Wartella, E., & Reeves, B. (1985). Historical trends in research on children and the media: 1900–1960. *Journal of Communication,* 35 (2), 118–133.

Whitney, D. C., & Wartella, E. (1992). Media coverage of the "Political Correctness" debate. *Journal of Communication,* 42(2), 83–95.

IDA B. WELLS-BARNETT (1862–1931)

Dorothy Zeccola

"Miss Ida B. Wells (Iola) has been called the 'Princess of the Press,' and she has earned the title" (Beasley & Gibbons, 1977). If Ida B. Wells-Barnett was a princess at 26, then she was surely a queen when she died. Born to slave parents on July 26, 1862, she overcame racism and sexism to become one of the most outspoken women of the nineteenth century (Schilpp & Murphy, 1983). Although most well-known for her crusade against lynching, Wells-Barnett supported several causes, including a woman's right to vote and women's clubs. "Throughout her life, she responded to lynching and violence, Christian duty and responsibility, leadership, and the role of religion out of the stance of her early years" (Townes, 1993, p. 115).

Wells-Barnett had an unusually "normal" and grounded childhood for an African American growing up in the late 1800s (Schilpp & Murphy, 1983). Wells-Barnett's life began in Tippah County, Mississippi. Her father, unlike many slaves, learned a trade working as a carpenter's apprentice. As a skilled craftsman, her father was able to provide for Wells-Barnett and her seven younger siblings after they were freed. Her mother attended school in addition to caring for the family (Schilpp & Murphy, 1983). After the family received its freedom, they moved to Holly Springs, Mississippi. Wells-Barnett attended the primary school at Rust College, where her father served on the first board of trustees (1983).

Unfortunately, her happy childhood ended in 1878 when yellow fever took the lives of her parents and her 10-month-old brother. In order to prevent her brothers and sisters from being separated and placed in foster homes, Wells-Barnett, at the age of 16, dropped out of school to raise them (Duster, 1970). The local Masons supplemented her small inheritance until she was able to take the district teaching exam. For the next few years, she supported the family by teaching in a one-room school house six miles out of town (Schilpp & Murphy, 1983).

In 1883 Wells-Barnett decided to move to Memphis, Tennessee, when an aunt who lived there offered to help her care for her younger brothers and sisters. Wells-Barnett continued to teach in rural schools while she waited to take the teaching exam for city schools. In the summers Wells-Barnett attended Fisk University (Schilpp & Murphy, 1983).

As a teacher, Wells-Barnett was a member of "the small emerging Black middle class in Memphis" (Townes, 1993). She became a member of the local literary society where she met the editor of the *Evening Star,* whom she later replaced. The paper as well as her own popularity grew, and soon she also became a columnist for another paper, the *Living Way.* Using the pen name Iola, Wells-Barnett wrote about schools, churches, and any relevant issues concerning African Americans in Memphis during the 1880s (Townes, 1993).

Wells-Barnett was no stranger to the one major issue of the time, discrimination. In 1884 she rode the Chesapeake and Ohio Railroad to her school. As usual, she sat in the ladies' car. When the conductor came around to take the tickets, he asked her to move to the smoking car. She refused. To keep the conductor from physically removing her from her seat, Wells-Barnett bit him on the hand. It took three men to finally remove her from her seat. Upon leaving the train, she immediately hired a lawyer and sued the railroad (Duster, 1970).

Wells-Barnett, at 22 years of age, brought a suit against the railroad for failing to provide "separate but equal" accommodations (Schilpp & Murphy, 1983). Awarded $500 by the circuit court, the decision was overturned by the supreme court of Tennessee. She had to return the money plus court costs. In her autobiography, she recounted her disappointment when she noted that even though the supreme court said she could go to the state courts to redress grievances, the civil rights bill enacted during the Reconstruction period provided very little, if any, justice for Negroes (Duster, 1970).

This early brush with injustice helped fuel Wells-Barnett's passion to use her writing to point out discrimination against African Americans. She received national attention for her articles concerning her court case against the railroad (McKerns, 1989). In 1889 she invested her savings and became part-owner and editor of a small paper, *Free Speech and Headlights,* whose name she shortened to the *Memphis Free Speech* (Schilpp & Murphy, 1983).

By 1891 her passion resulted in both favorable and unfavorable reviews. The Memphis Board of Education fired her because she wrote articles describing the "poor and neglected conditions of the black schools" (Schilpp & Murphy, 1983, p. 125). However, by this time the loss of her teaching position could be weathered because she was able to support herself from subscriptions to *Free Speech* (numbering about 4,000) (McKerns, 1989).

No longer needing to teach, Wells-Barnett had numerous other projects waiting for her attention. By 1981 she was a "regular correspondent" to the *Detroit Plaindealer, Christian Index,* and *The People's Choice* as well as a "regular contributor'' to *The New York Age, Indianapolis World, Gate City Press* (Missouri), *Little Rock Sun, American Baptist* (Kentucky), *Memphis Watchman, Chattanooga Justice,* and the *Fisk University Herald* (Townes, 1993, p. 10).

The following year tragedy forced Wells-Barnett to begin what was to become her life's work. One of her dear friends, Thomas Moss, along with two of his friends, was lynched. His death sparked her antilynching crusade, which would make her name known to people in the entire Untied States as well as in England (Townes, 1993).

Wells-Barnett's factual and terrifying accounts of lynching angered many in and out of Memphis. While in New York on business, she learned that the offices of the *Free Speech* had been destroyed (Schilpp & Murphy, 1983). An anonymous note had been left at the scene warning death to anyone who tried to publish the *Free Speech* again (McKerns, 1989).

The setback made Wells-Barnett more determined than ever to fight against lynching or any other form of injustice against African Americans (Schilpp & Murphy, 1983). She relocated to New York and before long was a part-owner of the *New York Age* (McKerns, 1989).

Wells-Barnett worked furiously over the next three years to inform the world about the horrors of lynching. She published a biweekly column for her paper and wrote two pamphlets (''Southern Horrors: Lynch Law in All Its Phases'' and ''The Reason Why the Colored American Is Not in the World's Columbian Exposition'') (McKerns, 1989). She traveled to Great Britain twice, both times for antilynching speaking tours. During the second tour she also wrote an ''Ida B. Wells Abroad'' column for the ''white'' journal *Chicago Inter Ocean.* In between her speaking tours she moved to Chicago and began writing for the *Chicago Conservator;* she also became more involved with women's issues (McKerns, 1989).

Surprisingly, during this time she also had a social life. On June 27, 1895, she married Ferdinand L. Barnett, an attorney as well as owner of the *Conservator* (McKerns, 1989). She was so busy, however, that the wedding date had to be changed three times (Duster, 1970). Interestingly, she was one of the first African-American women to keep her maiden name.

Wells-Barnett's public was not as happy for her as she would have liked, and she faced some rather severe censuring in the press. Many believed, unfortunately, that, with her marriage, she had deserted both them and the cause. One of those people was her friend, Susan B. Anthony:

I had been with her for several days before I noticed the way she would bite out my married name in addressing me. Finally I said to her, ''Miss Anthony, don't you believe in women getting married?'' She said, ''Oh, yes, but not women like you who had a special call for special work. I too might have married but it would have meant dropping the work to which I had set my hand.'' She said, ''I know of no one in all of this country better fitted to do the work you had in hand than yourself. Since you have gotten married, agitation seems practically to have ceased. Besides, you have a divided duty. (Duster, 1970, p. 254)

Wells-Barnett continued to work after the birth of her first child. She bought the *Conservator* outright and was its editor. She also spoke to women's clubs and acted as president of the Ida B. Wells Woman's Club. When the Women's State Central Committee asked her to do a tour of the state, she tried to refuse by requiring a nurse to take care of her 6-month-old son. When the Central Committee agreed, she stated that she believed she was the only woman with a nursing baby who traveled through the country making political speeches (Duster, 1970).

Wells-Barnett decided to stop working after the birth of her second child. Although it was an easy decision for her to make, she did so with great thought. A spiritual woman, she based her decision largely on her Christian beliefs: "Wells was clear about the correct behavior God expected from a faithful Christian" (Townes, 1993, p. 110). Her autobiography has an entire chapter, "A Divided Duty," dedicated to her thoughts on the subject of working mothers. In short, she stressed that motherhood was as much of a profession as school-teaching and lecturing and that one had to become proficient in this endeavor as in the others. She strongly believed that women have been given a special place in the overall scheme of life and that they owe it to themselves (as well as their children) to take advantage of the ways in which motherhood can help them develop their own womanhood (Duster, 1970).

Wells-Barnett returned to work with a vengeance after her last child's eighth birthday: "She used the lecture podium and newspaper articles to bring the injustices and outrage of bigotry before the public eye in an uncompromising and clear manner" (Townes, 1993, pp. 12–13).

In 1915 Wells-Barnett met with President Woodrow Wilson to speak about segregation in his administration (Townes, 1993). She continued to write, covering the 1919 riots of Chicago and the riots of Phillips County, Arkansas (Townes, 1993). Her final cause was a new one: politics. She ran for the state senate as an independent candidate in 1929 (Townes, 1993).

Although never ending her crusade, Wells-Barnett remained in the Chicago area for the rest of her days. She became involved with the suffrage movement, urging African-American women and men to register and vote. She worked with W.E.B. Du Bois and the initial founders of the National Association for the Advancement of Colored People. In founding the Negro Fellowship League, she wanted to focus on the poorer African Americans in Chicago. It was in this endeavor that she was the most disappointed, "She became vexed at their middle-class friends who were unwilling to work among the poorer blacks. . . . Too many wealthy blacks, she declared in frustration, lacked compassion" (Schilpp & Murphy, 1983, p. 129).

"Wells-Barnett provided an invaluable gift to African-American society when she began to unmask the double standards of southern society" (Townes, 1993, p. 210). She continued to do just that until 1931, when she died from uremic poisoning. One wonders how much credit Wells-Barnett actually gave herself for her lifetime of hard work. She once told Frederick Douglas: "I am only a mouthpiece through which to tell the story of lynching and I have told it so often that I know it by heart. I do not have to embellish; it makes its own way" (Duster, 1970, p. 231).

REFERENCES

Beasley, M., & Gibbons, S. (1977). *Women in media: A documentary source book.* Washington, D.C.: Women's Institute for Freedom of the Press.

Downs, R. B., & Downs, J. B. (1991). *Journalists of the United States.* Jefferson, N.C.: McFarland & Co.

Duster, A. M. (ed.). (1970). *Crusade for justice: The autobiography of Ida B. Wells.* Chicago: University of Chicago Press.

McKerns, J. P. (ed.). (1989). *Biographical dictionary of American journalism.* Westport, Conn.: Greenwood Press.

Schilpp, M. G., & Murphy, S. M. (1983). *Great women of the press.* Carbondale: Southern Illinois University Press.

Townes, E. M. (1993). *Womanist justice, womanist hope.* Atlanta, Ga.: Scholars Press.

APPENDIX: SHORT BIOGRAPHIES OF NOTABLE WOMEN IN COMMUNICATION

CONTENTS

ALBRECHT, TERRANCE (April 2, 1953–   ), Professor of Communication and Chairperson, Department of Communication, University of South Florida.

Terrance Albrecht, the daughter of William and Lorraine Albrecht, was born on April 2, 1953, in Fort Eustis, Virginia. She has a daughter, Ellen Lorraine. She completed both her undergraduate and graduate studies at Michigan State University. She received a B.A.

in communication in 1974, an M.A. in communication in 1975, a Master's degree in labor and industrial relations in 1978, as well as her Ph.D. in communication in 1978. In addition to her position at the University of South Florida, she is the co-director of the Medical Interaction Research Group at the H. Lee Moffitt Cancer Center and Research Institute in Tampa, Florida. Her mentor was Richard V. Farace. She received the International Communication Association's W. Charles Redding Dissertation of the Year Award in 1979.

Albrecht has been on the editorial boards of several journals including *Communication Research, Communication Monographs, Human Communication Research, Social Marketing Quarterly,* and *Organizational Communication: Emerging Perspectives.* She also served as the associate editor of the *Western Journal of Speech Communication.*

Her research has focused on medical interaction, social support, and organizational innovation, and she has had 11 convention papers ranked as a "Top 3 paper." She has edited two books on social support, the most recent of which was published in 1994 by Sage Publications. Her most significant publications include

Burleson, B., Albrecht, T., & Sarason, I. (eds.). (1994). *The communication of social support: Messages, interactions, relationships and community.* Newbury Park, Calif.: Sage.

Albrecht notes, with regard to her career, that

(t)he most important aspect of my professional life has been the opportunity to work with numerous outstanding graduate students (from diverse fields) at six universities. Working with these students in the classroom and research settings over the years embodied for me a true appreciation of the interdependence of teaching, research, and service. It has been a treasured privilege.

ALEXANDER, ALISON (October 21, 1949–). Professor and Department Head, Department of Telecommunication, Henry W. Grady College of Journalism and Mass Communication, University of Georgia.

Alison Alexander, the daughter of Leason and Andella Alexander, was born on October 21, 1949 in West Virginia. She is married to James Owers and has three children, Katherine, James, and Victoria Owers. She received her B.A. (magna cum laude) in 1971 from Marshall University, majoring in education. In 1974 she completed an M.A. in communication at the University of Kentucky and in 1979 received her Ph.D. in communication from Ohio State University. She was mentored by Ellen Wartella.*

Alexander has been very active in the field, serving as a member of the board of directors of the Broadcast Education Association between 1993 and 1996, editor of the *Journal of Broadcasting & Electronic Media (JOBEM)* from 1989 to 1991, as well as book review and criticism editor, for *JOBEM* from 1984 to 1988. She is a member of the editorial board of six journals. She has also been an active member of several professional associations, including the Eastern Communication Association, the Speech Communication Association, the International Communication Association, and the Association for Education and Journalism.

Alexander's research interests center on audience research, with a focus on media in the family, including family use of media. Current research includes a project examining industry and societal definitions of quality in children's programming. Her work in children's uses of the media has ranged across topics as diverse as children's viewing of soap operas to the place of sibling interaction in the television viewing context. Her teaching interests reflect these interests, concentrating on audience research, children and television, media theory, research methods, and writing.

Alexander is an active scholar; she has co-authored two books, contributed numerous chapters to edited collections, written a large number of journal articles, as well as consistently presenting papers at professional meetings. She cites the following as her three most significant publications:

Alexander, A. (1990). Effects of television on family interaction. In J. Bryant (ed.), *Television and the American family*. (pp. 211–226). Hillsdale, N.J.: Erlbaum.
Alexander, A., Fry, V., & Fry, D. (1990). Textual status, media consumption, and the stigmatized self. In J. Anderson (ed.), *Communication yearbook 13*. Newbury Park, Calif.: Sage.
Alexander, A., Ryan, M. S., & Munoz, P. (1984). Creating the learning context: Investigations on the interaction of siblings during co-viewing. *Critical Studies in Mass Communication*, 1 (4).

Alexander notes that the most significant thing about her career is:

[m]y diverse background in the discipline of communication has given me a broad perspective on our field. In my research and teaching, as well as in my administrative positions, I have been able to synthesize differing academic perspectives and also work with diverse individuals and programs. This breadth of perspective has been an important attribute of my career.

BAVELAS, JANET BEAVIN (February 12, 1940–   ). Professor, Department of Psychology, University of Victoria, Canada.

Janet Bavelas was born on February 12, 1940 in Portland, Oregon. She has since become a Canadian citizen. She completed her undergraduate and graduate degrees at Stanford University; she received her M.A. in communication research in 1968 and her Ph.D. in psychology in 1970. Her mentors include Paul Watzlawick, John Weakland, Don Jackson, and Alex Bavelas.

Bavelas' research and teaching interests include interpersonal communication, conversation, discourse analysis, nonverbal communication, and research methods. The following are her most significant publications.

Bavelas, J. B., Black, A., Chavil, H., & Mullett, J. (1990). *Equivocal communication*. Newbury Park, Calif.: Sage.
Watzlawick, P., Beavin, J. H., & Jackson, D. J. (1967). *Pragmatics of human communication*. New York: W. W. Norton.

BEASLEY, MAURINE (January 28, 1936–   ). Professor of Journalism, University of Maryland, College Park, Maryland.

Maurine Beasley, daughter of Dimmitt and Maurine Hieronymous Hoffman, was born on January 28, 1936 in Sedalia, Missouri. She is married to Henry (Hank) R. Beasley and has one child, Susan Sook Beasley Kim. She received her B.J. in journalism and her B.A. in history from the University of Missouri-Columbia in 1958; her M.S. in journalism from Columbia University in 1963, and her Ph.D. in American civilization from George Washington University, Washington, D.C., in 1974. Her mentor was Dr. Letitia Brown, her dissertation adviser at George Washington.

Beasley has received numerous awards, including the Haiman Award for Distinguished Scholarship in Freedom of Expression in 1995 and the Distinguished Service in Local Journalism Award from the Washington Chapter of the Society of Professional Journalists in 1994. She was also honored in 1994 with the Outstanding Woman Educator Award from the Commission on the Status of Women, Association for Education in Journalism and Mass Communication (AEJMC). In 1993 she was named Outstanding Woman, University of Maryland–College Park. Her book on the history of women and journalism was designated Notable Academic Book of 1994 by *CHOICE,* the journal of academic libraries.

Beasley is also very active in the field. She was president of AEJMC in 1993–1994; regional director and national board member, Society of Professional Journalists from 1991 to 1992; president, Washington Professional Chapter, Society of Professional Journalists, 1990–1991; and president, American Journalism Historians' Association, 1989–1990.

Beasley's research and teaching interests focus on women, the media, and journalism history. Her most significant publications are:

Beasley, M. (1987). *Eleanor Roosevelt and the media: A public quest for self-fulfillment.* Urbana, Ill.: University of Illinois Press.
Beasley, M. (1993). *Taking their place: A documentary history of women and journalism.* Washington, D.C.: American University Press.

Beasley notes that the most significant thing about her career is her hiring at the University of Maryland in 1974 under affirmative action.

BROWN, JANE D. (August 22, 1950–). Professor and Director of Graduate Studies, School of Journalism and Mass Communication, University of North Carolina, Chapel Hill.

Jane D. Brown, daughter of Clarence and Florence Brown, was born on August 20, 1950 in West Chester, Pennsylvania. She is married to Jim Protzman and has a daughter, Lillian Delano Brown, and a stepson, Alexander Protzman. She completed her undergraduate degree at the University of Kentucky, Lexington, in journalism, and received her M.A. in 1974 and Ph.D. in 1978 from the School of Journalism and Mass Communication, University of Wisconsin-Madison. Her mentor was Jack McLeod.

Brown is very active in the field. She is chair of the standing committee on research at the Association for Education in Journalism and Mass Communication (AEJMC) and is the current chair of the faculty at the University of North Carolina, Chapel Hill. She is a member of the editorial board of the *Journal of Broadcasting & Electronic Media, Journal of Communication, Newspaper Research Journal,* and *Health Communication.*

Brown's research has focused on adolescents, the mass media, identity development, and health behaviors. Her teaching typically focuses on the processes and effects of the mass media as well as health communication. Her most significant publications include

Bauman, K. E., LaPresse, J., Brown, J. D., Koch, G. G., & Padgett, C. A. (1991). The influence of three mass media campaigns on variables related to adolescent cigarette smoking: Results of a field experiment. *American Journal of Public Health,* 81(5), 597–604.
Brown, J. D., & Schulze, L. (1990). The effects of race, gender, and fandom on audience interpretations of Madonna's music videos. *Journal of Communication,* 40(2), 88–102.
Greenberg, B. S., Brown, J. D., & Buerkel-Rothfuss, N. (1992). *Media, sex and the adolescent.* Cresskill, N.J.: Hampton Press.

Brown writes that the most significant thing about her career is her ability to combine teaching and research about significant social issues such as adolescent girls' sexuality and the role of the mass media.

DATES, JANNETTE L. (March 17, 1937–). Acting Dean, School of Communications, Howard University, Washington, D.C.

Jannette L. Dates, daughter of Moses and Iantha Lake, was born on March 17, 1937, in Baltimore, Maryland. She is married to Victor H. Dates, Sr., and has four children, Karen, Victor, Matthew, and Craig. She completed her undergraduate studies at Coppin State College, majoring in education. She completed her M.A. in 1964 at Johns Hopkins University and her Ph.D. in 1979 at the University of Maryland at College Park. Her mentors include John T. Splaine, Thomas Cripps, Orlando L. Taylor, and Maurice T. Wilson. She was a fellow at the Freedom Forum Media Studies Center in 1992–1993 and in February 1991 received the Young, Gifted and Black Distinguished Resident Scholar award from California State University at Dominques Hills. Her 1990 co-edited book, *Split Image: African Americans in the Mass Media,* was winner of the Gustavus Meyer National Award for the best book on human rights in the United States (announced November 10, 1992).

Dates has had considerable experience in broadcast communications, recently serving as a television panelist on Media and Popular culture ("Close-Up" on C-Span), on the Clarence Thomas/Anita Hill Hearings—A Year later (Crier & Co., CNN), and as a radio panelist on the weekend edition of "All Things Considered" (National Pubic Radio). She is a member of the city of Baltimore's Mayor's Cable Communications Commission and during 1988–1990 served as chairwoman of the education task force, Mayor's Cable Advisory Commission.

Dates has been active in the Broadcast Education Association, serving as a Board of Trustees Task Force Member and Publications Committee Member, as well as chair-woman of the Multicultural Studies Division and the Leadership Challenge Division. In addition, she was the newsletter editor for the Gender Issues Division. She is a member of the Association for Education in Journalism and Mass Communication (AEJMC) Commission on the Status of Minorities and has been a member of the Women's Studies Division, the Research Division. She has been active in the Black Caucus of AEJMC as well as the Speech Communication Association (SCA).

Dates has written extensively on the the African American's image in the media, including a number of newspaper editorials and magazine articles as well as several scholarly publications. In addition, she has made numerous convention presentations on this topic. Her most significant publications include

Dates, J. L., (1991). Cultural diversity in American media history. In J. E. O'Connor & G. Bush (eds.), *Film history,* Vol. XXI, Nos. 2 & 3. The Historians Film Committee of the Smith-sonian Institute Media Studies Project.

Dates, J. L. (in press). Caroline Jones. Cindy Lont (ed.), *Women in media.* New York: Macmillan Press.

Dates, J. L., & Barlow, W. (eds.). (1993), *Split image: African Americans in the mass media.* 2nd edition. Washington, D.C.: Howard University Press.

Dates, J. L., & Cosby, C. (1992, October 11). For African Americans, television is, literally, "a different world." *The Philadelphia Inquirer.*

Dates notes that the most significant thing about her career is "being able to focus on the issues of concern to an often excluded or misrepresented group. I enjoy working with people and trying to make good things happen."

DORR, AIMEE (September 20, 1942–). Professor, Graduate School of Education and Information Studies, University of California, Los Angeles.

Aimee Dorr was born in Pasadena, California, on September 20, 1942. She is married to Donald Simpson and has two biological children (Simeon and JT) and two stepchildren (Daniel and Genevieve). She received her B.S. in mathematics from Stanford University in 1964; both of her graduate degrees are in developmental psychology from Stanford—an M.A. in 1966 and a Ph.D. in 1970. Her mentors were Eleanor Maccoby, Nathan Maccoby, and Gerald Lesser.

Dorr's research has focused on children's and teenager's interactions with the media and technology. Throughout her career she has been active in the public policy arena, serving on the Committee on Television and Social Behavior of the Social Science Research Council from 1975 to 1988 as well as a reviewer of grant applications as a member of the National Institute of Mental Health's Mental Health Behavior Sciences Research Review Committee. She also has served as an adviser to or evaluator of numerous children's programs such as "Sesame Street" and "The Big Blue Marble" and a consultant for the Disney Channel and PBS stations, including KCET and WGBH. She has also served on the editorial board of the *Journal of Communication, Communication Research,* and the *Journal of Broadcasting & Electronic Media.* She is a prolific researcher; her most important publications include

Dorr, A. (1986). *Television and children: A special medium for a special audience.* Beverly Hills, Calif.: Sage Publications.

Dorr, A., & Rabin, B. E. (1995). Parents, children and television. In M. H. Bornstein (ed.), *Handbook of parenting,* vol. 4: *Applied and practical considerations of parenting.* Mahwah, N.J.: Erlbaum.

Leifer, A. D. & Roberts, D. F. (1972). Children's responses to television violence. In J. P. Murray, E. A. Rubinstein, & G. A. Comstock (eds.), *Television and social behavior,* vol. 2, *Television and social learning.* (pp. 42–180). Washington, D.C.: Government Printing Office.

Palmer, E. L., & Dorr, A. (eds.). (1980). *Children and the faces of television—teaching, violence, selling.* New York: Academic Press. (Second printing, 1981).

Dorr has been working in the area of children and media for 30 years. She notes that the most significant things about her career are her continual effort to move back and forth between basic research and her use of research to inform practice and policy.

FAIRHURST, GAIL (October 9, 1951–   ). Professor and Head, Department of Communication, University of Cincinnati.

Gail Fairhurst, daughter of Albert and Agnes Theus, was born on October 9, 1951 in Cleveland, Ohio. She received her B.A. in 1973 from Bowling Green State University, majoring in English education. She received her M.A. degree in communication from Ohio State University in 1975 and her Ph.D. in communication from the University of Oregon in 1978. She is married to Dr. Verne Fairhurst, and they have three children, Katherine, Thomas, and Kelsey. Her mentor is L. Edna Rogers.*

Fairhurst has been active in the discipline's professional organizations, serving as chair (1992–1994) and vice chair (1990–1992) of the organizational communication division of the International Communication Association. She is on the editorial board of *Communication Monographs,* the *Journal of Communication, Management Communication Quarterly,* and *Communication Studies.*

Fairhurst studies internal organizational communication processes and specializes in the study of leadership, power, and control in organizations. She has published regularly in communication and organizational science journals and is known for the study of actual talk between leaders and employees, using conversational analysis as an assessment tool. Her most significant publications include

Courtright, J. A., Fairhurst, G. T., & Rogers, L. E. (1989). Interaction patterns in organic and mechanistic systems. *Academy of Management Journal,* 32, 773–802.

Fairhurst, G. (1993). The leader-member exchange patterns of women leaders in industry. *Communication Monographs,* 60, 1–31.

Fairhurst, G. T., Green, S. G., & Courtright, J. A. (1995). Inertial forces and the implementation of a socio-technical systems approach: A communication study. *Organization Science,* 6, 168–185.

Fairhurst, G. T., Green, S. G., & Snavely, B. K. (1984). Face support in controlling poor performance. *Human Communication Research,* 11, 272–295.

She notes that the most significant thing about her career is that her

research program has focused heavily on actual talk in organizations. This has spurred an interest in many forms of both quantitative and qualitative discourse analyses. A second notable feature of my research program is consistent cross-publishing within the Communication and Organizational Sciences.

HASLETT, B. J. (October 8, 1945–   ). Professor, Department of Communication, University of Delaware.

B. J. (Beth) Haslett, daughter of Clifford W. and Edna Stoeckmann Bonniwell, was born on October 8, 1945 in Hutchinson, Minnesota. She is married to David W. Haslett and has two children, Heidi Christine and Erik David. She completed her undergraduate education in speech communication at the University of Minnesota (Minneapolis); she received her M.A. in communication from the University of Wisconsin-Madison in 1968, and her Ph.D. in communication from the University of Minnesota (Minneapolis) in 1971. Her mentors include Dr. James J. Jenkins (psycholinguistics), Dr. William S. Howell (Communication), Dr. Gene Piche (sociolinguistics), and Dr. Frederick Williams.

Haslett's research has articulated and developed a pragmatic approach to the study of communication processes; she defines pragmatics as the use of language in context. Her research typically explores communication processes from an interdisciplinary base incorporating linguistics, psychology, and sociology. She has also made a significant contribution to the literature on gender issues in communication, particularly in organizational settings. Her most significant publications include

Haslett, B. J. (1984). Communication development: The state of the art. In R. Bostrom (ed.), *Communication yearbook.* Vol. 8. (pp. 198–267).

Haslett, B. J. (1987). *Communication: Strategic action in context.* Hillsdale, N.J.: Erlbaum.

Haslett, B. J., Geis, F. L., & Carter, M. R. (1992). *The organizational woman: Power and paradox.* Norwood, N.J.: Ablex Publishing Corp.

Haslett notes that the most significant aspect of her career has been her attempt to advance pragmatics as an important theoretical approach to communication. In addition, she believes that her book integrating social science research on gender issues in organizations is an important step in improving women's professional lives. She also believes that ''it is important to be well-read in your areas of research and teaching expertise, and that means reading *outside* of your own paradigm or theoretical preference. Another important skill is to be open-minded and learn from others' expertise throughout your professional career.''

JAMES, NAVITA (February 16, 1952–   ). Director of African Studies and Associate Professor of Communication and Mass Communications, University of South Florida.

Navita James, daughter of Major Herndon M. Cummings and the late Mildred Pearson Cummings, was born on February 16, 1952, in Columbus, Ohio. She is married to Julius

E. James and has two daughters, Erika Nicole and Jessica Erin. She completed her undergraduate and graduate education at Ohio State University; she received her B.A. in 1973 in speech communication, her M.A. in 1975, and her Ph.D. in 1981. Her mentors include Thomas A. McCain, Leonard C. Hawes, and Frank Hale.

James has been active in professional organizations and the community. She served as president of the Southern States Communication Association from 1993 to 1994 and has also been very active in the Speech Communication Association, serving as chair of the Mass Communication Division and as a member of the Legislative Council and numerous other committees. She has just been named chair of the Florida Commission on the Status of Women.

James' research interests have focused on the interconnection of mediated and interpersonal communication. Her research has also examined gender, race, class, and identity particularly as they relate to the mass media. Her most significant publications include

James, N. (1994). When Miss America was always white. In Alberto Gonzalez, Marsha Huston, & Victoria Chen (eds.), *Our voices: Essays in culture, ethnicity, and communication.* Los Angeles: Roxbury Publications.

James, N., & McCain, T. A. (1982). Television games preschool children play: Patterns, themes and uses. *Journal of Broadcasting,* 26(4), 783–800.

James notes that the most significant thing about her career is "liking the way my personal, professional, and community lives have nourished one another."

KRAMARAE, CHERIS (March 10, 1938–   ). Professor, Department of Speech Communication, and Director, Women's Studies, University of Illinois, Urbana–Champaign, Illinois.

Cheris Kramarae, daughter of Deda Rae Smits and William H. Gamble, was born on March 10, 1938 in Brookings, South Dakota. She is married to Dale Cramer and has two children, Brinlee and Jana Cramer. She received her M.S. in journalism/English from Ohio University in 1963, and her Ph.D. in speech communication and sociolinguistics from the University of Illinois, Urbana–Champaign, in 1975. Her mentors were the feminists of the nineteenth century.

Kramarae has published extensively in the areas of language and gender, gender and technology, and sociolinguistics. Her most significant publications are

Kramarae, C. (1986). *A feminist dictionary.* London and New York: Pandora Press/Unwin & Hyman, HarperCollins. (New edition, *Amazons, Bluestockings and Crones.* San Francisco: Harper [1992].)

Kramarae, C. (ed.) (1988). *Technology and women's voices.* London and New York: Routledge.

Kramarae, C., Thorne, B., & Henley, N. (eds.). (1983). *Language, gender and society.* Rowley, Mass.: Newbury House.

Kramarae has been very active in the academy, serving on the editorial or advisory boards of eight journals and as the editor (or co-editor) of four journals and one book series. She has planned numerous conferences dealing with feminist scholarship and has given numerous invited lectures both here and abroad. In 1992 she was awarded the Frances Merritt Award from the Speech Communication Association.

She writes that one of the most significant things about her career

is that it happened at all. When I married, all the clues around me indicated that I was to cook, clean, and child care. And I did—but I also went to classes, working toward the Ph.D., while initially teaching with temporary contracts. Like many U.S. women who were lucky enough to be able to participate in the Women's Movement of the 1970s, I have worked double-time for the past 30 years in order to survive in academe while helping establish Women's Studies courses and programs. They have been exciting, if often frustrating, years, and I've had the chance to work with amazing women. I think many of the 19th century suffragists felt the same way. I've learned that many of them said and wrote things that were much more radical and to the point than what most of us dare say today in academe.

KRENDL, KATHY A. (July 26, 1950–   ). Dean, School of Continuing Studies, and Professor of Telecommunications, Indiana University.

Kathy Krendl, the daughter of Karl and Mary Krendl, was born on July 26, 1950 in Celina, Ohio. She is married to Richard Gilbert and has two children, Claire and Thomas. She received her B.A. in English in 1972 from Lawrence University, her M.A. in journalism in 1977 from Ohio State University, and her Ph.D. in communication in 1982 from the University of Michigan. Her mentors are Stephen Withey and Wilbur Shramm.

Dean Krendl is a member of six professional organizations and has served as program chair for the Mass Communication Division of the Speech Communication Association (SCA) and for the Theory and Methodology Division of the Association for Education in Journalism and Mass Communication (AEJMC). She is on the editorial board of the *Journal of Broadcasting & Electronic Media,* and is a reviewer for several journals, publishers, and professional associations.

Krendl is a prolific scholar whose research interests center on the learning processes in formal and informal education contexts, particularly in relation to the media. She is also interested in the effects of media campaigns. Her teaching interests include media and society, social action and media, as well as learning and media. Her most significant publications are

Krendl, K. A. (1986). Media influence on learning: Examining the role of preconceptions. *Educational Communication and Technology Journal,* 34(4), 223–234.
Krendl, K. A. (1988). Two roads converge: The synthesis of research on media influence on learning. In B. Dervin & M. Voigt (eds.), *Progress in communication sciences,* Vol. 9. (pp. 105–122). Norwood, N.J.: Ablex.
Krendl, K. A., Clark, G., Dawson, R., & Troiano, C. (1993). Preschoolers and VCRS: A multiple methods approach. *Journal of Broadcasting & Electronic Media,* 37(3), 293–312.

When asked about the most significant thing about her career she wrote,

My mentors trained me to think broadly and openly about the role of media in people's lives. They focused on the importance of thinking carefully about media and their influence on people rather than following dominant research traditions or rigid hypotheses. I learned from them that it is more important to struggle to identify important questions, though they may be unanswerable, than to address questions that can be answered but are not interesting or helpful in the long term.

MEADOWCROFT, JEANNE M. (June 12, 1950–   ). Assistant Professor, Agricultural Journalism, University of Wisconsin–Madison.

Jeanne Meadowcroft, the daughter of Ruben and Frances Meadowcroft, was born on June 12, 1950 in Madison, Wisconsin. She is married to Stephen C. Smith. She completed both her undergraduate and graduate education at the University of Wisconsin–Madison. She received her J.B.A. in journalism and mass communication in 1979, her M.A. in journalism and mass communication in August 1981, and her Ph.D. in mass communications in 1985. Her mentors include Steve Chaffee, Jack McLeod, Mark Miller, and Byron Reeves.

Meadowcroft is active in the profession. She was the head of the Communication Theory and Methodology Division of the Association for Education in Journalism and Mass Communication (AEJMC) during the 1993–1994 academic year and the research program chair for this same division during the 1991–1992 academic year. She was a member of the editorial board of the *Journal of Broadcasting & Electronic Media* from 1991 to 1994, and continues as a member of the advisory board for the Council on International Nontheatrical Events.

Meadowcroft's publications and convention presentations date from the mid-1980s. Her research has focused on the media, cognition, and youth, and her teaching interests lie in media theory and research methods. Her three most significant publications are

Meadowcroft, J. M. (1986). Family communication patterns and political development: The child's role. *Communication Research,* 13(4), 603–624.

Meadowcroft, J. M. (in press). Attention span cycles. In J. H. Watt & A. VanLear, Jr. (eds.), *Cycles and dynamic patterns in communication processes.* Newbury Park, Calif.: Sage Publications.

Meadowcroft, J. M., & Reeves, B. (1989). Influence of story schema development on children's attention to television. *Communication Research,* 16(3), 252–274.

MONTGOMERY, KATHRYN CHRISTINE (January 30, 1947–   ). President, Center for Media Education, Washington, D.C.

Kathryn Montgomery, daughter of Robert L. and Ellen Rose, was born on January 30, 1947 in Riverside, California. She is married to Jeffrey Chester, her professional partner and co-founder of the Center for Media Education. They have one daughter, Lucy Chester. She received her B.A. in American Studies in 1973 from California State University, Los Angeles; her M.A. in mass communication in 1975 from California State University, Northridge; and her Ph.D. in motion pictures and television in 1979 from the University of California, Los Angeles. Her mentors are Erik Barnouw, Peggy Charren,* and George Gerbner.

Kathryn Montgomery has been active in the area of media policy and history; children's television; minorities and the media; emerging new technologies; and the institutional analysis of media industries. She has been a consultant for a number of organizations, including the United States Civil Rights Commission, and the Office for Substance Abuse Prevention, U.S. Department of Health and Human Services. Her most significant publication is

Montgomery, K. C. (1989). *Target: Prime time. Advocacy groups and the struggle over entertainment television.* New York: Oxford University Press.

Montgomery is the co-founder and president of the Center for Media Education (CME), a Washington-based public interest organization devoted to promoting the democratic potential of the electronic media through public education, research, policy analysis, and outreach to the press. CME is currently coordinating two major projects: The Campaign for Kids' TV (aimed at improving children's television and educating the public about the Children's Television Act) and The Future of Media Project (focused on fostering and creating a vision of how America's twenty-first century telecommunications infrastructure can serve the democratic and social needs of our society.

Montgomery writes that the most significant thing about her career is that

After 15 years as a university professor and scholar, I moved to Washington and co-founded CME (1991). In a short time, CME has become a leading public interest group in Washington. We are playing a critical role in promoting policies designed to bring about a more democratic, diverse, and equitable media system.

MURPHY, SHARON M. (August 2, 1940–   ). Provost, Academic Vice President, and Professor, Bradley University, Milwaukee, Wisconsin.

Sharon M. Murphy was born on August 2, 1940 in Milwaukee to Adolf and Margaret Hirtz Feyen. She was married to the late James E. Murphy and has two children, Shannon L. and Erin A. Murphy. She completed her B.A. in journalism at Marquette University in 1965, and her M.A. (1970) and Ph.D. (1973) at the University of Iowa. Her mentors include Dr. Malcolm Machean, Jr., and Dr. Richard Budd. She was a Fulbright senior lecturer in mass communication at the University of Nigeria during the 1977–1978 academic year.

Murphy has been very active in the discipline, serving as vice president of the National Accrediting Council on Education in Journalism and Mass Communication from 1983 to 1986, president of the Association for Education in Journalism and Mass Communication from 1986 to 1987, and has been a member of a number of committees for AEJMC and the Association of Schools of Journalism and Mass Communication. She received a Women in Communications, Inc. National "Headliner Award" in 1965 and a 1991 minisabbatical grant from the Freedom Forum. She is on the boards of directors of the Dow Jones Newspaper Fund, the Youth Communication/North American Center, the Milwaukee Press Club Endowment, Ltd., the Greater Milwaukee Chapter-American Red Cross, the Newspaper Association of America Foundation, and is a member of the Human Rights Committee of the Milwaukee Humans Relations Radio-Television Council.

Murphy has been a public relations director, magazine editor, and a newspaper reporter. She has conducted research in the history of women and minorities in the mass media, and her teaching interests include report writing as well as the history of women and minorities in the mass media. Her most significant publications include

Murphy, J., & Murphy, S. M. (1981). *Let my people know: American Indian journalism 1828–1978.* Norman: University of Oklahoma Press.
Murphy, S. M. (1974). *Other voices: Black, Chicano & American Indian press.* Dayton, Ohio: Pflaum.
Murphy, S. M., & Scalp, M. (1983). *Great women of the press.* Carbondale: Southern Illinois University Press.

She believes that the most significant thing about her career is that it has been focused on issues and history of diversity, internationalization, and multiculturalism in mass communication. Her career has included teaching at all levels from primary schools through doctoral programs. Most importantly, it was supported and enriched by a loving and brilliant scholar/editor/husband/fellow parent of two gifted and caring daughters.

O'KEEFE, BARBARA J. (July 4, 1950–   ). Associate Professor, University of Illinois, Urbana–Champaign.

Barbara O'Keefe, the daughter of Keith and Geraldine Jackson, was born on July 4, 1950 in Granite City, Illinois. She is married to Daniel J. O'Keefe. Her undergraduate and graduate degrees are from the University of Illinois–Urbana. She completed her A.B. degree in speech in 1971, graduating with High Honors and Distinction in speech. She received her A.M. degree in speech communication in 1973 and her Ph.D., also in speech communication, in 1976.

O'Keefe is an active member of the Rhetorical and Communication Theory Division of the Speech Communication Association, serving as a referee for convention papers over the past 15 years. She is also a member of the International Communication Association, serving on the 1992 Nominating Committee. She is an associate editor of *Communication Monographs, Human Communication Research, Communication Studies,* and the *Journal of Applied Communication Research.*

For the past six years, O'Keefe has been the director of the University of Illinois, Urbana–Champaign's (UIUC's) Verbal Communication Program. This has entailed the supervision of 35 sections of a two-semester course in oral and written composition to satisfy the freshman rhetoric requirement. This work has also been instrumental in setting up the Center for Writing Studies at UIUC.

O'Keefe's most significant contribution is the development of the theoretical and methodological foundation for a message-centered approach to communication research. Her research has focused on communication theory and research, including message production and effects, face-to-face interaction processes, written communication, and computer-mediated communication. She has published extensively in numerous journals and is now in the process of completing three co-authored books. Her most significant publications are

O'Keefe, B. J. (1988). The logic of message design: Individual differences in reasoning about communication. *Communication Monographs,* 55, 80–103.

O'Keefe, B. J., & Delia, J. G. (1982). Impression formation and message production. In M. Roloff & T. Berber (eds.), *Social cognition and communication.* (pp. 33–72). Beverly Hills, Calif.: Sage Publications.

O'Keefe, B. J., & Shepherd, G. J. (1987). The pursuit of multiple objectives in face-to-face persuasive interactions: Effects of construct differentiation on message organization. *Communication Monographs,* 54, 396–419.

PEARSON, JUDY C. (September 2, 1946–   ). Professor, School of Interpersonal Communication, Ohio University, Athens, Ohio.

Judy Pearson, daughter of Joseph D. and Sophia C. Forman, was born on September 2, 1946. She is married to Paul Edward Nelson and has four children—Christopher John, Kathryn Cornelia, Benjamin Joseph, and Rebekah Kristina. She completed her undergraduate degree from St. Cloud State University in 1968, majoring in speech communication and philosophy. She received her graduate degrees from Indiana University: her M.A. in rhetoric and public address in 1973 and her Ph.D. in speech communication and the history and philosophy of education in 1975. Her mentors are Paul W. Batty and J. Jeffrey Auer.

Over the years, Pearson has received numerous awards. She has been listed in several editions of *Who's Who,* has served on the editorial board of *Communication Studies, the Journal of the International Listening Association,* and *Communication Education,* and has served as a guest, consulting, or associate editor of numerous publications.

Pearson's research interests include gender and communication, family communication, and interpersonal relationships. Her research focuses on some of the basic tenets for effective communication, particularly in relation to gender differences and effective marital and family relations. Her work has been popularized on national television, including "CBS This Morning," the "Jenny Jones Show," and a PBS special, "Love and Marriage," and in over 250 newspapers and magazines. Her most significant publications include

Pearson, J. C. (1989). *Communication and the family: Seeking satisfaction in changing times.* New York: Harper & Row Publishers.
Pearson, J. C. (1991). *Gender and communication.* Dubuque, Iowa: William C. Brown. (2nd edition).
Pearson, J. C. (1992). *Lasting love: What keeps couples together.* Dubuque, Iowa: William C. Brown.

Pearson notes that the most significant thing about her career has been ''the influence I have had on women both personally and professionally.''

PERSE, ELIZABETH M. (July 29, 1949–   ), Associate Professor, Department of Communication, University of Delaware.

Elizabeth (Betsy) Perse, daughter of Virginia P. and Edward A. Moyer, was born on July 29, 1949 in Cleveland, Ohio. She is married to Jeffrey A. Bergstrom and has two children, Rebecca and Jonathan. She received her B.A. degree in English literature from Northwestern University in 1971. She completed her M.A. degree in 1985 and her Ph.D. in 1987 from Kent State University in communication studies. Her mentors include Alan M. Rubin, Rebecca B. Rubin, Nancy Signorielli, and John Courtright.

Perse's research interests include the uses and effects of mass communication and are grounded in a uses and gratifications perspective. She was listed in 1993 among the top 3.6 percent of active prolific scholars in communication and in 1992 was named the thirteenth most prolific active woman scholar in communication. In addition, in 1991 she was named the twenty-second most productive television researcher between 1985 and 1990. Her most significant publications include

Perse, E. M. (1990). Audience selectivity and involvement in the newer media environment. *Communication Research, 17,* 675–697.
Rubin, A. M., & Perse, E. M. (1987). Audience activity and television news gratifications. *Communication Research, 13,* 58–84.

Perse has been an active member of the Mass Communication Division of the Speech Communication Association. She served as secretary of the division from 1987 to 1988, as a member of the research committee of the Mass Communication Division from 1991 to 1993, and as chair of this committee during 1993–1994. She currently is the review and criticism editor for the *Journal of Broadcasting & Electronic Media.*

PINGREE, SUZANNE (June 5, 1945–   ). Professor, Agricultural Journalism, University of Wisconsin–Madison.

Suzanne Pingree was born on June 5, 1945 in San Francisco, California. She is married to Robert Hawkins and has three children, Paisley, Ray, and Haley. She received her B.A. in art history from the University of California at Santa Barbara and her Ph.D. in communication research from Stanford University in 1975. Her mentors include Aimee Dorr,* Mary Ann Yodelis Smith, and Brenda Dervin.* She teaches research design and media effects.

Pingree's research has focused on viewing activity and patterns, psychological processes in constructing social reality, as well as children and television. Her most recent research is exploring issues in health communication. Her most significant publications include

Hawkins, R. P., & Pingree, S. (1990). Divergent psychological processes in constructing social reality from mass media content. In N. Signorielli & M. Morgan (eds.), *Cultivation Analysis:*

New directions in media effects research. (pp. 35–50). Newbury Park, Calif.: Sage.
Pingree, S., Hawkins, R. P., Rosengren, K. E., Johnson-Smaraggdi, U., & Reynolds, N. (1991). Television structure and adolescent viewing patterns: A Swedish-American comparison. *European Journal of Communication,* 6(4), 417–440.

She notes that most significant thing about her career is "pushing the limits of collaborative scholarship with my husband, Robert Hawkins. Almost all of our publications are joint. We've been able to balance our careers with a great family life and have kept focused on what's really important."

PUTNAM, LINDA L. (August 10, 1945–   ). Professor and Head, Department of Speech Communication, Texas A&M University.

Linda L. Putnam, daughter of Etta and Allard Loutherback, was born on August 10, 1945, in Frederick, Oklahoma. She is married to Thomas M. Putnam and has one child, Ashley A. Putnam. She received her undergraduate degree in speech and theater from Hardin-Simmons University in 1967, her M.A. in communication from the University of Wisconsin–Madison in 1968, and her Ph.D. in speech communication from the University of Minnesota in 1977. Her mentors include Ernest G. Bormann, Emogene Emery, Rod Hart, and Kay Deux. She has received numerous awards, including the H. Woolbert Research Award from the Speech Communication Association in 1993, and was given the Outstanding Member Award for the Organizational Communication Association Division of the International Communication Association in 1993.

Putnam has been very active in the professional organizations of the discipline. She was president of the International Association for Conflict Management in 1993–1994, and she was an editor for the organization communication emerging perspectives series for Ablex Publishing from 1993–1995. She has been a member of numerous editorial boards, including, the Sage Annual Reviews of Communication Research, and a series editor in organizational communication for Lawrence Erlbaum Publishers. She currently is an associate editor for *Communication Theory* and *Management Communication Quarterly.*

Putnam's research is in the area of organizational communication, with special interest in negotiation and conflict management in organizations as well as group processes. Her teaching focuses on organizational culture, negotiation, and dispute resolution as well as communication and conflict management. She has an extensive publication record, including co-editing five books in organizational communication, a large number of chapters in books on organizational communication, as well as numerous articles in refereed journals. Her most significant publications are

Jablin, F., Putnam, L. L., Roberts, K., & Porter, L. (1987). *Handbook of organizational communication.* Beverly Hills, Calif.: Sage.
Putnam, L. L. (1983). The interpretive perspective: An alternative to functionalism. In L. L. Putnam & M. E. Pacanowsky (eds.), *Communication and organization: An interpretive approach.* (pp. 31–54). Beverly Hills, Calif.: Sage.
Putnam, L. L. (1990). Reframing integrative and distributive bargaining: A process perspective. In B. H. Sheppard & R. J. Lewicki (eds.), *Research on negotiation in organizations* (vol. 2) (pp. 3–30). Greenwich, Conn.: JAI Press.
Putnam, L. L., & Mumby, D. (1992). The politics of emotion: A feminist reading of bounded rationality. *Academy of Management Review,* 17, 465–486.

Putnam notes that the most significant thing about her career is "the support of family and friends and the desire to push the envelope or stretch the limits of the way we traditionally think about communication and organizing or about conflict management. The desire to make my work interdisciplinary rather than housed only in speech communication.''

RAKOW, LANA (April 17, 1952–   ). Professor and Director of the School of Communication, Associate Dean of the College of Fine Arts and Communication, University of North Dakota.

Lana Rakow, daughter of the late Vera and William Rakow, was born on April 17, 1952 in North Dakota. She is married to Tony Stukel, Library Network Director at North Dakota, and they have one child, a daughter, Caitlin Rakow. She completed her undergraduate degree at the University of North Dakota, with a double major in journalism and the humanities in 1974. She completed an M.A. degree in English at the University of North Dakota in 1977 and received her Ph.D. in communication from the University of Illinois, Urbana–Champaign. She is a member of Phi Beta Kappa.

Rakow was associated for many years with the University of Wisconsin–Parkside, as an assistant and later associate professor, as chair of the Communication Department, and as associate vice chancellor for undergraduate studies.

Rakow's research interests have focused on gender, technology, and feminist theory, and her publications mirror these interests. Her most significant publication, a study of women and the telephone, was named the 1993 Book of the Year by the Organization for the Study of Communication, Language, and Gender. The bibliographic reference for this book is

Rakow, L. (1992). *Gender on the line: Women, the telephone, and community life.* Urbana–Champaign: University of Illinois Press.

Rakow notes that the most significant thing about her career is ''being a feminist scholar at this point in time in the field'' and ''moving into administration and figuring out what it means to be a feminist administrator.''

RICHMOND, VIRGINIA P. Professor and Coordinator of Graduate Studies, Communication Studies Department, West Virginia University, Morgantown, West Virginia.

Virginia Richmond received her B.A. degree in 1971 from West Virginia Institute of Technology, majoring in language arts. She completed an M.A. in speech communication at West Virginia University in 1974 and her Ph.D. in speech communication, with a minor in management, from the University of Nebraska in 1977. She credits several mentors, including James C. McCroskey, John L. Petelle, Jerry Allen, Mark Hickson III, Raymie McKerrow, James Chesebro, Linda Lederman, Jeanne Lutz, Kathleen Jamieson,* and Gerald Ratliff.

Richmond has been extremely active in the Eastern Communication Association (ECA), receiving the distinguished service award in May 1994 in recognition of excellent professional achievement and service to the membership as well as the Donald H. Ecroyd/ Caroline Drummond Ecroyd teaching excellence award in 1993. She served as vice president of ECA in 1986–1987 and as president in 1987–1988 and was editor of *Communication Quarterly* in 1991–1993. She also was the founding editor of the World Communication Association's *Communication Research Reports* (1984–1988). In addition, in 1990 she was honored for outstanding achievement in instruction as a ''Master

Teacher'' by the Communication and Instruction Group of the Western States Communication Association.

Virginia Richmond has published extensively in the area of communication apprehension, avoidance, and effectiveness as well as in interpersonal, organizational and instructional communication. She was recognized as one of the most prolific active female scholars in the field of communication (see *Communication Quarterly*, 1992, 40(4), 350–356).

Her most significant publications include

McCroskey, J. C., & Richmond, V. P. (1993). Identifying compulsive communicators: The talka-holic scale. *Communication Research Reports*, 10, 107–114.
Richmond, V. P., & McCroskey, J. C. (1992). *Power in the classroom: Communication, control, and concern*. Hillsdale, N.J.: Lawrence Erlbaum Associates.
Richmond, V. P., & McCroskey, J. C. (1992). *Organizational communication for survival*. Englewood Cliffs, N.J.: Prentice-Hall.

SHOEMAKER, PAMELA J. (October 25, 1950–   ). John Ben Snow Professor, S. I. Newhouse School of Public Communications, Syracuse University.

Pamela J. Shoemaker, the daughter of Paul E. and Nettie K. (Steed) Shoemaker, was born on October 25, 1950 in Chillicothe, Ohio. She is married to John H. Parrish and has one son, John Shoemaker Parrish. She received her B.S. degree in journalism from Ohio University, graduating summa cum laude in 1972, and her M.S. in communication from Ohio University in 1972. She completed her Ph.D. in 1982 in mass communication at the University of Wisconsin, Madison. Her mentors include Steve Chaffee, Wayne Danielson, Guide Stempel, Ellen Wartella,* Dwight Teeter, and Max McCombs. She was the 1990 recipient of the Drieghbaum Under-40 Award from the Association for Education in Journalism and Mass Communication for outstanding achievement in teaching, research, and service.

Shoemaker has been very active in the professional organizations of the discipline. She is the current president-elect of the Association for Education in Journalism and Mass Communication and is the current chair of the Mass Communication Division of the International Communication Association. She has been a member of the editorial board of the following journals: *Communication Research, Political Communication, Journal of Communication, Journalism Monographs, Mass Communication Review*, and *Journalism Quarterly*.

Shoemaker's research has focused on the influences of media content, political communication, and deviance as a major part of newsworthiness. She has developed a course in critical thinking for mass communications, the goal of which is to increase the analytical skills of students early in their college careers. Her most significant publications include

Shoemaker, P. J. (1991). *Gatekeeping*. Communication Concept Series, Vol. 3. Newbury Park, Calif.: Sage Publications.
Shoemaker, P. J., with Mayfield, E. K. (1981). Building a theory of news content: A synthesis of current approaches. *Journalism Monographs*, 103.
Shoemaker, P. J., & Reese, S. D. (1991). *Mediating the message: Theories of influences on mass media content*. New York: Longman.

She notes that the most significant thing about her career is that she has ''helped call attention to 'the other half of the field'—the study of the forces that shape media content rather than the traditional study of media effects. I have contributed to theory building in this area by the synthesis of literature and the suggestion of hypotheses to be tested.''

SINGER, ELEANOR (March 4, 1930–   ). Research Scientist, Survey Research Center, University of Michigan, Ann Arbor.

Eleanor Singer was born on March 4, 1930, in Vienna, Austria. She is married to Alan G. Singer and has two children, Emily Ann Singer McCord and Lawrence Alexander Singer. She completed her B.A., summa cum laude, at Queens College in 1951, majoring in English, and was elected to Phi Beta Kappa in 1950. She received her Ph.D. from Columbia University in sociology in 1966. Her mentors were Herbert H. Hyman and Morris Zelditch, Jr.

Singer has been very active in the American Association for Public Opinion Research (AAPOR), receiving a special award in 1985 and serving as the Conference Committee Chair in 1984–1985, as councilor-at-large from 1985 to 1987 and 1991 to 1993, as vice president and president-elect in 1986–1987, and as president in 1987–1988. She also served as a member of a delegation of public opinion researchers to the USSR in 1990.

Singer served as editor of *Public Opinion Quarterly* from 1975 to 1986, noting that she "helped put *Public Opinion Quarterly* in a financially and intellectually secure position at a time when this was not at all a foregone conclusion." She continued as a member of this publications advisory committee until 1993. She has published extensively since the late 1960s, most recently focusing on issues relating to privacy and confidentiality and informed consent in survey research. She is also very interested in survey research methods and has edited (with Stanley Presser) *Survey Research Methods: A Reader* (University of Chicago Press, 1989). Her most significant publications include

Hyman, H. H., & Singer, E. (eds.). (1968). Readings in *reference group theory and research*. New York: Free Press.
Singer, E. (1978). Informed consent: Consequences for response rate and response quality in social surveys. *American Sociological Review*, 43, 144–162.
Singer, E., & Endreny, P. (1993). *Reporting on risk*. New York: Russell Sage Foundation.

When asked about the most significant thing about her career she wrote:

The fact that I've done mostly what I like for the past thirty or so years, and at a time when combining children and career was less common than it is today. And the fact that I'm beginning a new exciting and challenging career at the Survey Research Center at Michigan's Institute for Social Research at almost-retirement age. I've found out a few useful things in the course of my work, and have thoroughly enjoyed the process of doing so.

THOMAN, ELIZABETH (June 18, 1943–   ). Executive Director, Center for Media Literacy, Los Angeles, California.

Elizabeth Thoman, daughter of John and Gertrude Thoman, was born on June 18, 1943. Since 1964 she has been a member of the Sisters of the Humility of Mary, Davenport, Iowa, a Catholic religious order of women working for justice and educational empowerment for children and adults. She received her B.A. in English from Marycrest College (Iowa) and an M.A. in 1978 in communications management from The Annenberg School for Communication, University of Southern California. Her mentors include Everett Rogers, Richard Byrne, Marjorie Tuite, and Stewart Hoover.

Thoman is a leader of the growing media literacy movement. The founder of the Center for Media and Values (now the Center for Media Literacy), she was the founding editor and publisher of *Media & Values*, a quarterly magazine. Sixty-three issues of this periodical were published over a 16-year period, covering practically every major issue in the contemporary mass communication world. Some of the more significant issues were:

Militarism in the Media (no. 39/Summer 1987)
Redesigning Women (no. 49/Fall 1989)
Impact of Images (no. 57/Winter 1992)
Media and Violence (no. 62–63/Summer–Fall 1993)

The Center for Media Literacy, under Thoman's direction, also produces Media Literacy Workshop Kits. These provide a "startup" curriculum for media literacy in schools, religious organizations, and community centers.

Thoman notes that the most significant thing about her career is that because of her

strong social justice commitment and experience in community organizing that *Media & Values* was able to move the fledgling critical viewing-media education movement in the U.S. beyond intellectual understanding to a social change approach. Building our media literacy curriculum resources on social change theory was a fundamental shift in media literacy pedagogy as practiced in England and Canada that reflects the unique contribution the United States can make to the field.

THOMAS, SARI (July 25, 1950–). Professor and Chairperson, Mass Media and Communication; Director, Institute of Culture and Communication, Temple University, Philadelphia.

Sari Thomas, daughter of Abraham and Esther Tannenbaum, was born in Philadelphia, Pennsylvania, on July 25, 1950. She received her B.A. in 1971 in psychology from Temple University; her M.A. in 1973 from The Annenberg School for Communication, University of Pennsylvania, and her Ph.D. in 1977 from the Faculty of Arts and Sciences, University of Pennsylvania. Her mentors include Ray Birdwhistell, George Gerbner, Irving Goffman, Larry Gross, Dell Hymes, Robert Merton, Sol Worth, and Charles Wright.

Thomas has been active in the discipline, serving as the editor of *Critical Studies in Mass Communication* from 1990 to 1992, and on the editorial board of several journals, including the *Journal of Communication, Critical Studies in Mass Communication,* and *Philosophy of the Social Sciences.* She is director of the International Conferences on Communication and Culture, sponsored by the Institute of Culture and Communication at Temple University.

Thomas' research interests have focused on socioeconomics and the sociology of knowledge with respect to the place of the media in the social structure. Her most significant publications include

Thomas, S. (1980). Some problems of the paradigm in communication theory. *Philosophy of the Social Sciences,* 10(4), 427–444.
Thomas, S. (1986). Mass media and the social order. In G. Gumpert, and R. Cathcart (eds.), *Inter/ Media: Interpersonal communication in a media world.* (pp. 611–627; 664–666). New York: Oxford University Press.
Thomas, S. (1989). Functionalism revised and applied to mass communication study. In B. Dervin, L., Grossberg, H. O'Keefe, and E. Wartella (eds.), *Paradigm dialogs in communication, Vol. II.* (pp. 376–396). Beverly Hills, Calif.: Sage.
Thomas, S. (1994). Artifactual study in the analysis of culture: A defense of content analysis in a postmodern age. *Communication Research,* 21(6), 683–697.

TING-TOOMEY, STELLA (May 22, 1952–). Professor, Department of Speech Communication, California State University at Fullerton.

Stella Ting-Toomey was born in Hong Kong on May 22, 1952. She completed her B.A. degree in 1975 in mass communication at the University of Iowa and her M.A. degree in communication at the University of Iowa in 1976. She received her Ph.D. in 1981 in speech communication at the University of Washington.

Ting-Toomey was chair of the Intercultural and Development Division of the International Communication Association from 1993 to 1995. Her research and teaching interests lie in the area of cross-cultural communication, particular cross-cultural conflict management, and cross-cultural face-negotiation. Her most significant publications are

Ting-Toomey, S. (1988). Intercultural conflicts: a face-negotiation theory. In Y. Kim & W. Gudykunit (eds.), (pp. 213–235). *Theories in intercultural communication.* Newbury Park, Calif.: Sage Publications.

Ting-Toomey, S. (1993). Communicative resourcefulness: An identity negotiation perspective. In R. Wiseman & J. Koester (eds.), *Intercultural communication competence.* Newbury Park, Calif.: Sage Publications.

Ting-Toomey writes that the most significant thing about her career is "the development of the cross-cultural face-negotiation theory."

TRACY, KAREN (January 31, 1951–   ). Associate Professor of Communication, University of Colorado, Boulder, Colorado.

Karen Tracy was born on January 31, 1951, in Philadelphia. She is married to Robert Craig and has one daughter. She received her B.S. in speech pathology from the Pennsylvania State University in 1972, her M.A. in speech pathology from Bowling Green State University in 1974, and her Ph.D. in communication arts from the University of Wisconsin–Madison in 1981. Her mentors include Dean Hewes, Joseph Cappella, Mary Anne Fitzpatrick,* and Herb Simons. In 1982 she received the Speech Communication Association's Dissertation Award and in 1983, the Emerging Scholar Award from the Speech Communication Association of Pennsylvania.

Tracy's research has focused on discourse in institutional settings. She has edited three books and published numerous articles in this area. She is currently working on a book extending and reframing recent studies of intellectual discussion: *Talking about ideas: Dilemmas and discourse practices of academic discussion.* Her most significant publications include

Craig, R. T., Tracy, K., & Spisak, F. (1986). The discourse of requests: Assessment of a politeness approach. *Human Communication Research,* 12, 436–478.

Tracy, K., & Baratz, S. (1993). Intellectual discussion in the academy as situationed discourse. *Communication Monographs,* 60, 300–320.

Tracy, K., & Carjuzaa, J. (1993). Identity enactment in intellectual discussion. *Journal of Language and Social Psychology,* 12, 171–194.

Tracy has served on the editorial boards of a number of journals including *Communication Monographs, Discourse Processes, Communication Quarterly, Human Communication Research, Research on Language and Social Interaction, Text,* and the *Western Journal of Speech Communication.* She has been active in professional organizations, serving as chair of the Language and Social Interaction Division of the Speech Communication Association and chair of the Language and Social Interaction Interest Group of the International Communication Association.

Tracy believes that the most significant thing about her career is that "my research interests have been shaped by the practical communication problems I face in my personal and work roles.''

WILSON, BARBARA J. (November 27, 1957–   ). Associate Professor, Department of Communication, University of California, Santa Barbara.

Barbara J. Wilson, the daughter of W. R. Wilson and the late Joan Wilson, was born on November 27, 1957 in Wisconsin. She completed both her undergraduate and graduate studies at the University of Wisconsin–Madison. She received her B.A. in journalism, graduating with honors, in 1979, her M.A. in 1982, and her Ph.D. in 1985 in communication arts. She is married to John C. Lammers, assistant professor, Department of Communication, University of California, Santa Barbara. Her mentors include Joanne Cantor,* Edward Donnerstein, and Ellen Wartella.*

Wilson has been active in the professional organizations of the discipline. She served as vice chair (1991–1993) and chair (1993–1995) of the Instructional and Developmental Communication Division of the International Communication Association. She is on the editorial board of *Communication Reports, Human Communication Research, Journal of Broadcasting & Electronic Media,* and *Western Journal of Communication.*

Wilson's research interests focus on the social and psychological effects of the mass media, developmental differences in children's responses to the mass media, children's emotional and cognitive processing of mass media, and the media policy implications of social science research. Her most significant publications include

Wilson, B. J., Linz, D., Donnerstein, E., & Stipp, H. (1992). The impact of social issue television programming on attitudes toward rape. *Human Communication Research,* 19, 179–208.

Wilson, B. J., Linz, D., & Randall, B. (1990). Applying social science research to film ratings: A shift from offensiveness to harmful effects. *Journal of Broadcasting & Electronic Media,* 34, 443–468.

Wilson, B. J., & Weiss, A. J. (1993). The effects of sibling coviewing on preschoolers' reactions to a suspenseful movie scene. *Communication Research,* 20, 214–248.

She notes that the most significant aspect of her career

is that my research has practical implications that can help parents and children. Most of the studies I have conducted are aimed at testing theoretical propositions about child development and media effects. Some recent projects have focused on children's fear reactions to different plots and characters, children's understanding of emotions and humor in family situation comedies, children's comprehension of special effects in mass media programming, and children's reactions to toy-based advertising. But in addition to advancing theory, my goal is to identify and evaluate strategies for teaching children how to deal with the mass media. In some cases, my research also has had implications of public policy regarding mass media. Ultimately, I have strived for a balance between contributing to theoretical understanding and enhancing the everyday media experiences of American families.

AUTHOR INDEX

INDEX

Boldface page numbers indicate location of main entries.

Department of Health, Education, and
Welfare, 175
dependency theory, 14–15
depression, 132, 180
Depression. *See* Great Depression
Dervin, Brenda L., xxii, **103–117**, 455
desegregation, 16, 293
DeValera, Eamon, 274
developmental psychology, 433, 448; perspective, 55
Dewey, John, 95
Dewey, Thomas E., 317
Dickens, Charles, 357
Dickerson, Nancy, **118–123**
dictation skills, 370
dictators, 273
diets, fad, 71
diplomat, 67, 152, 313
direct effects models, 15
discrepancy arousal theory, 45
discrimination, 32–33, 68, 121, 151, 166,
254, 257–260, 294, 323, 375, 389,
419, 426–427, 439; discriminatory policies, 370
disk jockey, 370
Disney channel, 448
dissertation, 11, 52, 107, 144, 163–164,
166, 204, 230, 256–257, 294, 301,
331, 361; fellowships, 289
diversity, 57, 63, 109, 111–112, 209,
255, 307, 453
divorce, 2, 20, 25, 41, 122, 131, 155,
181, 213, 242, 247, 261, 286, 343,
377, 391, 409, 411, 421, 424, 427
Dix, Dorothy, **124–134**; *Dorothy Dix
Talks*, 124, 134
doctor, 330, 420, 430–431
Doctor of Humane Letters, 68
doctoral program, 222, 261; doctorate,
119; studies, 143, 229
documentary, 25, 71, 123, 422
Dollfuss, Engelbert, 274
domestic arts, 199; domestic life, 3, 6,
17, 191, 270, 314, 403; rhetoric, 199;
science, 195; skills, 265; violence, 298
Donaldson, Sam, 324
Donohue, Phil, 423
Dorr, Aimee, 447–448, 455

double binds, 232
double standard, 17, 74, 86, 441
Douglas, Frederick, 441
Downs, Hugh, 422, 426
Down's Syndrome, 292
Dred Scott decision, 394
drinking, 9, 177, 180, 251, 341; excessive, 247, 350–351, 353, 412
drugs: addiction, 376; amphetamines,
377; barbiturates, 243, 249; cocaine,
377; illicit, 251; marijuana, 377;
overdose, 243, 249
Du Bois, W.E.B., 441
Duke and Duchess of Kent, 245
dunking stool, 354
Dupont de Nemours, 206
DuPont, Ethel, 245
Durant, Michael, 73
dyslexia, 329

Earhart, Amelia, 319
Eastern Communication Association
(ECA), 444, 457
Eastman, Elaine Goodale, **135–141**
Eastwood, Clint, 425
eating disorders, 236, 239
Eaton, John H., 354
ecology, 207, 335–336; ecological metaphor, 328
economics, 88, 163, 165, 176, 178, 317,
330, 392, 426, 431; barriers, 339;
class, 314; factors affecting women,
391; forces, 435; issues, 155; problems, 205
Eden, Anthony, 277
editor, 35, 43, 144, 164, 297, 313, 323,
343, 389, 394; editing, 277; editorial
decisions, 173, 182 185, 312, 315; editorial duties, 194; editorial policy, 165,
177, 314; editor-in-chief, 36; female,
crusading, 349; service, 142, 193;
workers, 184; yearbook, 105
editorial advocacy, 188, 192; campaign,
193; consultant, 43; content, 37, 314;
excellence, 181
editorial board, 43, 144, 165, 218, 275,
297, 314, 383, 444

ABOUT THE EDITOR

Alan M. Rubin

The lives of all the communication scholars profiled in this book are marked by a series of important life-defining events and turning points. The same is true for the book's editor, Nancy Signorielli.

Nancy was born in New York City on July 29, 1943, to Marie and the late Anthony Signorielli. The world events that surrounded the Cold War of the 1950s, as well as her educational experiences, led Nancy to her interest in the scientific method of inquiry. She was in junior high school at a time when her country began to realize its deficiencies in science. She refers to herself as "a child of sputnik." At a time when high schools throughout the nation encouraged their students to consider the sciences, Nancy developed her interests in science and math.

Signorielli received her B.A. in 1965 from Wilson College, in Chambersburg, Pennsylvania, with a major in psychology and a minor in math. During her senior year, she was given a relatively free hand in designing and implementing a two-semester project examining conformity and response sets. This was a major turning point for Nancy. In an era before ready access to computers, she factor-analyzed her data with the assistance of a hand calculator. Nancy says that the analysis may not have been very accurate, but her love for the social sciences was cemented.

This, however, was an era when even those women who went to college were expected "to work for awhile and then get married, settle down, and have a family." No one spoke to Nancy Signorielli about going to graduate school. After graduation, she returned to New York and got a job in the Media Research Department of Compton Advertising. She followed media coverage, ad placements, and target audiences for certain products. Nancy was bored, though. A colleague at work had just begun a new doctoral program in psychology at the

City University of New York (CUNY). Over several lunches, she spoke with Nancy about the new program. Nancy began taking classes in experimental psychology at Hunter College and Queens College, and was admitted to the CUNY doctoral program in psychology with a research and teaching assistantship. The association lasted through the M.A. degree in psychology from Queens College in 1967, when Nancy decided she did not want to pursue further studies in learning theory or perception.

This time, Nancy got a media research position at Ogilvy & Mather in New York. The tasks were similar to those at Compton. Although she found herself training many young men who came into the company, she was not permitted to enter Ogilvy & Mather's management training program. The company justified this by telling her that she "would just leave to get married within two years." She was not excited by the tedium of her job, saw no room for advancement, and felt that a more advanced degree was "the key to be taken seriously." This, too, proved to be a turning point.

Conversations with a friend introduced Nancy to the field of communication. She met George Gerbner during a visit to the University of Pennsylvania, and learned about plans to develop a Ph.D. program at The Annenberg School for Communication. Nancy entered the M.A. program there in the fall of 1967, with the understanding that she would move into the doctoral program once it began. "It was the perfect move and fit."

The late 1960s, of course, were a time of extensive media coverage of important and tragic societal events: the assassinations of Martin Luther King and Robert Kennedy, the continuing importance of the civil rights movement, and the civil unrest surrounding the Vietnam War. A major question was whether the media contributed to the violence in society. The new President's Commission on the Causes and Prevention of Violence asked George Gerbner to conduct a content analysis of violence on television, and most of the faculty and students at Annenberg became involved in the project.

Signorielli began to work with George Gerbner on the Cultural Indicators (CI) project in the spring of 1969. At first, she guided the content analysis, and then, became a member of the CI team. She completed her doctoral classes three years later and began working on her dissertation, analyzing the characters on television drama. While doing this, she also taught statistics and experimental psychology at Chestnut Hill College, a small women's college in Philadelphia. In 1974, Nancy Signorielli Tedesco had her first, and possibly most cited publication, "Patterns in Prime Time," published in the *Journal of Communication*. The spring of 1975 saw the completion of Nancy's Ph.D. and the dissolution of her first marriage.

During the next 12 years, Nancy Signorielli continued with the CI project, serving as research administrator from 1977 to 1987. During this time, she authored or co-authored over 30 publications on the measurement of violence, the cultivation perspective, television content, demography of the television world, and media portrayals in books, reports, and articles in such journals as the *Journal of Communication, Journal of Broadcasting*, and *Journalism Quarterly*. The CI team also engaged in high-profile debates with academic colleagues (in *Communication Research* and *Public Opinion Quarterly*) and the television networks.

Nancy accepted a position as associate professor at the University of Delaware in the fall of 1987. She serves as graduate coordinator in the Department of Communication, and was promoted to full professor in 1992. She has continued her CI research with a flourish, seeking to learn how "what we see on television . . . may impact upon our beliefs." Of her many recent publications, she feels that her most significant ones are (a) those about violence and the violence profile, including a 1985 book chapter in *Broadcasting Research Methods* (Allyn & Bacon); (b) those about gender-role images on television, two of which are in *Sex Roles* (1989) and *Adolescent Medicine* (1993); and (c) two of her books, *Sourcebook on Children and Television* (Greenwood, 1991) and *Mass Media Images and Impact on Health* (Greenwood, 1993).

Her family has also increased her research resolve. Nancy wants children to be media literate, and even teaches a class in media literacy for teachers every summer. Nancy, who married Robert Penneys in September 1980, is a devoted mother to her two children, David and Laura Jane.

A string of professional accomplishments as a scholar, teacher, administrator, and consultant have surrounded Nancy Signorielli's life. Other professional involvements have included leadership positions at the University of Delaware and in the Mass Communication Division of the Speech Communication Association, reviewing activities both in the communication field and related disciplines, and consultancies for the U.S. Commission on Civil Rights, the Corporation for Public Broadcasting, and the National Coalition on Television Violence, among others. Nancy Signorielli, with her significant record of scholarly accomplishments, deserves to be a well-respected role model in our profession.

ISBN 0-313-29164-0

90000>

9 780313 291647

HARDCOVER BAR CODE